Linnen in the Press

pair of fine sheets,
Two pair of Servants Shee
pair of Ditto
Table cloths & Two Layovers
Dozen Napkins for Ditto — Dar
Cloth & a Layover, Star Pattern
Eyed Table Cloths & five Layovers
9 Napkins of Do.
Table Cloth old Damask for the
Dozen Napkins old Do.
Layovers — old Do.
Cloths Potatoe Pattern
Napkins Do. Pattern
Layovers of Different Sorts
Breakfast Table Cloths
Ten Napkins for Ditto
Room Table Cloth

GREAT IRISH
HOUSEHOLDS

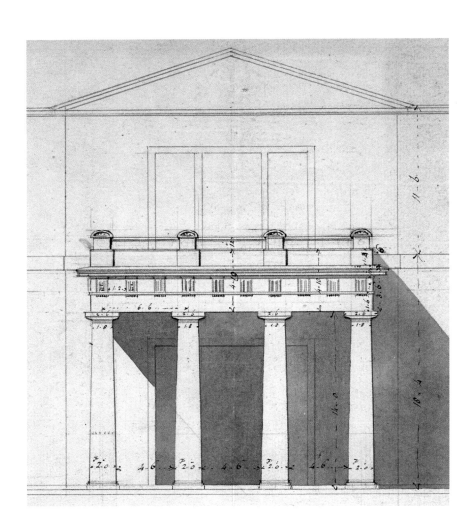

GREAT IRISH HOUSEHOLDS

*Inventories from the
Long Eighteenth Century*

Preface by Leslie Fitzpatrick
Foreword by Toby Barnard

Consultant editor Tessa Murdoch

TRANSCRIPTIONS BY
Jessica Cunningham and Rebecca Campion

WITH PREAMBLES BY
Jessica Cunningham, Rebecca Campion,
Edmund Joyce, Alec Cobbe and John Adamson

INDEX AND APPENDICES BY
John Adamson

A

John Adamson
CAMBRIDGE

Support for the publication of this book was
generously provided by

The Apollo Foundation

The Centre for the Study of Historic Irish Houses and
Estates (CSHIHE), History Department, Maynooth University,
Maynooth, Co. Kildare, Ireland

Irish Georgian Society
LONDON BRANCH

Marc Fitch Fund

The Silver Society

The Esmé Mitchell Trust
NORTHERN IRELAND

Edited, indexed and produced
by John Adamson

Copyright © 2022
Book: John Adamson
Inventories: see List of inventory sources
Contributions: their authors
Photographs: see List of plates

All the contributors have asserted
their moral right to be identified as
the authors of this work.

British Library Cataloguing in Publication Data
A catalogue record for this book is available
from the British Library.

Published by John Adamson,
90 Hertford Street,
Cambridge CB4 3AQ, England

First published in 2022

ISBN 978-1-898565-17-8

Designed by Philip Lewis
Maps on page 10 by Martin Lubikowski
Printed on Munken Lynx 120 gsm
and GardaPat 13 Bianka 135 gsm
by Opero S.r.l., Verona, Italy

All Rights Reserved.
No part of this publication may be reproduced
or transmitted in any form or by any means,
electronic or mechanical, including photocopy,
recording or any other information storage
and retrieval system, without prior permission
in writing from the publisher.

ENDPAPERS: After details of inventories
(from left to right) of Newbridge House,
Co. Dublin, 1821; Dublin Castle, Co. Dublin,
1707; Hillsborough Castle, Co. Down, 1777;
and Shelton Abbey, Co. Wicklow, 1816.
See List of inventory sources, p. 383.

FRONTISPIECE: Detail from George Dance
the Younger's elevation of the portico front
at Mount Stewart, Co. Down, 1803–8.
© Sir John Soane's Museum, London.
Photography by Ardon Bar-Hama.

CONTENTS

ACKNOWLEDGEMENTS 7

PREFACE 9

MAP OF IRELAND 10

FOREWORD BY TOBY BARNARD 11

NOTE ON THE TRANSCRIPTIONS 16

THE INVENTORIES

1 Lismore Castle, Co. Waterford, 1702/3 19

   THE ORMONDE INVENTORIES 25

2 Kilkenny Castle, Co. Kilkenny, 1705 31

3 Dublin Castle, 1707 55

4 The Duke of Ormonde's house at St James's Square, London, *c.* 1710 75

5 Bishop's mansion house, Elphin, Co. Roscommon, 1740 87

6 Captain Balfour's town house, Dublin, 1741/2 105

7 Hillsborough Castle, Co. Down, 1746 and 1777 123

8 Kilrush House, Freshford, Co. Kilkenny, 1750 147

9 No. 10 Henrietta Street, Dublin (Luke Gardiner's house), 1772 155

10 Morristown Lattin, Co. Kildare, 1773 165

11 Baronscourt, Co. Tyrone, 1782 177

12 Castlecomer House, Co. Kilkenny, 1798 187

13 Killadoon, Co. Kildare, 1807–29 201

14 Shelton Abbey, near Arklow, Co. Wicklow, 1816 227

15 Borris House, Co. Carlow, 1818 237

16 Carton House, Co. Kildare, 1818 247

17 Newbridge House, Co. Dublin, 1821 305

18 Mount Stewart, Co. Down, 1821 325

Glossary 351

APPENDIX I *Buyers at Captain Balfour's town house sale 1741/2* 365

APPENDIX II *Books in the second Duchess of Ormonde's closet at Kilkenny Castle, 1705* 368

APPENDIX III *Books in the study at the bishop's mansion house, Elphin, Co. Roscommon, 1740* 369

APPENDIX IV *Books at Newbridge House, Co. Dublin, 1821* 377

List of inventory sources 383

List of plates 384

Bibliography 390

Index of personal names 392

General index 397

This book has been published as a tribute to

DESMOND FITZGERALD,
THE KNIGHT OF GLIN (1937–2011)

ACKNOWLEDGEMENTS

WHEN SALLY CLEMENTS opened bedroom cabinet drawers at Killadoon House, County Kildare, to reveal an abundance of neatly folded pristine table linen dating from the early nineteenth century, it was a crowning moment. With Melanie Doderer-Winkler, I was leading members of the Furniture History Society on a study tour of selected great Irish houses. As we were guided, room by room, through the Clements family home, we felt we were tiptoeing through the pages of a late Georgian inventory. The thrill of being transported back into Irish history through its material culture strengthened my conviction that there should be a book of historic inventories to provide a primary resource and stimulus for further research into the great houses of Ireland.

At the farewell dinner at Carton House, Professor Terence Dooley, director of the Centre for the Study of Historic Irish Houses and Estates, agreed to offer sponsorship towards the publication, and Sally and her husband Charles, who were also guests, expressed a willingness to make inventories from Killadoon available for transcription. Edmund Joyce, a lecturer at what is now South East Technological University, who attended the dinner, was eager to be involved in the project too. It all boded well.

Our trip started at Newbridge House, County Dublin, led by Alec Cobbe, who grew up at this family home. He knew of the plans to bring out an Irish sequel to *Noble Households: Eighteenth-Century Inventories of Great English Houses* and demonstrated that he was keen to offer advice, to share inventories and pictures from the Cobbe collection, and to contribute an introduction to the Newbridge inventory.

The study tour included a visit to Abbey Leix, County Laois. There, Sir David Davies proudly demonstrated how one of Ireland's greatest houses had been brought back to life through sensitive restoration. At Leixlip Castle, County Kildare, we were reminded of the hugely important groundwork Desmond Guinness achieved from the 1950s to save for posterity the precious legacy of historic homes across the land, many dilapidated or under threat of being torn down. He and his first wife Mariga founded the Irish Georgian Society in 1958, and, like Desmond FitzGerald, Knight of Glin, did so much to help the preservation of this remarkable heritage over many decades.

The time was ripe to build on those solid foundations in a rather special way: through the publication of a book of inventories. I had persuaded John Adamson, the publisher of *Noble Households*, to join us on the Irish trip. He witnessed at first hand the groundswell of interest in the proposal and was soon fired with as much enthusiasm as I was to make it happen.

The following year (2015), David Wurtzel and Robert Wilson, inspired by the Irish study tour, led members of the Furniture History Society to Chicago, principally to view the remarkable exhibition curated by Christopher Monkhouse and Leslie Fitzpatrick *Ireland: Crossroads of Art and Design, 1690–1840* at the Art Institute. Viewing the exhibits with the expert curators and distinguished fellow traveller Simon Jervis (an authority on British and Irish secular inventories) brought home the breadth of interest in Irish material culture across the Atlantic, and the wealth of Irish artefacts to be found in private and public North American collections. The Krehbiels, keen collectors who had helped sponsor the exhibition, and John and Patricia O'Brien, welcomed us into their homes and encouraged me to take the book project forward.

I needed no second bidding. The Maynooth-trained scholar Jessica Cunningham was soon commissioned to help locate and make a representative choice of inventories from the town and country houses of leading families across Ireland. She unswervingly set about this task with the help, knowledge and contacts of Edmund Joyce, appraising material both in public and private archives.

Then the transcribing began. Rebecca Campion, also Maynooth trained, came on board to assist. A visit to Hillsborough and Mount Stewart in 2018 confirmed the inclusion of those two houses. We persuaded Toby Barnard, historian of Irish material culture, to contribute an introductory essay and Leslie Fitzpatrick to write the preface. John Adamson undertook to index the inventories. As the material came together, Philip Lewis embarked on creating the book's calm and highly readable design. We owe a great debt of gratitude to all the book's contributors, as we do to the Italian team at Opero in Verona, who undertook the pre-press work and oversaw the printing and binding of the book.

Much of the book has benefited from the advice, moral support and insights generously given by colleagues and friends. Among those who have helped in so many ways, we should particularly like to thank: Peter Adamson; Ellenor Alcorn; Flora Allen; Sophie Andreae; Marylyn and Tim Bacon; Frances Bailey; Lorraine Bourke; John Bowen; Ian Bristow; Margaret Brooks; Donough Cahill; the Cambridge University Library staff; Indigo Carnie; Christopher Catling; Charles and Sally Clements; Alec and Isabelle Cobbe; Hugh Cobbe; David Davies; Simon Dickinson; Terence Dooley; Cathal Dowd Smith; Arthur Drysdale; Glenn Dunne; Kate Dyson; Jane Fenlon; Alison FitzGerald; Olda FitzGerald; Leslie Fitzpatrick; Dolores Gaffney; Jeremy Garfield-Davies; †Nicholas Goodison; Gordon Hamme; James Harte; Mary Heffernan; †Della Howard; Simon Jervis; Paul Joannides; Morgan and Sara Kavanagh; Nicola Kelly; Claudia Kinmonth; William Laffan; Rob Lloyd; Lara L'vov-Basirov; Brian Mackey; George and Wendy Magan; Gilbert and Helen McCabe; Eddie McParland; Anthony Malcomson; Patricia Marsh; Fonsie and George Fonsie Mealy; David Mitchell; †Christopher Monkhouse; Christopher Moore; Lucy Morton; Karol Mullaney Dignam; David Murdoch; Patrick Murray; Jeremy Musson; David Needham; John Nesbitt; Charles Noble; Robert O'Byrne; Emma Paragreen; James Peill; Ugo and Chiara Pierucci; Timothy Rankin; John Redmill; James Rothwell; Melissa Ruddock; Richard and Sally St George; Rosalind Savill; Richard and Deirdre Serjeantson; Thomas and Nancy Sinsteden; Lanto Synge; Dora Thornton; Lucy Trench; Christopher Warleigh-Lock; Neil Watt; Bryan Whelan; Patrick White; Thomas Williams; and Lucy Wood. We should especially like to thank Philip Lewis, our designer, and the production team at Opero for bringing to fruition a book made to the highest standard.

TESSA MURDOCH

PREFACE

HOUSEHOLD INVENTORIES – whether undertaken at a pivotal moment in a family's history or as routine stocktaking – are increasingly understood as fundamental to disciplines as varied as gender studies and the history of collecting, not to mention their critical role in tracing provenance. Inventories hold particular importance in Ireland, which saw many resources for primary research destroyed in the economic and political upheavals of the late nineteenth and early twentieth centuries.

The eighteen inventories in this volume were selected to offer a broad picture of life in great houses in Ireland in the eighteenth and early nineteenth centuries. Inventories from counties across the country demonstrate that Belfast and Dublin were not the only sites of activity. Demesnes large, and, in some cases, viceregal or ducal – Kilkenny Castle and Carton House – compare with the more modest Kilrush House and Borris House, whereas the inclusion of town houses in Dublin and London reveals the contents of homes carefully furnished to entertain and impress. While in a distinct minority, the Lattins of Morristown, near Naas in County Kildare provide a glimpse into a prosperous Catholic household among the landed Protestant gentry.

Decorative arts specialists will read with great interest the increasing quantities of mahogany furniture in inventories as the eighteenth century progressed, as well as the appearance of Sheffield plate, and references to 'delf' and 'Chynah'. The ubiquity of these objects confirms Ireland's complex commercial relationships with countries near and far and helps explain the growth of domestic industries to meet consumer demand. Indeed, the Art Institute of Chicago's major 2015 loan exhibition *Ireland: Crossroads of Art and Design, 1690–1840*, which included objects from several of the houses represented here, explored the talent and ingenuity of native artists and this global reach of Irish entrepreneurs, collectors, and patrons. Held in a city with deep Irish roots and drawn almost exclusively from U.S. and Canadian collections, the exhibition highlighted the further migration of objects to North American shores.

The inventories, all but two of which are published here for the first time, are drawn from public and private sources. Several of the original documents are held in the collections of the National Library of Ireland and the Public Record Office of Northern Ireland, while a number have been provided by the families, trusts, or foundations that oversee the houses. Their generous participation will allow for new insight into Ireland's material culture in the long eighteenth century.

LESLIE FITZPATRICK
Former Samuel and M. Patricia Grober Associate Curator of European Decorative Arts
The Art Institute of Chicago

FOREWORD

THE VALUE OF INVENTORIES in charting how houses were arranged, furnished and used is now widely appreciated. Inventories were taken for a variety of purposes and on differing occasions: sometimes as the prelude to letting a property or to selling parts (or all) of its contents. Typically, the listings and valuations were occasioned by the death of an owner and the consequent need to deal with testamentary dispositions. Modest, even humble establishments – farmhouses and workshops – can sometimes be reconstructed on the basis of the surviving information. However, the weighting both in the documentation and in its analysis has favoured the grand and important, in short 'noble households'. The lists make it possible sometimes to trace the ownership of remarkable works of art, such as paintings and sculpture, and to chart the first appearance and increasing popularity of novelties, like oriental ceramics, tapestries to replace gilded-leather wallcoverings, and lacquered or caned furniture. Moreover, the names given to different rooms – 'breakfast' and 'library' for example – show how gradually they were reserved for particular purposes.

Pioneers, notably Peter Thornton and John Cornforth, have revealed the possibilities of studies anchored in inventories. The companion volume for eighteenth-century England showed in minute and fascinating detail what some of the grandest houses once contained. Now Ireland is set to benefit from similar scrutiny. The study of Ireland from this perspective has been hampered most obviously by the loss of much documentation, especially the lists compiled by appraisers before probate of wills could be granted. Most of this material was burnt with other legal records in 1922, although a little has been salvaged and may in time be conserved and become accessible. In addition, repugnance at the political, economic and cultural systems embodied in 'great' houses deterred sustained attempts to reconstruct how they had been arranged and used. Too reflexively, they were associated with the Protestant ascendancy which had prevailed from the seventeenth to the later nineteenth century and with other systems of economic and social discrimination. Only gradually was it realised that some mansions which were known from either surviving structures or documents had belonged to families of indigenous Irish stock or later settlers who did not conform to the stereotypes of boorish 'Cromwellians'. Furthermore, the lives of servants and tenants, as of women and children, might be illumined in fresh detail by an examination of such documentation. Similarly, light is thrown on the otherwise forgotten labours of artificers, many of whom were Irish.

Precocious toilers in what in Ireland, until recently, were lonely fields included the redoubtable Ada Longfield (later Leask) and Rosemary ffolliott. As well as seeing what could be gleaned from newspapers – particularly the advertisements for commodities – they edited several inventories. Building on and expanding their work, Jane Fenlon has been notable in exploiting the potential of inventories, most conspicuously relating to the pre-eminent ducal family between 1612 and 1716: the Ormondes. With country residences at Kilkenny, Dunmore, and Carrick-on-Suir, and regular occupation as viceroys of Dublin Castle, as well as appropriate establishments in and near London, they represented the acme of wealth and fashion. Dr Fenlon has presented a selection of mainly seventeenth-century inventories in *Goods & Chattels: A Survey of Early Household Inventories in Ireland* (Dublin, 2003). To these pioneering accounts can be added those by Desmond FitzGerald, Knight of Glin. Alert to the ways in which apparently ephemeral or trivial materials could yield unexpected insights – for example, the small printed trade cards distributed by specialist craftsmen and suppliers – he (in collaboration with James Peill) used inventories to show how houses were furnished, notably in *Irish Furniture*, published in 2007. Given Desmond FitzGerald's role in understanding how the apparently lost might be recovered, at least in outline, and the enormous encouragement he offered to others bent on similar quests, it is fitting that this collection should be dedicated to his memory.

A theme which runs strongly through these listings is a tension between the adoption of current fashions, usually derived most directly from England but frequently originating in France, Italy, the Low Countries and central Europe, and local idiosyncrasies. Individual proprietors and their immediate families stamped their own imprint on what might have been a common outline. Then, too, designers and artificers introduced their variations. Some had been lured, permanently or fleetingly, from abroad. Chambers's contribution to the Casino at Marino and to Lord Charlemont's other Irish ventures is now well-known, as are Gibbs's at Newbridge, Wyatt's (Castle Coole, County Fermanagh; Curraghmore, County Waterford; Mount Kennedy, County Wicklow; Slane Castle, County Meath) and Nash's Lough Cutra (County Galway) and Shanbally Castle (County Tipperary). Recent researches by Christine Casey, Conor Lucey and Joe McDonnell have uncovered the complex of classical and contemporary European sources which went into the decoration of both town and country houses across eighteenth-century Ireland. Similarly, the earl bishop of Derry, Frederick Hervey, enlisted and guided locals (notably Michael Shanahan from Cork) in the making of his prodigy houses at Downhill and Ballyscullion. The ease with which methods and styles current elsewhere could be imported into and adopted in Ireland is suggested by the efforts of the entrepreneurial Josiah Wedgwood and Matthew Boulton from the 1770s to vend their wares in Dublin.

Frequent travel between Ireland and Britain or further afield eased the acquisition or local reproduction of novelties. Against these external influences must be set not just the economic imperatives to favour the home-produced, but to cry up distinctive Irish features. The latter encompassed antlers and skulls of the giant elk, which might be mounted on walls, the commissioning of images of Ireland from artists such as Thomas Roberts, George Barrett, Jonathan Fisher and Thomas Malton, using local woods like arbutus or the preserved bog-oak, and patronizing potters, silversmiths and glass-houses operating in Dublin, Belfast, Cork and Waterford.

The ease with which artefacts could enter Ireland is revealed when the earls of Glandore, frequently staying in London, brought back to their seat remote in County

Kerry 'a monstrous picture of Macbeth' by Fuseli. Quickening traffic between Ireland and continental Europe explained how so much booty – busts, statuary, bronzes, cabinets, *pietre dure* and marbles – was crammed into Irish mansions. The craze for the foreign was lamented by patriots and stimulated some in Ireland to make cheaper versions, whether in wooden furniture, luxurious and utilitarian textiles, ceramics, glass and precious metals. Campaigns to buy Irish recurred. Lords lieutenant, like the Duke of Ormond in the 1660s or the Duke of Dorset in the 1750s, set examples. Institutions, notably the Dublin Society founded in 1731, furthered the schemes, through publications and through practical initiatives such as a silk warehouse which was opened in the capital and the establishment of a school of design. It was recognized that patriotic impulses were frequently outweighed by the craving to be in the pink of fashion. The latter led usually to preferring the imported – from Britain or continental Europe and the Orient – above the indigenous. In 1783, the Birmingham entrepreneur Matthew Boulton observed that 'most of the principal shopkeepers in Dublin come to England every year and know of the prices'. The Act of Union in 1800 strengthened the ties, economic and cultural as well as constitutional, between Ireland and Britain. On the one hand, it encouraged the adoption in Ireland of 'British' tastes. On the other, it intensified the wish among some, proud of a distinctive Irishness, to express this distinctiveness through possessions and ways of living. Inventories can help to assess these competing forces. In the earlier seventeenth century, appraisers distinguished between silver hall-marked in London and Dublin. One precious listing, first published by Miss ffolliott and now reproduced here (pp. 108–21), included a glass engraved to commemorate William III, lionized in Protestant Ireland for his victories over the Catholics, and baldly listed as 'the Glorious Memory'. This entry has extra resonances in that it is an item from the auction of the effects of Captain Balfour in his Dublin house following his death. Already, judging from its being singled out in the catalogue and from the price that it fetched, the glass was highly prized. It was bought by another member of the landed elite, Sir Laurence Parsons. While many of the Balfours' possessions were dispersed in the sale, some items were kept back, on behalf of the heir who was a minor.

Such explicit references that identify or imply place of manufacture are rare. It was relatively simple for the enterprising to have shipped in and to market goods from overseas. Equally it was easy to copy articles and designs popular outside Ireland: sketches and patterns arrived to guide copyists; artefacts could serve as prototypes; even memories of what had been admired abroad were enough to enable replicas to be made in Ireland. Commercial espionage and piracy were rife. Through similar processes the look of goods originating in Dublin was diffused into the provinces. Ideally, the terse entries in inventories need to be amplified with invoices and receipts, account books, and correspondence between traders and customers, or the recorded reactions of those who acquired or saw the pieces.

The houses which are covered are spread across Ireland, with some town houses in Dublin and others – the bishop's palace at Elphin in Roscommon, west of the River Shannon, and Baronscourt in western Ulster – relatively remote. Yet, it would be hard to detect any striking regional variations in the contents. No doubt much of the material had been bought locally, at fairs and markets and even from itinerants, or made by employees on the estate. The houses varied greatly in scale, with the ducal establishments of the Ormondes and later of the Leinsters at Carton perhaps in a league on their own. Only one belonged to a family which, notwithstanding the legal and economic pressures on Catholics, had not converted to Protestantism: the Lattins of Morristown. At least one belonged to a peer – the Earl of Cork and Burlington – now (by 1707) habitually non-resident in Ireland. Absence or presence, at least for part of the year, since all owners divided their time between the provinces, Dublin and England, may explain the comparative modesty of some listings. But, while variations can be discerned, at this elevated level of squires and peers, there was a standardization in furnishings: one, moreover, that was shared with Britain. What the inventories when probed minutely may show are changes over time, as new commodities became available and older ones fell from fashion. Furthermore, the financial circumstances of owners were not uniform, so that only the wealthiest could afford certain of the luxuries, although through cheaper simulacra the requisite show could be achieved at a lower price.

Three of the inventories include listings of books and, perhaps supporting the contention that the members of the Irish peerage and country gentry were not notably bookish, had in two instances been assembled by bishops (Howard at Elphin and Cobbe at Newbridge). The books in the Duchess of Ormonde's closet at Kilkenny Castle are listed, but those in the duke's are 'as by Catologe' and thus are not itemized. There is a plethora of bookcases to be found in the inventories but almost nothing to suggest what books had been bestowed on their shelves. Several of the inventories include much agricultural equipment, stock and produce: a valuable reminder that these establishments were frequently at the centre of working farms and that mundane activities had not been banished totally from view. There is an echo of the turbulence which could still disturb the countryside and destroy property when it is noted that the inventory taken at Castlecomer was in the wake of the violence of 1798. There were mechanisms through which owners hoped to be compensated for their losses.

Light is also cast on the process by which the valuations were made: at Morristown: if Bryan Dunne supervised proceedings, seven others, including two women, helped. At Hillsborough in 1747, Mrs Crosley, perhaps the housekeeper, was solely responsible. Specialized knowledge could be pooled, although minute detail, which would assist precise identification, for example of artists or of the sources of ceramics, is rarely offered. Thus, there are simply 'paintings' over doors, china on chimney-pieces, and prints, maybe in black frames or glazed. At Borris House, 'one painting in oil' is noted. In contrast, textiles were more frequently distinguished, or at least the 'Irish' from English. At Lismore, for example, some blankets were confidently described as 'North Country Cloath Sheets', perhaps from Cork and Burlington's Yorkshire estates, and reserved for the judges when they stayed on circuit. They were differentiated from the coarse ones for the servants' beds.

So far as paintings are concerned, the two inventories from Hillsborough (County Down) offer helpful detail. Hanging in the dining-room were portraits of named individuals. A full-length of the proprietor was flanked by forbears and kinsfolk. Why Sir Thomas Roe and the Duchess of Marlborough were also present is one of many questions prompted by the material. Moreover, the dozen prints of 'the Prodigal Son' or 'Rake's Progress' and four more, 'Morning', 'Noon', 'Evening' and 'Night' may have been among the twenty-four by Hogarth in the library, listed in 1777. We can only speculate whether the twelve pictures of 'birds and flowers' found in 'Lady Cranborn's room' may have been those in gouache and embossed paper of Samuel Dixon, who is known to have dedicated one of his compositions to Lady Hillsborough. By the later date, nine views of Naples had been added: presumably souvenirs of Lord Hillsborough's sojourn there in 1765–6. The prospects were displayed in the 'breakfast room', evidence in itself of the new specialization in the use and naming of rooms. At Hillsborough, too, there seems to have been a penchant for painted wooden furniture, specified as white or blue. A closet contained two glass cases of shell-work – virtuoso constructions associated particularly with Mary Delany, who resided intermittently not far away, and included the Hills family within her circle. These examples are merely a few of the many which are stimulated by the availability of so much hitherto largely unknown evidence.

This collection is focused on an elongated eighteenth century, stretching in effect from 1702, the year William of Orange died, to 1821, the year before George IV acceded to the throne. The period, although in Ireland interrupted twice by widespread and destructive unrest, was in other respects relatively placid, and with palpable improvements in the material conditions of at least a minority of the population. As has been stressed, more and more varied commodities entered Irish houses. The period, moreover, is the one onto which the Knight of Glin directed his penetrating gaze. In time, it may be that the documentation of his own collections at Glin – the topographical paintings fully described in *Painting Ireland* (2006) and some of the contents catalogued by Christie's for a sale in 2009 – will allow an illuminating reconstruction of a later twentieth-century successor to the cognoscenti whose establishments are opened up in this volume.

TOBY BARNARD
Emeritus Fellow in History at Hertford College,
University of Oxford

NOTE ON THE TRANSCRIPTIONS

While the transcriptions are faithful to original
spelling and punctuation and use of superscripts,
they are not facsimiles. There has been no revision of
spelling to conform to modern usage or any attempt
to make either spelling or punctuation consistent.
Striking through is also faithful to deletions in
the original documents. Inserted words are
shown in superscript.

Contemporary or later undated annotations
and commentaries are differentiated typographically,
using additional fonts to the main text typeface:
semibold, italic and tone. Very minor annotations
deemed to be ephemeral have been omitted.

Editorial annotations have been kept to
a minimum and are shown in square brackets.
A contextual interpretation has been given for
the few indecipherable words occurring. Some of the
inventories transcribed are clearly fair copies of drafts.
This has led at times to the anomalies in the spelling
of names and unusual words as recorded here.

The headings at the tops of pages in the original
manuscripts have been omitted or moved, and,
where needed, modified slightly to match the
column breaks in the transcript.

For ease of reading, dittos in the transcripts
are shown throughout in italic whenever they
are abbreviated.

The transcribers are identified in the List of
inventory sources on p. 383.

THE INVENTORIES

PLATE 1
Samuel Alken (1756–1815), after a drawing by
Thomas Sautelle Roberts (*c.* 1760–1826):
Lismore Castle, County Waterford, 1795, aquatint

1

LISMORE CASTLE,
COUNTY WATERFORD
1702/3

REBECCA CAMPION

IN 1602 RICHARD BOYLE, one of the most successful of the Elizabethan adventurers, bought Lismore Castle and 42,000 acres in counties Waterford and Cork from Sir Walter Raleigh for £1,500. The magnificent situation of Lismore Castle, above the Blackwater river, was originally the site of the seventh-century Lismore Abbey, onto which King John had a castle built to guard the waterway. The Great Earl (Boyle became first of Earl of Cork in 1620) made Lismore Castle his principal residence, adding the main living wing in the 1630s and a great terrace terminating in two turret-like summer houses.

The fortunes of Lismore Castle reflect the turbulence of this period. In the 1641 Rebellion, Lismore Castle was forfeited, and then sacked in 1645. It was confiscated again in 1689. The Great Earl's heir managed to recover the castle but the family never lived there again. This inventory was taken in 1702, during the brief tenure of Charles Boyle (second Earl of Burlington and third Earl of Cork), who lived on his Yorkshire estates, was made a Privy Councillor in London in 1702 and died in 1704.

The Boyle family were not regularly resident in Lismore Castle after the death of the Great Earl in 1643. In the 1702 inventory, one room is described as 'the little Parlour called My Lords Study', suggesting that rooms were reserved for the Boyle family. Two rooms are labelled as Mr and Mrs Congreve's rooms. Colonel William Congreve, originally from Yorkshire, was the long-standing estate agent for the earls of Cork. The four 'Judges Roomes in the Long Gallery' indicate that the castle continued to function as an administrative centre for the area.

Throughout the inventory, items are described as old and occasionally worn. The detail given in the linen inventory indicates careful cutting down and repurposing, with old sheets becoming tablecloths. The hierarchy of cloth is evident in the 'North Country Cloath Sheets' for Congreve and the judges whereas the servants had 'little course Sheetes'. New entries are listed but all are of a humble nature like close-stools or drinking-glasses. The residents dined off pewter plates, used brass candlesticks and cooked in iron saucepans. No china or silver appears on the inventory.

The Great Earl kept a diary or remembrancer from 1611 to 1642, which documented lavish purchases for Lismore Castle. By contrast, the inventory records a sparsely furnished house. In 1624 he paid £57 to a Dublin merchant for tapestries for the dining-chamber. In the 1702 inventory only two tables and the fire dogs are recorded in that same dining-room. In 1630 he spent £103 on eighteen tapestries from the Duke of Ormonde, which arrived in the same boat from Bristol as state beds with matching chairs and stools in crimson velvet finished with silk and silver fringe.

Beds were status symbols in the early seventeenth century and many beds, several with sets of matching chairs, were purchased. Turkey-work chairs, stools and cushions were brought from London where this knotted fabric was manufactured. Possibly some of the Great Earl's huge campaign of consumption survived the political upheavals of the 1640s and the bequests to his many children in his will, and still lurk among the beds, 'old Turkey worke Chaires' and the 'old Tapistry hangings' in the Congreves' rooms.

Lismore Castle was inherited by that champion of Palladio, Richard Boyle, third Earl of Burlington, but his interests were in England. The castle passed to the dukes of Devonshire in 1753. Lismore Castle, as it stands today, owes most to the sixth Duke of Devonshire, who from 1811 and for the next fifty years rebuilt the castle in Gothic style with magnificent interiors by A. W. N. Pugin and J. G. Crace.

The 1702/3 inventory is in the National Library of Ireland.

An Inventory of goods belonging to the Right hon^{ble}, the Earle of Burlington

In the Judges Roomes in the Long Gallery – vizt, in the roome at the Staire-head

1 Feather bead & bolster, 1 high bed Stead
1 pr blanketts new
1 White New Rugg
1 Sute of red Clouded Stuffe
  Curtaines & hangings
  of the Same
1 Suite of window Curtains
  white fflocking
1 Small Table
5 Cane chayres
1 New Close Stoole
1 white Chamber pott
1 white Bason
1 little Lookeing glasse
1 old pillow
1 Shovell & tongues
1 Iron back & fender

In the Middle roome

1 feather Bed & bolster
1 high bed stead
1 paire & ½ of New blancketts

1 New white Rugg
1 Suite of blew Clouded Stuffe
  Curtaines
1 Counterpan, & Table Cloath of
  the Same Stuffe
1 Suite of blew Kittermaster
  hangings
1 Small Table
1 Suite of white fflannele
  window Curtaines
5 Cane – Chayres
1 Elbow – Cane Chayre
1 Chamberpott
1 Bason
1 New Close-Stoole
1 ~~Iron back~~
  fire Shovell & tongues
1 ffender

In the Inner roome

1 ffeather bed & bolster
1 Bed-stead
1 Suite of Serge Curtaines
1 Counterpan of the Same,
1 paire of Blancketts,
2 Chaires cover'd wth ye Same
  Stuffe belonging to the Bed
1 old Close-Stoole,
2 old pillowes
1 Small Table

In the roome at ye end
of the Gallery

1 ffeather bed & Bolster
1 Bed-Stead
1 Suite of Stuffe Curtaines
1 Counterpan of the Same
1 white Rugg,
2 low Chairs cover'd with
   Serge,
3 Stooles coverd with ye Same
1 old glasse-Case

In the Dineing roome

2 Tables
1 pair of Iron Doggs
1 Iron back

In the Comon hall, formerly
the Kitchen

1 old dresser
1 ffoarme
1 Iron dogg
1 Iron back

In the Little Pantry

1 Table, & Shelves

In the little roome neare
My Lords Chamber

1 little feather bed
1 white Rugg
1 ffield Bedstead,
1 Curtaine

In Mrs Congreve's roome

1 ffeather bed & Bolster
1 high bed stead
1 Suite of Serge Curtaines
   lin'd wth Silke green
2 Cane-Chaires
1 Elbow-Cane Chaires
1 Chest of Drawers,
1 Shovell, ffender & Iron back
1 Couch
1 paire of white Callico windo Curtaines
   ~~In the Closett~~

1 quilt betwixt ye bed & ye Matt
3 ~~Suite~~ ∧^pieces of ∧^old Tapistry hangings
1 paire of bellowes
1 Turky worke Cushion
4 blancketts

In the Closett

1 Table
1 Cane Stoole
1 Turky-worke Stoole
1 rowe of Shelves
1 Close-Stoole

In Mr Congreve's roome

1 feather bed & bolster
1 Bed Stead
4 blancketts
1 old Callico Quilt
1 Suite of Serge ~~blew~~ Curtaines
1 Suite of Tapistry hangings vizt
2 pieces
3 Tables
2 Window Curtaines green Serge
1 Elbow Cane Chaire
4 ~~Cane Chaires~~ flag-bottom'd Chaire
1 old Turky worke Chaire,
1 Close Stoole & pan
1 Shovell & tonges & Iron back
   a Sett of Shelves
1 Iron ffender
1 old Screen

In the house keepers roome

1 feather bed & bolster
1 high bed stead
2 old blancketts
1 old Rugg
1 Counterpan
1 ~~Flock & Hair~~ [?] feather bed & bolster
1 low Bed Stead
1 blanckett
1 Caddow
1 large Linnen Chest
1 little Candle Chest
1 Clothe fflaskett
2 Curtins

Lismore Castle, County Waterford

In yᵉ Closet in yᵉ Gallery

    a double rowe of Shelves
1 Cane Stoole
1 Cupboard

In the little Parlour called My Lords Study

2 round Tables,
1 square Table
8 flagg bottom'd Chaires
1 Elbow Cane Chaire
1 Iron back
1 Shovell, tonges & fire forke
1 Iron ffender

In the passage

1 Large Cubbord
1 Table

In yᵉ little Study

1 Table wᵗʰ 2 drawers
2 old Turky worke Chaires
2 or 3 Small Shelves

Pewter

31 dishes, great & Small
4 doz: & 1 new plates
1 doz & 10 old plates
1 pye-plate
1 pr 2 Stands.
    an old round pye ∧cheese-plate
3 porringers
1 Bason
1 pewter Still
1 Bed-pan

Brasse

5 paire of Candlesticks
1 paire of flatt Candlesticks
2 paire of Snuffers,
1 Snuff dish
1 Ladle,
2 Skimers
1 kettle great
1 little Kettle
2 Fork meate skewers
1 Pepper pott

1 Walsh Kettle
1 warmeing pan

Iron

2 potts
1 Stew pan
1 Sauce-pan
1 frying Pan
1 paire of Racks
2 paire of pott hangers
1 fire-forke
1 flesh-forke
1 Shovell
1 paire of tonges
2 Spitts
1 Grid-Iron
2 pott hangers
1 Toaster
2 other Racks
2 flatt Smothing Irons
1 Cleaver
1 Iron back
2 pott lidds

Tinn

1 large pasty pan
1 little pasty pan
1 Dripping pan
1 Collender
1 Cover

Wooden vessells &c. in yᵉ Kitchin

1 Coop
1 Trencher Case
2 Salt boxes,
1 long dresser
3 Shelves
1 long Table
2 Chopping blocks
2 ffoarmes
1 Rack
3 pailes
2 other Racks
1 rouleing pin
1 powdering Tubb
4 Treas

In the Cellar

1 Cheese presse
3 Tables
9 halfe barrells
3 barrells
6 Keelers
1 dresser
1 drainer
4 Stellings

In the Brew house

1 large brewing pan
1 little brasse brewing pan
1 Iron kettle
1 Kieve
1 Stilling
1 old Iron pott
1 brand Iron
3 Corall
  waste tubb
1 tuning Tubb
2 Ladeing pailes

In the Lodge

1 bed – old & bolster
1 low Bed-Stead
1 paire of blanketts
1 Caddow
1 muskett

In the men-Servants room

1 flock bed and Bolster,
1 low Bed-Stead
1 paire of Blancketts
1 Caddow

new goods delivered M.\! *Knight*

1 Table baskett
1 Large glasse baskett
1 littel glasse baskett
10 drinking glasses
1 voyder
2 wooden Cans
14 Knives
10 fforkes
1 Viniger Caske

Linnen

6 paire of North Country Cloath Sheets for the Judges	}	whereof 2 paire given Col[nl] Congreve, 4 paire remaineing
2 paire of little course Sheetes for Servants	}	whereof one paire cutt out for Table Cloathes – 1 paire remaineing
7 old Pillow boards		These were made of old Sheets
3 Diaper Table Cloaths		
2 Little Table-Cloathes		Made out of a pr of old Sheetes
2 paire Bandle-Cloath, Table Cloathes	}	These were made out of an old paire of Sheets
2 old Side-board Cloaths		
3 Doz: of Diaper Napkins		Whereof 9 worne out – &
1 paire of Bandle Cloath Sheet		2 doz: & 3 remaineing

Inventory of the goods in y[e] Castle 1702/3

Lismore Castle, County Waterford

PLATE 2
Attributed to the Gouda workshop of Pieter de Cracht (*c.* 1600–1662), woven from designs by Sir Peter Paul Rubens (1577–1640): *Marcus Valerius consecrates Decius Mus*. One of a set of tapestries telling the story of the Roman consul Decius Mus, *c.* 1648, linen and wool.

THE
ORMONDE
INVENTORIES

Kilkenny Castle, County Kilkenny
1705

Dublin Castle
1707

St James's Square, London
c. 1710

JESSICA CUNNINGHAM

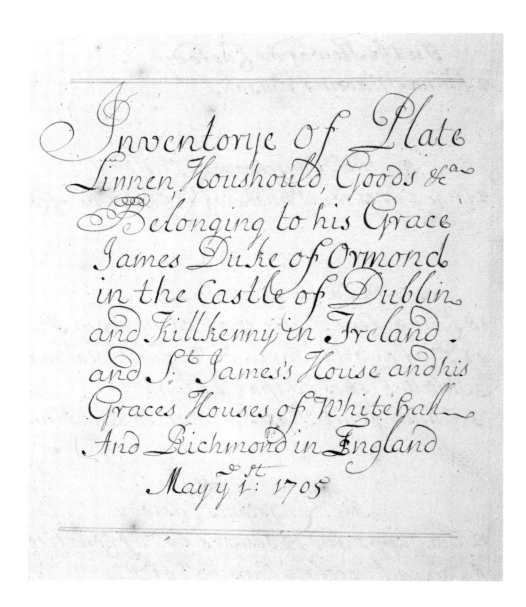

PLATE 3
Title inscribed on the front page within the bound
volume of manuscripts containing the 1705 inventory
of Kilkenny Castle transcribed here

NO COMPILATION OF great Irish household inventories would be complete without the inclusion of one or more relating to the various residences of the dukes of Ormonde. Jane Fenlon's edited volume of inventories, *Goods & Chattels* (2003), includes several seventeenth-century inventories of Ormonde properties: Ormonde Castle (1626), Kilkenny Castle (1629; 1630; 1639; 1684), Dunmore House (1675; 1684) and Dublin Castle (1678). These documents richly recount the interior worlds of the tenth Earl of Ormond, Thomas Butler, and those belonging to his successors, Walter Butler, the eleventh Earl, and James Butler, the twelfth Earl and first Duke of Ormonde (1610–1688) who inherited the title in 1632. Upon his elevation to duke in the English peerage, in 1682, an 'e' was added to the older name of Ormond.

James Butler married his cousin Elizabeth Preston, thereby solidifying his claims to Butler lands and, with his young bride, lived primarily in two of the Ormonde residences – Kilkenny Castle and Ormonde Castle, in Carrick-on-Suir, County Tipperary. From 1660 onwards the first duke and duchess undertook the refurbishment of their ancestral properties as well as their temporary accommodations at Dublin Castle and the viceregal lodge in Chapelizod outside the capital during the duke's tenures as lord lieutenant in the 1660s and 1670s. In addition, they acquired new properties in England, including a large town house in St James's Square in London. Their grandson, James Butler, who succeeded to the title in 1688 and under whose term the ensuing transcribed inventories were drawn up, carried out further refurbishments and acquisitions to these properties in the 1690s and in the first decade of the eighteenth century. With extensive properties serving diverse familial and political functions in Leinster, Munster and England, detailed household inventories were, perforce, regularly drawn up. Most of these inventories are now incorporated within the Ormonde Papers in the National Library of Ireland.

The inventories transcribed in this volume represent three distinct aspects of the second Duke of Ormonde's unique role in early eighteenth-century Irish society: his position as a leading member of the Old English elite with his family seat at Kilkenny Castle; his political prominence as the queen's representative in Ireland as lord lieutenant at Dublin Castle; and as a member of the peerage in England, with military, political, familial and social allegiances necessitating his presence in that country. Like his grandfather, James Butler distinguished himself with his loyalty to the crown and in his military leadership. He declared for William of Orange shortly after inheriting his dukedom and fought on the side of William III in the 1690s and as commander-in-chief of the British Forces during the Wars of the Spanish

The Ormonde Inventories

Succession against the French the following decade. During Queen Anne's reign he served as lord lieutenant for two periods: from 1703 to 1707 and from 1710 to 1713. His loyalty to Anne and the Jacobite cause precipitated his downfall. On the accession of George I in 1714 he was removed from his command and, the following year, was implicated in the Jacobite rising and impeached. He fled to France where he remained in exile until his death in 1745. Stripped of his title and his properties, these inventories, taken at the height of his career, remain a lasting snapshot of the lofty height from which he fell.

Each of the inventories here is notable for the volume of paintings adorning the walls of public and private spaces in the Ormonde households. This much is evident from page one of the 1705 inventory of Kilkenny Castle where, in the 'Supping Roome' alone, six portraits, one scene hung over the chimney-piece and two paintings positioned over each of the doors, decorate the room. Landscapes, portraits (of full or half size), still-life scenes, battle scenes, biblical and historical scenes, floral pictures and maps, many in carved or gilt frames, are in profusion in the dozens of rooms and stairways in the castle. The full range and variety are itemized on each of the four walls of the impressive Gallery, which includes portraits of Charles I and II, Ormonde ancestors and contemporary family members, biblical scenes – 'The Virgin Mary & Our Saviour in her lap' – and whimsical pictures including 'A piece of ffruite & a Munkie'. More indicative of a fashion from the previous period are the tapestries found in abundance in principal chambers at Kilkenny Castle: in the duchess's drawing-room '4 pieces of Tapestry hangings', measuring '10 foot deep', tell the story of Diogenes, while in the room over the so-called 'Councell Chambr', five tapestry-hangings, described as being from Antwerp, depict the story of Cyrus. Large volumes of silver equipped and ornamented these public and private spaces. The silver inventories are not reproduced here as they have been comprehensively analyzed and transcribed by Thomas Sinsteden in his excellent article 'Household plate of the dukes of Ormonde' (*Silver Studies,* no. 23, 2008). Besides the art and silver in Kilkenny Castle, opulence on a large-scale is communicated from the list of furnishings and equipage in the reception rooms and family bedchambers – the duke had a bathing-room adjacent to his bedroom containing a lead-lined bathing-tub. However, a degree of shabbiness is also evident: blankets and bedding are often referred to here as 'very bad' and other instances can be found describing fabrics and furniture as 'very old', 'broken' or 'worne out'. In the lobby outside the duke's bedchamber the curtains are described as being 'much too scant'. When compared with the household at St James's Square, it would seem that the Ormondes chose to spend more maintaining the condition of their London home than their ancestral Irish seat.

The Dublin Castle inventory of 1707 was drawn up at the end of the second duke's first viceregal tenure. A valuation inventory, for the most part appraised by the upholsterers John French and Stephen Finckley, it reflects the usual practice by outgoing lords lieutenant to sell on items from state apartments to their successors, or, as expressed in this instance, 'for the use of her Majesty', by way of the Earl of Pembroke. Not everything was retained in Dublin Castle, however; we can see that many items – mostly paintings – were transported to Kilkenny and England while items of silver worth £277 were sold to Dublin's leading goldsmith Thomas Bolton. Nonetheless, what remained at Dublin Castle indicates that during the duke's four years in office he evidently disbursed funds to furnish and equip the apartments in a fashionable and comfortable manner befitting the monarch's representative in Ireland: one of the drawing-rooms was furnished with ten armchairs upholstered in blue velvet and trimmed with silver lace and matching satin curtains while the secretary-general's office was equipped with a 'japanned' pier table and looking-glass.

Much of the contents of the principal inventory referred to the several bedrooms, which were replete with chests of drawers, sconces, tables, curtains, carpets, hangings, bedsteads of varying proportion, blankets, quilts, feather bolsters and counterpanes. Indicative of the working household are the lists of pewter, copper, brass and iron. The real ornaments at Dublin Castle can be detected in the inventories of items retained by the duke: numerous portraits of family members and other eminent figures, some of which are noted to be in gilt frames; a Madonna and Child attributed to Correggio; numerous floral and still-life scenes; maps, landscapes and paintings depicting naval battles; musical instruments; books; silverwares; marble and gilt tables; 'japanned' and silver-mounted items of furniture; and gold-trimmed and crimson damask upholstered armchairs.

The duke and duchess's London town house at St James's Square arguably exhibited the greatest opulence and grandeur they could muster. Like their other residences, most of the principal chambers, the hallways and stairways were adorned with tapestries and a vast array of full or half-length portraits, landscapes and floral, still-life or allegorical religious paintings, maps and pastoral scenes. The duchess's bedchamber and dressing room alone, for instance, had thirteen paintings and several tapestries. Besides these valuable adornments, notable items of decorative and fashionable equipage and furniture included a 'Tea Table with 10 Tea Dishes & Sasers Milk pote and Tea pote' in the duchess's dressing room, a large japanned Indian chest with a gilt frame and covered in leather, along with a pair of silver fire dogs in a drawing-room, and nineteen chairs covered in 'Turkey leather' and laced with gold in the duke's dining-room. Like all substantial households of the period, the lists of secondary bedchambers belonging to other family members and senior staff, along with the rooms accommodating the lesser staff – here, ranging from housekeeper to the laundry maid – convey the wide scope of the town house's operations.

The inventories of Kilkenny Castle (1705), Dublin Castle (1707) and St James's Square (c. 1710) are held in the National Library of Ireland.

PLATE 4
Francis Place (1647–1728): *Kilkenny Castle and Saint Canice's Cathedral*, 1699, ink and wash on paper (detail)

2

KILKENNY CASTLE, COUNTY KILKENNY

1705

*An Inventory of his
Grace yᵉ· Duke of Ormonds Goods
Att Killkenny Taken*

In yᵉ Stone Lobby

12 Wainscott Chaires & 2 painted Chaires
5 Lackered Sconces
A fixed Sideboard

In yᵉ Supping Roome

A Weather Glass not in Order wanting
Quick Silver, Two dozen of Cane Chaires
2 paire of Window Curtins & Vallens to yᵉ Windᵂˢ:
of Irish Stuff
One Table Bedsted, One Small Feather Bed & Bolster
Three Small Blankets, Part of a Turkey workt
Carpet on the Bedsted, Three Lackerd Sconces,
One Grate
One Iron Back, One paire of wrought Hand Irons
a paire of Tonges & ffireshoell wᵗʰ: brass knobs,
The Lady Dutchess of Ormond, & Earl of Ossory
The Lady Thurles   The Lady Chesterfield
The Lady Cavendish   The Earle of Pembrock
The Lady Fitzpatrick
A Chimney piece of Robery & 2 Small Pictures
over the Doores

In his Graces Dressing Roome

Hung wᵗʰ: 3 Pieces of fine Tapestry Landskip &
small figures hangings 8 foot deepe & lined wᵗʰ
Canvas, 12 blew damask Chayres wᵗʰ: black
frames, One Jappand Table & stands
One Lookeing Glass gaurnished wᵗʰ Brass the
glass 32 inches
Foure brass Sconces washt wᵗʰ Silver

Seven knotts belonging to yᵉ Sconces & glass
One Grate for Wood or Charcole
One Payre of hand Irons washt
One Iron Back
One Small brass Fireshovell & Tonges
One hearth Broome
Two payre of Window Curtins and Vallen of
Irish Stuff
Two Curtin Rods
One Picture of Fishermen over the Chimney
in a narrow guilt frame
Three Small Pictures over yᵉ Doores

In his Graces Bedchamber

Hung with 3 Pieces of Tapestry Hangings
Landskip & Small figures 8 foot deepe
There is 3 pieces moore of these hangings in
the Wardrobe, A Piller Bedsted with a
Riseing Teaster and Sackcloth Bottem, wᵗʰ
Foure guilt feete
One ffeather Bed & Bolster
One Holland Quilt
Foure Blanketts
Three pillows
The ffurniture of the Bed of Crimson & white
damask Trimed wᵗʰ Crimson, black & white
fringe, Containing Cantoon Curtins, Ariseing
Tester and a little inward Vallen
A gather'd headcloath headboard, Counterpaine
& bases
foure Cupps
Seven Payre of Tassells
One Case Curtin Rodd
foure Case Curtins of Crimson Serge
Six Arme Chayres & 4 black Stooles
Ten Damask & 10 Serge Cases Suitable to yᵉ Bed
a Pair of thrid Damask Window Curtins wᵗʰ: a rodd

One Jappan'd Table & Stands
One Lookeing Glass of ye same 32 Inches
One Grate, One Dressing Stoole w^th: an
old Taffety Case
One payre of Brass hand Irons
One payre of Brass Tonges and ffireshovell
one Needleworke firescreene in a black frame
Three Curtins, Vallens & Cornices to ye doores
of Silver Tabby fringed w^th: green fringe
A Landskip Picture & Carved frame over ye Chimney
Three Pictures in Pannells over ye Doores

In y̆ Baithing Roome

A Baitheing Tubb lined wth Lead
A Leaden Cester'n w^th: two brass Cocks

In y̆ Lobby Beyound y̆ Chamber

One Press bedstead w^th: Cord & Matt
One Small Table
The place hung wth Indian Callicoe
Two Curtins & Vallens of ye same of ye Curtins
much too Scant
One Old Serge Curtin to ye Window w^th: a Rodd
A Small Feather Bed & Bolster
A Small Old Rugg
A Smale Old Blankett
A smale bell w^th: a string into his Graces Chamb^r

*Att y̆ ffoot of y̆ Great Staires
and Upwards*

One Glass Lanthorn
One Pendulum Clock
3 Lackered Sconces
a Smale grate fixed on an Iron pan w^th: foure
long feet

In y̆ Stewards Eating Roome

One folding Ovall Table uppon Tressells
One Side board Table
18 Turkey workt Chaires
4 very Old red base Curtins & 2 Curtin Rodds
a pair of And Irons w^th: double Brasses
One Landskip over the Chimney

In y̆ Clossett

One Little Table
One Leather Stoole
One Curtin Rod & 2 old Curtins
A Pair of Smale Fireshovell & Tonges

In y̆ Great Dineing Roome

Compleatly hung w^th: gilt Leather
One Smale Table & frame
Two Side board Tables
A Carpett to each Side Table ye same of ye hangings
of ye Roome
32 Chaires w^th: black frames ye Same of ye hangings
3 Window Curtins of Striped Stuff Indian, fringed
wth thred fringe & strings & tassells to draw y^m up
2 paire of Stuff Curtins wth. rods to ye inner part
of ye Windows
One Iron Back in ye Chimney
A Large Grate
One Iron fender
A paire of Tonges & fireshovell w^th: brass knobbs
One pair of Large brass And Irons
One Six leav'd Screen painted w^th: Flowers and
flower potts, One Picture of ye Chimney
of Severall figures
A Piece of my Lord Strafford Over ye Doore
Eight Lakerd Sconces

The Clossett in y̆ Dineing Roome

One Old Candle Chest
One Old Brass Sconce
An End of a Table y^t: was to Lengthen a Long Table

In y̆ Clossett neare y̆ Dineing Roome

part of it hung wth. green Kidermaster
One Large Oglesbyes Bible covered w^th: blew
Turkey leather
7 Large Comon Prayre Bookes in fol^io
5 of a Lesser fol^io
7 in Octavio
One old one in Quarto coverd w^th: Turky leather
One Smale folio Covered w^th: blew plush
2 Long figured Crimson Caffa Cushions for
the Church
One Velvett Carpett fringed w^th: Crimson fringe
4 Smale figur'd Caffa Cutions
2 Smale Old Crimson Velvett Cutions

11 Smale Damask Cutions
One wrought Crostich Cution
6 Crimson Taffety Curtins Severall Sises
3 Old Crimson Serge Curtins
One Bassett Table Leafe Cover'd w[th]: green Say
One Black Play Table cover'd w[th]: Figur'd Velvett
One Umbro Table covered w[th]: green Cloth
A Smale Card Table cover'd w[th]: Velvett
One Jappan'd Tea Table
A Chynah plate
An Earthen Tea pott
Eight smale painted Chinah Sawcers &
Eight Tea Cupps Suitable, One of y[e] Sawcers
a piece broke of
a Chynah Cupp to hould Sug[r]

Her Graces Dressing Roome
Neare ẙ Dineing Roome

2 Arm'd Chaires & 7 backt Chaires of blew
figur'd Velvett w[th]: black frames
One Ebony Cabinett w[th]: a black frame
One writeing Desque covered w[th]: black Velvett
King Charles y[e] 2[d]: his Head
King James. his Head
The Princes Royall
The Old Duke of Ormonde & Mezendeere
One Smale Dutch piece w[th]: figures
One Smale Landskip
One flock workt Picture
One Smale picture wth flowers
One Landskip over y[e] Chimney
All y[e] above Pictures have Carved Guilt frames
One Charcole pan
One Paire of Smale brass And Irons & Chimny
hookes, A Smale paire of brass Tonges and
fireshovell, One Table w[th]: a blew Velvett
Carpett Suitable to y[e] Chaires
One gilt Leather Closestoole & pan

Her Graces Lodging Roome

Hung w[th]: 4 Pieces of Antwerp hangings
the Story Pollyphemees 10 foot deep
One Bed=Stead w[th]: a riseing Tester and Sacking
bottom, One ffeather Bed & Bolster
of fflanders ticking
One fustian pillow
Three Blanketts
One flock Mattress

The ffurniture of y[e] Bed of purple Moheare
Containing Six Curtins. 2 Cantoones. Double
bases, The Curtins lined w[th]: rich Venetian
Silk, Inner Vallens, Tester, headcloath
head board, The Counterpaine & Cases of y[e] posts
all of y[e] Same Silke, The top of y[e] Tester, the
head board & y[e] Counterpaine Richly Emboder'd
and fringe of y[e] Bed Suitable
One Case Curtin Rod
Foure purple Serge Case Curtins
One Old Tangeer Matt under y[e] Bed
A Table & a pair of Stands of Counterfiet
Inlayed Stone
A Lookin Glass 30 Inches deep y[e] frame Suitable
4 Armed Chaires w[th]: Carv'd & guilt frames
4 purple & Moheare Cases & 4 Serge Cases
2 Wind[w]: Curtins of white Damaske 2 breadths in
Each Indian, 2 Curtin Rods
One Iron Back in y[e] Chimny, & a Grate
A picture of Flowers over y[e] Stoole [*recte* Steele?] Doore
A Red Leather Closetoole & pan

In the Draweing Roome

4 pieces of Tapestry hangings the Story of
Dyogines 10 foot Deep
3 paire of white damask Window Curtins
3 Curtin Rods
6 Arm'd Chaires & 6 back Chaires of green
& gold colord Damask w[th]: black frames
12 Stuff Cases for y[e] Chaires
6 Red Velvett round Stooles
One Rich Needleworkt round Stoole border'd
wth Velvett
A Large Hazerd Table of Dansick Oake
A Percian Carpett 1 y[rd] & ½ wide & a little
above 3 y[rds] long
One Cristiall Shambileire w[th]: 10 Branches
& guilt Socketts w[th]: 2 knots of Ribands
One Large Lookinglass, the frame garnish'd
w[th]: Silver 37 Inches deepe & 3 knots of Riband
over it
One Large Cabinett garnish't w[th]: brass &
inlay'd wth Tartle Shell
One Iron Grate in y[e] Chimney
One paire of Marble And Irons & One paire
of Doggs Richly garnisht wth Silver
One fire Shovell & Tonges garnisht w[th]: Silver
A History piece of 3 figures Over y[e] Chimney
in a guilt frame A Landskip of

Kilkenny Castle, County Kilkenny

Fishing over yᵉ Doore in a smale guilt frame
Titian & Aritin in a guilt frame
3 Smale heads of Ladys in guilt frames
& 2 Landskips between them
Over yᵉ Windows 3 long pieces of Polodore

Chynah in ẙ Same Roome &c

One Large flowerpott
3 Large Jarrs whole at the Topps
5 Round Dᵒ: wᵗʰ Covers
1 Large Tea pott garnisht
2 Smale Bakers
2 Smale Deep Jarrs
1 Chinah Tea Kettle
1 Smale Tea pott garnisht
18 other pieces of Chynah

In ẙ Aulcove

5 Pieces of Tapesty Hangings Story of
Backonells 9 foot deep
5 pieces of green Damask Hangings
fringed Round wᵗʰ: Copper fringe
2 green Damask drawup Window Curtins
part Copper & some gould & Silver fringe
& Cornices to them
Two white Damask drawup Window Curtins
fringed wᵗʰ Silk fringe & Cornuces to yᵐ
A Bed-Stead wᵗʰ: a riseing Tester richly
Carved.
A Pair of black Balls
A Green Damask Beds ffurnitᵉ richly made
up wᵗʰ gold & silver fringe all much tarnish'd
8 Carved guilt Chaires frames Stuft they
did belong to yᵉ purple Moheare Bed . . . . .
8 purple Serge Chayre Cases, 8 green damaske
Chaire Cases fringe Suitable to yᵉ green Bed
10 round Stooles wᵗʰ: black frames & false
bottoms made of yᵉ Same Damask & fring'd
wᵗʰ Edging fringe
A Feather Bed & Bolster of Smale Stript
Flanders tick,
Two Blanketts
A Counterpan & 2 Smale pillows of
Indian worke finely wrought
2 quilt squobs wᵗʰ Cane bottoms
2 Jappand Scqobs wᵗʰ: gilt feet
One Old Tangeer Matt fix'd to yᵉ Alcove
Two Jappan'd Cabinetts wᵗʰ: Carved frames

One Table & stands very well Carv'd &
Silver'd wᵗʰ: leafe Silver & some part Coper
One Lookinglass 46 Inches deep, the frame
richly Carv'd & Silver'd wᵗʰ: leafe Silver
One Grate in yᵉ Chimney
A Picture over yᵉ Chimny of yᵉ 3 Young
Ladies, One paire of Lakerd And Irons
One pair of Smale Stands Silver'd
ffive large Chynah Dishes
Two High Round Chynah potts
Two Smale Chynah Basons wᵗʰ: Covers
Two Large Chinah Bakers
Two Large 8 Square botles
Two other Bottles not fellows
2 Paire of Small Botles
A Paire of 4 Square Bottles
A paire of Lesser Square Chynah Bottles
A paire of Smale flatt Bottles
A paire of halfe Bottles
2 Smale Deep Jarrs, one of them lesser
then yᵉ other
Two flaggons garnisht, they have been broke
but are mended
a blew bason garnisht wᵗʰ handles
a Cristiall glass wᵗʰ: a Cover garnisht
Two white Tea Kettles wᵗʰ: handles
18 other Pieces of Chynah
Severall of yᵉ above Chynah has been broke
but are Mended

Upstaires from ẙ Alcove
to her Graces Clossett

One yᵉ Right hand two Smale Landskips
Up yᵉ Staires a flower piece, Under that
a fruit piece, Under that a Landskip
Under that a piece wᵗʰ: Smale figures, by that
a Larg picture the Sacrifise to Jupiter
Under it a piece of Maskeraide
A Piece of King Ashures
Under it a Landskip of Smale figures
A Large Picture of Venus & Addonais
in a Large frame

Over ẙ Doore Entring into ẙ Clossett

A Long narrow Landskip of each side a Smale One
Under each of them a Large narrow Landskip
Under them two Square Landskips under yᵐ
two Smale Landskips

On the Right Hand

3 Landskips & a very Smale One all one over
another

Over y̆ᵉ Doore to y̆ᵉ Terriss

One Large narrow Landskip & one Smale one
on each Side
Two upright Landskips to each side of yᵉ Doore
Two Smale Ones Under them
Two Carv'd & gilt Sconces wᵗʰ Sockets

In Her Graces Clossett

All hung wᵗʰ Crimson & white Damaske fring'd
all round about wᵗʰ: green Silke fringe
One Coutch, the head board & foot Coverd & guilt
One Canvis Quilt, One ffeather Bed & Bolster
fill'd with curl'd haire, The Counterpan & bases
and Tenn Cusons all of Silver & green Silk &
Velvett fringe wᵗʰ: green Silk fringe & 2 little
pillows wᵗʰ Tossells Suitable to them,
One Guilt Pedistall for Chynah
One Cabinett frame garnisht wᵗʰ Brass
Six gilt frames for Cushons,
One Smale Wallnuttree Table
One Smale dressing Lookinglass garnisht
wᵗʰ brass, Two Paire of white Damask
Window Curtains & Vallens fringed round wᵗʰ
green Silk fringe & brass Rods
One Lookingglass 26 Inches deep & a gilt
frame, yᵉ frame much damaged & the
glass Milldewd
One Pan for Charcole & one Iron Back
in the Chimney,
Two Pair of Steele And Irons garnisht wᵗʰ
brass & guilt, One Pair of Tonges
& fireshovell
Over against & by the Glass Cupboard
Elizabeth Dutchess of Ormondes Picture
A History Piece of foure figures
in yᵉ Window on yᵉ left hand
Over yᵉ Chimney a Landskip of Building
over against yᵉ Chimney 2 round figures &
4 Landskips in guilt frames & One print
in a black frame about the Dutchess of
Richmonds Picture

In y̆ᵉ Windʷ: Opposite y̆ᵉ Doore

A Large Piece of yᵉ first Lady Arran
One Ovall Picture of Our Saviour at
the River Jourdan
The Earle of Arrans Picture
The Countess of Longford
Two Smale Landskips in Ovall frames
Our Saviour & the Virgin Mary a
Smale Picture
A Smale Picture done Upon Aggot
One each Side of that a Smale Picture
Some of the Ancestors of the ffamily
Three Smale Landskips under them
Six Smale Landskips & figures by the Lady
Arans Picture
The Old Duke of Ormonde in Cryans
King Charles yᵉ first in Needleworke
The Earle of Ossory in Cryans
Under that a Smale Landskip

Over y̆ᵉ Clossett Doore

One Piece of Building wᵗʰ Smale figures
Under that a Smale Piece of a Prospect of a Church
One yᵉ Left hand the Picture of Sophynizbah
Under that Sᵗ: Katherine

Over y̆ᵉ Little Clossett Doore

A Piece of Prospect wᵗʰ Small figures
Uppon yᵉ Doore a piece of ffruite
A Landskip of a fountain over yᵉ Chimney
Sᵗ Katherine in Silk by it
A Magdallen
Uppon yᵗ 8 pedestall 19 Pictures in Square
gilt frames
Within yᵉ Clossett Doore a Deaths Head
Over the Doore in yᵉ little Clossett a Dutch
Piece

*One the Left hand going in to the
Little Cossett*

A Landskip & on yᵉ Doore a Landskip
ffive Smale Pictures on yᵉ left hand
Over yᵉ Window a Picture wᵗʰ: 3 figures
On yᵉ Right hand two Copper Pieces One
of them Susanah & the Elders & one of
David & Goliah

Kilkenny Castle, County Kilkenny

A Smale Pictur of King Charles ye 2^d: and
three others under it
A smale Wallnuttree box garnisht wth Brass
One Small Indian Cabbinett
One Table Cover'd wth: Silver
One Guilt Table cover'd wth Velvett

Chynah in her Graces Clossett

5 large Jarrs wth Lids 3 of y^m: has Silver Tops
3 Paire of Lesser Jarrs
7 Large dishes of w^{ch}: two is broken & one broke
& mended
One Large Olivecolor Punch bole garnisht wth
brass guilt
Two Large blew & white punch bowles
One Large blew Chinah Dish
One white Chinah Cup wth: a Cover
Two paire of Large Bakers

Chynah Over ẙ Chimney in ẙ bigg Clossett

14 Smale Pieces of Chynah & 2 figures & a red Earthen
Cup on a foot ye Cup Crakt & mended

Over ẙ Chimney wth: in ẙ Glass Doores

10 Pieces of Chynah and a Large Bloodstone
upon a Pedistall
9 Smale Agatt Cups one of y^m: upon a foot
52 other pieces of Chynah of Severall Sorts & sises
2 painted glass sweet Bottles

Bookes in her Graces Clossett

One Bible in q^{rto} in two p^{rts}
Two Large Comon Prayre Bookes richly bound
wth Cutts
Two other Comon prayre Bookes richly bound
Two comon prayre Bookes in q^{rto} in blew turkey
leather
D^r: Littletons Sermons in fol^{io}
The Tryall of Mr Morden in fol^{io}
D^r: Masons Booke ⎫
Mr Eulin Siluia ⎬ Small Fol^{io}
The Saveing Star ⎭
The Treaty of a Minister ⎫
Woodfords Psalms. ⎬ In Quarto
A Dromatick Romance ⎭
Doct^r Cunings Lent fast
Mountagues Devout Esayes

The Parable of ye Pillgrim
Dr Ashtons Seasonable Apology
The Wonders of the Peake
The Ladyes Calling
The Government of ye Tongue & ye art of
Contentment
The Lively Oracle
The decay of Christian Piety
God the King and ye Church
S^r: Wm Temples History of ye Netherlands
Doc^r. Stillingfleets Anime Devertions
A Discourse of ffriendship
Doc^r Saules Catholick Faith
Faire warneing to ye World
Andrew Saules Sermons
The Coronation Sermon
ye Cases of Scandell

In ẙ Passage goeing to ẙ Teriss

In M^{rs}: Butlers Lodging Roome

Hung wth: Stript Drugitt
6 board bottom Chaires & six Cushons of the same
of the Roome
One Table Bed: stead
One Feather Bed & Bolster
One Quilt
4 Curtins & a Counterpan & Carpet of ye Same of y^e
Hangings
A hanging Shelfe
One Payre of And Irons wth Brasses
One Smale ½ round Grate
One little Table
One Old Brockadell Carpett white & Green

In ẙ Clossett

4 Drugitt Curtins Suitable to ye Hangings of
ye Roome & 3 Rods

*Pictures in ẙ Passage goeing to
ẙ Draweing Roome*

Two Long Picture of Pollodore
8 Square Landskips of Buildings

The Passage up to ỹ Gallery

4 Pictures of the Sences
One other Large Dutch Piece
Eight Landskips in Black frames
One Picture of a Ship
A Piece of Prospective of a Church
The Story of Syrus
One Old man Suckin very old & p^rt: broke
A Whinged Cupid
A History piece of ffive figures
One of ye Sences of feeleing
A Landskip of One of ye Kings Houses

In ỹ Gallery

13 Ellbow Chaires Stufft
24 Bak Chaires of ye Same all Cased w^th: yallow
& red figured Velvett
37 yallow Serge Cases for them all
10 Paire of yellow Searge Curtins
One p^r: of Large Curtins of ye Same of ye End Wind^w
11 Lakered Curtin Rods
3 Cristiall branches hung w^th: three chaines
Severall of ye Drops lost & most of ye branches
of One of them Broken
11 Carv'd guilt Sconces w^th: Birds p^rt: of y^m: broke
2 Lookeing Glasses 30 Inches deep, each w^th
guilt frames much damaged
Two paire of Old guilt Stands
One Large Cradle Grate in ye Chimney
One p^r: of Large Marble And Irons Black and White
One Large guilt Pedistall w^th: 3 Carv'd Rams heads
One very Large Jarr Covered & garnisht w^th: the
figure of Neptuan on ye Cover
One Large Cestern Containing 40 Gall^s:
3 guilt Pedistalls for Chynah to Stand on
5 Large Irons w^th: Covers & brass figures on ye Covers
of 4 them
One other Jarr or Tunn
One Large Chynah blew & white dish
One green Chynah Dish a bitt of it broken off
One blew & white Chynah bason a piece of it wanting
One paire of Wooden Japan'd Bakers wth Loose
pewter Insides

Pictures

The halfe Circle att ye upper end of ye Gallery a
flora & little boyes

A Large Picture of Venetian Senators
A picture of ye Jew of One Side
A picture of Still Life on ye other Side
Two Landskips under them

On ỹ South Side & to ỹ great Window

King Charles ye 2^d. at Length
S^r: Anthony Vandike on ye One Side
Under it a narrow Picture of Jno: Baptist
Duke Hamilton on ye other Side
Under it a picture of Our Lady & Saviour in
a Garland of Flowers
King Charles ye 1st
King Charles ye 1^d [*recte* st] his Queen ⎫
The L^d: D^ke. of Ormonde   ⎬ att Length
The Lady ffrancis Buttler   ⎭
The Young Dutchess of Richmond ⎫
The Old Earle of Ossory |
The Duke of Richmond |
The Dutchess of Richmond   ⎬ att Length
The Earle of Strafford in Armor |
The Earle of Dezmond |
The Hylander in Scotch Habitt   ⎭

Thomas Earle of Ormond in Scotch Armor
The Lady Pagetts Daughter under it
Prince Henry at Length
Thos Earle of Ormond in another Dress
Under it ye Lady Hasteings Mother
Mercury & ye Sabian woman at Length
Judeth & holy fernuses head
Under it James Earle of Ormonde
Over ye Lookinglass a piece of Prospective of
a Church

On ỹ North Side to ỹ Great Window

Queen Katherine at Length
The Former Dutchess of Yorke on ye one Side   ⎫
The Lady Dowager of Ossory on ye other Side   ⎬ ½ Lengths
Under them the Queen of Bohemia and the   ⎭
Earle of Ossory in Ovall fframes
The Late Duke of Yorke at Length
The Late Dutches of Yorke at Length
The Earle of Strafford & Mr Phillip Maneren
in one piece
The Lady Chesterfield on one Side
Lord Ossory on ye other Side

Kilkenny Castle, County Kilkenny

Pictures Continues in ỹ Gallery

Under Lady Chesterfield Joanes ffrobenius
Under L^d: Ossory . . . . S^r: Nicholas Poyntz
The Earle of Devonshire & Countess ⎫
Lord Beaverwart   ⎬ halfe Lengths
Lady Arlinton
Earle of Aron   ⎭
Under them an Old woman fleaing a Shock Dogg
Two Old mens heads
A Piece of ffruite & a Munkie
Lady Mary Hamilton
S^t. ffrances Head
A Piece of ffruite
Over ye Doore an Italian Woman
One Each Side a fflower Piece
Near them a Smale Piece of Our Lady & Saviour
And a Smale piece of an Old mans head
The Virgin Mary & Our Saviour in her Lap &
3 other figures in a Large piece
Under it two Pictures of ffowles
A Large piece of Malchizadeck & other figures
Vulcan & Venus & Severall Cupitts ⎫ from
trying Armor, this is onely a Strainein frame ⎬ Dunmore
Underneath a Picture of King Charles the 1st.'s
three Children
A Large piece of Vanity being a Woman Playing on a
base Viall & a boy on ye other Embleins of Vanity this
is in a white frame from Donmore
Underneath St Jno Baptist's head in one Piece & a
little boys head in another piece
All ye forementioned pictures in ye Gallery Except 2 are
in Carved & guilt frames

In ỹ Clossett in ỹ Gallery

One Smale Table
5 Crimson Velvett Chaires w^th: old bayes Cases
One ffrench Carpett of Crimson Velvett
One Paire of Old Callicoe Curtins & Rods
Over ye Table a Landskip Mildyed
One Each Side a Smale Picture wth figures &
Glass before them.
The head of Mr Hobbs on a Coper Plate
A Smale Landskip over ye Chimney
A Picture of fflowers before ye Chimney
A Firepan
A Large Earthen Jarr & two double Bottles
one of them broke

10 Pair of yallow Damask Curtins for ye Windows
& one Larg p^r for ye End Window

*In ỹ Roome att ỹ North
End of ỹ Gallery*

Hung w^th: 4 Pieces of Fine forestwork Tapestry
hangings wth Smale figures 7 foot & ½ deep
One Bedstead w^th: a riseing Teaster & a Sackcloath
bottom
One flock Mattress
One Feather Bed & bolster of Striped tickin
One Holland Quilt
Three Blankets very Old
The ffurniture of ye Bed of Arora & white
Damask containing 4 Curtins, 4 Cantoones
head cloath & Counterpaine, riseing Teaster,
head board & headcloath Embroider'd w^th: Smale
                                          fringe
Cases of ye Same Damask for 4 Elbo Chaires
& six backt Chaires
10 Taffety Cases for ye Chaires, ye ffurniture
garnish'd w^th: black blew & white fringe
4 Cups wth Sprigs to ye Bed
4 guilt feet
10 Chaires w^th: Carv'd guilt frames formerly
belonging to ye Allcove
One Grate in ye Chimney
One Iron Back
One Pair of Tonges & ffireshovell of
brass but broken
One Large Landskip over ye Chimney guilt fram'd
One other Landskip Over ye Doore
One paire of white Damask Window Curtins
3 y^rds & ½ deep & a Rod
One black Table & stands garnisht w^th: brass
One Lookeinglass of ye Same 31 Inches Deep
In ye Clossett all hung w^th: green Drugitt
One Cross footed Bedstead in ye other Clossett
One Quilt and Bolster
One Blankett & one white Rugg

In ỹ Roome at ỹ Top of ỹ Great Staires

Hung w^th: green & white Drugitt
One Canipie w^th: a folding Bed: stead
Two Curtins of ye Same, One Rod
One Feather Bed & Bolster
3 Old Blanketts very bad
One Little Table
3 Cushons

One Carpett & Counterpan Suitable to ye Bed
One Old Callicoe window Curtin & rod
One firepan & fireshovell
3 black board bottem Chaires

In Lady Marys Roome

One Bed:stead & a Sackcloath bottom
One ffeather Bed & Bolster
3 Large blanketts
One pillow
The Roome hung w^th: yellow Indian Sattin
printed wth black very Old & faded
The ffurniture of ye Bed of ye Same Containing 4
Curtins 4 Cantoones headcloath, Tester headboard
& Counterpan the Curtins lined w^th: yellow Sasnett
bases & 5 Cushons of ye same, fringed w^th: black and
yellow fringe, ye Top fringe lost
4 Clawes & 4 Cups much decayed
5 Black board Bottom Chaires
One Olive wood Table & Stands, ye Stands broke
One Lookinglass 25 Inches
4 Old yellow Serge Window Curtins & 2 rods
One Iron Back & doggs
One paire of Smale brass And Irons, one of them
broke
One ffireshovell & Tonges
Two Landskips over ye Doore & Chimney
One Redleather Closetoole & pan wants hinges
One little Armed Chaire
One pair of bellows & a hearth brush

In my Lady Elizabeths Roome

One Bed.stead and Saking bottom
4 blanketts
a good Feather bed & bolster
One pillow
The ffurniture of ye Bed very old Skye blew
Tabby containeing 4 Curtins head cloath tester
and Quilt of ye Same
4 Serge Case Curtins & 3 Rods
6 paire of buttons & Stringes
4 Smale Cups at ye 4 Corners of ye bed
The Roome hung w^th: old Stript Stuff
6 black board bottom Chaires w^th: 2 Cushons the
Same of the Bed
5 other Chaires covered wth blew Silke
One Stoole covered w^th: yellow Sattan
One Smale Table w^th: an Old Silke Carpett
One Old Table & Lookinglass 26 Inches deep

2 pair of Old Sasnett Window Curtins at ye Windows
lined w^th: blew Serge very bad
A pair of brass And Irons
One Fireshovell & a pair of Tonges w^th: Chimney
hookes
One paire of doggs
One paire of Bellows & Brush
Two Landskips in black frames

In y̆^e Lady Hariots Roome

One Bedstead w^th: a Sackin Bottom
One Feather Bed and bolster
One Mattress
4 blanketts and two pillows
The ffurniture of ye Bed of blew & white Drugitt
6 Cushons of ye hangings of ye Roome of ye same
6 black board bottom Chaires
One Olivewood Table & stands w^th: black leather
Covers
The Stands Covers wanting
Two paire of Old Sasnett Window Curtins lined w^th
blew Serge & 2 Curtin rods the Curtins very bad
One Glass in ye Chimney
One paire of Low And Irons & a paire of Doggs
One paire of Tonges & fireshovell
A Wicker Screen & Iron Stand
A Landskip over ye Chimney
One Little Stoole

In y̆^e Clossett

One Bed.stead w^th: a Sackin bottom
One Smale Feather bed & Bolster
Two Blanketts very bad
One Old Mattress Quilt
The Curtins & Counterpaine, headcloath & Tester
of Drugitt
One Smale Table
One board bottom Chaire
One Cubord wth turn'd doores
In ye little Clossett a Closetoole & pan

In y̆^e Roome Over Lady Marys Roome

One Bed.stead w^th: a Sackcloath bottom
One flock Mattress
One Feather Bed & Bolster
Two paire of blanketts One p^r: of y^m very bad
The Roome hung wth Drugitt
The ffurniture of ye Bed, 4 Curtins, headcloath

Kilkenny Castle, County Kilkenny

Teaster & Counterpan & six Cushons of yᵉ Same
Drugitt, 6 board bottom Chaires
One Armd Chaire of Brockadella
One Old Walnuttree Table wᵗʰ: a Carpett the Same
of yᵉ roome wᵗʰ: Stands
One Large Wallnuttree box upon a frame lined
One Old firescreen
One Grate
One fireshovell Tonges & fender
One paire of brass And Irons
One paire of Callicoe Window Curtins
One Old Serge Curtin in yᵉ Window
A Landskip over yᵉ Chimney

In ẙ Clossett

The Clossett hung wᵗʰ: Drugitt very Old & decayed
One Close Stoole & pan
One Smale Table
A Smale Cubert fixed in yᵉ Clossett

In ẙ Roome where ẙ Housemaids Lay

One Bed.Stead Matt & Cord
Some Old Cloath Curtins very bad
2 Old Banketts
One ffeather Bed & Bolster, One Sadcolord Rugg
A Smale Table
2 Leather Chaires, yᵉ bottom of one out
2 guilt Leather Chaires
One Smale Old Grate & A Fireshovell
A Landskip Over yᵉ Chimney
One Joynt Stoole

The Top of ẙ Territt

One Bed.Stead Cord & Matt
2 Old Serge Curtins on yᵉ Bed-stead
One flock bed & bolster
2 old blanketts
One good Cadow
One Table
3 Leather Chaires
One fixed grate & a fender

The South End of ẙ Gallery

One Japand Table & Stands & a Deale Cover
One Lookinglass 32 Inches but broke
2 paire of white Damask Curtins to yᵉ Windows
One pʳ: of 2 breadths & one pʳ: of 3 breadths and

3 Lakerd rods
One Iron back & Grate
One pʳ: of Tonges & fireshovell of brass
One Brass fender
One Picture of Europia over yᵉ Chimney
One Picture over the Doore of 3 figures & a shipp
The Roome hung wᵗʰ: 4 pieces of Tapestry hangings
large figures 13 foot deep yᵉ story of Detious
One Bed.stead wᵗʰ: a Sacking bottom
4 guilt feet
An Ordinary Feather Bed bolster & pillow
3 good Blanketts
One Holland Quilt
One Crimson & Goldcolord Damask ffurniture
garnisht wᵗʰ tuffted Silke fringe containing 4
Cantoone Curtins A Tester Inward Vallens
headcloath head board counterpaine & bases
8 damask Chaire Cases Suitable 9 paire of buttons
& 8 Strings
4 Cups & Sprigs
One Case Curtin Rod
4 Red Serge Case Curtins
8 Chaire Cases of yᵉ Same Serge
One Tangeer Matt under yᵉ Bed very much worne
The Clossett hung wᵗʰ Drugitt
One Close Stoole & pann
One paire of bellows & a brush for yᵉ hearth
2 Armd Chaires & 6 bakt Chaires

The Drugitt Roome Oposite ẙ Wardrobe

One Bed.Stead wᵗʰ: a Sacking Bottom
One Feather Bed & Bolster
3 blanketts
The ffurniture of yᵉ bed of green & white Drugitt
4 Curtins Counterpaine, headcloath & tester
A Carpett & 5 Cushons
yᵉ hangings of yᵉ Roome of yᵉ Same all very bad
One Table & 2 Stands
5 black board bottom Chaires
One Old Close Stoole & Pan
A firepan wᵗʰ: brass knobs
A Paire of Tonges fireshovell & Poker

In ẙ Clossett

Hung round wᵗʰ red & white Drugitt
2 Cushons of yᵉ Same
One Smale Table & Carpett of yᵉ same
2 black bottom Chaires & a hanging Shelfe

Goeing Down Staires

4 Landskips; 3 in black & Lackered frames
and one in black

A : G
The first Roome in the
Round Tower

Hung wth: 5 pieces of Old Tapestry hangings
One yall^w harnum Cushion
One Grate
a fireshovell Tonges & fender
A Table & a red Cloath Carpett
One Bed-stead wth: a Sackcloath bottom
A Suite of Curtins headcloath & baces of Old
Indian Silk very Old & much broken and a
Callicoe Tester
One Feather Bed Bolster & pillow
Three Old blanketts bad Ones
One white Rugg
Eight Old gilt leather Chaires Some of them
very bad ye frames broken
One Old Brockadella Arm'd Chaire
One O^{ld}: Japan'd Arm'd Chaire & Damask Cushon
Two Smale Pictures
Two Old Darnix Window Curtins
A Smale Lookinglass
An Old Wallnuttree Cabinett on a frame
One Close Stoole, Chaire & a pan

A : H
In y̆^e Next Roome in y̆^e Round
Tower

One Bedstead Cord & Matt & part of a
broken Old holland Quilt
One Old Feather Bed & Bolster
One White Rugg
Two Blanketts one of y^m very bad
One Table & 2 Old Chaires
4 Curtins of Coper Color'd printed Stuff wth
fringe a Top

A : J
The Next Roome

One Bedstead Cord & Matt
One Feather Bed & Bolster
Two Old Blanketts very bad Ones
One Red Rugg

4 Curtins of green printed Stuff
A Table and two Old Chayres
One furme

A K
The Councill Chamber

Hung wth: 5 Pieces of Tapestry hangings the
Story of Donquicksott lined wth: Canvis
4 Old Callicoe Window Curtins & 2 Rods
One Grate the Back burnt out
A Brass Fireshovell & Tonges
A Lookinglass 39 Inches deep in a black frame
A black Table & stands ye Stands wants mending
12 Silke Brockadella Chaires & Old Serge Covers
A Valvett Easey Chaire & Damask Cushon
A Landskip of Beasts over ye Chimney

In y̆^e Clossett

hung wth: gilt Leather
Three gilt Leather Chaires
A Smale Table
One Smale Spanish Table Cover'd

The Bedchamber

Hung wth: 2 pieces of Forest worke Tapestry
hangings lined wth: Canvis 9 foot deep
One Olive wood table & paire of Stands wth
leather Covers
One Bedstead wth: a Sacking bottom
One Feather Bed & Bolster
One Holland Quilt
One Paire of Large Blanketts
One Clouded Satten Beds ffurniture wth: Silke
fringe containing 4 Curtins headcloath Tester
double bases 4 Cantoones the Bed lined wth
a Cherry Color'd Sasnett & a Quilt Suitable
much decayd
9 paire of buttons & Strings to ye Curtins
One Carved head board washt
4 Chaires
4 Color'd Satten Cases
4 falce Cases for ye Serge of red Serge
a Case Curtin rod & 4 Case Curtins of ye Same Serge
4 Cups Covered wth Clouded Satten
4 midle pieces wth fringe & Tasells Suitable
to the bed
4 Sprigs of fflowers for ye Tops of ye Cups

Two Window Curtins of blew Taffety Old and much broken lined wth: blew Serge
One Curtin Rod
One gilt leather Close Stoole & pan
One Grate ye Bottom Worne out
A Brass fireshovell & Tonges
A Paire of Brass And Irons
3 Pictures fixed over ye doores & Chimney

In ẙ Clossett wth: in this Roome

p^{rt}. hung wth: Old Indian Silk very much worne out & broken
4 black boarded bottom Chaires & 4 old Cushons
A Smale Old Table
A pair of Low old Stands inlay'd wth: tortisshell

His Graces Clossett in M^r: Martin Baxters Charge

One Table
One green Cloath Carpett
One Grate fireshovell & Tonges
4 Back Chaires wth: gilt frames & blew Damask Cases
One paire of Bellows
The Books as by Cataloge

In ẙ New Passage

Seven Landskips 4 in black frames & ye other 3 in black & Lacker'd

The Roome over ẙ Councell Chamb^r

5 Pieces of Antwerp hangings, the Story of Cyrus lined wth: Canvis
A Beadstead wth. a riseing Tester & sacking bottom
A Feather Bed & Bolster
One paire of Large Blankets
The ffurniture of ye Bed of haire Camblett lined wth Straw Colered Taffety Containeing 4 Curtins, Vallans, Teaster, headcloath Quilt
headboard
and bases
4 gilt feet & Cups & Spriggs
Cases for 2 Arm'd Chaires & 6 backt Stooles of ye same Camblett much worne
Eight Chaires wth a wallnuttree frames
One Black Table & Stands

A Lookinglass 26 Inches deep in an Ebony & tortishell frame
2 yallow Sarge Window Curtins and 2 Rods
One firegrate & a p^r: of Tonges and Fireshovell
One Large Picture of S^t: John & a Lamb over the Chimney
A Close Stoole & pan

In the Clossett

Hung with Drugitt
A Folding Bedstead Coard & Matt
A Canopy frame and a Curtin Rod wth: a Vallen & headcloath of Old yallow Serge
A Feather Bed and Bolster
One Old Blankett and a Caddow
One Table
A Window Curtin & A Rod

The Roome Over the Bedchamber

One Bedstead wth: a Sackin bottom
One Feather Bed, Bolster and pillow
A Paire of Large Old Blanketts
The ffurniture of ye Bed of green & white Druggitt containeing 4 Curtins headcloath Teaster & Counterpaine
The hangings of ye Roome & Window Curtins and a Carpett of ye Same
One Curtin Rod
One Old Table
6 board bottom Chaires One of them broken
One Smale halfe round Grate
One paire of brass And Irons
One paire of Tonges and Fireshovell

In the Clossett

One Folding Bedstead Cord & Matt
One flock Bed & Bolster
Three Smale Blankets
A Canopy & 2 Curtins of harnum Damask
One Curtin Rod
One Deale Press
The Clossett hung wth: Indian Callicoe p^{rt}: broke
One Close Stoole & pan

The Roome Over his Graces Clossett

hung with 4 pieces of Antwerp hangings
One Bedstead wth: a Sackin Bottom

Three Old Blanketts two of them Large the other
a very bad One
One holland Quilt
One Feather Bed and Bolster
One Old Crimson Damask ffurniture containing
4 Curtins headcloath Teaster, Baces & Counterpaine
4 Cups & plumes of Feathers Smale & Old
One paire of white Serge Window Curtins two
breadths in One & One in ye Other
One Curtin Rod
One halfe round Grate
One Old Picture of Flowers, ye frame in pieces
and the Picture verry foule
One Old Gray Cloath Chaire
Two foulding Elbow Chaires & One Stoole Suitable
to ye Bed
One little foot Stoole of guilt Leather
One Old Ebony Table
One Old Arme Cane Chaire & a Stuff Cushon

The Passage on ye Same floore

3 Pictures being 2 Landskips & a ffaulkner in
black frames

Upermost Story ẙ^e 1st Roome

One Bed.Stead Coard & Matt
One fflock Bed & Boulster very Bad
One Caddow
One Blankett
One Gilt Leather Chayre

2^d Roome Upermost Story

One Lath Bottom Bedstead
One Old Straw Bed
One Smale Feather Bed Bolster & pillow
Two Smale Blanketts
One White Rugg
One Suite of Curtins of red Cloath and Brockadell
Striped
A Deepe SIlk fring round the Top
The Roome all hung w^{th}: gilt Leather
4 gilt Leather Chaires
One Table & a Carpett ye same of ye Curtins
Two Smale Window Curtins
One fixed Grate
A fireshovell & Tonges
One Wainscott Press

In the third Roome

two halfe headed Bed-Steads
two flock Beds One flock Bolster
3 Blanketts
One Red Rugg & One red Caddow
One Large Canopy & two Curtins
One Table
One guilt Leather Chaire & one other Chaire
One Paire of Doggs wth Brasses

In ẙ^e 4th Roome

One halfe headed Bedstead
One flock Bed & Boulster very bad
One Blankett
One Caddow
Two gilt Leather Chaires
One Little Table
One little Canopy w^{th}: 2 red Serge Curtins

In ẙ^e 5th Roome

Hung w^{th}: gilt Leather
4 Gilt Leather Chayres
One Bed-stead, Cord & Matt
One Feather Bed and Bolster
One Blankett a very bad one
One yallow Quilt very Old & broken
One White Rugg
The Curtins headcloath & ~~two~~ Teaster of green
printed Stuff
One Payre of Doggs w^{th}: Brasses
One Payre of Tonges & fireshovell
One Deale Table

In ẙ^e 6th Roome

One halfe headed Bed-stead Cord & Matt
One Flock Bed & Bolster
One Old Red Counterpaine
One Blankett very Bad
One Table
One Old Stoole & a Chaire

In ẙ^e Roome over ẙ^e New Larder

One Bedstead Cord & Matt
One ffeather Bed and Boulster
One Old Red Rugg
Two Blanketts

Kilkenny Castle, County Kilkenny

Two Leather Chayres
4 Curtins headcloath & Teaster of Orange & white Drugitt much worne & broken, the Teaster wore quite out
One little furme
One little Table
One Desque wth drawers
One Loose Grate mooveable

In ẙ Roome over ẙ ffrench Kitchin

One Bed.Stead Cord and Matt
One good ffeather Bed and Boulster
One Blankett
Two Caddows
The Curtins Quite Broke
One good Leather Chaire & 2 other Old Chaires
One Table
One Grate

In the Next Roome

One Bedstead Cord & Matt
One ffeather Bed & Boulster
One Blankett a bad one
One Old green Rugg
One little Caddow
Two Linnen Curtins
One Old Table
One Old Wooden Chaire

In ẙ Next Roome

One halfe headed Bed.Stead Cord & Matt
One flock Bed and Bolster
One Smale Blankett
One White Caddow & One green One
One Old boarded bottom Chayre

In ẙ Under Buttlers Roome

One Old Bedstead coard & Matt
One Feather Bed & bolster ye Bolster very bad
Two Caddows
One Old Blankett
Some Old Kidermaster nayled about ye Bed
One little Table
One Chayre

In ẙ Roome over ẙ Pastry (Viz^t)
the Clarke of ẙ Kitchins Roome

One Bedstead Cord & Matt
One good Feather Bed & Bolster
One good white Rugg
One Caddow
Two Blanketts
Two furmes
Two gilt Leather Chaires & one other Leather Chaire
One Table & a piece of an Old Turkey workt Carpett
One Suite of yellow Serge Curtins wth Silke fringes round the Top
One Grate & fender
One Smale box wth p^rtitions for writeings

In ẙ Usher of ẙ Halls Roome

One halfe headed Bedstead Cord & Matt
One very Old flock Bed & Bolster
One Caddow

In ẙ Roome over ẙ Clarke of ẙ Kitchins Roome

One halfe headed Bedstead Cord & Matt
One Very Old flock Bed & Bolster
2 Very Old Caddows & one Old Blanket worne out

In ẙ Scullery

One halfe headed Bed-Stead
One flock bed & Bolster
One Caddow
One blankett
One Cuboard and Rak to dry plates
One Large Coper fixed
One Little Iron Grate
One Oake Chest for plate
2 dressers Shelves & a joyne Stoole frame
One Large Tubb for wrenching of Plate
17 Large pewter dishes of w^ch: 6 is lesser then y^e rest
6 Lesser dishes of severall Sises
9 Intermesses
4 Lesser Intermesses
10 pye plates of Severall Sises
25 plates
9 Tinn Covers for dishes

In $\overset{e}{y}$ Pastery

2 Dressers
One Iron Colerake
One wooden Peile
One Iron Oven Stop^r
One Rowlin pinn

In $\overset{e}{y}$ Dry Larder

Two Dressers fixed
A Rayle wth Iron hookes to hang meat on
the Inner Roome done round wth Shelves

In $\overset{e}{y}$ Wet Larder

One Leadon Cestern
A Trough Covered Lead
One Old Dresser
A Standing Rack to hang meat on
a hanging Shelfe
a Chopping block

In $\overset{e}{y}$ Great Kitchin

One Large Iron Range & One Fender
One Lesser fender
4 Iron Rings & Grates to y^e Stove holes
One plate of Iron to hold before y^e Turnspitts
7 Large Spitts & one for a Chyne of Beefe
2 Smale birdspitts, One Leadon Cestorn
One very Large Dresser & a Smale loose Dresser
A Large payre of Iron Racks And a Lesser p^r
of Ditto

In $\overset{e}{y}$ ffrench Kitchin

One large Iron Stand to hold the Dishes
before y^e fire
One Iron Firepoker
One Large firshovell wth: a wooden handle
2 flesh forcks one of y^m Short for a wooden handle
One Iron Dripin pan
One very bad Small Dripin pan
2 paireing Shovells for Wooden handles
2 Iron Slicers
2 Iron Cleeves
11 Smale Tevitts to sett over ye stew holes
One Large Iron Trevitt y^t: holds a boyler
One Large gridd Iron & two lesser ones
One Bellmettle Mort & Iron pestall

One Coper boate fashon pan & 2 Covers
Two Brass Dishes & a patty pan
One Deep Brass Cullender
One brass bottom for a fish Kettle
One brass Scimmer
One Iron Ladle & a brass One
One Coper fixed y^e bottom worne very bad
One Coper Kettle wth: 2 handles
One Old brass Kettle y^e bottom worne out, quite
Useless

In $\overset{e}{y}$ Larder by $\overset{e}{y}$ ffrench Kitchon

One Large press & one Large Table
Dresser Shelves round y^e Roome
One furme & 4 hanging Shelves
2 Smale box wth p^{r}titions & a salt box
One Chopping Block

In $\overset{e}{y}$ Pantry

One Press for Lining
One Candle Chest
One Ring for Bread
A Cuboard against y^e wall to hold plate
One furme
One Large Dresser wth 2 drawers
One brass Sconce

In $\overset{e}{y}$ bigg Celler & $\overset{e}{y}$ little Roome by it

3 Rank's of Stillings
a Tubb wth: 3 feet to wash glasses, 2 Old black Jacks
a Deale Rack to dreyne Bottles
2 Smale Coper Cestrons
A Table & 3 furmes
A good face brush

In $\overset{e}{y}$ Great Hall

6 Tables
A Large Round Table wth: falling Leaves
A Large Table frame & a foalding Ovall Leafe
One Other Deale Table
10 Carv'd wooden Chaires
One Large Cuboard & a Small Cupboard
12 furmes Some of them broken
One Strong fixed grate
A fireshovell
An Old Baithing Tubb

Kilkenny Castle, County Kilkenny

In y̆ᵉ Roome Over y̆ᵉ Pantry

One Bedstead Cord & Matt
One Feather Bed and Bolster
3 Old Blankets
One white Rugg
A Suite of Old printed Stuff Curtins very bad
3 Old Rushy Leather Chayres
One little Table

In y̆ᵉ Darke Spicery

One Bedstead cord & Matt
One ffeather Bed & Bolster very Old & broken
One Blankett & a white Rugg
One Bad Chaire & a Stoole
One little Table fastned on Tressells
One wooden Stove Cubboard
14 red Earthen pans of Severall Sorts
12 Glass Salvers

In y̆ᵉ Confectionʳˢ: Roome

3 Wooden Stoves
2 Old Wooden Chayres & a Stoole
2 Old Leather Chayres Broken
one Grate   One pʳ of Tonges
one little Table
3 Trevitts one Trevitt grate Over yᵉ stove hole
A Wooden Squirt for yᵉ Confectionʳˢ Use
A Large Cubboard to hold Desarts

The Kitchin Doore & y̆ᵉ Back Staires

3 Glass Lanthornes

In y̆ᵉ Porters Lodge

One Bedstead Cord & Matt
One Old Feather Bed & bolster
One White Ruge very bad
2 Caddows One of them very bad
One Red Chayre & 2 Joynt Stooles
One Table
One furme
A suite of Old Curtins & headcloath of green printed Stuff
One little Table One Old Chayre in yᵉ out Lodge
One Grate fireshovell, Tonges & fender
One Muskett

2 Blunderbuses, one of yᵐ wants a lock
2 Large round Lanthornes one of yᵐ Broken

In y̆ᵉ Housekeepʳˢ: Lodging Roome

One Bedstead Cord & Matt
A Suite of Old green Cloath Curtins, headcloath Teaster & Vallens & Curtin Rods
One Feather Bed Bolster & pillow
2 blanketts
One Silke Blanketts
One Green Rugg

{ *The Roome hung wᵗʰ: 3 Sumpture Cloaths wᵗʰ his Graces Armes, & one Piece Tapestry hangings The Story Ahashuarus*

One Small Table
Six Old Silk Brockadella Chayres
One Lookinglass wᵗʰ a black & Tortishell frame the glass 20 Inches deep
A fixed Grate
A fireshovell Tonges & fender
One paire of green Serge Window Curtins & a rod
Two Old Quilted Cushons

In y̆ᵉ Next Roome on yᵗ floore

A halfe headed Bedstead Matt & Cord
An Old Feather Bed & Bolster
2 Old Blanketts & a white Rugg
A flock Bed & Bolster
A White Rugg & a Caddow
One Cubboard
One grate fixed
One fender
4 brass Candlesticks
54 other brass Candlesticks of Severall Sorts
6 Tinn Candlesticks
4 brass Snuffer frames & Snuffers
22 white Earthen Chamber potts
20 Ditto Earthen Basons
4 Other Earthen Basons

In y̆ᵉ Roome over y̆ᵉ last Roome

A flock Bed & Bolster
an Old Red Rugg
2 Old white Ruggs very bad
3 Old matted bottom Chayres

The Kitchon belonging to y̆ᵉ Housekeepʳ

One Grate wᵗʰ Cheekes yᵉ Cheekes very bad
One Gridle fireshovell & a pʳ: of Tonges
2 Trevitts for Stove holes
2 Old brass warming pans
frames of 2 Old Red Cloath Chayres, one of
them the bottom is boarded
One little Table
One Old Sauce pan & one little Kettle
One Iron pott
Two Old Still Topps
Two Old Pewter Salt Sellers

In y̆ᵉ Halle belonging to y̆ᵉ Housekeepʳ

Six Rushey Leather Chayres
One Deale Table
2 Old Elbo Chayres of blew figured Velvett
One Horse to dry Cloaths on
A fixed Grate
A paire of Tonges & a fireshovell
A paire of Smale green Serge Window Curtins
and a rod
A Press to hold Linnen

Linnen in y̆ᵉ Housekeepʳˢ: Charge

2 narrow Dutch Diaper Table Cloathes 5 yʳᵈˢ: _ long
2 broad Dutch Diaper table Cloathes 4 yʳᵈ & ½ long
3 Diaper table Cloathes 2 of yᵐ 3 yʳᵈˢ & ¼ yᵉ other
four yʳᵈˢ & a ¼ long
5 Diaper Side board Cloaths
7 Paire of Course Irish Sheetes
5 Paire of finer Sheetes
12 Corse Rubbers

In y̆ᵉ Roome Over y̆ᵉ Gate House﹍

One Bed.stead Cord & Matt
One Feather Bed Bolster & pillow
One Blankett
One white Rugg
A Sute of Old yellow Serge Curtins, headcloath
Teaster, Vallens & Baces
Two Tables
One Large Iron bound Trunke
Two Brockadella Chayres
One Old Arme Cane Chayre & Cushon﹍
One Old Am'd Searge Chayre
One Old Red Cloath Chayre

One Fireshovell & Tonges
One Large Map of yᵉ World much decayed
One yellow Serge Curtin & rod for yᵉ Window

In y̆ᵉ Outward Clossett

A Smale Table & Chayre

In the Next Roome

One Bed-Stead Cord & Matt
4 Curtins headcloath & teaster of Irish Stuff
fringed round wᵗʰ: worsted fringe
One Feather Bed and Bolster
One payre of Blankets
One White Rugg
One Old Blanket very bad
4 guilt Leather Chaires & One Stoole
One Stoole of Stuff yᵉ same of yᵉ Bed
One Table & old Greene Carpett
The Roome all hung wᵗʰ gilt Leather
One Grate fireshovell & tonges
A Paire of Smale yellow Serge Window Curtins
& a rod

In y̆ᵉ 1ˢᵗ Roome on y̆ᵉ Uper floore

A Bed-stead Cord & Matt
Some Old Stript Stuff about yᵉ Bed-stead & a
bout part of yᵉ roome
An Old flock Bed and Bolster
A Rugg A Blankett & an Old Caddow
A Smale Grate & a fender
A Smale Table & 2 old Chayres

In y̆ᵉ 2ᵈ Roome

One Bed-Stead, coard & Matt
One flock Bed & Bolster
One Old Blankett & A Caddow
One old Chayre

In y̆ᵉ 3ᵈ Roome

6 Armd Cane Chaires
3 Old Brockadella Chayres
7 Old Gilt Leather Chayres
6 Old Chayres wᵗʰ Damask Cushons most
of them broken
One Bigg Table
A Long Squobb frame & Couch frame wᵗʰ: one End
2 Long Cushons for yᵉ Squobb

Kilkenny Castle, County Kilkenny

In ỹ Bakers Lodging Roome

One Bed=stead Cord & Matt
One Sute of Old Kedermast[r] Curtins
One bad Old feather Bed & 2 flock bolsters
One Rugg
One Blankett
One Wooden Chayre One Settle Bed=Stead

In ỹ Bake House

One Wooden Beame & Scales w[th]: Cords
4 Leaden half hundreds
One Leaden q[r]: a hund[d] weight
One 14[℔] weight
One 7[℔] weight
One 4[℔] weight
One 2[℔]: weight & one 1[℔]: weight
One old Iron Grate
2 Payles
2 Earthen ᵖᵃⁿˢ & one other Vessell
One Short Tubb
2 Old Silke Sives
One Trewell
5 Iron Rasps, One Iron to prick bread w[th]
One peck & a halfe peck
4 Iron Candlesticks   One Salt box
One box for Eggs   3 Wooden Peeles
One great Iron forck & one Smale One w[th]:
                               Wooden handles
One Lanthorne
One Leather Chayre, One Stoole & one
                               Wooden Chayre
2 Large Basketts & one Smale One
A peell of smale boards to lay cakes on
A Doughing kniufe, & a Cutting kniufe
One great Ring
2 Large Dough Troughs & one Smale One
One Rolling Mill
One fine Rolling Cloath & one Corse One
One Wooden Shovell

In ỹ Wash House

One Coper fixed w[th]: a frame & 4 loose Iron bars
One Old Table

In her Graces Laundry in ỹ Laund[ry]: Maids Roome

One Bed Stead Cord & Mattt
One Sute of Red Cloath Curtins

One feather Bed & bolster of flanders ticking
One white Rugg
5 Old Chayres, One halfe round Grate

In ỹ Laundry Roome & Clossett

One Long Deale Table two Short Ditto
One horse to dry Cloaths on 3 wooden Stooles
One Buckett, One fireshovell & a p[r]: of Tonges
One Large Grate wth Cheekes & one large fender
A hanging Iron to hold Smoothing Irons on

In ỹ Roome Over ỹ Bake house

One Bedstead w[th]: a Sacking bottom
A Sute of blew Curtins head cloath & Teaster
a feather Bed Bolster & pillow
One White Rugg, & a very Old Blankett
4 gilt Leather Chaires & a Smale Oake Table
One Grate, One Oake Close Stoole very bad
The Roome hung wth Kidermaster Stuff

*In ỹ Office Over ỹ Bake House, M[r] Sweet
has the key of it*

In ỹ Roome at ỹ Stairehead

One halfe headed Bedstead Matt & Cord
One flock Bed and Bolster
2 Old Caddows very bad
2 Wooden Chayres

In ỹ Next Roome

One halfe heade Bed-stead Coard &Matt
One flock bed & bolster very bad
2 Old Caddows very bad

In ỹ 3[d] Roome from ỹ Afores[d]: Office

Hung w[th]: Old Kidermaster hangings
Two Window Curtins of y[e] Same
A Bedstead Matt and Coard
A Sute of Kidermast[r] Curtins head Cloath & teaster
a good feather Bed & Bolster Lank
a good white Rugg & 2 good blankets
4 Leather Chayres, & one Oake Table
One Grate

In y̆ͤ Little Roome that y̆ͤ Clerkes
write in

A Writeing Table
2 Furmes
2 Leather Chayres

In y̆ͤ 1ˢᵗ Roome on y̆ͤ Uper floore

One Bedstead Matt & Cord
Some Old Kidermaster Nailed about yᵉ Bed
One Old Feather Bed & flock Bolster
A Blanket & one Old Rugg
3 Old Leather Chayres
One Iron Grate wanting a Barr

In yᵉ Scond Roome

One Iron Grate

In y̆ͤ 3ᵈ Roome

One ½ headed Bed-Stead Matt & Cord
One good Feather bed & bolster, One good blankett
        & one new Caddow
One Deale Table, 2 Old Chayres & one Joynt Stoole
One Iron Grate

In his Graces Comssʳˢ: Office

The Roome hung wᵗʰ gilt Leather
A Table covered wᵗʰ green Say
8 gilt Leather Chayres
A Gilt Leather Chayres
A fixed Grate an an Iron fender

In his Comissoʳˢ: Office

The Roome hung wᵗʰ: gilt Leather
A Table coverd wᵗʰ: green Say
8 gilt Leather Chayres
A fixed Grate & an Iron fender

In y̆ͤ Next Roome to his Graces Comisoʳˢ: Office

In y̆ͤ Receiver Genˡˢ: Office

In y̆ͤ Roome over y̆ͤ S:ᵈ Office & two
other Garrett Roomes

These are Used to putt Distresses in

In y̆ͤ first Roome in y̆ͤ Little House
in y̆ͤ hay Yard

5 Old leather Chaires very bad ones
One Deale Table
One fixed Grate & one pʳ: of Tonges

In ye 2ᵈ: Roome

One Press cubboard, one Joynt Stoole
One Table wᵗʰ: a Drawer

In y̆ͤ first Roome above Staires

One Bed-Stead coarded
A Sute of green Cloath curtins, headcloath, teaster
and Vallens, A Feather Bed & bolster & 2 Old blankets
One Rugg, One Oake Table, 3 leather Chayres bad ones
One Iron Grate, a fireshovell and Tonges

In y̆ͤ Little Roome Next it

One Bed-Stead Cord & Matt
A Sute of Old yellow harnum Curtins headcloath
and Teaster
One yellow Serge Counter paine
A good Feather Bed & 2 feather Bolsters
Two Blanketts, & One pillow
Two gilt Leather Chayres

In y̆ͤ little Roome by the Granery

One Grate

In y̆ͤ first Quarter of y̆ͤ Stables on
the right hand Comeing from yᵉ Street

One Oake Settle Bed
One Binn for Oates

In y̆ͤ 2ᵈ Quarter on y̆ͤ right hand

One Settle Bed, A Flock bed and bolster
2 Caddows
A Binn for Oates

In y̆ͤ 1ˢᵗ Quartᵉʳ: on y̆ͤ Left hand

One Settle Bed, A Flock bed & bolster
Two Caddows
A Binn for Oates

In y̆ 2 Quarter on y̆ Left hand

One Settle Bed-stead
One flock Bed & Bolster
2 Caddows bad ones
1 Binn for Oates

In y̆ Stable in y̆ hay Yard

One Binn for Oates

In y̆ first Roome Over y̆ Stables

One Bed-Stead Coard & Matt, One Feather bed
         & bolster
Two Blankets very bad ones
One Deale Table, one Brass Candlestick
One Grate fixed

In y̆ 2ᵈ: Roome Over y̆ Stables

One Bed-Stead Cord & Matt
One Sute of Old Curtins
One flock Bed & Bolster
One Old Blankett & one Caddow
One little Table
Two Leather Chaires very bad ones

In y̆ 3ᵈ Roome

One Bed-Stead. Coard & Matt
One Old flock bed & bolster, yᵉ tikein much broken
One Rugg & 2 blanketts
2 Leather Chayres very bad Ones
One Deale Table
One Grate fixed

In y̆ 4ᵗʰ Roome

One Bedstead Cord & Matt
One Old flock Bed & Bolster
2 Smale Blanketts & bad Caddow
Some Old Broken Kidermaster Curtins teaster
        & headcloath
2 wooden Chayres

In y̆ 5ᵗʰ Roome

One halfe headed Bedstead Coard & Matt
One flock Bed & Bolster, 2 Smale Blanketts
One Old Silke Caddow, One Old Chayre

In y̆ 6ᵗʰ Roome

One halfe headed Bedstead Matt & Cord
Some Old Kidermaster nayled for Curtins
One feather Bed & Bolster
One Blanket, One white Rugg
One Red Caddow, One Old Chayre, & one Old Table

In y̆ 7ᵗʰ Roome

In y̆ 8ᵗʰ Roome

The roome humg wᵗʰ gilt Leather much broken,
      One Bedstead, Coard & Matt
One Feather bed bolster & pillow, one White Rugg
       & 2 blanketts
The Curtins of yᵉ Bed of yellow Serge, 3 gilt leather
      Chayres & one Stoole
A fireshovell & tonges, An Old Carpett of gilt Leather
One Large Table

In y̆ Gardners House

One Bedstead Cord & Matt
One Sute of old Cloath Curtins, Vallens
headpiece & teaster
One halfe headed Bedstead & Cord
One good feather Bed Bolster and pillow
One very Old Feather Bed & Bolster
One Old flock Bed & Bolster
One Old Red Rugg & a white Rugg
2 good Blanketts & 4 Old Blankets
6 Turkey workt Chaires
One Red Cloath Chayre yᵉ bottom Boarded
A Grate in one of yᵉ Chambers
A Fireshovell & Tonges
A Large Grate in yᵉ Kitchon wanting one barr
A Smale draw up Jack
One dozen of Old pewter plates

In y̆ Gaurd House

A Bedstead Matt & Coard
A Sute of Blew Kidermaster Curtins headcloath
       & teaster
A Canvis Mattress & a Chequer'd Quilt, & 2 Smale
       blankets
2 Old Leather Chayres
A Smale Table
Two fixed Grates

In his Graces Brewhouse

A Large Coper fixed wth: 13 barrs under it & a
frame & Doore
A Long Gridle fireshovell and Poker
A Cole Rake & a Cole hamer
5 Wooden Gutters
3 Oares & 2 Wooden Pumps for wort
A float & a Trough
2 Tunns fixed
4 Coolers fixed
ye above Wooden Vessells are much decay'd

In y̆^e Wash House Over y̆^e Water

One Large for Linning wth Screws & an Iron barr
to turn them, the Iron pinns of ye Screws out of Ord^r
a smale board wth. Handles to carry Linnen on
One broad thick planke Table
One Long deale box
One Long deale Table
another Old Table ye leafe broken
2 deale Dressers
one Low frame of a screen 4 Leaves
A Large deale Rack fastned to ye cealing
Two washing Tubb & an Old wrenching Tubb
One Leaden Pump wth: an Iron handle & a Sucker
not in Order
One Coper fixed wth: a Grate & Iron Dore under it
2 Iron frames of Casements not hung
a Long Iron grate in ye Chimney wanting one barr
a Lock & key to ye Street Doore

Above Staires

One little Oake Table fixed to ye Wall
A Lock & key to one of ye Doores

In y̆^e Drying Roome

Poles fixed for drying Large Linnen &
Deale Laths fitted & fixed on both sides of y^e
Roome for drying of Napkins

In y̆^e Warderobe in y̆^e Round Tower

One Percian Carpett 4 y^{rds} & ½ long 3 y^{rds}: & ½ wide
One Ditto 5 y^{rds} & ½ long 3 y^{rds} wide
One Turkey worke Carpett 4 y^{rds} & ½ long ¾^s wide
One Percian Carpett 7 y^{rds} long 2 y^{rds} & ½ wide

One Smyrnah Carpett 5 y^{rds} & ½ long 2 y^{rds}: & ¼ wide
One Percian Carpett more 5 y^{rds}. long 1 yrd & ¾^s wide
One Ditto 4 y^{rds} ¾ long 1 yrd ¾^s wide
One Ditto 3 y^{rds} long 1 yrd ½ wide
One Ditto 2 y^{rds} & a ¼ long 1 yrd & ½ wide
Two very Old Smale Carpetts very foule & bad &
a Piece of a Carpett

Tapestry Hangings

3 pieces of fine Antwerp hangings 8 foot deep
lined wth Canvis
3 Pieces of Antwerp Hangings Landskip & Smale
figures 8 foot deep unlin'd, Suteable to 3 Pieces
in his Graces Bedchamber, in Killkenny
3 pieces of fine hangings ye Story of Bachonells
9 foot deep
3 pieces of fine Tapestry hangings ye Story of
Decious 13 foot deep Suteable to those in ye roome
at ye South end of ye Gallery lined wth Canvis
5 Pieces of Mohare purple hangings lined with
Canvis formerly for the Inner part of ye Alcove
most of ye fringe taken of to putt on the green hangings

Some very old hangings of red Cloath painted
wth: gilt Leather near 11 y^{rds} in Compass & 2^{yds}: deepe
part of a Sute of gilt Leather hangings Suteable
to ye Chaires in ye great dineing Roome
Severall Pieces of gilt Leather hangings
Containeing about 100 Skins all of One Sort
Severall pieces of gilt Leather hangings Suteable
to those in ye Clossett by the Councell Chamber
in ye round Tower
Severall Old Pieces of gilt Leather
2 Pieces of Leather hangings ⌃^{painted} part of ye borders
wanting
A Square Carpett of 5 figures ye Story of Pallace
Around gilt Leather Carpett ye Story of ye Nimphs
One Old gilt Leather Carpett wth: white Ground
Two other pieces of ye Same for Sideboards
One very Old gilt Leather Carpett gilt round &
white flowers
Two Old red Leather Carpetts
5 Old fashon Seats & backs for Chaires of
Clouded Sattin
5 Old Crimson Serge Cases Ditto
Severall Remains of Old Chaire Cases &c^a: for any
odd Uses

Kilkenny Castle, County Kilkenny

Two Old quilted Cushons of Striped Indian Silke
Two Old yallow Sattin Cushons painted wth black
6 Old tickeing Cushons
7 Old Cushons of Calicoe &c filled wth flox
One paire of yallow Serge window Curtins about
2 y^rds deep a breadth in Each
One paire of white wind^w Curtins

A Paire of Druggit window Curtins 2 breadths in Each
5 breadths of yallow harmum Damask about 2 y^rds deep
Part of 2 Old Setts of white feathers formerly used
                                                      on beds
& since taken to Pieces & used on other occasions
One Large Umbrello
part of gilt Cups belonging to Lady Mary's Roome &
4 feet

An Old blew Vellvett Chaire
The Picture of ye Old Princes of Orange at Length
One Old Picture of King Charles ye 2^d at Length
Six deale packin Cases & boxes & a Large flatt Trunke

In ẙ^e Long Wardrobe

One Dutch hearth wth brass handles & 4 brass balls
3 Smale brass branches & socketts for Candles
One Old Carved gilt head board decayed
A Large deale box to hold wax Candles
One other long Shiny box
Two Old Chaires w^th: gilt frames covered w^th:
                              Canvis the gilding decayed
One Old Silke Bockadell Chaire broken & a red Case

PLATE 5
Francis Place (1647–1728): *Kilkenny Castle and Saint Canice's Cathedral*, 1699, ink and wash on paper

36 Brocadell Chaires & old red Covers . . \
9 . . Ditto . . & yallow Covers . . \
11 Crimson Velvett Chaires & Red baces Covers \
3 Old Chaires covered w{th}: blew Silke & \
4 Stooles Ditto \
6 old gray Chaires Motheaton . . . . . \
2 Old Arm{d} Chaires of blew figured Vellvett \
8 broken Chaires y{t} came from y{e} North Roome by the Gallery \
Severall other Ruins of Chaires & frames & other Lumber y{t}: is only fitt to be burnt \
a peell of Old Curtin rods p{art} of y{m} from Dumore \
2 Old gilded Pedistalls to sett Chinah on \
One Old Coper pott worn out & some other Small matters of that nature \
A peell of Bedsteads posts & sides &c but never a perfect Bedstead amongst them from Dunmore

} all these from Dunmore ye cases very bad & Severall of the frames broken

One Cradle Grate \
One Square Ditto \
Nine halfe round Grates 6 of y{em}: wants bottoms

Pictures from Dunmore

My Lady Betty Cavendish at Length \
My Lady Betty Stanop in an Ovall frame \
The Old Duke of Ormond at Length but Shorter & less then the Life \
69 other Pictures of Severall Sises & sorts as Landskips History pieces, Smale Dutch pieces wth figures &c{a} most of them has only Straineing frames all of them wants cleaneing & severall of them are very much decay'd & 10 of ym: has neither frame nor Straineing frame

Kilkenny Castle, County Kilkenny

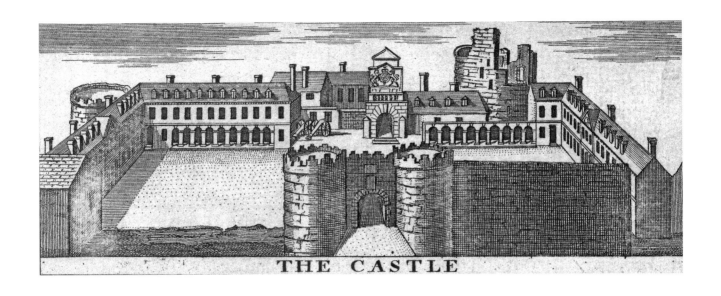

PLATE 6
Charles Brooking: *A Map of the City and Suburbs of Dublin*, 1728; detail showing a view of Dublin Castle

3

DUBLIN CASTLE
1707

An Acc,,ᵗᵗ of his Grace the Duke of Ormonds Household Furniture in yᵉ Castle of Dublin Appraized by two Upholsters for the Use of her Majesty

Nᵒ

5	*Two State Closetts*			
	Three Stuffe Window Curtains to draw up Eight black Stools of Stuffe, A Looking Glass 39 Inches, An Inlaid writeing Desk, Two Sconces, Two Window Curtains & Sconces in yᵉ Passage	17	10	--
6	*Secretary Genˡˡˢ Offices*			
	A Table & Glass Japan'd & 2 Chimney Sconces	6	10	--
7	*Dineing Roome*			
	Looking Glass 37 Inches & Table, Eight Velvett Chaires, A Chimney Glass & 2 Sconces	17	--	--
9	*Bedd Chamber*			
	One Standing beds Furniture of Blew print, Three blanketts and an Indian Quilt, Feather bed and bolster	5	--	--
		£ 46	--	--
10	*One pair of Stairs first Street Roome*			
	Five Oval Sconces, Two long Sconces over the Chimney	3	16	--
11	*Anti Chamber*			
	One Oval Sconce, & Two Oval Tables	1	15	--
12	*Second State Roome*			
	Ten Oval Sconces, & Two long ones over the Chimney	7	·4	--

13   *Drawing Roome*

Ten Armed Chaires of Blew Velvett, Trimed
with broad Silver Lace, Eleven back Stools D^o,
Three blew Sattin Window Curtains Furbelowed
with the same lined with blew Serge, Cornishes
Trimed with Silver Lace   83   .5   --

                £ 96   --   --

15   *Bedchamber*

A Genoway Damask bed, Gold Coul^d Scarlett
& Green, 12 ffoot high, Feather bed & bolster
of Flanders, three English Blanketts, a thick
Quilt and Holland Quilt, false Curtains of
paragon, Six Chaires with Damask cases
a White Indian Upper Quilt ...   £ 40 : 00 : 00

A Looking Glass 41½ Inches by 28
inlaid table and ye frame of ye Glass
Chimney Glass 5 foot by 14 Inches   10 : 15 : 00
wide, pear tree frames

Two Sconces, two old Window Curtains   5 : 00 : 00
of Damask and Tea Tables

                55   15   --

16   *Dressing Roome*

Three Doore Curtains, One pair of Window
Curtains lined with the same, four chaires —
two Stooles of the same Stuffe   6   --   --

17   *Closett*

A plad Couch, and three Pillowes, 6 Stooles,
two dore and one Window Curtains, two peices
of hangings lined with the same   10   10   --

                £ 72   .5   --

18   *Bed Chamber*

Two Suits of yellow Popling Wind^o Curtains
lined with the same   3 : 10 : 00
Eight Velvett Chaires   8 : 00 : 00
A looking Glass 41½ Inches, Table.
with a black frame   8 : 00 : 00
a black Japan Chest of Drawers.   3 : 10 : 00
a Wainscott Table and Drawer   0 : 04 : 06

                23   .4   .6

19   *Bed Chamber*

A Feild bed and Sacking bottom Furniture of Gold
Col.ᵈ & Scarlett wosted damask lin'd with a Strip'd
Persian, quilt of the same. feather bed & bolster
& Fustian Pillow, a quilt and Matress, 2 blanketts

2 window Curtains & 5 Chaires	£ 16 : 00 : 00	
a black Japan'd Chest of Drawers	2 : 10 : 00	
a Wainscoate Close Stool	0 : 07 : 00	
	18	17 --

20   *Drawing Roome*

Two Window Curtains of Stuffe, six Armed
Chaires, one Small Chest of Drawers a
small Wainscott Table

4	15
£ 46	16 .6

21   *Bed Chamber*

Hangings of Orange Coloured Flowerd
Stuffe, a Standing beds Furniture of Figured
Indian Stuffe A Feather bed bolster & pillow
One Rugg & 3 blanketts, A pair of Window
Curtains of Indian figured Stuff   9   10 --

22   *Bed Chamber*

Two bedsteads of Green Furniture, Feather
bed. bolster, 2 Ruggs & 5 blanketts   7   10 --

23   *Bed Chamber*

A Feild bedstead, and Stuffe Furniture
Feather bed, bolster, two blanketts and a
Rugg, yᵉ hangings of blew print   4 .5 --

24   Hangings of Orange Coloured print, a
plad bed lined Feather bed, bolster & pillow
four blanketts and Counterpaine, a Holland
Quilt, Two Window Curtains and Valens
furbuloed

13	-- --
£ 34	.5 --

25   *Bed Chamber*

Hangings of yᵉ Roome of blew Stuffe, a
Standing beds Furniture of blew and white
plad, Feather bed bolster and Pillow, Three
Blanketts one Rug and a Counterpaine   6 .5 --

Dublin Castle

27	*Bed Chamber*			
Hangings of the Roome of Green print a				
Standing beds Furniture of Stuffe, Counterpain				
Feather bed, bolster and Pillow Three blanketts				
and One Rugg	£ 7 : 03 : 00			
A Wainscott Table	0 : 04 : 00			
A Chest of Drawers	0 : 15 : 06			
		£ .8	.2	.6

30	*Bed Chamber*			
Standing beds Furniture of blew Kettermatter				
Feather bed, bolster and pillow, Three blanketts				
and One Rugg		3	--	--
		£ 17	.7	.6

34	*Bed Chamber*			
Standing Beds Furniture of Blew print,				
Feather bed, bolster, three blanketts, One Rugg.		.3	--	--

35	*Bed Chamber*			
Beadstead, a blew Furniture, Feather bedd,				
bolster, a pair of blanketts and a Rugg.		3	14	--

36	*Bed Chamber & Clossett*			
Standing beds Furniture of Checard Stuffe				
Feather bed, bolster, three blanketts, 2 pillowes				
Rug and Counterpan		5	.2	--
In ye Clossett a Flock bedd, 2 blanketts & a Rug		--	15	--

40	*Porters Lodge*			
Standing beds Furniture of green printed				
Stuffe with a Counterpan, Feather bed, bolster				
three blanketts and a Rugg		4	.8	--

D.^o	*Bed. Chamber*			
Standing beds Furniture of Green Searge				
Feather bed, bolster and 3 blanketts & a Rug.		3	12	--
		£ 20	11	--

41	*Bed Chamber*			
A Feather bed, bolster, Pillowes and				
three blanketts	£ 3 : 02 : 00			
Fire Shovell, Tongs, Poker & bellowes	0 : 01 : 09			
A p.^r of Window Curtains & Vallens	1 : 15 : 00			

A Close Stool & White Earthen Pan	0 : 07 : 00			
Two Window Curtains & a Red Case	0 : 04 : 06			
		5	10	.3

42 *Bed Chamber*

Blew Hangings to the Roome, Standing beds Furniture of blew print, Feather. bed, bolster and pillow, three blanketts and a Rugg	7	14	--

43 *Bed Chamber*

Beds Furniture of Green print, Feather bed, bolster, one blankett and Counterpan	3	18	--

44 *Bed Chamber*

Two Standing beds Furniture of Blew print, two Flock bedds, Two pair of Blanketts, two Ruggs, halfe headed bedstead.	3	--	--
	£ 20	.2	.3

46 *Bed Chamber*

Standing beds Furniture of Fillomatt Kitterm[r] Flock bed, bolster, three blanketts and a Rugg	1	.6	--

47 *Bed Chamber*

Standing beds Furniture of Fillomatt Kitterm[r] One flock bed, bolster, 3 blanketts and a Rugg	1	10	--

48 *Bed Chamber*

Standing beds Furniture of blew print Flock bed & bolster, Three blanketts and a Rugg	1	18	--

49 *Bed Chamber*

Standing beds Furniture of Fillomatt Stuffe Feather bed, bolster and Pillow, three Blanketts and One Rugg	4	--	--

50 *Bed Chamber*

Standing beds Furniture of Blew Print — Feather bed, bolster, two blanketts and a Rugg	2	10	--
	£ 11	.4	--

51 *Bed Chamber*

Standing beds Furniture of blew print, Flock bed, bolster and pillow 2 blanketts & one Rug.	3	11	--

52	Standing beds Furniture of blew print — Flock bed & bolster, 3 blanketts one Rugg.	1	10	--
53	Standing beds Furniture of blew print, Matt and Cord, Flock bed and bolster 3 blanketts and one Rugg	1	18	--
54	Standing beds Furniture of Green print Flock bed & bolster 3 blanketts & one Rugg	1	10	--

56   *Bed Chamber & Clossett*

Hangings of yellow print, Standing beds Furniture of ye same, Feather bed, bolster and 2 Pillowes 2 blanketts & one Rugg	6	15	--
A Feild bedstead and Furniture of Stuffe with a Counterpan, Feather bed, bolster and 3 blanketts	.4	--	--
	£ 19	.4	--

57   *Bed Chamber*

Standing beds Furniture of Green print Feather bed, bolster, two blanketts and one Rugg, & hangings to the Roome	.4	.2	--

58   *Bed Chamber*

Standing Beds Furniture & hangings of the Roome of ~~th~~ blew print, Feather bed, bolster and pillow, 2 blanketts and one Rugg	5	12	--

59   *Bed Chamber*

Halfe headed bedstead, Matt and Cord. Two blanketts and one Rug and bolster.	3	--	--

60 Flock bed and bolster, two blanketts and one Rugg	--	15	--
	£ 13	.9	--

63   *Bed Chamber*

Standing beds Furniture of Cheq^d Stuffe Feather bed, bolster and Pillow, 3 blanketts One Rug & Counterpan, Hangings of ye Room Curtains and Window Curtains	£ 7 : 5 : 0			
D^o Rug 3 blanketts, Flock bed & bolster	0 : 16 : 0			
		8	.1	--

		£	s	d
64	*Bed Chamber*			
	A Feild Bedsteads Furniture of Plad Feather bed, bolster and Pillow, 2 blanketts. Hangings and Plad Window Curtains, and one Rugg	5	--	--
65	Standing beds Furniture of Plad, lined with Red and White wosted Stuffe, Feather bed bolster and Pillow, three Blanketts one Rugg and Counterpan Window Curtains and hangings of the same	7	15	--
66	Hangings	--	.7	--
67	*Bed Chamber*			
	Standing Beds Furniture of Chequerd Stuffe Hanings of Kittermast[r], Feather bed, bolster 3 blanketts and a Rugg	.4	12	--
		£ 25	15	--
69	*Bed Chamber*			
	Standing beds Furniture of blew print Feather bed, bolster, 3 blanketts & a Rugg	3	14	--
70	*Bed Chamber*			
	Standing beds Furniture of green print Feather bolster, two blanketts & a Rugg	2	12	--
71	Feather bed and bolster, three blanketts. One Rugg, some blew print	3	--	--
72	*Bed Chamber*			
	Standing beds Furniture of plad lined with Stuffe, Feather bed, bolster & pillow Holl[d] and Indian Quilt 3 blanketts & hangings y[e] same.	13	12	--
	Twelve Chaires	1	--	--
	Two Tables	--	14	--
73	Standing beds Furniture of Print, Feather bed, bolster 2 blanketts and one Rugg	2	15	--
74	A Feild bedstead & Furniture lined, Feather bed, bolster & Counterpan & 2 blanketts	.8	--	--
		£ 35	.7	--

75	*Bed Chamber*			

Standing beds Furniture of Stuffe, Feather
bed bolster and Pillow, Two blanketts, one
Rugg and Counterpan — .6 .2 --

D.° A halfe headed Bedstead, Feather bed,
bolster & Pillow, 2 blanketts & One Rugg — .2 16 --

76	*Bed Chamber*

Standing beds Furniture of plad, Feather
bed, bolster & pillow, Two blanketts, One Rug
& Counterpan of ffillomatt — .7 .2 --

77	*In the Stables*

Six Flockbeds and bolsters four pair of
Blanketts & four Ruggs — .3 -- --

78	*Bed Chamber*

Standing beds Furniture of blew print,
Feather bed, bolster and Pillow two blanketts
and One Rugg — .3 10 --

£ 22 10 --

79	*Bed Chamber*

Two Standing beds Furniture, two Feather
beds, two bolsters, two pair of Blanketts &
Green Hangings to the Room — .8 -- --

Abstract of y^e foregoing Acc.^{tt}

$N.^o$				
1	46	--	--
2	96	--	--
3	72	.5	--
4	46	16	.6
5	34	.5	--
6	17	.7	.6
7	20	11	--
8	20	.2	.3
9	11	.4	--
10	19	.4	--
11	13	.9	--
12	25	15	--
13	35	.7	--
14	22	10	--
15	.8	--	--

Total of y^e household Furniture — £ 488 16 .3

An Acc.tt of Sizes Numbers and weight
of his Grace the Duke of Ormonds Pewter
Copper, Brass, Iron &c In the Castle of Dublin
Appraised as ℔ y.e following Acc.tts for y.e use
of his Ex.cy the Earl of Pembrook

English Pewter

		C	q.rs	℔	£	s	d
28	Seven pound Dishes weighing	100	.3	.1			
25	ffive pound Dishes weighing	100	..	11½			
15	Dozen and 4 plates weighing	100	.3	13			
19	Dish Covers weighing	..	.2	.9½			
10	Rings weighing	..	..	.9			
1	Seven pound dish & 3 five pound Dishes	..	..	21			
2	Dish covers weighing	..	..	10			
	Total of the English Pewter weighing	635 at 13.d ℔			£ 34	.7	11

Irish Pewter

		C	q.rs	℔	£	s	d
27	Five pound Dishes weighing	100	.1	.6			
10	Four pound Dishes						
8	Two pound Dishes						
2	Dozen of Plates — all weighing	..	.3	11			
6	Salts						
5	Stands						
2	Dishes One p.d: & ½ each						
30	plates						
5	Salts	..	.1	14			
1	Five pound Dish						
3	Three pounders						
		200	.2	.3			
	Total of the Irish Pewter weight makeing 283.℔ at 1.s ℔ pound				14	.3	--
					£ 48	10	11

Acc.tt of the Copper

		C	q.rs	℔	£	s	d
5	Sauce Pans						
2	Cullinders.						
5	Patty pans. — weighing	100	..	.8			
5	Stew Pans						
5	Potts with Covers weighing	..	.2	20			
4	potts with Covers weighing	..	.3	15			
1	large Fish pan and bottom						
2	Fish boats						
1	Dutch Oven — weighing	100	.1	.1			
1	Juren Pott and bottom						
2	Dripping Panns	..	.2	--			

Dublin Castle

Belonging to ye Confection.^r

1	Dutch Oven			
4	Preserveing Pans	weighing	-- .2 15	
1	Pott and Cover			
2	Plates belonging to ye Oven			
3	Fire Pieles 2 of Copper & one of brass		-- .1 11	
2	Frying Pans			
4	Small Ones	weighing	-- .1 --	
2	Skimmers			
2	Sadles [*recte* Ladles]		570 -- --	

Pounds 630 att 18^d ℔ pound   £ 47 .5 --

An Acc.^tt of the Iron

14	Large Spitts	weighing	
4	other large Spitts		200 .2 .3
2	Grid Irons 3 Clevers		
1	Kitchen Fork & Fire shovell		100 -- .6
1	Minceing Knife 2 Flesh Forks		
1	Slice 2 Fryen Pans		
10	Trevitts and 2 Slices		-- .2 --
			409 -- --

475^℔ [*recte* 457^℔] weight at 3^d ℔ pound   £ 5 14 .3

      Carried Forwards   £ 101 10 .2

Three Marble mortars one Valued att   -- 12 --
The other two at   .1 10 --

An Acc.^tt of what things the
Butler had in the Cellar

A Can & Funnell wth. Iron hoops, two Iron Screw
hoops & a p^r Stills, 4 Cell.^r Tubbs, Six dozen of
glass bottles, 4 flint water bottles and two
brass Cocks   .2 -- --

Confectionary things

42	Dozen great & Small Saucers	
17	doz: of Glass Stands, preserveing, Creame, Comfitts Ratifia & Jelly Glasses	.4 .4 .6

      In all £ 109 16 .8

Old Pewter & Brass returned to
Mr Johnson

3 Dozen and 7 plates	
9 Dishes	w.^{tt} 88^{pds} at 11^d ℔ p^d - 4 : 0 : 8
2 Dishcovers	
3 boat Covers of Copper	
5 patty pans Covers	
2 Copper Dishes	w.^{tt} 64^{pds} at 10^d ℔ p^d. 2 : 13 : 4
1 Sauce Pan	
1 Fish plate, Scimer, Slice	

July 25 more a Dish w.^{tt} 6 p^d & a halfe   0 : 5 : 11½

                                                          £.6 19 11½

Abstract of ye Valuation of the
Foregoeing Pewter, Copper, Iron & brass &c.

	€	q^{rs}	p^d				
English Pewter Weighing	5	.2	19	makes			
635 pound weight at 13^d ℔ pound					34	.7	11
Irish Pewter weighing	2	.2	.3	makes			
283 p^d weight at 1^s ℔ pound					14	.3	--
Copper & brass weighing	5	.2	14	makes			
630 p^{ds} weight at 18^d ℔ p^d					47	.5	--
Iron Wares weighing	4	--	.9	makes			
457 p^d weight at 3^d ℔ p^d					.5	14	.3
Three Marble Morters Valued at					.2	.2	--
Utensills belonging to ye Wine Celler Valued					.2	--	--
D^o. belonging to ye Confectioners Office					.4	.4	.6

                                          Total £ 109 16 .8

	£	s	d
Pewter and Brass	109	16	.8
Concordatum	488	16	.3
Hay	61	.8	.9
Coach & Horses	500	--	--
Wines	176	--	--
Total Reced of Ld Pembrook	£ 1336	.1	.8

Oct. y^e. 20th 1707
Wee Doe hereby Certifie that wee have
Valued All the Within mentioned Goods
to ye best of our Skill and Judgment

            John French
            Step: Finckley   } Upholsterers.

Dublin Castle

An Acc.^{tt} of more Goods Disposed
of since the first Valuation

These bo^t by Mr Peter Goodwin	Two Copper Cesternes & 2 Copper pailes weight 65 pounds at 18^d ℔ pound	4 17 .6
	A Tea Table, two little Oak Tables, a Table without a Drawer Two Stands and a p^r of Bellowes.	1 .8 .7½
	A Flock bed, bolster, three blanketts, Rugg and Matt 0.12.0 An Old Carding Table 4^s	-- 16 --
	Mr Goodwin	£ .6 12 .1½ [*recte* £ .7 .2 .1½]

Two Flock beds & bolsters, 4 blanketts, 2 Matts and two Ruggs — .1 .4 --

A pallat Bedstead — -- .3 .6

Two feather beds, bolsters, 4 blanketts, 2 Rugs and furniture to them — 4 .5 --

A Small Oak Table and a Card Table — -- .8 --

An Iron Stand to Warm Plates on — -- .4 --

Six Red Caphoy Cushions, & 6 Old Frames Chaires — .1 14 --

A Matress and an Old Blankett — -- 16 --

23 peices of China, basons dishes, plates, Coffe Cupps and a pair of Bellowes — .1 13 --

a ffender and two Glass Sconces — -- 12 --

These bo^t by Mr Pacy

Mr Pacy — £ 10 19 .6

Left with Mr Pacy ye following things
4 Rushia leather Chaires, 2 large Turkey work't
Carpetts, a large Map of flanders, One *D^o* large
of England, Scotland & Ireland, One *D^o* of Corke
Harbour, The Edisstone Lighthouse & 1 Small
Mapp. & the plan of Namure
more a bathing Tub and a broken Close Stool,
Two Wraught Stools by ye young Ladies
Two brass Candlesticks, & an Old Writeing Desk
& ye Oval Table y^t was in Sr And^r: Fountains Roome

Memorandu^m the large Map of flanders, The large Map of
great Brittain, the Plan of Corke Harbour and Namur
left with Ld Inchequeen

Bo^t by Mr French & Mr Finckly	A Feild bed and beding	3 -- --
	Eleven Flock beds, & six bolsters, 4 Ruggs some Matts, 3 little Square Tables, Old. Curtains and Hangings, Green blew and Gold Colour, a Corded bedstead	.4 10 --

12 Ivory handle Knifes and Eleven forks
12 black handle knives and 12 forkes
Two Water Tubbs a Tinned Baskett, another

-- 13 --

with out Tinn, and a Wooden Cistern   -- .7 .6
A Beam Scales, 4 halfe hundred weights of
Iron, one quarter of a hundred, one Seven
pound, one four pound one one p^d and
a halfe pound weight all Lead   .1 .3 .6
Three Trapps, four Milkpans, 14 tart
pans, 29 patty pans & one flower Tubb   .1 .2 --
Three leather Jacks for Beer, 3 Glass
basketts and a Tub   -- .9 --
Six pair of Standing brass Candlesticks
and 3 Flatt ones   -- 16 --
18 Tinn Covers and an Old Tinn Baskett   -- .5 --

                                  Finckly   £ 12 .6 --

Sold to Mr Audly one Chimney Glass att   .3 -- --

                        John French)
                        Step: Finkley)

Sent to Mr Fitz Gerald one of ye Bureaus)
that was in my Lord Dukes Clossett   )   .2 10 --

Remaining Still at Dublin Castle
Oct. 15th 1707

All the Prints in ye Drawing Roome Valued
by Mr Felster & Sold to my Lord Inchaqueen att   26 .4 --
Six Cane Chaires y^t were in Cole Gores Roome
Six Oaks Chaires y^t was in ye Stew^{ds} dineing Room
One Oval Table in Sr And^r. Fountains Roome
A Small Oval Table in ye Stewards Office
A Square Oak Table in Mr Smiths Room that
was Mrs Parkers and a Close Stool
One Steel hearth and Doggs in Ld Pembrooks
Anti Chamber
Three Bells and Pullies in the Lodgings.
400 load of Old Hay in the Lower Yard

Goods Wanting

A Large black Japan'd Skreen bo^t of Ld Rochester
The Red and White Striped Curtains in ye Closett
where his Graces Armes was kept
A Close Stool   ) What things were in
Several Pillowes   ) La Coudriers Roome
Two Carding Tables) a Chest of Drawers, a Glass
A Screwtore   ) & Close Stool that was in Mr
                      Romeius Room and an Easie
          Chair y^t was disposed of by Mr Richardson

The peice of Trophies   )
and ye large hazard Table) gone to Kilkeny

Wine Sold and the mony not yett
Received

	£	s	d
To my Lord Cutts 4 Hogsheads	52	--	--
To Leiu.^t Gen.^{ll} Eckling One hhd of whi: wine	11	--	--

Left with Mr Hester the Clockmaker one
Standing Clock made by Tompion

Mr Southwell is Debt.^r

	£ s d
For ye Furniture of Mr Young my Lord Rochesters Pages Roome. vizt	
Hangings to the Roome	2 : 0 : 0
A halfe headed bedstead wth Curtains of Printed Stuffe	1 : 0 : 0
Feather bed, bolster and Pillow	4 : 0 : 0
One Rugg, 3 blanketts and a Counterpan	1 : 3 : 0
	.8 .3 --

This mony I have Reced from M^r
Dawson y^e 8^t November 1707 of w^{ch}.
I shall give my Lord an Acc^{tt} in
England —
The above 8 : 3 : 0 is bro^{tt} in to M^r.
Pacy's English Acc^{tt} Comenceing y^e 1st.
of November 1707 —

PLATE 7
Unknown artist but said to be after Carlo Dolci (1616–1686): *Madonna and Child*, oil on canvas. This painting, now at Kilkenny Castle, may be a copy of the 'Virgin Mary with our Saviour in her Armes' attributed to Correggio, which was among the pictures and furniture shipped from Dublin to England by the 2nd Duke of Ormonde.

A acc.^{tt} of Pictures and other Furniture of
his Grace the Duke of Ormonds Ship.^d on board
the Betty Galley, Owner Briscoe Master

N.º

1 Virgin Mary with our
Saviour in her Armes by
Correggio,

2 One Spinnett Frame 12
Oval Pictures y.^t were in
his Graces bed Chamber
One is the Du.^{ks}: of Ormonds
2 peices of the Children.
one Emty frame,

3 One Harpsecale,

4 One Spinnett,

5 One large Indian Skreen

6 One other Skreen of y.^e
same bredth & Length

7 One Short Fire Skreen
with a Case,

8 3 Flower peices, 3 Lady's
Duke of Bewford, Lord
Rochester and the Earl
of Ossery,

9 One Strong box of her
Graces,

10 Fine Flower p.^s D.^s of ~/~
Sommerss'.^t Ld Capele, fine
Mapps,

11 A Picture that was in y.^e
State Chamber over the
Chimney,

12 Five p.^s of Sea Fights,

13 A large p.^s of Thos Duffe & the
Case rode,

14 A P.^s of St John the Baptist &
Virgin Mary, & our Saviour
in her Armes, was over the
Chimney in the drawing Room
from Kilkenny, Furniture of
the State bed, head board, 3 —
out side Valense. 4 in side Valans
Counterpan, 4 Damask ∞//∞
Curtains with gold Trimming
two Window Curtains of the
same, and 2 blanketts,

15 Four Case Curtains of Lewtstring
headcloth 3 p.^s of Damask
hangings w.th gold trimming
Frame to Shape ye Counterpan

16 A Picture of Vantrumph De ~
Ruter, one Lady, one Flower
p.^s a p.^s of a Henn at Roost
and a p.^s of Still life,

17 Three p.^s of State bed Cornishes
3 p.^s of Bast Mouldings, 6
Window curtains, 2 w.th out
lace, 2 patern Cases 4 little —
p.^s belonging to the bed —

18 The State bed w.th Sacking
bottom and posts bound
with Cord.

19 My Lord Dukes Feild ~
bedstead pack't, up in
Old portingale matt.

20 One Easy Chair of Crimson
and gold twelve balls, 2
Japan boxes, Seventeen –
little Pictures.

21 One Marble Table

22 four Square Sools of —
Crimson damask. 2 Round
Stools, 4 luetstring Covers

23 Two Crimson damask —
Chaires, with gold Trimming

24 Two more Chaires of the
same,

25 Two more Chaires all w.th
Crimson Damask & Gold

26 Two holland Quilts, one
white Satin Quilt, three
Stich't blanketts one ~
Camp Chaire with Damask
& Gold Colour Covers of
the same for 6 little Chaires
Teaster and headcloath
of Damask and Gold
4 Curtains of damask for
the feild bed, 2 Curtains for

ye windowes, 2 Valens of the
same, 2 bolsters & one small
Picture of my Lady Dutchess

27 Two Guilt Stands, Two
Marble Tops and 2 Gilt
Images,

28 Seventy fine Table cloaths
of all Sorts in the Chest

29 One Chest with 15 pair
of Sheets, 4 doz: of Old ~
Napkins, Sixteen Table Cloaths
of 3 Sorts,

30 A black Japan'd Chest with
Silver Furniture, two p^s
of Silver wanting, two ~
Corners, two blanketts,

31 Frame of ye Japand Chest
with two Doggs and a
large prospect. Glass,

32 Writeing Desk wth a Cabenett

33 A Chest with Cloaths

34 One large Gilt Dish, two
Flaggons, One Cup with a
Cover, one Salver, 2 Fireshovels,
and 2 pair of Tongs with
Silver belonging thereunto,
Silver belonging to 3 pair of
glass Sconces, 2 Iron Doggs
with plate Tops, 10 p^s of ~
plate belonging to AndIrons
very large and hallow, two
Silver Images for ye fire stead
8 pair of plate Sconces with
Socketts wanting, some Screws
Six knifes with Silver handles
2 China Candlesticks with
Silver Socketts,

35 Books ~
Eighty Seven books
5 paper books —

36 a low fireScreen

37 An Indian Corner
Cubbart

38 One other Cubbart
of the same

} belonging to my Lady Dutchess

3 p^s of my Ladies work
one Dressing box, a gold
Tissue Pin cushion upon
it,

Three Cases put on ~
board by Maj^r Masclary
Two Marked. D: O: w^thout
numbers, One that a blew
Velvett Sadle, hooseing
and Caps, and all other
Furniture belonged to
it never used, two p^r
of my Lord Dukes Pistolls
and two Caparison ~
Cloaths in ye other Case,
Twelve Mule Cloaths, one
case that seven Guns.
of his Grace and 2 p^r
of Serv^ts. Pistolls,
Forty five China Plates
and ye Allyblaster bowle
and Salver sent over
by Ward ~

Dublin Castle

Plate belonging to his Grace the Duke
*of Ormond Sold to Alderman Tho*ˢ*. Bolton*
*the 29*ᵗʰ *of July 1707*

	oz	pwᵗᵗˢ
2 Ovall dishes wᵗᵗ	254 -- 15	
6 Round Dishes wᵗᵗ	654 -- 4	
1 Old Skillett and pʳ of } handIrons wᵗᵗ	71 -- —	
	979 : 19	

979: ozˢ & 19 pennwᵗᵗˢ at 5ˢ : 8ᵈ ℔ Oz   277 13

I Doe Certifye that I was present when
yᵉ above Plate was wayed & delivered
to Aldᵐ Thomas Bolton at the Price
above moñconed ~

          Pe: Goodwin

Remaining of Plate in Mʳ Pacys hands
which he carries to England, one Silver
Tankard, 6 Silver handled Knifes ~

What the Several Boxes Contains
of Mr Portlocks

Nᵒ

1 The Top of the Screwtore
2 The bottom Part of it
3 large Mapps and Prints
4 Maps & prints & 6 Tea Cups
5 books and Top of a Tea Table
6 I Supose to be Empty never
    haveing had the Key.

D:O.

7 a Case that 10 Window Curtains
    a Gilt hearth, fender, fireshovele
    & Tongs, yᵉ large red Tea Tables
    3 blanketts to Wrap yᵉ Curtains
    in & 21 Mapps Roul'd up.

8
9 Three large Panell Glasses
10

11 Two Chimney Glasses
12

    The Frame of yᵉ Tea Table

These sent on } Owner
Board yᵉ   Briscoe
Pearle of Chester } Master

An Acc.^{tt} of Pictures Returned from
Dublin Castle to Kilkeny ye 24th of July 1707

The Story of Jacob painted by Jn° Victoria
The Persecution by Rosick —
The Story of Jupiter and Juno
A Large hunting p^s of a boar by hounds.
The Story of Phæbus and phæton
A Large hunting p^s of a Stagg.
A Seap^s of Shipps Unladeing
a Colation and Singing
a p^s of Birds and Bird Cages
A horse battle
A peice of Neat heard
An Old woman fleeing a Shock Dogg
A Cock and a Catt
A p^s of fruit Selling by a young woman
A p^s of fruit Selling by an Old woman
A p^s of Windsor Castle
a Landskip of a Garden
A p^s of Sheep goeing over a bridge
A Landskipp,

Two small Landskips in Gilt Frames
A Picture of a Lady in a Gilt Frame
A p^s of Vigo (vid) a Sea Skip
A bad Indian Picture of a Tyger
A painted Congratulatory speech on his
Graces comeing to Ireland,

these Six were not at Kilkeny or Dunmore formerly

An Acc.^{tt} of Pictures that were ∞//∞
formerly at Dunmore and Kilkeny and are
not Returned ~

A Peice of Hens Setting & at Roost
A p^s of Still Life (vid) Carrotts in a Wheelbarrow & c
A p^s of our Lady and St Luke
Cornelious Vantrump
Michae'l De Ruber
The Virgin Mary & our Saviour in her Armes
A Large History p^s of fine figures,
His Graces Picture at length ⵓ Van Treat

PLATE 8
Sutton Nicholls (fl. 1680–1740): St James's Square,
c. 1725, engraving. Ormond House (9–11 St James's
Square, London) is on the north side of the square
to the west of Duke of York Street.

4

THE DUKE OF ORMONDE'S HOUSE
AT ST JAMES'S SQUARE, LONDON

c. 1710

*The Furniture in
Her Graces Apartment
and the Two Floors
above*

*Her Grace the Dutches of Ormonds
Apartment.*

Dineing Roome

4 Peices of Tapstry Hangings representing Fire, Earth, and Air.
3 P.ʳ of Window Curtins Valence and Cornishes green Stuff
2 Marble Tables
2 Looking Glasses
2 Pair of Bracketts
2 Sconces with guilt Frames Branches & Nosells Silvered
22 Chairs covered with Green Coifoy & green Serg cases
1 Grate Fireshovell Poker Fend.ʳ bellows & brush.
1 Large Glases Chandelier with glass Drops.
1 Folding Fire Skreen of Indien paper.

Pictures

Landskip over yᵉ Chinmey
3 Flower peices over yᵉ Doors
Lady Northumberland ⎫
Prince's of Orange   ⎭ Halfe Lengths.

Her Graces Bed Chamber

Hangings of the Roome
1 Beddstead and Furniture Compleate wᵗʰ Counterpan
6 Chairs
2 p.ʳ Window Curtins with Valence and Cornishes all Crimson Damask trimed with D.º Lace
Cases to yᵉ Bedd and Chairs of Crimson paragon

1 Feather Bedd and Bolster
2 Pillows, 3 Blanketts, 1 Matriss Quilt, 1 Holland D.º
1 Peer Glass in a glass Frame
1 Chimney Glass and
4 Glass Sconces
1 Japan Writing Table covered with green ~~Table~~ Velvet
1 ~~Black Indian Chest and Frame~~
1 Writing Table with Drawers inlaid
1 Strong box and Frame
2 Japan Stands
1 Steel Hearth with Doggs fire shovell Tongues Brush and Bellows. &c.
1 Scrutore dore with glass Doors inlaid.

Pictures

Late Duches of Ormond. — in full Length
Present Duke of Ormonde
Lady Mary Saxfeild
Earl of Ossery
Lady Mary Buttler
Lord Caple
Lord Ossery and Lady Harriet Buttler in Minim Lands.ᵖ over the Doore.

Her Graces Dressing Roome

3 Peices of Tapstry Hangings
2 Pair of Indien Yellow Damask Curtins Vallence and Cornishes.
4 Elbo Chairs ⎫
3 Small Ditto ⎬ Green and gold couler Damask.
1 Sattee. and ⎪
2 Stoolls   ⎭
~~Green~~ Cases to yᵉ Chairs &c. Yellow Serge
1 Japan black Table
2 Stands D.º
1 Looking Glass with a black Frame
1 Chimney D.º

4 Glass Sconces with Silver Branches & Nosells
1 Little Indien Chest and Frame
1 *D.º* Fire skreen
1 Fire Hearth with Silver Frame and Nibbs
1 Pair Doggs *D.º* with Fire Shovell & tongues
  Bellows and Brush
1 Vmber Table covered with Green Cloth
1 Indien Japan corner Cubbord & Frame
1 Little Table Fire skreen
1 Cheny Jarr
2 Ditto with a Cover
1 Tea Table with 10 Tea Dishes & Sasers Milk
  pote and Tea pote
1 Dressing Glass with Japan Frame & Furniture

Pictures

Dutches of Sommersett ⎫
Late Earl of Arran   ⎬ Halfe Lengths
Dutches of York   ⎭
Lady Chesterfeild
Lady Westmorland in oval
Present Dutches of Ormond — Small Length
Flower Peice

Her Graces Drawing Roome

4 Peices of Tapstry Hangings *y.ᵉ* History of
  Diogenes
1 Large Fine black Japan Indien Chest with a
  Guilt Frame and Leath.ʳ Cover
2 P.ʳ of Window Curtins Valence and Cornish
  Trimed with ~~Green~~ Lace Blew
1 Small Black Japin Table with guilt Frame
1 Chimney Glass *D.º*
6 Glass Sconces with guilt Frames Brass Nosells
  and panns. Silvered
4 Carved Bracketts with Silver Nossells & panns
6 Elbo Chairs ⎫
2 Sattees.   ⎬ with guilt Frames
2 Window Cushions all of blew Velvett
  Serge Covers to *y.ᵉ* Chairs & Sattees
2 P.ʳ of Silver Doggs
1 Wrought Fire skreen in black Frame
  Flower Peice to Stand in *y.ᵉ* Chimney bellows &c
1 Large Indien Skreen with 6 Laves
1 Large Hanging Looking glass.

Pictures

Queen Ann   ⎫
Queen Mary ⎬ Whole Lengths
Late Duke of Ormond   ⎫
Late Duke of Beauford ⎬ Halfe *D.º*
Pres.ᵗ Duke of Beauford ⎭
Peice over *y.ᵉ* Chimney.

Her Graces Great Bed Chamber.

Hangings of the Roome
High Standing Bedd Furniture and counterpan
all of crimson and gold coulered Damask.
7 Elbo Chairs   ⎫
1 Easy *D.º*   ⎬ *D.º* Damask case Curtins &
2 Square Stools ⎬ covers to *D.º* of Yellow Serge
2 Window Seats   ⎭
2 P.ʳ of White Damask Window Curtins Valence &
  Cornishes.
1 Feather Bed and Bolster
1 Square black Japan Table covered with Leath.ʳ
1 ~~Large Looking Glass with a glass Frame~~
1 Repeating Clock and Stand
4 Little Glass Sconces with Silver Frames &
  Nosells
5 Larger Ditto
1 Chimney Glass
1 Iron Hearth with a Silver Frame and Nobbs
  and Tongues
1 Pair of Doggs Fireshovell brush and bellows
1 Small Indien Tea Table
1 Dressing Glass and stand.
1 Large Peer glass in guilt Frame

Pictures

⎫ Halfe Lengths
History peice over *y.ᵉ* Chimney.

The Great Stair Case

Pictures

1 Large Hunting Peice of Hungoes
1 Landskip   ⎫
1 Man in Armour   ⎬ over *y.ᵉ* Doors
1 Lady *w.ᵗʰ* Fruit ⎭
1 Large Lands.ᵖ with a Monum.ᵗ
1 Small Peice of Fergusons

1 Bore Hunting of Wykes
1 Large Peice of King Charles on Horse back
1 Large *D.º* of Flora.
1 S.ᵗ Cathrine
1 Lands.ᵖ of Ruin
1 Little *D.º*
1 Ditto with Figures
1 Peice of the Holy Family
1 Long Flower Piece
1 Baskett maker and Woman
1 Turkish Port
1 Lands.ᵖ of Cattle
1 Ruin with Shipping
1 Flora with Septers & Crowns
1 S.ᵗ John
1 Marige of S.ᵗ Cathrin
1 Hunting the Wild Bore
  /Caried over/

The Great Stair Case Continued

1 Judith with Holly Furne's Head
1 Peice of Cocks and Henns
1 Hern Hawking
1 Lands.ᵖ with Figuers
1 Ruin of Fergusons
1 Conversation
1 Battle
1 Lands.ᵖ– Geese
3 Pictures in y.ᵉ Cellings
6 Glass Sconces.

Lady Amilia Butler's Apartment

2 Peices of Tapstry Hangings of Landsp.ˢ
3 Cubbords.
3 Rush Chairs
1 Grate Fire Shovell and Tongues

Bed Chamber

2 Peices of Tapstry Hangings Green Work.
1 Standing Bedstead Furniture & Counterpann
2 P.ʳ of Window Curtins Valence and Cornishes
6 Elbo Chairs all Yellow Mohair, Cases of serge to *D.º*
2 Feather Bedds, 2 Bolsters 8 Blanketts 2 pillows
  3 Quilts 1 Matriss 2 Holland Quiltts
1 Truckle Bedd Stead.
1 Grate Fire Shovell Tongues poker and Fender
1 Old Skreen

Lady Amilia's Dressing Roome

2 Peices of Tapstry Hangings Men on Horseback
6 Elbo Chairs of Flowered Damask.
  Lands.ᵖ over y.ᵉ Chimney
2 Window Curtins of ~~Stripe Anterine~~ Damask
  Serge Cases to y.ᵉ Chairs
1 Iron Hearth Doggs Tongues & Fireshovell

Clossett

Hangings Window Curtins and Doore Curtins
of ~~Irish Plad~~ Worsted Damask.
1 Iron Harth Tongues and Fireshovell.

The Passage one pair of Stairs

1 Talle Beddsted
3 Blanketts
1 Rugg
1 Small oval Table
2 Glass Lanthorn's

M.ʳ Kennedyes Roome.

4 Peices of Tapstry Hangings
1 Feild Bedd with green Damask Curtins
1 Feather Bed and bolster 2 Pillows 3 Blanketts
1 Holland Quilt
1 Old Easy Chair
5 Elbo Chairs covered with French Silk
1 Fire Skreen
1 Large Looking Glass
1 Table inlaid
1 P.ʳ of Bracketts
1 Large Scrutore
1 Grate Fender Tongues Fire Shovell poker
  Bellows and Brush.
2 Glass Sconces
1 Wainscote Writing Table
2 ~~Blew Calico Window Curtins~~ p.ʳ green striped
  window ∧Curtins
1 P.ʳ of Brass Candlesticks with Snuffers & pann

Pictures

Mons.ʳ Overkirk in Halfe Length.
Dutches Sommersett. ⎫
Lady Cath: Hyde ⎭ Ovells guilt
Mary Queen of Scotts in black Frame
Lands.ᵖ in a Lackered Frame

Mrs. Butlers Roome.

Old Tapstry Hangings
1 Feild Bedd with Plad Curtins
1 Feather Bedd Bolster and Pillo
3 Blanketts and
1 Rugg.
1 Small Ovall Table
4 Cane Chairs
1 Elbo *D.º*
2 Round Stoolls
1 Wainscote Press.
1 Press with glass Doors
1 Grate Fireshovell Tongues Fend.^r & poker
  Bellows and brush
2 Brass Candlesticks and 1 p.^r Snuffers.
1 Silver Warming Pann

Lady Elizabeth Butler's Apartm.^t Two Pr Stairs.

Dressing Roome

Hangings of the Roome
2 Window Curtins
3 Rush Chairs with Cushions *D.º*
2 Indien Pictures
1 Lands^p
1 Small Sea piece
1 Stove Grate
1 Corner Cubbord.

Lady Bettyes Bedd Chamber

3 Pices of Tapstry Hangings Forest Work
  Standing Bedsted with green Damask Furniture
  Complete Case Curtins of green paragin
2 Feather Bedds 2 Bolsters 1 Matriss
6 Blanketts 2 Window Curtins ye same of ye bed
8 Cushions *D.º*
8 Cane Black Chairs
1 Dutch Chair
1 Large Glass
2 Stands and black Table
1 Dressing Table and Glass
2 Small Sconces
2 Pictures over ye Doors
1 Grate Fire Shovell, Poker Tongues, Fender
  Bellows and Brush

Margrates Roome.

2 Peices of Tapstry Hangings
6 Cane Chairs
1 Velvett Elbo Chair
3 Tables
1 Fixed Grate Fire Shovell, Tongues, Poker
  and Fender.
  Tea Table &c
1 Brass Candlestick and Snuffers.

The Stewards Roome.

2 Peices of Tapstry Hangings Figured Work
1 Standing Bedd with Crimson Paragon Furniture
1 Callico Quilt
1 Feather Bedd and Bolster
2 Large Blanketts
1 Small *D.º* 1 Pillow
1 Olive Tree Square Table
2 Stands
1 Large Looking Glass in a black Frame
1 Round Folding Table
1 Square Table of Cane
7 Cane Chairs
1 Grate Poker, Fire Shovell, Tongues, Fender
  Bellows and Brush.
2 Brass Candlesticks and snuffers.
1 Deal Press for Close
1 Old Velvett Chair
1 Little Writing Table with Drawers.

Mrs Parkers Roome

3 Peices of Tapstry Hangings. Forest Work.
1 Standing Beddstead of Blew Paragon
1 Feather Bedd and Bolster
3 Blanketts and 2 Pillows
1 White Callico Quilt
1 Olive Wood Table
1 Little Ovall *D.º*
1 Chest of Drawers
6 Dutch Rush Chairs
2 Cane *D.º*
1 Easy *D.º*
2 White Window Curtins
1 Large Wainscote Press
1 Stove Grate Fire Shovell Tongues, and Fender
2 Brass Candlesticks and Snuffers.
1 Indien Corner Cubbord

1 Black Stand
1 Old Fire Skreen.
1 Crimson Mohair Complete with green Lace
1 Hanging Glass.

The Valet D.ᵉ Chambers Roome

1 Peice of Tapstry Hangings
1 Standing Camlet Bedd with Yellow Lace
1 Square Table
2 Chairs and 2 Presses
1 Grate
1 Feather Bedd Bolster 2 Blanketts & 1 Rugg

Chaplins Roome

3 Peices of Tapstry Hangings with Forest Work
1 Feild Bedstead with red Damask Curtins & Furniture
1 Feather Bedd and Bolster 1 pillow 3 Blanketts
1 Matress
4 Arm Chairs covered with French Silk
6 Cane Chairs
1 Small Oake Table
1 Grate Fire Shovell, Tongues, poker, bellows & brush
1 Large Looking glass
1 Table
2 Stands
1 litte *D.ᵒ*
1 Pʳ. Brass Candlesticks and Snuffers.

The Middle Roome

1 Peice of Tapstry Hangings
1 Chandeleer.

M.ʳ Kennedyes Roome 2 P.ʳ Stairs

Hangings of Tapstry Forest Work
1 Large Looking Glass
1 Square Foulding Table
6 Old Dutch Chairs
1 Landsᴾ over yᵉ Chimney
1 Grate Fire Shovell Tongues and poker
1 Large Mapp of Flanders.

The Housekeepers Roome.

Hangings of Tapstry
Standing Beddsted with Drugett Plad & Valence
1 Feather and bolster 2 Pillows 3 Blanketts

1 Old Counterpann
1 Linnen Press
1 Little *D.ᵒ*
1 Oval Foulding Table
2 Old Elbo Chairs with Serge Covers
4 Other Old Chairs
1 Old Curtin
1 Square Table
1 Long Dresser
1 Stand and Cheafing Dish
2 Skilletts 1 Small Pote
1 pʳ of Brass Skeals and Weights
5 Pewter Ice Potts
1 Standing Grate Tongues Shovell, poker Fend.ʳ Bellow and Brush
1 Mapp of Hounslow Heath
2 Hand Candlesticks and Snuffers.

M.ʳ Desma's Roome

5 Peices of Tapstry Hangings
1 Feild bedstead with Furniture of blew yellow Checkered Stuff.
1 Feather Bedd and Bolster 1 Pillow
3 Blanketts and 1 rugg
1 Square Table
6 Cane Chairs
1 Elbo *D.ᵒ*
1 Fixed Grate and Fender
1 P.ʳ of White Callico Window Curtins
1 Carved Sangolier
1 Brass Candlestick.

Passage 2 P.ʳ Stairs

2 Glass Sconces.

The Appartments Three P.ʳ of Stairs

Wardrobe

1 ~~Bedstead with red Cloth Curtins and Valence~~
1 ~~Feather Bedd 1 Bolster 2 Blanketts 1 rugg~~
1 Feild Bedd with Blew Damask Furniture
1 Feather Bedd 1 bolster 2 Blanketts and a Rugg. *1 White Quilt*
1 Fixed Grate. Old
2 Cushions and 1 Vallence of White & purple Mohair
2 Crimson Cofoy very old Carpitts
5 Mule Cloths
1 Old Turky Work Carpitt

At St James's Square, London

His Graces Small Feild Crimson Harriteen Feild
Bedd and Bolster
1 Counterpann
1 Small White old Quilt of Silk
1 Case of a Chair Belonging to her Graces bed chamb.ͬ
2 Backs and Seats of Chairs of old French
Silk. Some new blew Lute String
2 Peices of Tapstry the Same of Her Graces
Dineing Roome
1 Holland Quilt belonging to his Graces Bed
and 2 Vallies
2 Pillows 1 Blankett

The Wardrobe Continued

4 Pieces of Tapstry Hangings y.ͤ History of Alexand.ͬ
1 Large Press
5 Peices of Tapstry Hangings } *2 at white hall* *1 in Lady Amely's Roome* *2 in M.ͬ Rodgers & Cross*
3 Large Boxes
4 Large Hair Trunks came from Flanders
1 Old Bedstead and old Drugett Curtins
6 Old Vmberclows.
1 Chimney Glass
  Camp of Hounslow Heath Rotten
  a parcell of old Lumber fitt for nothing
  but to Burn
9 Peices of Tapstry Hangings of Severall Sorts.
5 Chairs y.ͤ Same of Same Her Graces Dineing
                                 Roome.
2 Large Looking Glasses & inlaid Frames T
2 Tables D.ͦ
1 Spinnett & Frame 2 old Chairs 2 old Stools
2 Lady's in Guilt Frames. Halfe Length
2 Mapps ̷21 Flower Peice.

The Passpages Roome

4 Peices of Tapstry Hanging
1 Small Standing Bedd with Striped Irish Curtins
2 Feather Bedds Bolsters 4 Blanketts. & 2 Quilts
1 Old Quilt
1 Old Bedstead Feath.ͬ Bed 2 Blanketts and
1 Rugg
3 Old Tables
2 Old Chairs
1 Tinn Candlestick with a Stand
1 Lands.ͬ over the Chimney
1 Press For Close

The Maids Roome.

2 Bedsteads.
2 Feather Beds
2 Bolsters
4 Blanketts
3 Ruggs
2 Old Square Tables
6 Old Cane Chairs
1 Old Chest
1 Large Grate and Fender
3 Hand Candlesticks
1 Camlet Cur.ͭ & Furniture
1 Printed Stuff

His Graces Landry Maids Room

2 Peices of Tapstry Hangings
1 Standing Bedstead with Green Serge Curtins
1 Feather Bed and Bolster
1 Callico Quilt
3 Blanketts
1 Old Chest of Drawers
2 Cane Chairs
3 Old Rush Chairs
2 Old Stools
1 Small Sawce pann
1 Grate Fire Shovell and Poker
2 Tables
4 Smoothing Irons.

M.ͬ Crosses and M.ͬ Rogers roome

1 Old Plad Feild Bed
2 Blanketts
1 Matriss Quilt
1 Bolster
2 Old Leather Chairs
1 other D.ͦ
2 Old Tables
1 Fixed Grate
2 Flatt Small Candlesticks
2 Peices of Hangings.

Her Graces Landry maids room

1 Bedstead Feather Bed Bolster
2 Blanketts and 1 Rugg
2 Old Chairs and 1 Stooll
1 Old Stand

1 Close Horse
5 Smoothing Irons
1 Fixed Grate and Fender Fire Shovell
and poker
1 Old Sawce pann
2 Long Dressers
1 Small Little Table
Serge Curtins

John Huttes Roome.

1 Standing Bed with Old Serge Curtins
1 Feather Bedd and Bolster
2 Blanketts and 1 Rugg
2 Square Tables with an old Carpitt
5 Rushia Camp Chairs
1 Old Cane Chair
1 Velvett Elbo Chair
1 Grate Fender and Fire Shovell
1 Old Print
1 Small Peice of Tapstry.
Plad Curtins &c

His Graces Footman's Roome

2 Bedsteads with printed Stuff Curtins
2 Feather Bedds
2 Bolsters.
4 Blanketts
2 Ruggs.
Old Chairs
1 Old Table

The Blacks Roome.

1 Bedstead
1 Flock Bed and Bolster
2 Blanketts.

Walter Walshes Roome

1 Bedstead Feather bed and Bolster
2 Blanketts and 1 Rugg
1 Stooll
1 Brass Candlstick.

Her Graces Footmens Room

2 Bedsteads and Curtins. 1 Red Cloth & yᵉ other
printed Stuff
2 Feather Beds

2 Bolsters
1 Pillow
5 Blanketts
4 Old Chairs
1 Iron Harth & Doggs
1 Square Table

A Roome next the Footmens

1 Old Yellow Damask Teaster and Cornish &
Bedstead yᵗ came out of Lady Emelyes Bed
Chamber.

Mʳ Kennedyes Mans Room

1 Bedstead Feather Bed 2 Blanketts 1 Bolster
and 1 Rugg
2 Tables
2 Camp Chairs
3 *Dᵒ* Stoolls
2 Old Cane Chairs
1 Large Press
1 Hand Brass Hand Candlestick
Stuff Curtins &c

The Passage 3 Pʳ Stairs

1 Ladder

The Back Stairs

The Furniture in My Lord Dukes Apartment

His Graces Apartment

Dineing Roome

19 Chairs covered with Turkey leather & laced with gold
2 Square Tables with Leather Covers
2 ~~Inlaid Tables~~ *Marble Tables wᵗʰ wallnut Tree Frames*
2 Large ₐ^{Hanging} Looking Glasses ~~of the Same~~ }
wᵗʰ Glass & carved guilt Frames
1 Chimney Glass and
2 Sconces
2 Shandeliers
3 Pʳ Window Curtins Cornishes of Crimson
Lutestring ~~Mohair~~ Trimed with ^{crimson}~~green~~ Lace

At St James's Square, London

1 Stove Grate with Fire Shovell Tongues Poker &c
3 Cane Shashes.
1 Indien Skreen of 6 Leaves

Pictures

King Charles yᵉ 1ˢᵗ
His Queen.
King Charles 2ᵈ
King William.
Late Duke of Ormond
Earle of Ossory.
} Whole Lengths & guilt Frames

1 Large Picture of Venus over the Chimney
2 Three quarters Lengths Admirels of France
1 Earle of Ormond Halfe length.
1 Head of Chav! Montaigne
2 ~~Ladyes over the Glasses~~
3 Landsps over the Doors

The Drawing Roome Next his Graces Dineing Roome

2 Sattees
14 Chairs Window Curtins and Hangings all of Yellow Caffoiy
1 Fire Skreen Needle Work
1 Hearth with Iron Back Fire shovell Tongues Bellows and Brush.
1 Peer Glass
1 Chimney *Dᵒ* in Guilt Frame
2 Glass Sconces.
1 Black Square Table
2 Bracketts
1 Indien Tea Table
2 Kane Chasses in yᵉ Windows

Pictures

1 Landskip over the Chimney in guilt Frame
2 Ditto over the Doors.

Blew Roome

10 Elbo Chairs with Serge Covers
1 Sattee with *Dᵒ*
2 Pair Window Curtins Cornishes & Hangings of Blew Mohair
1 Marble Table with guilt Frame
2 Stands *Dᵒ*
1 Large Peer :Hanging Glass in Glass Frame
1 Chimney *Dᵒ*

2 Carved guilt Sconces over the Chimney
1 Large Double Movement Clock.
1 Brass Hearth with Fire Shovell Tongues bellows &c
2 Cane Chashes in the Windows

Pictures

1 Large Histirocal peice over yᵉ Chimney
1 Large Magdellon
  Modona.
  Cores
  Royall Family
2 Flower Peices over yᵉ Doors

  Dutches of Ormond
  Dutches Graffton
  Dutches Mazerin
  Lady Rochester
  Lady Amilia Buttler
  Lady Grantham

The Waiting Roome

1 Table Bedstead Feather Bed and bolster
2 Blanketts and
1 Rugg.
4 old Elbo Velvet Chairs
1 Grate Shovell Poker Brush and Iron to Sett the Chocolat pott on &c.
2 Black Stands For Tea

Pictures

Sʳ Neil O'Neil
Sʳ Mungo Murrey
} Whole Lengths
Six Peices of Sea Fights in guilt Frames

His Graces Dressing Roome

1 Square Wallnutt Tree Table
1 Small oval Wainscote *Dᵒ*
1 Large Indien Chest
1 Glass Press for Books
1 Peer Glass
1 Chimney *Dᵒ*
2 Glass Sconces
2 Wall Nutt Tree Bracketts.
1 Steell Hearth Fire Shovell Tongues Bellows & Brush
6 Flowered Silk Elbo Chairs
1 Pair of Crimson lute string with green lace ~~Indien Blew~~ Silk Curtins Valence Cornishes

PLATE 9
John Michael Wright (1617–1694): *Sir Neil O'Neill as an Irish chieftain*, 1680, oil on canvas. Sir Neil O'Neill (*c.* 1658–1690) died after fighting at the Battle of the Boyne. Note the Japanese *dō-maru* armour lying at his feet.

Pictures

1 Landskip over ye Chimney
1 Halfe Length of Queen Ann
1 Ditto Dutches of York.
1 Ditto Rossomonde
1 ~~Large Mapp of Flanders~~
2 Peices of ~~Landskip Hangings~~ Tapstry air
  & water.

His Graces Closset

Hangings of Velvett Crimson laced with Gold
5 Chairs ⎫
3 Stoolls ⎬ of *D^o.* Velvett *D^o.*
1 Saffoiy ⎭
1 Chimney Glass
3 Corner Cubbords with Glass Doors
1 Stove Grate
3 Pair Curtins Valence and Cornishes
1 Foulding Writing Table and Scrutore

Pictures

2 Landskips and Figures of Wykes 3 p^s in
  Guilt Frames
1 Small Ditto … in *D^o.*
1 Ditto Head after Geordon in *D^o.*
2 Draughts of Sea Fights in Black Frames
1 Peice of Flowers in the Chimney

Bathing Roome

1 Large Square Wainscote Table with a green Cloth
  Carpett.

His Graces Bed Chamber

Hangings of the Roome
2 Pair of Window Curtins
2 Ditto of Doore Ditto Valence
5 Chairs — 4 Back and 1 Easy
1 Feild Bedd all of Crimson Damask Trimed with
  Gold Lace.
1 Check Matriss Quilt.
1 *D^o.* Fustian
1 *D^o.* Holland
1 *D^o.* Silk
4 Stitched Blanketts
1 Crimson Damask Counterpann
1 Feather Bolster

3 Pillows
1 Black Japan Square Table
1 Looking Glass *D^o.*
1 Chimney Glass
1 Glass Sconces
1 Weather Glass
1 Iron Hearth and Bellows
1 Fire Skreen

Pictures

1 Landskip over ye Chimney
2 Flower peices over the Doors.

The Valet D'Chambers Roome

1 Standing Beddstead with ~~Plad Curtins~~ Yellow
  pasion Curtins.
1 Feather Bedd
1 Bolster
3 Blanketts and
1 Rugg
1 Doore Curtin
1 Glass Press
1 pair of Doggs
2 Peices of Tapstry Hangings
1 Flower peice of the Chimney
4 Leather Trunks belongs to ye Berliene
2 Hair *D^o.* for his Graces Close
1 Callico Quilt

The Plump House

1 Blew Silk window Curtin
2 Round Stoolls
1 Wainscote Close Stooll
1 Leaden Cistorn.

The Great Passage

1 Large Oake Ovall Table
1 Oyster Table
2 Glass Lanthorns
1 Standing Ladder
1 Print of a Ship.

Pictures

1 Large Land^sp
1 Queen Elizabeth Half Length.
1 Peice Still life over ye Doore
1 City of London in Flames.

1 Citty of Killkenny.
1 Sacrifice to Jupiture
5 Landsps.

The Hall next the Porters Lodge

6 Halberts
26 Fusies
1 Pipe Belonging to ye Water Ingien
1 Great Glass Lanthorn
3 Small Lanthorns
1 Fixed Grate

Porters Lodge

1 Chair and
1 Seate to Sitt on
48 Bucketts
3 Glass Sconces
1 Porters Staff with a Silver Head
1 Fixed Grate Fire shovell poker and Fender
1 hand Brass Candlestick and Snuffers.

The Stewards Office

1 Scrutore
1 Box for papers
2 Small Tables
5 Chairs
1 Picture over y^e Chimney
1 Grate Fire shovell & Tongues
1 Mapp of all y^e World

Porters Roome

1 Feather Bedd Bedstead & Curtins
1 Bolster
2 Blanketts and
1 Rugg.
1 Table &
1 Stoolle.

At St James's Square, London

PLATE 10
John Brooks (*fl.* 1730–56): *Right Reverend Dr Robert Howard (1683–1740), Lord Bishop of Elphin (1730–40)*, mezzotint after a painting by Michael Dahl (1656/1659–1743)

5

BISHOP'S MANSION HOUSE, ELPHIN, COUNTY ROSCOMMON

1740

JOHN ADAMSON

A CURSORY GLANCE at the 1740 inventory of the goods and chattels held at the palace at Elphin and belonging to the Rev. Dr Robert Howard, lately dead, and we could be forgiven for thinking that this Church of Ireland bishop was a somewhat otherworldly man (see his portrait on facing page). Was it for lack of resources or through some kind of asceticism that he had apparently decked the see house with only the most utilitarian of furniture and fittings? The impression that latterly the interior of this palace might even have had a slightly woebegone aspect is strengthened when we read the addendum at the foot of the first folio. There, George Manby, the appraiser, admits having overlooked a mistake made by the transcriber: the value of the stair-head room had been wrongly entered at £6 instead of at £2 6s, 'ye Curtains being much damaged & torn'. Furthermore, the breadth and depth of learning held between the boards of Robert Howard's 380 or so books ranged on shelves in his study and listed in a separate inventory of the same month indicate that he was perhaps more interested in bookishness than in the comforts of the home.

Yet in truth, the bishop's affairs at the time of his death on 3 April 1740 were not what they might seem at first. When his father died in 1710 he had been left £750 and later had become a successful landowner, having acquired lands either through purchase for £40,000 at Carlow or by his marriage in 1724 to Patience Boleyn, and when his elder brother Hugh died in 1738, he had inherited vast tracts of land, mainly around what became known as Shelton Abbey in County Wicklow (see inventory on pp. 229–34). He was also the owner of a smart town house in Dublin's newly created Dawson Street.

Nevertheless, throughout his episcopate, first at Killala, County Mayo (1727–30), and then at Elphin (1730–40), he exhibited great restraint and railed against any conspicuous display of wealth. 'Luxury and the rage of profit hath got into all orders and degrees of men,' he once wrote to his brother Hugh, the painter, collector and connoisseur, 'and how can it be otherwise when finery ... is looked upon as the chief distinction and felicity'.

At the same time, he was a man who believed in the benefits of education for both the clergy and laity of his bishopric. The stock of books lining his study served as a local library, for it was kept for his visitors' enlightenment and edification as well as his own. Venturing far beyond a mere gathering of theological and devotional works, the choice of books is remarkably eclectic, albeit rather old-fashioned, with only a sprinkling of titles from the early eighteenth century. One of these newer works was Ephraim Chambers's *Cyclopædia* (London, 1728), which Robert Howard, writing to his brother Hugh, described as 'a sort of library in one volume' (though in fact published in two). That book was kept in the parlour, 'for the instruction and amusement of country gentry and parsons' and so does not appear in the inventory of books in the study. With the help of modern information technology, it has been possible to identify, or conjecture the identity of, most of the books listed. The outcome is shown in an index sorted by author (see Appendix III). The inventory of the books was done on 12 June 1740, almost a week before the general inventory was drawn up, and in a different hand. However, no value is given for the books, and in reckoning how much his successor Bishop Edward Synge was to pay Bishop Howard's widow in total for the contents of the house and outhouses and for the livestock the appraiser does not itemize a sum for them.

Although Bishop Howard during summer sojourns had rebuilt the palace at Elphin, Bishop Synge, his successor, was to bring about a sea-change, replacing the house with an Irish Palladian-style dwelling into which he moved in 1749.

A scion of a well-educated and successful Dublin family, Robert was the second son of Ralph Howard, a leading physician. Born in 1683, he attended Mr Jones's school in Dublin and studied at Trinity College, where he obtained a fellowship in 1703. In 1705 he was ordained in the diocese of Meath. On 19 March 1727 he was consecrated bishop of Killala, but on 13 January 1730 was translated to the see of Elphin. Robert's eldest son Ralph, who inherited the family estate on his death, was created Baron Clonmore of Clonmore Castle, County Carlow, in 1776, and in 1785 was made Viscount Wicklow (see his portrait as a young man, page 258, plate 41). In 1793, Ralph's widow became Countess of Wicklow in her own right, and when she died in 1807, their eldest son succeeded as second Earl of Wicklow.

The inventories of the Bishop's Mansion House, Elphin, County Roscommon, dated 1740, form part of the Wicklow Papers held at the National Library of Ireland.

*An Inventory of the household Goods belonging
To Docter Robert Howard Late Lord Bishop
of Elphin taken this 21st day of June 1740*

N°1   The Closset Inside the Nursery

    a Little Read Bead & Bed Stead
    a Bed & Boulster
    a Pair of Blankets
    a white Quilt   2   18   1½
    a Small oak table Bed
    a Bed & Boulster
    a pair of Blankets
    one Under ~~Quilt~~ Blanket

N°2   The Nursery left hand

    a blue bed & bed cloths
    one Oake table bed
    a feather Bed Boulster & pillow
    one pair of Blankets & Under Blanket
    2 Rush Bottomed Chairs
    Tongs fire Shovell & fender   5   11   0
    an old Chest of Drawers
    an Iron Lock on the Door
    one Bolt on Inside Door
    a Small oake Dressing table
    2 Counterpains
    a Blew Bed & Bed Cloaths

N°3   My Lords Bed Chamber

    a Yellow Stuff bed & Curtains
    a feather Bed
    a Boulster & pilloe
    a pair of Blankets & Under Blanket
    a Mattress & Quilt
    5 Rush Bottomed Chairs
    one Oake Chest of Drawers wth Locks & Keyes   8   0   0
    one Oake Dressing table
    one Brass Lock
    one Stock Lock on the Closet
    a Chimney Glass
    a Grate fender fire Shovell & Tongs

N°4   My Lords Studdy

    an oake writeing table & greene Cloath
    an oake arm Chair & one plain Chair
    a Large Chest of Drawers
    a Craked Looking Glass   3   5   0
    a Pewter writeing Stand
    one Stock a^{lock} on the Door
    In the Lobby one glass Lantron
    a Stock Lock on the Closset

N°5   The Stair Head Room

    a Bed Stead & Bed Curtains
    a feather Bead Boulster & pillow
    a pair of Blankets & Under Blankets   6   0   0
    one Oake Chair
    an Old Lock on the Door
    a white tufted Quilt

N°6   Blew Room

    one New Standing bed
    a feather Bed & Boulster
    2 pillows & Mattress
    2 Blankets & Under Blanket
    one White Quilt tufted
    Carried on   25   14   1½

The Am^t of the other Side   25   14   1½

    one oake Dressing table
    one Blew field Bed
    one feather Bed Boulster & pillow
    a pair of Blankets & Under Blanket
    a White quilt tufted
    4 Dressing Glasses
    a fender tongs & fire shovell   20   17   8
    one pair of Bellows
    Eight wraught Chairs
    the Room New Hung
    a Brass Lock on the Door
    an old Card table in the Closset
    a Cloce Stool & pewter pan
    an Iron Lock on the Room

Bishop's mansion house, Elphin, County Roscommon

N° 7   In the Store Room

A Pewter Still & Iron pott
3 Groce of Corks
a Stone Bottle
a Tarrier to broach Wine
7 New Bed Cords
one New Stock Lock wth two Keyes
                Bolts & old locks
one Copper Chaifeing dish
a Dale Box wth a number of Candles
a pair of Iron Racks
a Pistle & Mortar
a Little Dale table   8 18 0
Severall Sorts of Cords
New Bed Bottoms & Cloaths Baskets
old Curtin Rods
a New Iron Coale Box
Sive Bottoms & a brass plate Stand
Brush Heads
a Large parcell of Nailes   3 17 0
a New Caple roape
an Iron Lock on the Door
A Hammer

N° 8   In the Closset

Earthen ware of All Sorts
0„ 2„ 6 Soape
Some tin ware

N° 9   Red Room

Red Bed & Bed Curtains
a feather Bed & Boulster
2 pillows Mattres & a Callicoe quilt
2 Blankets & Under Blanket
a Settee & tea weater
a Chimney glass & 2 brass Sconces
a pair of Bellows & 2 hand screens
a Brass fender fire shovell tongs   10 19 3
                & poker
a Dale Dressing table & an arm Chair
7 Chairs a Mohogany tea teable &
                tea Chest
2 Screenes & Window Curtains

N° 10   In the further Clossett

a Cloce Stool & pan
In the Next Clossett a field Bed &
                Red Curtains
a feather Bed & Boulster   3 8 1½
a pair of Blankets Under blanket & quilt
2 Bolts on the Closset Doors & A brass Lock
on the Room Door Red Window Curtains

In the Hall a Lantron

N° 11   In the Parlor

A Clock A Card table a tea teable
an Oake Dressing table a side Oake table
a Mohogany round table
ten Leather Bottomed Chairs   12 1 0
a Loeking Glass & 2 Sconces a Brass Lock
                on the Door
an Iron grate tongs fire Shovell & fender

Carried on	85	15	2
The Am^t of the other Side	85	15	2

N° 12   In the Drawing Room

4 oake Chairs one arm Chair
an oake table bed a Brass Lock
a tongs fire Shovell & fender   2 5 0
an Iron Lock & an Iron Lock on the Closset
a Lock on the Closset in the passadge

N° 13   In the Large Dineing Room

2 Large oake tables
15 leather Bottomed Chairs A Screen
a Looking Glass & 2 pair of Glass Arms   11 15 3
a grate fire Shovell tongs poker & fender
2 pair of yellow Windoe Curtains
a Brass Lock

N° 14   Pantry

Shelves & Dressers 2 & a halfe Dozen of   1 12 0
Ivery Knives & ~~forks~~ & *D.°* of *D.°* forks

N° 15   The Larder

a Pikling tub & bread Rasp   0 5 0

N° 16 The Little Hall

a Large Deale Bin & pad Lock	
a Little oake table & six oake Chairs	1 10 0

N° 17 Serv.ts Hall

a Settle Bed & Long table & 2 forms	
a horse to dry Cloaths on	1 5 0

N° 18 The Kitchen

A Bell over the Kitchen
23 pewter Dishes 3 Dozen of pewter plates
1 Dozen of Soop plates 1 pewter tun dish
1 pewter Stand & Cullender
2 Copper Kettle pots & Covers
3 Copper toss pans 3 Copper pudden pans
3 Copper Sauce pans 2 Copper pots for Drink
2 tea Kettles 2 Coffee potts 1 Chocolat pott
1 Copper Warming pan 1 Copper Drainer
1 Brass pepper Box 1 Brass Mortar & pestill
2 tin pudden pans   18 2 10
2 Iron Skivers w.th Lead heads 2 plain Iron D°
2 Kleevers 1 frying pann 1 Brass Skimmer
1 Grid Iron 1 Iron Croe 2 trippits
1 hanging Iron 1 old fire Buket 5 Spitts

Jack useless till mended
1 Jack & 2 Chains 1 Coffee Roaster 1 Salt Box
2 Hogs In Bacon w.t 1.2.26   2 8 6
7 Brass Hand Candle Sticks
1 pair Kitchen tongs 2 pair tall brass Candle
Sticks a Deale teable Dresser & Shelves
a Grate   2 10 0

N° 19 The Room over the Kitchen

one Red Deale Chest one old Oake Chest
lock & Key a haire Line 1 Silk Serch[?]
a Haire Sive a feather bed & boulster
a pair of blankets & Under Blanket
a Bed & boulster 1 pair of blankets
an old flock Bed & Boulster   4 7 0
a Box Smoothing Iron & 2 heaters
5 Cloaths baskets a plate Basket
3 flatt Smoothing Irons a Deale press for
Grocerys an old fender a Jelly Stand
a Stock Lock on the Door
1. 2. 8 wrought Iron of All Sorts   2 8 9

Carried forward   134 4 6

Carried forward	134	4	6

N° 20 China ware

2 Craked Dishes	0	16	0
2 Large Dishes	1	10	0
7 of a size	2	16	0
7 more D°	1	15	0
2 more Craked			
4 Small Dishes	1	0	0
3 Dozen & 3 China plates	2	19	3
4 Bowles	0	8	0
12 Coffee Cups	0	8	0
20 tea Saucers & 19 tea Cups	0	19	6
a plate Basket	0	1	1

N° 21 The Glasses

3 Dozen & 3 Wine Glasses	0	15	0
2 large Beer Glasses	0	1	0
4 pair of Crewetts for oyle & Ving.r	0	2	0
17 Water glasses	0	5	8
2 Decanters	0	2	8
3 Water Bottles	0	2	0
12 Whip Silly bub Glasses	0	3	0
16 Jelly Glasses	0	4	0
1 Glass Bowle	0	1	0
Sweet mate glasses	0	2	0
1 Glass Stand 1 Bowle for Wine			
3 Dozen of tin patty pans	0	14	0
	£ 149	9	8

*I certifie y.t upon a Revisal of the within
Valuation I perfectly recollect & am certain
y.t the furniture of y.e Stair head room was va-
-lued only at two pounds six shillings ster, y.e
Curtains being much damaged & torn, & y.t by
a mistake of y.e transcriber it was made in this
paper six pounds, & the mistake was overlookd
by me at our Signing it Geo. Manby
July y.e 9.th 1740*

Bishop's mansion house, Elphin, County Roscommon

An Inventory of Goods Belonging to the Late
Lord Bishop of Elphin taken this 21st June 1740

$N^o 1$ *The out Apartm^{ts} The Store Room Over the work house*

2 plough tree wth the takling for one	
2 Harroes wth Iron pins 1 four horse Swingle tree	
bound wth Iron 3 pair 2 horse trees bound	0 8 0
wth Iron	
4 pair of Leather treaces Iron Chains for 2 harrows	
5 Aulder poles	0 2 6
8 Ash Axell trees for wheele Car^s	0 5 4
22 wheele Carrs wood bars	0 1 0
46 whole Deale boards	2 17 6
400 Shingles	0 16 0
12 Brooms	0 1 0
500 Gads	0
6 Bailes for the Stable Horses	0 6 0
5 pitch forks	0 3 4
4 hay Rakes	0 1 0
5 Stradles	0 0 10
5 Hains	-- -- 10
1 hand barrow	0 0 3
2 Stock Locks one Store room & Worke house	
Some Lumber in said apartments	0 1 0

$N^o 2$ *Coach house*, a Bin to hold Corn a Lock to
y^e Door   0 10 0

$N^o 3$ *The Lower Stable & Tumblers*   0 8 0
A stock lock to the Door & D^o to the other Door

$N^o 4$ *The Hay yeard*

4 Wheel Cars	2 0 0
4 turf Keshes	
a Cock of Hay 1 D^o of Straw	7 0 0
4 oake posts in the bleach yeard & horse Locks	
1 Stock lock to the Slaughter house	

5th *Dary* eight Keelers   0 12 0

6 Milk Earthen panns	0 7 0
4 Wooden Milk bowles	0 4 0
1 Churn	0 3 6
4 Gallons for Milking & 2 Verry bad	0 1 8
1 Small tub	0 0 8
1 flower tub	0 0 8

1 Candle Box wth 12 Moulds	0 12 0
1 Oake Chair	0 1 6
3 Small Wooden Bowles	0 1 6
5 — — D^o Trenchers	0 0 6
1 Strainer for Milk	0 0 6
3 Cheese fatts & Skimmer	0 2 0
1 Broaken Dale table Lafe	
1 Stock Lock on the Door	

$N^o 6$ *Brew house*

1 Large Copper fixed in furnis	10 10 0
1 Small D^o	3 10 0
1 Large Keeve	0 12 0
5 Stans	0 12 6
8 Washing tubs	0 12 0
1 Standing D^o	0 2 6
1 Tundish	0 0 6
2 Small poles	0 3 0

Carried Over   33 12 7   033 12 7

Carried forward   33 12 7

1 Keeve Stoole	
1 Washing Dresser	
2 Coops for poultry	0 5 0
1 Stock Lock on the Door	

$N^o 7$ *The Guile Room*

5 Hheads filled wth table Beer	1 5 0
4 Tierces filled wth the same	0 16 0
1 Wheate Steele Millen	1 10 0
1 Stock Lock on the Door	

$N^o 8$ *In the Court*
a Bottle Drain wth & Locks   2 0 0

$N^o 9$ *The Table Beer Cellar*
Eight Heads of table Beer   2 0 0
1 Empty Cask a Filter & Lock to
the Door

N° 10 Wine Cellar

1 Bin 6 Dozen of March Beer & Lock on the Door	2	14	0

N° 11 The Ale Cellar

10 Hheads Under Ale	2	10	0
1 Droper 3 Brass Cocks & Lok on the Door	0	4	6
In Office 1 Oake Chair Lock & Key	0	1	0

N° 12 M.r Holdings Room

4 Oake Chairs	0	6	0
1 Small oake table 1 Deale table	0	2	6
A Bed Stead a Bead Boulster pillow			
3 Blankets Quilt a pewter Chamber pott			
A Stock Lock to the Door & one on the Closset	2	10	0

N° 13 The Gardners Room

Bed Stead Bed & Boulster 1 pair of blankets			
1 Rug 2 Oake Chairs 1 Stock Lock to the Door	1	10	0

N° 14 The Serv.ts Room

3 Bed Steads 3 ffeather beds Boulsters			
3 pair of blankets & 3 Rugs	4	10	0

N° 15 The Granerry

1 Stable Buket	0	2	6
Empty Bottles 60 Dozen Q.rts 4 D.o pintes	6	6	0
1 Screene for Claining Corn	1	2	9
A Parlament barrell & peck	0	2	6
16 Barrells of Oates	4	16	0
Wheate 9 barrells	10	16	0
A Winnoing Cloath	0	7	6

Abroade

A Long Ladder a Short one In the Pidgeon house			
1 Short one In the hay yeard one hay knife	0	12	0
All Locks In & Aboutt the house	2	0	0
Garden Tools of All Sorts w.th Glasses & Wheel Barroes	2	2	0
A Roleing Stone	1	10	0
Bee Hives	0	5	0
Old Iron 1. 2. 14	0	15	2
New D.o 2. 3	0	11	10 ½
Gardners Weages	3	6	8
Leaborers	2	2	8
Carried over	92	15	2 ½

Carried on	92	15	2 ½
Garden Seeds	3	8	5
Weeders	0	13	0
Spring Corn	8	10	0
Winter Corn the Worst I Ever Saw	5	0	0
for 48½ Barrell.s of Malt & 72½ p.d of hopps	20	7	5 ½
160 Turf	0	13	0
48 Mens Labar at 5[d]	1	0	0
3½ barrells of Potatoes	1	10	0
The Black Cattle 2 Stall fed Bullocks	10	0	0
6 Milks Cows	15	0	0
4 Strappers 1 of w.ch is dry	8	0	0
1 Bullock 4 yeare old	2	10	0
2 D.o 3 yeare D.o	4	0	0
2 D.o 2 yeare D.o	3	0	0
2 heaffers 2 yeare D.o	3	2	0
a Bull 7 y.r old Irone in			
1 heafer 1 y.r old	0	12	0
1 Bullock 1 y.r old	0	10	0
40 fatt Weathers & the Ram	16	0	0
a Black Filly 3 y.r old	4	10	0
1 Black Sadle Mare	4	0	0
4 Plowgh Horses	12	0	0
1 old Grey Mare	0	18	3
	£ 217	19	4
	149	9	8
	367	9	0

The Above is an Acc.t Settled by Us this day Amounting in the Whole to three hundred Sixty Seven pounds Nine Shillings Ster.g Dated this 21 day of June 1740

Blandford

Geo Manby

I Patience Howard One of the Ex.rs of Robert Howard Late <u>Bp</u> of Elphin do hereby Acknow==ledge to have Rec.d of the Right Reverend D.r Edward Synge now <u>Bp</u> of Elphin the Sume of 302,,6,,2 which together with an Allowance Claim'd by him for Repairs to be made in and about the Mansion House and out Houses be==longing to the See of Elphin is in full Satisfaction for all the Household Goods and other Chattles mentioned in the above And Annext Inventory and for the Books in the Said Mansion House

£	s	d
302	6	2

Bishop's mansion house, Elphin, County Roscommon

of Elphin at the Death of the Said Late Bp &
in Consideration thereof, I Doe hereby Bargain
and Sell unto the Said Edward Lord Bp of
Elphin all the Said Household Goods Books
and Chattles, and in Consideration of y^e p^remisses,
I the Said Edward Lord Bp of Elphin Doe
hereby Acknowledge to have Rec^d full Satis=
=faction from the Said Patience Howard for
All Claims Challenges and Demands whatsoever which
I Can or May have against the Said Patience Howard &
Other the Execu^trs of the Said Dr Robert Howard for or on
Account of all Repairs to be made in or about the Mansion
House or Out Houses belonging to the Said See, or on any
other Account whatsoever Witness Our hand this Twenty
first Day of ffeb^ry 1740

       Pat Howard Edw: Elphin

'An Acc^t of Goods
Sold at Elphin with
ye R^t Revd Dr Edward
Synge Act: for
ye Same
£302:6:2

Bishop's mansion house, Elphin, County Roscommon, books in the study, 1740

For suggested identifications of books listed in abridged form in the list below, see Appendix III, pp. 369–76.

A List of the books in ye Studie att Elphin

1st Shelf.

The Devout Christian by D. Pat^k	1
Des Erasmi Roterodami doctissimaComentaria	2
Ethica Eustachii	3
An Abridgem^t of Ld Cookes comentaries upon Littleton	4
Dr Burnetts Travels 1. Vol. old, out of ye Binding	5
institutio Græcæ Gramatices Compendiaria	6.
Marcelli Palingenii Stellati Poetæ Doctissimi Zodiacus Vitæ	7.
Acute Dicta omnium Veterum Poetarum Latinorum &c	8.
two Dialogues in English between a D. of D^{ty} & a Stud^t in ye Law	9.
Dryden's English juvenal in Verse – *Octav. mins part*	10.
Machiavelii Florentini Disputaõnes	11.
The Young Clerk's Tutor by Edwd Cocker	12
The court keeper's Guide	13.
Justi Lipsii tractatus peculiares. &	14.
Pharmaco Poeia Collegii Regalis Londini ⨏ Shipton	15.
Bellarminus Enervatus in quatuor tonos divisus	16.
Willis's Pharma – 2 Vol.	17.
Lexicon Medicum Blancardi	18.
Oeuvres Diverses Le Traite du Sublime	19.
Taylor's Discourse on ye Liberty of Prophesying	20.
Ward's Mathematician's Guide	21.
a Collecõn of Articles &c belonging to ye Church of England	22.
Shakesspears Works 3 Vol *out of eight*	25.
a French book on ye Festivals 2 Vol	26.
Bray's Bibliotheca Parochialis Vol 1.	27.
A. B. Usher's Dissertaõn on on Polycarp & Ignatius	28.
Discorsi Dinicoloma Machia Velli	29.
Philosophical Transacõns	30.
Lucubraõnes omnes Judæi Philonis – Octavo	40.
Tomus tertius continuaõnis Joannis Sleidani & Michaelem Casparum	41.
Theocritus	42.
Ben John'stons Comedies & Tragedies 2 vol. *a miscellaneous collection Oct*	43.
Barronii Annales *a little Abridgm^t not worth a penny*	44
Machivel's Discourses upon ye 1st Decade of T: Livius	45.

Catechismus ad Parochos jussu Pii Pont. Max. promulgatus	46.
M: T: Ciceronis Lib. Philosophicorum Vol. 1^{mum}	47.
A Collec͠on of Sermons by Several hands	48.
A book ~~on life~~ call'd ye Educa͠on of young Gentlem^n in 2 parts.	49
Relec͠ones Hyemales de ra͠one & Methodo Legendi Historias.	50.
a French book De la Conformite Des. merveilles Modernes	51.
Aristoteles Poetry	52.
Sansovinus's treatise on Governm^t in French	53.
Rela ͠one Della Corte alias De Roma	54.
Bennetts Discourse on Schism	55.
Ristretto Dell Historie Del Mondo Del Padre	56.
Athenagorus Libellus	57

The 2^d Shelf.

Hierocles Philo.	58.
Polydori Vergilli Urbinatis de rerum inven͠oribus	59.
Hieronomus Cardanus de Subtililate	60.
Plutarchi Moralia *Latin*	61.
Memoires Historiques 2 Vol	63.
The Ladie's Library 2 Vol	65.
Cornelii Taciti Opera – *2 mighty bad Editions*	66.
Chronicon Carionis a Philippo Melanchthone	67.
institutiones Linguæ Grecæ a Nicholao Cleonardo	68.
Robertus Sanderson De juramenti Obliga ͠one. *out of binding*	69.
New Testament in French	70.
Selden De Dis Syris	71.
Ray's Wisdom of God	72.
Schola Salernii	73.
Erasmi Colloquia Notæ Bin.	74.
Julius Caesar Scaliger de causis Linguæ Latinæ	75.
Mechanicall Geometry by J. w:	76.
Comedies De Plaute	77.
Galliæ Descrip͠o a Joanne Sleidano	78.
Ritratto De Roma Antiqua	79.
Edmundus Richerius De Historia conciliorum 3	82.
Francisci Sanctii Minerva	83.
~~Taei~~ Opera Lucii Cælii	85
Thesaurus Gramaticus	86.
Arnoldus De justi͠a & jure	87.
An introduc͠on to ye Italian tongue	88.
ye whole Duty of Man	89.
Bellarminus De Scriptoribus Ecclesiasticis	90.
Barth. Cor[r]anza De concilius a S: Petro usque ad julium *Octavo*	91.
La cour Saincte ou institution Chrestienne	92.
Le Decameron De Maistre Jean Bocace	93.
Josephus Scaliger De Propert Catulli Tibulli	94.
Antiquitates Rom: a M: Friderico Hilde brando	95.

an History of ye original of Ecclesiastical Revenues	96.
Ray's travels	97.
Fragmenta Antiquitatis ℔ T: B.	98.
The Repertoire of Letters	99.
The Pastoral care by The Bp. of Sarum	100.
Lucretius de Rerum Natura	101.

The 3^d Shelf.

Steel's Connick Secõns	102.
Cumberland de Legibus Naturæ	103.
Bacons councils Civil & Moral	104.
Fleetwood's Sermon's 1. vol	105.
A Dissuasive from Popery by jer^y Bp of Down	106.
Pearson's Exposiõn of ye Creed in breif	107.
Strada De Bello Belgico	109.
Legrand Philosophia	110.
Legrand Sacra Historia	111.
Stillingfleete's Divine Right	112.
Socratis Memorabilia	113.
Petronius Arbiter Variorum	114
Taylor's Living & dying	115.
The Mystery of Jesuitism	116.
Apologia Catholica	117.
Petty's Political Arithmetick	118.
Du P. Rapin's Reflecõns. 2. Vol	120.
La Cour de Rome La Saincte	121.
Macrobii Opera	122.
Bp jewel's Apology of ye Church of England	123.
Siden Hami Observaõnes	124.
Stillingfleet's Origines Sacræ	125.
The Perambulaõn of Kent	126.
Le Moven De Parvenir	127.
Gramatica Latina ℔ Sam^m Pratt Dec. Roffens	128.
Wells's Astronomy	129.
Stultitæ Laus	130.
Bladen de curiis Ecclesiasticis al^s Clark's Praxis	131.
G. Cheyn on Health	132.
Theatrum Historicum	133.
Analysis Methodica juris Pontificii ℔ Dan^m Venatorium	134.
Didacas Stella de Vanitate Mundi	135.
Rous Mella Patrum	136.
Fisonomia Della Porta	137.
Calvini instituõn	138.
M: T: Ciceronis de officiis	139.
The free holder	140.
Plato De Repu. Divin	141.
Vareni Geographia	142.

Bishop's mansion house, Elphin, County Roscommon

Ciceronis Orationes 3. vol *Octavo*	146.
King deorigine Mali	146.
Hunts Abridgem.ᵗ 2 Vol	1478
Meritons Abridgem.ᵗ of yᵉ Irish Statues	149.

4.ᵗʰ Shelf.

The Rights of yᵉ Church	150.
Gedde's upon yᵉ Adoraõn of Images	151.
Alingham's Treasury of yᵉ Mathematicks	152.
Gibson's Anatomy	153.
Borelii Observaõnes	154.
The compleat Horse Man by S.ʳ W.ᵐ Hore	155.
Dupin's Method of Studying Divinity	156.
An Exposiõn of yᵉ Church Catechism by Gilb.ᵗ B. of Sarum	157.
Wake's Exposiõn of yᵉ Catechism	158.
Vitæ German Philoso.	159.
Bull's Vindicaõn of yᵉ Church of England	160.
[fully erased title]	161.
Erasmi Colloquia	162
Whiston's Mathematical Prælecõns	163.
Tyrrel's Law of Nature	164
Gastrel's Sermon's	165.
Maurice's Defence of Diocesian Episcopacy	166.
Lock's Abridgem.ᵗ on Humane Understanding	167.
Synodus Anglicana	168.
The Faith Religion &c profess'd & protected in England	169
Gravesande's Mathematical Elements	170
Ecclesiæ Anglicanæ Articuli 39.	171.
Appiani Alexandrini Romanarum Historiarum 2 Vol	173.
Law Quibbles comonly used in yᵉ Profession of yᵉ Law	174.
The Irish Historical Library	175.
Bennetts Essay on yᵉ 39 Articles	176.
Plinii Epistolæ	177.
La Geneologia ₍Glin Dei	178.
Eng. Statues Abr. 1. Vol. 8.ᵛᵒ	179.
Duncombe's Law of England concerning juries	180.
A Survey of Trade &c.	181
The Law of Masters	182.

ye 4th Shelf continued

term [ink mark] of ye Law	183
Mathesis juvenilis 3 vol	186.
Cæsar Variorum 2. Vol.	1876.
Quincy's Dispensatory	189.
Hudibras	190.
Dr Wicliffs Life	191.
A Treatise of Affairs Maritime	192.
Rohaults Physicks	193.
Kettlewell's Christian Obedience	194.
Hobbs De Legibus Naturæ	195.
Lucretius Creech	196.
Quincy's Medicina Statica	197.
Tanners History of ye Religious Houses in England & Wales	198
A Defence of revealed Religion by Conybear	199
The History of Charles ye twelfth	200.

ye 5th Shelf

Bacon's Adv. of Learning fol	201.
Strabonis Geographica fol *1. **Vol. a very old Bad Edition***	202.
Grew's Anat: of Plants fol	203.
Chillingworths works fol	204.
Stilling Origines Britan: fol	205.
Platinæ de Vitis Pontificum Romanorum L 4to	206.
Belon Observ. L 4to.	207.
Origines Contra Celsum a Spen^d Edit L 4to	208.
Historia Del concilio Tridentino L 4to	209.
Dictionarium Historicum Geographicum L 4to	210.
Natural History of Ireland L 4to	211.
Pancirolii Rerum Memorabilium L 4to	212.
Boter Rela õni Universi L 4to.	213.
Antiquitates Romanorum L 4to.	214.
Boxhornii His: Univ: L 4to	215.
Christiani Eberhardi introducõ 2 Vol. L 4^{to's}	216.
Le Vite De Pittori Scultori L 4to	217.
Pemberton's Veiw L 4to.	218.
Stillingfleet's Separaõn L 4to	219
A breif Treatise of Testaments & last Wills	220.
officium Clerici Pacis 8vo	221.
Spanhemii Dissertaõnes L 4to	222
Zenophon Gr. 8vo a School boy's	223.
Horatius in Usum Delph	224.
juvenal in Usum Delph	225.
A Bible	226.
Sault's Chronology	227.
Sturmius's Mathematicks	228.

Bishop's mansion house, Elphin, County Roscommon

Opuscula Mythologica	229.
Monsieur Le Clerc's Supplem^t to Dr Hamond's Paraphrase	230.
Grotius de jure Belli ac Pacis	231.
Foster's Sermons	232.
The fairee Queen *old*	233.
Godwin's Moses & Aron	234.
Taylor's Episcopacie	235
Apparatus Latinæ Locu õnis	236.
Biblia Græca 8vo	237.
Diodatii annotaõnes	238.

The 5th shelf continued

~~Euclidis Opera~~ *Hieronymi Opera* 3 Vol folio	241.
M: T: Opera 2 Vol folio 1680	24~~2~~3.
Liber De Piscibus folio	244.
Scapula Lexicon	245.
Historiæ Rom: Scriptorum Latinorum Veterum 2 Vol. Folio	247.
A Bible L 4to	248.
A New Dictionary in five Alphabets L 4to	249.
Lexicon Pentaglotton folio	250.
Pearson's exposition of ye Creed. *miserably abus"d* folio	251
Cave Historia Litteraria	252.
Athenæus Gr: Lat: Casaubon 2 vol folio	253.
Aquinatis Sum̄a Theologica folio	254.
Lock of Humane Understanding folio	255.
Bolton's justice of Peace folio	256.
Fullers Ch: History folio	257
Wood's institute folio	258.
Cabasutitii Notitia Ecclesia folio	259.
Gilberts Exposiõn of ye 39 Articles folio	260.
M. Antonii in Livium Annota õnes folio	261.
Procopii Cæsariensis Historia Arcana folio	262.
Barrow's Works *1. Vol. only* folio	263.
~~Sir James Wares History of Ire~~land &c folio	264.
Bennett's His: of Council Trent folio	265
A Synopsis of Papism folio	266.
Pausanias Græco. La. folio	267.
The Oceana by Mr Harrington folio	268.
Robbins's Abridgem^t of ye Statues folio.	269.
Spelman's concilia & decreta	270.

in Little shelfs

1ˢᵗ shelf

Lexicon Manuale 8ᵛ·ᵒ	270.
Lucretius de rerum Natura Duodecimo.	271
a Copious & exact Dictionarie in Italian & English	272
The Clergy Man's Vade mecum	273.
Novum Testamentum Græcum	274
Liber precum com̄unium	275.
Lexicon Græco Latinum in Testamentum Novum	276.
Compendium Græcum	277.
yᵉ Parson's Guide	278
Articuli 39 ℀ Jo Elis	279.
Clavis Græca Novi Testamenti	280
Græca Gramatica	281
Il Trionfo Del Pennello Di Guido Reni	282
Rice's Guide to persons concern'd in yᵉ Bp's court	283
Rapin de Hortis	284
Celsus de Re Medica	285.

2ᵈ shelf. yᵉ Back part

Thuanus *a Vol. 8ᵛ·ᵒ not worth 2ᵈ*	286
Vitæ Germanorum Medicorum a Melchiore Adamo	287.
De Synederiis Veterum Ebræorum 2 Vol	289
Eccl Brit Anti:	290.
Hutton & Croke's Argumᵗˢ	291.
Errour convicted	292
Sulpitii Severi Historia Sacra	293.
Zouchei Elementa	294
Thomæ Smethi Angli de Republica Anglorum	296.
The occasion of yᵉ Contempt of yᵉ Clergy *1ˢᵗ + worst [?] Edit*	297.
Bulleri Monarchia fæminia Sive Apum Historia	298.

The front part of yᵉ 2ᵈ shelf

Duodecimo's

Plat's jewel house of Nature	299.
Newton's Chronology	300.
Ireland's Natural History by Boate	301.
Le Maitre Italien	302.
M. Porci Catonis de Re Rustica Liber	303.
The Lady's Religion	304.
Beveridge's Explanãon of yᵉ Catechism	305
La minte du Tasse Pastorale	306
Sandersoni Prælecõnes	307.
Acts for improving Hempen & flaxen Manufacturies	308.

Bishop's mansion house, Elphin, County Roscommon

Harveus De circulaõne Sanguinis 309
Hippocrati's Aphorismi 310.
Leicester's com̄on Wealth by Parsons 311.
S^r. Francis Bacon's Essays 312.
Liber de Statica Medicina 313.
Dupins His: of ye Church 2 Vol 8vo ***imperfect*** 315.
Demosthene's Oraõnes in English 8vo 316.
Aulus Gellius 317.
Anacreontis Ode 318.
Mores & Leges & Ritus omnium Gentium 319.
M: T: Ciceronis Epistolæ 320.
Roma Antica E Moderna 321.

ye 3^d Shelf

Molyneuxi's Case of Ireland 322.
Huygen's Cælestial worlds discover'd 323.
The Romish Doctrine plainly discover'd by Bp Usher 324.
Pomponius Mela de Situ Orbis 325.
Tractatus de Visitaõnibus Episcopalibus 326.
Rice's Discourse of Coin 327.
Aurelii Augustini Episcopi Liber 328.
Helvetiorum Respublica 329.
M. T. Ciceronis Epis. 330.
jocorum atque Seriorum cum Novorum Memorabilium Liber 331.
Ovidii Epistolæ 332.
Hieronomi Arcana Politica 333.
Tacitus 334.
La Regle Des Mœurs 335.
conservandæ bonae Valetudinis præcepta 336.
Deur De Molier 3 Vol. ***1. Wanting*** 337.
Antoninus De Seipso 338.
Milton's Paradise regain'd 339.
Willis's Anatomy 340
an Hebrew Gram̄ar 341
Virgilii Opera 342

4th Shelf

R: ~~R~~P: Famiani Stradæ E Prolusiones Academicæ 343.
Descripõ Regni Japoniæ 344.
Ausonii Burdigalensis Opera 345.
Arnoldi Corvini Digesta p̄. Aphorismos Strictim explicata 346.
Apologia Eccl. Anglicanæ 347.
Contracõn rerum Gallicarum 348
Jani Anglorum facies altera 349.
Polydori Virgilii Urbinatis de rerum inventoribus 350.

	M: T: Ciceronis Epistolæ ad familiares	351.
	De Obligaõne conscien᷈æ ℔ Sanderson	352
	Suetonius	353.

yᵉ 4ᵗʰ Shelf continued

	Tractatus de Corde &c ℔ Rich. Lower	354.
Latin	Polybii Megalopolitani Historia Nicholao Perotto interprete	355.
	M: T: Cice: De Philosophia	356.
	Wollebius's Abridgemᵗ of Christian Divinity	357.
	De L'Usage Des Passions par Le Francois Senault	358.
	prælec᷈ônes de obligaõne conscientiæ ℔ Sanderson	359.
	Caii julii Cæsaris comentaria	360.
	Liber continens Hebræa Chaldæa Græca & Latina nomina Virorum &c quæ in Bibliis leguntur	361.
	Euripedes tragedies *mighty bad*	362.
	Julius Cæsar de Causis Linguæ Latinæ	363.
	M: T: Ciceronis Opera *an odd Vol of Epistles 8ᵛ·⁰*	364
	Grotius de veritate Religionis	365.
	Disputaõnes Anti Bellarminianæ	366.
	Sophoclis Tragædiæ *very bad*	367.

yᵉ 5ᵗʰ· & last Shelf

	Novum instrumentum diligentes ab Erasmo recognitum ^folio^	368.
Eusebuis translated by Hanmer	Hanner's ancient Ecclesiastical History folio	369.
	Montaigne's Essays folio.	370.
	Morney's Mysterie of iniquitie ie, yᵉ His: of yᵉ Papacie ^folio^	371.
	Helvici Theatrum Historicum L 4ᵗᵒ	372.
	Pyrchass's Pilgrimage *1. Vol*	373.
	Spencer De Legibus Hebræorum L 4ᵗᵒ·	374.
	Paraphrases in omnes Psalmos L 4ᵗᵒ·	375
	Tithes too hot to be touch'd by Hen: Spelman 4ᵗᵒ	376.
	A Latin Bible	377.
	Caroli Siconii Historia de Occidentali imperio 4ᵗ·⁰	378.
	Biblia ad vetustissima exemplaria castigata	379.
	Petri Bellonii observaõnes de Græcia aliisqᵤₑ provinciis	380.
	The Evangelical Harmony	381.
	Mundus imperiorum a Joanne Botero	382.
	Mainwayrings Progress of pains inflamaõns &c	383.

This list ^taken^ june yᵉ 12ᵗʰ 1740

Bishop's mansion house, Elphin, County Roscommon

PLATE 11
John Rocque (*c*. 1704–1762): *An Exact Survey of the City and Suburbs of Dublin, 1756*; detail showing the area around St Stephen's Green, Dublin. It is not yet known where Captain Balfour lived, but his house may well have been in Dublin within easy reach of St Stephen's Green, an already fashionable residential area.

6

CAPTAIN BALFOUR'S
TOWN HOUSE, DUBLIN
1741/2

EDMUND JOYCE

THE HOUSE REPRESENTED in this inventory is believed to be a Dublin town house belonging to a Captain Balfour.

This inventory differs from the usual format and function, for it is the catalogue of a house clearance sale, and may subsequently have been used for probate purposes. Normally, the figures given in probate inventories are notional values, but those recorded in this inventory are the prices realized at the sale. The room-by-room list documents what must have been the entire contents of a relatively large town house, the price paid for each item, and the name of the buyer. Despite the welter of detail on offer, the exact location of the town house has yet to be determined. There is, however, a note in the inventory that refers to the sale of the guns and swords from the collection at 'Geminijany's Room'. The scholar Rosemary ffolliott conjectured that this was the Great Room set up by Francesco Geminiani (1687–1762), the Italian violinist and composer, in Spring Garden, a court off Dame Street, and used for concerts and art sales. This adds to the likelihood that the house was in the Dublin area. The broad cross-section of society which attended the sale would also suggest that the location was readily accessible, again placing it within the greater Dublin area. Assuming this to have been where the dwelling stood, the document offers an insight into the social history of 1740s Dublin and highlights the market for second-hand goods amongst Dublin society.

It is not known whether the captain had owned the property or had lived there on a long-term lease, but judging by the quality of much of what was put up for sale, the Balfour household's goods and chattels betoken more than a fair degree of prosperity. The furnishing, and the sequence, of the rooms are those of a relatively large house amply fitted out for receiving guests in style. The extensive array of furniture in mahogany (a timber which had been in circulation only for some twenty years), indicates a relatively recently furnished interior.

The introductory note refers to the 'Late Cap.ᵗ Belfourt', indicating that the sale was called after his demise. The sale may have been required for a number of possible reasons: money may have been needed to clear debts, the house might have been leased for his life, and – most compelling – his heir, according to a reference at the end of the document, was a minor and had no immediate use for a house in Dublin. It seems, since a number of items are listed as 'reserved for the minor', that the house had not been purged of family items prior to the sale, but that these heirlooms remained *in situ* at the time the inventory was taken. They are listed in an addendum to the main inventory, an unusual feature in either an auction catalogue or a probate valuation. Altogether, this supports the notion that the inventory could be regarded as a full record of the goods and chattels of a fairly substantial town house in 1740s Dublin. No item, not even the stock of 'coale', escapes the auctioneer's gavel; and there is hint of finality to the auction in the sale of the mahogany-cased locks, fashionable door-furniture in Ireland at that time.

The inventory shows that care has been taken with the grouping and cataloguing of lots, and that the sale has been designed to maximize return. Bed-sheets, for instance, have been paired up and separated out into forty-seven consecutive lots. Those viewing the auction have been allowed access to every last corner of the property. The market for plate was typically stronger than that for furniture, as plate is catalogued in special detail with the weights of each lot being recorded in the inventory. The result of the sale justified this approach, as the value of the plate constitutes a high proportion of the total of £992 8s 5d which was realized.

The Irish-silver historian Thomas Sinsteden suggests that Mr Walker who bought several items of plate at the Balfour sale was Thomas Walker, the Dublin goldsmith, who two years later was to appraise the silver belonging to Blaney Townley Balfour at Townley Hall. He also believes Mr Putland, who bought some silver items, was John Putland, the successful landowner, collector and bibliophile of Bray, County Wicklow, and Merrion Square. Silver historians are still on the lookout for an item that can be identified as having been in Captain Balfour's possession.

In addition to plate, always a high-status possession, personal items such as a collection of jewellery, which included 'a Goold watch & Chane', featured in the sale. This would suggest that there was a financial imperative to release capital in order to cover the cost of legacies and/or clear outstanding debts. Such practices were not unusual.

The list of successful bidders (though some of the names are spelt unfathomably) offers an insight into the cross-section of Dublin society consuming second-hand goods. Noticeable amongst the auction attendees are several clergymen (or their wives). These, including 'Archde[a]con He[a]rne' of Cashel', who bought a cupboard with shelves, some curtains and a clock, and Louis Saurin, dean of St Patrick's Cathedral, who bought some chairs, were busy buying practical items with which to furnish half-empty rectories and deaneries.

Amongst the clergy represented was a 'Mrs Easte', probably the wife of Charles Este (1696–1745), then bishop of Ossory. Although she only bought some towels, her presence like that of other female bidders is noteworthy. Other women buying at the sale included Lady St Leger (of Doneraile Court, County Cork) and Lady Maude (wife of Sir Robert Maude, baronet), who both bought china-ware, and a Mrs Warburton, who was by far the most prolific of all the bidders on the day. She was clearly furnishing a house, buying a total of thirty-four separate lots, including a collection of mahogany furniture, a fire grate, an array of linen and bedding, glassware, a large amount of coal and more. It seems likely, considering the extent and diversity of her purchases, that Mrs Warburton was either living nearby or that she was to be the future occupier of the house.

Other noteworthy bidders include a 'Mr Gardiner' who purchased '20 prints of the fortifications', a set of rush-bottomed chairs and a bed. This was most likely Luke Gardiner (*c.* 1690–1755) of No. 10 Henrietta Street (see page 155). The results also reveal that bidding at auctions was not an elitist activity alone, for 'Bell. ye maid' successfully purchased several lots including blankets, candlesticks, copper ware, pewter plates and numerous bed-sheets. On a separate note, a Mr Townl[e]y, presumably a kinsman of Captain Balfour, had bought a gun from the specialized sale of military items at Geminiani's. The attendance of family and/or friends at such sales is not unusual, as many, whether for sentimental reasons or other, often try to acquire items from a collection that they have an association with.

In reckoning totals the compiler has omitted both halfpence and farthings.

Sales by buyer at the auction are listed in Appendix I on pp. 365–7.

The inventory is in the collection of Townley Hall papers at the National Library of Ireland.

Captain Balfour's town house, Dublin

Capt; Belfour Acc^{tt} ——

1741/2
March·15·th·

An acc^{tt} of the Late Capt Belfourt, Hous^d Goods. Plate, China Linnin &c Sold by Auction,

In the Back Parlour,

		£	s	d
Mr Ward, —	1 · Mohoganey. Supper table,	£ —:	16:	6
Mrs Warburton,	1 · mohoganey. dineing table,	1:	15:	—
Mr Demsey:	1 · D^o larger,	2:	17:	—
Mr Moore, —	1 · mohoganey. Cestron,	—:	16:	—
Mrs Warburton,	1 · mohoganey. Side board. table,	3:	15:	—
Mrs Brown. —	2 · Pair Scarlet window Curtains,	3:	9:	—
Dean . Soren. —	12 · Chairs wth leath^r Seats & 1 armd D^o at 10^s/3^d	6.	13:	3
Mr Moore. —	1 · Sconce in. a Gilt frame.	5:	7:	6
D^o —	1 · Pair. gilt branches,	—:	17:	6
D^o —	1 · Chimney. glass. in a gilt frame.	4:	7:	6
D^o —	1 · pair. gilt branches.	—:	18:	3
D^o —	1 · Moveing. Grate brass fender & Irons	1:	15:	—
Couns^r Smith,	1 · Landscape over the Chimney.	1:	11:	—
Mr Gardiner	20 prints of the fortifications,	1:	14:	—
Mr Scofier, —	1 print,	—:	—:	8
Mr Hoey. —	6 Pices of the Seeches at 8^s,	2:	8:	—
Mr Chapman:	4 hunting Pices, at 7^s/6^d	1:	10:	—
Mr Moore. —	1 · Press in the Closet,	—:	10:	—
Archdecon . Hyrne	1 Cubbard & Shelves in D^o	—:	2:	8
Mr Moore —	1 Scotch-Carpett,	·1:	3.	3
D^o —	1 Small green D^o	—.	7:	3

£ 42: 14: 4

Brought ov^r

Brought over. £ 42: 14^s: 4^d

Street, Parlour,

		£	s	d
ArchDecon Hyrne,	2 Pair Scarlet Camlet. wind^w Curtins at 35^s/6	£ 3:	11:	—
Couns^r Smith,	8. Chairs wth tapstry Seats & 2 armd D^o at 36^s,	18:	—:	—
Mr Tayler —	1. two-leafe. fire Screen.	4:	4:	6
Sq^r; Preston,	1. Sconce in a Gilt frame,	5:	12:	—
D^o —	1. Chimney Glass in D^o	4.	8.	—
Mr Lee. —	2. pair Double branches & Shades	1:	14:	—
Mrs Hamilton,	1. Turkey Carpett,	5:	—:	—
Mr Wesbit, —	1. Sea pice in a Goold. frame ov^r ye Chimney,	2.	18.	—
Mr Hoey, —	2. Landscapes. over the doors, at 47^s–	4.	14.	—
Mr Creagh. —	12 fruite pices at 8^s/8^d	5:	4:	—
Dean Hutchinson;	12. flower pices, at 7/4	4.	8:	—

Mrs Warburton,	1. mohoganey. card table,	1:	3.	6	
Sq^r; Bush, —	1. marble. table wth. a carved frame.	1:	15:	—	
Mr Hasale, —	1. Moveing grate and furniture,	2.	7.	—	
Mrs Warburton,	1. Scollop^d, mohoganey tea table,	1:	3:	6	
					£ 66: 2: 6

Bed Chamber one Pair, —— Brought. ov^r, £ 108. 16. 10

Mr Demsey.	1. Yellow Camlet: bed. & 1 p^{r.} wind^{w.} Curt^s,	5:	19:	—
D^o, —	1. feather bed. bolster & 2 pillows,	2.	10.	—
Mrs Coppinger,	4 blankets & a manchester quilt,	2:	10:	—
Mr Moore. —	6. Chairs, 1 Elbow D^o & 2 Stooles. at 10^s/10^d.	4:	17:	6
Mr Baldwin,	1 mohoganey. tallboy.	2:	10.	—
Mrs Warburton;	1. Moveing grate brass fend^{r.} & Irons.	1:	12:	6
Mr. Kenedy,	2 Pictures of the kiss returnd,	—:	16.	—
Mr Thomas,	1 pair brass branches	—:	4.	2

Brought. ov^r, £ 20: 19. 2

Brought. over £ 108: 16: 10

Bed Chamber one Pair Continu^d,,

Brought ov^{r.} £ 20: 19: 2

Mrs Owens, —	1 oak dressing table,	—.	3:	9
Mrs Troy —	1 dressing glass,	—.	6:	2
Mrs. Hern. —	2 Velvet cussions. for kneeling on.	—:	3:	4
Mr. Smith,	1 mohoganey bason. stan,	—:	10:	—
Sq^{r.} Cole, —	1 Marble Chimney pice & Cove^g Stones,	4:	5:	—

£ 26: 7: 5

Dineing Roome,

Mrs Johnson:	1 wallnut Chest,	£ 2:	4:	—
Mr. Gardiner, —	1 wrought bed & Counter pan.	7:	15:	—
Mrs Warburton,	1 feather bed bolster & 2 pillows,	4:	1:	—
Bell. ye maid	2. blankets & one under D^o	—.	13.	6
Mrs Warburton,	3. Pices of tapstry hangings,	7:	—:	—
Mr. Fairbrother,	1 Marble chimney pice & coveing Stones	4:	11:	—
Mr Nenoe,	2. marble. table tops,	2:	1:	—
Mr Bolton,	1. Turkey Carpett.	9:	6.	—
Mr. Hannel, —	1 dressing glass,	—:	8:	6
Mr. Hannel, —	8. mapps.	—.	12:	—
Mr. Reily, —	1. oak. dineing table,	—.	7:	6
Mr Gardiner, —	6 Rush bottom chairs, at 2^s	—:	12:	—
Mr Nenoe, —	1 Small oak desk.	—.	1:	2
Mr. Bolton, —	1 mohoganey. kettle Stan,	—:	7:	8

£ 40: —: 4

Captain Balfour's town house, Dublin

Hall. and Stairs, —

Archdecon Herne, —	1 Clock.	£ 6: 14: —	
Mr. Bolton, —	1 hall lantron,	1: 4: 9	
Mr. Bush —	oyle cloath for the Stairs,	1. 11: —	
			£ 9: 9: 9

Brought, over,   £ 184: 14: 4

Brought, over,   £ 184: 14^s: 4^d

Street Roome 2 pair, —

Mr. Spring,	1 Cloath cullar 4 post bed, & 2 pr wind:w Curtins	£ 6. 13, —
Mrs. Warburton,	1 feather bed bolster & 2 pillows,	3: 3: —
Mr Moore. —	3. blankets, 1 under Do a green quilt, & matrass	3: 3: —
Mrs. Warburton,	1, wallnut Chest,	1: 11: —
Do —	1, moveing Grate. and furniture,	1: 10: —
Mr. Bush. —	1, mohoganey tallboy.	1: 13: —
Mrs. Coope, —	1 pair brass. branches	—: 4: 1
Mrs. Johnson	1 oak dressing table,	—. 6: —
Mrs Warburton,	1 dressing box	—. 11: 8
Mrs Dogan —	1 Small dressing glass.	—. 3: 4
Mr Reeves. —	6. Rush chairs, & – 1 Elbow Do at 2 3^d	—. 13. 5
Do —	3. mohoganey. locks on the doors at 5/6	—. 16. 6
Mr. Moore, —	4 Iron locks on Do at 2/6	—. 10. —
		£ 20. 18: —

Back Roome. 2 pair,   Brt ovr — £ 205: 12: 4 —

Mr Nenoe, —	1: oak Chest drawers.	£ 1: 18. 10
Mr Asdle, —	1 wallnut Cabinet,	2: 5: —
Mr. Moore, —	1 moveing grate & furniture,	1: 5: 9
Mr Dwire, —	1 green Calamencoe bed.	1: 5: —
Mrs Troy. —	1 feather bed bolster & pillow,	1. 10. —
Mr. Moore, —	3 blankets and. a white quilt,	1: 6: —
Mrs Troy. —	1 feather bed. & bolster,	1: 2. 8
Mr. Moore. —	1 Cloose Stoole	—. 4. 11
Mrs Troy, —	3 blankets,	—: 9: 8
Mr. Dogan.	1 pair green window Curtains,	—. 5. 10
Mrs Troy, —	6 Rush Chairs broake at 9^{d}½	—. 4. 9

Brought ovr £ 11: 18: 5

Brought over.   £ 205: 12^s: 4^d

Back Roome 2 pair Continu:d

Brought over. £ 11. 18^s. 5^d

Miss Acton, —	1 Small dale table,	—. —. 7
Mr Gormon. —	1 Do,	—. —: 5
Mr. Ewing, —	1 Do,	—. 1. 1

Mr Spring, —	2 Small carpetts.	—.	4:	6
Mr Moore, —	1 dale chest drawers in the closet	—.	8.	1.
D^o —	1 dresser in D^o	—.	2:	—
D^o —	1 Iron lock. on the closet	—.	1:	6

£ 12. 16: 7

Street Garret,

Mr Ewing, —	1 blue bed,	—:	15:	—
Mrs Carr, —	1 feather bed bolster 2 blankets & a rug.	1:	4:	6
Mr Moore. —	1 blue bed faceing the door.	—.	15.	9
D^o —	1 feather bed. bolster 2 blankets & rugg	1:	14.	6
Catty Reilly, —	1 small dressing glass.	—:	3.	6
Mrs Dogan. —	1 flock bed bolster 2 blankets & quilt, in $_\wedge$ the hall	—.	4.	8

£ 4. 17. 11

Back Garret,

Mr Gormon:	2 blankets & a rug.,	£—.	2.	—
Mr Dogan	bed stead, feather bed bolster 2 blankets & quilt	1:	—.	—
Mrs Warburton,	1 twig flasket	—	2.	8

£ 1: 4: 8

Yard,

Dean Hutchinson.	1 bottle drane,	£—.	14.	6
Mr Reeves:	3 water casks.	—.	5:	2
Mr Delahunty,	1 bucket	—.	1.	1
Mr Muny —	1 Chicken coope	—.	3.	4
Mr Fenlon	2 brocken coale boxes	—.	1.	—

£ 1. 5. 1

Brought ov^r — £ 225: 16: 7

Brought over. £225: 16^s: 7^d

Kitching, —

Mr Moore	2 flat candle sticks,	£—.	4^s:	6^d	
D^o —	2 D^o	—.	4.	4	
D^o —	2 D^o	—.	3:	3	
Bell, —	1 pair of high D^o	—.	1:	5	
Capt Levison, —	1 small brass mortar	—:	3.	4	
Mrs Vandeleur, —	1 copper lamp.	—:	7:	—	
D^o —	1. copper gallon.	—:	7:	—	
Mr Marshal, —	1 Jack. &c	2.	17:	6	
Mr Murry, —	3. Jack Spitts,	—.	8:	3	
D^o —	1 pair standing racks.	—.	7:	2	
Mr Marshal, —	1 Crane & hooks. w^t 61^{lb} at 3^{d}¼	—.	6:	6	[recte 16 6]
D^o —	1 pair niggars, 39^{lb} at 3^{d}¼	—.	10:	7	
Mr Murry, —	tongs fire shovel. & poker.	—.	7:	—	
Mrs Hutchinson:	2 smoothing Irons & 1 box D^o	—.	3.	6	

Captain Balfour's town house, Dublin

Mr Smith, —	1 pair bellows.		—.	4:	5
Mr. Marshal, —	1 copper druging box & basting ladle		—.	4:	—
Mr. Muny	1 grid Iron & 1 frying pan		—:	4:	4
Mr Moore, —	1 Iron driping pan broake & frame.		—.	1:	10
Do. —	1 copper ladle & brass skimmer,		—:	3:	8
Do. —	1 brass ladle skimmer & flesh fork		—.	3:	2
Mrs Hutchinson:	1 copper cheese. toaster.		—.	3.	—
Mrs Brown. —	1 brass skillet,		—.	4.	5
Mr. Marshal,	1 copper stew pan.		—.	8.	10
Do. —	1 Do.		—.	8:	4
Capt Levison, —	1 coppr, coffee pott		—.	4.	—
Bell. —	1 copper tea kettle.		—.	7:	—
Mr Gormon	1 Do. broake	wt 4lb at 9d	—.	3:	—
Mr Seamor —	1 copper knive box,		—.	19.	—
Mr Marshal,	1 copper cullinder,		—.	8.	10

Brought ovr. £ 10: 19 2

Brought over. £ 225. 16. 7

Kitching Continud.

Brought ovr. £ 10. 19. 2

Mrs Warburton,	1 copper Sauce pan.		—:	6.	—
Bell, —	1 Smaller Do.		—.	4.	6
Mr. Marshal,	1 larger Do. & cover.		—:	12.	6
Mrs Brown —	1 Copper fish pan.	wt 31lb at 17d½	2:	5:	2
Mr. Marshal, —	1 Copper kettle & Covr.	33lb at 10d	1.	19:	6 [recte 1 7 6 ?]
Do. —	1 Smaller Do.	15lb at 15d½	—.	19:	4
Mr. Moore. —	1 broaken warming pan.		—:	2.	6
Mr Marshal, —	1 brass mortar	wt 28lb at 7d½	—.	17:	6
Mr Cromie,	1 copper knive basket	12lb at 20d¾	1:	—.	9
Mr Moore —	1 Globe & Iron at the door		—.	9:	8
Mr. Marshal —	1 pair Scales & wts,		—.	6.	1
Mr. Nenoe, —	1 doz. of English pewter plates,		—.	17.	3
Do. —	1 doz Do.		—.	17.	4
Mrs Peters, —	1 doz Do.		—.	17.	3
Mr. Gormon:	1 doz Do.		—.	17:	9
Do. —	1 doz Do.		—.	17:	2
Mr Nenoe, —	10 plates Do.		—.	14:	2
Mrs. Warburton	1 pewter fish plate	wt 3lb½ at 2/4	—:	8:	2
Mr. Murry	9 pewter dishes	25lb at 14d¾	1.	10.	8
Mrs Brown —	1 brass plate warmer.		—:	15	—
Bell. —	10 old. pewter plates at 7d		—.	5:	10
Mr Gormon:	10 Ivory knives 11 forks,		—	8:	3
Do. —	12 knives 8 forks black. hafts,		—.	5.	—
Do. —	1 knive basket.		—.	2.	1
Do. —	pasty pan greater & rowlin pin		—.	1.	3
Mrs. Warburton, —	a glass basket.		—.	2.	11

Brought ovr. £ 29: 2. 9

						Brought ov.^{r}	£ 225: 16^s: 7^d

Kitching Continu^d

				Brought ov^r	£ 29.	2.^{s}	9^d
Mrs Warburton;	1 Iron pott,				—.	3:	4
Dean Coppin:	1 D^o				—.	9:	—
Mr Gormon:	1 dale table,				—.	2:	3
Mrs Warburton	2 tripets,				—.	1:	3
Mr Murry, —	1 plate drane.				—.	2.	9
D^o —	1 chopper & Salt box,				—.	1:	1
D^o —	2 forms.				—.	1:	9
Mrs Warburton,	2 D^o				—.	1:	2
Mr Murry:	2 treas & a bowle.				—.	4:	8
Mrs Warburton,	4 oak chairs broake at 19^d				—.	6:	4
Mr Rogers, —	5 crocks.				—.	1:	6
Mr Gormon:	1 poudering tub.				—.	5.	6
Mrs Troy, —	1 D^o				—.	5:	—
Mr Murry:	1 D^o				—.	3:	3
Mr Byrne, —	4 butter casks. all broake				—.	1:	—
Mr Nenoe, —	2 washing tubs & a pale.				—.	—	11
Mr Marshal —	7 pewter dishes. English	w^t 33^{lb}	at 14^d ¾		2.	—.	7
D^o —	1 Soope dish	4^{lb}	at 14^d ¾		—.	4.	11

£ 33: 19: —

					Brought ov^r.	£ 259: 15: 7
					Brought over.	£ 259: 15^s: 7^d

Linnin &^{c}

					£	^{s}	^{d}
M^{rs} McMullan:	N.1,	12 Diap^r Napkins & 1 table Cloath			£ 2.	12:	—
Mr Marshal, —	1,	12 D^o & 1 table cloath			2.	11:	—
Mrs Vandeleur,	2.	20 fine napkins,			2.	—.	—
Mrs Warburton,	2.	2 fine Diap^r table cloaths.			1:	—.	6
Mr Marshal, —	3.	1 doz. napkins 2 table cloaths			1.	19.	—
Capt Levison, —	3.	1 doz. napkins 2 table cloaths			1.	18.	—
D^o —	3:	5 napkins 1 table cloath.			—.	16.	6
Mrs Walsh —	4.	2 table cloaths,			—.	13:	—
Mrs Bligh, —	4,	2 D^o			—.	11:	—
Mrs Sanford, —	4.	16 napkins,	at 21^d		1:	8:	—
Mrs Bligh —	5.	2 table Cloaths.			—.	6.	10.
Mr Brown. —	5.	1 D^o			1:	5:	—
Miss Roberts, —	5:	1 D^o			—.	14.	6
Mrs Helsham, —	5:	22 napkins,			1:	17.	—
Capt Levison, —	6.	23 napkins,	at 10^{d}½		1.	—.	1
Mrs Warbuton,	7.	2 table cloaths 11 napkins,			1:	13.	—
Mrs Kenton, —	8.	6 napkins.			—.	6.	6
Mrs Harmon,	9.	3 doz. napkins	at 7^d		1:	1:	—

Captain Balfour's town house, Dublin

			£	s	d
Mrs Kenton.	10.	1 doz. napkins, 1 table cloath	8.	15.	—
Mrs Harmon.	11:	1 doz. napkins 1 table cloath	8.	18.	—
Mr Brown:	12.	1 dozen napkins,	—.	4.	8
Mr Longfield, —	13.	1 dozen. D^o	—.	7.	2
Mrs Barlow,	14.	6 table cloaths	1:	10.	0
Mr Longfield,	14.	5 D^o	1:	12.	6
Mr Gooding, —	14.	4 D^o	—	14.	—
		Brought ov^r	£ 45:	14.	3
		Brought. over.	£ 259.	15.	7

Linnin Continu^d

			£	s	d
		Brought ov^r	£ 45:	14:	3
Mr Walker, *N.*	15:	2 table cloaths.	1.	—.	6
D^o —	15.	1 D^o	—.	10:	3
Mrs Warburton,	16:	3 D^o	2.	19.	—
Mr Bonnom:	16.	3 D^o	2.	8.	6
Mr Preston:	17.	3 D^o & 2 lay overs.	2.	5.	6
Mr Walker:	18.	2 table cloaths	—	10.	3
M^{rs} O Hara, —	19.	1 large & 2 Small.	—.	15:	3
M^{rs} M^c.Mullan:	20.	2 table cloaths	1.	9:	—
Mr Marshal, —	21.	3 table cloaths	2:	14.	—
Mrs Gormon:	23:	1 table cloath	1:	11.	6
M^{rs} M^c.Mullan:	23:	3: D^o	1:	5:	—
Mrs Burton, —	24.	7 table cloaths,	1:	12:	—
Mr Ward, —	25.	6 Small. D^o	—.	17:	—
Mrs Carr, —	26.	6 D^o	—.	6:	9
Mr Feild, —	27:	23 p^r pillow Cases	1:	1:	6
Mrs Gormon:	28:	2 pair Sheets.	1.	16.	6
Mrs Vandeleur,	28.	2 pair D^o	2:	7:	—
Mr Muny:	28.	1 pair D^o	1:	9.	—
Bell, —	29.	5 pair Course.	2.	—	6
Mrs Byrne. —	30.	2 doz. towels,	1:	3:	—
Mrs Corker. —	30.	2 doz D^o	1:	2:	—
Mrs Easte,	31.	2 doz french D^o	1:	4.	—
Mrs Vandeleur, —	31.	2 doz. D^o	1.	6.	—
Mrs Warburton	32.	2 doz 8 D^o	1.	10.	—
Mr Calahan —	34.	2 doz. towels,	—.	13:	—
		Brought ov^r	£ 81:	11.	3
		Brought. over.	£ 259.	15.	7

Linnin Continu^d

			£	s	d
		Brought ov^r	£ 81	11:	3
Mr Ward., — *N.*	34.	2 dozen towels,	—.	9:	6
Mr Caterwood,	34.	1 doz ½ D^o	—.	8:	—
Mrs Easte, —	35.	2 doz. 3 D^o	—.	15:	—

Mrs Warburton,	36 & 43:	13 tea napkins,	—:	11:	6
D^{o} —	37:	6 tea napkins.	—.	8.	6
D^{o} —	38:	11 tea D^{o}	—:	14:	6
D^{o} —	39:	2 doz. 5: napkins,	—.	15:	—
D^{o}.	40.	6 layovers.,	—:	7:	9
Mr Brown. —	40:	7 D^{o}	—:	5:	—
Mrs Warburton:	41:	4 D^{o}	—:	10.	10
Mr Wilcocks,	42.	6 napkins	—.	2:	—
Mr Caterwood, —	44.	1 table cloath	—.	2:	—
Mr Walker, —	46.	1 pair Sheets	—.	7:	—
Mr Marshal, —	46.	1 p^{r} D^{o}	—.	16.	4
D^{o} —	46.	1 p^{r} D^{o}	—.	18:	—
Bell —	46.	1 p^{r} D^{o}	—.	7.	6
Mr Moorehead,	47.	1 p^{r} D^{o}	—.	6:	—
Mr Marshal, —	47:	1 p^{r} D^{o}	1:	—:	—
D^{o} —	47:	1 p^{r} D^{o}	—	16	3
D^{o} —	47:	1 p^{r} D^{o}	1:	1:	—
Mrs Sands. —	48.	1 p^{r} D^{o}	—.	6.	6
Bell, —	48.	1 p^{r} D^{o}	1:	7:	—
Mrs Burton.	48:	1 p^{r} D^{o}	1:	—.	—
Mr Brown. —	48.	1 p^{r} D^{o}	—.	10.	—
Mrs Warburton, —	49.	1 p^{r} D^{o}	—.	11.	4.
Mr Walker	49.	1 p^{r} D^{o}	—.	12.	3
D^{o} —	49.	1 p^{r} D^{o}	—.	17:	6
D^{o} —	49.	1 p^{r} D^{o}	—.	18	6

Brought ov^{r} £ 98. 16. —

Brought. over.   £ 259: 15. 7

Linnin Continu^{d}

Brought ov^{r} £ 98: 16: 0

Mr Caterwood:	N 50:	1 pair D^{o}	—:	12:	3
Mr Walker:	50.	1 p^{r} D^{o}	—.	12:	3
Mrs Corker. —	50.	1 p^{r} D^{o}	—.	17:	3
Mr Marshal,	50:	1 p^{r} D^{o}	—.	14:	6
Mrs Corker, —	51.	1 p^{r} D^{o}	—.	15.	—
Mr Walker.	51.	1 p^{r} D^{o}	—:	13:	6
Mrs Gormon.	51.	1 p^{r} D^{o}	—.	15.	6
Mr Walker:	51.	1 p^{r} D^{o}	—.	14:	3
D^{o} —	52.	1 p^{r} D^{o}	—.	8:	—
Mr Marshall D^{o}, —	52.	1 p^{r} D^{o}	—.	14.	—
D^{o} —	52.	1 p^{r} D^{o}	—.	14.	—
Mr Marshal,	52:	1 p^{r} D^{o}	—.	12:	3
Mr Moorehead	53.	1 p^{r} D^{o}	—:	12:	3
Mr Murry:	53.	1 p^{r} D^{o}	—.	14:	6
Mr Caterwood,	53.	1 p^{r} D^{o}	—.	9:	9
D^{o} —	53.	1 p^{r} D^{o}	—.	7:	3
Mr Moorehead	54.	1 p^{r} D^{o}	—.	5:	—

Captain Balfour's town house, Dublin

					£	s	d	
M.r Caterwood, —	54.	1 p.r D.º			—.	7.	<u>6</u>	
M.r Murry	54.	1 p.r D.º			—:	7.	6	
M.rs Corker, —	54.	1 p.r D.º			—.	11.	4.	
M.r Marshal	55.	1 p.r D.º			—.	3.	9.	
M.r Walker	55.	1 p.r D.º			—.	4:	—	
M.rs Troy, —	55:	1 p.r D.º			—.	2:	2	
D.º —	55:	1 p.r D.º			—.	4.	—	

Brought ov.r £ 111 7 9

Brought. ov.r £ 259: 15 (s) 7 (d)

Linnin Continu.d

Brought ov.r £ 111: 7: (s) 9 (d)

					£	s	d
M.rs Gormon	56.	1 pair D.º			—.	8.	6
M.r Marshal	56.	1 p.r D.º			—.	9.	6
M.rs Troy	56.	1 p.r D.º			—.	7:	3
M.r Moorehead	56.	1 p.r D.º			—.	3.	3
M.r Walker:	57.	1 p.r D.º			—.	5.	7
D.º —	57.	1 p.r D.º			—.	8.	6
Bell —	57.	1 p.r D.º			—.	6.	—
M.r Walker —	58.	3 napkins,			—.	5.	3
M.rs Warburton,		2 pices. of french quilting			2:	7.	—

£ 116: 8: 7

Plate &.c

Brought ov.r £ 376: 4. 2

		oz	d		£	s	d	
M.r Preston:	4 tea Spoons.	w.t 0:	11½	at 7/2	£ —	11.	4	[recte 1 oz 11½ d]
Cap.t Levison:	12 larger D.º	7:	19	at 6/6½	2.	12.	—	
D.º —	11 D.º	4:	9	at 6/10	1.	10.	5	
M.rs Troy. —	1 pair tea tongs,	1:	4½	at 8/2½	—.	9.	10	
M.rs Walsh:	1. p.r Salts & 2 Salt Spoons,	5.	10	at 6/2	1.	13:	11	
M.r Spring, —	1 p.r D.º & 2 Spoons.	4.	19	at 6/3	1.	10.	11	
Sq.r Preston,	1 Chamber. pott.	23:	10	at 6/5	7.	10.	9	
D.º —	1 tea kettle & lamp	71.	10	at 6/4	22:	12.	4	
D.º —	1 Cup. & Cover.	52.	10	at 6/9	17:	14:	4	
M.rs Warburton,	2 Decanters,	119:	5	at 6/9	40:	4:	11	
M.r Hunt,	1 Montaafe,	97.	0	at 6/9	32:	14:	9	
M.rs Stuard, —	1 Stan & lamp,	28.	0	at 6/4	8.	17:	4	
M.r Putland	1 Cup & Cover.	32.	0	at 5/11	9.	9.	4	

Brought ov.r £ 147 12 2

Brought over   £ 376: 4: 2

Plate. &ᶜ. Continu,ᵈ

Brought over.   £ 147. 12. 2

			oz d		£	s	d
Mʳ Hunt,	1 Coffee pott,	wᵗ,	30: 0	at 7/3	10:	17.	6
Dᵒ, —	1 large Salver.		43: 0	at 6/5	13:	15.	11
Mʳ Walker,	3 Castors,		26. 15	at 6/4½	8:	10.	6
Sqʳ Preston,	2 pʳ Candle Sticks,		63: 15	at 8ˢ—	25:	10.	—
Mʳ Marshal,	Snufers. & dish.		11: 0	at 6/2½	3:	8:	3
Mʳ Gooding,	2 Canns.		16: 10	at 6/9	5:	1:	3
Mʳ, Hunt,	2 Sauce-boats,		31. 5	at 7/4	11:	9:	2
Mʳ Baillie,	1 tea dish,		15. 5	at 6/7	5:	2:	4
Mʳ Hunt,	1 Sugar bowle.		4:15	at 6/10	1.	12:	5
Mʳ Caufield	1 punch ladle.		2. 9	at 6/4	—:	15:	6
Mʳ Hunt,	1 Dᵒ,		2. 11	at 8/4	1:	1:	3
Mʳˢ White,	1 Soope ladle		9: 15.	at 7ˢ—	3:	8.	3
Mʳˢ Staples,	1 Straner,		4: 0	at 7/3	1:	9.	—
Mʳ Hunt, —	12 Saucers.		40. 0	at 7/5	14.	6.	8
Mʳˢ Atkins,	6 butter cups.		9. 5	at 7/8	3.	10.	11
Sqʳ. Preston,	1 marrow. Spoon.		2. 0	at 7/3	—:	14.	6
Mʳ Walker,	1 Extinguisher,		1: 4	at 7ˢ.—	—:	8.	4
Dᵒ, —	12 forks 12 knives 12 Spoons		79: 1	at 6/2½	24:	10	9
Mʳˢ Fits Gibbon	12 knives 12 forks		52: 4	at 7/6	19.	11	6
Mʳ Walker,	12 Spoons.		29. 10	at 6/3½	9:	5.	7
Mʳ Feild,	1 pair Salvers		11. 0	at 6/4	3.	9.	8

Brought ovʳ —   £ 315: 11. 5

Brought over   £ 376: 4. 2

Plate. &ᶜ. Continu,ᵈ

Brought over.   £ 315. 11. 5

			oz d		£	s	d
Mʳˢ Adams:	1 Cream Sauce pan	wᵗ,	5. 5	at 6/3	1	12.	9
Mʳ Hoey:	1 tankard,		40. 0	at 6/7	13.	6:	7
Mʳˢ White, —	1 pair Salvers		10. 15	at 6/2	3:	6.	3
Mʳˢ Atkins,	1 pair Dᵒ, larger		31: 0	at 6/6	10:	1:	6
Mʳ Putland	1 Scollopᵈ dish.		15: 6	at 6/7	5:	—.	9
Mʳ Bonnom:	1 tea-pott. & Sockets		12. 0	at 6/2½	3.	14.	6
Mʳ Calahan:	1 ¹ pair Candle Sticks		25. 19	at 7ˢ—	9.	1:	8
Mʳ Baillie,	1 pʳ Dᵒ & Dᵒ		25: 4	at 6/9	8.	10:	1
Mʳ Walker	1 hand. Candle. Stick,		6. 15	at 6/3½	2.	2.	5
Dᵒ, —	1 hand Dᵒ		7. 3	at 6/4½	2.	5.	7
Mʳ Baillie,	1 Cruit Stan & Castor,		20. 10	at 7/3	7.	8.	1
Mʳ Calahan:	1 Slop bowle.		13. 10	at 6/5	4.	6.	7
Mʳ Walker:	1 Sauce pan		14. 10	at 6/1½	4.	8.	9
Mʳ Bonnom.	1 dish Stan		23. 8	at 6/6	7.	12.	1
Mʳ Walker:	1 Cream. Yore		5. 14	at 6/11½	1:	19.	7
Mʳ Clifton, —	1 Soope. Spoon.		8. 1	at 6/8	2.	13.	8
Mʳ Marshal,	1 Soope dish		47. 10	at 5/11	14.	1.	1

Captain Balfour's town house, Dublin

Mr Walker	1 Coco. cup.				1.	5.	3
Do —	1 Do				1.	12.	9
Mr Nenoe	1 Do				1.	13.	3
Do —	1 Do				1.	13:	9

Brought ovr — £ 423 8 4

Brought ovr £ 376. 4. 2

Plate &c Continud

Brought ovr — £ 423 8 4

Mr Hunt,	1 Scollop Spoon. trea,	wt 4: 4	at 6/10	1.	8.	8
Mr Mane. —	1 pr Shew buckles & 1 pr knee	2. 1½	at 7s	—.	14.	6
Mr Ward, —	1 pr Do & Do	1. 18.	at 5/10	—.	11.	1
Mrs OHara, —	1 pr Do & Do	2: 6	at 5/10½	—.	13.	6
Mr Vickers, —	1 Stock buckle			—.	4.	6
Miss Maude,	1 Ebeny toaster,			1:	7.	—
Mr Bolton,	2 Spoons	4: 6	at 6/3	1.	6.	10
Mr Walker,	1 Cane wth a goold head			2.	11.	6
Mr Bolton:	a Goold watch & Chane			20:	—.	—
Mr Marshal.	1 goold, Snuff box	4: 0	at 85s	17.	—.	—
Mrs Corker —	1 wax Candle Stick	3: 6	at 6s	—.	19.	9
Mr Hoey, —	2 Sales			2:	—:	—
Mr Mane —	1 turkey-Stone ring,			1:	15:	—
Mr Caterwood	1 goold ring,			1.	16:	6
Mr Marshal,	1 Deamond Ring,			3.	9.	6
Do —	1 Diamond hoope ring,			14:	—.	—
Mr Walker:	1 Diamond ring,			22.	17.	—
Do —	1 Diamond buckle.			30:	5	—
Mr Mane.	1 mother pearl Snuff box			—.	14.	6

£ 547: 3: 2

Brought. ovr £ 923: 7: 4

Brought. over. £ 923: 7. 4

China. &c

Mr Caterwood,	1 Red. China tea pott.	£ —:	7:	9
Mr Walker. —	1 blue & white. Do	—.	8.	3
Do	1 goold & white Do	—:	13.	6
Do	1 tea pott & dish cullard,	—.	8.	1
Mr Tayler, —	1 Yore wth a Silver Spout,	1.	19.	6
Mr Walker,	2 China canisters,	—:	13.	6
Mr Tayler, —	4 small. Aget cups.,	1:	14:	—
Mrs Croaker,	11 white & goold tea cups. 8 Saucers	1:	—.	6
Mrs Gorge, —	1 Small. china Jarr	—.	4:	—
Mr Gledstones,	1 blue & white. bowle. & dish,	—.	9.	2
Mrs Brooks:	4. brown Jacolet cupps 4 Saucers	—.	6.	6
Mr Cash:	2. Coffee. cups. 3 tea Do & 1 hartly cup, Some of Do crackd	—:	3:	—

Mrs Johnson:	9. blue & white plates,		—:	7:	10
Mrs Gorge, —	11. blue &. white Soope plates.		—.	15:	6
Mr Tayler—	2. plates Goold & white,		—:	13:	3
Lady Maude,	8. white plates,		—:	8:	—
Capt Levison	3 dishes blue & white,	at 5/9	—:	17:	3
Lady. St Leger:	4 small Do	at 2/8½	—.	10.	10
Mrs Baker, —	4 cups. 1 Saucer & a bowle.		—:	7:	—
Miss French:	1 Safran pot and Saucer.		—:	7:	—
Mr Gledstones,	9 Cullard dishes & 3 doz. plates,		7:	—.	—
Mrs Gorge, —	11 cullard custard cupps.		—.	9:	2
Mr Walker —	1 large china punch bowle		3:	15	—
Mrs Baker, —	1 cullard porringer,		—.	2.	—
Mrs Gorge —	4 cullard coffee-cups.		—.	4.	4
Do —	1 blue & white crackd punch bowle		—:	3.	6

Brought ovr   £ 24   8   5

Brought. ovr   £ 923:   7:   4

China. &c. Continud,

Brought ovr   £ 24:   8:   5

Sqr Parsons,	1: Quaderelle. box.	—:	10	10
Mrs Bags, —	1 Do	—:	·3	3
Mr Woulfe —	2 cups. 2 saucers. & 1 delf bowle	—:	1:	1
Mr Hoey —	1 Indian hand board,	—.	2:	—
Sr Richd Butler:	1 box of Counters,	—.	2:	2
Sr Lau: Parsons:	1 box Do	—.	2.	2
Mr Woulfe —	1 Coco cup. broake	—.	—.	6
Miss. Pearson:	broaken. china,	—.	6.	—
Sr Richd Butler:	1 Mohoganey tea Chest.	—.	16.	3
Mr Nenoe, —	1 Do	—.	5:	5

£ 26. 18. 1

£ 950: 5: 5

Glasses. &c.

Brt ovr   £ 950: 5: 5

Mrs Warburton:	8 water tumrells	at 3½d	£ —.	2.	4
Do —	6 Sweet meat Stans	at 4d	—.	2:	—
Mrs Gibbons	6 glass baskets 1 of Do crackd		—.	1:	3
Mrs Gorge —	6. C**d Sweet-meate glasses		—.	6.	—
Mrs Warburton	26 Sweet-meate glasses & Saucers		—.	2.	8.
Miss Putland	6 water tumrels	at 6d	—.	3.	—
Mr Calahan —	2 water glasses		—.	3.	6
Mrs Warburton	1 glass Rumer.		—.	1.	8
Dean. Coppin:	1 tea-bell.		—.	1.	5
Miss Groves:	1 glass. Jug.		—.	—.	7
Mr Calahan:	1 Do		—.	—	4
Mrs Warburton	2 water-glasses		—.	4:	4
Do —	2 Do		—.	5.	6

£ 1: 14: 7

Captain Balfour's town house, Dublin

	Brought. over.	£ 950: 5: 5

Glasses &c Continu^d —

		Brought ov.^r	£ 1: 14: 7
Mrs Gibbons	1. glass. plate. & Salver	—.	1: 10
Sr Lau Parsons.	21. wine glasses.	—.	10. —
Mr Putland.	9. wine D.^o	—.	2. 3
Sr Lau. Parsons.	5 wine D.^o	—.	2. 6
Mrs Gorge. —	2 water bottles.	—.	1: 4
Sr Lau. Parsons.	2 Decanters.	—.	2. 2
Mr Walsh —	1. glass. mug.	—.	1. 1
Mrs Gibbons	2 Decanters.	—.	3: 4
Mrs Rudgate	2 D.^o	—.	3. —
Mrs Gorge. —	2 D.^o	—.	3. 6
Mrs Gibbons, —	2 D.^o	—.	2. 9
Mrs Warburton,	1 D.^o	—.	2. 8
Mrs Sanford, —	1 glass. Jug.	—.	1. 10
Mrs Warburton,	2 beer. glasses.	—.	2. —
Mr Shouldam:	2 D.^o	—.	1. 10
Sr Lau Parsons:	1 Glass. the Glorious. Memory.	—	9, —
Mrs Warburton:	3 water-glasses. 1 bowle. & 1 p.^r Salts	—.	3. 2
Mrs Gibbons, —	1 pair cruits.	—	1. 4
Capt. Levison	1. mohogany. tea board.	—.	3. —
D.^o —	1 Cruit frame.	—.	2. 8
Mrs Rudgate, —	6 collom casters & 1 wood.^n D^o	—.	3: 4
Mrs Gorge —	1 blue Jug & 1 white mug.	—	2: —
Mrs Warburton:	1 white Damask. quilt.	2:	6: —
Mr Caterwood, —	1 high.land pistol		8. 6.
Mr Gormon:	1 bullet gun.	2.	18. 6
Mrs Warbuton:	1 Screw barrel. bullet gun	2.	—. —

		£ 12: 14. 2
	Brought. over —	£ 962: 19: 7

	Brought. over.	£ 962: 19: 7

Mrs Warburton,	4. hun.^d of kennel. coale.	£ —.	5: 4
D.^o —	6 brass. locks on the doors at 10.^s/6	3:	3. —
D.^o —	2. D.^o	—.	16. —
D.^o —	3 ould. table cloaths & 2 p.^r Sheets	—.	4. 4
D.^o —	some. old Canisters., Sug.^r mallet & hammer	—.	4. —
Mr Marshal,	1 hanging rack in the kitching.	—	16 3
D.^o —	1 Plate-trunk.	1.	9. 3
Mr Barnwell,	Some ould ticking	—.	6. 8
Mr Moore —	a brass. knocker. & handle, a Rowlin Stone, and a binn.	1.	6 11
Mrs Warburton	2 tuns coals. wont.^g a barrel.	1:	—. 7
Mr Marshal,	1 Pillion & Shag cloath.	1.	2. 9

		£ 10: 15. 1
	Totall, —	£ 973: 14: 8

Goods Sold before at Geminijany's Room*

Mr Ribton —	1 Blunderbuss	—:	16.	3
Mrs Hern —	1 D^o	1:	8:	—
D^o —	1 Case of Pistols	—:	17:	6
Mr Townly —	1 Gunn	2:	15:	—
Mrs Harvy	2 smale Blunderbusses	1:	7:	—
Mr Stradwell	1 Cutteau	1:	11:	—
Mrs Harvey	1 Gunn	3:	3:	—
Mr Rieves	1 silver Hilted Sword	2:	4:	—
Mr Ivres.	1 D^o	2:	2:	—
Mrs Gash.	2 broad swords	1:	1:	6
Mrs Ivres.	1 mourning Sword	—:	3:	—
Mr Walsh	1 silver hilted sword	1:	5:	6

18: 13: 9   £ 18: 13: 9

Totall   £ 992: 7: 5

[recte £ 992 8 5]

Brought over 992 7 5   992: 7 5

[heavily scored line – illegible])
a Coach & 6 Harness (50 ——

by some famaly Pictures & books
reserved for the minor vallued.   37: 11: —

* In the MS it is not possible to tell whether the title of
  some of the buyers who bought goods at 'Geminijany's Room'
  is written Mr or Mrs.

992 7 5
50 .

Captain Balfour's town house, Dublin

PLATE 12
Robert Furze Brettingham (1750–1820): Hillsborough Castle,
drawing of the west front, 1788

7

HILLSBOROUGH CASTLE, COUNTY DOWN

1746 and 1777

REBECCA CAMPION

THE TWO HILLSBOROUGH CASTLE inventories are of particular interest because they are both associated with the same patron, Wills Hill (1718–1793), who was second Viscount Hillsborough (1742), and later first Earl of Hillsborough (1751), in Ireland. He became first Earl of Hillsborough in the peerage of Great Britiain in 1772, and first Marquess of Downshire in the peerage of Ireland in 1789. The first inventory of 1746 records a rather modest house, which Mrs Mary Delany, the letter writer and artist, described after her visit there in 1758 as 'not extraordinary, but prettily fitted up and furnished'. She went on to outline the earl's plans to build a 'magnificent' house 'in a finer situation than the one he at present inhabits, and about a mile from it', once he had restored the old fort. The 1777 inventory is of the new house, built from about 1760 and continually augmented over the next eighty years. This house was part of an ambitious and handsome scheme for a designed model town, with Hillsborough Castle positioned in relation to a square with a market house, restored fort and greatly expanded church in Gothic style, which, Hill hoped in vain, would be upgraded to cathedral status.

Comparing the two inventories, the number of rooms increased dramatically in the second house and room names reflected both changing fashion and added grandeur. The ground-floor rooms in the 1746 inventory comprised the drawing-room, large parlour, little parlour and hall. The principal rooms of the new house, as recorded in 1777, also included the drawing-room and 'great' hall, but the parlours had been replaced by the breakfast-room, dining-room and library. The functions of rooms were more carefully demarcated as indicated by the changing names and purpose-specific furniture. Leisure activities had also expanded in variety: card-tables and a mahogany backgammon table were recorded in both houses while a pianoforte and billiard-table appear only in the later inventory.

More pictures appear in the second inventory. As in many houses, the dining-room was the display space for portraiture. The dining-room of Hillsborough Castle had sixteen portraits, dominated by a large full-length likeness of Wills Hill himself (see plate 16), and five pictures of birds, beasts, fruits and flowers. Grand tour views of Naples hung in the breakfast-room and twenty-four Hogarth prints (perhaps including the twelve *Rake's Progress* prints noted in the great parlour of the earlier house) were in the library. Unusually, no pictures were listed in the drawing-room, which was often where the most valuable artwork was displayed.

A taste for chintz fabric is common to both inventories. Two bedrooms in the first house were described as the 'Great Chince' and 'Little Chince' rooms, with bed-hangings, window curtains, wallpaper and upholstered chairs all matching. The inventories do not confirm which furniture and fabric were moved to the new house; thirty years later, however, the new house also had a 'small Chince Room' upstairs. The 1777 inventory gives detail for the bedroom of Lady Mary-Emilia (Emily Mary) Cranborne (second daughter of Wills Hill), listing delicate finishes: a four-post bed with 'Chints Furniture' or hangings, 'an India Cabinett', an inlaid writing-table, six painted chairs and twelve pictures of birds and flowers. Oriental patterns were not restricted to the bedrooms; there were green Chinese chairs in the drawing-room and painted chairs with chintz covers in the breakfast-room.

The short inventory of blue-and-white china and 'Other things' written on the verso of the last page of the 1777 inventory is dated 15 January 1776 but may in fact have been drawn up in January 1778, unless both inventories were fair copies not entered in chronological order.

Twelve miles south-west of Belfast, Hillsborough Castle became the official British government residence in Northern Ireland when the 3rd Duke of Abercorn, as the first governor of Northern Ireland, moved in with his wife in 1925.

The inventories are located in the Public Record Office of Northern Ireland, Belfast.

Inventory

Goods in Lord ᵒᶠ Hillsborough's house at Hillsborough 10ᵗʰ February 1746
Taken By Mʳˢ Crosley

In the Little Parlour

A Couch Bed, 3 pillows wᵗʰ Cheque Covers, a Cheque Mattress and, Blue Harrateen Curtains

These Curtains in the Chest up
Two pair of Stairs & are Entred so —

2. Window Curtains of the same
1. Cherry Tree folding Oval Table
1. Looking glass with Walnut Tree frame
1. Large Elbow Chair, cover'd with Leather
6. Black Leather Chairs
1. Claw Breakfast Table
13. Hudibrastick Pictures
1. Of Sʳ Thomas Roe
1. Of James Annesley
1. of Mʳ Mᶜkercher
2. Brass Arms
1. Grate with Broken back, fire shovell, Tongs,Bellows & Tin Fender
3. Oak Chests with Papers, standing one upon another
2. Mahogony Corner Stands
1. Hair Broom

In the Great Parlour

1. Folding Table	of Mohogony
2. Sideboard *Dᵒ*	of *Dᵒ*
1. Plate Tray	of *Dᵒ*
1 Tray for Botles	of *Dᵒ*
6 Botle Stands	of *Dᵒ*
1 Round Dining Table	of *Dᵒ*

12 Black Leather Chairs
1. Eight day Clock on a Black Pedestal
2. Blew Chamlet Window Curtains
1. Marble Chimney piece & Slab (crack'd

Great Parlour continued

2 Brass arms gilt
1. Mohogony Cupboard For a Chamber pot
1. Grate (Back crack'd thro'
1. Tin Fender wᵗʰ Fire Shovell, Bellows, Tongs and Hearth Broom

12 Prints of the Prodigal son or Rake's progress. wᵗʰ black frames gilt & glas'd,
4 Prints of Morning, Noon, Evening and night, fram'd
1. *Dᵒ*: over the Chimney piece wᵗʰ Black frame and gilt

In the Drawing Room

1. Black Chimney piece with a Crack'd Slab
1. Grate … (Back Broke)
1. Broom
1 pair of Bellows
Fire shovell & Tongs
1 Hand Skreen,   2. small fire Skreens & 2 Brass arms
1. Card Table,   1. Large Dining Table &   1. Backgamon *Dᵒ* all Mahogony
7 Large Green Damask Chairs,   2 *Dᵒ*: Settees all wᵗʰ Cheque Covers
1 Large Turky Carpet   1. Scotch *Dᵒ*   1. Tin fender
2. Green Damask Window Curtains

In the Hall

1 Large Glass Lanthorn & 6. Large Mapps
4 Windsor Chairs — Note 1. *Dᵒ* at the office & 1. at Mʳ Benson's

Up Stairs. First Floor

Great Chince Room

1. Bedstead with Curtains To match the paper
2 Window Curtains of *Dᵒ*
2 Barrack Mattresses,   1. fine Dimety Mattress,
   3. Blankets one
      Bolster Two pillows, and one white Quilt
1 Tufted Cotton Counterpane
3 Large Chairs cover'd wᵗʰ same as the Curtains (one of 'em Elbow'd)
1. Mohogony Buero.   1. glass over it wᵗʰ Carv'd frame
1. Small deal dressing Table.
1. Grate fire shovell, Tongs, Tin fender, Hair broom and Bellows
2. Black Leather Chairs

Hillsborough Castle, County Down

Little Chince room

1. Bedstead with Chince pattern hangings &
   a window Curtain of D^o
1. Hair & 1. Wool Mattresses, 1. Bolster, 1. pillow,
   3 Blankets & 1. White Linnen Quilt
1. Small deal dressing Table & stand glass over it

Red Damask room

1 Crimson Damask bed, 2. Window Curtains of
D^o 2. Barr^k mattresses
  1. feather bed, 1. fine Dimitty mattress,
   3. Blankets, 1. Bolster,
  2. pillows &. 1. white Quilt
1 Mohogony Scruitore, 4. Chairs (Seats cover'd with
Red Damask) 2.
Black Leather D^o: 1. Large Chair with Cheque cover
1 Little Tea Table
1. Pier glass with a carv'd frame & 1. Dressing glass
1. Grate, fire shovell, Tongs, Broom & Tin fender
1. Chair with Close Stool & Pan

In My Lord's Bed Chamber

1. Bed with Green Worsted Curtains & Window
   Curtain of the same,
   Feather bed, a Wool mattress, 3. Blankets,
   1. Colour'd Quilt
   1. Bolster & 1. pillow.
1. Large Cloaths Chest, 1. Dressing Table &
   a Swing glass
1. Wash hand Mohogony Stand, 3. Rush bottom'd
   Chairs
1. pair of Bellows, Tongs, fire Shovel and Tinfender

In the Study

1. Mohogony Cabinet, 1. D^o Table, 3 Rush bottom'd
   & 1. Elbow Chair
1 Grate, hair Broom, pair of Bellows
1. Little Walnut tree Box & Oak shelves for Books
2 Large Black Trunks & a gilt
   picture frame.   *In the passage*

In Lady Rawdon's room

1. Bed with yellow Harrateen Curtains, feather bed,
   1. Linnen Matress One Dimitty D^o: 3 Blankets,
   1. Bolster 1. pillow & Colour'd Quilt
1. Wainscot Chair & Close stool, 1. Leather ^{bottom'd}
   Chair with Elbows
4 Matted Chairs, 1. Mohogony Buero 1. Little table
   for a Candle, one deal dressing Table & Swing glass
2 yellow Stuff window Curtains
1. Stool Cover'd with green Damask
1. Grate with fire shovell, Tongs, Bellows, Fender
   and Brish.

In Mrs Johnson's room

1 yellow Harrateen bed with Feather bed Bolster,
pillow, 3 Blank^{ts} & White Quilt.
1 Mohogony Tall boy, 1. deal dressing table &
Dressing glass over it.
1 Stuff window Curtain
2 Matted Chairs & 1. work basket

Aleck's Room

1 Brown Stuff bed, wth feather bed, Bolster, Two
Blankets & a Quilt
1 Tin fender, 1. hand brush, 1. Black Hair Trunk,
2. Rush bottom'd Chairs & 1. pair of Bellows

Dark Closet, up one pair of Stairs

1. Great Looking glass with a Black frame, 9. hearth
brooms, 3. Large Hairbrooms, 5 Maps and
5. Canisters

Kitchen

Pewter

21 Dishes, & 32 at Mr Benson's
3 Dozen of plates
64 plates at Mr Benson's

Coppers &c

10 Stewpans
2 fish kettles & plates for 'em
10 Covers. & 1. Chang'd away
3 Gravey pans
1 D^o.. us'd by the Brazier
4 Saucepans
3 Soop pots
5 petty pans
1 Copper Dispatcher
2 pulpetoon pans
1 pot for pease
4 pudding Coppers
1 Ladle
2 Skimmers
1 Soop Ladle
1 flat Copper
2 flesh forks
1 Driping pan
1 Iron frying pan
1 Basting Ladle
1 Tin Spice box
1 Dutch Oven
2 Tin Cullenders
14 Petit pattee pans
12 Tin petit pattee pans
1 Grid Iron
3 Spits
1 Salamander
1 pair of Tongs
2 pair of mincing knives
2 Iron Cleevers
1 Copper Cann . . Large
1 Mortar & pestell
4 Trippets for Stoves
1 D^o.... for the Grate
1 Crane
3 Loaded Iron Skewers
1 Brass Candlestick & Snuffers
1 Tin D^o
1 Meloniere

1 pair of Tongs, fire shovell and Poker
3 Iron pins for the Spitts
1 pair Iron Racks for 3 Spitts
1 Kitchen Table
2 Tubbs
2 Large Black Leather Jacks
3 Drinking horns
1 p^r of Bellows
1 Brass Chaffing dish
15 potting pots

Scullery

1 Table
1 Plate rack

Larder

2 Tubs for Salting meat in – wth. Covers
1 Hog Tub in the yard

Dairy

2 Churns
2 Milking pails
1 Cann
3 piggins
1 Butter bowl
4 pails
11 Earthen Milk pans
1 Large Iron pot
1 pair wooden Scales
2 Small Cheesefatts
11 Black Butterpots

Landry

8 Washing Tubs
1 Large Pail
1 Cooler for holding water
1 Horse for Drying Cloaths
1 pair of Tongs
4 Cloaths Baskets
4 Deal Tables
1 Pot and pair of Pot hooks

Magarry's bed in Spencer's

1 Blanket & a Rugg
1 Blue & White old mattress

Hillsborough Castle, County Down

Housekeepers room

1 Oak folding Table
1 Arm'd Chair wth Cheque Covers
12 Beech Chairs
3 Oak *D^o*
3 plate Baskets
3 Sieves
2 Lanthorns
1 Tea kettle Japan'd Lamp & Stand
1 Tallboy, Coffee pot & Chocolate pot
3 p^r Brass candlesticks
7 flat *D^o*
3 pair Steel Snuffers
1 pair Brass *D^o*
2 Carving knives and forks, never us'd
2 knife baskets

China &c

4 Soop dishes .. 2. of 'em crack'd,
3 Sallad dishes
17 Dinner dishes
9 new *D^o*.. for 2^d Course
3 *D^o*.. Wash hand basons
1 Doz Desert plates
1 Doz 11. new plates (one was broke in carriage.)
5 Litle blue & white desert dishes
4 China Mugs – 2. of 'em Crack'd,
2 doz 11. Comon plates
11 Soop plates
8 Supper dishes
2 Baking *D^o*....Burnt China
3 punsh bowls (one of 'em Join'd)
3 Little breakfast plates
8 Coffee dishes
4 Chocolate Cups and Saucers
12 Gilt Tea Cups – 11 Saucers
2 China Teapots – one of 'em ~~broken~~ brown
the other blue & white

2 pair Stone boats
2 Equipages. 1. of 'em tip'd wth Silver & Cut glass
4 China Basons
7 Argentee Candlesticks

In *D^o* Room

1 Jelly stand
1 grate, Tongs, Tinfender
1 fine Gun in a Case
1 Chocolate pot
2 Black Tea kettles
2 Box Irons & 3 heaters
1 Japan'd pint Cann
10 flat Smoothing Irons

In the Brewhouse

3 Coolers
1 Tub for Carrying Drink to Ton
1 great Kieve, 1 Runing Tub
1 Copper, 1 Large Oak Table, Two large
Deal tables, two Deal forms, 1. Barrel
Churn, 2 Canns, 1 pail, 1. Wort sieve.
3 Tables in the Turf room
14 Iron Bound hogsheads
2 Hogsheads in the Cellar   *Full*
4 Pipes in *D^o*.   *Full*
1 pair of Tongs

Stables

3 Beds
2 Mattresses
1 Double blanket, 1. single *D^o*
2 Suits yellow Harateen Curtains
3 Rugs
3 Bolsters

PLATE 13
Michael Dahl (1656/1659–1743) (attributed to)
Charles Boyle, 2nd Earl of Burlington and 3rd Earl of Cork (c. 1662–1704)
detail, oil on canvas

PLATE 14
Sir Godfrey Kneller (1646–1723)
James Butler, 2nd Duke of Ormonde (1665–1745)
oil on canvas

PLATE 15
Artist unknown, follower of
Michael Dahl (1656/1659–1743)
Mary Butler (née *Somerset*) *(1665–1733),*
2nd Duchess of Ormonde
oil on canvas

PLATE 16
Pompeo Batoni (1708–1787)
*Wills Hill, 1st Earl of Hillsborough,
later 1st Marquess of Downshire (1718–1793)*
1766, oil on canvas

PLATE 17
Sir Joshua Reynolds, PRA (1723–1792)
*Luke Gardiner, the Younger,
later 1st Viscount Mountjoy (1745–1798)*
oil on canvas

PLATE 18
Thomas Gainsborough (1727–1788)
James Hamilton, 8th Earl of Abercorn (1712–1789)
oil on canvas

PLATE 19
Frank Lydon (1836–1917)
Baronscourt (c. 1876), from Rev. F. O. Morris: *The County Seats of the Noblemen and Gentlemen of Great Britain and Ireland*, printed by Benjamin Fawcett

PLATE 20
Hugh Douglas Hamilton, RHA (1739–1808)
Susan Frances Elizabeth (Anne) Butler (née *Wandesford*),
Countess of Ormonde (1754–1830)
oil on canvas

Inventory
Hillsborough Lodge
November 20th 1777.

The Purl Pattern Room; *Attick Story.*

A four Post Bedstead, Cotton furniture)
   lined with a Green lutestring Silk)
6 Chairs, Walnutree cover'd with Cotton.
a Feather Bed Bolster & 1 Pillow
a Wool Matrass & Cotton *D?*
White Linen Quilt
4 Blankets
4 Cotton Window Curtains lined)
   with White Linen)
a Mahogany dressing Table & Glass
a Mahogany Writing Table.
a spice chest
a Mahogany night stool
a small Landskip Picture, plain frame.
1 Brass Stove Grate
Fire shovel and Tongs
Pair of Bellows & Brush.

The small Chince Room; *Attick Story*

A Four Post Bedstead and Curtains
a Feather Bed Bolster and Pillow
a Wool Matrass
3 Blankets
a White Cotton Rug
1 Window Curtain
an Oak dressing Table & Glass
an oak chest of Drawers
2 Rush bottom'd Chairs
a Bedside Carpet

Purple & White Room *Attick Story*

A four Post Bedstead & Curtains
a Feather Bed, Polster & Pillow
4 Blankets
a White Linen Quilt
2 Matrasses
2 Window Curtains
a Mahogany Dressing Table & Glass
Chest of Drawers Mahogany
8 Pictures

3 Rush bottom'd Chairs
a fixed Grate
Fire shovel Tongs & Tin Fender
a Pair of Bellows.

The Green Room *Attick Story*

A Four Post Bedstead & Curtains
a Feather Bed, Bolster & Pillow
2 Mattrasses
3 Blankets
a White Cotton Rug
a Window Curtain
1 Oak Chest of Drawers
a Glass
3 Rush bottom'd Chairs
a Bed Carpet
a fixed Grate
a shovel Tongs & Tin Fender
a small folding Table

Blue checked Room

2 Fourpost Bedsteads, Check furniture
2 Feather Beds Bolsters & Pillows
4 Matrasses
6 Blankets
2 Cotton Quilts
1 Window Curtain
1 Oak Chest of Drawers
1 oak Table
2 Chairs
a Glass
a fixed Grate
pair of Tongs & shovell
a Brush & Bellows
a Bedside Carpet.

Lady Charlotte's Room *Attick Story.*

a 4 Post Bedstead & Curtains
a Feather Bed Bolster & Pillow
2 Matrasses
3 Blankets
a White Linen Quilt
2 Window Curtains
a Walnut dressing Table
a Mahogany Beaureau
Ditto Drawers

Hillsborough Castle, County Down

a Ditto
2 looking Glass
6 Painted chairs, with Bottoms   } arm'd Chair
   & Cotton Covers & Cushions }
a Stool
a fixed Grate
a Pair of Tongs Fire shovel & poker
3 Mahogany Shelves
a Pair of Bellows
a Bedside Carpett
a Fire Screen.

Lady Cranborn's Room   Attick Story

a Four Post Mahogany Bedstead & Curtains
   with Chints Furniture
a Feather Bed, Bolster & 2 Pillows
a Wool Matrass
a Cotton Ditto
4 Blankets & 2 Bedside Carpetts
2 Window Curtains
a Mahogany Beaureau
a Mahogany Chest of Drawers
an India Cabinett
a Small inlaid writing Table
a Mahogany night Table
Mahagony shelves with Drawers
a walnut folding Table
a Fir dressing Table & Glass
Boxes Ditto
6 Chairs Painted rush bottoms &
   Cotton Covers & Curtains. an arm'd Chair
12 Pictures, Birds & flowers.
a fixed Grate
a fire shovell Tongs
a pair Bellows & Brush

Lord Cranborn's Dressing Room.   Attick Story

a four post Bedstead & Curtains (cotton)
a Feather Bed Bolster and pillow
a Cotton Rug
3 Blanketts
   Cushions
2 Mahogany chests of Drawers
   Mahogany Shelves with drawers
an oval dressing Glass
3 Rush bottom'd Chairs
a fixed Grate
a fir dressing Table

In the Passage

A Japan Table.

The Blue Dressing Room   Middle Floor

An India Chest and Leather cover for Cloaths
a new Deal Table & Glass and 7 dressing Boxes
an oval Pier Glass carved & Gilt Frame
2 Blue Silk Damask Window Curtains
a small 2 leaved writing Table
4 Blue and White painted Chairs rush bottoms }
   Silk Damask Cushions & cheque Covers. }
a Fire Screen
a pair of Tongs Fire shovell & Poker
a Fixed Grate & Tin Fender
a half Length Portrait picture of a Lady.

Blue Damask Room ....   Middle Floor

a Four Post Bedstead blue silk Damask Curtains
A Counterpane D^o and white silk night Quilt
a white Cotton D^o
a Feather Bed Bolster and 2 pillows.
2 Mattrasses & 3 Blankets
3 Window Curtains blue Damask
4 Painted Chairs Cushions & Covers
A Mahogany Bureau and Bookcase
A D^o Dressing Table & D^o chest of Drawers
2 oak night Tables and a Carpet
A fixed Grate & Tin Fender
a Pair of Tongs Fire shovell & Poker
A pair of Bellows & Brush
2 oval Glasses, carved & Gilt frames
2 Glass cases of shellwork in the Closet
a night stool.

Lord Fairford's Room   Middle Floor

a four Post Oak Bedstead, blue & white Linen Curtains
3 Matrasses
A Feather Bed Bolster & Pillow
a white Linnen Quilt
3 Blankets
2 Bedside Carpetts
a Mahogany Bookcase
a Small Mahogany Writing Table with Drawers
A D^o wash hand stand.
a small looking Glass
a D^o Swing
6 Rush Bottom Chairs

A night Stool
an oak chest of Drawers
a Fixed Grate
a Fire shovell & Tongs
a pair of Bellows & Brush.

Lady Kildar's Room ... Middle Floor

a 4 Post Mahogany Bedstead yellow silk damask Curtains
a Feather Bed Bolster & 1 Pillow
2 Matrasses
3 Blanketts
a white Quilt Muslin
A chints Counterpane
A Gent.s Dressing Table & Glass
a Mahogany folding Table
a D.º Beaureau
6 white painted chairs Cushions & white cotton Covers
2 yellow silk window curtains
a white silk night Quilt.
2 Bedside Carpets
a Floor Ditto
a Small pier Glass
An Oval D.º over the Chimney cracked.
a fixed Grate
a Pair of Tongs fire shovell & Poker
a Pair of Bellows & Brush & Tin Fender.

In the Closet.

A Deal Dressing Table & set of Japan Boxes & oval Glasses.
A Mahogany Horse for night Cloaths.
a Basket for foul Linen
A Set of Oak Shelves.

In the Passage

A Mahogany Beaureau & Bookcase
An Oak Chest for Blankets & Turf Baskets
2 Blankets in D.º

My Lord's Bedchamber, Middle Floor

A 4 Post Bedstead, white Dimity Curtains lined with
   blue Silk
a Feather Bed Bolster and 2 Pillows
2 Mattrasses
a Cotten Counterpane
a Dimity Ditto
2 fixed night Tables
2 Chinese painted Commodes

2 Dressing Tables Mahogany
a small Mahogany Table
a Small Mahogany writing Table
4 blue painted chairs rush bottoms & white dimity Covers
a fire Screen
2 Window Curtains Dimity
a Wilton Floor Carpett
2 White Stools Dimity Covers

In the Writing Closet

a writing Desk
an armed Chair, Cane Bottom.
a Small round claw Table
2 set of shelves & a Floor Carpet.

In the Bed Closet

an Oak Cloaths press and Drawers
a Mahogany Night Table
a Tambour Frame.
a Small Mahogany Box.

Stair Foot

a Glass Lanthorn
a Chamber 8 Day Clock
a Turf Basket

Breakfast Room .... Ground Floor

a Dozen of Painted Chairs Rush Bottoms ⎱
   Hair cushions & chints Covers.   ⎰
2 Mahogany Card Tables
a Round Table Ditto
a 2 leaved dining Table
a Smaller Ditto
A Backgammon D.º
2 Fire Screens Mahogany
a large Pier Glass gilt Frame
9 Pictures views of Naples.
15
A Family
A Mahogany side Board
a Wilton Floor Carpet
A Piano Forte

The Drawing Room Ground Floor

12 Arm'd Chairs (Chinese) Green silk Damask
   Cushions & Cotton Covers

Hillsborough Castle, County Down

6 more Chairs, not armed,
2 Window Curtains
2 Pier Glasses Marble Tables Leather Covers and
2 Glass cut Lustres
an oval Glass
2 Mahogany Writing Tables
2 Fire Screens
a Steel Stove Grate
Fire shovel Tongs & Poker
a Hearth Brush & Bellows.

Dining Room

24 chairs rush Bottoms
2 Mahogany side Board Tables
A large Mahogany dining Table in 3 Parts.
a Round Ditto
a Cistern *D?*
a ~~Round~~ ₙ^{Dumb} Waiter *D?*
A Fire Screen
a large Whole Length Picture of Lord Hillsborough
a Half Length Picture of Lord Dungannon
a *D?* Dutchess of Marlborough
a *D?* Sir W^m. Cooper
D? Col. Hen. Rowe
D? W. Hill Esqr.
D? Marcus Hill Esqr.
D? Anthony Rowe Esqr.
D? Sir Thos. Rowe
D? Mich^l. Hill Esqr.

Dining Room continued

a Half Length Picture S^r. Henry Rowe Kn^t.
D? Arthur Hill Esqr.
D? S^r. Moses & Lady Hill
D? S^r. Thomas & Lady Rowe
D? Anne Viscountess Middleton
Mary Viscountess Hillsborough
D?
A Picture of Birds Beasts Fruit & Flowers
a *D?* of Birds
D? Birds & Flowers
a *D?*
a *D?*

My Lord's Library

4 Oak Book Cases with Glass Doors.
a Writing Table

a round Mahogany Claw Table
a Commode.
3 Green & white check Window Curtains
A Black Leather arm'd chair
a Writing Chandelier
a small Looking Glass
a Hand *D?*
a Mahogany Bason Stand
2 armd Chairs Green & white Covers
2 *D?* . . . . . . *D?*
a Backgammon Table
a Mahogany Writing Table with Drawers
A *D?*
A Perpetual Almanack
24 Prints, Hogarth,

My Lord's Library continued

a fixed Grate
Tongs, Poker, Fire shovell, Brush & Bellows
4 Guns, 2 Blunderbusses
2 pair Pistolls Brass mounted.
1 pair *D?* Silver & Steel.
a pair Small *D?*
1 Small *D?*
1 Gun sm. half stock.
3 Broad Swords.

The Great Hall

A Monthly clock
a Billiard Table
a Card Table
2 Globe Lamps
a Map of the County of Down.
an Iron Grate
a broken fire screen.

The Housekeeper's Room.

a large Linen Press
a warming Pan.
a Deal Table
a *D?* with flaps
2 Japanned Teaboards
2 India *D?* Square
1 oval *D?*
2 large Japan *D?*
2 waiters *D?*
2 chairs.

Steward's Room

A large Oak dining Table
a Deal side Table
a Mahogany claw Table
a Small Deal Table
a large Mahogany Tea Board
12 walnut tree Chairs Rush Bottoms
2 Landskip Pictures
a Looking Glass.
a Fixed Grate
a Fireshovell Tongs & Poker
a Hearth Brush.

Butler's Pantry

A Press Bedstead
a Featherbed Bolster & Pillow
a white Quilt
    Blankets
an Oak Beaureau
a New Deal Table with 3 Drawers Locks & Key.
an arm'd Chair.

In the Passage

a Deal Table with a Drawer for cleaning Plate
2 Glass Lanthorns

Servants' Hall

2 Deal Tables
6 Deal Forms
3 Horns for drinking

Linnen in the Press in ye Housekeepers Room

Thirty pair of fine sheets.
Thirty Two pair of Servants Sheets .. old
Eleven pair of Ditto ..   New
Two Table cloths & Two Lay overs, Damask, for the
    22 Table.
Two Dozen napkins for Ditto – Damask.
One Table Cloth & a Lay over, star Pattern, Damask for
    14 Table
five Bird Eyed Table Cloths & five Lay overs for the
    14 Table
four Dozen & 9 Napkins of D^o for Ditto
Twenty six Table Cloths old Damask for the 10 Table
Thirteen Dozen Napkins old D^o for D^o
Twenty Lay overs ...   old D^o for D^o

Seven Table Cloths Potatoe Pattern
Two Dozen Napkins D^o Pattern
four old Lay overs of Different Sorts
Twenty three Breakfast Table Cloths
Six Dozen & ten Napkins for Ditto
Twelve steward Room Table Cloths
Six Stewards Room Breakfast Cloths
Eight Dozen & eleven Towells
Three Dozen Pittow Cases,
Three Huckaback Round Towells
Two plain ~~Huckaback~~ Ditto.
~~Six Stewards Room T~~
Six Servants Hall Table Cloths
Three Dishing Cloths.

First Room   *over the Pantry*

a 4 Post Bedstead, Cotton Curtains
a Feather Bed Bolster & Pillow
a Straw Matrass
4 Blankets
a Cotton Quilt
The upper part of a Mahogany Writing Desk
a chest of Deal Drawers
a Looking Glass
a Fir Table
an oak night chair

Second Room   *over D^o*

a 4 Post Bedstead, Cotton Furniture
an Oak Table   a Feather Bed Bolster & Pillow
a Looking Glass   3 Blankets & a small Cotton quilt
a Chest of Drawers   a straw Matrass.
2 viewes of the Thames   a wool Matrass.
a Rush Bottom Chair
a fixed Grate.

The Bedchamber   *over the Servants Hall*

a 4 Post Bedstead Blue Stuff .... Furniture.
2 Feather Beds & Bolster & 2 Pillows
2 Mattrasses, 4 Blankets & a Cotton Quilt.
3 Rush Bottomd Chairs & a night chair.
a Deal Table and Looking Glass
2 Bedside Carpetts
an Oak Beaureau
a Grate.

Hillsborough Castle, County Down

The Footmen's Room.

2 Four Post Bedsteads Oak with Cheque Furniture
2 Feather Beds and 2 Bolsters
2 Straw Matrasses
6 Blankets
2 Cotton Quilts
an Armed Chair
a writing Desk ~~for~~ fir,
an old Trunk.

Bedchamber   *over the Steward's Room*

a four Post Bedstead, Cotton Furniture
a Cotton Quilt
a Feather Bed Bolster & Pillow & 2 Matrasses
a Fir Table & Glass
a Bedside Carpet
an old Leather Trunk
an old Hair Trunk
a Wooden Chair
a Broken Mahogany Tea Kettle stand.

In the Passage

a Soap chest of Deal
a Deal chest with church Cushions
a *D.º* with paper Hangings
a Box with a Bedstead in it.
an old Hair Trunk
~~a Coffee~~

The Kitchen

a large Deal Table with 8 Drawers
2 Dressers
6 Shelves
a Deal Box standing on the Dresser
a Salt Box
a Skreen lined with Tin
a Broken windsor chair
a chopping Block.
a Deal Jelly stand.
a Pump.

Iron Furniture

a Range
2 Iron Spit Racks
3 Pins for *D.º*
a Pair of Tongs & poker

a Pair of Stake Tongs
a Smoak Jack
3 chains to *D.º*
2 Beef Forks
5 Spits, & a Coffee Roasting Spit
1 Double Grid Iron
2 Single *D.º*
5 Mincing Knives
2 Loaded Scivers
4 Scivers
a Wafer Iron
2 Iron holdfasts for the Spits
6 Trivets
2 Crowes for the Grates
an Iron Rod & Hooks for the Trivets
an Iron Frying Pan.

Kitchen Furniture continued

Copper

a large Tea Kettle to serve the Kitchens
2 small Kitchens
1 Large *D.º*
1 old *D.º* broken.
25 Stewpans with Covers
3 Ditto without Covers
1 large Soop pot & Cover
3 Small Ditto with Covers
1 oval Soop pot with Cover
7 Small Saucepans
2 larger Sort *D.º*
2 Fish Kettles with plates & Covers
1 Oval Doving pan & Cover
5 Common pots with 4 Covers
~~1 Copper Triping Pan larg~~
1 Large Copper Dripping Pan
a Copper Cullender
2 Beer Coppers
a Basting Ladle *D.º*
2 Copper Ladles
2 preserving Pans
2 Coffee Potts
one chocolate Pott
1 Steel
2 Graters
2 Paste Brushes
2 pair Fish Sheers
2 Baking Plates Copper
11 larding Pins.

Kitchen furniture continued

7 Turnip Scoops
4 Paste Cutters & a Roler
2 large Mellon Molds
6 Small Ditto
1 Pig Mold
3 Turks Cap Molds
a large Grape Mold
2 round Crocant Molds
4 Oval Ditto
2 oval ribb'd Molds
1 Cherry Mold
2 small Grape Molds
1 Small Turk's Cap
25 Small common ribb'd Molds Copper
6 Snuff Box Copper Molds
6 Heart Copper Molds
6 Walnutt Copper Molds
5 Scollop shells, copper
8 large Patty pans D^o
12 Thimble molds D^o
15 Small round patty pans D^o
3 Dozen & 9 more patty pans of diff^t sorts D^o
3 more Small Turks Caps D^o
5 more Small ribb'd Flower'd patty Pans D^o
1 Basket patty pan D^o
a handle Turner
a Church Mold in 4 pieces Copper
a Drudging Box Copper.

Kitchen continued

Tin

a Heart & a round Paste cutter
12 Heart Molds
14 Small round molds
8 molds of different Sorts
2 Pudding molds.

Pewter

22 Dishes
3 Dozen Plates

Prass [recte Brass]

16 flat candlesticks
2 High Ditto.

Silver Scullery

a Deal Table
a Plate Drainer
1 Iron Pott Set
2 Shelves

Kitchen Scullery

a Deal Table
a Plate Rack

2 Boyling Coppers with Cocks
a Jack multiplying Wheel & Lead Weight
a Pump.

Dry Larder

2 Dressers
3 Shelves
a Chopping Block
a step Ladder.

Wet Larder

a Powdering Tub lined with Lead
2 Ditto
a Tub for Salt

3 meal Baskets
a Box with Handles for fat or Kitchen Stuff
2 Vinegar Casks.

The Yard

A Pump
a Water Tub
a large Iron Pot 3 feet
a large Copper for Water
A Bottle Rack
a D^o with Doors Lock & Key

The Laundry 1st Room

2 Bedsteads Deal & yellow Furniture
2 Feather Beds & Bolsters
8 Blankets
2 Cotton Quilts

2^d Bedchamber

an Oak 4 post Bedstead, blue Camblet Furniture
a Feather Bed Bolster & 2 Pillows
2 Matrasses, 1 straw, the other flock.
4 Blankets
1 Cotton Quilt
1 Chair
1 Small looking Glass
a moving Grate

3 Bedchamber

2 four post Bedsteads Deal, old Cheque furniture
3 Feather Beds 2 Bolsters
1 straw Matrass
6 Blankets,
a Cotton Quilt, A stuff.

Hillsborough Castle, County Down

a small oak press Bedstead
a Feather Bed & pillow
3 Blankets & a Cotton Quilt
a Folding Table
1 chair

The Laundry continued.

A Mangle by Peter Lyon
2 Fixed Dressers
1 Large Table, Deal
1 Small Ditto
2 Folding Cloaths Horses
2 Stools
3 old Wooden Bottom Chairs
1 Rush *D.*
A Ceder chest with Blankets.
a large Travelling Plate Chest.
2 Large Packing Boxes
4 long Cloaths Baskets
3 Round *D.*
1 old Copper Tea Kettle
a Pair of Tongs & shovell.
an old Tin Fender.
3 old Box – Irons
16 flat Irons all good
3 stands for *D.*
1 old Ironing Blanket
2 Tin Candlesticks flat.

Wash House

4 Small Tubs & 1 large *D.*
a Wet Horse
2 Lading Pails & a stand *D.*
a Deal Table
1 Fixed Iron Boiler

Laundry continued

a Cedar Chest containing Furniture
as follows
a set of Red & white cheque Bed Furniture compleat
3 Red & white flower'd Cotton window Curtains
2 Blue Mohair & silk window Curtains
3 Green stuff window Curtains, belong'd to the Library
2 Green Mohair & silk window Curtains
6 Blankets
2 window Curtains flowerd Cotton red.
A Red & white cheque cushion Cover

24 yards of yellow Camblette ½ Ell wide
a Piece of blue & white cheque
about 2 yards of Carpett
a piece of
a Cover for an arm'd chair red &
    white Cotton, matches with the }
    furniture of the stair Head Room
5 Cotton Quilts.
1 need work'd *D.*
A set of flower'd Tafty Bed
= furniture complete & Quilt

In the Laundry

A large Iron bound chest formerly used for Plate
containing Furniture as follows
10 yards of purple & white Cotton
4½ y^{ds} *D.* coulourd
A Green & white cheque 6 y^{ds}.

The Brew House

a fixed Copper Boyler
a Mash Tub
2 Coolers & Spout
a Steel Mill for grinding Malt

Dairy

2 Leads for Milk
3 ~~Churns~~ 3 Churns
a Scalding Tub.
1 Peal, 2 Cans
3 Piggins,
1 Bowl,

over the Stables.

2 Bedded Room

2 Oak 4 Post Bedsteads blue & white cheque furniture
2 Feather Beds 2 Bolsters & 1 pillow
2 Straw Matrasses
2 Cheque Quilts
2 large folding Screens
a Deal Table with Drawer
a Deal Corner Cupboard with Shelves
a Settee Green chair
2 blue & white window Curtains
A walnut Settee.

2d Room

A 4 post Oak Bedstead blue & white cheque furniture
a Feather bed, Bolster & a Pillow)
1 Quilt) at Mr. Slade's
3

3d Room at the stair Head

a four Post Bedstead blue & cheque furniture

4th Room

a 4 post Bedstead, green stuff Curtains
a Feather Bed, Bolster, Pillow & straw Matrass
3 Blankets

5th Room over the Stables

A 4 Post Bedstead, blue cheque Furniture
A Feather Bed

6th Room

3, 4 post Oak Bedsteads blue cheque furniture
3 Bolsters
3 straw Matrasses
9 Blankets
2 Cotton Quilts
1 Green D?
a Stettee
a Wooden Chair
an Oak Bedstead press
an Oak chest
an old Grate
a Small looking Glass.

Porter's Lodge

a Deal Bedstead
a Feather Bed & Bolster
3 Blankets
a Stuff Quilts
a Deal Table with a Drawer
2 Deal Forms & a Chair
a fixed Grate.

Hillsborough Castle
Janry 15th 1776

Blue & White China.

4 Tea Potts
3 Sugar Dishes with Covers
2½ Dozen Cups & Saucers
2 Cream Potts (Glass)
4 Slop Basons (large)
6 Ditto, Small
2 Dozen Coffee Cups
1 Tea Board and waiter
3 Dozen Plates.
a Tea Kitchen

Other things

32 Arm'd Chairs (Green)
1 Carved Cycamore Arm'd Chair
1 Mahogany claw Table
1 old writing Table
1 Small Carpet
2 flower Baskets

Hillsborough Castle, County Down

PLATE 21
John Brooks (*fl.* 1730–56): *Richd St George Esqr Brig.^r Genl in his Majesty King George the II^ds Forces*, mezzotint after a painting *c.* 1730 by Francis Bindon

8

KILRUSH HOUSE, FRESHFORD, COUNTY KILKENNY
1750

EDMUND JOYCE

AT THE TIME THE INVENTORY was made, Kilrush House was owned by Major-General Richard St George (1670–1755). The property had come into St George's possession a generation earlier, when Richard's father, Henry, was granted the lands by Charles II in 1666. The house recorded at this time was an extended medieval tower-house which had at one time been a stronghold of the Shortall family. A primitive representation on a cartographer's map contemporary to 1755, illustrates a castle adjoining a two-storey range. According to documents at Kilrush, Richard St George, who like many of his ancestors had pursued a successful military career, had ambitious plans to replace this earlier house.

The extent of this plan, according to an undated drawing in the family archive, inscribed 'A perspective of new improvements to be executed for Richard St George Esq., at Kilrush' and drawn by John Kennedy Gardner, was to build a large eight-bay three-storey house. The proposed house does not appear to incorporate the old tower-house, and although it is a relatively artless representation, the overall composition and massing of the house is attributable to the Irish architect and painter Francis Bindon. A portrait by Bindon of Richard St George painted around 1730 confirms that the two were at least acquainted. Another architectural drawing, also by Kennedy, contemporary to this period, is for a monumental 'Green House and ... two pine stoves'.

In preparation for funding the realization of his grand scheme, Richard had disposed of his interest in a fashionable town house in Henrietta Street, Dublin, and more damagingly, had leased his lands at Kilrush on a long-term lease at a fixed rent. When he died a few years later his plans remained on paper, and the estate, now without a reliable income, passed to his younger brother Arthur. Under his tenure, Kilrush remained largely unchanged; his energies were focused on a legal wrangle concerning the reclaiming of the family land.

In general, the sparse furnishing represented in the inventory reflects the relatively small spaces in the tower-house as well as an eighteenth-century fashion for order. With such inventories, the valuations are not the only measure of the significance of items in a family collection: the positioning of such items indicates their uniqueness and importance. The tapestries, which command the highest valuations, occupy prominent rooms. Their use as a wallcovering, by 1750 already out of fashion, suggests an archaic approach to interior decor and a collection replete with inherited items. However, such pieces, which were large and pliable, were conducive to tower-house occupation as they were easily carried up the winding stairs which serviced the upper levels.

The most valuable piece in the hall at Kilrush is one of two 'Mohogney Oval table[s]'. Its oval form contrasts with the rectangular nature of plank-topped pieces generally associated with Irish tower-house furnishing. More important, however, is the use of mahogany in a regional house; in 1750, this was a relatively new material, having been introduced to Ireland *c.* 1725. The presence of just three mahogany items in the entire house reflects the very gradual introduction of new pieces to already established collections. The positioning of two of these pieces in the hall was deliberate; it gave visitors an immediate impression of contemporary fashion. The identification of the timber as mahogany, and the lack of identified materials in so many of the descriptions elsewhere, suggests that the remaining pieces were mostly made of more readily available native timbers such as oak, elm and other indigenous woods.

The chimney-pieces are another prominent feature of the inventory. Their values indicate quality and craftsmanship. The 'Flowered' chimney-piece in 'The Grate Parlour' evokes an image of a similar one attributed to Richard Cassels at Strokestown Park, County Roscommon.

The room titles themselves are a point of interest. The 'Stococo' room conjures an image of a space richly ornamented with decorative plasterwork. The presence of a 'Yellow Room' and a 'Crimson Room' suggests an adherence to the mid-Georgian fashion for strong bold colours. 'The China Room', although a bedroom, may have contained chinoiserie decoration in either the form of China-ware or Chinese-inspired wall coverings. Chinoiserie decoration from the 1730s and 1740s is sometimes seen as a veiled criticism of the pacific administration of Sir Robert Walpole and an expression of the arguments for active imperialism. Whether or not this was the case at Kilrush will remain conjecture as explicit details extending to the trinkets and wares at Kilrush are lacking.

The house recorded in the 1750 inventory was eventually abandoned and in the later eighteenth century a modest, pedimented house was constructed on a height of ground facing towards the old tower-house. Shortly later, in the early nineteenth century, the Kilkenny-based architect, William Robertson, was commissioned to aggrandize this house. A large villa was attached to the earlier range and this amalgamation is the Kilrush House extant today. Some very good quality chimney-pieces of early to mid-eighteenth-century origin were incorporated into the earlier of the two schemes, suggesting that at least some of those which feature in the inventory moved with the St Georges to their new home. The tower-house still exists, albeit in an abandoned and much dilapidated state. Surrounding it, on a southerly prospect from its successor, are the remnants of a once-grand seventeenth- or early eighteenth-century planned landscape of straight canals and lime avenues.

This manuscript remains in the collection of the St George family at Kilrush House.

Kilrush House, Freshford, County Kilkenny

*An Account of
The Goods and
particulars belonging
to Gen^{ll} St George
in his House at
Killrush*

[from the back page (f. 2v; sideways script)]

N° 1   *The Grate Parlour*

12 Chairs at 10^s: 10^d ⅌	6:	10:	0
1 Glass	3:	8:	3
1 Chimney piece flowered	2:	5:	6
1 Marble Chimney piece & hearth Stone	3:	0:	0
Window Curtains / Viz^t 27y^{ds} at 1^s: 4^d ⅌	1:	16:	0
	16:	19:	9

N° 2   *The Col^s Room*

One Chimney peice	1:	16:	6
6 Chairs at 10^s: 10^d ⅌	3:	5:	0
1 Bedstead and Curtains	6:	0:	0
Window Curtains	2:	8:	0
1 Oak Chest of Drawers	1:	2:	9
2 Glasses	9:	2:	0
2 Sconces	0:	6:	6
1 Tea table	0:	8:	1½
1 Grate	0:	16:	3
1 Hanging glass and Walnut frame	1:	2:	9
2 3 Swinging glasses at 8^s: 1½ ⅌	1:	4:	4½
	27:	12:	9 [*recte* 27: 12: 3]

N° 3   *In the Hall*

1 Mohogney Oval table	4:	11:	6
1 *D^o*	1:	2:	9
1 Grate	0:	16:	3
1 Hall Dale table and Cloth	1:	2:	9
1 Chimney piece	2:	5:	6
	9:	18:	9

N° 4   *In the Little Parlour*

1 Chimney peice	2:	5:	6
1 Arm Chair	0:	8:	1½
	2:	13:	7½

No.5	*In the Stococo Room*			
1 Grate		0:	16:	3
1 Table Viz.ᵗ a Card Sideboard table		5:	0:	0
1 Looking Glass		4:	0:	0
1 Tea and Card table &c now in the Parlor		3:	0:	0
		12:	6:	3 [*recte* 12: 16: 3]

The Chimney piece not Valued

No.6	*In the Yellow Room*			
1 Mohogony Chest		4:	0:	0
1 bedstead and Curtains		3:	8:	3
1 Bed at 6½ ᵈ ℔ [?]		2:	10:	0
Window Curtains		1:	4:	0
Tapestry		6:	16:	6
1 Grate		0:	4:	4
6 Chairs at 10ˢ: 10 ℔		3:	5:	0
1 Arm'd Chair		0:	6:	6
1 fram'd table		0:	4:	4
1 Tea table		0:	4:	4
		22:	3:	3

No.7	*The Closett of the Yellow Room*			
The Tapestry		2:	0:	0

No.8	*The Dressing Room*			
1 Chimney piece		2:	5:	6
The Slab		0:	8:	1½
The grate		0:	16:	3
Four pannells of Cuffoy		3:	9:	4
Two Stools		0:	16:	3
1 Arm'd Chair		0:	11:	4½
1 Cuffoy Settea Bed		6:	8:	2
		14:	18:	0 [*recte* 14: 15: 0]

No.9	*The China Room*			
The Bedstead and Curtains		2:	5:	6
Tapestry		6:	16:	6
1 Dressing table		0:	4:	4
The Chimney piece and Slab		3:	8:	3
		12:	14:	7

No.10	*The Crimson Room*			
1 Chimney piece		6:	0:	0
6 Chairs at 10ˢ: 10ᵈ ℔		3:	5:	0
1 Grate		1:	2:	9
		10:	7:	9

1 Tea Table not Valued

N.º 11   *In the Gen.ls Room*

1 Tea table	0:	3:	3
1 Grate	0:	16:	3
1 Chimney piece	3:	8:	3
1 Arm'd Kane Chair	0:	4:	4
	4:	12:	1

N.º 12   *In the Gen.ls Closett*

1 Chimney piece	1:	10:	0
1 Table	0:	11:	4½
	£ 2:	1:	4½

N.º 13   *In the Brewhouse*

1 Brewing furnace	20:	0:	0
1 Large Kieve	4:	11:	0
1 Small Kieve	1:	10:	0
1 Large Cooler	2:	10:	0
7 Hogsheads at 4.s: 4.d ⅌	1:	10:	4
1 Malt mill	0:	16:	3
1 Guiling Tub	0:	3:	3
In the Wash house one Large Boiler	3:	0:	0
3 Guiling Tubs	0:	9:	0
4 three quarter Casks at 2.s: 2.d ⅌	0:	8:	8
	34:	18:	6

N.º 14   *The Nurses Room*

1 Bed Bedstead & hangings	2:	0:	0
1 Press	0:	18:	3
1 Small Press Bed	1:	0:	0
1 Small Cupboard	0:	4:	4
	£ 4:	2:	7

N.º 15   *In the Maids Room*

1 Bed and Bedstead	1:	2:	9

[N.º 16]   *The Boot Room*

1 Bed and Boulster	1:	0:	0
1 Table	0:	8:	1½
	1:	8:	1½

N.º 17   *In the Still Room*

1 Still	4:	11:	0

The grate, Crane, Niggers, Pott, Hangers
Table &c in the Kitchen not Valued or
Charged

N.º 1	16:	19:	9
2	27:	12:	3
3	9:	18:	9
4	2:	13:	7½
5	12:	16:	3
6	22:	3:	3
7	2:	0:	0
8	14:	15:	0
9	12:	14:	7
10	10:	7:	9
11	4:	12:	1
12	2:	1:	4½
13	34:	18:	6
14	4:	2:	7
15	1:	2:	9
16	1:	8:	1½
17	4:	11:	0
£	184:	17:	7½

The Jack, Crane, grate, Niggards pott hangers and Boyler Dressers and Kitchen table	0:	0:	0
the Chimney piece in the Stuco Room	0:	0:	0
	184:	17:	7½

Deduct for the Tapestry in the Closett	2:	0:	0
	182:	17:	7½

An Account of The Goods and particulars belonging to Gen.ll St George in his House at Killrush

Black Cattle According to Valuation	39:	0:	0
the Expence of plowing and Sowing three Acres and a half of Wheat and Eight Acres of Oates	9:	19:	6
	231:	17:	1½
Deduct more for the tapestry	13:	13:	0
	218:	4:	1½

Received the Contents of the above Inventory
this 7.th of July 1750

         R. S.t George.

PLATE 22
John Brooks (fl. 1730–56): *Richard St George Esq.r Major General in his Majesty King George the II.ds Forces*, mezzotint after a painting of 1744 by Stephen Slaughter (1697–1765)

PLATE 23
Mountjoy House, No. 10 Henrietta Street, Dublin, engraving from the *Dublin Penny Journal*, 13 February 1836

PLATE 24
John Rocque (1704?–1762): *An Exact Survey of the City and Suburbs of Dublin*, 1756; detail showing the area around Henrietta Street, Dublin

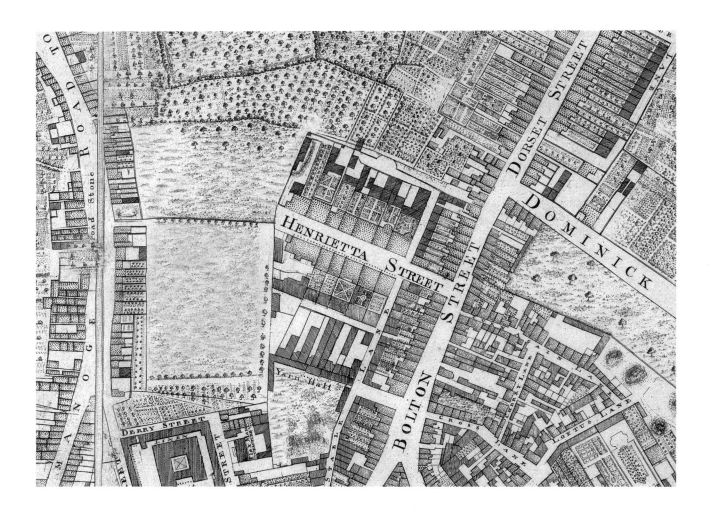

No. 10 HENRIETTA STREET, DUBLIN:
LUKE GARDINER'S HOUSE
1772
WITH INVENTORIES OF SILVERWARES 1755 AND 1773

JESSICA CUNNINGHAM

THE 'HENRIETTA STREET HOUSE' to which the 1772 inventory refers is the town house at number ten Henrietta Street on the north side of Dublin city, the home of Luke Gardiner (*c.* 1690–1755) (see plate 25). Together the three inventories serve as a valuation schedule to a detailed indenture. The circumstances surrounding the drawing up of this indenture some eighteen years after the death of Luke Gardiner are interesting. Gardiner had bequeathed the house at Henrietta Street and all its goods, furniture and silver to his second son, Sackville Gardiner. However, on his death in 1755, his elder son, Charles Gardiner MP (1720–1769), took up residence in the house. The indenture established that the property and its contents belonged to Sackville Gardiner and, accordingly, Charles 'did yield up' the house to his younger brother. In 1773, the year of the indenture, the house at Henrietta Street was sold by Sackville to Charles's son, Luke Gardiner (the younger) (1745–1798) for the sum of £1,598 3s 10d (see plate 17). The main inventory, drawn up the year before the indenture, lists and values the goods and furniture still at the house from the time when the elder Luke Gardiner was living there. The two silver inventories relate to a portion of Luke Gardiner's silver sold in 1755 and the valuation of the remaining silver in 1773.

The Gardiners' legacy to eighteenth-century Dublin's political, economic and built landscape cannot be overstated. The first Luke Gardiner charted an impressive career in Dublin Corporation, in the Irish Treasury, and also as a banker and major property developer. He was singularly responsible for the creation of north Dublin city's pioneering architectural transformation during the early Georgian period. In the early decades of the century he had piecemeal acquired extensive tracts of land north of the river Liffey. The earliest plan in his grand vision for the urban development of his land was a cul-de-sac street of brick-fronted, terraced houses, each occupying very large sites. The construction of this street began in the late 1720s and it is said to have been named Henrietta Street after the second Duchess of Grafton. On elevated land, it benefited from pleasant views and avoided the clutter and cramped conditions of the older residential areas in Dublin city. Over a twenty-year period, the construction of these enormous houses was gradually completed, and Gardiner succeeded in attracting important members of the establishment to acquire leases, among whom were peers, members of parliament, a judge and an archbishop.

At number ten Luke Gardiner set up his own home, the design of which has been attributed to the young architect Sir Edward Lovett Pearce (1699–1733), who was simultaneously engaged with the construction of the new Parliament House on the city's south side. The first four bays on the right of the house's front elevation belong to the original structure; in 1755, Charles Gardiner added four more, as well as a Venetian window on the first floor. The vast scale of this town house, built on three storeys over a basement, is evident from the inventory which, among other rooms, accounts for the furnishings in the Great Hall, Breakfast Parlour, Street Parlour, Gilt Parlour, Yellow Drawing Room, Blue Drawing Room and Ball Room. The contents of these rooms, however, and indeed the other rooms in the house – bedchambers, the nursery, servants' rooms, the kitchen, pantry and other service rooms – indicate a sparsely furnished and equipped home. However, it is unlikely they were thus during Luke Gardiner's occupancy or that of his son, Charles, but rather that large volumes of furniture had been removed, repurposed or sold since the elder Gardiner's death. What remains are reminders of the original grandeur and opulence of the interior of this house. In the Breakfast Parlour, for instance, there are no chairs, sofas or occasional tables, as one would expect, yet there are crimson curtains, a looking-glass and gilt-framed paintings. Similarly, in the Ball Room are numerous pictures and portraits on the walls, and two mahogany card-tables and two marble table tops, but again no seating furniture. In the Yellow Drawing Room there are just three items: a pier-table mirror, an Italian marble table and a framed painting depicting a biblical scene. In the second and third schedule of the inventory – the silver sold by Charles Gardiner to the goldsmith Robert Calderwood in 1755 and the remaining silver weighed and valued in 1773 – are further clues to the original richness of the interior of this house, where entertainment was provided on a grand scale. Several dozen silver-handled knives and silver forks and spoons along with silver plates, tureens, dishes, sauce-boats, a cruet frame, salvers, cups, candlesticks and an epergne are indicative of a well-equipped and lavish dining-table. A silver chamber pot and shaving basin, meanwhile, speak of real luxury and show that little expense was spared when it came to items of intimate use. That Charles Gardiner sold a large proportion of his father's silver in 1755 might suggest he also sold off several pieces of furniture too or transferred these to another residence, though there is no reference to such activity in the inventory or the indenture. The inventories of number ten Henrietta Street conjure up a palatial urban dwelling-house which, now with its scant furnishings, had been reduced from the grandeur it undoubtedly enjoyed during the residence of Luke Gardiner, its first inhabitant. Together with the indenture, they are contained in the National Library of Ireland's Gardiner Papers.

No. 10 Henrietta Street Dublin, 1772

*Deed relative
to the Plate and
ffurniture in Hen:
rietta Street House.*

*The first part of the Schedule to which the
Annexed Deed referrs containing a list of the Goods at Henrietta
Street House which did belong to the late Luke Gardiner
Esq.ʳ taken and valued by Joseph Ellis and J: Kirchhoffer
November the 9ᵗʰ 1772*

House Keepers Room

1 Deal press Bed	1	0	0
1 Feather bed bolster & one Pillow	4	0	0
3 Blankets one Cotton Quilt	1	1	0
1 Double deal press one Single	1	15	0
1 Deal Table	0	2	4
4 Old Chairs	0	6	0
3 Painted Pictures	1	14	6
1 Old Baize Screen	0	4	0
2 Blue paragon Curtains	0	3	0
1 Old Candle Chest	0	2	0
1 Sett of Fire Irons one brass Fender	0	8	0

Butlers Pantry

1 Deal press Bed	1	0	0
1 Feather bed and bolster	1	10	0
3 Blankets 1 Quilt	1	0	0
All the deal presses dresser and shelves	4	4	0
1 Deal Table	0	2	8
4 Old Knife Cases	0	12	0
1 Copper Capuchine plate warmer	0	18	0
2 Square Mohog.ʸ treas	0	8	0
1 Square Mohog.ʸ Bucket	0	9	0
1 Round Brass mounted Bucket	0	10	0
1 Mohogony Knife box	0	5	0

Maids Room

2 Deal box bedsteads	1	10	0
2 Feather beds and 2 bolsters	2	0	0
6 Blankets two rugs	1	8	0
1 Deal press	0	7	0

China Room

1 Deal press	0	7	0
1 Wallnutt Corner Cup board	0	10	0
12 Enamelled china dishes one broke 5 plates 3 broke	1	18	0

Servants Hall

2 Large deal Tables two formes	2	0	0
1 Deal sofa one deal press	0	10	0

Servants Room over the Coach House

3 Bedsteads	0	13	0
1 Wallnut Table	0	2	0

Stable

1 Settle Bed	0	12	0
1 Oat Binn	0	8	0

Kitchen

1 Jack mettle Weights	2	5	6
4 Spits	0	12	0
1 Copper Kettle and Cover	0	15	0
1 Copper Cheese toaster	0	3	3
1 Copper fish kettle and cover.	1	12	0
1 Brass scillit	0	6	0
1 Copper baking dish	0	3	6
1 Deal fire screen	0	2	0
1 Old deal table	0	1	6

Back Hall

1 Eight day Clock	6	0	0

Great Hall

2 Deal Seats	1	10	0
17 Musquets repeaters [?] bayonets	5	19	0
4 Bell lamps two of them broke	1	4	0

Breakfast Parlour

1 Marble Table top	1	0	0
1 Chimney Glass	1	15	0
1 Pair double brass branches	1	6	0
2 Crimson paragon window Curtains	1	4	0
1 Large fruit piece in a Gilt frame	5	0	0
1 Dutch Masacre in D^o fframe	7	0	0
3 Landscapes over the doors	5	0	0
3 Family pieces	3	0	0

Street Parlour

1	Marble table top	1	0	0
1	Large pier Glass in a white carved frame	7	0	0
1	Mohog.ʸ Dining Table	2	8	0
1	Chimney Glass	6	0	0
1	Round Mohog.ʸ pillar table	0	13	0
1	Needle work screen	0	12	0
1	Landscape of Powerscourt waterfall	3	8	3
2	Pictures King William Queen Mary	7	0	0
2	Sea pieces over the doors	1	10	0
1	Large History piece	3	8	3
2	flower pieces 1 Conversation piece in gilt frames	7	0	0
1	Portriat by candle light	1	2	9

Gilt Parlour

1	Large pier glass in a white carved frame	10	0	0
1	Marble table on Iron brackets	1	10	0
2	Killkenny ∧Marble Sideboards on Iron brackets	2	16	0
1	Mohogony dining table	1	10	0
1	Landscape in a Gilt frame over the Chimney	0	15	0
2	Pictures over the doors	0	10	0
1	Needle work fire screen	0	12	0

Yellow Drawing Room

1	Large pier Glass in a white carved frame	12	10	0
1	Italian Marble table on a D.ᵒ frame	4	0	0
1	Scripture piece with all the carved round it over the Chimney	5	0	0

Blue Drawing Room

1	Large pier Glass in a red and gold frame	9	0	0
1	Marble table with a Griffin in Gilt frame	3	0	0
2	Whole length pictures of Ladys and one three Quorto in Gilt frames	21	0	0

The Anty Chamber

2	large Landscapes in Gilt frames	22	15	0
1	D.ᵒ a Dutch Market	7	0	0
1	Mohog.ʸ Dressing Table.	0	15	0

Ball Room

2	Marble table tops with brass borders	9	0	0
2	Pictures of the Cartoons gilt frames	50	0	0
2	Whole lengths of George the first and the Duke of Bolton gilt frames	17	0	0
1	D.ᵒ Lord Stafford and his Secretary	7	0	0

No. 10 Henrietta Street, Dublin

2 Mohogony Card Tables	1	16	0
2 Glass plates in the late Mr Gardiners frames	17	0	0

Closet

1 large Wallnut burew	2	10	0
1 Old Tea kettle Stand	0	3	0
1 Old Corner table	0	7	0
1 Two leaf Needle work screen	1	10	0

Mrs Barnet's Room

1 Easy Chair	1	2	9
1 Oak Chest of drawers	0	15	0
1 Deal press	0	8	0
1 Large Mohog^y dressing table	0	18	0
1 Round Mohog^y Tea table	0	12	0
1 Old Settee	0	15	0
1 Elbow and two small Mohog^y Chairs	0	18	0
1 Sett of fire Irons and fender	0	5	0
1 Night Chair	1	0	0

Nursery

1 Wallnutt desk	0	15	0
1 Dressing table	0	3	0
2 Old Chairs	0	3	0
1 Wallnutt dressing glass	0	9	0
1 Sett fire Irons	0	2	6
1 Six leaf gilt leather screen	1	0	0
1 Old oak Chest of drawers	0	15	0

Mrs Gardiner's dressing Room

1 Small mohog^y $_\wedge$^{Dressing} table	0	12	0

In the Passage

1 Mohog^y cloaths chest	3	0	0

Mrs Gardiner's bed Chamber

1 Mohog^y tall boy	2	10	0
1 Mohog^y book case with glass door	2	5	6
1 Small Mohog^y desk & book case looking glass doors	5	0	0

Miss Norman's Room

1 Mohog^y four post bed with chintz Curtains	6	0	0
1 Pair Chintz Window Curtains	0	8	0
1 Chimney Glass in a Gilt frame	2	5	6
1 Sett fire Irons	0	4	0

2 Elbow with 6 other Chairs	3	12	0
1 Wallnutt chest of drawers	2	10	0

Late M.ʳ Gardiner's bed Chamber

6 Mohog.ʸ Cha_ᴀⁱrs & one Elbow one	3	3	0
1 Mohog.ʸ Squob	2	0	0
1 Mohog.ʸ pillar table	0	14	0
1 Old Wallnutt chest chest of drawers	0	5	0
1 Chimney Glass plate cracked	1	0	0

His Dressing Room

6 Mohog.ʸ & two Elbow chairs	6	0	0
1 Double headed squob two bolsters and two Cushions	3	10	0
1 Mohog.ʸ dressing glass	1	0	0
8 Mohog.ʸ Chairs needle work seats	8	0	0
A Rowling Stone	0	5	5

The Second part of the Schedule to which
the Annexed Deed referrs being an Account of Old plate received from Charles Gardiner Esquire 17.ᵗʰ October 1755 by Robert Calderwood

		Oz	pts
2 Sauce boats	W.ᵗ	33	5
1 Gilt porringer and Cover		26.	11
1 Large Cup		46:	4
4 Cans		31:	8
1 Large Salver		25:	4
4 Small Ditto		16:	18
6 Salts and four shovels		26:	4
1 Cross Stand		22:	15
1 Crewet frame 3 Casters & 2 Crewet Caps		38:	7
1 Tundish			
1 bell		8:	4
2 Juggs and Covers		85:	7
6 Small Candlesticks		46:	0
1 Tea kettle stand and lamp		93:	0
1 Coffee pot		24:	10
1 Shaving bason Water Ewer wash ball & Spung box		83:	12
1 drinking horn and Cover		10:	16
1 Cheese toaster		11:	11
1 Chamber pot		28:	1
65 Large knife hafts		151:	0.
10 Small Ditto			

No. 10 Henrietta Street, Dublin

62 Large three pronged forks ⎫				156:	10
11 Small Ditto ⎭					
2 Soup Spoons				13:	0
14 Table Spoons ⎫					
11 Desert *D?* ⎬				48:	10
1 Marrow Spoon ⎭					

$$\text{Oz } 1026: 17 \quad \text{at } 5:10 \quad \overset{s\ d}{} \quad \overset{£\ s\ d}{299:\ 9:\ 11}$$

The third part of the Schedule to which the
Annexed Deed referrs being an Account of Plate Weighed
at Luke Gardiner's Esqre 24th May 1773 by John Locker
and Alexander Lilly

		Oz	pwts
2 Large Ovil dishes	W^t	147:	0
4 *D?* next size		173:	0
4 *D?* *D?*		138:	0
4 *D?* *D?*		107:	10
4 Round dishes		128:	0
4 Sallett *D?*		85:	0

Oz	dpts	s d		£	s d
778: 10	at	6/6		223:	0: 3

		Oz	dpts		s d	£	s d
5 Dozen Pleats		1158: 10	at		*D^o*	376:	10: 3
2 pair of cheas'd Candlest^{ks}		130: 0	at		*D^o*	42:	5
A Turreen Ladle		6: 10	@		*D?*	2:	2: 3

		Oz	pwts				
1 Turreen & Cover	W^t	113:	0				
1 Epergne		197:	0				
2 Beaking dishes		31:	10				
10 Square dishes		234	0				
6 Candlesticks		72:	0				
2 Fish pleats		40:	10				
1 Gilt Cup & Cover		80	10	768: 10 at 6/0		230:	11: 0

$$£\ 904\ \ 8\ \ 9$$

Signed sealed & delivered ⎫
in the presence of <u>*us*</u> *by* ⎪
the within Named Sackville ⎬
Gardiner & Luke Gardiner ⎭

Thos Bracker
Willm Leysted

PLATE 25
John Brooks (fl. 1730–56): *The Right Honble Luke Gardiner Esqr*, mezzotint after a painting by Charles Jervis

PLATE 26
M. J. Smith (draughtsman); J. Cooke (lithographer):
South Front of Morrastown, Lattin. Cº Kildare [*sic*], lithograph

10

MORRISTOWN LATTIN, COUNTY KILDARE
1773

JESSICA CUNNINGHAM

MORRISTOWN LATTIN WAS not the grandest house in late eighteenth-century Ireland but this household inventory and valuation drawn up on the death in 1773 of George Lattin, the proprietor, do, however, merit inclusion for a number of reasons.

This document offers a rare glimpse of the interior space and material wealth of a prosperous Roman Catholic family who retained prominence during the era of the Penal Laws. Despite the rise of the Protestant ascendancy, whose power and position were visibly evident in several neighbouring County Kildare households – notably, the Connollys of Castletown House and the FitzGeralds of Carton House – the Lattins of Morristown, near Naas, succeeded in continuing the maintenance of a 650-acre estate as they had done since the sixteenth century. Survivors of seventeenth-century sectarian clashes, their construction of Morristown in 1692 in the immediate aftermath of the Williamite War signalled unusual confidence.

The 1773 inventory presents a modestly proportioned Jacobean manor home. The 1692 house was a two-storey construction with two deep bays on either end of the façade and attic dormitories. The Lattins' continuing prosperity and confidence in the early decades of the Georgian period saw further development of the property with the addition of a four-storey tower rising from the middle of the front. The simple arrangement of the principal rooms is conveyed in the inventory. A hall, big parlour, little parlour and breakfast room provided dining, leisure and entertainment spaces. The remainder of Morristown Lattin's rooms – four bedrooms, office, nursery, attic bedrooms and kitchen – accommodated family and staff. The household's larger scale, however, is communicated by the inventory's lists of ancillary buildings and agricultural outhouses. Additional staff lived in a separate servants' lodge while a cart house, coach-house, stables, brewhouse, beer cellar, dairy, granary, poultry yard and extensive stocks of timber all indicate a household working on a larger scale.

Few inventories from this period supply a complete view of a late eighteenth-century Irish domestic interior. Fewer still reflect the tastes, comforts and conveniences of Irish Catholic gentry. At Morristown Lattin confessional status is far from evident in the furnishings or equipment. The principal bedrooms and reception rooms were arranged in the style of the period, albeit on a modest scale. Mahogany tables, several sets of chairs – leather-bottomed, mahogany-framed – card-table, tea-table, sideboards, fire screens, numerous hanging prints, gilt-framed mirrors, carpets and curtains all articulate ease, quality and leisure. China coffee-cups, delftware sweetmeat stands and champagne glasses indicate refined, fashionable palates and regular entertainment. Economies were made in less visible spaces; the nursery's furnishings include oak and deal, and rush-bottomed chairs equip sparsely equipped bedrooms.

Morristown Lattin's 1773 inventory conveys a lived-in, comfortable and working household. It is neither ostentatious nor shabby and, as such, sits in between grandeur and practicality. The house was remodelled in 1845 following the passing of the property to the Mansfield family. The inventory, archived with the Mansfield Papers in the National Library of Ireland, remains a fitting snapshot of the house's eighteenth-century incarnation.

Morristown Lattin, Co Kildare
29 July 1773

An Inventory	*Valued*			*Sold*		
	£	s	d			
Brew House						
1 Copper Boylor wth a Copper cock & Wooden Cover						
1 Iron Fork for *D?*						
1 Kieve & two Mashing Shovels and a Copper Cock		10				
2 Sieves broke			4			
8 Coolers		12				
1 Two handle Tub one Wooden Ladle		2	2			
1 Small Wooden Bowel, Barm Can & Wooden Tun dish		1	6			
3 Barrels Casks 16 half *D?* 1 quarter Cask & Cock	2	3	4	*1 Barrel & 1 Half Barrell B? by M? Rielly*		5
1 Pair of Slings		1	6			
3 Stillens		6	6			
1 Malt Ben & Hangen Lock		6	6			
1 Wooden Streamer			3			
1 Pair Scales Iron Beam & Chain 21 10 Mettal Weights	1	14	1½			
1 Large Kennal Pot		5	5	*1 Large Kennal Pott sold to Gale*		12
Cart House						
2 Carts	2	16	10½	*2 Carts Sold to M? Gale*	4 11	0
1 Pair Cart Wheels & Axeltree		16		*1 P? Cart Wheels & Axle trees*	1	4
1 Carr one Tumbrel box		9		*1 P*		
1 Pair Carr Wheels & Iron Gudgeons		5		*1 P? Car Wheels & Iron Gudgeons*		7
2 Iron Backbands 2 Stradles 2 Collars & 2 pair Haims		8				
1 Large Rolling Stone & Wooden Carriage	1	5				
1 Small *D?* with an Iron Handle		11	4½			
2 Long Slateing Ladders one Short *D?*	1	4	-	*one Short D? 10ˢ - 10ᵈ*		
4 Short *D?*		8	8	*4 Short Ladders one Short Ladder Jaˢ - Lyons 4ˢ*		
1 Box Barrow with Iron Wheel & Axeltree		4	-			
1 Rack for hanging Geers on		1	6			
1 Large Garden Seat & two Turn Stiles		6	6			
1 Grinding Stone with Iron Axeltree & Handle		1	1			

	Valued				Sold		

1 Large Wooden Dog Trough	1 6	1 Large Wooden Dog Trough Ja.^{s} Lyons	1: 8
4 Doors **Rotton**	2 6	4 Doors Sold 2 to Magee 3^s – one to Gale 2:8½ $^{s\ d}$	
		one to Mar: Nowlan 1^s 2^d	0 6: 10½
1 Post for a Stable	2 6	1 Stable Post	2 6
1 Preak with a Steaple and Hook	2 2	1 Preak with a Staple & Hook	3
1 Tail Board for a Cart	6	1 Tail Board for a Cart	1
1 Old Cart Shafts & old Sticks.	1	1 Old Cart Shaft & Stick	2
		2 Pair of Cart Shafts Enterd in its own Place	

Coach House

1 Four Wheel Capriole & Harness for one Horse	25 - -	
1 Small *D.^{o}* with four Wheels & Harness for one Horse & Horse	20 „ „	
2 Small Wheels for *D^o*	2 2	
1 New Set of Post Chaise Wheels & Coach Pole	2 5 6	

Six Stall Stable

2 Old Sadles w.th two good Sadles in the House	1 6	One of House saddles sold for 14^s
1 Snaffle Bridle one Crub *D.^{o}* 1 new Crub *D.^{o}* in y.^{e} House and old Leather for Mending Harness§	8 1½	
2 Oaten Bins	18	
Ra$_∧^c$ks	3	
Waleran [*recte* Wateran] Bridle	1 6	

Three $^{Stall}_∧$ Stable

2 Racks	1 6

Common Stable

3 Racks	2 6

Beer Seller

2 Hogsheads one three q.^{r} Cask	- 8 -	1 Hogshead to Darby Duggan 4^s - 6^d
1 Large Powdering Tub & Cover	3	1 Large Powdering Tub & 1 Small D.^{o} to Mr Reilly 6 ^{s}
1 Stillen	1 1	
4 Standing Step Ladders	8 -	1 Step Ladder 2^s - 2^d
1 Chopping Block one Table	2 6	
6 Pieces of Timber	2 -	6 Pieces Timber Sold Ja.^{s} Lyons & some Lumber in Cow yard 2: 6

Garden Tools

1 Spead
1 Large Coper Watering Pot
1 Garden Iron reel & line
3 Hoes 1 Iron reak 1 Wooden *D^o* w.th Iron Teeth
1 Box Barrow
2 Garden Seats

Edge Tooles in Brew House

1 Hatchet	1 6
2 Fauling Axes	2 8
2 Pair of Garden Sheers	3 3

Morristown Lattin, County Kildare

	Valued				Sold	
1 Augur	0	4				
1 Beef Ax	2	2				
1 Crascut Saw	4	4				
1 Iron Sledge	4	4				
3 Iron Pickaxes	2	–				
2 Iron Madox	1	8				
1 Handsaw broke	0	6				
1 Billhook	0	6				
1 Iron Anker & Some plow Iron				*Iron Chain w.t 8^{ll} at 3^d 2^{sh} D^o 2^s:2^d } Firrall sold 24^{ll} Iron for 3^d – six shil*	

Fir deal Timber
In Brew House

	Valued			Sold	
7 Leaves Slit Deal *dō@sd* [?]	3	6		*Sold to John Rorke for*	*4 : 6*
10 Slit *D.º*	5	–		*Sold to Danial Magee of Naas*	*5 : 4*
16 Slit *D.º*	5	4		*16 Slit D.º to Daniel Magee Sold for*	*6 : 0*
4 Slit *D.º*	1	4			
18 Outsides Slab *D.º*	2	2		*18 out side slabs Sold to Dan: Magee*	*2 : 6*
10 Short Boards Deal	1	8		*10 Short Boards Deal Sold to D.º*	*2 : 2*
1 Piece Scantlen	2	2		*1 Piece of Scantling*	*2 : 6*
1 Short *D.º*		10			
3 Short Pieces Scantlen Elm		9			
1 Whole Deal Board	1	6			
1 Deal Plank	2	–			
1 Short *D.º*	1	2			

Little Parlor

	Valued		
1 Moving Grate Tong's and poker	1	2	9
1 Dineing Mohoganey Table & Green Cloth Cover	1	2	9
1 Side Board Table	–	4	4
1 Dozen Leather bottam^d Chairs	3	–	–
1 Lucking Glass with a Guilt Frame	2	10	
16 Prints	2	16	10½
4 Small *D.º*		1	8
1 Mohogany Shelf		4	4
1 Turf Box		2	–
3 Window Curtains	1	2	9

Big Parlor

	Valued		
1 Moving Grate Tongs & Poker		13	–
2 Side board Tables	1	6	
1 Tea *D.º*		11	4½
1 Card *D.º*		14	
1 Dozen Worked Chairs wth Mohogany Frames	5	–	
1 Fire Skreen		5	–
15 p^r Prints	1	10	
8 Small drawings		2	2
1 Turf box		2	–

4 Window Curtains	1	2	9
1 Carpet	1	8	
2 Small *D?* for side boards		3	–

Hall

1 Marble Side board Table		11	4½
5 Green Chairs		8	1½
1 Mohogany dineing Table & blue Frise Cover	1	8	–
1 Glass Bell		9	
1 Copper Plate Warmer & Mohogany bucket	1	2	9
1 Tea Board		2	6
1 Wine Cooper		8	

Office Room

1 Camp Bed & Curtains	1	6	–
1 Matrass	–	4	–
1 Rush Bottom,[d] Chair		1	6

In y? Room over office Room

1 four Post bed with blue & white Curtains	1	15	–
1 Matross feather bed Bolster & pair of Pillows	3		
1 Under Blanket 1 pair Eng. *D?*		16	3
1 Tufted Quilt		15	–
1 Dressing Table Glass & boxes	1		
1 Bason Stand			6
4 Rush Bottom,[d] Chairs		6	–
1 Close Stoole & Pewter pan		5	–
1 Tinn Fender Moving grate & Tong's		9	
2 Window Curtains		12	–

Red Room

1 Camp bed with red & White Curtains	1	10	–
1 Feather bed Bolster ~~& Paillasse~~	1	18	–
1 Pair Eng. Blanket & under *D?* 1 Cottan Quilt	1		
1 Dressing Table & Glass		8	1½
1 Beason Stand			6
4 Rush Bottom'd Chairs		6	–
1 Close Stoole & Pewter pan		5	
1 Window Curtain		6	
1 Tong's		1	6

Middle bed Chamber

1 Camp bed wth Cotton Curtains	2	15	
1 Matrass & Feather bed Bolster & six Pillows	3	8	3
1 Easey Chair wth a Blew & White Cover		11	4½
1 Feather Cushon wth a Blew & White Cover		2	

NOTE

Right-hand column empty on this page and the following two pages of this transcript, since no sales recorded on the MS.

Morristown Lattin, County Kildare

1 Red Ditto		1	6
1 Table & Drawer		4	–
1 Dressing Glass		6	6
5 Rush Bottom'd Chairs		7	6
1 Small Cupboard		2	6
1 Print		2	8½
2 Window Curtains		12	–

Break Fast Room

1 Chest of Drawers	1	2	9
1 Round Tea Table		11	4½
1 Small Spider *D⁰*		1	6
5 Rush Bottom'd Chairs		7	6
1 Cain *D⁰*		1	6
1 Fire Skreen		4	–
1 Small Shelf		1	6
9 Prints	1	4	
3 Window Curtains		18	
1 Tongs		1	6
1 Turf Basket		1	–

In Pasage

2 Weather Glasses		16	3
Stair Carpeting & rods		12	
In Bow Lobby 4 Green Chairs		6	6
2 Small bed side Carpets		6	6
1 Old Strip of *D⁰*		3	3

Miss Lattins Room

1 Chest of Drawers		8	1½
1 Table & Drawer		4	
1 Small red Table		1	6
1 Shelf		1	6
1 Camp bed wth red & white Curtains	2	–	–
1 Feather bed & Matrass	3		
1 English Blanket		8	–
1 Under *D⁰*		3	
1 Pair Irish *D⁰*	–	9	
1 Tufted Cotton Quilt		16	3
1 Camp Bed wth Green & white Curtains	1	2	9
1 Feather Bed & Matrass	2	10	–
1 Pair of Irish Blankets		11	4½
1 Under *D⁰*		3	–
1 Cotton Quilt		6	6
1 Cloas-Stool Chair & white Delf pan		6	–
1 Dressing Glass ₍Crack^d₎ one Parogan window Curtain		8	1½
1 Tong's		1	6

4 Rush Bottom'd Chairs	6	–
1 Chest	4	4
3 Small Pictures	2	0

Nursery

1 Cloas Press		1	
1 Small *D?*		10	
1 two Posted bed & half Curtains Feather bed & Bolster	2	5	6
1 Pair of Irish blanket & under dito		9	–
1 Check Quilt		6	6
1 Press bed, Feather bed & Bolster	2	10	–
1 Pair of Irish Blankets		7	
1 Small round Oak Table		5	5
1 Small Deal ~~red~~ Table		1	8
4 Oak Chairs		8	–
1 Fourm		1	4
1 Small dressing Glass		2	–
1 Pair of Tong's		1	6

Garetts

2 Boarded beds with half Curtains		16	3
2 Feather beds and Bolsters	4	–	–
2 Pair of Irish Blankets		14	–
1 Green Baise Quilt		3	3
1 Small old Oak Table 1 Iron bound Chest 1 fourm		7	7
1 Boarded bed ~~& Matrass~~ half Curtain		8	1½
1 Picture Box 1 oak Chest 1 deal *D?*		11	4½
1 Iron Chest		11	4½
1 Leather Trunk		4	–
1 Hair Ditto		3	–

Kitchen

1 Large Pewter Dish 1 soupe *D?* 1½ Dozen pewter plates	1	4	–
1 Tin Cover 1 Water plate & plate for Dito	–	2	8½
1 Tin Cullender 1 Tin baking pan 3 Small *D?*		1	6
1 Pewter Bason 1 Slice, Fish plate, Basteing Ladle drudging box		2	6
1 Copper & Cover 1 Copper Coffey pot 1 Coffey Roaster & Mill	1	–	–
2 Large Mettal pots 2 small ditto 2 pothooks 1 Flesh fork		16	3
1 Iron Ladle 1 Tin ~~Basteing~~ ᴬ Grater		–	4
3 Copper Toss Pans 1 Copper Cover 1 large Copper Sauspan	1	4	–
3 Small Copper Sauspans 2 pewter Quarts 1 Tin *D?*		8	8
2 Brass Skillets 1 rod spit 1 small *D?* 2 frying pans		18	–
1 Pair of Iron racks 1 Dripping pan		3	6
1 Mettal Pot Oven, 1 Griddle, 1 Trippet, 7 Iron Candlesticks		8	–
1 Tong's 1 Steak *D?*		2	8½
1 Copper Buckett		8	1½
1 plate Draen			

Morristown Lattin, County Kildare

		£	s	d
1	Small Table		1	6
2	Meal Hgsheads		4	4
1	Servants Table		6	6
1	Settle bed, Feather bed, & Bolster	2	15	–
1	Coper Warming Pan		2	8½
1	Pestle & Mortar		2	
1	P. Smoothing Irons		2	6
10	Molds		10	10
1	Tea Kettle		2	–
1	Iron Chafing Dish		1	6

Ash

		Valued	£	s	d			Sold	
15	Carr Slats		–	3	9	15	*Car Slats to D: Wogan Cara*		*5 : 0*
22	Short *D.*		–	3	8	22	*Short D. to D.*		*4 : 7*
1	Ash Board		–	–	8	1	*Ash Board sold with 17 outside Slabs*		
							See 8th Article		
3	Pair Carr Sides ash		–	6	6	3	*P. Car Sides ash to D: Wogan Cara*		*7 : 6*
2	Pair Cart Shafts		–	3	8	2	*P. Cart Shafts Sold to Gale*		*4 : 4*
6	Axeltrees for Carrs		–	6	6	6	*Axletrees for Cars*		*7 : 0*
1	Pair Cart Soals		–	2	8	1	*P. Cart Soals*		*3*
17	Out Side Slabs *D.*		–	2	4	17	*outside Slabs & one Ash board*		*4 : 2*
1	Short block Ash		–	1	–	1	*Short Block Ash*		*1 1*
3	Swinging Beals		–	1	4	3	*Swinging Bales Gale*		*1 :*
1	Pair Window Shut		–	–	10	1	*P. of Window Shuts Mart: Nowlan*		*1 : 4*
1	Small *D.*				4	1	*Small D. to Gale*		*8*
7	Old Carr Slats		–	–	7	7	*old Car Slates [recte Slats]*		*1 4*
1	Bed Side		–	–	4				

Oak

			£	s	d				Sold
4	Short Pieces of oak Scantlen		1	4		4	*Short Pieces of Oak Scantling*		*2 : 6*
	old Lumber		2	6			*old Lumber Sold to Martin Nowlan*		*3 : 6*
300	Plastering Lats		3	6		300	*Plastering Laths*		*3 : 9*
3	Dozen Small Rubberys		3	3		3	*Dozn Small Ribberrys sold to Mrs Kenedy*		*3 : 3*
1	Pair of red Window Shuts		1	6			*Sent to town*		

Timber in Hay Yard

			£	s					Sold
1	Piece of Ash		4	–		1	*Piece of Ash to Dumphy Naas*	⎫	
4	Short *D.* Ash		5	–		4	*Short D. to D. Sold together*	⎬ *10 : 6*

Oak

5	Pieces	12	–
3	Pieces Bog *D?*		10
1	Elm Fork 4 Short *D?*	8	
1	Ladder Pole	4	
4	Short fir Deal	2	8
1	Piece of Aspin	1	6
7	Pieces of Cherry Trees	15	
	Parcel of Aple Trees	5	5
1	Ash Tree a.t the Turf yard	13	–

5 Pieces Oak 4 to Gale at 14.sh. – one Piece Magee 2.s:p.d — 16 0
1 Elm fork Mate Carriage Harpsichord, 2 short D?. Posts for Gate

1 Ladder Pole Sold M.r Rielly — 4 4
4 Short fir Deal Ja.s Lyons — 3 : 4
1 Piece of Aspin W.m Griffen — 1 : 8

Parcell Aple Trees sold to Henigan — 5 : 11½
1 Ash Tree Sold to M.rs Kenedy — 13

Grannery over Dairry

3	Meal Hg'sh'ds with Covers	7	6
1	Large Chest	2	–
1	Small *D?*	2	6

Dairry

1	Pump, Churn dash and Cover	6	–
1	Small *D?* dash and cover	4	–
1	Cream Tub	1	1
1	Milk *D?*	1	6
3	Milk Pails	2	2
2	Keelers	2	–
2	Butter Bowels	1	6
2	Skiming dishes	0	3
2	Streaners and Streanerstand	0	9
5	Large ~~Delf~~ Milk Pans	4	2
4	Small *D?*	2	2
5	Large Butter Crocks Crack'd	7	
1	small Bowel		2
1	Milk Tub [almost entirely erased]		

Grannery over Lodge

3	Dozen and 4 New rackstaves	9	–
3	Dozen Old *D?*	2	
20	Old Wainscot Pannels & one Frame	2	6
5	Packing Boxes	2	6
10	Oars	2	6
	Old Lumber Boards	2	6
1	Close Stand		3
1	Case of a Hgsh'd		6

Morristown Lattin, County Kildare

Servants Lodge

4	ᵖʳ ₙBed Stedds	12	–
1	Rack	1	
1	Lime Riddle	1	4

Grannery *over Beer Celler*

1	Winnow Sheet 4 Sacks	10	0
1	Wheat Screen	2	–
	A Parcel of Old Sashes & a dome Glass	4	–

Poultry Yard

1	Bottle Drean	2	6

This Inventory with the annexed Valuation
Containing Eleven Pages begining at the Brew House and
Ending at the Poultry Yard Was made at Morristown
By me this 29ᵗʰ Day of July 1773

Bryan Dunne

We Beleive the above to be an Exact Inventory
and a Just Valuation Morristown this 29ᵗʰ of July 1773

Rich Ferrall
James Archbold Esq.
William Eustace
Robert Ferrall
John Reilly

Besides the above Subscribers there were Present Mʳˢ
Christian Kennedy of Littel Morristown & Mʳˢ Elizabeth
Archbold Eadstown

Morristown Lattin, County Kildare
Supplementary document to 1773 household inventory.

A List of China & delf

7 China Cups 9 Saucers
3 Coffey Cans *D.º* 1 Crack'd *D.º*
1 Sugar Boul 1 Blue & White Slob Boul
4 Crack'd Cups & 3 Saucers
2 Two handle *D.º*
5 Fluted Coffey Cans
4 Chocolate Cups
3 Flat Bottom *D.º* 1 Crack'd *D.º*
3 China Mugs
1 Large Delf Mug
2 Small *D.º*
1 Blue & White China Dish
1 Large Blue & white Crack'd Saucer
2 Small Delf Jugs & Covers
2 Small delf bouls
1 Round delf Dish
2 Small Butter boats *D.º*
4 Crack'd blamonge Cups
3 Crack'd pattys
1 Delf sweetmeat stand 1 Tort. Cover
5 Crack'd delf fruit Baskits & 8 plates w.th 2 Covers
1 Large white delf dish
4 Small Blue & white *D.º*
3 Dozen & 5 Plates *D.º*
1 Jelly Glass Stand & Glasses
3 Small Pickle Stands & Covers
3 Crack.d *D.º*
1 Blue Crack'd *D.º* & Cover
1 Large Glass Punch boul Crack'd
13 Water Glasses
1 Dozen & 10 Wine Glasses
3 Crack'd *D.º*
1 Dozen & 1 Short *D.º*
11 Champaign Glasses
1 Tumbler Glass
1 Handle ditto
2 Long *D.º*
1 Crack'd *D.º* with a tin foot
3 Quart Dicanters
2 Pints *D.º*
1 Green Quart *D.º*
5 higo [*recte* Lrge?] Glass Salts 1 Crack'd *D.º*
4 Flat Salts

Butlers Pantree Continued

Plate

7 Pair of Plated Candlesticks
4 Plated Waiters
3 Doz. Silver table Spoons
8 Desart Spoons
6 Silver plated Salts, with Glass to D.º
4 Silver Salts Spoons, 2 Botte Stands
18 Tea Spoones
1 p.º of tea tonges
1 Soup Ladle
1 French plate dish ring
1 French plate Marrow Spoone
1 D.º Sugar Caster
1 Plated Pepper box
1 Plated hand Candlestick, with Estinguesher belonging to D.º
3 Silver Botte tickets
a pair of Patten Snuffers, a Doecter,
2 Snuffer Pans
4 Doz. Knives, & 4 Doz.ⁿ Forkes
2 Meat treas
1 D.º for Glasses
1 D.º holding Fowle plates
a Coper Plate Warmer
a Knife box
2 Windeer Chaires
a Sett Grate with fender fireshoole Pocker and tongs

Yallow Stone ware, Ovel

14 Large Dishes, 2 Soup D.º
4 a Size less ⎫ 17 Round Dishes
12 a Size less ⎬ 8 Baking Dishes
6 a Size less ⎭
16 a Size less
27 Second Coursse D.º
5 Small, 6 Pincushen Dishes
3 Turines, 2 Bread Baskets
4 Fish Drainers
5 long Sallad Dishes, 3 D.º Round, 2 Small long Sallad Dishes
11 Sauce botles
a Table with 2 Drawers in D.º
12 Soup plates, 8 Doz.ⁿ Comman D.º
2 Juggs 5 Muggs 2 Doz. New Knives never used

Kitchen

a Jack with Multiplying wheel, and all Compleat
a Range Compleat with fender Fireshoole Pocker & tonges
An Oven, broiling plate and six Stoves
a Table in the Midle of the Kitchen
An Eight day Clock, by Gregg
2 Large boilers with covers to D.º
1 Dish Kettle
1 Ovel Fish kettle with plate and cover to D.º
3 Large Sauce pans with covers to D.º
4 D.º Smaler
1 Large Stock pot with cover to D.º
1 Large Braze kettle with plate and Cover to D.º
1 Soup pot with cover to D.º
5 Old Stew pans with 3 Covers to D.º
16 New Stew pans with covers to D.º
1 Putter Colender
1 Copper Grater, 2 ladles, and Basting D.º
1 Marble Morter
1 Brass D.º, with pestel to D.º
1 Gridiron
1 Dripping Pan
1 Fire Screen lined with tin
2 Frying pans, one Salt box
2 Square Trivets, 2 Tryangle D.º
1 Pair of Belles, 3 Spitts
1 Chocholet pot with Stick to D.º
1 Chaffing Dish
2 Clivers, one Salamander
1 Round Fish plate
6 Round Pewter pans, 6 Ovel D.º
1 Flower box, a Choping block
2 Coper Blaemange moulds, 6 Putter Froal D.º
2 Tea Kettles, 31 Putter Dishes of differant Sizes
1 Coffea pott
a Warming pan

PLATE 27
(i) 'Butlers Pantree Continued: Plate'; (ii) 'Kitchen'.
Pages from the Baronscourt inventory of 1782

11

BARONSCOURT,
COUNTY TYRONE
1782

EDMUND JOYCE

IN 1612, DURING THE PLANTATION OF ULSTER, the Hamiltons from Renfrewshire in Scotland were granted 12,400 acres of land in County Tyrone. A survey undertaken in 1622 records that at Derrione (Derrywoone), within the current demesne of Baronscourt, Sir George Hamilton had begun to build a 'fair stone howse, 4 stories high'. The original house was subsequently replaced with a house built on a different site within the demesne. This new house, which was described by Alistair Rowan as a 'charming essay in rustic Palladianism ... [and] one of the most interesting small classical houses in Ulster and architecturally one of the more ambitious ...', was begun *c.* 1741 by the seventh Earl of Abercorn. On his death just three years later, the house, designed by James Martin, remained unfinished and its completion was left to his successor, his son James, eighth Earl of Abercorn. This Palladian gem was reduced in size in the 1780s, when the eighth earl embarked on building yet another new house on a green-field site below James Martin's, this time to the drawings of the Scottish architect George Steuart. Constructed between 1779 and 1782 this seven-bay three-storey neoclassical house, complete with three-bay loggia supported on paired Tuscan columns, below a shallow pediment, cost a total of £8,015 8s 7½d. The 1782 inventory describes its contents just after its completion.

The eighth earl already had building projects outside Ireland to his credit, notably his Scottish seat, Duddingston, near Edinburgh, which he had commissioned Sir William Chambers to design in the 1760s. By 1779 he was in his seventies, and was building for his family's dynastic future. Characteristically, he made light of this: '[A]t my time in life it is perhaps necessary to find excuses for engagements of this sort. Mine must be that it sets very many people to work, who would otherwise be idle.' However, the effect which the new house had on a visiting amateur architect, the Rev. Daniel Augustus Beaufort, who saw it just four years after its completion, shows that the eighth earl's architectural 'engagements' had had a serious purpose, which they had admirably fulfilled. Beaufort wrote: 'Through hills at the foot of Bessy Bell ... we come to Baronscourt, Lord Abercorn's magnificent seat ... the great number of fine oaks and three long narrow lakes which ornament this place give it an air of great grandeur.'

This inventory, like that of Borris House, County Carlow, catalogues the collection of a bachelor proprietor; in this case that of a bachelor earl with ample resources of cash at his disposal. The building of a new house at Baronscourt facilitated the purging of old and unfashionable items, with the few 'old' items mentioned being demoted to the service areas of the house. The inventory would have been needed to

177

keep track of his recently augmented collection and to record the new location of both new and old. The scale of his new house is conveyed through the arrangement and number of rooms. The contents of the main family rooms, and indeed the run of service rooms, indicate a house that was fully furnished and equipped by 1782.

The contents of the principal rooms bespeak an environment of comfort and fashion. The presence of '3 marble sideboards on frames' in the dining-room and the extensive service of flatware to include '3 Doz^n Silver table Spoons . . . 4 Doz^n Knives, & 4 Doz^n Forkes' are indicative of the numerous courses served and lavish entertainments held at Baronscourt during the eighth earl's regular visits. On closer inspection the 'Grate Hall' apparently served a double purpose and the presence of dining-tables would suggest an overlapping of function. Such arrangements were not unusual, but the contents allow an insight into how this homeowner perceived and occupied this newly created space. Although age and provenance are by no means explicit in the descriptions, the presence of 'A Marble Table, seported by an Egle' suggests that at least some of the more exquisite items from the 1740s Palladian villa were resurrected.

China is a common element of many pictorial representations of the eighteenth-century interior. These delicate pieces, often arranged and grouped for effect, reflected the owners' discernment and 'reach'. Such a demonstration of taste was conspicuous at Baronscourt, where the mantels in many of the principal rooms and bedchambers were adorned with collections and groupings of china. Such rooms, uninhibited by the constraints of previous arrangements, were a *tabula rasa* for fashionable, contemporary adornment. Having a newly built house to decorate also facilitated the streamlining of the chosen decorative schemes. This is evident in rooms such as the 'Yellow Damask Bed Chamber' and its adjacent dressing room, where the bed drapes and the numerous chairs and stools were all covered in the same 'Yellow' damask fabric.

The 1782 inventory is of great historical interest, because the eighth earl's nephew and successor, created first Marquess of Abercorn in 1790, almost immediately made it obsolete; he commissioned Sir John Soane to reorientate, remodel and enlarge the recently constructed house to which it related. Just five years after that, in 1796, the main body of this reordered house was destroyed by fire. The repairs, which were completed by 1810, reused the earlier forms but in a makeshift sort of way. With much of the interior gutted and its contents lost, a new internal scheme was called for, but was not implemented by the time of the first marquess's death in 1818, nor until after the coming of age and early marriage of his grandson and successor in the early 1830s. In 1835 James Hamilton, second Marquess (later first Duke) of Abercorn, commissioned William Vitruvius Morrison, and subsequently Sir Richard Morrison, to reimagine and aggrandize Baronscourt. The accomplishment of this commission is the Baronscourt extant today. It remains the seat of the Hamiltons and it is currently lived in by James Hamilton, fifth Duke of Abercorn, and his family.

The inventory is in the collection of Abercorn papers at the Public Record Office of Northern Ireland (PRONI).

Baronscourt, County Tyrone, 1782

Inventory of linen at Baron's Court

1 Large Damask table cloth, Mark! $\mathcal{P}$*
32 Damask table clothes, 21 Mark! $\mathcal{A}$. 10 Mark^t $\mathcal{P}$.
1 Small Damask Table Cloth.
1 Doz. fine diaper Napkens, Mark! 12, $\mathcal{A}$
9 fine Diaper Napkens Mark! $\mathcal{A}$, one table cloth
11 Deaper Napkens Mark! $\mathcal{P}$ N° 12, one table cloth
48 Damask Napkens Mark! $\mathcal{P}$
12 fine tea Napkens Mark! 12
6 Course tea Napkens Mark! $\mathcal{P}$.
1 Fine Deaper table Cloth, 12 Napkins to D^o
3 Diaper table Cloths, 35 Napkens to D^o
52 Diaper Napkens Mark! 54
12 Damask tea Napkins
4 Breakfast Clothes, Square patren
4 Diaper table Clothes, for the Stewards Room
5 Diaper table Clothes, for Breakfast for D^o—

Towiling

12 Damask Towles, Mark! $\mathcal{P}$.
12. Huckabeck Towles Mark! $\mathcal{P}$
30 Huckabeck Towles Mark! 30
36 fine Huckaback Towles Mark! 36
31 D^o Mark! 31

Sheeting

19 Pair of fine Sheets
2 fine Bowlster Cases
5 Bowlster Cases not so fine
30 fine Pillow Cases
5 D^o Course
9 Pair of upper Servents Sheets
10 Pair of Course D^o—

---

* The decorative $\mathcal{P}$ as marked on the table linen was also used in the inventory for the P in the entries for two Pictures, one over the chimney in the 'Breakfast Roome' (p. 180) and the other over the chimney in the 'Green Damask bed chamber' (p. 181).

Inventory of household Furniture at Baron's Court 1782

Grate Hall

2 Mahogney Dineng Tables
2 Mahogney Sircular Tables belonging D^o
2 Card tables
2 Large Marble tables on Frames
3 Side Lanthorns, Glaz^d with Plate glass with lamp^s to D^o—
1 Weather Glass
A Herpsicord with Stand to D^o
2 Heads and 4 Figures over doar Capes
a Mahogney Stool

Drawing Room

A Grate, with fender, fire Shovle, Pocker and tongues
A Large Turkey Carpet, 2 Small D^o—
A Marble Table, seported by an Egle
A Japan table, with a large China Jarr under D^o—
A Small Fly table
3 Chinea Jarrs over Chimley
3 Stooles
2 Screins
1 Half Settea
4 Elbo Chaires
7 Back Stool Chairs
16 Pictures
1 Pear Glass
3 Window Curtains
A harth brush

Dineing Room

A Grate with Fender fire shovle Pocker and Tongues
A Large Turkey Carpet
A Pier Glass
3 Marble side boards on Frames
2 Screens
A Picture over Chimney
A Brass Figure and 2 Yewres over Chimney
2 Elbow Chaires
11 Dineing D^o
2 Window Curtains
A Harth Brush

Breakfast Roome

A Fixt grate with Fender, fire Shovle, Pocker, and Tongues
A Turkey Carpet
A Picture over Chimney
2 China Jarrs, one Bottle & 2 Teapots
A Marble table on a Frame
An Ovil looking Glass in a Guilt Frame
7 Elboe Chaires, with red and white Check Covers
A Harth Brush —
A Mahogney pembroke table

Studey

A Grate with Fender fire Shovle Pocker and Tongues
A Turkey Carpett
A Piear Glass
A Mahogney Comode
A Picture over Chimney
7 Elbow Chaires with red and white Check Covers
2 Window Curtains
A Harth Brush
A Head over Book Case

Audience Roome

A Fixt Grate with fender fireshovle, pocker & Tongues
A Carpet
A Mahogney Book case a small Beawrow
A Marble table on A Frame
A Small Mahogney Dineing table
A Writting table
8 Stuft leather bottemud Chairs
A Harth brush
3 Fire Screens
A Hand bell
A Pier Glass
3 Window Curtains
39 Prints in black frames
A Lyon Over Book Case

Stewards Parlor

A Fixt Greate with Fender, fireshovel, Pocker, & tongues
2 Matts on the floore
A Pier Glass
A Mahogney Side board
2 Mahogney Dineing tables
A Small Round D^o_

2 Elbow & ten Chaires cover'd with Silk, with blue Check covers to D^o_
A Pair of Piller Candlesticks, with Snuffers & pan to D^o
A Bewrow for the use of the Steward
A Harth brush
2 Urnes over Cupboards
2 Cupboards with Glasses, Muggs, Knives & forks &c for the use of the Stewards Roome
36 Prints in Black Frames, A Canvas fire Screen
20 Punch glasses
2 Doz. wine D^o_
4 Salts
2 Jugges
5 Muggs
1 Decanter
2 Botle Sliders

A Copper Coal Scuttle belonging to this Floore

Chince Bedchamber Principal Story

A Fixt Grate with fender, fireshovle, Pocker and tonges
A Bed steed whith Chince Fourniture, D^o Counterpin
A Father bed with two Matresses 3 blankets
1 Bowelster and two Pillows
A Bid side Carpit
A Table and Pier Glass
7 Back Stools covered with Crimson Damask with linen covers to D^o_
A. Picture over the Chimney 9 Pieces of Chinea
A Night table
2 Window Curtains
A Botle and Bason
A Harth Brush
A Small Chist of Drawers

Dressing Room to D^o

A Sett Grate with Fender, fireshovle, Pocker & Tongs
A Small Chist of Drawers
A Couch & 4 Stooles cover'd with white Saten with Gold & Silver Stuff
A Couch bed and 3 Pillows coverd with D^o_
A Dressing Glass
A Bason & Bottle
A Close Stool
A Window Curtain
A Picture over Chimney
A Small turkey Carpet upon the flooer

Green Damask bed Chamber

A Sett Grate with Fender, fireshovle Pocker and tongs
A Bedsteed with green Damask Furniture
A Father bed with ʌ² Matreesses 3 Blankets
    A Cownterpen
    a Bowlster, A with 2 pillows
2 Bedside Carpets
2 Elbo, and Six Back Stooles covered with Damask,)
    and Covers for $D^{\underline{o}}$)
A Mahogney Dressing table and Dressing Glass
A Picture and Glass over Chimney
A Night table
2 Window Curtains
A Harth Brush
A Botle and Bason
4 Drawings in frames

Dressing Roome to $D^{\underline{o}}$

A Sett Grate with Fender Fireshovle Pocker and tongs.
A Small Mahogney Chist of Drawers
4 Elbow Chaires covered with flowered Silk, with
    covers to $D^o\_$
A Mahogney Dressing table & Dressing Glass
A Botle and Bason
A Small China botle over Chimney
A Small Carpet on the floure
A Harth Brush

Yellow Damask Bed Chamber

A Sett Grate with fender, fireshovle, Pocker & tongs
A Bedstead with Yellow Damask Furniture
2 Matresses a Faether bed bowlster and two Pillows
3 Blankets and Quilt, Two bedside Carpets, two Window
    Curtains
A Mahogney Chist of Drawers, A Pier Glass
A Picture over the Chimney, two Pictures of Sampson
    Over the Doars
An urn a two piecess of China over Chimney
2 Elbow, and 7 Back Stoles cover'd with Yallow Damask
    with Yallow covers to $D^o\_$
A Harth Brush
A Botle & Bason

Dressing Roome to $D^{\underline{o}}$

A Sett Grate, with fender fireshovle Pocker and tongs
A Picture and Chinea botle over the Chimney

5 Back Stooles covered with Yellow Damask with Yallow
    covers   to $D^{\underline{o}}\_$
A Mahogney Dressing table and Dressing Glass
A Close Stool
A Small walnut tree Chist of Drawers
A Botle and Bason
A Window Curtain
A Harth Brush
A Small Turkey Carpet

Blue Morine Bed Chamber

A Sett Grate with fender fireshovle, Pocker and tongs
A Bed Steed with Blue Morine Furniture
A Fether Bed and two Matresses a Bowlster & two
    Pillows,
3 Blankets and Quilt three Window Curtains
A Mahogney Chist of Drawers and Pier Glass,
A Mahogney Dressing table
two Bed Side Carpets
6 Chairs covered with blue Stuff
A Harth Brush
An Elbow Chaire cover with green Silk
A Botle and Bason

Dressing Roome to $D^{\underline{o}}$

A Sett Grate with fender fire shovle Pocket and tongs
4 Chairs
A Picture over the Chimney and Chinea botle
A Mahogney Dressing table & Dressing Glass
A Harth Brush
A Small Turkey Carpet
A Window Curtain
A Drawing in A Black Frame

Green Stript Bed Chamber

A Sett Grate with fender, fireshovle Pocker & tongs
A Bed Steed with Green & White Stript Furniture
A Fether bed and two Matresses, A Bowlster and two Pillows
3 Blankets and Quilt, two Window Curtains,
1 Elbow Chaire covered with flowered Silk
6 Common $D^{\underline{o}}$ covered with Green Stuff
A Chest of Drawers
2 Bed Side Carpets, and A Scotch $D^{\underline{o}}$ on the floure
A Mahogney table
A Pier Glass, a Pole $D^{\underline{o}}$
A Harth Brush
A Botle and Bason, 2 Weig Stands

Baronscourt, County Tyrone

A Picture and Glass over the Chimney
A Picture over the Doar

Attick Story
Blue Bed Chamber ʌ^{over} *Chince Roome*

A Sett Grate
A Bed Steed with blue Stuff Furniture
A Fether bed Bowlster and Pillow
3 Blankets & Quilt
A Chist of Drawers, a Table and looking Glass
6 Chaires covered with blue Stuff
An Elbow Chair covered with Check
A Carpet round the bed

Roome over Chince Dressing Roome

A Sett Grate
A Field bed with blue Stuff Furniture
A Fether bed, with bowlster and one Pillow
3 Blankets and Quilt
A Table and Print over Chimney

Camblet bed Chamber over Green Damask Roome

A Sett Grate
A Bed Steed with white Camblet Stuff Furniture
A Fether Bed, Bowlster and Pillow, A Matress
3 Blankets and Quilt,
A Chist of Drawers & Table, a looking Glass,
A Picture over Chimney
6 Chaires an Elbow *D*ọ A Turkey Carpet A *D*ọ round the Bed

Roome Over Green Damask Dressing Roome

A Sett Grate
A Field bed with blue Stuff Furniture
A Fether bed with Bowlster and one Pillow
3 Blankets and Quilt
A Table, and Settee covered with Green Silk
A Table and Picture Over Chimney

Roome over Yellow Damask Dressing Roome

A Sett Grate
A Bed Steed with green and white Stript furniture
A Fether bed Bowlster and one Pillow
3 Blankets and Quilt
A Bed side Carpet, 6 Chaires
A Table & Glass
A Picture over Chimney

Roome over Yellow Damask bed Chamber

A Sett grate, with fender, fire shovle pocker and tongs
A Bed Steed with blue Furniture
A Fether bed Bowlster two Matresses & A Pillow
3 Blankets and Quilt
A Table & five Chaires, A Mahogney table fixt to the winscott
A Chist of Drawers,
2 Bed Side Carpets
A Looking Glass, and Picture over Chimney

Roome over the blue Morine Dressing Roome

This is a Roome for all Gentlemen to Powder in, with a Table and one Chair and A Sett Grate

Roome over blue Morine Bed chamber

A Sett grate with fender fire shovle Pocker and tongs
A Field bed with green Morine Furniture
A Fether bed Bowlster and two Matresses, A Pillow
3 Blankets and Counterpin
A Chist of Drawers, two Tables A looking Glass
A Picture over Chimney
2 Elbow Chaires, and 5 Common *D*ọ
A Sid bed Carpet, A Harth Brush

Roome over Green & White Stript bedchamber

A Sett Grate, with fender fire shovle Pocker and tongs
A Bed Steed with Chince Furniture
A Fether bed Bowlster and Pillow
2 Matresses, 3 Blankets and Quilt
6 Chaires A Table and looking Glass
A Chist of Drawers
A Turkey Carpet 2 Side bed *D*ọ
An Elbow Chaire
2 Window Curtains
A Harth Brush
A Picture over Chimney

House Keeper's Roome

A Sett Grate with fender fire shovle pocker and tongs
2 Elbow Chaires, 12 Green Chaires
A Table and looking Glass, A Canvas fire Screen
A Tea Kitchen, Some Cupes and Sawcers
  for use of the house keepers Roome
  Some Jelley Glasses, a Cofea Mill
2 Pꭱ of Candlesticks; 1 pꭱ of Snuffers

House Keepers Store Roome

A Table and on Chair
6 Chania Dishes
11 Fruitt Dishes of *D<u>o</u>*
12 Cups & 12 Sawscers Nankeen 1 Bason to *D<u>o</u>* 1 Sugar Bason
13 Cups & 13 Sawscers of the walpole Chinea
8 Chinea Basons, 4 Tea pots
2 Tea Boards, 1 *D<u>o</u>* for Fruitt

Butlers Pantree,

Glass
12 Wash hand Glasses
13 Wine and Water *D<u>o</u>*
2 Doz and 10 Wine Glasses Cutt
9 Tumbler Glasses
2 Water Decanters
33 Wine *D<u>o</u>*—
4 Crafts
3 Cruites
1 Mustard pot
8 Glass Salts
4 Beer Glasses

Plate
7 Pair of plated Candlesticks
4 Plated Waiters
3 Doz<u>n</u> Silver table Spoons
8 Desart Spoons
6 Silver Plated Salts, with Glass to *D<u>o</u>*
4 Silver Salts Spoons, 2 Bottle Stands
18 Tea Spoones
1 p<u>r</u> of tea tonges
1 Sowp Ladle
1 French Plate dish ring
1 French Plate Marrow Spoone
1 *D<u>o</u>* Sugar Caster
1 Plated Pepper box
1 Plated hand Candlestick, with Estinguesher belonging to *D<u>o</u>*
3 Silver Botle tickets
A pair of Patten Snuffers, a Dowter,
2 Snuffer Panes
4 Doz<u>n</u> Knives, & 4 Doz<u>n</u> Forkes
2 Meat treas
1 *D<u>o</u>* for Glasses
1 *D<u>o</u>* holding Fowle Plates
A Coper Plate Warmer

A Knife box
2 Windser Chaires
A Sett Grate with fender fireshovle Pocker and tongs

Yellow Stone ware, Ovel
14 Large Dishes, 2 Sowp *D<u>o</u>*
4 A Size less   17 Round Dishes
12 A Size less   8 Baking Dishes
6 A Size less
16 A Size less
27 Second Courss *D<u>o</u>*
5 Small, 6 Pincushen Dishes
3 Turines, 2 Bread Baskets
4 Fish Drainers
5 long Sallad Dishes, 3 *D<u>o</u>* Round, 2 Small long Sallad Dishes
11 Sawce botles
A Table with 2 Drawers in *D<u>o</u>*
12 Sowp plates, 8 Doz.<u>n</u> Common *D<u>o</u>*
2 Jugges 5 Muggs 2 Doz. new Knives never used

Kitchen

A Jack with Multiplying wheel, and all Compleat
A Range Compleat with fender Fire shovle pocker & tonges
An Oven, broiling Plate and Six Stoves
A Table in the Midle of the Kitchen
An Eight day Clock, by Gregg
2 large boilers with covers to *D<u>o</u>*
1 Dish Kettle
1 Ovel Fish kettle with Plate and cover to *D<u>o</u>*
3 large Sawce pans with covers to *D<u>o</u>*
4 *D<u>o</u>* Smaler
1 Large Stock pot with cover to *D<u>o</u>*
1 Large Braze ketle with Plate and Cover to *D<u>o</u>*—
1 Sowp pot with cover to *D<u>o</u>*
5 Old Stew pans with 3 Covers to *D<u>o</u>*
16 New Stew pans with covers to *D<u>o</u>*—
1 Putter Colender
1 Copper Grater, 2 ladles, and Basting *D<u>o</u>*—
1 Marble Morter
1 Brass *D<u>o</u>*, with Pestel to *D<u>o</u>*
1 Grediron
1 Driping Pan
1 Fire Screen lined with tin
2 Frying Pans, one Salt box
2 Square Trivets, 2 Tryangle *D<u>o</u>*
1 Pair of Belles, 3 Spitts

Baronscourt, County Tyrone

1 Chockolet pot with Stick to *D⁰*
1 Chaffing Dish
1 Clivers, one Salimander
1 Round Fish Plate
6 Round Pewter Pans, 6 Ovel *D⁰*
1 Flower box, A Choping block
2 Coper Blamange Mould: 6 Putter Froal [*recte* froat (fruit)] *D⁰*
2 Tea Kettles 31 Putter Dishes of Differant Sizes
1 Coffea Pott
A Warming Pan
6 Doz Putter Plates
1 Doz Sowp *D⁰*

Scullery

A Large Devision Copper with three covers to *D⁰*
A Large boiler Sett for warming water to wash Dishes
A Sett grate

Servents Hall

A Sett Grate
A Long Table
6 Formes
A Lither Jack
2 Horns

Brew House

A Large Brewing Copper Sett

Wash House

A Sett Copper & 3 Tables

Lawrder

2 Tables for Salting Meat

Backi House

Lawndrea

2 Cloase horses & 3 Stools

Lawndree Maids bed Chamber

A Sett Grate
A Bed Steed with green Furniture
A Fether bed Bowlster
3 Blankets & Coverlid
A Table

House Maids bed Chamber

A Sett Grate
Two Beds with green Furniture
with two Fether beds two Bowlsters
two Coverlides, A Table
37 Prints without frames
4 Wooden Chaires
A Large Chist for holding Furniture

House Keepers bed Chamber

A Sett Grate
A Bedstead with blue Furniture
A Fether bed Bowlster and Pillowes
3 Blankets and Quilt
A Table & Looking Glass
A Winscott Chist of Drawers belonging to the House keeper
4 Wooden Chaires
An Elbow Chaire

House keepers Dressing Roome

Some Matting

Bed Chamber over Water Closett

A Sett Grate
Settiee bed with Check furniture
A Fether bed Bowlster
two Blankets and Quilt
A Table & 4 Wooden Chairs

Bed Chamber Over House keepers Roome

A Sett Grate
A Bed Steed with blue Stuff Furniture
A Fether bed Bowlster and Pillow
3 Blankets and Quilt
A Table & Glass with 4 Wooden Chaires
A Mahogney tal boy

Bed chamber over House keepers Store roome

A Sett Grate
A Field bed with blue Furniture
A Fether bed Bowlster & Pillow
3 Blanket & Quilt
A Table and looking glass
4 Wooden Chaires

Bed chamber over Butlers Pantree

A Sett Grate
A Field Bedsteed with Green Furniture
A Fether bed Bowlster A Pillow
3 Blankets & Quilt
A table & looking Glass
4 Wooden Chaires
A Winscot Beurow

Bed Chamber over Dairey

A Sett Grate with fender fireshovle pocker & tonges
A Bedsteed with green Furniture
A Fether bed Bowlster and Pillow
1 Matresses
3 Blankets and Quilt
A Bed side carpett
A Table and Glass
A Botle and Bason
4 Chaires

Bed chamber over Stewards Parlor

A Sett Grate with fender fire shovle Pocker & tonges
A Bed with red & white Chequer Furniture
A Fether bed with two Matresses A Bowlster and
    Pillow
3 Blankets & Quilt
A Winscott Chist of Drawers
A Looking Glass
A Table & Cloase Press
A Picture over the Chimney belonging to Mr Home
An Elbow Chaire, A Bedside Carpett
4 Green bottemed Chaires
2 Window Curtains
A Botle and Bason

Dressing Roome to D^o_

2 Tables, and looking Glass
A Horse for Brushing Cloase
A Matt on the Floor
A Close Stool

Foot Man's Bed Chamber

4 Bed Steeds with Six Fether beds
6 Bowlsters, 3 Blankets to Each bed, not good
A Sett Grate

Cooks Bed chamber over Scullery

A Bedsteed with green Furniture
Fetherbed Bowlster, 3 Blankets an Coverlid
6 Old Chaires & A Table
A Sett grate with fender fireshovle Pocker & tonges

Kitchen & Scullory Maids Bed chamber over Bake house

A Sett Grate
A Bed with green Furniture
Fether bed Bowlster 3 Blankets and Coverlid

A Side Lanthorn on the Back Stairs with lamp to D^o

3 D^o in the long Passiage with lamps to D^o_
1 D^o going down to Sellers with D^o_
1 D^o going to the Kitchen with D^o_
2 Spare lamps for lanthorns in the Butlers Pantree

At the Stables 4 Fether beds
4 Bowlsters, 4 Old Bed Steeds

PLATE 28

Unknown artist: *Castlecomer House*, engraving, frontispiece to Hardy Bertram McCall's book *Story of the Family of Wandesforde of Kirklington & Castlecomer*, 1904 (McCall). This is a view of the house built in 1802 to drawings by John Johnston (d. 1812).

12

CASTLECOMER HOUSE, COUNTY KILKENNY
1798

JESSICA CUNNINGHAM

WITHIN THIS VOLUME'S COLLECTION of household inventories, the context in which Castlecomer House's 1798 inventory was drawn up is unique. From May to September of that year the United Irishmen instigated an uprising against the crown's forces, with a concentration of conflict taking place in the counties surrounding Dublin and the greater Leinster area. The rebellion failed and the losses of life and property were significant. More lasting was the blow it dealt to political hopes for legislative independence; the rebellion accelerated the passing of the Act of Union, which came into effect in 1801, thus ending Ireland's parliamentary independence. In June 1798, the United Irishmen attacked the inhabitants of the town of Castlecomer, County Kilkenny, because, as the *Freeman's Journal* reported that month, the colliers of the local mines 'resisted every solicitation to join the assailants'. In revenge the rebels 'consumed to ashes' both the town of Castlecomer and the manor house. The destruction at Castlecomer House was indiscriminate with, as this inventory shows, and, as the *Freeman's Journal* put it, loss to 'all the furniture, paintings, family plate, and a most valuable library'.

Castlecomer House, in 1798, was the seat of Anne, the Countess of Ormonde, *née* Wandesford (1739–1830). Anne was the widow of John Butler, seventeenth Earl of Ormonde (1740–1795) and heir of the Wandesford Estate. The Wandesfords had arrived in Ireland in the 1630s; Christopher Wandesford, from Kirklington, Yorkshire, was a kinsman of Thomas Wentworth, Lord Strafford, who went on to become lord deputy of Ireland under Charles I. Wandesford bought the Castlecomer estate on 20,000 acres in 1637 and established several industries there, including the coal mines. The house to which this inventory pertains was built in this period. The titles Baron Wandesford and Viscount Castlecomer were created for Christopher Wandesford III as a reward for his support of William III in 1690. In 1758 the fifth viscount, John Wandesford (1725–1784), father of Anne, was created first Earl Wandesford.

The following inventory, with supplementary inventories of silver, linen, copper and wine, accounted for the wholesale losses at Castlecomer House following the June 1798 attack. Within the inventory are comments and adjectives which support the presumption that it was drawn up with a view to submitting a claim for compensation, as many did following the rebellion, and, therefore, sought to convey the full value of fixtures and furnishings lost. We can see that the stairs and lobby had Scotch carpeting 'very little used'. A similar carpet was installed in the dining-room along with five pairs of green curtains, all of which was 'but a few Months in use'. The mahogany pier tables, mahogany breakfast-table, music stool, 'conversation stools' and chairs in the drawing-room, meanwhile, were all specified as new and its sets of chintz curtains were 'not more than a year up'. The lists of other furniture, new and old, throughout the house convey an ample and comfortable home. Leisure is prioritized in this house: a billiard-room containing a twelve-foot billiard-table and a range of cues, while other games and equipment sit in a room hung with numerous caricature prints.

Further clues to the comfort and refinement enjoyed at Castlecomer House are to be found in the interesting inventory of silverwares. Of note, in the heading of this inventory, it is written that the list of 'plate' (the word was used in this period to refer to items of sterling silver) includes that which was 'taken or destroy'd' by the rebels, along with that which was recovered following the attack. The inventory details that more than 2,400 ounces of silver were retrieved from the ruins (valued at just over £730), while an additional £1,576 worth of wares were lost. Like most homes of the Irish elite in this period, most of these items were used in the dining-room. Dining wares here ranged from an extensive collection of plates and dishes – seven dozen dinner plates and twenty-four dishes – to smaller vessels and utensils serving particular purposes such as the pair of marrow spoons, the dish for the wine funnel and the lemon strainer. Every course, condiment, sauce and beverage had an associated tureen, salver, utensil, caster, jug or pot. Additional silver was to be found in the countess's dressing-room with boxes and pots used to contain tooth powder, tooth picks, jewels and pomades. Gold pieces of symbolic significance, among them a cup and cover, two corporation boxes (small, engraved boxes presented on behalf of civic corporations to honour the benevolence, achievement or patronage of an individual) and a gold medal, all together worth nearly £350, were especially big losses. The final section of this inventory lists 'plated articles' and refers to items made of the relatively new material Sheffield plate. Using only a fifth of the quantity of silver found in hallmarked, sterling silverwares, Sheffield plate was chiefly composed of copper with a silver coating. It looked like silver and was hard-wearing and affordable. This made it particularly suited to large domestic items like Castlecomer's ice-pails (wine-coolers) and those in frequent use such as the candlesticks.

In 1802, a mere four years after its destruction, Castlecomer House was rebuilt under the Countess of Ormonde's directive, this time as a larger and more imposing structure. Alas, this house became derelict in the mid-twentieth century and was demolished in the 1970s. The Prior-Wandesforde Papers, the archive to which this inventory belongs, are held in the National Library of Ireland.

Inventory of
Castlecomer House, 1798

An Inventory of the Furniture, and Effects, that was in the house of Castlecomer, in the County of Kilkenny, the property of the Countess of Ormonde, when Attacked, and burn'd, by the Rebels, on the 24th of June 1798

N.º 1
Hall

Cover'd with Oil Cloth   Bell = } 1-2-9
A Glass hall bell & Shade hung, with silk line & tassells
An Eight day Clock, with a good Mahogany Case 4 = 11
Two fram'd doors, cover'd on both sides, with green Cloth, & stuck with gilt Nails, had two long springs, and lacquerd pulling handles to them

N.º 2
Broad Stairs & Lobby's

Coverd with Scotch Carpeting, very little used
Two dozen of strong brass Stair Rods 2 – 9 long and brass screw staples for the Rods = 1 = 16 = 0
Four Stair Case Glass Bells – 0 = 16 – 0
A fine Chamber Clock with an <u>Alarm</u> to it

N.º 3
Breakfast Parlour

12 Fashionable Mahogany Chairs with /curld hair,/ stuffd bottoms, Upholsterd, with fine hair Silk, and two rows of Gilt Nails, very little used —
A Mahogany press Bed Stead, in form of a Desk, with sacking bottom,
A Feather Bed & Bolster, & Pillow
2½ pair of Blankets
One Mahogany table, about 5 feet in length
Two pier Glasses, about 9$^{In.s}$ broad & 6: high each, with a Narrow Gilt rope frame
3 Window Curtains of Callico, lind with white D.^{o}

N.º 4
Dineing Parlour

Cover'd with Scotch Carpeting, but a few Months in use
18 Mahogany Chairs, the same as in N.º 3 —
A fine Organ 9 feet high, at least, all Inclos'd with Mahogany
A large Mahogany Side board
A very large D.^{o} Northumberland dineing table of 7 Join^{gs}
A smaller   D.^{o} .   .   D.^{o} .   .   of 5 D.^{o}
Two large . D.^{o} Pier tables to join Occasionally
Two large . D.^{o} Dumb Waiters
A large   . D.^{o} Wine Cooper
A .   . . D.^{o} Wine Cellar, lin'd & divided with lead,
A large .   D.^{o} Sugar Store, on a Mahogany frame, with tin Cannisters, a Drawer &c
5 Green Moreen Window Curtains, upwards of 14 yards to each a very few Months in use. cost of Moreen
&c 11 – 14 – 6
A Set of fire Irons, & a large open work Wire fender

N.º 5
Drawing Room

A Turkey Carpet that nearly coverd the Room /very good/
Three Window Curtains, of Chintz Palampoes, lind with white Callico, trimd at sides, top, & bottom with Green lutestring, and a great quantity of fringe, lines, & Tassells not more than a year up
A Grand Piano Forte 60 Guineas
Two large New inlaid Mahogany pier tables
Two large pier Glasses in Gilt frames
Chairs & Conversation Stools made in Sepr 97
cost 32 – 12 – 4
A large New Mahogany Breakfast table
A New round   D.^{o} Musick Stool, Upholsterd with Green leather & Gilt Nails
A Mahogany Musick Stand
Musick — 15 Guineas, much under the Value
4 Mahogany Card Tables
A Backgammon table Complete
A Loto Box   .   . D.^{o}
A Chimney piece a few Months up Cost 23 – 5 – 4½
A Grate, fire Irons & fender D.^{o} .   .   .   5 – 11 – 0
The Room hung with very fine Indian paper /Sixteen Sheets at least/ only a few Months up

Castlecomer House, County Kilkenny

N.º 6
Lady Ormondes Bed Chamber

A four post Bed stead, Mahogany posts
Furniture Cotton Curtains, lin'd with Callico
A feather Bed, Bolster, & pillow
A Curld hair Mattrass
A Paillass
One & half pair of Blankets
One Quilt & Counterpane
Three Window Curtains the same as the bed
7 Curld hair stuffd bottom chairs,$^{12}_\wedge$ covers, the same of Cur,^{tns}
1 Large Mahogany Wardrobe, with Cedar shelves, hung with Green Baize
1 *D.º* . *D.º* Secretary
1 Chest of Drawers
1 Cabbinet
2 large hanging Shelves ⎬ all Mahogany
2 Work Boxes
1 Spider Table
1 Night Chair
1 Bason Stand
1 Set of fire Irons & Wire Workd fender
A Bed Carpet of Scotch Carpeting ¾ ^{wide} a few Months in use, coverd at each side, & feet,$^{of\ bed}_\wedge$ and Mitred at Corners

N.º 7
A Bedchamber

A four post Bedstead, fluted Mahogany posts
A feather Bed, Bolster, & two Pillows,
A Curld hair Mattrass, and a Paillass
1½ pair of Blankets
A Marseills Quilt
Bed Curtains of white Dimity, lind with Callico & trim'd with fine Muslin & Gymp
Three Window Curtains the same as the bed &c &c &c
Six large Chair Covers to Match the above
Six Mahogany fram'd Chairs, with stuffd Curld hair, bottoms,
A Spider table of Mahogany
A Night Chair . . *D.º*
Two Commodes . . *D.º*
Two Bason Stands . . *D.º*
One half tallboy . . *D.º*
One large swinging dressing Glass with a desk under
One *D.º* deal Toilet table
One fine Muslin Toilet, & Veil trimed with rich
/point lace

A Bed Carpet the same as in N.º 6
A Set of fire Irons, and Wire work'd fender

The furniture of N.º 7 put up in the Summer of 1797

N.º 8
A Bed Chamber

A four post Bedstead, Oak fluted posts
A feather Bed, Bolster, & two Pillows
A Paillass
1½ pair of Blankets
A Marseilles Quilt
The Bed Curtains, two Window Curtains, and 4 Chair Covers, the same as N.º 7 and put up same time
Four Mahogany fram'd Chairs, with hair stuffd bottoms
One Oak Night Chair
One inlaid Mahogany table with Cedar drawers
Two Commodes of *D.º*
One Bason Stand *D.º*
One Book Shelves
One Set of fire Irons & fender

N.º 9
A Bed Chamber

A four post Bed stead, fluted Mahogany posts
A feather Bed, Bolster, & Pillow
A Paillass
1½ pair of Blankets
1 Marseilles Quilt, & Counterpane
A Cannopy Bedstead
The Curtains of the Beds, and of three Windows, worn Chintz Pallampoes, lined with white Callico, and trimed with very handsome Notted fringe & Gymp
Two Mahogany Settees with stuffd bottoms
Seven *D.º* Chairs with stuffd backs & bottoms, and white Dimity Covers trim'd with fringe & Gymp
One round Stool, with stuffd seat, Mahogany
One Night Chair . . . . *D.º*
Two Commodes . . . . *D.º*
Two Bason Stands . . . . *D.º*
One Dressing Table & Glass with drawers . *D.º*
One deal Toilet Table, furniture fine Muslin trim'd with lace

№ 10

A Bed Chamber

A field Bed Stead — Mahogany posts
The Curtains Damascus . both New
A large Window Curtain of the same, /for a bow, containg.
four large Sashes/
A feather Bed, Bolster, & Pillow,
A Mattrass
1½ pair of Blankets
A Marseilles Quilt
A large Wardrobe of Deal, new. /painted Mahogany Col./
A Book Case Mahogany
A Table .   .   *Dº*
A *Dº* of .   .   Elm
Five Chairs stuffd with Damascus Covers
A Bason Stand Mahogany
Two looking Glasses
A Biddy Mahogany
A Set of fire Irons & fender

№ 11

A Bed Chamber

A field Bedstead Mahogany posts
A Feather Bed, Bolster, & pillow
The Curtains & one Window Curtain Damascus
1½ pair of Blankets
1 Quilt
A Mahogany Desk
Two *Dº* small tables
One dressing Glass
One Night Chair
One set of fire Irons & fender
One japand trunk and a frame

№ 12

Bed Chamber

Two field Bedsteads, posts Mahogany, damascus
Curtains, & three Window Curtains of the same, paid
for them in 1796 /at the time bought/ per Bill £16 – 4 – 0
Two feather Beds, Bolsters, & pillows
Three pair of Blankets
Two Quilts
One Mahogany Wardrobe
One half tallboy Mahogany
One Spider table . *Dº*
One Round Musick Stool Mahogany Coverd with green
leather & Gilt Nails .   .   .

One large Sally Desk
One small inlaid *Dº*
Fifteen Rush bottomd Chairs, quite new, cost 6/6 each
One Oak Night Chair
One painted table, One Bracket
One New drawing box
One set of Fire Irons, & Fender

№ 13

A Bed Chamber

One four post Bedstead Mahogany posts
Furniture Cotton Curtains to *Dº*
A feather Bed. Bolster, & pillow
1½ pair of Blankets, One quilt
One four post Bedstead Oak posts
furniture linen Curtains to *Dº*
One feather Bed Bolster, & pillow.
2 pair of Blankets & 1 quilt
3 Window Curtains of furniture linen
1 Oak tallboy,
1 small Writing Desk +
1 Dressing table & Glass
1 Spider table of Mahogany
1 Commode
6 Rush bottomd Chairs
1 Set of fire Irons & fender

№ 14

One press Bedstead of .   .   Mahogany
One four post *Dº* posts   .   .   *Dº*
One feather Bed two bolsters & two pillows
1½ pair of Blankets
1 Quilt
One large Mahogany dressing table & Glass +
One   .   .   *Dº* tallboy
One   .   .   *Dº* Spider table
Six   .   .   *Dº* Chairs with stuffd bottoms
The Curtains of the four post Bed, two Window
Curtains, & the Covers of the Chairs, was of
Callico, lind with white Callico, bound & fringd,
The Curtains to press Bed. Damascus.
One Mahogany Commode
Book Shelves of Mahogany
A Set of fire Irons & fender

Castlecomer House, County Kilkenny

No 15
Bed Chamber

One four post Bedstead, Oak posts Moreen Curtains
A feather Bed, Bolster, Pillow, & Paillass
1½ pair of Blankets. One quilt
One dressing table
One Oak Desk
Four Rush bottomd Chairs
Two looking Glasses
A Mahogany Screw press

No 16
Bed Chamber

A four post Bed stead, Oak posts, & paragon Curtains
A feather Bed, Bolster, Pillow & two Matrasses
1½ pair of Blankets. One quilt
One dressing table, & Glass,
One Japand Chest of Drawers
Three Rush bottomd Chairs
One Oak Night   . Do

No 17
Bed Chamber

Two four post Bedsteads, Oak posts, Paragon Curtains
Two feather Beds, two Bolsters, & one pillow
2½ pair of Blankets to each Bed
2 Quilts
One Mahogany Settee stuffd
Three   Do   Chairs . Do
Two   .   Do Commodes
One large trunk of Cedar, coverd with Seal skin,
containing 6 new Palampoes, several sheets of fine
Indian paper, an Entire set, of Valuable Needle workd
Chair Covers, with Eng:sh Worsteds on Canvas, also
   for two Settees
& Elbow Chairs and a large quantity of new Curtains
   line & Tassells

No 18
Billiard Room

A Billiard Table of Mahogany, 12 feet long, with 3 Sets
of Balls, a Number of Queues, Maces, &c all very good,
Three Mahogany Chairs, with stuffd Backs, Seats &
Damascus Covers. /the table had a drawer & Eng:sh
   stuff Cover/

A frame, with 12 new tin lamps, four burners to each.
Dials for Marking the Game, & a Number of Caracature
                                                    / Prints

No 19
Stewards Room

Two Mahogany Dining tables to join ~~to join~~ Occasionally
One   Do . . . small   Do with two Cants
One large Walnut dining table with broad Cants
Two small pier Glasses
Twelve Oak Chairs with Stuffd bottoms
One large deal press
One   Do paragon Window Curtain

Closet to Stewards Room

Had a long broad Bench, with lockers underneath,
& Shelves over it.
A large Corner press, the height of the Room

No 20
Servants Hall

One large deal Table
Two long   Do forms
One short . . Do
One long and broad side table, hung with hinges,
and fly feet, to raise occasionally
One large deal Corner press

Closet to Servants hall

A deal bench & Shelves

No 21
Butler's Pantry

One Oak tall boy Bed stead, with two drawers at top,
/furniture linen Curtains, quite new/
A feather Bed, Bolster, & Pillow
Two pair of Blankets
A White Marseilles quilt
A large deal press about 9 feet square, with folding doors,
Two large deep presses, fixed in Nitches, in a thick Wall
A large deal table, with drawers from top to bottom, at each end
A large   Do . Do
A high parcel of Shelves, the shelves to raise, or lower, Occas,ly
One deal Writing desk
One Carriage trunk, coverd with leather & Gilt Nails, as
good as when made

A Quantity of Decanters, Glasses &c, some fine Breakf.st
& Evening tea China, some dozens of Wax Candles,
Card table Cloths, pools, & Counters, plate Buckets
Trays /Mahogany & Japand,/ knife boxes, China & Delft
Jugs & Mugs, Green hafted knives & forks.

N.º 22
House keeper's Room & Store Room

A Long and broad bench, with lockers underneath, and
Shelves over it.
A Nest of Drawers for Grocery's &c
Two deal tables
Four Chairs
Two large presses, fix'd in Nitches,
One looking Glass
fire Irons & fender
A quantity of Grocerys, preserves & pickles, Soap
Candles, &c. &c. with many usefull and Necessary
Articles, such as Scales, Weights pickling & preserving
pots, and jars, Ice pots & buckets. Table China & Delft
pewter Dishes, plates, and Measures, Sugar & Tea
Cannisters

N.º 23
A Bed Chamber for Servants

One four post Bedstead, Oak posts, Paragon Curtains
A feather Bed, Bolster.
1½ pair of Blankets
1 Quilt
One field Bed stead, Oak posts, furniture linen
Curtains
A feather Bed & bolster,
1½ pair of Blankets.
1 Quilt
One deal table
2 Chairs
Two Chests containing four good Damascus
Window Curtains, twenty D.º Chair Covers, & some
new Damascus

N.º 24
A Bed Chamber for Servants

One four post Bed stead Oak posts, paragon Curtains
A feather Bed & Bolster
1½ pair of Blankets
1 Quilt
1 Oak table
One large deal Wardrobe the same as in N.º 10
One smaller deal press
Eight Chairs
One Arm D.º Coverd with black leather
Two large deal Boxes

N.º 25
A Bed Chamber for Servants

One four post Bedstead, Oak posts, paragon Curtains
A feather Bed, Bolster, & pillow
Two Oak Desks
Two deal presses
One Mahogany Table
One Deal   . D.º
Two presses in Nitches
Three Chairs

N.º 26
A Bed Chamber for Servants

A four post Bedstead furniture linen Curtains
A feather Bed, Bolster, & pillow
1½ pair of Blankets
1 Quilt
2 deal tables
1 Very large deal Store press
1 Very large Chest full of Carpeting /the most of it had
never been in use/ & a quantity of fine Old Tapestry
A Mahogany Bracket
A Swinging looking Glass
Four Chairs
One four footed Stool, Rush bottom

Castlecomer House, County Kilkenny

N.º 27
A Bed Chamber for Serv.ts

Two four post Bedsteads   paragon Curtains
Two feather Beds. & Bolsters
Three pair of Blankets
Two Quilts
One folding Bedstead, with Sacking bottom
One Oak Chest of Drawers
One large trunk
Two Chairs
One looking Glass

N.º 28
A Medicine Closet

A small Medicine Chest, new Cost   .   . £3 – 8 – 3
A parcell of Medicines just from Dub.n   7 – 8 – 0
China Ornaments & figures, with many
Articles of Value
A press with drawers & Nests for the Medicines of
Mahogany

N.º 29
Footmen's Pantry

Containing a Bench. drawers, Shelves, Cupboard
A Quantity of Breakfast & Evening Tea China
of Different kinds

N.º 30
A Very large Lumber & Store House

In it there was a very large linen Mangle, only a
short time home from the Maker, and was not fix'd up,
Cost Exclusive of Carriage from Dub.n
Many Grose of Bottles, /Scotch pints, full quarts, seald,
Burgundy & Champagne, ^{bottles} /Wine Merchants/
                                                Common bottles,
Seltzer Water bottles &c —
Several hundred Weight of Sheet lead, that was taken
off houses, in the Improvements, and Stord up, to
Secure it from the Rebels, on the Appearance of the
Rebellion
Two very large Cases full of Bacon, Hams, & Beef.
A Quantity of Ale, Beer, & Cyder, Stilns, Empty
Wine Vessels, Two large Strong Store Chests, A black
Marble Chimney piece, and a large Grate, with
brass faceings, that had been only a few Months in
use in the Drawing Room /N.º 5/ was taken down &
replaced by others,

Inventory of copper wares

June 26th 1798

List of the Coppers brought from Castle Comer
To Kilkenny Castle — Viz.

---

2 Large Oval Copper Briziers and Covers
1 Large Copper Soup Pot and Cover
1 Small Copper *D°* and Cover
2 Oval Copper Stew pans and Covers
19 Round Copper *D°* and Covers
1 Copper Coffee Pot and Cover
1 Large Oval Copper Dish
1 Small Oval *D°*
2 Round Copper Baking Sheets
1 Copper Cullender
1 Slice
2 Preserving Pans
2 Round Copper Shapes
1 Oval Copper Shape
1 Copper Butter Sauce pan
1 Grid Iron
1 Jack and 2 Chains

---

12 Copper Stew pan Covers
2 Copper Soup Pot Covers
1 Tea Kitchen and heater

---

1 Blue China Tureen Dish and Cover
12 Blue China Soup Plates
3 Desart Blue China Plates
7 Small Dishes Wedge wood,s Ware
24 flat Plates *D°*
4 Desart *D°*

Thomas Maguire

Articles found in the ruins in Castlecomer

a large Copper tea Kitchen for boiling
watter a Copper Soup pot 3 Copper
Cake pans 4 Stew pans 3 flat Copper
Candlesticks 1 hall Ditto —
one large Copper Dish 4 pewter Dishes
8 Ditto plates

An acc.[t] of linen of Lady Ormonde's, that was
burned at Castlecomber, 24th ~~May~~ June 1798.

Ten large damask Cloaths
Three pair of strips to match
Five dozen dinner damask Napkins } These are Damask *here*
Three dozen desert damask Napkins
Three layovers of damask to match
Thirteen Cloaths of different sizes. damask

. . . .

Six large diaper Cloaths } *neither here or Old*
Four layovers to match
One pair of Strips to match
Seven large star*e*'d cloaths
Six large star*ʳ*d .. *d°* .. old ones } These are Diapers.
Seven of a smaller size.
Six new breakfast Cloaths

. . . .

Five large diaper dinner cloaths Stewards room } not here
Six coarse diaper dinner cloaths. Servants hall. £ 2: 14: 2
~~Twelve~~ yards new linen 26 y[ds] at 2[s]:1[d] P[d] *for it* £ 1: 5

. . . .

Sixteen Pair best Sheets, *New*
Twelve Pair second best Sheets *New*
Thirtytwo Pair coarse Sheets ~~& old~~ *New & Old*

As to linen sent from Dublin My Lady has the bill of it and
and [sic] the Ticking all has been lost but Fifteen yards
which is safe with the white Pillow fustain. The Damascus
intended for the Cap[ts] Room is burned.

		yds	d		
Bill ~~for~~ of Ticken		73 19½		5:18:7½	Bill for Ticken
saved		10 —		16: 3¼	£ 7:—:8
Bill of D°	30 y[ds] 2:4[s]	3[:] 10[:] 0		5: 2: 4	Bill for 191½ of Linnen
saved	5 —	11 [:] 8		2 18 4	new £ 12: 15: 4
		£ 2: 18 [:] 4		7:—:8 [recte 8:—:8½]	

Ticken 30 yards at 2/4[s/d] . . . . 3 – 10 – 0
of *D°* 5 y[ds]. saved . . . . – 11 – 8
 2 : 18 : 4

Ticken 73 yards at 19½[d] ⅌ y[d]. . . 5 – 18 – 7½
of *D°* 10 y[ds] saved . . – 16 – 3
 5 : 2 : 4½
 2 : 18 : 4

Total Am.[t] of Ticken destroyed £ 8 : 0 : 8½

Inventory of household silver, 1798

Particulars of
Lady Ormonde's
Losses during
the Rebellion
of
— 1798 —

Mr Magowan Ballyragget

Plate Lists

An Account of The Plate & Gold Belonging to The R.^t Hon.
The Countess of Ormond Taken or Destroy'd By the rebbles at Her House in Castlecomer
on The 24.th Day of June 1798 with the Credit Given of what has Been recover'd from
The ruins &cc —

		oᶻ dwt		[£ s d]
7 doz. Gad.ᵈ Plates	w.ᵗ – 1508 – 10 ⎫	2222 – 15 —	8/–	888 – 16 –
24 — d.ᵒ — dishes	714 – 5 ⎭			
4 Compotee — dᵒ & Covers ⎫		314 – 14 —	9/6	149 – 10 –
4 Casserole dᵒ & dᵒ ⎭				
2 Soop Tureens & Covers		197 – 2	9/6	93 – 12 – 9
4 Sauce dᵒ & dᵒ		120 – 15	9/6	57 – 7 – 6
4 Cand.ᵏˢ & 2 Branches		208 – 8	10/–	104 – 4 –
1 Large Chas'd fruit dish		60 –		39 –
6 Salts & Spoons Chas'd festons Bro.ᵗ on		69 – 18		39 – 14 – 7
4 Gilt Basket Salts		16 –		10 – 17 – 9
1 Large Cup		40 –	8/–	16 –
2 Small d.ᵒ		30 –	8/–	12 –
2 dᵒ dᵒ		30 –	7/6	11 – 5 –
2 Coffee pots		44 –	6/–	13 – 4 –
2 Large waiters		120 –	8/6	51 –
4 Sauce Boats		60 –	9/–	27 –
1 Epergne		150 –	11/4½	85 – 6 – 3
1 round Salver		50 –	6/–	15 –
2 Eight Inch dᵒ		24 –	8/6	10 – 14 –
2 Seven dᵒ dᵒ		20 –	8/6	8 – 10 –

	2 Six d^o d^o	16 –	8/6	6 – 16 –
	2 Small d^o	8 – 10	6/–	2 – 11 –
	2 wine Jugs	50 – 9	9/6	24 –
	1 Coffee Bigon	20 – 10		12 – 7
*was there one _No_	1 Tankard			
	1 Kettle & Stand	100 –	6/–	30 –
	2 Tureen Ladles	12 – 9		5 – 13 – 6
	4 Sauce d^o	5 – 17		3 – 10 – 7
	4 Gravy Spoons	14 – 12		6 – 7 – 5
	7 Scuers	6 – 1		3 – 10 – 2
	2 Egg Cups			3 –
	2 Cans	18 –	6/–	5 – 8
	1 Tea Dish & 2 Butter Plates	26 –	6/–	7 – 16
	1 wine funnell plate	3 –		1 – 7 – 1
	1 Cream Jug	6 – 0	6/–	1 – 16 –
	4 Sauce Ladles	7 –		3 – 11 – 6
	18 Table Spoons	45 –		18 – 4 – 6
	5 Gravy d^o	15 –		6 – 10 –
	12 Tea d^o	6 –		3 – 3 –
	2 Marrow d^o	3 – 10		1 – 10 – 9
	1 Soop Ladle	7 –		3 – 1 – 9
	2 Cream Spoons	1 – 10		17 – 4
	2 doz. Knives & forks			13 – 13 –
	3 Caster Urns Sug^r Must^d & pepper	22 –	6/6	7 – 3 –
	1 pair Coasters	12 – 10		6 – 6 – 9
	28 Desert Spoons	28 –		11 – 18 –
	18 d^o Knives & forks all Silv^r	108 –	10/–	54 –
	24 Table Spoon forks	60 –		25 – 10 –
	12 Desert d^o — d^o	12 –		4 – 17 –
	10 wine Lables			3 – 5 –
	3 OEconomist Corks			– 14 – 7½
	1 mustard pot	3 – 18		2 – 8 –
	12 Knives	18 –	6/–	5 – 8 –
	A Sallad fork	4 –		2 – [0] – 3
	1 Table & 1 Gravy Spoon	5 – 10		2 – 3 – 9
	1 Large Soop — d^o	7 – 10	6/–	2 – 5 –
	1 Side Board Screw Silv Bow			16 – 3
	1 pint Can	9 –	6/–	2 – 14 –
	1 Slop Bowl	12 –	9/6	5 – 14 –
	1 Lemon Strainer	6 –	6/–	1 – 16 –
	1 Snuffer dish	8 –	6/–	2 – 8 –
*was there one _No_	*1 Tea Pot			

Dressing plate

1 Large Cut Glass Box Silv Top			6 – 16 – 6
2 Small d^o d^o d^o			6 – 16 – 6
2 Tooth powder d^o			3 – 8 – 3
1 Shaveing Brush & Case			1 – 14 – 1½

Castlecomer House, County Kilkenny

1 pomatom Box			2 – 5 – 6
3 Tops for Bottles	2 ——		12 – 0
3 Filagree Bouzu Boxes			3 – 8 – 3
1 *d⁰* — Tooth pick Case			16 – 3
*1 Chamber Cand^ks.			

Gold

1 Gold Cup & Cover	40 – 0 – 0	a 5 Gui ½ pr oz.	227 – 10 –
1 *d⁰* Corporation Box	7 ——	83/-	29 – 1 –
1 *d⁰* *d⁰* waterford City	5 ——		20 – 15 –
1 *d⁰* Enam^d. Box	6 ——		24 –
1 *d⁰* Trench *d⁰*	5 ——		20 –
2 Large *d⁰*			
1 Gold medal	5 – 6 – 12		21 – 6 –

whether Gold ⎞
or Silver ⎠ (bracketed beside "2 Large *d⁰*" and "1 Gold medal")

Plated Articles

4 plat^d. Ice pails	27 – 6 –
4 pair plated Candles^ks.	4 – 11 –
A p^r Steak Dishes & Stands	9 – 2 –
A p^r Horn Lin'd plate	5 – 5

Cash paid a Goldsmith & refiner for Going to weigh & Value ⎞ the recover'd plate & Examine The rubbish &cc. ⎠	11 – 7 – 6
Cash p^d for washing rubbish	
d⁰ — *d⁰* — for refineing	
	2360 – 5 – 4

2

(By Am⁼ of Silv^r recover'd from The ruins &cc.   2433 – 13 a 6/– ℔ oz.

£ 730 – 1 – 10½

By part of a Gold Cup recover'd   13 – 10 – 0 a 80/–   54

784 – 1 – 10½

£ 1576 – 3 – 5½

Lists of
Family Plate
Gold Cup &c

at C'Comer House
1798
Some taken & destroyed
by Rebels

Wine inventory, 1798

An Account of the Wines, the
property of the Countess of Ormonde,
that was destroyed by the Rebels, in
her Ladyships house at Castlecomer,
in the County of Kilkenny, in the
Month of June 1798

			£
	A But of Madeira		127 ~ 8 ~ 0
4	Dozen of Old *Do*	at 75	15 ~ 0 ~ 0
2	Hhd[s] of Port	at. 25	50 ~ 0 ~ 0
2	*Do* *Do* in bottle	a 26	52 ~ 0 ~ 0
5	Dozen of Hock	a 6 G[s]	34 ~ 2 ~ 6
16 ~~25~~	Dozen of *Do*	a 4 G[s]	113 ~ 15 ~ 0
21	Dozen of Red Hermitage	a 3 G[s]	71 ~ 13 ~ 3
21	Dozen of White *Do*	*Do*	71 ~ 13 ~ 3
4	*Do* of Champagne	a 5 G[s]	22 ~ 15 ~ 0
5	*Do* of Burgundy	a 4 *Do*	22 ~ 15 ~ 0
5	Hhd[s] of Claret	a 45 G[s]	225 ~ 18 ~ 9
5	*Do* of *Do*	a 40 G[s]	227 ~ 10 ~ 0
1	*Do* of *Do*	a 50 G[s]	56 ~ 17 ~ 6
10	Dozen of Sherry	a 34/1/~	17 ~ 1 ~ 3
70	Pints of Malmsey Madeira	at 4 G[s] ℔ Doz[n]	26 ~ 10 ~ 10
29	Dozen of Malaga	at 22/9	32 ~ 19 ~ 9
69	Bottles of Red Ravesatt	a 4 G[s] ℔ doz[n]	26 ~ 3 ~ 3
69	*Do* of White *Do*	*Do*	26 ~ 3 ~ 3
~~15~~	Dozen of Carcavilla	at 30 ~~℔ dozen~~	~~22 ~ 10 ~ 0~~
18	Gallons of Arack	at 30 ℔ Gal[n]	27 ~ 0 ~ 0
19	Dozen of Vindegrave	at 34/1½ ℔ doz[n]	32 ~ 8 ~ 4½
	Bottles on a Computation		34 ~ 2 ~ 6
			1336 ~ 7 ~ 5½

Castlecomer House, County Kilkenny

PLATE 29
One of a set of Irish George III mahogany hall chairs, painted with the crest of the Clements family

13

KILLADOON,
COUNTY KILDARE
1807–29

EDMUND JOYCE

IN 1764, ROBERT CLEMENTS (1732–1804), eldest son of the statesman Nathaniel Clements, leased the Killadoon estate near Celbridge in County Kildare from Thomas Conolly of Castletown House. The prime site on the banks of the Liffey, and within easy reach of Dublin, provided him with the ideal setting to establish a suitable family seat. The lease, which contains a map, indicates that there was already a house on the site. Between 1767 and 1771, Robert Clements embarked on creating a substantial five-bay, three-storey house. The earlier range was retained and utilized as a service wing for the new house. The principal rooms of the new range take full advantage of the topography, maximizing views across the Liffey towards Lyons' Hill and the Wicklow Mountains beyond.

The fashionable interior spaces created at Killadoon reflected the sensitivities and aspirations of Robert Clements. His aesthetic was shaped during his Grand Tour made in the 1750s. His Grand Tour portrait by Pompeo Batoni, of circa 1753–4, which is now at the Hood Museum of Art, Dartford, New Hampshire, represents a confident and fashionable young man (see plate 40). The portrayal of Robert Clements beside a bust of Homer (which references Rembrandt's *Aristotle with a Bust of Homer*), was significant as such a direct classical allusion had not previously featured in Batoni's work. The apparently early nineteenth-century series of watercolour sketches of the picture-hang (still in the Clements archive) shows that the Batoni portrait originally hung over the mantel in the dining-room.

In 1783, in response to long-running solicitation, and as a reward for providing a parliamentary seat for the lord lieutenant's chief secretary, Robert Clements was elevated to the peerage as Baron Leitrim, and was advanced to the earldom of Leitrim in 1795. His son, Nathaniel Clements, second Earl of Leitrim (1768–1854), married in 1800 Mary Bermingham, co-heiress with her sister, the Countess of Charlemont, to the Rosshill estate, County Galway. The newly-weds honeymooned at Killadoon, and took up permanent residence there when the first earl moved to England, where he spent the last four years of his life. According to the Knight of Glin and James Peill, Nathaniel and Mary undertook two phases of redecoration at Killadoon; the first between 1805 and 1810 and the second between 1825 and 1835.

The comprehensive Killadoon inventories document these phases of redecoration. By the time the first inventory was created in 1807, this large, bright house was filled with all sorts of fashionable objects. Between 1804 and 1807 the Killadoon collection had seen an influx of early nineteenth-century furniture and objects, 1807 being a particularly significant date because in that year Leitrim House, Upper Sackville

Street, the Dublin town house of the family, was let and its high-status contents were transferred to Killadoon. The initial inventory was needed in order to keep a handle on the extent and the positioning of this recently augmented collection, and was edited and enlarged in 1812 and again in 1829 to reflect additions, subtractions (mostly due to breakages) and the movement of pieces within the house. A study of the distribution of objects at Killadoon between 1807 and 1829, reveals that the major portion of the collection remained stationary. This in itself conveys a strong sense of stability. The broad range of key objects retained in the series of rooms, reflects the level of discernment practised in the procurement and subsequent placing of goods. Each layer of objects supplemented earlier schemes and subsequently became integral components of the Killadoon interior. The abundance of inventories at Killadoon, all created within a relatively narrow time frame, and almost entirely in Lady Leitrim's own hand, signifies the interest and pride which the Leitrims took in their collection.

The Leitrims also used the later editions, particularly those of 1829, to refine their descriptions. Additional detail was added to some of the earlier descriptions; for example, the entry of 'Four Fire Skreens' in the Drawing Room was extended to include 'views of Marino', the seaside home of the Charlemonts at Clontarf, County Dublin. Inherited items also featured in the collection. In both inventories, a bronze bust of Philip Stanhope, fourth Earl of Chesterfield (1694–1773), who was a patron of Nathaniel Clements, the second earl's grandfather, is listed as being in the Entrance Hall. The emotional attachment to inherited items was often further strengthened by an acknowledgement that they carried messages of lineage and longevity. The collection of busts grew between 1807 and 1829 to include numerous classical figures and, most notably, two busts of Lady Charlemont and one of Lord Leitrim. The growth of classical objects, marble statues, busts and table tops, reflects the extensive continental travels undertaken by the Leitrims in the early 1820s. The positioning of such items in prominent rooms heightened the status of the collection; here the family were actively reaffirming and demonstrating their lineage, connections and international sensibilities.

The 'Eagle room' at Killadoon, the epitome of an early nineteenth-century empire interior, was in fact present in 1807. The decorative scheme adopted is significant. The room is fitted with a 'Soffa Bed with blue & Pink calico Curtains', the drapes of which are supported from an 'Eagle & brass ring'. The design of the bed together with that of the 'Eight Hall Chairs' in the Entrance Hall are influenced by zoomorphic forms and by traditional French design. The vigour and robustness applied in their design echo the work of the contemporary designers Thomas Hope and George Smith. Killadoon had become a stage for design ahead of its time.

Writing to his son George in 1835, Nathaniel acknowledged that Killadoon 'is certainly not a fine place, nor can it ever be so, for it is not of sufficient extent … but … it is … a very comfortable place … and certainly it is now in a very different state from what it was when I first went to live there.' Architecturally, Killadoon has remained much unchanged since 1829; the spaces referred to in the inventory are thus easy to identify. Although the house was sold in 2019 by the Clements family, the two small notebooks which contain the inventories are still part of the Clements archive.

Inventory of Killadoon
1807 / overlaid with 1812

List of Furniture 1812

Hall

Two Curtains & Draperies
Eight Hall Chairs
One Foot Brush
One Sheep Rug
Four Mohogany Shutters
One Trou Madame Table
Two Card Tables
Three Large China Jars
Two smaller Jars with Saucers
Two smaller Jars on Chimney Piece
Bust of Mr Fox on d^o
Bust of Lord Chesterfield
Clock & Bracket
One Green Stool
One Sarcophagus Grate a fender & fire Irons
One Scarlet Hearth Rug
Five Brass Bell Weights
One Patent Lamp, with three Burners

March – 1812
Library

1 Library Table
1 Silver Ink Stand with sand Box with Bottle &
   bell seperate — One Bronze Paper Weight, one
   Bronze lamp. One Plated Stand for two
   Candles with Shade & doubter — one Card Rack
   One Red leather Letter Box
1 Round Table & Green Cloth Cover
2 Large Chairs with reading desks, & Candlesticks.
6 small Cane Chairs with Cushions & Calico covers
2 Roman Chairs
2 Window Stools & Cushions in Calico covers
2 Fire Screens
1 Greecian Soffa with Cushion Bolster & Pillow
   Calico Covers
1. Foot Stool
1. Small Claw Table
1 Register Grate, fire Irons & Steel Fender
1 Hearth Rug
1 Bronze Groupe on Chimney Piece two Bronze
   candlesticks Three China Ornaments Crackly China
   two Hand Screens with Transperancies

2 Black Velvet Bell pulls — two Enamelled Portraits
3 Drawings in Gilt Frames
3 Venetian Blinds
2 Calico Curtains & Drapery
1 Sheep Rug
1 Carpet
1 Thermometer outside Window
7 Bronze Figures upon one Book case. five
   Bronze Figure & 2 Wedgewood do upon
      the other.
2 Red Morocco – blotting Books – on Library Table.

Drawing Room

1. Steel Register Grate with Fire Irons & fender, one
   Hearth Rug
2 Fire Screens — two Hand Screen — two Round
   Foot Stools — Two Patent Lamps on Chimney Piece
   An Etruscan Vase & 8 China Ornaments on do
1. Round Claw Table — Two Soffa Tables, One
   Square Table — One small inlaid Table —
   One reading Desk
1 Large Soffa with four Cushions 2 Bolsters
   & two Pillows in Calico Cases
1 Greecian Soffa with three Cushions one Bolster
   & one Pillow in Calico Cases
2 Large Arm Chairs Calico Covers — Three Tapestry
   Chairs Calico Cover – Four chairs Gilt frames
8 Green painted chairs 2 of them with Arms
2 Inlaid Commodes
2 Pier Glasses
2 Etruscan Vases & 4 China Ornaments on Commodes
1 Marble & Or Moulu Ink Stand
1 China Ink Stand – Papiliotte case – one
   Candlestick – two Wafer Saucers, one Pen
   Tray – & 1 Case of Dictionaries on Soffa Table.
1. Six leaved Screen
1 Piano Forte & Leather Cover
1. Rack for Music Books
1. Axminster Carpet & two Slips
1 Large Portugal Mat
1. small Indian   d^o at Door
3 Venetian Blinds
3. Silk Window Curtains
1 Hearth Brush – one pair Bellows
1 Small Book Stand
2 Velvet & Green ribbon Bell pulls
2 Pictures
1. Red Morocco blotting Book on Soffa Table

Killadoon, County Kildare

List of Furniture in Killadoon
September the 26th 1807
In Leitrim [prob. Lough Rynn, Mohill, Co. Leitrim]

* In the MS this heading appears before 'Thermometer outside Window' in the 1812 overlay (*see* p. 203) and is struck through.

Library 26th September 1807

1. Library Table Rose Wood
1. Claw Table — Mahogany
1. Pillar Table Mahogany
1. Egyptian Soffa with Cushion Bolster & Pillow
1. Egyptian Footstool
2. Cane chairs with 2 Leather Cushions & a Mahogany reading desk & brass Candlestick to each
2 Gothic Chairs covered with blue Cloth
6. Mahogany & Cane Chairs with Cushions to each.
2 Window Stools with Cushions to each
1 Drapery & 2 Curtain's round the Bow
1 Bronze Group, 2. Bronze Candlesticks &
2 Crackley china Vases on Chimney Piece.
1 ornament to match Vases
1 Silver Ink Stand with sand box ink bottle & Bell seperate
1. Bronze Antique lamp ~~& Wedgwood Papiliotte ease~~, 1. China Wafer tray 1 Bronze lamp
1 Bronze Head Paper Weight — & 1 Mahogany railed stand for loose Papers
1 Plated reading Candlestick with two branches & 2 tin shades (& steel Extinguishes
1. Brussels Carpet
1 Hearth Rug
1. Steel Fender
1. Set of Fire Irons
1. ~~Hempen~~ Sheep Rug at Glass door
2. Red Morocco Bloting Books
2 Wedgewood Sphinx's over Bookcases
12. Bronze figures – Groups over Bookcases
1. Large Drawing in Gilt frame with plate Glass over Chimney Piece
2 Enameled Portraits in black & gold frames over Chimney piece
2 Black Velvet Bell pull's with gilt handles
3 Venetian Blinds

Killadoon Drawing Room the 26th September. 1807

1 large Soffa with 4 Cushions 2 Pillows & Chintz covers to all 2 Bolsters

2~~1~~. Grecian Arm Chair with 1 Cushion & 1 Chints Cover to all
~~2 Hunting Chairs with 3 cushions to each & Chints Covers~~
8 Green Painted Chairs cushions to each with clouded Green Silk covers
4 Gilt framed chairs with clouded green silk covers nailed on
3. Tapestry & Gilt Chairs with flannel & Chints covers to each
1~~2~~. Worsted Hassocks worked
1. Screen with six leaves
2~~1~~. fire Screen ~~claw Stand~~ Mahogany & Green silk
1. Grand Piano Forte — with leather Cover
1. Mahogany reading desk on Pillar
1. Round Claw Table Mahogany
1. Small inlaid Table on Claw
2. Rose wood Soffa Tables 2 drawers each baise covers each
1. Mahogany Spider Table
1. Satin wood Book shelf with drawer
2 Inlaid Commodes — with Leather Covers
3. Etruscan Vases
2. Colebrook Dale Flower Pots
2 Colebrook Dale Papiliotte cases
2 French China Cups with basket handles
2 very small Colebrook dale Candlesticks
1. Pen Tray & 1 Papiliotte case of Colebrook dale gold with white flowers — 1 Bronze & Gold China Candlestick & Extinguisher ~~1. white bronze & gold Inkstand Antique shape.~~
1 Cup & Saucer for Wafers
1. French China Ink Stand
~~1. Candlestick, 1 pentray, 1 Inkstand of Colebrook dale China Dragon Pattern~~
1. Bowl cover & Saucer French China
1. Cup with Gold handle 1 Saucer French China
2 small Wafer trays Colebrook Dale China
2. Hand Screens ~~with transperancies~~ Green
1. Picture in Gilt frame. Landscape Claude Lorrain
1. Carpet Axminster — & 2 side Slips *do*
1. Hearth Rug
1. Steel fender
1 Set of fire Irons
1. Inlaid Hearth Brush
1. Spa painted Bellows
3 Green Clouded Silk Curtains for Windows with Gilt Cornices
2 Peer Glasses in Gilt frames

1. small Mat
3. Venetian Blinds
2 Round Green Cloth Footstools
1. Chaise longue 3 Cushion's 1 Bolster 1 Pillow in Calico cases

Killadoon the 26<u>th</u> of September Furniture of Dining Room

2. Sideboard Tables — Mahogany
1 ~~Mahogany Table to dine 4 people~~
1. Mahogany Table to dine 8. people.
1. Set of Tables in three pieces with two seperate leaves — Mahogany
1 Mahogany Claw Table
3. Mahogany Dumb Waiters
1. Mahogany Canterbury with 3. Tin's
1. Mahogany Wine Cooper
1. Mahogany Stand for Cistern
1. very small Mahogany Chest
1. Mahogany Plate Bucket with brass hoopes
1. Mahogany Tea Chest on Stand
2 Red Leather Bergers
1~~2~~4 Red Leather & Mahogany Chairs
1. Mahogany & stuff fire Screen
1. Medusa in White Marble on Chimney Piece
2 Small Wedgewood Vases on *do*
2 Bronze Lions on *D°*
2 Mahogany & Cane Chairs screwed on Tables for Children
2~~1~~ ^Indian Screen*s* with ~~five~~ Six leaves each
1 Turkey Carpet with 2 side Stripes to match.
2 Stripes of Oil Cloth
1. Steel Fender
1 Set of fire Irons
4. Stripped Damascus Window Curtains
3. Venetian Blinds

Killadoon the 26<u>th</u> of September 1807 – Furniture of Entrance Hall

8 Mahogany Chairs with Crest painted
4 Mahogany Shutters for Doors & Windows
3 Mahogany & Green Cloth Tables
1. Painted Stool
1 Cut Glass & Brass Patent lamp with 2 lights
1. Foot Brush
1. Bronze Head of Ld Chesterfield on Stand
1. Or Moulu Clock
1. Set of Fire Irons

Killadoon the 26<u>th</u> of September Furniture in space under the Principal Stair Case

1. Mahogany writing Table with six Drawers covered with Green Cloth
2 portable garden Chairs
1. Glass Globe for Candle hung from Cieling
1. half circular Green Basket Stand for flower Pot.
2 Green Basket Stands in two tiers for *d°*
1 round Basket & Tin
4 Green Ba[s]kets for one flower pot each

China Vases in this & Entrance Hall

2 Very large China Vases coloured Flowers Gilt &^c
1 Very large Blue & White China Vase
2 large China Vases flower pattern & one Cover
1 China Vase Blue & grey
2 Cheasea China flower Pots with saucers to each
2 Green Red & blue Old China Vases & covers.
1. Blue & White Pot Pourris Pot & Cover
2 Old China Pot Pourris Pots coloured flower pattern
7 blue & White open flower Pots China

Killadoon the 26<u>th</u> of September 1807 Furniture in Butler's Pantry

6 Mahogany Chairs
1. Mahogany Step ladder
1. Deal Press Bed
1. large Soffa
1. Plate Bucket Mahogany – Square Shape
1 Press for Tools
1. Mahogany Supper Stand or Waiter Trays
at the door of this room is a Mahogany Table called the Hazard Table

Killadoon the 26<u>th</u> of September 1807 Furniture in Lord Leitrim's Dressing room

1. Dressing Table Mahogany with Mahogany Shelf – & drawer
1 Writing Table Mahogany
1 Inlaid Table with Drawer – lock & key
1 Mahogany table with Drawer lock & key
1 Mahogany Wardrobe

1 Mahogany Alphabet
1 Mahogany Bason stand with looking Glass
1. Mahogany & red Leather Bidee
1. Tunbridge Inlaid Cabinet
2 painted flowerpot stands
2 Inlaid brackets
1. low chair with 2 two cushions & chintz covers –
5 large Arm Chairs tapestry with flannel & damascus covers
2. Green & White Cane chairs
1 Old Rush bottomed Arm Chair
1. Ink stand with three glass bottles & plated stoppers
1 Mahogany Dressing Glass
2. Pier Glasses in gilt frames
15 Oil paintaings 11 Gilt frames & 1 drawing & Glass.
1. Carpet
1. Hearth Rug
1. Steel Fender with brass wire treillage
1. Set of fire Irons
1. Oil Cloth
1. small white Bason
1 Glass & 1 Glass Jug
1 yellow ware footpan
1 Weighing Machine Mahogany
3. Chintz Window Curtains
3. Venetian Blinds

Killadoon the 26ᵗʰ of September 1807
Furniture in Lady Leitrim's Bed Room

1. Four Posted Bed with Maronne & Yellow Curtains & trimmings
1. Palliasse
1. Feather Bed
1. Hair Mattrass
1. Bolster
2 Pillows
1. Under Blanket
1. pair of Upper Blankets
1. Marseilles Quilt
2. Mahogany Commodes
1. Bed Carpet
1. Large Wardrobe with Drawers &ᶜ
1. Set of Mahogany Drawers
2 Corner Mahogany Commodes
2. Mahogany inlaid Book Shelves
1. Mahogany folding Horse
1. Mahogany Dressing table with drawer & Shelf

1. Table & Shelf Mahogany for Bason's also wᵗʰ drawers
1. Soffa with 3 Cushions & 4 Pillows white calico covers.
1. low Chair with 2 Cushions & Chints covers
6. Rush bottomed Chair
2 Rush bottomed dressing Stools
1 round foot stool
1. Oil Cloth
1. Dressing Glass in japan frame
1. Pier Glass in white painted frame.
1. Steel fender
1. Set of fire Irons
1. Wocester China Bowl cover & Bason 4 blue & white China flower Pots & 1 cup cover & saucer on Chimney piece
1. Portrait in gilt frame
1. Yellow Ware Footpan
2 Chamber Vases – 2 large jugs – 1 small jug 1 plate 1 tooth brush tray & mug
1. Tin Kettle
1 Small blue mug Colebrook dale

Killadoon the 26ᵗʰ of September 1807
Furniture of Small front Dressing Room

1 Mahogany Dressing table Shelf & Drawer
1. Dressing Glass in Mahogany frame
1. large Mahogany Wardrobe
1. Small Mahogany Table & Shelf for Basons
1. Mahogany Commode
1. Mahogany Writing table & Drawer
1. Mahogany Set of Drawers
2. Mahogany Book Shelves
2. Mahogany Brackets
1. Mahogany Alphabet
1. Mahogany & red Leather Bidée
1. Mahogany folding Horse
2 small Mahogany brackets for papers
1. looking Glass in Gilt frame
1. Tapestry Soffa with flannel & Damascus covers.
2 Tapestry Arm Chairs with flannel & damascus. covers.
2 Painted Chairs with cushions & damascus covers
1. Old Rush bottomed Chairs
2 Rush bottomed dressing Stools
1. Oil Cloth
1. Steel fender with brass wire treilliage
1. Set of fire Iron's
10 Pictures

1 Iron stand for bars of grate
2. China flower Pots 2 cups & saucers – 4 Dresden figure & flower Pots
1 White dimity Window Curtain

Killadoon the 26th of September 1807
Furniture in Middle Bed room

1. Four Posted Bed with Chints Curtains & trimmings
1. Palliasse
1. Feather Bed
1. Hair Mattrass
1. Bolster
2. Pillows
1. Under Blanket
1 pair of Upper Blankets
1. Marseilles Quilt
2. Bed Steps Mahogany & Chints carpetted
1. Carpet all over the room
2. Mahogany Commodes
1. Mahogany Night Chair
1. Set of Inlaid & brass Drawers
1. Mahogany Wardrobe
1. Mahogany & red Leather Bidée
1. ~~Dressing~~ Toilet with a calico & a Muslin cover
1. Spa Dressing Glass – 7 Boxes & 2 Candlesticks
2 Chints Window Curtains & Draperies
2 Muslin Curtains
1. Soffa with 2 Cushions & 2 large Pillows Chints covers for all
1. Mahogany Dressing Table
1. Small Mahogany Table Shelf & Drawer
1. Mahogany Bason Stand
1. Dressing Glass in Mahogany frame
1~~2~~. Rush bottomed Dressing Stools
10 Rush bottomed green painted Chairs
1. Mahogany folding Horse
1. looking Glass in Gilt frame
1. Picture in gilt frame
2 China flower Pots
2 Wedgewood Candlesticks
1. Steel fender
1. Set of fire Irons

Killadoon the 26th of September 1807
Furniture in Venus Room

1. Four Posted Bed with yellow & blue Curtains & trimmings
1. Palliasse
1. Feather Bed
1. Hair Matterass
1. Bolster
2 Pillows
1. Under Blanket
1 pair of upper Blankets
1. Marseilles Quilt
2. Yellow & blue Window curtains & draperies
2. Muslin Curtains
1. Toilette Table with Calico & Muslin covers
1. Spa Dressing Glass with 9 Boxes 2 trays 2 Brushes & 2 Candlesticks
1. Brussels Bed Carpet
1. Square *do* for middle of the room
1. Soffa & two cushions with yellow calico covers
2. Mahogany Commodes
1. Mahogany Night Chair
2. Inlaid Corner Commodes
1. Inlaid & Brass set of Drawers
1. Mahogany Set of Drawers
1. Mahogany & Red Leather Bidée
1. Mahogany folding Horse
2. Bed Steps with yellow Calico Mahogany & Carpets.
1. Mahogany & Ebony Dressing table with 2 Drawers
1. Small Mahogany table & Drawer
1. Mahogany Bason Stand ~~& Drawer~~
1. Dressing Glass in Mahogany frame
1. Picture in Gilt frame
1. looking Glass in Pier Gilt frame
2 Wedgewood Candlesticks
3 Black Wedgewood Vases
1. Ink Stand
2. Rush Bottomed dressing Stools
8 Cane chairs Green & White
1. Steel fender with wire treilliage
1. Set of fire Irons
1. Yellow ware footpan
1. Tin Kettle

Killadoon, County Kildare

Killadoon the 26th of September 1807
Furniture in Eagle Dressing Room

1 Soffa Bed with blue & Pink calico Curtains
  & trimmings
1. Eagle & brass ring
2. Bolsters
1 Hair Mattrass
1 large Pillow – with blue covers for all.
1 Eagle for Window Curtain
1. Blue & Pink Window Curtain & pink Drapery
1. Mahogany Commode
1. Mahogany & red Leather Bidee
1. Mahogany folding Horse
1. Mahogany Dressing Table & Drawer
1 Small Mahogany Table & Drawer
1. Mahogany Bason Stand
2. Rush bottomed dressing Stools
8 Yellow painted cane Chairs
1. Set of Mahogany Drawers
1. Brussels Carpet
1 Steel fender with brass wire treilliage
1. Set of fire Irons
1 Iron stand to hang on grate
2 Cups Covers & Saucers.
1 french China Bowl Ewer & cup
2. Wedgewood Candlesticks
1. Boot Jack
1. Dressing Glass in Mahogany frame

Killadoon the 26th of September 1807
In the Lobby on the first Floor

1. Mahogany Desk
1. Mahogany Table

Killadoon the 26th of September 1807
Furniture in Bow Room in Atic Story

1 Four Posted Bed with Chints Curtains
  & trimmings
1. Palliasse
1. Feather Bed
1. Hair Mattrass
1. Bolster
1. Pillow
1. Under Blanket
1. pair of Upper Blankets
1. Marseilles Quilt
1. Soffa & 2 Cushions – *2 Pillows*

1. Mahogany Dressing Table with ~~**** & shelfs~~
  two Drawers
1. Mahogany Bason Stand
1. Mahogany Spider Table – *not here*
1. Octagon Mahogany Table
1. Mahogany Set of Drawers
1. Mahogany Commode
1. Mahogany Night Chair
1. Mahogany & Red Leather Bidée
1. Mahogany folding Horse
1. Boot Jack
1. Steel fender
1. Set of fire Irons
1. Bed Carpet
1. Oil Cloth
3. Chints Window Curtains
2 Mahogany bookshelves
1. Ink Stand
1. Picture in frame
1. Dressing Glass in Japan frame
8. Yellow painted Chairs & rush bottom's
2 Blue & White Bason's 2 *d*º Jugs – 1 small *d*º
  Bason 2 *d*º small Jugs – 1 Mug *d*º 1 soap stand
  1. tumbler glass
1. Tin Kettle
  two Beds with 2 Palliasses 2 Mattrasses
  two Feather Beds 2 Bolsters 2 under Blankets
2 pair Upper Blankets
1 Field Bed with Palliasse 1 Feather Bed 1 Mattrass
1 Under Blanket 1 Upper Blanket 1 Bolster
3 Quilts in this Room

Killadoon the 26th of September 1807
Furniture in First Nursery – Atic Story

2 Canopy Beds with White Calico Curtains
   & trimmings to each
2 Palliasses
2. Hair Mattrasses
2. Feather Beds
2. Bolsters
1. Pillow
2. Under Blankets
2. pair of Upper Blankets
1 Quilted Quilt
1 Old Tufted Quilt
2. White Calico Curtains for Window with Valences
2. Mahogany Sets of Drawers
1. Mahogany Book case – with 2 small Drawers

1. Mahogany Dressing Table Shelf & Drawer
1. Small Mahogany Table with Drawer
2. Mahogany Clothes Horses one folding 1 Uprignt.
1. Small Dressing Glass in Mahogany frame y̱ᵉ plate ᶜʳᵃᶜᵏᵉᵈ.
1 Small Mahogany Bason Stand
2. Oak Tables — very shabby
2. Oil Cloths
1. Stel̶el fire guard to hang on Grate
1 Steel wire Fender very shabby
1. Set of fire Iron's
1 Small Mahogany Childs Night Chair
3. Mahogany Chairs Mohair Bottoms
7. Green painted Chairs Rush bottomed
1. Rush Bottomed Dressing Stool
1. Plain White ware footpan
3. Yellow ware Bason's
2 Yellow ware Jugs

Killadoon the 26ᵗʰ of September 1807
Furniture in Lᵈ Clements's Room Atic Story

1. Canopy Bed with White Dimity Curtains & white Dimity Counterpan trimmed with Muslin
1. Palliasse
1. Feather Bed
1. Wool Mattrass
1. Bolster
1. Pillow
1. Hair Matterass × *not here*
1 Under Blanket
1. pair of Upper Blankets
1 M̶a̶h̶ tufted Quilt
1. Mahogany Dressing Table with Shelf & divisions & Looking Glass
1. Mahogany Commode
1. Mahogany very small Spider Table
1. Mahogany Spider Table
1. Mahogany Table & Shelf
1. Book Case with Glass doors — Mahogany
1. small Piano Forte
1. small Mahogany Horse
1. Rush bottomed Dressing Stool
1. Steel fender
1. Set of fire Irons
8. Green painted Rush bottomed Chairs
A Soffa Bed with 2 Straw Mattrasses – 1 Bolster –
2 Childrens Beds with Straw Mattrasses Palliasses

Pillow's under Blankets Upper Blankets &
Quilts to each
1 Childs Swing Bed with 1 Mattrass 1 Pillow
1 Under & 1 Upper Blanket 1 Quilt
1 Field Bed with Chintz Curtains 1 Palliasse
1 Feather Bed 1 Bolster 1 Pillow 1 under Blanket
1 Pair of Upper Blankets 1 Tufted Quilt

Killadoon the 26ᵗʰ of September 1807
Furniture in Second Nursery Atic Story

2. Canopy Beds with White Calico Curtains & trimmings
2. Palliasses
2. Feather Beds
2. Bolsters
2. Pillows
2. Under Blankets
2 pair of Upper Blankets
2. Tufted Quilts
2. White Calico Curtains & Valences for Windows
1. four Posted Childs Bed with 1 Palliasse 1 Hair Mattrass 1 Pillow 1 Under Blanket 1 double upper Blanket – 1 Calico Quilt – 1 Set of White Calico Curtains & trimmings
1. Large White Wardrobe & Drawers
1. Mahogany Corner Press
2. Bason Stands
1. Mahogany Horse
2. Oil Cloths
1. small Childs Mahogany Night Chair
1. Oak Table with Drawer
1. Shabby Oak Table
1 Steel Wire fender
1 Set of fire Irons
1. Dressing Glass Mahogany frame & Drawer very much cracked
1. Iron Stand to hang on Grate
1 Picture Frame & Glass
1. Black shade frame & Glass
2. low Rush bottomed Green Chairs
2. Rush bottomed Green Chairs
1. Yellow ware footpan
1. Copper Tea Kettle

Killadoon, County Kildare

Killadoon the 26th of September 1807
Furniture of Rose Room

1. field Bed with Chints Curtains
2. Palliasses
1. Feather Bed
1. Hair Mattrass
1. Bolster
1. Pillow
1. Under Blanket
1. pair of Upper Blankets
1. Marseilles Quilt
1. Chints Window Curtain
1. Mahogany Commode
1. Mahogany Dressing Table Drawer & Shelf
1. Small Mahogany Table & Drawer
1. Triangular Table with black leather cover
1. Mahogany Bidee
1. Mahogany Set of Drawers
1. Dressing Glass in Mahogany frame
1. Mahogany folding Screen
1. Rush bottomed Dressing Stool
2. Arm Chairs with Damascus Covers
1 Old Rush bottomed Arm Chair
1. Rush bottomed Green Chair
1. Steel Fender
1. Set of fire Irons
1. Soffa Bed with Chintz Curtains
1. Hair Mattrass
4 ~~3~~ Wool Mattrasses
1. Bolster
1. Pillow
1. Under Blanket
1. pair of new Upper Blankets

Ladies Maids Room

two Field Bed with Chintz Curtains, lined
2 Palliasses
3 Feather Beds
2 Hair Mattrasses
2 Under Blankets
2 pair Upper Blankets
2 Bolsters
2 Pillows
2 Tufted Quilts
1 Deal Table with Drawer
1 Spider Table
1 small Chest of Drawers
1 small Clothes Horse

4 Rush Bottomed Chairs
1 Carpet
1 Chimney Glass
2 Prints in frames with Glasses
1 looking Glass

Killadoon the 26th of September 1807
Furniture in The Ladies Maids Room

1. Four Posted Bed with Stripped Damascus
    Curtains & trimmings
1. Palliasse
1. Hair Mattrass
1. Feather Bed
1. Bolster
1. Pillow
1. Under Blanket
1. pair of Upper Blankets
1. Tufted Quilt a large size brought from Dublin
2. Camp Beds – one with Check one with
    Calico curtains
2 Palliasses
2. Feather Beds – 2 Bolsters – 2 Pillows
1. Mattrass which Belongs to second nursery
2. Under Blankets
2 pair of Upper Blankets
2 Tufted Quilts one extremely bad
1. Oak Press
1 painted set of ~~Oak~~ Drawers
1. Painted Horse
1. Oak Table & Drawer
1 Oak Spider Table
1 looking Glass in Mahogany frame
1. Steel Fender
1. set of fire Irons
4 ~~3~~ Green painted Rush bottomed Chairs
1. Yellow Ware Jug & Bason

Killadoon the 26th of September 1807
Furniture in House Keepers Room's

6 Stuffed back Chairs – 4 stripped damascus covers.
1 Arm Chair Mohair bottom
1 Mahogany Claw Table
1 large ~~deal~~ Oak Dining Table Oval
1. looking Glass Gilt frame
1. Wire fender
1. Set of Fire Iron's
1. Footman & 1 Copper Tea Kettle
1. Carpet

Killadoon the 26th of September 1807
Furniture in Stewards Room

1. Mahogany Arm Chair Mohair Bottom
11. dinning Chairs Mahogany & Mohair Bottom's.
1. Deal Table
2 Oval Oak Tables
1 Screen
1. Tea Tray Mahogany
1. Steel Fender
1. Set of Fire Irons
1. Deal painted Press
1. Turkey Carpet

Killadoon the 26th of September 1807
Furniture in Servants Hall

1 long deal Table
3 deal forms
1 Set of Fire Irons
1 Green Glass lamp

Killadoon the 26th of September 1807
Furniture in Footmans Bed Room

2 Deal Beds
2. Palliasses
2 Feather Beds
2 Bolsters
2 Under Blankets
2 pair of Upper Blankets
2 Blue Sarge Quilts lined with white
1. Deal Table
1 Oak Chair
1. looking Glass cracked

Killadoon the 26th of September 1807
Furniture in House Maids room

3 Beds with 4 Feather Beds – 3 Bolsters
3 pair of Blankets upper one's
3 under Blankets
23. Blue & White Sarge Quilts
1. Cotton Quilt
3 Oak Chairs
1. Oak arm Chair
2 Green painted Rush bottomed chairs
1 deal Table
2 Beds – 2 Palliasses
3 Feather Beds
2 Bolsters

2 Under Blankets 2 pair Upper Blankets
2. Quilted Stuff Quilts
2 Chairs
3 Deal Chairs
1 Stool
2 Rush Bottomed Stools Chairs
1 Deal Table

Killadoon the 26th of September 1807
Furniture in Cooks Room

2 Beds with Curtains
2 Feather Beds
2 Bolsters
2 Blue & White Sarge Quilts
1. Deal Press lock &
1 Deal Table
2 Green Rush bottomed Chair
1 Old Oak Chair

Killadoon the 26th of September 1807
Furniture in Bed room over Pump Room

1 Field Bedstead
1 Palliasse
1 Feather Bed
1. Bolster
1 Under Blanket
1 pair of Upper Blankets
1. Old Cotten Quilt
1 painted Press
1 Shabby Oak Table
2 Oldfashined Mahogany Chairs
2 Rush Bottomed Chairs
1. looking Glass

Killadoon the 26th of September 1807
Furniture in Butlers Room

1 Four Posted Bed Check Curtains
1 Palliasse
1 Feather Bed
1 Bolster
1 Under Blanket
1 pair of Upper Blankets
1 Cotten Quilt
1 Set of Mahogany Drawers with Desk
1 Set of Oak Drawers
1 Oak Table A Mahogany Table
1 Mahogany Table

Killadoon, County Kildare

1 ~~Deal Horse~~
2 Old fashioned Mahogany Chairs
2 Rush Bottomed Green Chairs
1. looking Glass
1 pair of Tongs & 1 Poker
1 *Press Bed with Feather Bed Bolster ~~& under~~*
1 *pair Blankets*

Killadoon the 26th of September 1807
Furniture in House Keepers Room

1~~2~~ Field Bed's Check Curtains
1~~2~~. Palliasses
2 Feather Beds
1~~2~~ Bolsters
1 Pillow – 1 Arm Chair with Damascus Cover
~~1 Hair Mattrass belonging to second Nursery~~
1 Set of Deal Drawers lock & Key
1 painted Press lock & Key
2 Oak Tables
1 Mahogany Table
2 looking Glasses in Mahogany Frames
                          1 Sent to the Landery
1 Oak Horse
4~~5~~ Rush bottomed Green Chairs
1 piece of Carpet
1~~2~~ Under Blankets
1~~2~~ pair of Upper Blankets
1~~2~~ ~~Cotten~~ Tufted Quilts
~~in this Room is a Feather Bed & bolster~~
~~& pair of new Blankets belonging to~~
~~Press Bed in Pantry~~

Killadoon the 26th of September 1807
Furniture in End Room Offices

1 Field Bed Stead with Check Curtains
~~2~~ Palliasses 1
1 Feather Bed
1. Bolster
1 Under Blanket
1 pair of Upper Blankets
1. ~~Cotten~~ blue Quilt
1. Painted Set of Drawers
~~1 Mahogany Deal Table with Drawer~~
1 deal Table & Shelf
1 looking Glass ~~hung up~~
2~~4~~ Old fashioned Mahogany Chairs
1 Rush Bottomed Chair

Store

4 *New Pillows*
3 *Old Do*
1 *Bed for Eagle Room 1 Bolster*
1 *Straw Mattrass*
1 *Hair Mattrass*
1 *Wool Mattrass*
4 *Feather Beds*
2 *Bolster covered with Blue*
1 *small Childs Mattrass*
4 *Childrens Blankets 1 under Blanket*
1 *large Tin Foot Pan*
1 *under & 1 pair Upper Blankets*
1 *pair & 1 under Blanket for Bed taken*
   from Dublin
1 *pair & 1 under Blanket for Eagle Room &* *Marseilles quilt*
   Calico Curtains for Soffa Bed
   Damascus Curtains for ᴧ² Beds from Dublin,
3 *Upper Blankets unpaired*
1 *Bolster*
1 *pair of Blankets 1 under Blanket*

   This is an Imperfect Inventory of
   things in the Store Room on this date

Large Room in Offices

1 *Four Post Bed Damascus Curtains*
1 *Palliasse*
1 *Flock Mattrass*
1 *Feather Bed*
1 *Hair Mattrass*
1 *Bolster 1 Pillow*
1 *Under Blanket 1 pair Upper Blankets*
1 *Cotton Quilt*
1 *Camp Bed Check Curtains*
1 *Palliasse 1 Wool Mattrass*
1 *Feather Bed – 1 Bolster 1 Pillow*
1 *Under Blanket 1 pair upper Blankets*
1 *Deal Dressing Table with looking Glass*
   in Mahogany Frame
1 *Spider Table Mahogany*
1 *Dressing Table with Glass – moved to the*
    Ladys room
1 *Painted Press*
1 *Mohogany Desk – moved to Lord Clement room*
2~~1~~ *Arm Chair 3 Chairs 2 Stools all*
   Rush Bottoms
1 *Clothes Horse*

1 Set of fire Irons
2 Window Curtains & Draperies
1 Bed Commode

Servants Hall

1 Long Table
43 Forums
1 Chair
1 Set of Fire Irons

Footmans Room

2 Deal Beds
2 Palliasses
2 Feather Beds – 2 Bolsters
2 Under Blankets
2 pair Upper Blankets
2 Quilted Stuff Quilts
1 Table

Butlers Room

1 Field Bed Check Curtains
1 Palliasse 2 Feather Beds – 1 under
  Blanket 1 pair Upper Blankets 2 Bolsters
1 Pillow
1 Table 1 Tool Press
2 Old fashioned Chairs
2 Mahogney Chairs
1 Set of Mahogany Drawers & Desk
1 looking Glass

Coach Mans Room

2 Beds
2 Feather
2 Under Blankets
2 Bolsters
2 Under Blankets
2 pair upper Blankets
2 Quilted Stuff Quilts
1 Chest of Drawers
1 Chair
1 Table

Laundery

4 new Tubs
1 Mangle — 4 Mangling Cloths
3 Horses
3 Tables
3 Chairs
2 Chests of Drawers
1 Mohogany Turnup Bed
1 Feather Bed ∧$^{1\ Bolster}$ 1 Under Blanket 1 pair
  Upper Blankets 1 Quilted Stuff Quilt
4 Baskets
7 Irons 1 Copper Skellet — 1 Iron for
  Blanket 1 under d^{o}

Inventory of Killadoon

1812, revised in 1829

Killadoon

10th of February
1812.

Hall

Two Curtains & Drapery
Eight Hall Chairs
One Foot Brush
One Sheep Rug
Four Mahogany Shutters
1829 One ~~Trou~~ Madame ~~Table~~ *Marble Table*
Two Card Tables
Three large China Jars
Two Smaller *Do* with Saucers
Two Smaller *Do* on Chimney piece
Bust of Mr Fox on *Do*
Bust of Lord Chesterfield *Bronze*
Clock & Bracket
one green Stool
One Sarcophagus Grate, Fender, & Fire Irons
one Scarlet Hearth Rug
~~Five~~ Six Brass Bell Weights 6
one Lamp, with three burners
two Brass Hoops in Corners for Umbrella's
1829 *one letter Box, Brass, & Tortoishell, inlaid*
1829 *2 Carved Battle Pieces in Brass & Ebony Frames*
1829 *3 White Marble Statues 2 Egyptian Granite Rochio's*

Library

One Library Table leather Top six Drawers.
One Silver Ink Stand
One Bronze Paper Weight
One Bronze Lamp
One Plated Stand for two Candles, with
    Shade, & Doubter
One Card Rack
One Letter box
One Round Table & green Cloth Cover
Two large Chairs, with reading Desks, &
    Candlesticks
Six Small Cane Chairs with Cushions
Two Roman Chairs
Two Window Stools & Cushions
Two Fire Skreens

One Grecian Sofa, with Cushion, Bolster & *(Pillow*
One Foot Stool
One Small Claw Table
One Register Grate, with Fire Irons, & Fender
One Hearth Rug
One Bronze Group on Chimney Piece
Two Bronze Candlesticks on *Do*
Three China Ornaments on *Do*
1829 ~~Two~~ Four Hand Skreens *4*
Two Black Velvet Bell pulls
Two enamelled Portraits in black & ormoulu frames
1829 *7* ~~Three~~ Drawings Gilt frames – *seven Drawgs*
Three Venetian Blinds   *frames do*
Two Callico Curtains & Drapery
One Sheep Rug
One Carpet
Thermometer outside the Window
Seven Bronze figures upon one Book
Case, Five bronze figures, & two Wedgwood
Do upon the other.
Two Red Morocco blotting books, on
Library Table
~~two Bister Drawings Gilt frames~~
1829 *4 Enamelled Portraits in Square Ormoulu frames*
    1 Sulphur Cameo Portrait of the late, Lady
        Landaff – in Brass, & Tortoishell frame
1829 *1 Verd antique Paper weight Bronze handle*
    1. lava Wafer Stand
    1 Square Mahogany Table
    1. Hearth Brush
    A Square Gibraltar Rock, Paper Weight, brought
    home by Sydney.

Drawing Room

One Steel Register Grate, with Fire Irons & Fender
One Hearth Rug
1829 Four Fire Skreens *views of Marino*
Two Hand Skreens, *Mahogany, with fluted silk*
Two Round foot Stools – ~~1 Hassock~~
Two patent Lamps on Chimney Piece
broken ~~One Etruscan Vase, & eight China Ornaments~~ *Do*
One Round Claw Table
Two Sofa Tables *with 2 Drawers each*
1829 One Square Table, *this Table is in the Library for*
    Maps books
One Small inlaid *Do*
One Reading Desk, leather Cushion to the stand
One Large Sofa, with four Cushions, two

PLATE 30
Antoine-Marie Melotte (1722–1795): *Battle of the Amazons*, battle-piece relief in wood after a painting attributed to Sir Peter Paul Rubens (1577–1640). See *Hall*, '*2 Carved Battle Pieces*', facing page, column 1.

	Bolsters, & two Pillows
	One Greecian Sofa, with three Cushions, one Bolster, & one Pillow
	Two large Arm Chairs a Cushion in each
1829	Five Tapestry Chairs.
	Four Chairs, Gilt Frames
	Eight Green painted Chairs *with Cushions covers &c.*
1829	Two Commodes Rose *Wood, Marble Tops, Plate Glass doors.*
	Two pier Glasses
	Two Etruscan Vases, & + four China Ornaments on Commodes
	One Marble Ink Stand, One China Ink Stand
	One Papillotte Case, one Candlestick, two Wafer Saucers, one Pen tray, & one Case of Dictionaries on Sofa Tables
	One Six leaved Skreen
1829	One Piano Forte – *NB. now, always hired*

One Rack for Music books *with Drawer*
One Axminster Carpet, & two Strips
One Large Portugal Mat
One Small Indian D⁰ at Door
Three Venetian Blinds
Three Silk Window Curtains   *Gilt Cornice.*
                              ∧ 6 Muslin Curtains
One Hearth Brush
One pair of Bellows
One Small Book Stand *with 2 shelves & Drawer*
Two Bell pulls *brass handles*
1829 ~~Five~~ Four Pictures – *in gilt frames*
One Red Morocco blotting book on Sofa Table
two Music Stools.
~~A Writing Table~~
two Rose Wood Stands for Books, with Busts on each of Lord Leitrim one of Lady Charlemont
2 Blue China Vases with Saucers.
1829 *1 inlaid French Commode under Claude Landscape*

Killadoon, County Kildare

1829 1. *French Clock with two figures on black stained*
          Stand, with Glass Shade
5. *Alabaster Vases on Chimney Piece.*
2. *China Flower Pots.*
2. *China Allumette Cases.*
1 *Alabaster Vase with four Pidgeons.*
1. *Green China Cup Saucer, & cover.*
2. *small China Figures*
1. *Gibraltar Rock Paper weight, brought by*
          Sydney. 1829
1. *Spring Sofa, seat Squab, 2 Pillows, calico*
          Covers lined.
          brought from Cheltenham 1826.
1. *Square stuffed Ottoman with Center, Calico*
          cover lined.
1. *Oblong Mahogany claw Reading Table on sliding*
          pillar.
1. *black stained flower table, with Tin center.*
1 *Gilt framed Tapestry Sofa.*
1829 2 *Feather hand Skreens.*
1829 1 *Square footstool shades of Green worked*
          by M^{rs}. B.
          2 *China Baskets with birds painted on them*
          twisted Ormoulu handles
          2 *Small China Candlesticks 1 extinguisher*
1829 *Green China Ink Stands of Carolines*
1829 2 *Cut Glass Eau de Cologne Bottles. 1 yellow*
          & white Glass bottle

Parlour

Sixteen red leather Chairs
Two *D^o* Arm Chairs
Two Sideboards
Three Dumb Waiters
One Canterbury
Two oval Tables
One Claw Table
One Set of Dining Tables, consisting of
          two ends, a Center & two leaves
One Cistern Stand
One Bottle Stand
One Tea Chest
One Sugar Chest
Two large China Jars
Two Indian Skreens *6 leaves in each*
One Fire Skreen
One Turkey Carpet, two bits, & a Hearth Rug

A Register Grate, Fender, & Fire Irons
One Marble Bust. *Medusa*
Two Bronze Lions
1829. M.L. ~~Two Wedgwood Vases~~ *NB these have been broken*
Two Patent Lamps
1829 Two Child's Chair & Table *in Store Room*
Four Window Curtains
Two pieces of Oil Cloth under the Side boards

Study

One Table Covered with Green Cloth 6 Drawers
One Mahogany Desk
One Ink Stand, with only two Bottles
One Small Mahogany table, with drawer
One Tapestry Sofa, with Cover
Two *D^o* Arm Chairs with *D^o*,
Five Rush bottomed Stools
One hair bottomed Mahogany Chair
One Carpet
One Bronze Boar
Two Allumette Cases
One Fender, & Set of Fire Irons
1829 6 *Rosewood stained Chairs Cane seats*
          2 *Crayon Drawings in Gilt Frames*
          1 *Moreen Curtain in two parts a Drapery &*
          3 *Brass Honeysuckle pin's*

Passage leading to the Offices

One Clock
One Mahogany table & drawer
Two portable folding up Stools
Two Mats
One Rug at the foot of the Stair Case
one Patent Lamp, with three Burners
One Window Curtain

Passage leading to the principal Stair Case

One Carpet
Three flower Stands
Two China Vases & Covers
Four China Flower Pots
One Barometer
One Patent Lamp with two Burners
One Sheep Rug

Stair Case

Carpeted, & brass rods
Two China Vases, & one Cover
One Patent Lamp, with two burners
Both Galleries Carpeted
One Table
Two Stools
One Window Curtain } in first Gallery
& Drapery
A Swing, in second Gallery
One Rug, & one China Vase in Water Closet
A Lamp with one burner in first Gallery
1829 *2 Oriental Alabaster Tables inlaid with*
Black Marble on Mahogany stands
1829 *1. White Marble Bust of Canova's Venus*

Lord Leitrim's Dressing room

One Carpet
One Hearth Rug
A Register Grate, Fender, Fire Guard, & Fire
Irons
Three Window Curtains
One Wardrobe
(*NB.* One Writing Table) one Ink Stand with three
in C.R. bottles
One Dressing Table
1829 one inlaid French Table *in Middle Bed Room*
One Bason Stand, & Looking Glass
A Silver bason & Ewer, Two Silver Wash ball
boxes, & four bottles with Silver Tops
A Glass Ewer & tumbler = A Spunge Saucer
One Alphabet Table
Two pier Glasses
Three Venetian Blinds
One Oil Cloth
One Dressing Glass
One Commode for Boots & Shoes
One Bidet
One Merlin Scales
One Fire Skreen
One Horse for Clothes
Two small book Shelves inlaid ~~with~~ ᵃ Drawer each
One Hunting Chair, with three Cushions, &
Callico Cover
1829 Three Tapestry Chairs with Covers
Four Cane Chairs
Two drawings in Gilt Frames
One Drawing in black frame

1829 Fourteen paintings in Frames 14
One Crayon Portrait in frame Glazed
1829 Twelve paintings without frames.
Two flower pots
Two Allumette Cases
One Thermometer
One Silver taper Stand
1829 A Square table with Drawer
a Yellow ware Feet Pan
~~a Square~~ Mahogany writing case brass clasps
1829 *a Square Library Table covered with Black leather with two*
kneeholes, & 18 Drawers, tumbler locks Key, Dᵒ
1829 *An Iron Chest*

Lady Leitrim's Bed Chamber

One Mahogany four post bed, on French Castors
with Chintz Callico Curtains, & Draperies, lined
with white – One Palliasse, one Feather bed, one
Mattrass, one Bolster, & Two Pillows – an Under
Blanket, a pair & a half of Upper Blankets,
a Marseilles Quilt, & an Eyder down Quilt
Two bed Steps
Two bed Commodes
Two Window Curtains, & Draperies matching bed
~~One Pier Glass~~
Two Spring Window Blinds
One Large Wardrobe
Two Corner Commodes
One Chest of Drawers
One Writing table with six Drawers
One Dressing table with Drawer
One Dressing Glass in Indian frame
One Bason table with Drawer
Two large Basons & Ewers
One Small Bason & Ewer
Two Soap Boxes } Blue & White
One tooth brush Stand
One Plate, one Mug
One Spunge Plate, Indian China
1829 ~~One Mug, Coalbrook Dale China~~ – *broken*
One pair of Snuffers & Stand
One Bidet
One hassock *or footstool, black, & red, upon*
black balls 1829.
A Six ~~Five~~ leaved Skreen *Moreen & Mahogany.*
One Sofa, with two Cushions, & two Pillows,
Chintz Callico Cover
One Grecian Dressing Stool, with Callico cover

Killadoon, County Kildare

One Hunting Chair, with Three Cushions,
    & Callico cover's
One Nursing Chair, with two Cushions,
    & Callico covers
Six Cane Chairs

1829. ML ~~A Small Writing table with Drawer~~
    one Ink Stand with three bottles – one blotting book
    Two Etruscan flower pot Stands
    One Horse for Clothes
    ~~one Pier Table~~
1829 ~~Two Book Shelves~~ *now in the Girls Room*
    One Register Grate, Fender & Fire Irons
    One Hearth Rug – one Hearth Brush
    One Brussells bed Carpet, & one Square *D⁰*
    Two Portraits, & two Landscapes
    One Wedgwood Déjeuné in tray
    ~~Four blue & white flower pots~~
    A pair of Derbyshire Spar Candlesticks
    One Caudle bason, stand, & Cover
    Eight Caudle Cups, Saucers & Covers
    Two plates to match *D⁰*
    One Cold Cream bowl, stand & Cover
    One Japanned Night Lamp
    One Foot Pan
    Two Night Vases, blue & white
1829 a Pembroke Mahogany Table with Drawer & Castors.
1829 a Mahogany Sécrètaire Brass Gallery & book case
    underneath
1829 a Bust of Lady Charlemont
1829 2 Blue Indian China Cups & Saucers
    2 Plumeaux for Dusting Furniture
    2 White & gold Allumette cases
    1 Green & bleu China ornamental bottle small.
    2 Paper hand Screens with prints
    1. Small Square Rug under Sécrètaire
    2. Green silk folding Screen's upon Brass, at each
        side of fire place.
    1. Small Oil Painting in Gilt frame Madonna
        & Child
    1. Drawing gilt frame glazed of M^rs. B.

Middle Bed Chamber

A Mahogany four post bed, on French Castors.
One Palliasse, one Feather bed, one Mattrass,
One Bolster, & two pillows – one Under blanket
one pair of upper blankets, & a Marseilles Quilt
Chintz Callico Curtains & Draperies, lined
with Blue

Two Window Curtains & Drapers to match *D⁰*
Two Spring Window blinds
Two Bed Steps
Two Bed Commodes, with Night Vases, blue & ^(brown
A Register Grate, Fender, & Fire Irons
One Hearth Rug
One Carpet
One Sofa, with one Cushion, two Bolsters, &
Four Pillows, in Callico Covers
One Dressing Stool, with Callico Cover
Eight Cane Chairs
One Foot ~~Stool~~ *Hassock*
One Dressing table & drawer, with dressing Glass
One large Dressing Glass, in Cheval frame, with
two Candlesticks, & Pin Cushion
One Wash hand Stand, with two large Basons,
   { Two Ewers, one Small bason & Liner, two
   } Wash ball stands, one tooth brush tray, all
     Blue & brown
one Small tumbler glass
One Foot pan
one Bidet
one Horse for Clothes
One Writing table, with drawer, an Inkstand
with three bottles, & Blotting book
One Wardrobe
One French Chest of Drawers mounted in brass
One night Table
On the Chimney piece, one French Bason,
Ewer & Cup – Two Caudle cups, Saucers, & Covers,
Two Wedgwood Candlesticks – Two Allumette
Cases, & two Flower pots.
A Small tin Kettle
1829 a Lavabo French Mahogany with White & gold
    Bason & Ewer – open cups – Almond Paste Pot
      & Cover
    cut glass tumbler, & cut glass bottle, with
      glass stopper.
1829 a French Mahogany Claw Table on Castor dove
    Marble Top
1829 from Lord Leitrims Dressing Room an Inlaid Table with
    Shelf Drawer lock & Key
1829 2 blue & gold Indian China broth basons Plates
    & Covers

Venus Room

A Mahogany four post bed, on French Castors
with Curtains & Draperies of yellow Callico
lined with blue – one Palliasse, one Feather bed,
& one Mattrass – one Bolster, two Pillows,
an under Blanket, a pair of upper Blankets,
& a Marseilles Quilt
Two Window Curtains, & draperies to match
the Bed
Two Spring Window blinds
A Register Grate, Fender, & Fire Irons
A Hearth rug, & Carpet
One Sofa, with two Cushions, & two pillows in
Callico covers
A Dressing Stool, with Callico cover
Eight Chairs with Cushions & Calico covers
Two bed Steps, & two bed Commodes with Night
1829 Vases, blue & white *Dove Marble Top & shelf to each*
~~A Night Chair~~ *Commode they [?] are French*
1829 Two inlaid Corner Commodes *one a night Chair,*
A Bidet
A Horse for Clothes
A Dressing Glass in Cheval frame, with two
Candlesticks, & a pin cushion
A Dressing table, with two drawers – *locks & Key.*
A Dressing Glass

1829 not here {
A wash hand Table, with two large Basons, two
large Ewers, one Small bason, two small Ewers,
two Soap Stands, one tooth brush tray, & one plate
Blue & White
}

One Foot pan, Yellow Ware
One Small Kettle
A Writing table, with Drawer, an Inkstand
Pen tray, & Candlestick, Coalbrook dale China
And a Blotting book
A French Chest of Drawers, mounted in brass
1829 A Mahogany Chest of Drawers – *French Marble Top*
One ~~Painting~~ Picture over the Chimney piece
On the Chimney piece – Three black
Wedgwood Ornaments, two Allumette Cases,
Two Delft Candlesticks, & two French China Cups
& Saucers — *a Bisciuit Group of four figures*
A Boot Jack
1829 *a pair of French gilt Candlesticks*
a French Mahogany Lavabo with Marble Top
White & gold Bason & Ewer open ditto cup, Almond
Paste Pot, & Cover – Glass Tumbler Glass Bottle
with Stopper

French Mahogany Claw Table on Castors Dove
Marble Slab
Hassock of Worsted work
a pair of Steel Snuffers Japanned tray

Eagle Room

A Sofa bed, with one Mattrass, two bolsters,
& a pillow in blue Callico covers, Curtains
Suspended by an Eagle blue & Pink
A Window Curtain & Drapery to match
Two Muslin Window Curtains on brass rod
A Register grate, with fender & fire Irons
a Hearth Rug, & Carpet
An oil Cloth
One Bed Commode, & Night Vase, blue & white
A Bidet
A Horse for Clothes
A Dressing table with two drawers
A Dressing Glass
A Bason Stand, with two large Basons,
two large Ewers, one Small bason, two Small Ewers,
one Mug, one Soap box, one tooth brush tray, one
Plate, blue & White, & one small tumbler Glass
One Washing Table
One Writing Table, with Drawer
An Ink Stand with three Bottles, & a blotting book
One Chest of Drawers
Eight Cane Chairs
A Chimney Glass, & a pair of Delft Candlesticks
A Boot Jack
A Rice Ornamented Cup on stand
2 Allumette Cases white & Gold

Dressing room to middle Room

A Register Grate, with Fender, & Fire Irons
A Hearth Rug
An Oil Cloth
A Large Wardrobe
Two Book Shelves
Two Brackets
An Alphabet Press
Eight Cane Chairs
Two Arm Chairs, with Cushions, in damascus Covers
One Tapestry Arm Chair in Damascus Cover
A Dimity Window Curtain
Two Muslin Window Curtains, on brass rod
A Dressing table & Drawer
~~A Dressing Glass~~

Killadoon, County Kildare

A Bason Stand, with looking Glass – two large
Basons, two large Ewers, one small bason, two
Small Ewers, a mug, a plate, a Soap Stand, a tooth
brush tray, A Night Vase blue & white, & a small
    tumbler Glass
A Bidet
A Small table
A Writing table & Drawer, an Ink Stand with
three bottles, & a blotting book
A Chimney Glass
Two Card racks
Nineteen Pictures
a Boot Jack
a Mahogany Clothes Horse on Castors with leaves
2 Old China candlesticks in the Shape of Monkeys
2 Derbyshire Spar Candlesticks mounted in White M.
1 Red & Black Wedgewood Tea pot with
Crocodile on Lid
1 Indian Chiny Broth Bason & Saucer
Drab colour with medallions of flowers
3 Small Indian China Cups & Saucers
3 Ditto Saucers & one Cover without a Cup
1 Bowl Cover & Stand of Embossed coloured
Indian China
1 Rice Chimney Ornament of Trees & Houses.
1. Mahogany Row of Pegs against the Wall
1. Mahogany Chest of five Drawers with locks & Key

Bow Window Room, Attic Story

A Four post bed, with Chintz Callico Curtains &
Vallances, a palliasse, Feather bed, Mattrass,
Bolster, Pillow, an under Blanket, a pair of
Upper Blankets, & a Marseilles Quilt
Three Window Curtains to match Bed
Two bed Commodes, with two Vases blue & white
A Bed Carpet, & a Square Carpet
An Oil Cloth
Two small bits of Carpet & a Hearth Rug
A Bath stove, Steel Fender, Fire Irons, & hearth brush
A Sofa, with two Cushions, two bolsters, & two
Pillows, in brown linen Covers
A Nursing Chair with two Cushions in Callico (Covers –
A Night Chair
A Dressing Stool with Callico Cover
Eight rush bottomed Chairs, two of them Arm Chairs
A Dressing table, with two Drawers
A Dressing Glass
A Horse for Clothes

A Bason Stand, with two large Basons, two
large Ewers, one Small bason & Ewer, a Mug,
a Soap box, & plate, a tooth brush tray, blue &
white, and a Spunge Saucer, Indian China
A Wardrobe
A Chest of Drawers
A Chimney Glass
A Portrait, & a Landscape
Two Book Shelves
2 blue & White indian China Flower Pots
2 blue & White English China flower Pots
2 White & Gold Allumette Cases

The Young Ladies Bed Chamber

Two Canopy Beds, with White Callico curtains
& Vallances, a Palliasse, a Feather bed, Mattrass,
Bolster, an under Blanket, a pair of Upper
Blankets & a tufted Quilt to each
A Waggon roof bed, with Chintz Callico Curtains
lined with White, a Palliasse, Feather bed,
Mattrass, Bolster, an Under Blanket, an
Upper Blanket, & a tufted Quilt
Three Bed Carpets
Two Window Curtains, & Vallances White Callico
Four Chests of Drawers
An Oval Table – An Octagon Table
An Oak Dressing table with Drawer
Two Mahogany Dressing tables with Drawers
A Small Mahogany table with Drawer
Two small Spider tables, & a Triangular table
A Tunbridge Ware Cabinet
Three Mahogany Stack Seats
Three Mahogany hair bottom Chairs
Two rush bottomed Chairs
One Mahogany Night box
A Looking Glass
Two Horses for Clothes
A Book Case *open with small shut ends*
A Wash hand Stand, Two basons & Ewers
& a foot pan, Yellow Ware
A Bath Stove, with Fire Guard, Steel fender
& Fire Irons
A Hearth Rug, & two Oil Cloths
Seven pictures in Frames
A Rush bottomed Dressing Stool
a looking Glass over Chimney Piece in White frame
a Mahogany book Case with Brass Trelace Doors.
a Mahogany Book Case between Windows with 2 Drawers

1829 a Bust or Cast of Apollo of Belvedere
a Mahogany Wardrobe with five Trays. – & four Drawers,
Tumbler locks & Keys – from Cheltenham

Lord Clements's Room

A Canopy bed, with White Dimity Curtains &
Vallance, a Palliasse, Feather bed, & Wool Mattrass,
A Bolster, an Under blanket, A pair of Upper
Blankets, & a Tufted Quilt — a Pillow
A Sofa bed, with two Palliasses, a Mattrass, & a
Bolster — *Calico Curtains & Bed posts in Store Room*
Two Children's beds, a Palliasse, Mattrass, Pillow
& White Callico Curtains & Trimmings to each
A White Callico Window Curtain & Vallance
Two Oil Cloths
A Deal table, & an Oak table with Drawer
An Oak Chest of Drawers
A Mahogany Child's Night Chair
T~~wo~~hree rush bottomed Chairs
A Horse for Clothes
A Looking Glass
A Mahogany Book Case
A Bath Stove, with Fender, & Fire Irons
A Portrait over the Chimney with Frame & Glass
a White Dimity Counterpan trimmed with muslin
belonging to Canopy Bed

Lord Clements's Room the 19th August 1829

A French Mahogany Bed with two Wollen, & 1 hair
Mattrass in White Bound Calico Cases.
a Round Mahogany Canopy with two Curtains,
  & valences of
White & blue Striped Calico lined with bleu,
  & bound, d.° d.°
French Window Curtain's in two parts to match
  Bed Valences
with Brass Rose Pins – & Japanned Leno Curtains in
  2 parts.
a Green & Black Carpet planned to Room
  a hearth Rug
a Bath Stove with Iron stand for Kettle a set of
  Fire Irons
steel with round nobs – a steel fender – Snuffers
  & Japan Tray
a Mahogany Dressing Table with Drawer lock &
  Key & Tray shelf
a Mahogany framed Dressing Glass
a Mahogany Writing Table with Drawer lock & Key

*a Mahogany Writing Table from L*d *L's dressing*
  R. carved legs, &
lift up Top on hinges Brass handles. 6 Drawers &
  on Castors
a Painted White & Green wash hand table with two shelves
  – 2 large
Basons & Ewers – 1 small Bason & Ewer, 1 soap stand
  1 Tooth Brush
Tray 1. Glass Decanter 2 tumbler Glasses – 1. Bed
  Commode & Vase.
1 Bidet – 2 Mahogany Chests of Drawers locks & Keys –
  brass handles.
1 Mahogany Clothes horse. 1 black stained ink stand
  3 bottles with
plated tops – 1. black painted chair on castors &
  2 Cushions Calico cases
1 Sofa with 2 squabs. 2 Bolsters. 2 Pillows in Calico cases.
  6 bleu painted
chairs. cane seats – 2 have cushions in Calico cases
  a Window seat with
cushion in Calico case – 2 bleu twisted Bell Pulls,
  with Tassels.
2 Allumette Cases
2 Glass bottles with Stoppers.
a Bronze Watch Stand an Indian Jos. a Globe in Case.
  a blue Footstool

The Nursery

2 Canopy Beds with white Calico Curtains &
  Trimmings
2 Palliasses 2 Feather Beds 2 Bolsters 1 Pillow, (there
are four Mattrasses & a pillow belonging to these two
Beds in store Room –) 2 under Blankets 2 pair of
Upper Blankets 2 Tufted Quilts.
2 White Calico Curtains & Valences for Windows
1. Childs Swing Bed with Dimity Curtains 1. Mattrass
1. Pillow – 1 under & 1. upper Blanket – 1 Quilt
1. Field Bed with Chintz Curtains – 1. Palliasse,
1. Feather Bed. 1 Bolster, 1. Pillow, 1 under Blanket
1. pair of upper Blankets 1. Tufted Quilt
One Grate with attached fire gard – 1. fender
1 set of Fire Irons
2. Oil Cloths
1. Oak Writing Table & Drawer One Oak Dressing
Table & Drawer, one Dressing Glass in Mahogany
Frame & Drawer the plate much cracked
2 oak Bason stands with yellow Basons & Ewers
a Yellow Ware Foot Pan

Killadoon, County Kildare

PLATE 31
Henry Bone (1755–1834), after unknown artist:
Nathaniel Clements, 2nd Earl of Leitrim (1768–1854), 1813,
pencil squared in ink for transfer

A Large White Wardrobe in three parts with Drawers in Center – Green Stuff Curtains to Glass doors.
1. Corner Mahogany Corner Press
1. Oak Chest of Drawers
2. Oil Clothes
1. Mahogany Clothes Horse
1. Crayon Portrait over Chimney piece. 1 *do do* opposite & a shade all in Gilt frames
There are six extremely old chairs

Rose Room

A Mahogany four post bed, with Chintz Curtains & Vallances, a Palliasse, two flock & one hair Mattrasses, a Bolster & Pillow, an under blanket, a pair of upper Blankets & a Marseilles Quilt
A Window Curtain to match Bed
A Bed Commode, & Vase blue & brown
A Sofa bed, with Chintz Curtains, hair Mattrass & bolster in Callico Covers
A Chest of Drawers
A Horse for Clothes
A Bidet – a Night Chair
Two bed Carpets, a Square Carpet, & an Oil Cloth
A Hearth Rug, a set of ʌ^{fire} Irons, & a hearth brush
Six ʌ^{rush} bottomed Chairs, one of them an Arm Chair
A Dressing table, with drawer – a small table
A Writing table & drawer
A Dressing Glass
Within the Sofa bed, four wool Mattrasses, Bolster, an under Blanket, & a pair of Upper Blankets

Ladies Maids Room

2. Field Beds with Calico Curtains – 2 Palliasses,
3. Feather Beds – 2. Bolsters, 2. Pillows, 2. Under Blankets 2. pair of Upper Blankets 2. Tufted Quilts
1. Deal Table with Drawer – 1. Spider Table
1. Small painted set of Drawers
1. Small Horse for Clothes
4. Rush bottomed Chairs
1. Iron swing footman on Grate
1. Set of Fire Irons – 1. Steel fender
1. Old Green Carpet
1. Looking Glass in White Frame over Chimney
2 Prints with Glasses & Frames
1. Dressing Glass

Pump Room

1. Stand for Brushing Coats
1 Deal Table & Drawers
1. Tin Bath

Bed Room Over Pump Room

1 Field Bed with Check Curtains, Palliasse Feather Bed, Bolster Under Blanket one pair upper Blankets a Stuff quilted Quilt
1. Oak oldfashioned fold up Chair
2. Rush Bottomed Chairs
1 Oak Table & Drawer
1. Painted Press
1 bed Carpet

2^d Spare Servants Room

1. Four Posted Bed Check Curtains – a Palliasse, Feather Bed, Bolster, 1 under Blanket 1 pair Upper Blankets – 1. Cotten Quilt – 1 Pillow
1. Mahogany Table with Drawer
1. Dressing Glass in swing frame
2. Old fashioned Mahogany Chairs
1. Rush Bottomed Chair
1. Bed Carpet
1. Oak Chest of Drawers
1. Pair of Tongs & 1. Poker
1. Oak Press Bed with Feather Bed Bolster under Blanket & one pair of Upper Blankets.
1. Clothes Horse

House Keepers Room

1. Field Bed Check Curtains – Palliasse, Bolster Pillow, Feather Bed, under Blanket, one pair Upper Blankets 1. Tufted Quilt
2 old pieces of Carpet
1. Deal Table & Drawer
1. Dressing Glass in Mahogany swing frame
1. small oak Table & Drawer
1. Mahogany Table & Drawer
1 Oak Chest of Drawers
1. Painted Press
1. Small oak Clothes Horse
4 Old Rush Bottomed Chairs
1. Arm Chair Damascus cover
1. Fender, 1, Shovel
1. Mahogany Press Bed 1. Feather Bed

Killadoon, County Kildare

3rd Spare Servants Room

1. Field Bed Check Curtains, a Palliasse Feather Bed, Bolster, Under Blanket pair of Upper Blankets, Stuff quilted Quilt
1. Small bit bed Carpet
1. Deal Table with Shelf
1. Dressing Glass swing Mahogany frame
1. Painted set of Drawers
2. Old fashioned Mahogany Chairs 1 Rush bottomed Chairs
1. Deal Press Bed a Feather Bed, Bolster under Blanket 1 pair upper Blankets

Large Room end of Offices

1. Four Posted Bed Green Stripped Damascus Curtains & Valences — Palliasse Feather Bed, Flock, & Hair Mattrasses, Bolster, Pillow, under Blanket 1 pair upper Blankets – 1. Cotten Quilt
1. Camp Bed Check Curtains — Palliasse, Flock Mattrass – Feather Bed, Bolster, Pillow, 1. Under Blanket 1 p^r upper blankets Chintz Quilt
1. Deal Dressing Table with Shelf
1. Swing frame Mahogany. Dressing Glass
1. Mahogany Dressing Table with looking Glass
1. Mahogany Spider Table
1. Mahogany Clothes Horse
1. Mahogany Desk Table
1. Bed Commode
1. Painted Press
2 Rush bottomed dressing stool's 2 Arm & 3 other Rush bottomed Chairs
1. Green Baize on floor
1. bit Carpet on hearth
2. Maroon & Yellow Window Curtains & Draperies
1. Oil Cloth in Passage to this Room

House Keepers Room

6. Stuffed back Chairs – Damascus covers
1. Arm Chair Mohair Bottom
1. Mahogany Claw Table
1. Large Oak Dining Table
1. Looking Glass Gilt frame over Chimney
3. Pictures in Gilt frames
1. Wire fender 1, set of Fire Irons
1. Footman, 1 Copper Kettle
1. Carpet
1. Window Curtain

Stewards Room

1. Mahogany Arm Chair Mohair bottom
11. Dining Chairs Mahogany frames Mohair bottomed
1. Deal Table
2. Oval Oak Tables
1. Mahogany Tea Tray
1. Steel fender. 1 set of fire Irons
1. Deal Painted Press
1. Turkey Carpet
1. Window Curtain
1. Looking Glass White Frame
6. Pictures Gilt Frames

Butlers Pantry

3 Painted Presses on Wall
2. Deal Supper Tables
3 Mahogany Chairs 1 Old fashioned Chair
1 Poker & Shovel – a Register Stove Grate

Servants Hall

1. Long Deal Table
4. Deal forms
1. Set of Fire Irons
1. Oak Chair

Butler Bed Room inside Pantry

1. Field Bed ~~Check Curtains~~ – a Palliasse Feather bed, under Blanket a pair of Upper Blankets – a Bolster, Pillow Cotton Quilt.
1. Table
1. Tool Press
2. Old fashioned Chairs 2 Mahogany Chairs – 1 Set of Mahogany Drawers & Desk
1. looking Glass hung up

Footmans Room inside Hall

2. Deal Beds – 2 Palliasses 2 Feather Beds,
   2 Bolsters 2 Under Blankets, 2 pair of
   Upper Blankets 2 Quilted Stuff quilts.
1. Table – 1 Looking Glass

House Maids Bed Room

2 field Beds & Curtains – 2 Palliasses
   3 Feather Beds. 2 Bolsters, 2 Under
   Blankets. 2 pair of Upper Blankets,
   2 Quilted Stuff Quilts
3 Deal Chairs, 1 Stool, 2 Rush Bottomed
   Chairs, 1. ~~Ta~~ Deal Table

Cooks – Room – beyond Kitchen

1. Four Post Bed with Green Stuff Curtains
   1 Feather Bed 1 Bolster. 1 under Blanket
   1. pair Upper Blankets – 1 Quilted Stuff Quilt.
1. Field Bed with Curtains – 1 Feather Bed,
   1 Bolster, 1 pair Blankets, 1 under Blanket,
   1 Quilted Stuff Quilt
1. Deal Press
2. Green Rush bottomed chairs
2. Tables
1. Looking Glass

Coach mans Room

2. Beds – with Feather Beds – 2 under Blankets
   2. pair upper Blankets 2. Bolsters, 2 Quilted
   Stuff Quilts
1. Chest of painted Drawers
1. Chair
1. Table

Laundry

4. New Tubs
1. Mangle – 4 Mangling Clothes
3. Horses
3. Tables
3. Chairs
2. Chests of Drawers
1. Mahogany Press Bed — with Feather Bed
   1 Bolster 1. under Blanket 1. pair of Upper
   Blankets – 1 Quilted Stuff Quilt
4. Baskets
7. Irons. 1. Copper Skillet
1. Ironing Blanket & 1. under *do*
1. Looking Glass hung up

Killadoon, County Kildare

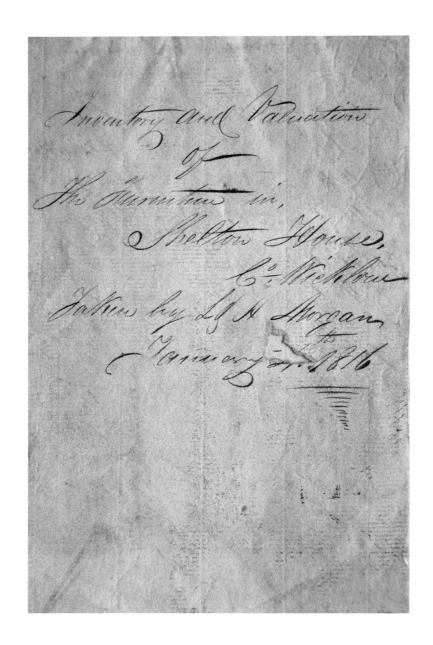

PLATE 32
Front page of the Shelton Abbey inventory, 1816

14

SHELTON ABBEY, NEAR ARKLOW, COUNTY WICKLOW
INVENTORY OF FURNITURE
1816

REBECCA CAMPION

THIS 1816 INVENTORY RECORDS a substantial Georgian house on the eve of its transformation into a fashionable Gothic 'abbey'. The Howards (earls of Wicklow from 1785) were a highly cultivated family, adroit at making advantageous marriages, and included politicians, collectors, soldiers, a bishop and a portraitist among their members.

Yet because this is an inventory of furniture and includes no books and a paucity of artworks, it gives little inkling of the unusually refined cultural and artistic interests of the Howard family. The collections at Shelton had been assembled over several generations, reflecting the particular interests or expertise of individual Howards. Dr Hugh Howard (1675–1737) travelled as a young man to Italy, where he studied under the Italian classicist painter Carlo Maratta (1625–1713) and on his return in 1700 established himself as a portrait painter in London. He also collected art and advised notable British patrons on their own collections. On his death, Hugh Howard's art collection and the house passed to his younger brother, Robert Howard, bishop of Elphin.

The bishop's remarkable book collection appears in this volume as 'A List of the books in yᵉ Studie att Elphin' (see pp. 95–103), but it seems that the books listed were left for his successor, Bishop Synge, rather than forming part of the library at Shelton Abbey. When a portion of the library at Shelton was sold by Sotheby & Co. in 1950, the sale catalogue included a manuscript list of books in the library of Ralph Howard, the bishop's eldest son, dated 30 December 1743. In their foreword to the sale catalogue the auctioneers wrote: 'The books at Shelton bear little definite evidence of previous ownership, but there can be no doubt that the major portion of this very interesting library has descended from Hugh Howard...' (Sotheby).

Ralph Howard, first Viscount Wicklow, undertook the Grand Tour as a young man in 1750–1 and, like more than two hundred other British and Irish grand tourists, sat to the leading portraitist Pompeo Batoni (1708–1787) in Rome (see plate 41). More unusually, Ralph Howard brought the artist Gabriele Ricciardelli to Ireland in the 1750s and commissioned views of Naples in rococo frames.

The portraits and picture collection were beyond the scope of this inventory, and many of the artworks recorded here not on display: in the 'Store Room', '30 old Oil paintings & 10 „ framed and glazied engravings' were valued at only £10 and in the 'Store Room over Kitchen', '4 oil paintings' were valued at £3 and '3 Engravings framed' at 18s. Traditionally the drawing-room was where the most valuable artworks were hung. Although this inventory does not list the pictures, it does record that the two most expensive items in the house were on the drawing-room walls: 'a large

Mirror in gilt frame' valued at £90 and 'a Large Chimney Glass' worth £50. The inventory also shows that the drawing-room was lit by two candelabra and two three-armed lustres, had a Brussels carpet the size of the room and extensive seating with three sofas, ten matching armchairs and ten painted cane chairs. Even without the paintings, the contents of the drawing-room alone represent a fifth of the value of the inventoried house contents.

The inventory records the eleven-bay, red-brick Georgian house just before its complete remodelling. The house had originally been built in 1770 by Ralph Howard with money from his advantageous marriage to the heiress Alice Forward. The substantial house was presumably part of his successful campaign to be elevated to the peerage. In 1818, only two years after this inventory was made, the 30-year-old William Howard, fourth Earl of Wicklow, inherited the long red house. Sensitive to the romantic potential of its site in the Vale of Avoca, he immediately commissioned Richard and William Morrison to create a Gothicized house with crenellated parapets and buttresses topped with pinnacles, arranged on each side of a Tudor-style porte-cochère (see plate 42). Entry was through a fan-vaulted 'Prayer Hall' and an octagonal tower contained the earl's study. The house was decorated with delicate Gothic plasterwork ceilings. In 1840 he added a second wing, 'The Nunnery', for his seven unmarried daughters.

After its brief spell as a hotel, the eighth Earl of Wicklow was forced to sell Shelton Abbey in 1950; the remaining contents and collections (excluding books) were dispersed in a thirteen-day auction (see plate 33), and, as we have seen, a portion of the books in a two-day sale later that year. The house is now an open prison.

The inventory is located in the Wicklow Papers in the National Library of Ireland, Dublin.

Shelton Abbey,
County Wicklow,
1816

Inventory and Valuation
of The Furniture in, Shelton House, Cº Wicklow
Taken by L & A Morgan, January 4th 1816

Breakfast Parlour

	£	s	d
Two Linen Calico window Curtains	3	"	–
A Mahogy Sofa uphd in Green leather	3	18	–
8 Arm Chairs to match	9	2	–
An Oval dining Table	4	10	–
One dº Smaller	2	5	6
A Green Ground Carpet	6	"	"
A Mahogy Card Table	1	4	–
A Dº pier Table	1	14	1½
2 fire Screens in Green Silk	1	16	–
A Chimney Glass	4	11	–
A Sett of Fire Irons & Wire fender and oil cloth Hearth Cover	1	16	–
59 framed and Glaized Engravings different Subjects	53	2	–

Drawing Room

	£	s	d
Two Window Curtains and Cornices	2	"	"
2 Window Stools	"	15	–
3 Sofas with Calico Covs	13	13	–
10 arm Chairs to Match	5	"	"
10 painted Cane Chairs 6s	3	"	–
A Mahogany voidore Table	2	10	–
A Dº Card Table	1	4	–
A Dº Spider Table	"	18	–
2 painted Chandelebra	6	18	–
2 Sattin Woodpier Tables & covers and 2 Marble vases	3	"	"
A large Mirror in gilt frame	90	"	"
A Large Chimney Glass	50	"	"

	£	s	d
Two fire Screens on poles and 2 painted dº on Stands	1	10	–
A Sett of Fire Irons and Steel fender & oil cloth Hearth cover	2	6	–
Two cut Glass Lusters with 3 lights Each	"	18	–
A Brussells Carpet to fit the Room	13	10	–
A Green Baize Cover	1	10	–

Bed Chamber Small Room off Breakfast Parlour

	£	s	d
A field Bedstead with calico curtains, a feather bed bolster and pillow hair Mattrass 1½ pr of Blanketts & Quilt	10	"	"
3 Rush Seat Chairs	1	1	–
A Spider Table	"	10	–
A night Stool	"	12	–
A Basin Stand	"	7	–
A Glass	"	10	–

Third Bed Chamber off Library

	£	s	d
A Waggon Roof Bed and Curtains palliss mattrass feather Bed and bolster and pillow 1½ pr of Blanketts and Quilt & 1 Window Curtain	13	"	"
A Mahogy Case of draws	3	"	"
A Dº night Table	1	10	–
7 rush Seat Chairs	1	1	–
A deal Dressing Table and Glass	2	10	–
A Mahogy Basin Stand	"	12	–
a Carpet Bedround	"	10	–

Shelton Abbey, near Arklow, County Wicklow

Second Bed Room off Library

	£	s	d
A Waggon Bed Calico Curt.^s palliasse Mattrass feather Bed Bolster and p.^r of pillows 1½ p.^r of Blanketts and Quilt	15	"	"
A Mahog.^y Case of drawrs	4	11	–
A Mah.^y night Table	1	10	–
A D.^o Circular Table	1	8	–
A D.^o Spider d.^o	"	16	–
A d.^o Bedside Commode	"	8	–
Seven Rush Seat Chairs	1	1	–
A Carpet Bed Round	"	15	–
A Sett of Fire Irons & fender and hearth cover	"	10	–
A Mahog.^y Cloaths airer	"	5	–
A deal Table and Dressing Glass	2	"	"
2 Calico Window Curt.^s	1	"	"
A Basin Stand	"	10	–

1.St Bed Chamber off Library

	£	s	d
A Waggon Bed and Curtains palliasse mattrass feather Bed and Bolster 2 pillows 1½ p.^r Eng.^l Blanketts & Quilt	16	"	"
A Mahog.^y Case of draw.^s	5	16	–
A d.^o Basin Stand	"	8	–
A D.^o Cloaths Horse	"	5	–
A d.^o Spider Table	"	10	–
A d.^o night Table	"	18	–
A d.^o Bidet and pan	"	15	–
A d.^o Bedside Commode	"	5	"
A Walnut Bed Chamebr [sic] Chest	1	18	–
A Barometer broken	"	10	–
6 Cane Seat Chairs	1	10	–
2 Calico Window Curtains	1	"	"
A Toilet Table and Glass	2	"	"
A Sett of Fire Irons and fender and Oil Cloth hearth cover	1	4	"
A Carpet Bedround	"	10	–

Bed Chamber Back of Library

	£	s	d
A Waggon bed and Curtains palliass mattrass feather Bed and bolster 2½ p.^r of Blanketts, bad 1 and Quilt	8	"	"
2 Window Curtains	"	15	–
A Carpet Bedround	"	5	"
A Mah.^y Secretary	2	10	–
A D.^o night Table	"	10	–
5 Cane Seat Chairs	"	15	–
A deal Table	"	5	

Bedchamber of [sic] Drawing room

	£	s	d
A Waggon Bed and Curt.^s Palliass and Mattrass feather bed bolster and pillow 1½ p.^r of Blan -kets and Quilt	15	"	"
A carpet Bedround	"	10	–
A Mahog.^y Case of d.^s	3	"	"
A D.^o Basin Stand	"	10	–
A D.^o Circular Table	"	18	–
Six Chairs upholst.^d St.^s	2	2	–
1 Window Curtain	"	10	–
A Toilet Table & Glass	2	"	"
A Bidet and pan	"	18	–
A night Table	"	19	6
a Fender	"	3	–

Best Bed Chamber over the Breakfast Parlour

	£	s	d
A 4 post Bed and Calico curtains palliass and mattrass feather bed & Bolster 2 pillows 1½ p.^r Blanketts & 2 Quilts	20	"	"
A Wilton Bedround	"	15	–
2 Window Curtains & cornices	2	"	"
A Mahog.^y Wardrobe	10	"	"
A D.^o Spider Table	"	10	–
A D.^o night Table	"	18	–
A 2 [sic] D.^o Basin Stands	"	15	–
A D.^o Bedside Commode	"	7	–
A D.^o Card Table	"	18	–
A D.^o Cloaths airer on Claws	"	7	–

A Bidet and pan	1	"	"
8 Chairs backs and seats upholst.ᵈ	4	"	"
2 large Arm Chairs	1	"	"
1 Easy Chair and Cover	2	"	"
A Toilet Table and glass	2	"	"
A Sett of Fire Irons and fender and Oil Cloth Hearth Cover	"	10	–
1 Looking Glass in Gilt frame	4	11	–
23 framed and Glazed Engravings	5	15	–

Bed Chamber (L.ᵈʸ Eleanors)

A Waggon Bed & Curtains Palliasse and mattrass feather Bed and bolster 2 pillows 1½ p.ʳ of Blankets & Counterpain	13	"	"
1 Window Curtain	"	15	–
A Mah.ʸ Case of draw.ˢ	2	18	–
2 A D. º Spider Tables	1	10	–
A Toilet Glass	"	15	–
A Basin Stand	"	7	–
3 rush Seat Chairs	1	1	–
A Bedside Carpet	"	2	–
A night Stool	"	8	–

Great Stairs

Six pieces of Wilton Stair Carpeting & 28 brass rods	8	12	–

Atticks 1ˢᵗ flight of Stairs

A field Bed Check curt.ˢ feather Bed and bolster 1½ p.ʳ of Blanketts and Blue Quilt	5	"	"
2 Chairs	"	6	–
A Walnut Case of drw.ʳˢ	"	5	–

Large Attick over State Bed Chamber

A 4 post Bed Crimson Morine Curtains 2 Mattrasses 2½ p.ʳ of Blanketts & Leige Quilt	2	"	"
A field Bed and Green Marine Curtains feather Bed and Bolster 1½ p.ʳ of Blanketts & Leige Quilt	5	"	"
Two Chairs	"	3	–

Store Room

30 old Oil paintings & 10 „ framed & Glaized Engravings	10	"	"
4 Horse Shuts	6	18	–
An Old Case of drawrs	"	10	–
2 old Chairs & Cushons	"	10	–
A Bidet	"	5	–
A night Stool	"	10	–
23 parts of delfe bed-chamber Ware	"	19	–

Store Room over Kitchen

2 Chamber Chests	4	"	"
A Small 4 post bed and check Curtains	2	10	–
Six feather Beds 8 bolsters 10 pillows	25	"	"
4 Chairs with cushons	1	4	–
A Sofa with mah.ʸ frame	3	10	–
A Walnut Sect.ʸ	2	10	–
A mah.ʸ night Table	"	10	–
3 Engravings framed	"	18	–
4 Oil Paintings	3	"	"
3 large Leather Trunks	3	"	"
A Camp Chair	"	5	"
Sundry Calico and Check bed and Window Curtains in 24 parts	2	"	"

Shelton Abbey, near Arklow, County Wicklow

Nursery

	£	s	d
Two field Beds with check curtains 3 feather Beds 1 mattrass 3 pair of blankets 3 White Quilts & 2 Bolsters	10	"	"
A Walnut Table	1	4	–
An Oak Case of drawrs	1	"	"
2 Rush Seat Chairs 2 large arm Chairs and 2 Window Seats	"	12	–
2 Mah^y Spider Tables	"	10	–
A looking Glass (broken)	"	5	–
2 Check Window Curt^s	"	8	–

Mens Servants Attick

	£	s	d
2 Field Beds and Check curtains 2 feather beds & bolsters 2 pair of blank-etts and 4 palliass covers	6	"	–
2 Deal Tables	"	8	–
5 Chairs	"	6	–
A press Bed	"	10	–
A Mahog^y Wine Cooler	"	8	–

Anteroom off Drawing room Leading to Back Stairs

	£	s	d
8 Chairs	2	"	"

House Keepes [sic] _bed_ Room

	£	s	d
A field Bed and Curtains feather Bed and bolster 2 pillows 1½ p^r of Blanketts & White Quilt	6	"	"
A Walnut Table	"	6	–
A Secretary	1	10	–
3 Chairs	"	9	–
1 night Stool	"	5	–
A Dressing Glass in Swing frame	"	18	–

Coachmans Room

	£	s	d
Two Standing Beds 2 feather Beds 3 blank^{ts} and 2 Quilts	6	"	"
A Circular Table	"	5	–
3 Chairs	–	6	–
1 Deal Table	"	2	–
A feather Bed and bolster 2 old Blanketts and Quilt and 2 old Chairs in Helpers Room	2	2	–

Grooms Room

	£	s	d
A feather Bed & Bolster	2	"	"

Servants Hall

	£	s	d
2 deal Tables	3	"	"
1 deal Cloaths Horse	"	10	–
2 Forms	"	10	–

Kitchen

	£	s	d
Thin Deal Tables	1	"	"
Thin forms	"	6	–
An Eight Day Clock	2	"	"
A Deal Cloaths horse	"	5	–
A Choping Block	"	5	–
1 – 2^{qr} – 12^{lb} Copper old & new – 1^{qr}. 21^{lb}. of Pewter 10 dish covers 6 brass flat Candlesticks 2 high Iron D^o 4 smoothing Irons a Kettle Stand a Tin Coffee pot a pair of Scales and Weights	10	"	"

House Keepers Room

	£	s	d
8 Chairs	1	4	–
2 Small Tables	"	18	–
2 Sq^r Tables	"	10	–
a Bread Box	"	8	–
A Calico Window Curtain	"	6	–
A deal Table	"	3	–
A Sett of Fire Irons and fender	"	5	"

China Closett

Tea China

17 Breakfast cups and Saucers (odd, ones)			
1 Slop Bowl			
2 Sugar Bowls			
2 Tea pots	"	16	3
1 China Cover			
2 Cake plates			

Blue & White China

10 Dishes			
2 Soup D^o			
44 plates	5	16	–
13 Soup plates			
1 Gilt dish			

Desert B^{lk} & yellow

20 plates			
6 Leaves			
2 Basketts & stands	2	5	6
2 Sugar Stands			
3 Fruit dishes			

Pink China

20 Dishes			
2 Terreens			
4 Sauce Boats			
3 Butter Boats			
1 Salad Bowl	22	15	–
8 Round Dishes			
56 Dinner plates			
18 Soup plates			
34 Small plates			

Brown Edge Delfe

15 dishes 4 Sq^r D^o & covers 46 Soup Plates			
10 Small plates 3 Sauce Boats 2 butter d^o 2 fish d^o 1 Terreen	2	5	6
2 Baking dishes 1 Salad Dish 4 pickling Saucers			

Dining Room

A Sett of dining Tables Thin Tables & 4 leaves	11	18	–
20 Mahog^y Chairs in hair Cloth at 13/-	13	"	–
2 Mah^y pier Tables	3	8	3
2 „ Side Board Tables	10	"	"
2 „ Pedestals	4	11	–
3 „ Knife Cases	1	"	"
1 „ Wine Cooler	2	"	"
1 Japan^d plate warmer	"	18	–
2 plate Bucketts	1	16	–
2 Mah^y Dumb Waiters	3	"	"
2 pole Screens	"	10	–
A Sett of Fire Irons and Brass fender a Hearth Brush and Oil cloth hearth cover	1	10	–
A Mahog^y bottle cooper	"	18	–
A Green Ground Carpet	11	10	
3 Marine Window Curts and Drap^s with Cornices (Grey)	1	16	–
17 Engravings framed and Glaized	101	14	7

Hall

6 Mahog^y Chairs crested	9	"	"
2 Side Tables marble Tops	6	10	–
1 Dining Table	3	18	–
4 Busts & Bracketts	4	"	"
3 Composition figures	1	10	–
A Flower Stand	"	18	–
2 Mah^y Card Tables	2	8	–
A piece of Oil Cloth	"	16	–

Library

2 Calico Window Curt^s and Drap^s	1	10	–
6 arm chairs in Leather	6	16	6
A Mahog^y Writing Table	2	"	"
A D^o Card Table	"	18	–

Shelton Abbey, near Arklow, County Wicklow

A Mah.^y Sect.^y and Bookcase	8	"	"
A piece of Carpet	"	7	–
2 paintings in Oil	5	"	"
A Sett of Fire Irons & fender	"	10	–
A walnut Table	1	"	"
A Circular Convex Glass	"	19	6

Butles [sic] Pantry

Thin Mahog.^y Trays 2 Japannd *D.º*	2	5	6
16 Glass Wine Coolers			
13 Blue finger Glasses			
1 White *D.º*			
8 Beer Glasses			
8 Ale *D.º*			
4 Decanters	4	"	"
1 Pint *D.º*			
12 Tumblers			
32 old Hobnob Glasses			
12 Champain *D.º*			
8 *D.º* Wine Glasses			
33 Case Knives			
24 Forks			
20 Small Knives			
24 forks			
3 Carving Knives & forks			
2 flat Candlesticks	5	"	"
1 Tea Urn			
2 Mah.^y bottle coopers			
1 Japan.^d Tray			

Total All £ 932 · 12 · 8½

We have carefully viewed
the furniture above stated
and certify thier value to be
Nine Hundred & Thirty two pounds
Twelve Shillings & Eight pence
Halfpenny ^Stg

Valuation Ffees

£ 100 at 5 pc.^t	£ 5 –
832 · 12 · 8½ at 2½ pc.^t	20 ‑ 16 · 2
832 · 12 ‑ 8½	£ 25 ‑ 16 ‑ 2

Louis & Anthony Morgan
Janu.^y 9.th 1816.

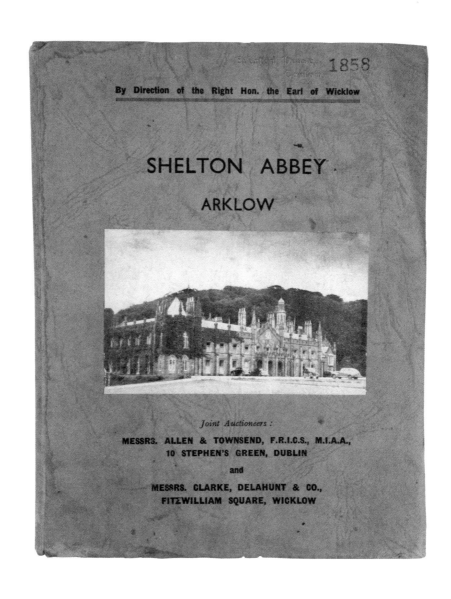

PLATE 33
Shelton Abbey, Arklow. Sale catalogue of the auction of the house's contents (excluding books) held jointly on the premises by Allen & Townsend, Dublin, and Clarke, Delahunt & Co., Wicklow, 16 October – 3 November 1950

PLATE 34
John Preston Neale (1780–1847) (draughtsman);
William Radclyffe (engraver) (1783–1855): *Borris House,
County Carlow*, published in 1819, engraving

15

BORRIS HOUSE,
COUNTY CARLOW
1818

EDMUND JOYCE

BORRIS HOUSE HAS BEEN the ancestral seat of the MacMurrough Kavanaghs, a family of ancient Gaelic origin, since at least 1570, and the importance of the house and of its survival into the twenty-first century in its original family hands cannot be overstated. The repeated confiscations and whittling down of Catholic-owned lands in Ireland down the centuries might have been expected to have eliminated, or at any rate decimated, those of the MacMurrough Kavanaghs. However, they succeeded in evading these threatening enactments, and preserved their estates by a combination of family solidarity, legal sleight of hand and prudential changes in their allegiances and (at least ostensibly) in their religion. Over the centuries, the Kavanagh estates expanded, peaking in the third quarter of the nineteenth century at 38,000 acres.

Borris House is an architectural palimpsest which has been reworked and extended on various occasions, including a reworking in the early 1660s and again in 1731. The most recent major makeover took place between 1813 and 1819, under the accomplished auspices of the architectural duo Sir Richard and his son William Vitruvius Morrison, and at the behest of Walter Kavanagh, a bachelor in his late fifties, who wanted to create an imposing family seat worthy of the ancestry and importance of the Kavanaghs.

Walter Kavanagh had been the owner of the house and estate since 1790. The house suffered external scarring following an attack by insurgents during the 1798 rebellion. But Walter seems to have been content to make good the limited damage caused at that time and to continue living in his largely unchanged ancestral home. The catalyst for the improvements of 1813 appears to have been an inheritance which he received *c.* 1812; this comprised the large Ballyragget estate, County Kilkenny, which had belonged to a Butler kinsman of his by then long-deceased mother, Lady Susannah. The Ballyragget Butlers had remained Catholic, and since all their Butler cousins were now Protestant, Walter, as their closest Catholic relative, was chosen as heir to the Ballyragget estate. (His Butler benefactor could not have foreseen that Walter's Catholicism would waver and that he would be buried in the Church of Ireland church at Saint Mullins, on the Kavanagh estate.) The prospect of a sizeable rental income from this estate allowed him to give immediate shape to ambitious plans for the house which he may have been harbouring for many years.

Work was in progress from 1813 to 1818, when Walter died unexpectedly. The Borris inventory is dated 1818 and is a probate inventory, one of a number of accountancy documents drawn up in connection with the winding up of his estate. Some of these others throw additional light on the inventory. Accounts of work done

237

by the Dublin cabinet-making firms of Morgan's and Preston's show that Walter had been busy adding to the collection at Borris up to the time of his death. Another account which appears in the probate documents is a charge from Walter's solicitor for his attendance at the premises of another such cabinet-making firm, Mack, Williams & Gibton of Dublin, to obtain an estimate of what fees they would charge for valuing the contents at Borris. This remit was subsequently given to Morgan's, who were the obvious choice granted that they already had a working relationship with the Kavanagh family, and were thus likely to be familiar with the house and the values associated with its contents.

Although the end of the Morrisons' improvements at Borris was within sight in 1818, the inventory captures a house which had not yet reached its final form. Nevertheless, it was not a building site, but a house richly fitted out for family living and entertaining. The luxurious bedrooms were fitted out with all manner of bedsteads, complete with drapes and dressings. The two drawing-rooms contained an array of seating furniture, from sofas to chairs to window seats. The dining-room was richly furnished with a multitude of mahogany pieces. The scarcity of precious metals and their association with coinage, placed silver on a pedestal when it came to the display of wealth. Values were based on weight, and despite the relatively modest array of 'solid plate' at Borris, it amounted to a value of £173 5s of the overall £1,056 5s 9d. By contrast, the Sheffield plate did not fare so favourably. Even though we know from Walter Kavanagh's diary for 1813 that some of it had been supplied by Edward Thomason of Birmingham at a cost of £150, the Birmingham pieces together with other lots of Sheffield plate were valued at a mere £50.

Considering the vast scale and endless wall space of Borris, it is surprising that a diminutive total of 5 oil paintings and 32 prints is recorded as adorning the principal rooms and passages. It is, however, possible that the bulk of the Kavanaghs' collection of paintings was stored elsewhere at the time of the valuation, and deliberately kept out of harm's way. The absence of paintings is comparable to the contemporary Carton inventory, both drawn up in houses that were in a phase of redevelopment. The lack of paintings at Borris may be explained by Lena Cowen Orlin's view in *Fictions of the Early Modern English Probate Inventory*, where she outlines that probate inventories may omit objects to 'which the deceased person did not have sole title'. These 'heirlooms', which may have included portraits, were often 'withheld from inventory and thus made unavailable to answer debts'.

The Borris inventory concentrates on the principal family areas of the house and excludes the service and ancillary workings of a by then sprawling mansion. As a result, the newly constructed chapel at the end of the main service wing does not feature. The house and its collection continued to evolve after 1818 and from the inventory it transpires that spaces such as Walter's 'Office' and 'Room over office' were precursors to the late 1820s double-height library which the Morrisons inserted at first-floor level.

A letter which accompanies the inventory, signed 'L & A Morgan', advises the wife of Walter's successor that the best way of 'keeping the S[t]eel work of Draw[g]. Room grate &c. is to rub them with Swee[t] oil & cover them well with powdered lime'. This inventory, in a notebook with a soft-bound cover, remains at Borris House in the collection of the Kavanagh family.

Borris House
1818

Furniture

[ROYAL HANOVERIAN ARMS]
MORGAN'S,
CABINET MAKERS & UPHOLDER'S,
To the Right Honble & Honble

The Commissioners of His Majesty's Revenue.
General Post Office, Board of Ordnance &c.&c.
N.º 21 Henry Street
Dublin

[Label pasted to inside front cover.
See plate 36, p. 245]

Henry Street
July 20th 1818

Sir

    We have the honor herewith
to send you the Inventory & Valuation
of the furniture of your House
the amount of which we consi
der as a fair value for the property
in question.

    We beg leave to acquaint Lady Eliz^{bth}
that the best mode of keeping the Seel [*recte* Steel]
work of Draw.^g Room grate &c is to rub them
with Sweel [*recte* Sweet] oil & cover them well with
powdered lime.

               We have the Honor to be
                     Sir
              Most respectfully
          Your most obedien[t]
T. Kavanagh Esq.   L & A Morgan

[Loose insert]

1

Abstract of the furniture &.^c
a Borris House and
Valuation thereof taken
July 16th 1818

Large Drawing Room

	£	s	d
two Square Sofas each with a Seat and 3 Back Cushions and two Bolsters also Calico Covers	11	7	6
8 Arm Chairs with cushions and Calico Covers	8	"	~
8 Small Chairs to Match (No Cushions) 10/~	4	"	~
2 Card Tables lined	4	11	~
3 Window Seats with Cushions	2	5	~
Two small Mahogany Pier Tables and Cabinet	6	16	6
	£ 37	0	~

2

	£	s	d
A Mahogany Tea store	2	"	~
A Square Mahogany pillar and Claw Table top to fold	6	"	~
A large Mahogany sofa Table	20	"	~
One Smaller *d.º*	4	16	~
A Grate Brass fender and steel fire Irons	22	15	~
A pair of painted Screens	"	10	~
3 Roller Blinds	3	"	~
one Hearth Rug	"	10	~

3

Small Drawing Room   96   11   ~

	£	s	d
3 Cained Arm chairs	2	5	~
4 Small *d.º* 10/~	2	"	~
A small step ladder	"	18	~
A Mahogany Circular Table	3	10	~
A Mahogany Dining Table	3	16	~
An upright Piana forte	15	"	~
A Brass fender and set of fire Irons	3	"	~

Cabinet

	£	s	d
a Circular Table	4	11	~
one Chair	"	15	~
2 Paintings in Oil	2	5	6

4

Hall — 134 11 6

10 Mahogany Chairs	5	*"*	~
2 Mahogany side Boards	1	10	~
A Maple stand	*"*	10	~
A Clock	2	10	~

Dining Room

3 Taboret window Curtains and draperies	3	4	9
2 Mahogany pier Tables	*"*	10	~
A Mahogany side Board	3	*"*	~
2 Mahogany dumb waiters 3 dishes each	3	*"*	~
12 Mahogany Chairs the Seats upholstered in leather	14	8	~
6 Arm Chairs to Match	10	16	~

£ 179 0 3

5

An oval Table on pillar and Claws	3	18	~
A Set of Imperial Mah*y* dining Tables	17	1	3
Two Mahogany Pedestals and Vases	3	*"*	~
A Set of fire Irons and wire fender and a Hearth Rug	1	6	~
A Circular Mahogany Table	2	18	~
A Mahogany sarophagus	2	10	~
A fire Screen with slides Covered in Moreen	2	*"*	~
2 Mahogany Supper Canterburys	2	4	~
7 framed and Glaized prints	3	*"*	~
2 paintings in Oil	30	*"*	~
2 Maps and a weather Glass	2	10	~

£ 249 7 6

6

Butlers pantry

6 Mahogany trays and one x stand	3	12	~
A press with 2 pair of doors	3	*"*	~

3 Mahogany Tables	4	*"*	~
1 deal *d*º	*"*	10	~
1 Oak *d*º	*"*	5	~
2 Chairs	*"*	3	~
Sundry Oil Lamps &*c*	1	10	~

7

Solid Plate — 263 7 6

2 Soup Ladles	
8 Gravy Spoons	
1 fish Trowel	
1 Salled fork	
6 dozen large forks	
3 dozen small *d*º	
1 dozen & 11 desart spoons	
2 dozen & 8 Tea spoons	
3 Sugar Spoons	
1 Marrow Spoon	
10 Wine Lables	
1 Sugar strainer	
10 Egg spoons	
1 dozen of Salt Spoons	
1 Tea pot	
1 Cream ewer	
6 oval Salt Cellars	

forward £ 263 7 6

8

Solid Plate Continued — 263 7 6

2 Wine funnells			
1 Butter Knife			
594 oz at 5/10	173	5	~

Plated Ware

1 Tea urn	
1 Coffey urn	
2 Coffey stands with Pots	
1 Tea Pot	
1 large Salver	
7 Small *d*º	
1 Sugar Bowl	
6 Wine Labbles	
1 Egg stand	
2 Ice Pails	
1 Cheese slaice	
4 Covered Dishes with stands	

forward £ 436 12 6

9

Plated Ware Continued

	436	12	6

2 Tureens with stands
4 Covered dishes
1 Apirn
2 Pair of Candle sticks
2 Pair of Cand d^o
3 Snuffers with stands
1 Bread Basket
6 Round Salt Cellars
2 Cruet stands
1 Tea Kettle with stand — 50 " ~
2 large Branches
4 Pair of Old Candlesticks
13 Bed Chamber Candlesticks
4 Sauce Boats with stands

£ 486 12 6

10

Principal Bed Chamber

A 4 Post Bed Mahogany Pillars
Cornice and footboard. A suit
of Morone Yellow Calico Curtains
A Palliass Curled Hair
Mattrass feather Bed bolster
and pillows a pair & half
of Blanketts a Marsellas — 50 " ~
quilt
3 Marone & Yellow Calico
Window Curtains Complete } — 18 " ~
3 white linen Roller blinds — " ~
3 Chairs upholstered Seats — " 10 6
2 Arm Chairs — " 10 ~
A Mahogany Wardrobe
with drawers in wings — 15 " ~
A d^o dressing Table and
Glass — 5 18 ~

tot wrong £3: —

£ 579 11 ~

11

A Writing Table — 2 10 ~
A deception Commode — 3 " ~
A Bidet — 1 " ~
A Chamber Table — 18 ~
A Case of Drawers — 5 18 ~
A washing Table and two
set of ware &^{c} — 2 10 ~

---

2 Bedside Commodes — 1 16 ~
Six Prints framed and
Glaized — 10 " ~
One Bedstep — 1 " ~
A Fender and set of fire Irons — 15 ~

£ 608 18 ~

12

Dressing Room

A sofa 2 Mattrasses a feather
bed and Bolster a pair of
Blanketts and a quilt — 15 " ~
A canopy and Curtains
to form a bed
A Window Curtain to Match
and a Roller Blind — 4 11 ~
A Mah^y Dressing Table — 2 " ~
1 Basin stand and ware — 1 " ~
A Mahogany Cloths press — 3 " ~
2 Chairs — 6 ~
3 prints framed & Glaized — 3 " ~
A fender — 5 ~
A Bedside stand — 5 ~

£ 638 5 ~

13

2nd Bed Chamber front

A 4 post bed a Suit of
Curtains and palliass fea
ther [sic] bed bolster & 2 pillows
a hair Mattrass a pair and — 22 15 ~
half of Blanketts and
a Marselles quilt
A dressing Table & Glass — 3 18 ~
A washing Table and ware — 2 " ~
A Chamber Table — 18 ~
A Chest of Drawers — 5 18 ~
4 Chairs — 1 " ~
2 Bedside stands — 1 " ~
A set of bedsteps — 1 " ~
A fender & set of fire Irons
and a hearth Rug — 1 10 ~
One painting in Oil 2 Prints
Glaized in Gilt frames — 12 " ~

£ 690 4 ~

14

Closet	690	4	~
A Camp Bedstead with Mattrass & Palliass	4	4	~

*Green Bed Chamber
and Dressing Room*

Dressing Room

A waggon Bed a suit of Curtains 2 Mattrasses a feather Bed & Bolster a pair of Blankets & a Counterpane	13	18	6
One Window Curtain and a Blind	4	18	~
A dressing Table & Glass	2	5	6
A Basin stand and ware		18	~
A Spider Table		10	~
3 Chairs		15	~
£ 717		13	~

15

A Cloths Airer		10	~
A Bedside stand		5	~

Bed Chamber Green Room

A 4 Post bed foot board and Mattrass & palliass feather Bed Bolster & pair of pillows 1½ pair Blanketts & quilt a suit of Curtains lined Green	45	"	~
A Mahogany Ward Robe on drawers	10	"	~
A Mahogany Deception Commode	3	"	~
A Cloths Airer	"	18	~
A Dressing Table & Glass	4	10	~
£ 781		16	~

16

3 Roller blinds	2	5	~
2 Bedside Commodes	1	10	~
2 Bed steps	2	"	~
3 Chairs		18	~
A Bedside Carpet		10	~

A Waggon Bed A Suit of Curtains a Palliass and Counter Pane	6	10	~
A Writing Table	2	16	~

Closet

A Washing stand and ware	2	10	~
A Bidet & Commode stand	1	"	~
2 Chairs		10	~
A dressing Glass	1	4	~
5 framed & Glaized Prints	10	"	~
£ 813		9	~

17

Matted Bed Curtains a 4 post bed a Suit of Cur tains a palliass a Mattrass a feather Bed & Bolster 1½ Pair of Blanketts and a Counter Pane	25	0	~
A Bed side Carpet		10	~
2 Calico Window Curtains	3	0	~
A dressing Table & Glass	2	5	6
A Basin stand & Ware		18	~
A Mah^y Case of drawers	5	18	~
A d^o Chamber Table	1	4	~
6 Chairs	1	16	~
2 Bedside stands & 1 Bidet	2	10	~
A fender & set of fire Irons		10	~
2 prints framed & Glaized	2	5	6
2 Bed steps		5	~
£ 859		11	~

18

Closet

A Waggon Bed Curtains & Palliass	4	11	~
A night Table and Commode Stand one Chair	1	16	~

Bed Chamber Governess Room

A 4 Post bed a suit of Curtains a palliass Mattress and feather Bed bolster 1½ pair Blanketts & Counter Pane	20	"	~

PLATE 35
Madame de Beaurepaire [Françoise-Cunégonde
Chacheré de Beaurepaire] (c. 1763–1856):
Walter Kavanagh, 1808, pastel

1 Bedside Commode		5	~
A Sofa & Cover	1	4	~
2 Window Curtains	4	"	~
A Dressing Table & Glass	4	"	~
A Basin Stand and Ware	"	18	~
A Shaving Stand & Ware	2	5	6
	£ 898	10	6

19

A Cloths Horse	"	12	~
7 Chairs and Covers	1	16	~
A Bed side Carpet	"	10	~
A fender and fire Irons	"	10	~
A spider Table	"	10	6
A night Table	1	16	~
A Mah^y Cloths Press on drawers	6	18	6

Bed Chamber

A Waggon Bed and Suit of Curtains 2 Mattrasses a pair & half of Blanketts and Counterpane a feather Bed and bolster and pillow	15	"	~
	£ 926	3	6

20

2 Mahogany Cases of drawers and a dressing Glass	5	18	~
A dressing Table	1	10	~
1 Basin stand		18	~
1 Small Mahogany Press	"	13	6
3 Chairs	"	7	6

Bed Chamber (Nursery)

A 4 post bedstead a suit of Curtains a Pallyass and Mattrass Bolster a Pair of Blanketts	10	"	~
3 Elm Tables	1	16	~
A Mah^y Spider Table	"	5	~
5 Chairs		10	~
3 Mah^y Cloths Presses	10	18	~
	£ 958	19	6

21

2 looking Glasses	2	10	~
4 prints		12	~
A Chamber Clock	4	10	~
A fender & fire Irons		3	6

School Room

A Waggon Bed 2 Mattrasses a feather bed and Bolster & a suit of Curtains	7	10	~
A Mah^y Voidore Table	2	5	6
A Case of drawers and a Book case	3	8	3
7 Chairs	1	1	~
1 dressing Glass		10	
	£ 981	10	9

22

Room Over Office

A Mahy Cloths Press	2	18	6
One Case of drawers	3	10	~
A Voidore Table	1	4	~
Sundry lumber & Boxes	2	5	6
An Arm Chair	"	3	~
A Medicine Chest & stand	1	10	~
2 Prints framed and Glaized	3	10	~
	£ 996	11	9

Office   23

A Mahogany writing table on Presses the top lined with Cloth & having two desks	10	"	~
3 Mah^y Bookcases & drawers	25	"	~
A Mah^y Case of Drawers	3	8	3
9 Chairs	9	"	~
A shoe stand	1	"	~
A Writing Table	2	10	~
A Voidore Table	"	18	~
A Sofa	"	16	3
Sundry small Boxes &c	2	10	~
A Basin stand & Table	"	10	6
A Cloths Horse	"	10	~
A framed & Glaized Eng^g	4	11	~
An Iron Chest	3	"	~
forward £ 1060		5	9

24			
Amount forw^d	£ 1060	5	9
Deduct			
Error in tot of page 6 £ 1 ~			
do " " 10 – 3			
	4		
	£ 1056	5	9

We have carefully viewed the furniture of the House al [*recte* t] Borris & have valued il [*recte* t] to the best of our judment, amo.^t One Thousand & fifty six pounds five Shillings & Nine pence

Lewis & Anthony Morgan

Henry Street
July 20th 1818.

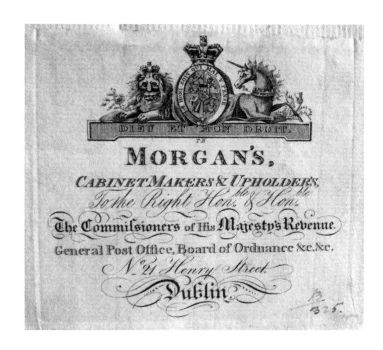

PLATE 36
Label of Morgan's, Cabinet Makers & Upholders pasted to the inside front cover of the inventory

PLATE 37
The Carton library bookplate showing the arms of the dukes of Leinster, pasted on the inside front cover of a copy of John Rocque's *A Survey of Kilkea: One of the Manors of the Right Hon*[ble] *Iames Earl of Kildare*, 1760

16

CARTON HOUSE,
COUNTY KILDARE
1818

EDMUND JOYCE

THE LANDS AT CARTON in County Kildare have, since Norman times, belonged to the FitzGeralds, earls of Kildare. Their principal seat until the mid-eighteenth century was at nearby Maynooth Castle. The lands were leased in the mid-seventeenth century to a junior branch of the Talbots of Malahide Castle, who built the first house on the site. After the Williamite victory in 1691, the leasehold was confiscated from James II's lord deputy of Ireland, Richard Talbot, Earl (and Jacobite Duke) of Tyrconnell. In 1703 the lease was sold by the trustees of the forfeited estates to Major-General Richard Ingoldsby, Master General of the Ordnance and a lord justice of Ireland. Under the tenure of the Ingoldsbys the house was enlarged and formalized. A large landscape by William van der Hagen, dated *c.* 1730, of Carton and its demesne, portrays an elegant nine-bay Palladio-inspired central block with flanking wings sitting comfortably in a formal park of parterres and avenues (see plate 49). The reversion of the lease was sold to the FitzGeralds in 1739 and Carton soon became their principal seat.

This 1818 inventory was created at a significant time in the history of the family and of Carton House. Augustus Frederick, third Duke of Leinster, then aged 26, was shortly to marry Lady Charlotte Augusta Stanhope, daughter of the third Earl of Harrington. Preparations for this must have necessitated changes at Carton, as did his recent sale of Leinster House, the family's Dublin town house, to the Dublin Society in 1815. Carton had now to become the sole architectural manifestation of his unique (in Ireland) status as a duke, the centre of his future marital and presumably family life, and the showcase of the now consolidated collection from both houses. Unfortunately, the £10,000 received from the sale of Leinster House went only a small way towards the vast improvements required at Carton. The value of Leinster House had plummeted following the Act of Union of 1801, and his father, the second duke, who died in 1804, had failed to act quickly enough to sell to greater advantage. The decision to sell had perforce been deferred until Augustus Frederick reached his majority, and the much knocked-down price received was an encouragement to him to economize by stripping the house of its most valuable chimney-pieces and other contents and to incorporate them into the ongoing reworking of Carton. Keeping an account of these ever-growing additions, which included the 'Leinster House Linen', was obviously an important factor in the inventory's creation. The inventory was also needed to keep track of the displaced parts of the established collection at Carton, which according to the displacement of 'old' items, were now relegated to the upper storeys and other less public spaces.

The most expensive and extensive aspect of the third duke's reworking of Carton was the dining-room and other new accommodation added by his architect, Sir Richard Morrison. The inventory throws new light on the precise timing and sequence of Morrison's work. A plan, watermarked either 1813 or 1815, by Robinson Carolin (who is assumed to be a draughtsman of Francis Johnston's) shows the house with the present arrangement of ground-floor rooms, excluding the wings designed by Morrison. Bryan Bolger's measured drawing of 1815 reaffirms this layout and that the quadrants linking the main block to the wings, were still in place in 1815. A subsequent survey of 1819, also by Bolger, documents the extent of Morrison's reworking of the house. It shows that the quadrants had been removed and replaced by two large volumes, one, the south wing, accommodating a suite of rooms, including the duke's study, and the other a large dining-room. Until now, architecturally speaking, the sequence of events in the four years between 1815 and 1819 has remained shrouded in speculation. The array of rooms documented in this 1818 inventory indicates that the south wing was in fact complete and fitted out at the time when the inventory was taken but that the north wing, which contained a new dining-room, was not yet complete. The new dining-room, and an anteroom already extant as part of the main body of the house and known to have been refurbished around this time (the extent of which was subsequently lost in a fire of 1857) are both omitted from the run of rooms on the ground floor, suggesting that both were still part of a building site. The dining-room which is included, complete with 'organ', is in fact the double-height, rococo-dressed parlour designed by Richard Cassels for the nineteenth Earl of Kildare in 1739. Bryan Bolger (d. 1834), measurer and architect, produced survey drawings for many of the Morrisons' commissions. His association with Carton, which began in July 1815 and continued until February 1825, saw the production of many measured drawings and copious survey notes.

The inventory represents many of the everyday routines of country-house living with no space escaping the eye of the assessor; from the parade of formal rooms down to the 'Bullock Yard', the 'Slaughtering House' and the 'Pidgeon Paddock'. It does not start, as might be expected, with the principal run of reception rooms but, instead, at attic level, descending floor by floor to the principal floor before exiting into the wings, the yards and the ancillary buildings beyond. The utilitarian nature of the service areas at Carton provides a sharp contrast to the richness of goods found in the family areas. All manner of art objects adorn the grand parade of reception rooms.

Despite the considerable content and the magnitude of this tome, the inventory lacks information about the collection of paintings at Carton. The very few paintings that are mentioned throughout the house are grouped by subject, such as '5 Portraits, Gilt frames, Glazed' with no mention made of either the sitter or the artist. Room No. 4 of the attic storey is described as 'full of paintings and prints', which would indicate that the bulk of the collection may have been relocated there for safekeeping from what must have been pretty much a building site. The only painting in which the subject is identified, is a miniature of Augustus Frederick's great aunt 'Lady Louisa Connolly [Conolly]', who was by then 74 and still living at Castletown House (see plate 45).

Ownership of Carton left the FitzGerald family in the 1920s. By the early twenty-first century the house, now restored, had been subsumed into a large hotel complex.

The inventory is the property of the Castletown Foundation and is held in its archive.

Carton House
1818

[TABLE OF CONTENTS]

A

Attic Story	*Page* 1 to 21, [253–4]
Attic (Old or Middle Story)	23 to 49, [254–6, 265–7]

B

Bed Room, Summer	55 [268]
ditto, Autumn	57 [268–9]
ditto, Spring	67 [270]
Billiard Room	89 [274]
Brew House	187 [289]
Bake House	189 [289–90]
Bacon House	189 [290]
Barrack Rooms	195 to 203 [290–2]

C

Cellars	161, 175 [285, 287]
Cellar, Store	173 [287]
Coal Vaults	187 [289]
Chip House	225 [297]

D

Dressing Room, Summer	*Page* 51 [267–8]
ditto Autumn	59 [269]
ditto Winter	63 [269–70]
ditto Spring	65, 71 [270, 271]
ditto adjoining study	77 [272]
Dining Room	87 [273–4]
Dillons M.ʳ Room	193 [290]
Dairy &c	211 to 215 [293–4]

E

Engine House	209 [293]

F

Forge	*Page* 217 [295–6]
Rooms attached	219 [296]
Farmyard	227 to 237 [297–9]

G

Groom of the chambers Room	93 [274]
Granary	209 [293]
Garden	241 [300]
Gardiners House	243, 245 [300–1]
Green House & Pinery	245 [301]
Garden Lodge	249 [301]
Gate Lodges	263, 265 [303]

H

Hall and Stairs	91 [274]
Hall, outside and Passage	93 [274]
House Stewards Room	95 [274–5]
House Stewards office	97 [275]
House Maids Room	99 [275]
ditto 1.ˢᵗ and 2.ⁿᵈ	177 [288]
ditto Lists	179 [288]
House Keepers Rooms	111, 113 [276]
ditto Storeroom	117 to 125 [277–9]
House linen	127 to 141 [279–82]
Hall, servants	157, 159 [285]

I

K

Kitchen Storey	*Page* 95 to 107 [274–6]
Kitchen	147 [283–4]
Kitchen Boys Room	185 [289]

L

Library, Small	81 [272]
ditto Large	83, 85 [272–3]
Larder	155 [284–5]
Lamp Room	169 [287]
Laundry & Rooms attached	181, 183 [288–9]
Lead House	225 [297]

N

NOTE

The page numbers shown in this table of contents refer to the original manuscript. Page references for this transcript are given in square brackets.

PLATE 38 (overleaf)

Sir Richard Morrison (1767–1849): Engraved plan and elevation of the garden front at Carton after Morrison's additions of *c.* 1815

PLAN AND ELEVATION OF CARTON TH[E]

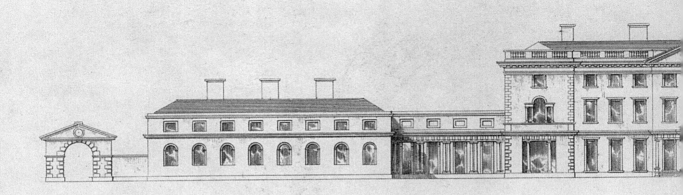

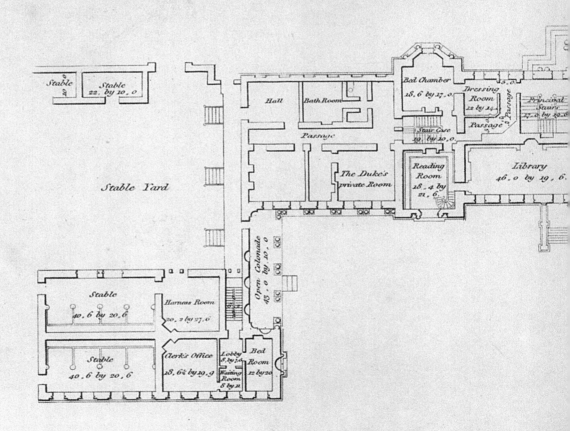

EAT OF THE DVKE OF LEINSTER.

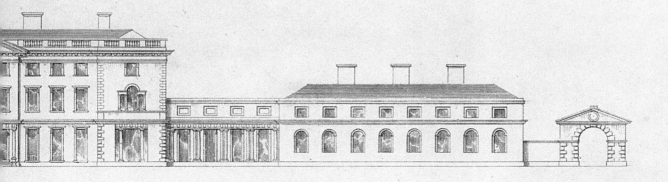

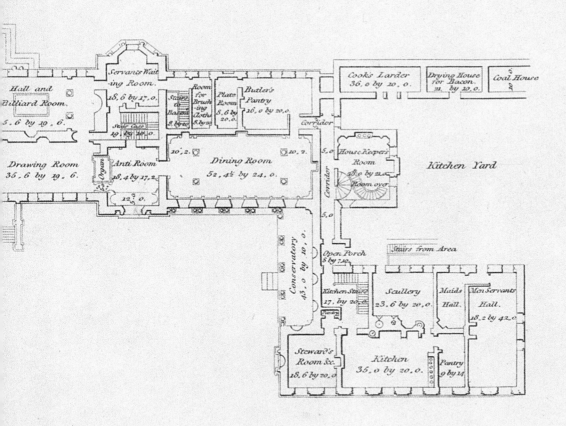

O		
Own Mans Room & Closet		171 [287]
Office	his Graces	225 [297]
d°	Carton	191 [290]
P		
Passages	Lumber	109 [276]
d°	closet	115 [277]
do	to Housekeepers room	125 [279]
do	to Servants Hall	159 [285]
do	to cellars	175 [287]
do	to M.ʳ Dillons room	189 [290]
Pastry		151 [284]
Pantry,	Glass	163 [286]
d°	plate	167 [286]

S		
Sitting Room, Spring		*Page* 73 [271]
Study, His Graces		75 [271–2]
ditto old		79 [272]
Stewards Room		143 [282–3]
Scullery		153 [284]
ditto to Glass Pantry		165 [286]
Stillroom		175 [287]
Sheals, M.ʳ Room		185 [289]
Stables &c		205, 207 [292–3]
Stewards House		217 [294]
Ditto Old		239 [300]
Shepherds House		239 [299]
W		
Watchmans Room		187 [289]
Workmens Shops &c		221, 223 [296–7]
Waterstown		251 to 261 [301–3]
Y		
Yards		223 [297]

PLATE 39
Mack, Williams & Gibton (attributed to):
Rosewood-banded mahogany dining-table, *c.* 1815,
probably commissioned by Augustus Frederick
FitzGerald, 3rd Duke of Leinster (1791–1874) for
the newly built dining-room at Carton House

Inventory of Furniture
& of Carton House
January 1st 1818

Attic Story
Room Nº 1

One deal Bedstead painted
One feather Bed and Bolster Cotton Tick
One pair of English Blanketts
One under Irish Blanket
One cotton quilt lined
One small Bit of carpet
One deal painted press   (Lock and Key)
Two deal painted Tables with drawers
One dressing Toilet Glass Mahogany frame
One White Bason Ewer And Vace
One old Chair covered in silk and Brass Nailed
One lock and Key to Door.

3

Room Nº 2

Two painted cradle Bedsteads with deal sides
Two feather Beds and Bolsters with cotton Ticks
One English Blanket   2¼ yards wide
One under Irish   do   1¾   „   do
One Cotton quilt lined
One Chcker   do   do
One deal painted press   (Lock and Key)
One deal painted Table and drawer
One Old Chair covered in Silk and Brass Nailed
Two Water Jugs and Two Vaces
One Lock and Key to Door

5

Room Nº 3

Two deal Bedsteads painted with sides
Two feather Beds and Bolsters cotton Ticks
One pair of Irish Blankets   1¾ Wide
One under   do   1¾   do
One pair of English Blankets   2¼   do
One under   do   do
Two checker quilts lined
Two deal presses painted with locks and Keys
One deal Table with drawer painted
Two old Chairs covered in silk with Brass Nails
Two small Bitts of carpits ¾ square
One Bason Ewer And Vase
One Lock and Key to Door.

Room Nº 4

Full of paintings And Prints

7

Room Nº 5

2 deal cradle bedsteads with sides painted
1 feather bed & bolster cotton tick
1 Borderd   Do Do   linen tick
1 Single english Blanket 2¼ wide
1 Under Irish   Do   1¾ Do
1 English Blanket (an under one)
1 Pair ditto   2½ wide
1 Cotton Quilt lined
1   Do   lined
2 deal painted Presss with locks & Keys
1 deal painted Dressing Table & Drawer
1 old Toilet Glass
1 Bason 2 Ewers & 1 Vase
1 white
1 old chair coverd in silk & brass nails
1 old Rush chair
   Lock to the Door
   Two panes Glass broken in Window

9

Room Nº 6

1 Cradle bedstead with deal sides painted
1 Feather bed & bolster cotton tick
1 Plain Wool & Hair mattrass
1 pair English Blankets 2¼ wide
1 Single Irish   Do   1¾ Do
1 Feather Pillow
1 Cotton Quilt lined
1 painted deal Press with lock & key
1   ditto   Table with Drawers
1 piece old Carpet ¾ square
2 old chairs covered in silk & brass nails
1 old arm chair & case
1 Toilet Glass
1 White Ewer Bason & Vase
   Lock & key to door

11

Room Nº 7

1 Cradle bedstead with deal sides painted
1 Feather bed & bolster cotton tick
1 Pair Irish Blankets 1¾ wide
1 under   Do   1¾

Carton House, County Kildare

1 Cotton Quilt lined
1 Painted deal Press lock & key
1 old chair
1 Painted deal Table with drawer
1 Shaving Glass
1 White bason Water Jug & Vase
Lock & key to Door

13

Room Nº 8

1 Cradle bedstead deal sides painted
1 Feather bed & bolster cotton tick
1 Pair Irish Blankets 1¾ wide
1 under *Dº* 1¾
1 Painted deal Press lock & key
1 *Dº* Table & drawer
1 old Chair coverd in Silk & brass Naild
1 old rush chair
1 Small bed Carpet
1 Bason Water Jug & Vase
1 Cotton Quilt lined
Lock & key to Door

15

Room Nº 9

1 Cradle bedstead deal sides painted
1 Feather bed & bolster
1 Pair Irish Blankets 2¼ wide
1 Irish under *Dº* 〃
1 Chequer Quilt lined
1 Painted deal Press lock & key
1 old arm chair gilt
1 old chair coverd in Silk & brass naild
1 Painted deal Table & drawer painted
1 Toilet Glass 14 × 10
1 White Bason & Vase
Lock & key to Door

17

Room Nº 10

1 Cradle bedstead deal sides painted
1 Feather bed & bolster cotton tick
1 Pair Irish blankets 1¾ wide
1 Under *Dº* 1½ 〃
1 Cotton Quilt lined
1 Piece of old Carpet
1 deal Press painted no lock or key
1 Painted deal Table with a drawer
1 old chair cover^{d} in silk & brass naild
1 Frame of Shaving Glass
1 White Bason Jug & Vase
Lock & Key to Door

19

Room Nº 11

1 Cradle bedstead deal sides painted
1 Feather bed & bolster cotton tick
1 Pair Irish Blankets 1¾ wide
1 Under *ditto* 1¾ 〃
1 Cotton Quilt lined
1 Painted deal Press & lock & key
1 *Dº* *Dº* Table with drawer
1 old chair coverd in silk & brass naild
1 Small bit Carpet
1 White Bason & Jug
Lock & Key to Door

21

Room Nº 12

1 Cradle Bedstead deal sides, painted
2 Feather Beds and two Bolsters
1 Single Blanket 1¾ wide
1 Under Irish Blanket 1½ wide
1 Cotton Quilt, lined
1 Piece of old carpet
1 Painted deal press Lock & Key
1 *Dº* ~ *Dº* Table with drawer
2 Pieces of Old Carpet
1 White Bason, Jug and Vase
Lock and Key to door.

Attic Story Corrodore

1 Painted Deal press, Lock & Key
1 Cupboard, Lancewood
2 Bed Airers and pans

23

Old Attic or Middle Story

Room Nº 1

1 fourpost bedstead, fluted pillars, Buff Chintz and Calico Curtains, lined White,
1 Bordered Paliass
1 Bordered feather bed, Bolster and one pillow, Linen Tick

1 Bordered Hair Mattrass
1 pair of English Blankets   2½ wide
1 Under Irish D^o ~   2 wide
2 Chintz festoon Window Curtains lined,
1 Mahogany Wardrobe, wire doors at Top and
     Pannel^d d^o at bottom
1 Lancewood Chest of Drawers
1 Oak Press, lock and Key
1 Tambour Writing Tables, inlaid
1 Painted deal dressing Table
1 Old Chinese Table
1 Elm Spider Table
1 Toilette Glass   16 × 13
1 Mahogany Bidet and Delph Pan
1 Mahogany Commode, Broken pan
1 Japan^d foot Pan
1 Mahogany Clothes Horse
1   D^o ~ D^o with Boot Jack
3 Painted cane Seat Chairs
1 Old arm chair in Tapestry,
1 large wire fire guard, Brass mounted,
1 Sett of fire Irons and hearth brush
1 Copper Kettle
1 piece of Oil cloth 5 feet Square
1 Venitian Bedround Carpet
1 Round Shaving Glass
7 Prints, black frames, glazed
3 White Basons, a large Water Jug & Ewer
1 Small Water Jug, a Brush Stand, Gilt Chinese
1 Saucer, an Eye Cup, Croft and Tumbler & 1 Vase
     Lock and key for door

25

Room N.º 2

1 Small four post Bedstead 3 .. 6 wide, Chintz calico
     curtains, lined white
1 Bordered Paliass
1 D^o Hair Mattrass
1 D^o feather Bed, Bolster and pillows
1 Single English Blanket 3¼ wide
1 Under Irish Blanket 1½ wide
1 Marseilles Quilt   3 wide
2 festoon Window Curtains to match bed
1 Mahogany Wardrobe, Pannel doors
1 Oak Chest upon chest drawers
1 Painted Deal dressing Table
1 Elm D^o ~ D^o
3 Painted cane seat chairs

1 Old arm chair in Tapestry,
1 Mahogany Bidet & delph pan
1   D^o Night commode
1 Glass   16 × 12
1 Elm Candle Stand
1 Airwood Writing table
1 Mahogany Chamber Airer
1 Mahogany clothes horse with Boot Jack
1 large wire fire guard, brass mounted
1 Sett of fire Irons and Brush
1 Copper Kettle Nº 2
1 Venitian Bedround carpet
1 piece of Oil cloth 5 feet square
1 Tin Japan^d foot pan
3 white Bason, large and small Jugs and
1 Water Ewer, Brush Stand and Soap d^o
2 Delph candlesticks, Gilt, Tumbler & Croft
1 Tin shaving Pot, Stand and Vase
2 large old paintings in Gilt frames.

27

Room N.º 3

1 French Bedstead, Pallempore Calico curtains,
     lined Green,
1 Straw Paliass
1 Bordered hair Mattrass
1   Wool D^o
1 Bordered feather Bed, bolster and 2 White pillows
1 pair of English Blankets, 3 wide
1 Single D^o D^o
1 Marseilles Quilt D^o
1 Venitian Bedround Carpet
2 Buff calico chintz festoon Window Curtains,
     lined White,
1 Mahogany chest of Drawers, banded and Strung
1 painted deal dressing table
1 Elm D^o with drawers
1 D^o Voidore Table
1 Mahogany Bedstep, lined with Brussels carpet
2 painted cane Seat Chairs
1 Arm chair covered in Tapestry,
1 Mahogany Bidet and delph pan
1 D^o Chamber Airer
1 D^o Clothes horse with Boot Jack
1 Toilette Glass   14 × 13
1 large Wire fire guard Brass mounted
1 Set of fires Irons and Brush
1 Copper Kettle

Carton House, County Kildare

4 prints, black frames, Glazed
1 Tin Japan^d foot pan
1 Tin shaving Pot and Stand
3 white Basons and large Water Jug
1 Small Jug. 1 Water Ewer and brush Tray
   China Lancer [*recte* Saucer] and two china
      candlesticks, white and Gold
   Croft Tumbler & Vase
   One piece of Oil cloth 5 feet Square

29

Room N⁰ 4

1 Camp bedsteads and buff chintz calico curtains,
   lined White, 3 feet wide,
1 Old hair Mattrass
1 Bordered feather Bed & Bolster & pillow
1 Single English Blanket 2¾ wide
1 Old Irish under   *D⁰*
1 Very old Counterpane
1 festoon chintz calico Window Curtain, lined White
1 Mahogany Dressing Table, with drawer
1 Narrow   *D⁰*   *D⁰*
1 Toilette Glass   17 × 9
1 Painted Cane seat chair
1 Camp Arm Chair
1 Mahogany clothes horse with Boot Jack
1 piece of Oil cloth 5 feet square
2 white Basons, 1 Ewer, 1 Vase, Soap Stand, Tumbler
   & Croft
   Lock & Key to door

31

Room N⁰ 5

1 fourpost Bedstead & Buff Chintz Calico Curtains,
   lined White, 5 feet wide,
1 Bordered Paliass
1 *D⁰* hair Mattrass
1 *D⁰* feather Bed & bolster and Pillows
1½ pair of Old Blankets,   different Sizes
1 New ¹²⁄₄ Counterpane
1 Venitian Bedround Carpet
2 Buff chintz window Curtains, lined White
1 Oak Press, deal shelves (No lock or Key)
1 Oak chest of Drawers
1 Mahogany Dressing Table
1 Deal   *do*   painted
1 Cheval dressing Glass, Mahogany frame 28 × 48,
   2 Brass branches

1 Toilette Glass 13 × 16
1 Mahogany Night Table & Pan
1   *d⁰*   chamber Airer
1   *d⁰*   clothes horse & Boot Jack
2 painted cane seat Chairs
2 Arm chairs covered in Tapestry,
1 Large wire fire guard, Brass mounted
1 Sett of fire Irons
1 Copper Kettle
6 prints, views of the Lake of Killarney, Black
   frames, Glazed
1 Mahogany Bidet & Pan
1 Tin Japan^d foot pan
1 piece of Oil cloth 5 feet Square
3 White Basons, water Jug and Ewer
1 Brush tray, Soap pot, cover, Small Jug, Vase, croft
   & Tumbler
2 Delph candlesticks, Gilt edges

33

Room N⁰ 6

1 fourpost Bedstead, Oak pillars, 4 feet wide, Buff
   chintz calico curtains, lined white,
1 Bordered Paliass
1 Bordered hair Mattrass
1 Bordered feather Bed bolster and One pillow
1 P^r of English Blankets   2½ wide
1 Under Irish Blanket   2 wide
1 Marseilles Quilt   2¾ wide
2 Chintz calico Window Curtains, lined, White
1 Venitian Bedround Carpet
1 Mahogany Chest of Drawers (No Locks or handles)
1   *d⁰*   Spider Table
1   *d⁰*   Night Table (No pan)
1   *d⁰*   Bidet with Delph pan
1   *d⁰*   Clothes horse with Boot Jack
1   *do*   Chamber Airer
1 Deal dressing Table (painted)
4 painted cane seat Chairs
1 Arm chair covered in Tapestry,
1 Wire fire guard brass mounted
1 Sett of fire Irons and Brush
1 Copper Kettle
1 piece of Oil cloth 5 feet Square
1 Japan^d tin foot pan
1 Toillette Glass 16 × 13
6 Prints, black frames, Glazed,
3 White Basons, large and small water Jug

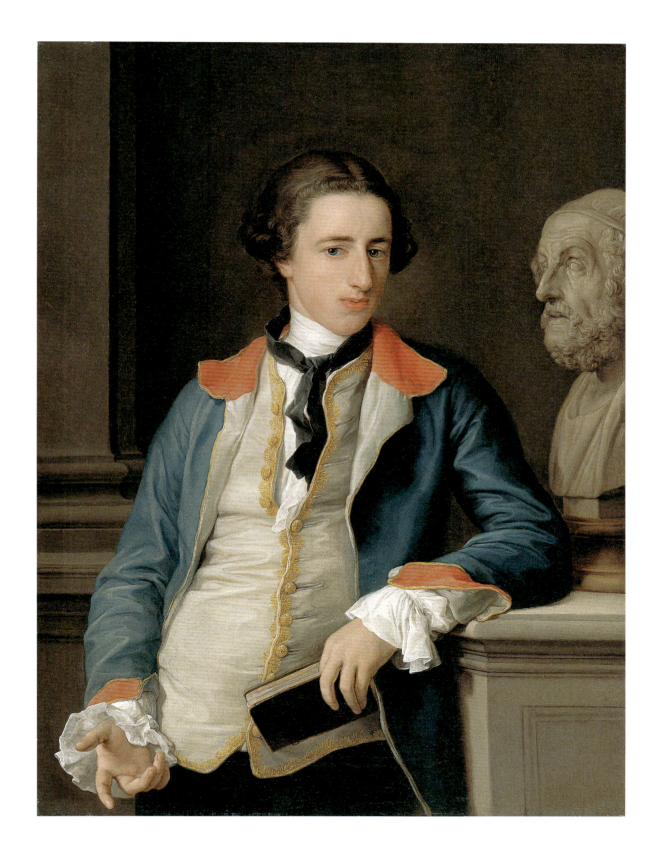

PLATE 40
Pompeo Batoni (1708–1787)
Robert Clements, later 1st Earl of Leitrim (1732–1804)
1754, oil on canvas

PLATE 41
Pompeo Batoni (1708–1787)
Ralph Howard, later 1st Viscount Wicklow (1726–1786)
1752, oil on canvas

PLATE 42
John Preston Neale (1780–1847) (draughtsman)
Engraved by William Radclyffe
Shelton Abbey
1820, engraving

PLATE 43
Artist unknown
Portrait of Walter Kavanagh (d. *1818*) *of Borris House, County Carlow*
oil on canvas

PLATE 44
Charles Robertson (1759–1821)
Charles Cobbe (1781–1857)
miniature in watercolour on ivory

PLATE 45
Hugh Douglas Hamilton, RHA
(1739–1808)
Lady Louisa Conolly (1743–1821)
1785, pastel on paper

PLATE 46
Gédéon Gaspard Alfred de Grimaud
[Alfred Guillaume Gabriel],
comte d'Orsay (1801–1852) (after
an original work attributed to)
*Augustus Frederick FitzGerald,
3rd Duke of Leinster (1791–1874)*
1830s, lithograph

PLATE 47
Hugh Douglas Hamilton, RHA
(1739–1808)
*Robert Stewart, 1st Marquess of
Londonderry, MP (1739–1821)*
oil on canvas

PLATE 48
Sir Thomas Lawrence, PRA
(Bristol 1769–London 1830)
*Robert Stewart, Viscount Castlereagh,
later 2nd Marquess of Londonderry,
KG, GCH, MP (1769–1822)*
1814, oil on canvas

PLATE 49
William van der Hagen (*fl.* 1720–1745)
An extensive view of Carton House, County Kildare, with Maynooth in the distance
oil on canvas

Water Ewer, Soap tray, Vase, croft & Tumbler
2 delph Candlesticks, Gilt edges
Lock & Key to door

Room Nº 7

1 fourpost Bedstead, with Canopy top 4 „ 6 wide
A suit of Buff calico chintz curtains, lined white
1 Bordered Paliass
1   *d*º   hair Mattrass
1   *d*º   feather Bed, bolster and Pillows
1½ pair of Old English Blankets, different Sizes
1 Old Counterpane
1 Feild Bedstead with chintz curtains 4 „ 6 wide
    lined white,
1 Bordered hair Mattrass
1   *d*º   feather Bed, bolster and pillow
2 old Blankets
1 old Counterpane
2 Buff Chintz calico festoon window curtains,
    lined white
1½ Yds Venitian carpet
1 Childs cott and Dimity Curtains
1 Hair Mattrass
1 Pillow
2 Blankets
1 Mahogany Chest of Drawers, Banded & Strung.
1 Deal painted dressing Table
1 Elm dressing Table with drawer
1 Toilette Glass 13 × 16
3 painted cane seat Chairs
1 Arm Chair & Cushion, Gilt
1 Cane seat childs chair
1 dressing stool covered in Carpet
1 Mahogany Chamber Airer
1   *d*º   Clothes horse with Boot Jack
1 Footstool covered with Carpet
1 Wire fire guard brass mounted
1 Sett of fire Irons and brush
1 Copper Kettle
1 piece of Oil cloth 5 feet Square
1 Small deal Spider Table
2 White Basons, 1 Water Ewer, 2 Vases, Croft
    & Tumbler.

Room Nº 8

A Fourpost Bedstead 4 „ 6 wide, Oak pillars, Chintz ⎫
    calico curtains   ⎬
    Lined with white   ⎭
1 Bordered Paliass
1   *d*º   hair Mattrass
1   *d*º   feather Bed, bolster and pillow
1½ pair of old English Sundry Blankets
1 Counterpane 2½ yds wide
1 Small 4 post Bedstead 3/6 Mahogany Pillars
    Buff Chintz calico curtains, lined white,
1 Bordered paliass
1   *d*º   Hair Mattrass
1   *d*º   feather Bed, bolster and Pillows
1 old English Blanket 3 yds wide
1 old Irish under *d*º.
1 old Counterpane
2 Buff Chintz calico festoon window Curtains,
    lined white
1 Oak Press with 2 inside drawers
1 Deal dressing Table (Top Split)
1   *D*º   *D*º   painted
1 Toilette Glass (frame Broken)
1 Mahogany Night Table (no pan)
3 painted Cane Seat Chairs
1 Mahogany chamber Airer
1   *do*   Bidet & delph Pan
2 pieces Venitian carpet 2 yds each
1 Tin foot Pan Jap^d
1 Wire fire guard brass mounted.
1 Sett of fire Irons and brush
1 Copper Kettle
2 Basons, two water Jugs, 1 Ewer and broken
    Brush Tray
1 Croft and tumbler
1 Tin shaving Pot, 1 Vase.
1 piece of Oil Cloth 5 feet square
1 Clothes Horse with Boot Jack.

In Room Nº 8 belonging to
Winter Bed room

A Bordered feather Bed, bolster and two festoon Pillows
3 English Blankets   3½ yds wide
1 Old Counterpane   2¾ „ wide
1 Sett of fire Irons

Carton House, County Kildare

1 Copper Kettle
1 Mahogany clothes horse with Boot Jack
1 Venitian carpet for Bed
1 Bordered Hair Mattrass.

Room N.º 9

1 Small four post Bedstead 3 ,, 6 wide with }
  Chintz Calico curtains lined white
1 Bordered Paliass
1 Bordered hair Mattrass
1 Bordered feather Bed, bolster and Pillow
1 Single English Blanket 3 wide
1 under Irish d^o 1¾ wide
1 Counterpane   2 wide
1 Venitian Bedround Carpet
2 Buff Chintz Calico Window Curtains, lined White,
1 Oak Press (No Lock)
1 Small Mahogany Press (no shelves, no Key)
3 painted cane Seat Chairs
1 Arm chair covered in Tapestry,
1 Deal dressing Table painted
1 Mahogany Spider Table
1 Toilette Glass 13 × 16
1 Mahogany Chamber Airer
1   d^o Clothes horse and Jack
1   d^o Bidet and Delph Pan
1 Japaned Tin foot pan
1 Wire fire guard, brass mounted
1 Sett of fire Irons and Brush
1 Copper Kettle
1 piece of Oil cloth 5 feet square
1 Bedside Commode
3 Basons, large water Jug and Ewer
  Small Jug, Soap Stand, Brush tray and Croft & 1 Vase
2 Delph Candlesticks, Gilt edges
1 print, Black frame, Glazed,

Room N.º 10

1 Field Bedstead and Buff Chintz Calico Curtains,
  (lined white)
1 Bordered Paliass
1   d^o hair Mattrass
1   d^o feather Bed, bolster and Pillow
1 pair of English Blankets 2½ wide
1 Single d^o 2¼ wide
1 Counterpane   2½ wide

2 Buff Chintz window Curtains (lined)
1 Old Oak Chest of drawers
1 deal dressing Table Painted
1 Elm d^o
1 Dressing Glass 13 × 16
1 Mahogany Bidet, delph pan
1   d^o Clothes horse with Boot Jack
2 Painted cane seat chairs
1 Arm chair covered in Tapestry,
1 Venitian Bedround Carpet
1 Japand Tin foot Pan
1 piece of Oil cloth 5 feet square
1 Mahogany Bedside Commode
1 Wire fire guard, brass mounted
1 Sett of fire Irons and Brush
1 Copper Kettle
3 large Basons, One Water Jug, One Small d^o
1 Water Ewer, Soap Stand, and Brush Tray
1 Croft, one tumbler and One Vase
2 Delph Candlesticks, Gilt edges,

Room N.º 11

1 Field Bedstead 4 ,, 6 wide }
  Chintz calico curtains, lined white
1 Bordered Paliass
1   d^o hair Mattrass
1   d^o feather Bed, bolster and Pillow
1 pair of English Blankets 2½ yds wide
1 Single Irish d^o 1¾ ,, wide
1 Counterpane   2¾ ,, wide
1 Venitian Bedround Carpet
2 Buff Chintz calico Window Curtains, (lined White)
1 Oak press 2 drawers inside
1 Mahogany dressing Table
1 Elm Voidore Window Table
1 deal dressing Table painted
1 Toilette Glass 16 × 13
1 Bedside Commode with drawer
1 Mahogany Chamber Airer
1 Clothes horse with Boot Jack
1 Mahogany Bidet delph Pan
1 Japaned Tin foot Pan
3 Painted cane seat chairs
1 Arm chair covered in Tapestry,
1 piece of Oil cloth 5 feet square
2 Prints, black frames, Glazed,
1 Wire fire guard, brass mounted

1 Sett of fire Irons and Brush
1 Copper Kettle
3 Basons, Water Jug and Ewer, Soap stand, One Vase
    Brush Tray, Tin Shaving Pot, Croft & Tumbler
2 Gilt edged delph Candlesticks

47

Room N<u>o</u> 12

1 Small low post Bedstead 3 „ 6 wide   }
  Buff chintz calico curtains, lined white   }
1 Bordered Paliass
1   *d.º*   hair Mattrass
1   *dº*   feather Bed, bolster and Pillow
1 pair of Eng.ʰ Blankets   2½ wide
1 Single   *dº*   2½ wide
1 Counterpane   2¼ wide
1 Venitian Bedround carpet
2 Buff chintz calico Window Curtain, lined,
1 Oak chest of drawers
1 Painted deal dressing Table
1 Mahogany Dressing Table
1   *dº*   Bidet and delph Pan
1 Japaned tin foot Pan
1 Mahogany chamber Airer
1   *d.º*   Clothes Horse with Boot Jack
2 Painted cane seat chairs
1 Arm chair covered in Tapestry,
1 Mahogany Night Table and Pan
4 prints, Black frames, Glazed,
1 piece of Oil cloth 5 feet Square
1 Wire fire guard, Brass mounted
1 Sett of fire Irons and Brush
1 Copper Kettle
3 Basons, large and small Water Jugs, Water Ewer,
    Soap Stand, Brush tray, Tin Shaving Pot, Croft,
    Tumbler & Vase
2 White & Gold china candlesticks
1 Dressing Glass 16 × 13,

49

Room N<u>o</u> 13

1 four post Bedstead 6 feet   }
  Striped calico curtains, lined white,   }
1 Bordered Paliass
1   *dº*   Hair Mattrass
1   *dº*   feather Bed, bolster and 2 festooned pillows
1 pair of English Blankets 2¾ wide
1 Single   *dº*   3¼ wide

1 Marseilles Quilt
1 Venitian Bedround Carpet
2 Buff Chintz festoon Window Curtains (lined white)
1 Bedstep, covered with Brussells Carpet
1 French Chest of Drawers, Brass mounted
2 Deal Tables
1 Deal dressing Table painted
5 Cane Seat Chairs
1 Toilette Glass   16 × 13
1 Camp Arm Chair
1 Mahogany Bidet and delph Pan
1 Japann.ᵈ Tin foot Pan
1 Mahogany Chamber Airer
1   *dº*   Clothes horse & Boot Jack
1 Piece of Oil cloth 5 feet square
5 Portraits, Gilt frames, Glazed,
1 Print   *dº*   *dº*
1 Wire fire guard brass mounted
1 Sett of fire Irons and Brush
1 Copper Kettle
3 Basons, 2 water Jugs, one Ewer, Brush tray,
    Soap Stand, Tin Shaving Pot and Stand ~
2 Delph candlesticks, Gilt.

51

Summer Dressing Room

1 Wardrobe Bed, Mahogany Pannell doors 3 „ 6 wide
  a Suit of Cheque red curtains
1 Bordered feather Bed, Bolster and Pillows
1 English Blanket   2¼ wide
1 under   *dº*   2   wide
1 Striped calico festoon window curtain
1 Sloping Mahogany Desk with drawers
1 Mahogany folding Top writing desk Table
1 Deal dressing table, two drawers
1   *Do*   on castors, no drawers
1 Toilette Glass   16 × 13
1 Cheval Glass, Mahogany framd 41 × 21 brass branches
2 Mahogany cane seat chairs, Cushions and Cases
1 Arm chair covered in Damask in Gilt frame
1 Mahogany chamber Airer
1   *dº*   Clothes horse and Boot Jack
1   *dº*   Bidet and Delph Pan
1 Japaned Tin foot Pan
1 Old Irish carpet 3¼ by 4
1 piece of Tapestry lined with linen 2¾ × 2¾
1 large Painting in Gilt frame
1 old   *dº*   Boys and Grapes

1 Wire fire guard, brass Mounted
1 Sett of fire Irons and Brush
1 Copper Kettle
2 White Basons, green edges, 1 Ewer and Vase
1 Water Jug and Ewer, tray stand, soap pot and cover
  Eye cup, Large white Bason and Water Jug
1 Tin shaving Pot, Croft and cut Tumbler
1 piece of Oil cloth 5 feet square

Closet of Summer dressing Room

6 Rush light Lanthorns
2 Japand tin foot Pans
1 Copper Bed Warmer
1 New sett of Steel fire Irons
24 plated Snuffers, Extinguishers and Tray
8 Chair Bottoms worked in Silk & Worsted (unfinished)
1   *d^o*   *d^o*   in Tambour frame
4 pieces of work for fire screens
2   *d^o*   Striped chair Bottoms
1 Sattin counterpane white lined, red silk fringed
33 yards of Stuffing Canvass
1 White sattin Mantle embroidered with white Sarsnet,
                     fringed with Gold
1 Small   *d^o*   & silk fringe
2 White Sattin cradle quilts (quilted)
1 Scarlet Velvet Mantle, embroidered with Gold and }
     Silver and lined with Scarlet Sarsnet.
1 Christening Pin Cushion
1 White Sattin christening Robe, trimm^d with point }
     Lace and lined with white Sarsnet
2 Caps, a Bib, a pair of Cuffs, a pair of Gloves of point lace
1 under Cap, a Shirt trimmed with Point lace
5 Caps, 1 Bib and 1 p^r of cuffs.
1 Small Basket
1 India Chest, Lock and Key
1 Painted Velvet stool cover
1 Looking Glass in Gilt frame, Centre plate 28 × 48
1   *d^o*   *d^o*   *d^o* 26 × 48
1 Small Glass round the plate of the above
2¼ yds of 4/4 Working Canvass
1 Tambour frame in Green Silk Bag.

Summer Bed Room

1 Large 4 post Bedstead 6 feet wide, Palampore
  Calico curtains, lined white,
1 Small Paliass
1 Old Plain hair Mattrass
1 Bordered Hair Mattrass, covered in Holland
1   *d^o*   feather Bed, Bolster and 2 fustian pillows
1 p^r of English Blankets   14/4
1 Single   *d^o*   13/4
1 Marseilles Counterpane 13/4
1 Venitian Bed round carpet
2 yds of *d^o* for dressing Table
2 Mahogany Bedsteps covered in Brussells Carpet
2 Festoon Window curtains
1 Mahogany Wardrobe, Wired doors at top, and Mahog.
                     pannelled doors }
     at bottom, with deception Commode   }
1 french chest of drawers, Ornamented with Brass
1 Elm dressing Table with drawers
1 Small Mahogany Table
1   *d^o* Spider Table
1 Cheval Glass, Mahogany frame 16½ × 41
1 Toilette *d^o*   19½ × 15½
2 Mahogany cane seat Chairs, Cushions & Cases
2 Old Arm Chairs, covered in Damask, Gilt frames
1 Mahogany Bidet and delph pan
1 Jap^d tin foot Pan
1 Mahogany Chamber Airer
1 piece of Oil cloth 5 feet sq^u
2 portraits in Gilt frames
2 Prints in Black frames, Glazed, An Old painting
  (Boys & Grapes)
1 Wire fire guard, Brass mounted
1 Sett of fire Irons and Brush
1 Copper Kettle
2 white Basons, green edges, 1 Jug & Cover, Soap
  stand and brush tray
1 Water croft & Cut Tumbler, large white water Jug
  and Bason
2 Green edged Vases.

Autumn Bed Room

1 Four post Bedstead, with Dimity curtains, fringed
1 old Paliass
1 Bordered hair Mattrass
1   *d^o*   fustian *d^o*

1   *d°*   feather Bed, Bolster and 3 fustian pillows
1 pair of English Blankets   14/4   1815
1 Single   *d°*   14/4   1815
1 Marseilles counterpane   15/4
1 Venitian Bed round carpet
1 piece of Tapestry   5½ × 3
2 Mahogany Bedsteps covered in Brussells Carpet
2 Dimity Window curtains & draperies, fringed &
     deal cornices
1 Indian Japan^d chest (lock and Key)
1 Small Indian cabinet on a frame
11 Indian dressing table ornaments
1 Tambour Airwood writing Table
1 Mahogany dressing Table 5 drawers
1 Deal dressing table on castors
1 Elm   *d°*
1 Mahogany Bidet and delph Pan
1 Cheval dressing Glass, Mahogany frame   27½ × 47½
1 Toilette Glass   14½ × 17½
3 Mahogany cane seat Chairs, cushions & dimity Cases,
1 Arm chair, covered in Damask, Gilt frame
1 Japaned tin foot Pan
1 Piece of Oil cloth 5 feet square
2 Large paintings in gilt frames   (Rivers)
4 Spar chimney Ornaments
4 China cups & saucers
5 Ornamented china Cups with handles
1 Mahogany chamber Airer
1   *d°*   clothes horse with Boot Jack
1 Wire fire guard, brass mounted.
1 Sett of fire Irons and Brush
1 Copper Kettle
2 Blue Basons, 1 small Jug & cover, 1 soap stand &
     Cover, 1 Brush Tray.
1 Eye cup, 1 cut croft and Tumbler, 1 large white Bason
1 Tin shaving Pot, 2 Vases.

59

Autumn Dressing Room

2 Dimity curtains & draperies, fringed, & Deal cornices
1 Sofa with cushion, 3 back cushions, 2 hair bolsters,
                     2 feather Pillows }
      one calico case and one dimity case
1 Scarlet India cabinet on Black frame
1 Gilt Table frame and Marble Slab 3 ft 7 × 2 ft 3
1 Airwood Tambour Writing Table
1 deal dressing Table
1 Cheval glass in Mahogany frame   25 × 42

1 Toilette glass   19 × 17
1 Mahogany Oval Table
1 Small Mahogany Table with one leaf
1 Mahogany Night Table
1   *d°*   Bidet and delph pan
1 Japann^d tin foot Pan,
1 piece of Oil cloth 5 feet square
2 Mahogany chairs, with cushions &
     dimity cases
1 piece of Tapestry 2¾ × 4½
1 Mahogany chamber Airer
1   *d°*   clothes Horse with Boot Jack
3 paintings (views) Gilt frames
3 portraits in gilt frames
1 painting (Boys & Music)
1 Arm chair covered in Damask, gilt frame
1 Wire fire guard, brass mounted,
1 Sett of fire Irons and Brush
1 Copper Kettle
2 Blue Basons, 1 water Ewer, 1 Jug and cover, 1 Eye cup
1 cut croft and Tumbler, 1 White water Jug and Bason
1 Tin shaving Pot and Stand,
1 Blue Vase:

Drapery and cornice belonging to Music Room

1 Sett of steel fire Irons to ditto
1 Brass fender ~ to ditto

63

Winter Dressing Room

1 Bookcase Bedstead and Suit of Curtains
1 Bordered feather Bed, Bolster and fustian Pillows
1 Old English Blanket   11/4
1 Under Irish   *do*
1 Counterpane   8/4
1 piece of Venitian carpet 2 yards
1 Striped calico festoon window curtain
1 Mahogany Sloping desk and drawers
1   *do*   round Table on pillar and Claws
1   *do*   Night Table
1   *do*   Wash hand Table
1   *do*   small round pillar and claw Table
1 Elm Table
1 Mahogany Bidet and delph Pan
1 Japan^d Tin foot pan
1 piece of Oil cloth 5 feet square
1 Cheval dressing glass, Mahogany frame   20 × 41
1 Toilette   *do.*   17 × 11

Carton House, County Kildare

1 Mahogany cane Seat chair, cushion & Calico case
1 Arm chair covered in Damask, gilt frame
1 Mahogany chamber Airer
1 Wire fire guard, Brass mounted
1 Sett of fire Irons and Brush
1 Copper Kettle
2 Basons with red edges, & 1 water Ewer
1 Water Jug and cover, Soap stand & Cover, 1 Brush Tray
1 Eye Cup, large white water Jug and Bason
1 Tin shaving pot and Vase,

65

Spring Dressing Room

1 Large Couch Bed, with Paliass, Hair cushion,
          feather pillow ⎱
  and green furniture calico cases, lined white ⎰
Window curtain of green furniture Calico, drapery
          lined with Pink ⎱
  Brass rods, curtain Pins and painted Cornices ⎰
3 Linen Blinds
1 Mahogany sloping Desk and drawers and small ⎱
  Book Case on top with looking Glass pannells ⎰
1 Mahogany Tambour Writing desk
1   *do*   chamber Chest
1   *d°*   Breakfast Table and drawers
1   *do*   Round Table on pillar and Claws
1 Gilt frame and Marble Slab 3 ft 5 × 2 ft 2
1 Narrow Elm Table
1 Cheval dressing glass, with branches 42 × 21
1 Toilette Glass 14 × 12
1 Chimney Glass, gilt frame, Diamond Plate 31 × 20
  (plate Bad)
1 Dressing room Commode
  Mahogany Bidet and delph pan
1 Japan^d tin foot Pan
1 Mahogany Chamber Airer
1   *do*   clothes horse and Boot Jack
1 old carpet 2 yards by 3.
1 piece of Oil cloth 5 ft square
2 Bamboo Chairs
1 Arm chair, covered in Damask, Gilt frame
2 Marble chimney urns
1 Black Italian *do,*
4 China cups and Suacers
1 Fowling piece inlaid with Pearl
1 Case of Pistols mounted with Silver
1 Desk [*recte* Dirk (prob.)] and case, Silver mounted
1 Basket handled sword, Silver Mounted

1 Sword Blade
7 Prints, Black frames Glazed
2 Portraits, Black frames *do.*
1 Wire fire guard, Brass mounted
1 Sett of fire Irons and Brush
1 Copper Kettle
2 Blue Basons and water Ewer
1 Blue Jug & Cover
1 Soap Stand
1 Cut croft and Tumbler
1 Tin shaving Pot
1 Large white water Jug and Bason
1 Vase

67

Spring Bed Room

1 Four post Bedstead, Mahogany carved cornices,
          and pillars & footboard ⎱
  Green calico curtains, lined Pink, and Draperies ⎰
1 Bordered Paliass
2   *do*   hair Mattrasses
1   *do*   feather Bed, bolster and 2 pillows
1 pair of large English Blankets 14/4   1815
1 single   *d°*   13/4   1815
1 Marseilles Quilt   15/4
2 Bedsteps covered in Brussel carpet
1 Venitian Bed round carpet
2 Green furniture calico window curtains ⎱
  lined with pink and deal cornices complete ⎰
2 linen roller blinds
1 French chest of drawers, brass Ornaments and
  Mouldings
1 Elm dressing table and drawers
1   *d°*   *d°*   with leaves
2 hollow stuffed seat chairs and calico cases
1 small stuffed seat chair, Chinese back
1 Arm chair covered in Damask & Gilt frame
1 Cheval Dressing glass 24 × 45
1 Toilette Glass 21 × 17
1 old fire screen
2 Spar chimney Ornaments
2 Small paintings in Gilt frames

69

3 Small Drawings, Black frames, Glazed
1 Wire fire guard, Brass Mounted
1 Sett of fire Irons and Brush
2 Blue Chamber Vases

Spring Dressing Room

71

1 Green furniture Window Curtain and drapery,
lined with pink }
and deal cornice &c complete

1 linen roller Blind (Slip broken)
1 Gilt frame and Mantle Slab 3 ft 5 × 2 feet.2
1 Bamboo Arm chair Stuffed Seat
1 Mahogany Bidet and Delph Pan
1   *d⁰*   chamber Airer
1   *d⁰*   corner shelf
1 Japanᵈ Tin foot Pan
  Oil cloth to fit room and Water Closet
2 Small Portraits in Gilt frames
1 Landscape (composition) Gilt frame
2 Oval Medallions
3 China Cups and Saucers
1 Wire fire guard, Brass mounted
1 Sett of fire Irons and Brush
1 Copper Kettle
2 Blue Basons & one Ewer
1 Water Jug and cover
1 Soap Stand and cover, one brush Tray
1 croft and Tumbler
1 large white Jug and Bason

Spring Sitting Room

73

2 Green Calico window Curtains and Draperies,
lined pink, with cornices }
rods and Pins, & 2 Linen spring Blinds, complete, }

1 Grecian couch and cushion, round hair Bolster
and pillow }
With green furniture calico Cases }

3 Hollow seat stuffed chairs & Calico cases
1 Bamboo chair, stuffed seat
1 Arm chair covered in Damask and Gilt Frame
1 Mahogany Bookcase, wire doors at top, panelled *d⁰*
at Bottom }
With wings and drawers underneath }

1 Mahogany Voidore Table, with drawer & Stamped
green & yellow cloth cover,
1 Cabinet with composition Stone pannels
1 Inlaid tambour airwood Writing Table
1 Airwood Book Stand and Drawers, foot work guard,
2   *do*   Bookshelves, with drawers, & fluted
pink calico at back
1 Horse Reading Stand.

1 Folding paper fire screen, with prints   &c   &c
1 Marble Vase
1 French china figure
4 China cups
2 Large Gilt china cups and saucers
1 china cup with handle, cover and Stand, (coronet
in centre)
2 Chinese composition cannisters
1 Wedgewood Medallion of Earl Cooper
1 Round china Bowl & Cover
1 Old carpet 3¾ × 5
1 Wire fire guard, brass mounted.
1 Sett of fire Irons and Brush

His Graces Study

75

1 Library Table with drawers and enclosed doors
lined with }
Black leather, with Skeleton on Top }

1 Mahogany Chest of drawers
4   *do*   Bookcases with Glass doors at Top and }
Mahogany pannelled doors at Bottom }

1 Mahogany Office chair
4 Large Arm chairs in Black leather
1 Mahogany Reading Stand, On pillar and Claws
1 Cane Seat chair
1 Pianoforte and Leather cover by Broadwood & Sons
1 Elm Spider Table with shelf
1 Show Box and Lamp
1 Comfort and ease covered in drab Cloth.
2 Stools covered in carpet
2 fire screens
1 Hearth Rug
1 Scarlet Morine window curtain and drapery,
fringed & Brass Rods
2 Pair of caned blinds, Mahogany frames
1 Chimney Glass, 3 Plates, in carved fretwork gilt frame,
2 Glasses in Window recess   36 × 20
1 Barometer
1 Thermometer
1 Map of Kildare
  Carpenters corporation Box (Oak, with case of
Mathematical instruments
1 Yew letter Box
1 Twine Box
1 Messengers Box (Red Morrocco)
2 Mahogany Gun cases
       do   Drawing Box

Carton House, County Kildare

1 Backgammon Box (Red Morrocco)
1 Long Mahogany case
2 Small Mahogany Boxes
1 Japaned tin Box for Harp strings
1 Yew ink stand with drawer and Bottles &c
1 Brass fenders, fire Irons and Brush
1 Tomahawk

Dressing Room adjoining Study

Scarlet Morine Window curtains & draperies
1 Couch covered in grey linen
1 Bench, with Vice & Anvil
1 Mahogany clothes Horse with Boot Jack
1 Tool chest
1 Deal Wash Table
1 Arm chair covered in Damask, gilt frame
1 Wire fire guard, Brass mounted
1 Sett of fire Irons and Brush
4 China cups and saucers
2 d^o Green Bowls
1 Copper Kettle
2 Prints (Lord Holland and Judge Fox)
2 Brown edged Basons
1 Water Jug and cover
1 Soap Stand & Cover
1 Brush Tray
1 Cut croft and Tumbler
1 Large white water Jug and Bason
a Quantity of Paintings
3 pieces of Metal Trellice work
a pair of Antique Spurs
Deers Horns

Old Study

1 Old Couch
3 Sattin wood Canterburys
1 Mahogany chamber Horse
3 do Bidets (no pans)
1 Wire fire guard, Brass mounted
1 Brass grate
2 do Window rods
6 Curtain Pins
1 Old wire fire guard
1 pole screen
1 Mopes head
A quantity of Marble figures and Vases

2 pieces of old carpet
1 Drum & Sticks
1 Tamborine, frame and Triangles
1 Pipe clay Sauce pan
2 Small deal boxes (one locked)

Small Library

1 Mahogany Library Table, pannelled doors on One Side
and brass lattice doors, covered with black leather
1 Round Library Table, Sattin Wood draw front on Pillar &
claws, lined with green cloth, and a p^r plated
branches in centre
2 Library chairs, covered with green cloth,
with back & seat Cushions
2 Comforts & Ease to Match
1 Reading chair covered with black leather and
Mahogany Desk attached
4 Mahogany Cane Seat chairs
1 Large sofa , one seat & three back Cushions
2 Mahogany Candlestand on Pillars and claws
1 Inlay^d Airwood Work Table
1 Turkey Carpet 17 f^t. × 14 f^t.
1 Rug to Match
2 fire screens, brass poles and Mahogany bases, Shield
cov^d in tapestry,
1 do in Bronze and Gold, with fancy designs,
Varnished,
1 Painting on Marble
1 Marble Vase with rich Brass mounting,
4 Stone Cups
1 Ivory d^o cyphered
1 Green Damask Window Curtain, lined with green
Silk persian, with
Draperies, Rich gilt cornices &c, Silk fringe & bordering
3 Linen Window blinds
1 Brass fender
1 Sett of Steel fire Irons
1 Silver Ink Stand
1 Indian leather cushion
1 Small Box, pannels of composition Stone.

Large Library

5 Green Damask Window curtains, lined with green
Silk persian
with draperies, rich gilt cornices , Silk fringe and
bordering

5 Roller Blinds of white holland
2 Large sofas, Mahogany frames, covered with drab
Cloth, with)
cushions, Bolsters and 2 pillows each)
2 Library chairs covered with drab cloth, back &
seat cushions,
2 foot rests covered to match
1   carpet 17 ft. × 15 ft.
1 Hearth Rug
8 Mahogany cane Seat chairs
2   *do*   Sofa Tables claw feet on castors
2 Crimson Table covers Border.ᵈ
1 Mahogany chess Table on claws and castors, inside
lined with)
Morrocco & Men with chess &c)
1 Grand Pianoforte, (By Broadwood)
2 Mahogany Whatnots
1 Stool covered in needlework
1 Mahogany card Table, lined
1 Airwood Spider Table
1 Small Mahogany *do.*
1 Musical chronometer and rosewood case
2 Gilt frames with Marble Tables 36 × 24
2 Cabinets of curiosities
1 Painted flower Stand
2 Oval looking Glasses
2 Bronze, patent lamps, Glass dish and bronze rim
& Chains
2 fire Screens, brass poles and Mahogany bases)
Shields covered in Tapestry)
1 Foot stool covered in carpet
1 Small Mahogany Childs Table
1 Yew letter Box inlaid
1 White Sheep Skin Matt
2 Tanned Sheep Skin *do.*
1 Rich Tortoise shell Table inlaid with brass
1 Brass fender
1 Sett of Steel fire Irons
1 Chamber clock
1 Small Mahogany cabinet & drawers inside
2 Blue china Jars
2 White and Gold China urns
1 large china Vase
2 Small *do.*   *do.*
1 White french china figure
1 Wax figure (children & Dog) & Glass cover
2 Ormolu Candlesticks
2 Stone blue china Ewers, Mounted in Ormolu
1   *do*   *do*   Centre

1 Reclining Venus on Marble plinth

85

2 Ormolu Candlesticks
1 Bronze Hercules, on a Marble plinth
2   *do*   figures   on   *Do*   (Venus & Adonis)
2   *do*   Groups of figures on   *Do*
2 Red Stone Jars, Mounted in Ormolu
2 Heads painted on Copper
2 Brass Candlesticks
2 Silver Ink Stands
2 frank Weights
2 China Match Stands
1 Stone Cup
2 Yew Boxes, carved tops
1 Miniature (Lady Louisa Connolly)
4 Marble Busts
1 Porphery Jar,
2 large Shells
1 Model of a canoe
5 Shells
1 Portrait, 1 Print
1 ruin of a Castle cut in Wood

87

Dining Room

4 Drab Moreen Window Curtains and draperies,
Silk fringe & rich Gilt Cornices
4 White Holland blinds
17 Two slatt Mahogany Parlor chairs, in hair cloth,
2 Mahogany frames, with Marble Slabs at Top
1   *do*   pedestal lined with Tin for plates
2 Bronze and Gold frames & rich embossed
Marble Slabs
1 Small Mahogany Voidore Table
1 Mahogany Octagon Bottle Cooper
Grey drugget for floor 4 by 5¾ yds
1 Turkey Rug
1   *do*   carpet
2 Tanned Sheep skins
1 Sett of Mahogany Pillar Tables (Consisting of 8
3 Basket servers covered in scarlet Morine
1 Brass fender
1 Sett of Steel fire Irons and brush
1 piece of 8/4 green cloth 3¼ yds long
2 Grecian Lamps, large Glass dishes, Bronze rims
& Chains
1 Stool covered in Carpet

Carton House, County Kildare

1 Large China Jar & Cover
1 Small *do* *do*
1 Large China Bowl
1 China Baker
1 Striped Blue & white Baker
1 french time piece in Ormolu frame & Glass case
2 Ormolu figures on white Marble plinths
2 Brass Cranes on Wooden plinths
2 Stone color china Ornaments, on brass plinths
2 Bronze Dogs on Marble plinths
1 Minute Glass
1 Large Organ

89

Billiard Room

1 Large Billiard Table 12 ft 8 × 6 ft 8 and Ticken cover
2 Mahogany cue presses, with brass Markers on Top
4 flower Damask festoon Window curtains
4 Linen spring Blinds
1 Large India Chest, raised brass work
2 white carved frames with composition slabs
1 French Inlaid cabinet, Sweep^d Front
1 *do* *do* cove top & Silver Moldings
2 *do* *do* Corner
2 *do* *do* Smaller
1 Mahogany Oval Table
1 smaller *do*
8 Mahogany × Chairs
1 plain Hearth Rug
1 Brass fender
1 Sett of fire Irons brass mounted
1 Chamber Clock, Mahogany case
4 Deal Brackets for lights
1 small Bronzed figure on Marble plinth
1 Bust (plaister of Paris) Bronzed,

91

Inside Hall & Stairs

4 Drab morine curtains and cornices
1 Large Hall Lanthorn, Brass mounting & Chains
1 Glass Lamp
2 Dinner Canterburys
2 Small Dumb waiters
1 Large Oval Mahogany table
2 Mahogany Wine Tables
1 *do* Step Ladder
1 Brass fender
3 Bronze figures, Boar, Bull & Lion

1 Sett of Steel fire Irons & Brush
1 Deal Harp Case
1 Tanned sheep skin Matt
2 Ranges of Brass hat hooks

93

Passage outside Hall

1 Drab Moreen Window curtain
1 Glass Lamp
1 Mahogany Oval Table
1 Tanned Sheep Skin Matt
2 Mahogany cross seats
1 Foot Brush

Groom of the Chambers Room

1 Mahogany Oval Table
1 Backgammon & Chess Table
1 Porters Chair
1 Mahogany Pole screen
1 Old Brass fender
1 Old sett of fire Irons and Brush
1 Japanned plate warmer
1 Eight Day Clock
2 Oak falling leaves, (fast)
1 Copper coal Box (new)

95

Kitchen Story
House Stewards Room

1 Fourpost Bedstead and old Morine Curtains
1 Old Paliass
1 *do* hair Mattrass
1 feather Bed, Bolster and pillow,
1 Single Eng^h. Blanket 12/4
1 Under *do* 9/4
1 Counterpane 10/4
1 Old couch and hair cushion
1 deal office Stool
1 Mahogany chamber Airer
1 Oak Chest of Drawers
1 Elm *do*
1 Oak clothes Press
1 Deal Table & drawer
1 *do* Bason Stand
1 *do* Stool
4 Old chairs
1 Mahogany Night Stool

1   *do*   Round pillar & Claw Table
1 old Toilette glass
1 Mahogany sloping desk on a frame
1 White Bason & Vase
1 Sett of old fire Irons,

97

House Stewards Office

1 old Arm Chair
1 deal clothes horse
1 deal Office Table with Book rack and shelves
1 Nest of Drawers and shelves fastened to wall
1 Old plated candlestick
1 Box with Old Lumber &c
2 White Jugs
1 Japanned Can
3 Silk Sieves
1 Hand Saw
1 Sugar Nippers
1 Iron coal Scuttle,

99

House Maids Room

3 Deal Bedsteads, deal Testers and headboards
3 Suits of blue cheque curtains
3 Straw Paliasses
1 Bordered feather Bed and bolster
2 plain   *do*   & bolsters
3 pair of Old Sundry Blankets
3 wider [*recte* under?] *do do*
3 Cotton Quilts
1 large deal table
2 Small   *do*
8 Old chairs
2 deal forms
1 large deal press painted
1 Old chamber Airer
1 Smoothing Blanket
1 Dressing Glass
1 Deal clothes Horse

101

Room Nº 7

1 four post Bedstead and Old Chintz curtains
1 Bordered Straw Paliass
1 Plain Hair Mattrass
1 Bordered Feather Bed & Bolster

1 pair of Old English Blankets
1 under   *dº*
1 Cotton quilt, lined
1 Mahogany card Table, lined
1 Old Chair
1 Mahogany chest with drawers
1 White water Ewer and Bason
1 Old Toilette Glass
1 Deal form
1 Vase
1 Suit of Bed curtains (Chintz)

103

Room Nº 4

1 old fourpost Bedstead and Morine curtains
1 old Hair Mattrass
2 feather Beds 1 Bolster and 2 Pillows
1 pair of Irish Blankets 8/4
1 under   *dº*
1 green serge quilt
1 Oak chest of drawers
2 old window curtains
1 Stamp Leather cover for Grand piano
1 Deal Table with drawers
1 Old chair
1 Toilette glass
1 white Bason, Ewer & Vase, Soap Stand & brush tray
1 Saucer and Tumbler
1 Shelf fastened to the Wall
6 Rugs
2 pieces of haircloth
5 Worsted Brussells quilts.

105

Room Nº 5

1 four post bedstead and Morine Curtains
1 Straw Paliass
1 feather Bed, 2 Ticken pillows & Bolster
1 pair of Old Eng^h Blankets
1 Bed Airer and Pan
1 Old Mahogany Drawers
1 Old Chair
1 deal Table with drawer
1 White Bason, Ewer and Vase

Carton House, County Kildare

Room No 6

1 old fourpost Bedstead & Curtains
1 do Straw Paliass
1 Border^d Hair Mattrass
1 feather Bed & Bolster & Pillow
1 Single Blanket
1 under Irish *do*
1 Deal Sloping desk and drawers
1 *do* Table and drawers
1 Small glass
1 old cane seat chair
1 Old Bason, Ewer and Vase
1 Tumbler,

Lumber Passage

1 Old Deal Chest
2 deal clothes Horses
3 old chairs
1 old Stool
1 Spinning Wheel
1 feather Bed and Bolster
1 pair of Irish Blankets
1 Cheque Quilt, lined
2 Packs of Old Wool and hair

House keepers Sitting Room

2 Range of deal Presses
1 Mahogany Table, falling leaf & Drawers
1 *do* Oval Table
2 *do* Voidore Tables
1 *do* Sloping desk & drawers
1 Deal Table & drawer
1 Small Mahog. Spider Table
1 Deal *do*
1 deal Step Ladder
1 Mahogany Bookshelf
2 *Do* *Do* on top of Press
4 *Do* Parlor Chairs
1 Rush chair
1 Bamboo chair, stuffed seat
1 old chair and Damascus Case
1 Sofa, 2 Bolsters & Damascus case
2 Tin canisters
2 Brass Candlesticks

1 Brass flat. Extinguishers & Snuffers
1 Snuffers & Tray
1 Copper coal scuttle, 1 Metal Kettle
1 Sett of fire Irons & Brush
1 Looking Glass
35 Prints & paintings
1 Stool covered in Needlework
1 Gilt picture frame, Glazed
3 Tall Brass Candlesticks
1 Tin *Do* Snuffers & Exting^{hrs}
2 Pewter wine Measures (half pint & Naggin)
2 pair of Sugar Nippers
2 Coffee and 3 Tea Canisters.

H. keepers Bed Room

1 Camp Bedstead & Cheque curtains
1 Hair Mattrass
1 Bordered feather Bed, Bolster & pillow
1 Wool Mattrass
1 pair of Blankets
1 Large single Eng^h. Blanket
1 Old white Counterpane
1 Mahogany sloping desk with Book case on Top & }
    Mahog. pannel doors }
1 Oak Chest of drawers
1 Large deal dressing table with drawers
1 Deal Cupboard
1 Mahogany Bookshelf
1 deal shelf with sides
1 Deal Nest of small drawers fastened to Wall
2 old dressing Tables
1 old oval Toilette press
1 dressing Stool
3 Prints
3 white Basons, 2 Water Ewers,
1 croft and Tumbler
1 Brush Tray, 1 Soap Stand
1 Bedside carpet
1 Mahogany Night Table
1 Small Japaned Indian Cabinet
1 Vase
1 Blue & White cream Jug
1 Large Bason

115

Closet in Passage   № 8

1 Brass fender
4 old steel *d°*
7 setts of old broken fire Irons
1 Wafer Tongs
1 Fumigating Bellows
2 pair of chamber Bellows
3 Tin candlesticks
5 water Ewers
2 Vases, 3 white Basons
5 Small Jugs and Covers
5 Large white Jugs
31 white Plates
27   *d°* Dishes
2 cut crofts, four Wine glasses
1 Salt
1 Metal Bell, 1 Black
1 pickling crock
1 Large pickling Pan
19 Pewter Plates, 1 Dish
1 Plaister of Paris pannell
1 Old Japann^d Tray
4 Hanging dressing glass, (Mahogany Japan^d frames)
1   *d°*   *d°*   Gilt frame
1 Looking glass plate
1 Boot Jack

117

House keepers Store Room
China Desert Service

9 Doz. and 6 Plates
5 Small round Dishes, 6 large   *d°*
4 Shallow   *do* ,   7 Square *d°*
7 Shell   *do* ,
4 Ice pails and covers
4 Suace Boats and Stands
4 Muffin dishes & Covers
8 round cups & Covers and four Stands
2 Sallad Bowls
25 Custard cups & Covers & 6   *do* ~ *do*
6 Wine coolers & Cups

Rose Bud Desert Service

25 Plates
2 Oval dishes
2 Square *d°*,

4 Round *do,*
4 Shell *do*
2 Turreens & Covers
2 Ice Pails & Covers
2 Large Oval dishes

Rose Bud Breakfast Service

36 Cups and 36 Saucers
24 Coffee cups
20 Saucers
6 Sugar Bowls
4 Sweet Meat cups, Stands & Covers
2 Cream Ewers
1 Large & 2 small Bowls
4 Muffin Plates & Covers
35 Breakfast Plates
2 Sallad Bowls
2 large Milk Jugs
1 Coffee Pot
4 Cake dishes, 1 Beef steak dish
5 China Egg Cups
2 White china Match cups
1 Blue Wedgewood Sugar Bowl & cream Jug
12 White & Gold custard Cups

119

Colord Tea Service

6 Cups and 6 Saucers
7 coffee cans
2 Cake Plates
1 Bowl

White, Gold & scarlet Tea service

1 Tea Pot
6 Cups & 8 Suacers
6 coffee cans
1 Sugar Bowl
1 Cream Ewer
2 Plates
1 Bowl
11 Brown china saucers
8 Cups
9 China Saucers
4 Cups and 4 cream Ewers } Cypher ℒ & coronet
1 Bowl, 1 china Broth Bason
1 old china Tea pot.
1 China sugar Bowl

Carton House, County Kildare

1 old china Plate
2 Blue china Bowls
5 Large round china dishes, Scarlet & Gold
8 Octagon china   *d?*
6 French round china *d?*
2 Blue   *d?*   *d?*
1 Blue china Baker
6 old Flower Pots
15 old china Dishes
1 Fish Ornament (Brass mounted)

Blue edged Breakfast Service

1 Saucers, 15 cups, 11 coffee cans
9 Saucers
4 Sugar Bowls & Covers
4 cream Ewers
1 Jug, 1 Honey Bowl & Cover
13 Egg cups, 2 Glass cups
3 Bowls & 4 cake Plates
27 Plates (sundries)
4 Muffin plates

121

French China

2 Oval dishes
3 Square *d?*
2 Tureens
6 Plates
2 Cups, belonging to Ice Pails
1 round, color^d Antique Dish
4 large cut glass sweetmeat dishes
4   *D?*   *D?*   smaller
2 Jelly stands and 6 Glasses
2 crofts and 2 Tumblers
15 Glass Jars
12 Sundry white round Basons
5   *d?*   *D?*   Bedroom Basons
8 Lip^d: Basons
2 Brown edged Basons
3 Jugs and one cover to match
1 Soap Tray, 3 chamber Vases
2 Red striped Basons
2   *d?*   Jugs 1 cover
1 Water Ewer & Cover
1 Soap and 1 Brush Tray
2 Chamber Vases, 1 green edged Cup
1   *d?* ~
3 Large water Jugs

3 Night Pans

Staffordshire Dinner service

5 Oval dishes
1 Square dish & 2 covers
1 Soup turreen & Cover
5 Sauce turreens and 2 ladles
13 Dinner Plates
16 Soup   *d?*
7 Blue   *d?*
7 Blue dishes
5 Blue Oval   *d?*
1 Large white Butter Pail & cover (Marked Dairy)
6 Blue Bowls
8 Plates (Sundries)
12 Small Delph shapes
2 Bread Pans
1 Delph Ice Pail
2 Baking dishes
3 Sandwich Dishes and 1 centre
3 Black Teapots, 1 Japanned *d?*
4 White Dishes

123

Sweet Meat Pots

122 Sweet Meat Pots   (empty)
147   *d?*   (full of Preserves)
39 white cups and 9 saucers
2 Soup Pots
3 Blue Knife rests
a Quantity of Raspberry Vinegar Bottles
a Hamper of Broken china
a Hamper of Glass
2 Brass wire Seives
4 Lawn   *D?*
9 Hair   *D?*
1 New canvass   *D?*
5 Slat Sieves
13 New Sweeping Brushes
2   stair   *d?*
5   Dusting   *d?*
3   Painting   *d?*
1 Carpet Brush (Twig)
5 Scrubbing and 1 dry rubbing brushes
1 Dust Pan
1 Chestnut Shovel
1 Stove Tongs
2 Lemon Squeezers

3 Straining Ladders
2 Mallets and 2 Rolling Pins
8 Wooden Spoons
1 Silver Toasting Fork
2 p.r scales, chains & Beams
1 Tin Kettle
1 China Dog pan
1 Lumber box
1 Bronzed figure on Marble plinth
2 *d⁰* *d⁰* (Buffalo & Lion)
2 chinese Stone Ornaments
   Shaw & Pelham
1 chinese figure (broken)
1 composition Vase (Broken)
2 Pewter pints, 1 Quart
1 copper sauce pan & 2 Kettles
1 Brass Skillet
6 Pewter Ice moulds
2 *D.º* freezing pails
2 *D.º* *D.º*
2 *D.º* Ice moulds
1 Silver sauce pan & spoon
2 Stone flags
a Tin cullender, Grater and 2 dredging boxes
a Marble Mortar and Glass Pestle
2 Flour Tubs
2 Watering *d⁰*
11 Candle Boxes

125

1 Soap Box
6 Jars
2 Smoothing Irons and stands
1 Tin Tundish
1 Deal press
1 Deal Shelf
3 Large deal Tables
1 Small *d.º*
1 Old chair
3 Wooden Bowls
1 Mahogany Tray
1 Old Japann.d Tray

Passage to H„keepers Room

a Beam & Scales with copper Bottom
a Sett of Brass weights 7 lbs„
1 14 lb *D.º* as a case for *d.º*
a Set of weights (imperfect)

1 Deal Table fastened in Wall
1 *d⁰* Press with Lock & Key
1 Mahogany chamber Airer with 2 folds
1 Deal Table
1 Oil Lamp
5 Copper preserving Pans
1 Slop Tub
1 china Tub
5 Pickling crocks

127

House Linen
Damask Table Linen

4 Cromaboo Table clothes 5 yds × 3 yds
4 *d.º* Slips 3⅜ ~ 3 Napkins
1 Kildare cloth 5 yds × 3
1 *d.º* 4 „ × 3
2 Damask cloths mark*d* N.º 2 = 77 .. 5 × 3 yds..
2 *d.º* *d.º* 1.2 „ 76 .. 2⅞ × 2¼
1 *d.º* *d.º* 3 „ 76 .. 3½ × 2¼
1 *d.º* *d⁰* 4 „ 76 .. 3⅜ × 2¼
1 *d.º* *d⁰* 5 „ 76 .. 3½ × 2¼
1 *d.º* *d.º* 2 „ 77 .. 2⅞ × 2¼
1 *d.º* *d.º* 2 „ 76 .. 3⅜ × 2¼
1 *d⁰* *d.º* 2 „ 76 .. 2⅞ × 2¼

Leinster House Linen

5 Damask clothes, bound & marked n.º 9 „ 76 .. 4⅛ by 3 yds
4 *D.º* *D.º* „ 9 „ 76 .. 2⅞ × 2⅜
7 *D.º* *D.º* „ 1 „ 76 .. Viz..
                               4 of 2½ × 2⅜
                               1 of 3⅜ × 2⅜
                               1 of 2⅞ × 2⅜
                               1 of 4⅛ × 3
4 Table clothes n.º 2 „ 76 Viz 2 of 3½ by 2⅜
                                        2 of 2⅞ by 2¼
8 Lay overs 1⅜ × 1½

129

Napkins

45 Napkins Bor*d* N.º 45 × 76
34 *d.º* not bor*d* 34 × 76
11 *d.º* bor*d* 11 × 76
21 *d.º* *d.º* 21 × 76
12 *d.º* *d.º* 12 × 76
23 *d.º* *d.º* 23 × 76

Carton House, County Kildare

20 dº dº 20 × 76
24 dº dº 24 × 76
24 dº dº 24 × 76
24 dº dº 24 × 76

26 Cromaboo Napkins Nº 1 .. 78
26 dº dº 78
18 Kildare dº 93

6 Lay overs 1⅜ by 1½ yds n°s 1. 2. 3. 4. 5. 6. year 76
26 Breakfast Napkins nº 78

72 New Damask Napkins from Boyle 72 ~ 1816

12 Diaper dutch matting Table clothes Viz..
6 of 2¾ × 1⅞ mark^{d} 79
5 of 2½ × 1⅞ 〃 〃
1 of 2 × 1⅞ 〃 〃

5 Striped Diaper Table clothes Viz .
4 of 3 × 2⅜ marked 94
1 of 2⅞ × 2¾ 〃 〃

137 Diaper Napkins Marked 1801
60 Dutch Matt^{d} patt napkins
71 Dutch Matt Breakfast *dº*
36 *dº* *dº* cut off Table clothes nº 36
8 Table clothes, Stewards room 2½ yds each
30 Old Waiting Napkins
5 Gentlemens night caps

131

Studderts Linen

20 pair of sheets of 5/4 sheeting 12½ yds each, marked 1. to 20
18 pillow cases to match nº 1 to 18
18 pair of sheets ⅝ sheeting 3½ yds 14 yds each, 2 to 20 (1812)
7 pair dº 5/4 fine 3 breadths 4½ yards long }
3 dº dº 3 dº 4⅝ 〃 long } N°s 1 to 10
35 pillow cases nº 2 to 36 (1812)
5 yds 5/4 sheeting
12 pair of sheets ⅝ sheeting 2 breadths 3 yds long N°s 1 to 12 (1812)
6 pair twilled dº ~ 2 dº 3 yds 〃 to 18 (1812)

Bird Eye Diaper ¾ wide

39 Towels (1812)
76 Waiting Napkins ½ breadth each (1812)
67 Huckaback Towels Mark^{d} 1812 ℒ. N°s 18 to 51

⅝ Drogheda linen〃

12 pair of sheets 4 breaths [*sic*] in each 1813 3 yds long
2 Basket clothes for laundry
18 Towels of grey linen
2 Bottle clothes
10 pair of sheets 4 Bd^{ths} each 3 yds long n°s 1 to 10 (1813) mark^{d}
28 Towels
2 pillow cases
27 Spoon clothes ½ Brd^{ths}
2 Round Towels

19 House maids dusters of Dowlas linen 1813

80 Towels mark^{d} in red Nº 81, 1813, of ¾ Bird Eye diaper @ 3/3
24 dº dº 〃 25 dº @ 2/8½
82 dº dº 〃 82 dº @ 2/2

7 Table clothes, 1 Breadth of 7/4 diaper mark^{d} nº 7 { 3 of 1⅞ long; 4 of 1⅝ 〃 }
6 dº 〃 1⅓ 〃 dº 2½ yds long
3 dº 〃 dº 〃 dº 4 〃 long

4 Servants Hall clothes, Strong diaper 2 Brd^{ths} 4¾ long }
4 dº dº dº 4¼ 〃 }
2 Laundry Maids Dº dº 1¾ 〃 } 4/4
2 Servant Maids Dº dº 2⅝ 〃 }
2 Breakfast Dº 1½ dº 2⅜ 〃 }
2 Kitchens Dº 2 dº 1⅜ 〃 }

133

52 Towels, mark^{d} M. K. 52, 1813 ¾ diaper

6 pair of sheets 4 Brd^{ths} 4½ yds long Nº 1 to 6 1813
18 flounced Pillow cases n°s 1 to 18 1813
7½ yds of 4/4 linen

68 Towels Marked 68, 1813, ⅝ huckaback
50 dº 〃 50, 1813, ¾ dº
15 Knife clothes
10 Candlestick dº }
14 China dº 2 yds long 1½ Breadth } Grey linen
2 dº dº dº }
6 House maids clothes dº }

12 trimmd pincushions & Covers
17¾ Yards of dimity and some stripes
3¾ *do* Coarse linen
4 pair coarse sheets nos. 1 to 4, 1815, 12 yds each
6 House Maids clothes, 2 Brdths. each grey linen sheeting
31 House dusters
33 *do* Dowlas @ 20d
10 Glass clothes
1⅞ Yds of a remnant
22 diaper Towels marked 22, 1815
11 pair of fine sheets 5/4 sheeting 2½ brdths. 3⅞ long no. 1 to 11, 1815
4 Pillow cases marked 1 to 4, 1815
2½ yards in 2 remnants to match
50 Towels, marked 50, 1815,

5/4 Boyle Sheeting

5 pair of Sheets	5 breadths each		4⅜ yds long	
3 *Do.*	2½	*do.*	4	*do.*
1 *Do.*	2	*do.*	4	*do.*
9 *Do*	marked 1 to 9,		1816	
3 pillow cases	〃 1 to 3,		1816	

3¾ yds Linen to match

Strong Mill Yarn

11 pair of sheets 2 Breadths 3¼ long
1 pair to Simpsons Lodge No. 8 〃 1816
6 Stable Rubbers,

135

Boyle Dowlas linen 〃

48 Glass clothes marked 48, 1816 } S
20 *do* 〃 72, 1816 } S
14 footmans clothes } F 1816
14 *do* 〃 1½ long } F 1816
14 Groom of the chambers clothes G 1816
6 Coachmans *do.* S 1816
6 House keepers *do.* H 1816
1 Remnant 9½ yds long
1 *do* 3¾ 〃
1 *do* 1½ 〃
1 *do* 3 〃
1 *do* ¾ 〃

6 Table clothes	3¼ yds long	12/4	Sup. Diaper
4 *do*	3⅛	〃	〃
1 *do*	3¾	〃	〃
4 *do*	2⅞	〃	〃
3 *do*	3	〃	〃
2 *do*	3¾	〃	〃

20 Marked 20, 1816 in red

4/4 Strong Diaper

48 plate clothes 1½ yds long No. 48, 1816
6 Servants hall *do.* 2 Brdths marked 6,
2 yards sent to the Poultry Maid
14 round Towels
6 Table rubbers marked T, 6, 1816
13 Lamp clothes *do* 14 1816
1 *Do.* common plaisterer
4½ yds grey linen left from Mr Dillons bed
26½ yds. white calico
48 Towels, marked 48 × 1816
24 Milld yarn Oyster clothes
1 remnant ¾ yd
17 Knife cloths of Drogheda linen
1 Remnant of *do.* 4 yds
14 Aprons for cook
6 Diaper Kitchen Table clothes, 2 Breadths
6 Diaper *do* 1 *do*
6 *Do* *do* 1½ *do*
3 Servants Hall clothes 2 *do* 2¼ long
2 Remnants 2 yards
14 Kitchen Rubbers, (drogheda linen
12 *do.* *do.* } grey
2 Marrow bone cloths } grey
2 Pudding *Do* } grey
6 Cooks Rubbers

137

8 Round Towels Marked 4 ~ 1812
8 Knife clothes } of ⅞ grey linen
2½ yds, a remt. } of ⅞ grey linen
22 Glass clothes
6 Slaughter house Do
7 yds of ticken in 2 remnants
9 yds printed calico
1 Hexagon Quilt of silk patch work, unfinished,
1 Palampore Quilt fringed
12 yds Drab Moreen
10¾ 〃 Buff ground fur. Calico
36 〃 in sundry remnants of pink calico
4 Groce chintz Binding

3 Short remts. of Black & Scarlet fringe
1   *D⁰*   white cotton   *d⁰*
1   *D⁰*   Lace Binding
4½ yds green Persian
1 Damask festoon curtain, lined with crimson Stuff
    Some color^d paper and Ornaments for making
        Desert Boxes
    a Quantity of Threads, Tapes, Silks, cottons,
                                    pins & needles
            D⁰   of old bits of Tickens, Carpets &c no value
2¾ yds Welch Flannel
6 Hearth Brushes
1 Green ground furniture calico window curtain for ⎫
        Winter Bed room   ⎭
1 Drab Morine   *d⁰*   for Music room
4 Scarlet Morine   *d⁰*   for Old Study
1 Suit of palampore curtains for a Bed. (complete
        except Tester & headcloth)
1 *D⁰* of Window curtains
    Linings of *d⁰.*
1 Remnant of Pillow fustian
1 Chair cover for Spring room
5 Palampore chair covers
2 Remnants of Blue cheque
1   *d⁰*   green Calico
1 Bale of white and 1 of crimson line
1 Remnant of Buckram
5 Screens & 6 Medallions

Quilts and Counterpanes

1 Marsielles Quilt   14/4   n⁰. 1   „ 1814
1   *d⁰*   „ 2   „ 1816
1   *d⁰*   „ 3   „ 1816
1   *d⁰*   „ 4   „ 1816
1   *d⁰*   13/4   no mark
1 Counterpane   14/4   N⁰. 1   „ 1816
1   *d⁰*   12/4   „ 2   *d⁰*
1   *d⁰*   12/4   „ 3   *d⁰*
1   *d⁰*   12/4   „ 4   *d⁰*
1   *d⁰*   12/4   „ 5   *d⁰*
1   *d⁰*   14/4   „ 6   *d⁰*
1   *d⁰*   12/4   no mark
1   old Counterpane   12/4
1   *d⁰*   small size
    remnant of grey linen about 1 yard
        D⁰   of Dowlas   2¼ *d⁰*

Old Damask Linen &c

24 Damask bird eye   Napkins Marked   76
18   *d⁰*   *d⁰*   „   1769
12   *d⁰*   *d⁰*   „   L 3
12   *d⁰*   *d⁰*   „   6 D 4
72   *d⁰*   *d⁰*   24 Mark^d 2, 1769,
                                48 mark^d 4, 1769
3   *d⁰*   Table clothes, Bird eye marked 76
2   *d⁰*   *d⁰*   „ 76
3   *d⁰*   *d⁰*   no mark
2 Small diaper   marked 94
3 pair of sheets 3 Breadths each
3   *d⁰*   2½   *d⁰*   each
1 Single   *d⁰*
1 old 11/4 counterpane
1   *d⁰* ¾   *d⁰*
36 Bird eye diaper Towels, 1801
84 glass clothes and Rubbers
15 round Towels ;

Stewards Room

17 White dishes dif^t sizes
2 Soup Turreens 1 Ladle
32 Dinner Plates
15 Supper   *d⁰.*
13 Soup   *d⁰*
3 Small   *d⁰*
3 Blue Butter Boats
5 Blue Jugs
1 Ice pail
1 Blue Salad Bowl
1 Japan^d cocoa pot and cover
4 Salts
3 Vinegar cruets
1 Mustard pot
3 Doz. new Knives and 20 forks
8 old dinner Knives and 15 forks
4 Carving Knives, 6 forks
1 Round of Beef carving Knife and fork
19 Breakfast Knives
24 Silver Table spoons
1 large Gravy spoon
1 Small *do* with grater
2 Sugar Tongs
19 Tea spoons
2 Silver teapots

2 plated goblets
1 Japanned Tea Canister
1   *d^o*   Tea Urn
12 Blue saucers & 11 Cups
3 Bowls to match
8 Blue saucers and 9 cups
2 Black cream Ewers
14 Beer glasses
13 Wine   *d^o*
1 Decanter
4 Silver candlesticks
1 flat tin   *d^o*
1 Japan^d Knife
1 Snuffers & Stand
1 Coal Scuttle
1 Old Plate Basket
1 Mahogany Knife *d^o*
1   Deal   *D^o*
1   Basket   *D^o*
1 Mahogany Glass tray.
1 Jap^d Tea Tray, 1 old *D$^{o.}$*
1 Copper Gallon
1 Wooden Bowl
1 Sweeping Brush

145

1 Steel fender
1 Sett of fire Irons & Brush
1 Mahogany Table
3   Oak   *D^o*
1   deal   *D^o*
1 Mahogany BackGammon *d^o*
1   *D^o*   Round Table on pillar & Claws
13 old Chairs
1 Eight Day Clock
1 chimney glass with two Diamond plates
2 old Paintings
2 old prints
2 Gilt picture frames
2   Black   *d$^{o.}$*
1 corner cupboard (deal)

147

Kitchen

1 Large Oak Table
1   *d^o*   with drawers and shelves
1 fire screen lined
1 Smoke Jack and Chain

3 Hand spits
1 Cradle *d$^{o.}$*
12 Round stew pans and covers
8 Oval   *do*   *&* *do*
15 round   *do*   *&* *do*
17   *d^o*   *do*   *&* *do* 2$^{nd}_{,,}$ Size
14   *d^o*   *do*   *&* *do* 3$^{rd}_{,,}$ *d^o*
2 large soup potts and covers
2 Small   *do*   *do*
4 Smaller   *do*   *do*
1 flat pan & Cover
3 Omilet Pans
2 Soutiers
6 Oven sheets
2 Copper cullenders
1   *d^o*   Gallon
4 pudding pans
1 copper dredging box
3 copper fish Kettles plates and covers
1 copper heater for stew pans
10   *d^o*   dishing spoons
11   *d^o*   fish slices
6   *d^o*   Ladles
1 Brass Grater
7 Wooden Spoons
1   *d^o*   pestle
8   *d^o*   Trenchers
4 Larding pins
1 Steel
1 Metal Oven, made fast
7 Grates and Stoves
2 Gridirons
1 Kitchen poker and 2 shovels
2 Meat saws
1 Large chopper
5 Small *d$^{o.}$* 1 a Mincing Knife
1 Cutlet Beater
1 Hot plate
1 pestle and Mortar
1 Large copper dripping$_x$ & Iron stand   ($_x$Pan)
10 Tripods
9 Pewter dishes
1 Tin Can   (very bad)
3 Kitchen Knives
2 Delph Tubs

149

26 Iron Skewers
1 Frying pan
2 Tin spice Boxes
1 Silver sauce pan and spoon
1 Eight Day clock
1 small deal table
1 Broken Chair
8 Tin coffee pots
3 Metal sauce pans & 2 copper covers
1 Copper Basting Ladle
1 Iron *d°*
1 large Metal Boiler
1 old Tin Pot
4 Odd copper stew pans and covers
1 Large Tin Tray
1 Brass Cock for Pipe
1 Steak Tongs
1 deal Twine Box
3 Tin candlesticks
1 House Bucket
1 Clothes Basket
2 Tawney clothes
1 Vegetable Brush

151

Pastry

26 Tartlet Pans ⎞
8 Large *d°* ⎠ tin
10 fluted Jelly pans or Moulds
5 Plain *d°*
1 Elephant *d°*
⎧ 1 Mellon *d°*
⎩ 2 large Jelly Moulds
1 Partridge Shape
Quere where 1 Copper Toss pan
are the
ditto —— 4 Small stew pans and covers
6 Small Jelly shapes
12 *d°* *d°*
1 Brass Scales
1 Tin Bread cullender
3 Tin Shapes
2 Small Wooden Bowls
6 Tin toast Pans
2 Wooden Bowls
2 Brown Pan crocks
14 lip^d Bowls
1 Bread rasp

1 Brass candlestick, snuffers & Extinguisher
3 Boxes of Tin paste cutters
1 Tin Vegetable cutter
1 Tin Sconce
1 Broken Looking Glass
2 Wafer Tongues
1 deal hanging shelf
1 Small deal Table
1 Flour Tub
1 Small *d°*
1 Elm Table
2 deal dressers painted
1 paste Board
1 Coffee Mill
8 Hair sieves
1 old Chair
1 Salt Binn
6 Tawneys
2 Wooden Butter slices
2 Paste Brushes
3 Carved Stamps

153

Scullery

1 Plate Drain.
1 Grease Tub (lock & Key)
1 large deal Table
1 copper Pan
1 sheet Iron Beef Boiler [*recte* Broiler (?)]
1 Griddle
1 Sallamander
1 Goffrey
2 Stools
3 Water Tubs
1 Large deal dresser
4 Black crocks
1 Wooden Bowl
2 Boiling Vats
1 Jelly Stand

155

Larder

1 Beef Tub lined with lead
1 Oak Table
1 Small powdering File [or Tile?]
1 Step Ladder
4 Black crocks
2 Pewter dishes

1 Marble slab
1 Beam and chains & Wooden scale bottoms
1 Weight 6 s^t
15 ½ cw^t. w^{ts}
1 Stone w^t
1 half *do*
1 4^{lb}.. *do*
1 frame with hooks

Servants Hall

1 large Oak Table
7 formes
1 large Press
1 Elm Table
1 Tub
1 Plate Basket
1 Mop and Brush
1 cloth roller
23 Japan^d Pints
52 Forks, 24 Knives
2 carving Knives & forks
16 Iron spoons
37 Pewter dinner plates
18 *do* soup *do*
2 long Iron candlesticks
2 Japan^d Trays and 2 snuffers
1 Wooden Knife Box
3 Trenchers
2 wooden Bowls
1 Spade and fire shovel
1 Old fender
1 poker and 1 shovel
1 5 Gallon copper can
2 2 Gallon *d^o-*
1 1 Gallon *d^o-*

Servant Maids Hall

1 Oak Table
3 forms
1 deal press fitted to Wall
1 Metal Kettle
1 Poker and 1 Tongs

Passage

1 Large Bacon chest, (lock and Key)
1 Old chair
1 Corner cupboard fast to Wall
1 deal side Board leaf
1 Bread cupboard (lock & Key)

Beer Cellar

4 Stillions
2 Hampers
1 Small Basket
1 Copper half Gallon
1 Pewter quart
2 Barrel Racks
2 Brass cocks
1 form

Inside Cellar

3 Beer stands
A Large quantity of Bottles
1 Brewers Sling

Ale Cellar

1 Deal Bottle Stand
1 Glass Lanthorn
1 Hogshead

Inside Cellar

1 Deal Rack with hooks
1 Old Board
1 Green Lanthorn

Large Ale Cellar

4 large Stillions
4 Pipes
1 Brass cock
1 Tin Tundish
1 pitcher
2 Barrel Racks

Carton House, County Kildare

Glass Pantry

18 Cut quart Decanters
20 cut water crofts
7 cut Pint decanters
1 Sallad Bottle
2 cut Butter coolers & stands
1 Sugar Bowl
8 Ale glasses
13 Beer cans
16 Wine & Water glasses
22 cut wash hand D^o
17 lip^d wine coolers
3 odd wash hand glasses
15 large cut Dinner d^o
21   Wine   do
25   do   dinner glasses
23 Liquiere Glasses
2 Chamber Vases
2 White Basons
1 White and Brown Stone Jug
1 Glass Bucket
1 old plain decanter
7 Mahogany Dish Trays
2   d^o glass d^o
5 Tubs
2 plate Baskets lined with Tin
1 plate Drain
1 form, 1 sconce
1 Deal Table
2   do presses
2 Plate chests
2 Leather cases
1 Oak turn up Bedstead
1 Old hair Mattrass
1 feather Bolster,
1 Large Old English Blanket, 1 under d^o (Irish)
1 Blue Serge Quilt
1 Blunderbuss
1 Table   }
1 Dresser } with drawers fast to Wall
1 Oil Lamp & Cover
5 Decanters, 1 Stopper
2 Pickle glasses
14 Hobnob   do
8 Liquire   do

Scullery to Glass Pantry

3 old Deal Tables
2 old Boxes
4 copper dishes with handles (plated)
3 Glass Lanthorns
12 old tin Dish covers
20 pewter water plates
5 Tin water dishes
8 Brass ormolu candlesticks 4 lights
8 Small d^o
1 Tin sconce
2 Mops
1 Metal Pot
1 Iron Spoon
1 old Knife Box
1 old Mill
1 Knife Board
1 range of Shelves
1 Old Mahogany Gardevine
1 old deal Table
   Old Boxes & Bottles
3 old Copper Ice pails
2 Japan^d Bottle coopers
2 Hanging shelves
1 New Iron coal box
1   d^o coal shovel
1   d^o tin 2 gallon Can
1 white delph Jug.

Plate Pantry

1 Range of Presses with drawers inside
1 Range of Shelves
1 Mahog. Oval Table
1 old deal   do
1 deal clothes horse
1 old Stuffed back and seat Chair
3 old Stools
1 poker and tongs
1 Copper Boiler
1 Sweeping Brush
1 Coffee Mill
1 Pewter Bason
1 Toilette glass
1 Tin Sconce

¹⁶⁹

Lamp Room

1 Old Mahogany Oval Table
3 old deal Tables
2 corner presses, fast
3 old chairs
3 old Deal Boxes
2 old footmen or Kettle Stands
a Butt of Oil
a Large Tin Oil Vessel, with 3 cocks and Stand
2 Tin^d Lamp trays
3 Oil cans
1 Oil figure
1 Brass cock (perfect)
3 old *d^o*
1 Brass 6 Burner Lamp
6 *do* 2 *Do*
4 *do* 1 *Do*
2 *do*   with glass round Tops
2 old tin lamps Painted
4 Japan^d.. *Do*
1 old reading *Do*
3 Brass branch lamps
1 old painted cupboard
1 copper coffee pot
1 Tin   *do*
1 Tin flat candlestick and Snuffers
4 glass Lanthorns
1 Deal Table

¹⁷¹

The Dukes own mans Room

1 Mahogany Half talboy
1 Deal Table
3 Small *do*
1 Mahogany chair covered in hair cloth
3   *Do*   old chairs
2 Yds Venitian Carpet
1 Elm Voidore Table
1 old Large Stuffed back & Seat chair
1 Oak Hall chair
1 old wire fender
1 Sett of Old fire Irons & Brush
3 white Basons,   Ewers & Vase
1 Soap tray
1 Japan^d footpan
1 Small dressing glass

Closet

1 Long deal Table
1 clothes Horse
  Old Boxes &c

¹⁷³

Store Cellar

2 Vinegar Hogsheads
4 Stillions
1 form
1 Brewers Sling
3 Small Kegs
4 old Baskets
2 Oil cans
1 Jar
1 Hanging Shelf
1 Wooden dish

¹⁷⁵

Still Room

3 deal Tables
3 deal presses
1 Paste board
2 old chairs
6 Tubs, 20 Mops
36 old sweeping Brushes
4 Jars, 1 Copper Kettle
3 Casks, 1 Brass cock
5 Balls of Mop Yarn
10 pickling crocks
10 Baskets
1 Sweeping brush
1 Small Basket, New,

Cellar

46 Bottles of Ginger Spruce
19   *D^o*   *D^o*   (not fit for use)
19   *D^o*   ginger wine
1 Stillion
1 Lot of old Mop handles
1 Mopes Head
1 Glass Lanthorn
1 clothes Horse (broken)

Passage to Cellars

1 Old Bottle Drainer

Carton House, County Kildare

First Housemaids App^ts

- 1 Carpet Broom
- 1 Sweeping Brush
- 2 House Buckets
- 2 Coal Boxes
- 1 Stair Brush
- 1 dusting *d^o*
- 1 Crevice *d^o*
- 2 Iron coal scuttles
- 1 Black Pitcher
- 1 Black lead Kettle and brush
- 1 Copper coal Box (New)

Second House^mds App^ts

- 1 New Copper coal Box
- 1 Sweeping brush
- 1 Carpet Twig
- 1 Dust pan, 1 Stair brush
- 1 Table Brush, 1 dusting *d^o*
- 1 crevice *D^o*, 2 House Buckets
- 1 Iron coal Scuttle
- 1 Black Lead Kettle and Brush
- 5 Brass candlesticks 4 Extinguishers
- 6 pair of Steel Snuffers
- 1 Steel candlestick and Snuffers

Still room Maids List

- 1 Tin candlestick
- 1 flat Brass *d^o*
- 1 dust Pan, 1 Brush

Barrack room Maids List

- 1 House Bucket
- 1 Dust Pan
- 1 Dust Brush
- 1 Sweeping *d^o*

House Maid of Attic Storys list

- 2 House Buckets
- 1 Tin house pan
- 1 Sweeping Brush
- 1 dusting *d^o*
- 10 Tin Candlesticks
- 9 pair of Snuffers & 10 Extinguishers
- 1 New copper coal Box

Laundry
Smoothing room

- Large Table with 5 Drawers
- 15 Smoothing Irons & 4 Stands
- 1 coal shovel, 2 old stools
- 2 Smoothing Blankets
- 1 old Arm chair
- 5 Deal folding Horses
- 6 hanging racks for drying clothes
- 2 long copper steam pipes

Small Bedroom adjoining smoothing room

- 1 old deal Bedstead
- 1 old Mattrass
- 1 old deal Table & Chair
- 1 Cupboard fast in wall
- 1 old Tongs, fender & Brush
- 1 New Ironing Blanket 1¾ yds by 1¼

Mangle Room

- 1 Large Mangle, Oak Beds & 4 Poles
- 4 Holland Mangle clothes
- 1 Deal Table
- 5 Leg boards

Washing Room

- 1 Copper Boiler
- 1 Iron *d^o*
- Leaden pipes with 20 Brass cocks
- 2 Washing Tubs (1 broken)
- 1 Step ladder
- 1 Shovel and poker & Coal Box
- 1 Tin can
- 2 Wooden bowls & 2 spoons
- 1 Brass Skillet
- 3 white Basons
- 1 Metal Kettle
- 2 tin candlesticks
- 9 clothes Baskets (2 broken)
- 1 Hair sieve
- 1 Scrubbing Brush, 1 sweeping *d^o*

Bed Room (off Mangle room)

1 old 4 post Bedstead and Blue cheque curtains
1 old straw paliass
1 Bordered feather Bed & bolster
1 old English Blanket
2 old Irish d^o
1 Serge Quilt
2 Deal Tables
5 Chairs
1 Japan^d tea tray
1 old Looking glass
1 small Deal hanging shelf
1 old Tin fender
1 Sett of fire Irons & hearth brush   „

185

Kitchen Boy^s Room

1 old four post Bedstead
1 old sloping d^o
1 old stump d^o
3 old Paliasses
4 feather Beds and 3 bolsters
3 old Blankets on each bed
2 Brussels quilts
3 Serge d^o
4 old stuffed back and Seat chairs
2 Caned D^o
1 Rush D^o & 1 Oak d^o
1 Small deal Table
1 Deal press
2 Tin candlesticks
1 deal clothes Horse

Mr Sheals Room

1 Tent Bedstead & Green Morine Curtains
1 Bordered Paliass and hair Mattrass
1 Feather Bed, bolster and Pillow
3 Blankets, 1 Counterpane
1 piece of carpet
1 Sloping Desk and Drawers & Keys
1 Deal corner cupboard
1 Oak Press
1 Cheque curtain
1 Oak Table & Drawer
4 Chairs, 1 Stool
1 Looking glass, 1 Toilette d^o
1 Tea cadea,   1 wire fender

1 Sett of fire Irons and brush
1 copper coffee pot
1 Deal coal box
1 Mahog. Night stool
8 Tin canisters
1 Brass footman
1 Brass & 1 tin candlestick
1 Bason, Ewer and Vase

187

Watchmans Room

1 old Bedstead & Straw Paliass
2 old feather Beds and 1 Bolster
2 old Blankets
1 Serge quilt
4 old chairs & 1 Table
1 Sconce, 1 old cupboard fast to wall
1 Oil sconce & Candlestick
1 Gun & Bayonet
1 Brass Barrel Pistol
1 Large old Lanthorn
1 Earthen Dish
1 old Sweeping Brush
1 Tin lanthorn, 3 tin Oil cans
1 Tin fender, 2 Jars
1 Tin Oil Tray
10 Tin Sconces
2 Mops
1 Tin Quart
6 new green lamps, glazed
6 Burners for *ditto*

Coal Waults

1 Copper coal Box
3 Iron d^o

Brew House

1 Copper Boiler
1 Lead pump
1 Shovel

189

Bake House

2 deal Tables
1 Salt Box
1 old Binn
1 Losset and 2 Stands

1 deal press, 2 Jars
a lot of Window Sashes & leads
a large Quantity of deal pannels & Lumber
a large Powder Horn
1 deal Step Ladder
2 Garden Matts
a Lot of broken tiles
Some old Iron
Part of a leaden Spout

Bacon House

1 Chair & Stool
1 Hatchet
5 Wooden racks with Iron hooks
a Quantity of Wooden Lumber

Passage to Mr Dillons room

1 Deal Table
2 forms with lockers
1 Eight day Clock
1 Saddle tree
1 Lamp.

191

Carton Office

1 Deal office desk, counter and drawers
1 Mahogany Sloping Desk with Book case on top
1 deal press
1 office stool
1 Nest deal drawers fastened to wall
1 French Weather Glass
1 plain   *d^o*
1 Mahog. × Stool
14 Maps, Large & small
a Rack for *d^o*
1 deal Alphabet
2 leather letter Bags
1 Iron safe
1 Tin Tun dish & leather case
1 Hammer Cork Screw for bottling wine
1 Boring Brace & 4 gimblets
1 copper coffee pot
1 Oval Oak Table
1 old leather bottom^d chair
9 cord racks
1 old tin fender
1 Sett of fire Irons & Brush

1 Pewter Quart, pint and half pint
1 oak Skeleton desk
1 deal fire guard
1 Japan^d Snuffers and Tray

193

Mr Dillons Bedroom

1 four post Bedstead ～
1 new suit of check curtains
1 Bordered Paliass
1 feather Bed, bolster & pillow
4 English Blankets   11¼
1 old   *d^o*
2 fringed Counterpanes   11¼
1 chest of Drawers (oak)
1 Deal press fast to wall
1 pair of Pistols brass mounted
1 Elm Table
1 Small Mahogany   *d^o*
2 deal   *d^o*
4 leather Bottom^d Chairs   (1 broken)
1 Messengers Box, red,
1 paint   *D^o*
1 hanging Bookshelf
1 Festoon window curtain, blue check
1 Dressing Glass
1 Blue bason, Ewer & white Vase, 1 Soap Pot
2 Glass Tumblers
2 long brass candlestick
1   *D^o*   *D^o*
1 old green Morine curtain
1 white Teapot, 1 Jug, & 1 white Cup
1 Tin Fender
1 Sett of fire Irons & Brush
1 Small piece of Carpet

195

Barrack

Coachmans Room n° 1.

1 Stump Bedstead and Straw Paliass
1 Old feather Bed & Bolster
2 old Blankets
1 Worsted Brussels Quilt
1 large deal press
4 old chairs
1 deal Table with drawer
1 Toilette glass
1 Tin candlestick & Extinguisher
1 White Vase, Jug and Bason

290

Room nº 2„

1 Iron Bedstead and Paliass
3 feather Beds & 1 Bolster
3 Small old Blankets
1 Worsted Brussels quilt
1 deal chest of drawers
1 *dº* Table
2 Old chairs
1 Tin candlestick
1 White Vase

Room nº 3„

1 4 Post Bedstead & Curtains
1 Paliass
1 feather Bed and new Bolster
3 old Blankets
1 worsted Brussels Quilt
1 deal press
1 *dº* Table
1 Chair
1 Bason, Ewer & Vase

197

Room nº 4

1 4 post Bedstead & Morine curtains
1 Paliass
1 feather Bed and Bolster
3 old Blankets
1 Worsted Brussels Quilt
2 old chairs   (1 broken)
1 deal Press
1 *dº* Table
1 Vase

Sportsmans Room

1 Iron Bedstead & Paliass
1 Feather Bed and Bolster
3 Blankets
1 Worsted Brussels Quilt
2 old chairs covered in Tapestry,
2 cane seat *Dº*
1 Deal Table
1 *Dº* Press
1 white Vase, bason & Water Jug
1 Tin Candlestick

Net Room

1 Deal Table
1 Large deal Press
1 Draft net
2 Eel Nets
2 landing *dº* (broken)
1 Thread casting Net
1 Silk   *dº*
1 Canoe
3 Cat Traps, 1 Man trap
6 Kite Traps
1 Map
1 Mallet, Wadding & punch lead
1 Garden Mat

199

Store Room nº 6„

a Case of Stained glass, 10 pieces (1 broke)
1 Horn drawing Board
1 Stool and Cushion in Morine
13 Crimson Morine cushions
3 Scarlet cloth   *dº*
1 Small Mahogany work table
4 Gilt pier table frames
2 *dº* white frames
   part of (Trou Madam) Table
   Oak top of *dº* —— *dº*
1 Narrow Mahogany
2 Gilt leather Church screens
6 Japan.ᵈ   *dº*
2 Old gilt chairs covered in leather.
1 Broken Night Table and Stool
1 library Desk and Ladder
1 Large old Trunk
6 Mahog. Boot Jacks
1 Hair cushion covered in Damask
1 Small corner cupboard
2 Tent poles and Marquee cover
2 old Halberts
1 French horn
1 old fishing rods
1 painters frame
parts of 5 old Bedsteads
2 old Backgammon Boxes
2 old Damask curtains
1 old Mattrass
1 Oak Bed Table

Carton House, County Kildare

1 Large glass dish, with bronze mounting }
weights & Chains for Lamps }
68 Deal frame picture backs
60 print frames, glazed
6 old paintings in frames
3 old Gilt frames, not glazed
5 old blind frames;
1 glass Still
A quantity of useless lumber,

Store Room nº 7

2 green wire fire guards
2 deal Presses
1 Mahogany Bidet and delph Pan
2 old Broken   *dº*
2 Japan^d foot pans
1 Mahog. horse drawing board
1 Turkey Carpet
1 old Trunk
1 old gilt sofa, cover^d in Damask & Case
1 Mahog. Toilette frame with^t glass   18 × 17
1 old Gilt chair
1 p^r of new Mahogany Bedsteps, cover^d in Brussels carpet
a Mahogany cornice of Organ
1   *dº*   Chamber Airer
1 old Chart frame
3 Mahog. O. G. Bed cornices
1 Gilt wyat window cornice & 2 brass rods
4 rolls of Oil cloth
    part of a Bedsteads broken
    a quantity of Old deal Boards

Room nº 8

1 Iron Bedstead
2 Bordered Paliasses
1 feather Bed & Bolster
3 old Blankets
1 worsted Brussels Quilt
2 old chairs, 1 deal Table
1 deal press
1 Tin candlestick

Room nº 9.

2 old chairs   (Broken)
1 Bordered Paliass   (Cut)
1 Deal press
1 old Bedstead,   (Mr. Scotts room)

Room nº 10.,

1 Iron Bedstead
2 Bordered Paliass   (Cut)
3 old chairs   (broken)
1 Deal Press
1   *dº*   Table

Post Boys Room nº 11.,

2 Iron Bedsteads
2 Border^d Paliasses
4 feather Beds, 2 Bolsters
6 old Blankets
2 Worsted Brussels Quilts
2 old chairs
1 Deal Table
1   *dº*   Press
1 tin candlestick
1 white Vase
1 dressing glass

Room nº 12.,

1 deal Stump Bedstead
1 Paliass
2 feather Beds and 1 bolster
1½ p^r of old Blankets
1 worsted Brussels Quilt
1 deal Press
1   *dº*   Table

Coach Horse Stable

5 Stable Buckets
1 corner Oat Binn painted
1 tin Sconce
1 Step Ladder
1 Nose Bag
2 curry combs and Brushes
1 Water Brush
4 horse collars
1 deal press fitted to wall
3 forks 1 broom & 1 Shovel
    Racks fastened to Wall
2 new stable Buckets

Old coach horse Stable

1 Chaff cutter
2 old Binns
1 Press
1 Lanthorn

Hack Stable

1 Oat Binn
1 Seive

Saddle horse stable

1 Oat Binn

[207]

Coach House

1 Summer Carriage
1 Snow   *D°*
1 Childs   *D°*
1   *d°*   Pheaton
1 Caravan with Cushions & Tarpaulin
1 Jaunting Car & Cushions
1 Tilbury
1 Chariot
1 Horse Break
2 Trunk covers & straps

Saddle room

4 double Rein Bridles
4 Snaffle   *d°*   (2 old)
4 Saddles   (1 stirrup Iron wanting)
1 Side Saddle
4 Suits of Horse clothes
5 pair of Girths
1 Water deck
1 pair of Holsters
1 Rigger
1 pair of coach Harness complete, (plated mounting)
1 Set of Gig Harness
1 Set of Jaunting Car *d°*
1 Table
1 Stool and Chair
3 Saddle Racks
   Harness Racks round the room
1 Old Stove

Stable Yard

1 old Harness Stand
1 Carriage Setter

[209]

Engine House

1 Large fire Engine
1 Small   *d°*
   Suckers, Tubes and Pipes
1 Old deal table & Trussells
6 Leather Buckets
2 old shutters
3 Harness Racks

Granary

1 old Mahogany Oval table
1 Leather Trunk
a Table frame
1 old Table, Mahogany top on deal frame
a Windlass
1 Step ladder
a long pole
2 Shovels
1 Bushell
   Sack car
1 Winnowing Sheet
10 old Sacks
a Scoop & Basket
1 Brush
1 Beam & Scales
2 weights of 28^{lb} each
1   *D°*   „   14 „
2   *D°*   „   7 „
6 half Cw^t.

[211]

Dairy Kitchen

1 deal dresser and drawers
24 white plates & 4 dishes   (8 cracked)
3 deal Tables
5 old Chairs
1 Metal Boiler
3 Churns and 2 dashes
2 Washing Tubs
1 form
1 Tin can
1 Tin candlestick
1 Copper coal Box, 1 wooden *d°.*

Carton House, County Kildare

1 old Sofa
1 metal Kettle
2 Sweeping brushes
2 Mops

Bed room

1 old Stump Bedstead, & Paliass
1 feather Bed and bolster
1 old English Blanket
5 old Chairs   (3 broken)
1 old Deal press
1 old frame Bedsted

Stairs

An Eight day clock
A deal Horse

213

Winter Dairy

21 Small black pan crocks
3 Large   *D^o*
4 Butter   *D^o*
4 large pan *D^o*   (3 broken)
3 Milk pails
1 Small piggen
2 Butter Buckets
1 Small childs churn
1 Butter scales   deal, 2.½^{lb} w^{ts} 1 – ¼^{lb} *d^o*
2 Strainers, 3 Keelers
2 wooden Bowls
1 Strainer ladder
1 deal table top with Iron frame
   Deal shelves round the room
2 Print cutters
1 Silver Spoon

Summer Dairy

A Marble Fountain
Marble Slabs, fitted on Iron frame, all round
10 Venitian Blinds
5 White delf urns and covers
1 delph Churn
1 white round delph Butter Pan   (cracked)
1   *d^o*   delph strainer
2   *d^o*   sauce pans
1   *d^o*   Noggin
6   *do*   delph milk pans
1 wooden churn

Yard

A churn drainer
A Stone Trough
A wheel Barrow

215

Hen house

1 old Bedstead
1 feather Bed & Bolster
2 old Blankets   } all bad & Worn
1 Quilt & 1 Rug
1 old Chair
1 Deal Table
1 Tin can
1 Iron Pot
1 Sweeping brush
1 Smoothing Iron
2 linen feather Bags
1 old sett of fire Irons
1 old Candlestick
1 Heater
1 Dish, 1 Knife & fork
2 Wooden Bowls
1 large chicken coup
1 old deal Press
2 old forms
3 old Boxes
1 Washing Tub

Yard

1 Large Bird house
1 Hamper
2 Wheelbarrows
1 Iron shovels

217

Stewards House

1 deal Settle Bed
1 Large deal Table
1 Small   *d^o*
2 old chairs

Stewards Bed room

2 old feather Beds and 2 bolsters
2 pair of old Blankets
2 old Chairs
1 Deal chest

Forge„

	✓	2	Pair of forge Bellows
	✓	2	Anvils and blocks
	✓	1	Bench with drawers
	✓	3	Vices
	✓	1	Bucket
	✓	1	Water trough
	✓	1	upright drill, with ½ cwᵗ. & ¼ cwt wieghts, Brace & 3 bits
	✓	1	old Stool

Mettal ✓ 1 Mandrill for rounding hoops *Gᵗ Large one*

13 new 12 Botting Tools

9 Dogs or Ties ✓ 7 Shewing *dᵒ*

2 4 Wrenches (1 broke)

old & Broke 1 Bit & Brace *put with old Irons*

not yet [?] to be found ✓ 1 travllʳ for wheels *kept and amongˢᵗ old Iron*

5 Screw Taps and 5 plates *has 6 Plates 14 Screw Taps*

3 Tap wrenches

✓ 9 pr of fire tongs *has 13 Tongs*

2 Shovels *2 Shovells for Fire*

Irons ✓ 1 Cutter and 1 Fuller *has 2 Horse shears Fullers* *has 5 Cutters has 3 Bottoms & 3 Top Fullers*

4 Top and 7 Bottoms 6 Suages

6 Fullers *has 3 Bottoms & 3 Top Fullers*

has 6 & 6 of 2 wedges

them all Mandrells 1 Mandrel for Axes | *Peter Wise* |

has 28 ✓ 24 Punches

219

only one 2 Tin Mans Sheers *the other Broke up –*

✓ 1 Straight edge

✓ 1 pʳ. Compasses

✓ 6 small hand punches

✓ 1 Metal sack Mandrill

has 9 4 Dogs for cart Wheels *Good & Bad*

has 4 5 only 11 files different sizes

✓ 1 large stake & 1 small *dᵒ*

✓ 2 Sledges

has 8 4 Hammers

✓ 2 Sett Hammers

✓ 1 *Dᵒ* without handle

has 2 1 cutting block *or Dalston has one for axe & 1 large*

✓ 1 Small Hand vice

1 Stamp (K) | *not to be had* |

1 chissell *has 2 hand Chissells*

1 Breast plate for drilling | *none to be had* |

has 2 1 Pritching

✓ 1 Coal Shovel

Carton House, County Kildare

2 Tripods   } Kitchen;   /none/
2 Spits   /none/
12 Flat Files
2 Tack Drills

Iron Shops

2 Beams
6 Molding Planes
1 Bench, with desk on Top

Black Smiths Rooms

inside rooms

	✓	1 Deal painted press upon press
has 2 now		1 deal Table
vy old	✓	1 Settle Bed
1 only		2 forms
	✓	16 plates of Glass, (Some Broken)

2 peices of old Chmy Peice
1 old brass Candlestick
1 Wooden Box - old
1 Bed stead from Carton House
1 Chaff Bed - old & Bad
5 very bad sheets
45 Blanktts Doubles
2 old Bed Ticks
one of these
2 old Bolsters both ∧ Halm [?] Chaff
2 old Chairs bttm cane
1 Iron fire Shovell
1 Iron flesh fork vy bad
1 Iron Pot
1 old Buckett

Bed Room

1 Deal Stump Bedstead
1 chaff Bed in Ticken & 2 feather bolsters
2 Pᵣ Blankets, 1 Rug.
2 Pᵣ sheets 2ys breadths
1 Deal Table
1 Old Arm chair

221

Coopers Shop

1 Flower Tub
1 Coal Measure
1 Wine Tub
1 Deal case
6 Garden Matts
33 Hampers
1 coopers Stake
1   *Dᵒ*   Mace
1 Augur
   Some Lumber

Paint Shops

7 unfinished Rakes
4 cross cut saws
12 crow bars
2 Mullets, Flag & Stand
2 10 Gallon Oil Kegs

4 Tin paint Pots
1 Deal cupboard
1 old Stool
1 Bench with drawers
10 pᵣ of shears

Carpenters Shop

2 Benches
4 Molding planes
1 small Turning Leaths
1 cheval fire screen
1 Bottle cooper
1 lamp Tray
1 Organ Barrel
1 chamber airer
3 old chairs
1 Tenon saw
10 Buckets 5 Hods   } Plaisterers &
5 Mortar Boards, 1 Stone trough } Labourers &c

223

Wheelers Shop

1 Bench hold fast
2 Working Benches
2 Wheeling pits
1 Boring Block
1 Turning leath

2 Gauges
2 Chissels
1 Step Ladder
4 pair cart wheels, (unfinished) with stocks, spokes & felloes
2 Small harrows
1 pump rod for drawing boxes
1 Callipers
1 training block

Yard *inside carpenters Shop*

full of Lumber

Iron room in Yard
some square & rod Iron
Hoop Iron & Lumber

Large Yard

11 Iron Gates
1 grinding stone
1 old winnowing Machine
8 old Hothouse Sashes
1 old Water Barrel
1 hand Barrow
1 old leaden cistern, ornamented
1 Whip saw
1 cross cut saw
1 Step ladder
1 Snow breaker

225

Lead House

a quantity of old Lead
   Some pitch & Tar
1 Man Trap
a Basket of illumination sconces
2 plain cisterns
1   *D.º*   ornamented

Chip House

full of wood for fire

His Graces Office

a Turning Lathe & bench & brasses (compleat)
1 Bench Vice
1 pʳ of Sticking bolts
a Chest of Tools

2 Cases of turning chisels containing 92
a Surveyors chain (Brass) and Triangle & Measures
a Deal press
1 14ᵇ weight
1 old seat
a nest of small drawers
1 Deal alphabet
1 Nail Box
1 Hand stove ⎫
1 Glue pot   ⎬ loft over office
2 Scrapers   ⎭
1 Ladder
   A quantity of Lumber

227

Farm yard

3 New drays, rails framed on
1 old   *Dᵒ*
6 Carts with Sides
2 Mules   *Dᵒ*
1 Bomb cart
1 Timber Truck
1 Stone Slide
6 frames for carts
1 Hay sweep
1 Hay horse rake
3 Sett of side ladders for drays
1 Turnip wood on roller ⎫
1 Grass seed   *Dᵒ*   ⎬ with carriages
2 Bush Harrows
1 Stone Roller
2 large Metal rollers
1 small   *dᵒ*
11 cart Ropes
4 pʳ rope plough reins
1 Saw
1 Scrub
18 Hay rakes
2 pʳ flails
3 Shovels
6 Sling forks
2 Sod Irons
2 corn weeders , wooden
1   *Dᵒ*   , Iron
7 hay forks
1 Edging Iron
7 Grass pickers
5 Dung forks
7 Potatoe *dᵒ*

17 Turnip scufflers
6 Mattocks
1 Iron rake
2 dung drags
3 Brick cleaners
2 Bullock scrapers
2 Bill hooks
4 Rope Twisters
4 falling Axes
2 Small D^o_-
1 Dung Knife
3 p$^r_-$ Hedgesheers
1 Thatching fork
1 Sledge
4 Stone hammers
3 Hay Knives

229

3 Pick Axes
1 Line & Reel
2 Road rakes
4 crow Bars
1 Ice Mallet
9 Wheel Barrows
1 hand D^o
20 Potatoe Baskets
1 Kish
1 Metal roller (for Mule)
3 long red Ladders   about 30 feet
1 short D^o about 20 feet
2 Scotch wheel Ploughs
3   d^o (no wheels)
1 Double drill plough   (imperfect)
1 Scuffling d^o
1 Moulding d^o
1 Break Harrow
2 Turnip Barrows
2 double Harrows
22 Swinging Bars
1 Large Hay Tether
1 Winnowing Machine
2 Sowing Sheets
4 Sheep Racks
1 Scutch harrow
1 deal Table   } in the Barn
2 Ladders, made fast
a quantity of Lumber
2 old short ladders
1 oval Tub
1 charcoal half Barrel

231

Carters Room

1 Deal Table
2 forms, 1 Garden seat
2 old deal Bedsteads
2 chaff Beds
4 old Blankets
2 old Rugs
2 Broken Sheets
1 Deal Box
1   d^o door

Harness Room

5 Setts of Plough harness, Iron chains & brass Ferrules
1 Sett of Mules Plough harness with ropes
1 patent feeding tube
1 Sett of Mules leather Boots
2 p^r of Shears
1 Leather fire Bucket
1 Cart hammer
2 pair of Iron Tandem chains
6 Waggoners Whips
2 Grease boxes, 3 tin lanthorns
1 Oil feeder, 2 oil pans & 2 brushes
2 Water Brushes, 1 Oil can & 2 Jars
7 feeding Bags
1 Collar block
2 deal Tables
1 desk covered in cloth
2 Stools
5 Ridders and 2 Seives
1 Straw Basket
a Quantity of old cart Harness
1 Ladder – (a fixture)
5 Setts of Trace harness
13 Cart Straddles, 12 setts of Britchers
19 Collars & harness
17 p^r Winkers, Iron chains & Bits
4 p^r Blinds for Horse Mill
3 Awl blades 1. Hammer. 2 Knives   }
1 pincers 3 Punches, 2 Collar Needles } Workmens Tools
1 collar stuffer, 2 p^r Clambs   }

233

Tool House

2 paviours Hammers
2 Trowels
5 chissels
1 Plaistering Board
  Birch Brooms

Stewards Stable

1 Saddle & Bridle
1 Collar
1 Peck

Two cart horse Stables

12 Head collars

Shrubbery

1 Grass Barrow
1 Wheel *do*
2 Scuffles
2 Rakes
1 Small Saw

Bullock Yard

20 Cribs

Slaughtering House

1 Tackle & Rope
1 Hatchet
1 Pritch
2 Knives
1 Steel & Pouch
2 Beef saws   (one bad)
2 Butchers Aprons
1 Beef tree
1 *D^o* hook
1 Swivel *D^o*
3 Barrels
1 Large Tub
2 Buckets
2 horn Brands
10 Sheep *d^o*
1 Step ladder
1 Tar Pot
1 Mortar & Pestle
1 Stone Jar
1 Bushel
1 Chopper
1 Sheep crook
3 half cw^t weights
1 14$^{lb}_{,,}$ *D^o*

237

Pidgeon Paddock

1 Water Barrow
1 Lime Screen
1 Water Barrel on a Large carriage
1 Tundish for   *d^o*

Pig Yard

1 oat chest
1 Boiler
1 Iron Potatoe Shovel
3 Water troughs
1 hand Water Barrel on a small carriage
1 Large water Vessel
1 Block
12 Metal troughs
2 Stone   *d^o*
1 Hatchet
1 Riddle

Dog Kennel

Wooden Dog beds
1 fork
4 troughs
2 Buckets
1 Meal Tub
10 p^r of couples
1 dog Muzzle
2 Rat traps
4 Puzzling pins
1 Cat trap (broken)
1 Chair

239

Shepherds House

2 deal Tables
2 chairs   (1 broken)
1 Settle Bed
1 Mahogany Table
3 Cherry wood chairs
1 Deal Bedstead
1 old fourpost Bedstead

Carton House, County Kildare

Old Stewards House

1 Moving Grate
1 deal Table with 2 drawers
1   *d⁰*   no drawers
1 Oak Chair
1 Iron Bedstead
4 Cherry wood chairs
1 deal Table with a drawer
1 Wash hand Stand   (broken)
1 old wire fender

Garden

9 Garden Spades   (2 broken)
1 Water Barrow with Barrell
4 Wheel Barrows   (1 broken)
6 Mignionette Boxes
1 Boat rest
1 old Cyder Trough
6 Large Watering pots   (2 useless)
2 Small   *D⁰*
8 pushing hoes
4 drawing   *d⁰*
5 Iron rakes
2 Wooden *D⁰*   (broken)
5 Hammers
2 Pruning chissels
3 Bill hooks
1 Hatchet
2 p.ʳ Shears, for clipping
4 Dung forks
3 Small   *D⁰*
1 Verging Iron
1 p.ʳ edging shears
1 p.ʳ lopping   *d⁰*
2 Hand syringes
2 Pine watering Tubes (Tin)
1 old Wire sieve
10 Scythes, put together for cleaning Pond
5 Scythes for moving, & 3 boards
2 p.ʳ Grape scissars
2 Garden Reels, & 1 Line
   part of a gate
2 old Barrels
5 forcing Mignionette boxes
1 old cyder Press
2 Broken ladders
1 old water vessel

3 Shovels
3 light frame
32 Caulyflower boxes with sashes
1 light frame & Sash
9 Melon frames with Sashes
64 Sashes in bad repair
49 Flower pots with sweet Marjoram
2 Bee stands
8 *d⁰* Hives,   (4 alive)

Melon Ground

46 Old Sashes
1 old door
1 Wire Screen

Gardiners House
Parlor

1 Oak Table with leaves
1 small Mahogany Table
1 Mahog. Sloping desk, with drawers
1 Deal desk on a frame
3 oak chairs
4 Mahogany stuffed seat *d⁰*
1 8 Day clock
1 old looking glass
1 Corner press
   Millers Gardiners Dictionary 2 Vols:
1 Tin fender
1 Sett fire Irons & brush
1 Tea tray
1 Ink stand
4 white Jugs, 1 blue *d⁰*
6 Blue Tea cups & saucers, 2 slop bowls
1 Black Tea Pot & Cream Ewer
2 Sauce Boats, 1 blue Plate
8 Wine glasses, 6 Egg cups
7 Tumblers, (2 broke)
1 Mustard & Pepper Stand

Kit[c]hen

1 painted deal dresser and Drawers
1 large deal Table
1 Small   *d⁰*
2 Oak chairs
1 Washing Tub

1 Sweeping brush
13 white plates & 3 dishes, 1 broken Bason,
2 Metal top pans & Covers
1 oval Metal Pot & cover
1 Metal tea Kettle
1 Tin   *do*
1 copper coal Box
1 Gridiron
1 Frying Pan
1 pr Tongs
1 pr Bellows
1 Small Basket
1 Brass candlestick
1 Small old Stool
1 Knife Board

Bed Room

1 fourpost Bedstead & old cheque curtains
1 Hair Mattrass
1 Feather Bed, (new tick, bolster & pillow)
1 pair of Irish Blankets
1 old under   *do*
2 pair of sheets   2 breadths 3 yds long
1 Rug Quilt,   1   *D̲o̲*
1 Pillow case
2 odd chairs
1 oak Press & small drawers on *do.*
1 Mahogany dressing Table
1 small Glass
1 White Vase
1 old nest of drawers
2 Diaper Table cloths,   2 breadths 2½ long

247

Lock Up Room

1 Deal Table
2 chairs
1 corner cupboard
1 old Barrel
3 large flower Pots
3 preserving Jars

Seed Room

Shelves and Drawers for seeds   (drawers not here)
18 Garden Nets for Wall trees

Greenhouse „

637 green House plants
23 Pots of carnation pinks
63   *do*   chinese Rose

Pinery „

353 Succession Pine plants
35 plants in fruit

249

Garden Lodge

1 Deal dresser
1 deal Table
1 Glass Lanthorn
2 forms
1 Pewter plate
1 deal desk painted
1 Settle Bed
1 fourpost bedstead
1 Paliass
2 feather Beds & 2 Bolsters
3½ pair of Old Blankets
2 Serge quilts

251

Waterstown

Kitchen

2 deal dressers
1 old Table & leaf
2 deal stools
1 8 day clock
2 old Chairs
    Shelves &c
      Do in, inside Kitchen;

Bed Room

1 old four post Bedstead
2 old chairs
1 Mahogany Table
1 Carbine & Powder Horn
2 pints
2 Chairs

Carton House, County Kildare

253

Cottage Barn

1 Large Metal roller
1 Watering Barrow
1 large Grass Barrow
2 wheel Barrows
1 Grind stone
1 Reel & Line
2 Stone rollers
1 hand barrow
3 Scythes
1 Wire riddle
3 dung forks
4 Scuffles
2 Garden Rakes
1 draw Hoe
1 Axe
2 Mallets
2 chissels
1 Billhook
1 Slashing hook
2 Wooden rakes
4 Watering Pots   (2 old)
1 Small d^o
2 Shovels
3 Spades
1 pruning chissel
1 Ladder
1 Small d^o
1 cross cut Saw
1 clipping Shears
4 garden Seats
1 pick Axe
1 hand saw

255

Cottage Garden

8 Flower Pots
1 Three light Box and Sashes
3 One light d^o
1 Weeding Trowel

Kit[c]hen

3 dozen & 9 green Plates	1 broken	} Desert Service
6 fruit Baskets	2 broken	

24 Green Saucers

12 Tea cups   } different Patterns
3 coffee Cans   2 broken
2 White sauce Boats
2 Blue fruit Bowls
1 White Bowl with green edge
24 white Plates
5 Large Dishes & 1 Small d^o 1 broken
2 Butter Buckets   1 D^o
16 Fruit dishes
1 old tea Pot
2 White flower Pots
1 Green Ink stand
6 small Wine glasses
35 Larger D^o
6 Salts
2 Odd Tumblers, (1 broken)
4 wooden Bowls
2   d^o Noggins
1   d^o Cooler
20   d^o Trenchers
1 Tin Kettle and Stand
1 Wooden Bucket, Iron hoops & handle
1 painted Deal dresser
1 Large deal Table
1 Kitchen Seat
2 deal Tables, fast to wall
Small deal painted shelf

257

1 Oven
1 Stove
1 Hot hearth &c

Passage

Deal shelves &c
1 plate drain
1 form
3 Stuffed Ottas

Stewards Room

3 Chairs, (2 broken)
Oak shelves and deal stand
1 Deal Table

Red Cottage Room

- 1 Large oak Table with narrow leaves
- 1 deal Table and drawer
- 7 deal chairs ⎞
- 2 conversation deal seats ⎠ Matted
- 1 Wooden clock
- 1 deal dresser with shelves
- 1 corner cupboard
- 1 Iron Fender
- 1 Sett of fire Irons
- 1 Old Pole screen & 1 Basket *d⁰*
- 1 Twig Book case
- 4 delph candlesticks
- 4 Box *D⁰* (1 broken)
- 1 Blue china Urn
- 1 Cocoa Shell
- 1 Bread Basket
- 1 Glass *d⁰*
- 73 Trenchers
- 9 Wooden Bowls
- 1 *d⁰* Strainer
- 5 *d⁰* Buckets
- 5 Madders
- 2 Dishes (Wood)
- 12 Spoons *d⁰*
- 7 Knives *d⁰*
- 2 Skimmers *d⁰* (1 broken)
- 1 Churn & Dash (no lid)
- 2 Mustard Pots
- 20 Wooden cups & Saucers
- 1 *d⁰* Tea pot
- 1 Spinning Wheel
  Deers Horns & Shells

Ball Room

- 1 Large deal Table
- 1 Oak *D⁰* with 2 leaves
- 1 pʳ Mahogany card tables
- 1 Mahogany Tea table & Drawer
- 5 Deal chairs
- 9 Seats covered in Morine
- 2 Tin branches for lights

Grand Lodge

- 1 Dresser with drawers &c
- 1 Settle Bed & 6 Stools
- 1 deal Table & drawer
- 2 old Bed Ticks and 4 bolsters (empty & Bad)
- 1 pair Old Blankets and quilt
- 2 Iron fire grates

Dairy

  Shelves all round
- 1 Wheel Barrow
  pair of Gates and Door

Carton Lodge Gate

- 1 Deal dresser
- 1 old four post Bedstead
- 1 case Pistols (brass barrels)
  A Double Gate
  Small gate, the lock out of Order

Kellys Town gate lodge

- 1 Dresser (new)
- 2 old stools & 2 forms
- 1 Barrow
- 1 Bill hook
- 1 Hoe and old spade
  pʳ of Gates ⎞
  small *D⁰* ⎠ locks out of order

New Gatehouse

- 1 Pair of Iron Gates with locks & Keys
- 1 Pair of Iron doors

Maynooth gate House

- 1 Deal dresser
- 1 Wheel Barrow (new)
- 1 deal form
  Iron gate, with padlock
  Small gates, (the locks Bad)

Carton House, County Kildare

PLATE 50
Unknown lithographer: *New Bridge, Co. Dublin*, *c*. 1860, lithograph
after a drawing by Frances Power Cobbe (1822–1904)

17

NEWBRIDGE HOUSE, COUNTY DUBLIN

1821

ALEC COBBE

NEWBRIDGE HOUSE IS ONE of a dwindling number of country houses in Ireland where the historic contents are still in place and where the original family is still in residence. The former Stuart-era house was bought by Archbishop Charles Cobbe (1686–1765) in June 1736 and a decade later he embarked on rebuilding it as a Palladian villa, for which James Gibbs (1682–1754) provided two alternative designs, one of which was executed. The archbishop bestowed his considerable estates and the nearly finished house on his only surviving son, Thomas, on his marriage to Lady Elizabeth Beresford in 1755. They continued the work and enlarged the house by adding a wing for a sculpture vestibule and picture gallery to the north, still employing Gibbs's designs in the interiors. Thomas Cobbe also built a large town house in Palace Row, Dublin, in 1768, a few doors from Charlemont House (it was sold twenty years later and, in the 1860s, demolished to make way for a church). Meanwhile, further establishments were maintained in Bath from the 1780s until 1836. The family archives are rich in letters, diaries and account books, which document purchases of furniture, Old Master pictures, statuary and the formation at Newbridge of a cabinet of curiosities, referred to as 'ye Ark' in the 1760s and as 'the China Room' in 1821 on account of the 1760s Chinese painted-paper panels with which the room was hung.

The earliest complete inventory of Newbridge is dated 1821. There are earlier lists of the archbishop's silver dated 1730 and from 1748 or thereabouts, and later inventories, sometimes only partial, taken at intervals through the nineteenth century and beyond (1839, 1852, 1898, 1901, 1914).

The 1821 inventory, here transcribed, was drawn up for Charles Cobbe (1781–1857), the archbishop's great-grandson. It was a time, as Charles's daughter, Frances Power Cobbe, the social reformer and author, would later write, when much in the house of the furniture and decorations belonged to the previous century. The inventory is unusual in not being occasioned by either a death or a marriage; no values are given. Its commissioning may have been preparatory to Charles's intended sojourn of some years with his family in England to attend to his children's education. A name inscribed at the end of the inventory, 'Mr McCabe, Peter's Place, Mount St', may possibly identify the compiler, but that name does not appear in family accounts or in Dublin directories of the time. The document was supplemented with a list of plate in Bath, drawn up by Charles himself in November 1821. The young Frances Power Cobbe annotated it in 1839, and in 1848 added 'New Lists'.

During 1821, Cobbe was High Sheriff of County Dublin, in which capacity he greeted King George IV when he landed in and departed from Ireland and conducted him to and from the boundaries of the City of Dublin. Perhaps because of Cobbe's shrieval year, the English sojourn was delayed until August 1823, lasting, with intermittent visits to Ireland, until May 1828. Curiously, this interrupted a major redecoration of the 1760s great drawing-room picture gallery. This room is still hung with Charles's grandfather's notable collection of Dutch and Italian Old Masters. In 1821 it included a superlative landscape by Meindert Hobbema, which, in 1839, Charles would sell in order to further his programme of rebuilding labourers' cottages throughout his estates. Charles embarked on the redecoration in October 1822 when the Drawing Room was hung with crimson flock paper supplied by the Dublin wallpaper manufacturer Patrick Boylan, and fitted with an Axminster carpet, sent over from Bath in March 1823. However, the sumptuous gilt poles and red silk curtains made by Messrs Mack & Gibton, an integral part of the scheme, had to wait until the family's return from England in 1828. Charles's refurbishment of what is generally considered among the finest eighteenth-century interiors in Ireland, survives unaltered to this day.

The inventory deals with contents of each room individually, commencing with the 'Middle Floor' (*piano nobile*). The room nomenclatures in the inventory are mostly self-explanatory, such as the 'Entrance Hall' and 'Dining Parlour'.

In 1823, however, the 'Sitting Room' was fitted out as the present library. This presumably replaced an earlier library, which disappeared in 1800 when Thomas Cobbe, then in Bath, directed that all the books of his father, the archbishop, should be sold by Vallance, the Dublin auctioneer. The books listed in the inventory are chiefly, then, what remained after that sale and the personal books subsequently acquired by Charles Cobbe. The list cannot be a complete inventory, for it leaves out a considerable number of seventeenth- and eighteenth-century volumes still in Newbridge which, from their inscriptions or bookplates, are known to have been in continuous family ownership. A significant proportion of those listed do survive. It would be surprising if the '2 large bibles' at the head of the list were not those of the archbishop which are still extant. The list includes some notable rarities such as the two volumes of 'New Fairy Tales', being the first edition of *A New System of Fairery*, published in Dublin in 1750 (plate 55). This is not merely rare, but the Newbridge copy is the only one known, although only the second of the two volumes can at present be found. The Æsop's Fables in prose by Sir Roger L'Estrange seems to have been lost but the archbishop's very scarce duodecimo edition of *Fables Choisies* put into verse by Jean de La Fontaine, Paris 1668, although not listed, survives. The Library would grow exponentially over the nineteenth century. The first wave of books to arrive after this inventory was taken resulted from the early death in 1823 of Charles's learned and artistic youngest brother the Rev. Henry William Cobbe, and that may have been the catalyst for fitting up the new library. An annotation at the end of the book list, in Charles's hand, states that his brother's books are distinguished in a separate catalogue (no longer believed extant).

The 'China Room' can only be the present-day 'Museum', hung in the 1760s with Chinese wallpaper panels (sold in 1961; replicas instated in 1985). It embraced a multitude of curiosities including the archbishop's collection of Swiftiana and his son's, of South Pacific material gathered on Cook's voyages, as well as the contributions made in the next generation by Charles and his brothers. Yet the inventory makes no mention of the 1762 museum display furniture, rather simple plain painted cases, almost certainly made by the estate joiner. Were these omitted, like the chimney-pieces, because they were largely immovable fixtures? It seems unlikely they had been temporarily removed to storage, since Frances, Charles's wife, was particularly interested in the cabinet of curiosities, which was later referred to by her children as their 'mother's museum'.

The bedrooms are mostly referred to by their colours (red, green, purple, white); however, the rooms of the master and mistress of the house, who occupied the two south-facing chambers at the top of the 'Broad Stairs', are 'Mr Cobbe's Dressing Room' and 'Mrs Cobbe's Bedroom', though from these titles one might not guess that the first is the larger room of the two. The chamber occupied by the archbishop, traditionally known as the 'Bishop's Room' appears as the 'Red Bedroom' while the room over the Drawing Room bay is the 'Bow Room' which was distinguished by its door and window-shutter panels being extra-ornamented with egg-and-dart carving. This room contained the 'Large Baby House', a Palladian doll's house standing eight feet high (a rare loss from the house and now at Leixlip Castle).

As its title implies, the inventory records the (mostly Irish) furniture, and includes carpets, window-curtains and the undetailed number of 'Pictures on the walls', with separate lists for books, linen, crockery, plate and sundries. There is also a separate section devoted to 'china' that records the 'Peacock' dinner and dessert service of Worcester porcelain, commissioned in 1763 by Thomas and Lady Betty Cobbe. Originally comprising more than 400 pieces, this is believed to be the largest recorded service to be supplied by an English china manufacturer at that time. It uniquely included steel and silver cutlery with matching porcelain handles, the latter separately listed in the 'Plate' section (see p. 316). There are items of plate that with certainty can be identified with pieces in the archbishop's lists. Many survived because they were in his silver chest lodged in 1909 at the Bank of Ireland, where it remained until withdrawn in 1959 and its contents sold. With its own compartment in that chest there had been a pierced basket of 66 troy ounces by John Hamilton of Dublin (*fl.* 1709–*d.* 1751), which was soon noticed in the London press and migrated to the United States. Forty years later, the piece returned to Ireland and was bought back. Made for the archbishop, it must date from between 1749 and 1751, since it is not on his 1748 list. In the present inventory it is described as a bread-basket (plate 52). In some cases, the inventory has confirmed tentative identifications of original functions of pieces of furniture, such as the 'Oyster table' listed in the 'Sitting Room' (now Library) and the 'Spirit Case' in the 'Dining Parlour' – both pieces extant today. Indeed, it is noteworthy that much of the contents of the principal rooms of Newbridge, as listed, survives intact and *in situ*, nearly two hundred years on.

The 1821 inventory is in the Cobbe Papers: Hugh Cobbe Division, private collection.

NOTE

The headings at the tops of pages in the original manuscript have been moved and, where needed, modified slightly to match the column breaks in the transcript.

Newbridge House
1821 inventory

House Lists.
Furniture.
Plate. Linen. Glass.
℘. ℘. ℘.
Newbridge
1821

1821 ## Furniture ~ Middle Floor

Entrance Hall
Remarks

1 Billiard Table with Cover, balls &.
1 Mahogany dining Table & Cover
1 Mahogany Consol Table & Marble Slab
1 Bronze figure with lamp Complete
10 Mahogany Hall Chairs with crests.
1 Green Baize Curtain for door &
1 Stove *Wants a Poker*
1 Hemp Mat

Middle Hall
Wants a Curtain

1 Round Oak Table with baize
1 Small Mahogany Table for lamp
1 Trouve-Madam Table
1 Barrell Organ
1 Bronze figure with lamp Complete
6 Mahogany Chairs (crested)
1 Clock, 1 Hat stand, 1 flower stand
1 Sheep rug 1 Bell lamp
1 Painted deal Table [*blot*] 1 Step ladder
17 Pictures on the Walls.

Inner Hall

1 Red Cloth Window Curtain
2 Marble figures (in nitches)
2 Hemp Rugs ~ 2 flower Stands.
1 long Mat. *1 Large Dining Table*
1 Card Table. 1 Marble Table. 1 Sheep Rug.
4 Pictures on the Walls

Study
Remarks

1 Mahogany Writing Table
2 Study Tables (Mahogany)
1 Small Table with drawer (*do.*
1 Mahogany Pier book Case with }
– Marble Slab and figure
Mahogany Wash and Stand with
1 —— Bason, Ewer, small Jug, Soap
—— stand, chamber &
1 Fire skreen
1 Reading desk
2 Large Book Cases
1 Iron Chest with Papers
1 Terrestrial Globe
1 Study Chair
1 Merlin Chair with Jacks
4 Mahogany Chairs
1 Carpet & Rug
1 Mahogany cloaths Horse
1 Fender & fire Irons & hearth brush
1 Pʳ Bellows
1 Boot Jack
4 Marble figures (Mantle piece)
2 Window blinds
1 Barometer
14 Pictures (on the Walls)

Dining Parlour

2 Mahogany Side boards
3 Mahogany Dining Tables
2 Dumb Waiters
14 Mahogany Chairs
1 Large Pier Glass
2 Window Curtains
1 Carpet with Covering & oil cloth
1 Green Baize screen
1 Hearth Rug. fender. fire Irons & brush.
1 Wine Cooper
2 Mahogany Tubs under Sideboards
1 Mahogany Wine Carrier *Note the dinner*
1 Commode (complete. *Trays, Plate Basket*
1 Mahogany Tea Chest *& Knive Trays*
1 Plate Warmer *are marked in Pantry*
4 Chimney Ornaments *below stairs*
1 Marble figure – Jupiter
1 Spirit Case

PLATE 51
Frances Power Cobbe (1822–1904): *The Drawing Room at Newbridge House*, 1840s, ink on paper

Furniture ~ Middle Floor

Large Drawing Room

- 1 Mahogany Round Table & Cover
- 1 Tea Table with drawer
- 1 Sofa Table with drawers
- 4 Half round Pier Tables
- 2 Square Pier Tables with drawers
- 2 Large Sofa's with Covers
- 2 Small *Ditto* . *do*
- 5 Window Curtains
- 1 Druggett Carpet & Rug
- 2 Indian Cabinets with china
- 1 Large Chair & Cover
- 1 Crimson Cloth Chair.
- 6 Tapestry Arm Chairs & Covers
- 2 Arm Chairs & Covers
- 1 Piano Forte
- 4 Fire Screen Tapestry
- 4 Looking Glasses
- 1 Green baize Screen
- 1 Fender, fire Irons, & brush
- 2 Ornaments for Chimney Piece
- 1 Marble figure for *do*. Marcus Aurelius
- 1 Musick Stand & Musick books.
- 1 Childs Chair & Table
- 4 Small Mahogany Tables   1 painted
- ~~2 Tapestry Screens~~
- 2 Card Tables. 2 Red cloth Stools
- 10 Mahogany Chairs
- ~~2 Arm Chairs & Covers Green~~
- ~~2 Large China Jars, 2 Long *do*. 2 Bottles.~~
- 31 Pictures on the Walls
- 1 Tea Chest
- 1 Backgammon box 1 Chess board

Newbridge House, County Dublin

Furniture ~ Middle Floor

Sitting Room

Remarks

1 Carpet & Hearth Rug
1 Sofa Couch & Cover
10 Mahogany Chairs
1 Oak ditto with Cushion
2 Looking Glasses
1 China Painted Table
1 Backgammon Table
2 Card Tables
1 Backgammon box
1 Work Table
1 Indian Cabinet
1 Ornamental Table
1 fire Screen
1 Brass fender, fire Irons & brush   *No shovel*
1 Oyster Table
3 China Jars (blue)
4 China Flower Pots . *do.*
1 Case Shells
3 China boxes for Counters
Green baize over Carpet
36 Pictures on the Walls

China Room

1 Dining Table Mahogany
6 Blue Chairs
2 Looking Glasses
1 Glass Book Case
1 Mahogany screw reading Desk
1 Peice of Carpet   *no fender or Irons*

Broad Stairs

1 Red Cloth Curtain
1 Bell Lamp

Lobby up Stairs

2 Gilt Brackets with china figures
1 Druggett Carpet

Mr Cobbe's Dressing Room

1 4 Post Bedstead with chintz Curtains
1 Palliasse. 1 Feather bed. 1 Mattrass hair.
1 Pr Blankets   *1 Under Blanket*
1 Bolster   *Wanting*
1 Pillow^s   *2.*

Furniture ~ Upper Floor

Mr Cobbe's Dressing Room Cont^d.

1 Indian Palampore
2 Window Curtains
1 Bed Side Carpet
2 Peices of Carpet to Match.
1 Mahogany Wardrobe
1 Mahogany chest of Drawers
2 Painted Dressing Tables
1 Dressing Box
1 Cloaths horse
1 Boot & Shoe Rack
1 Night Stool
1 White foot Tub
2 Blue Jugs & Basons
1 Water Croft and Tumbler
1 Hot Water Jug & tooth brush Case
1 Tin Kettle
1 Fender fire Irons & brush
6~4~ Chairs
1 Sawcer for Soap

Mrs Cobbe's Bedroom

1 4 Post Mahogany Bedstead, with Curtains
1 Bolster. 2 Pillows. 1 Small round *do.*
3 Blankets
1 Counterpayne
2 Window Curtains
1 Dressing Table & Looking Glass
2 Looking Glasses
1 Tortoice Inlaid Table
1 Bedside Carpet
1 Bedside Chamber Stand
1 Cloaths horse
1 Small Mahogany Table
1 Mahogany Wardrobe
1 Small chest of Drawers
1 White dressing Table & looking Glass   ×
2 Pier looking Glasses   ×
1 Fender fire Irons & brush
1 Small Kettle
1 Indian Trunk Cabinet
2 Gilt Bracketts
1 Chamber Clock
2 Chambers
6 Chairs

Furniture ~ Upper Floor

Closet to Bed Room

Remarks

1 Small Table with drawers
1 Bedside chamber stand
1 Chamber
1 White Cloaths press
1 Mahogany box of Small drawers
2 Blue Jugs & Basons
1 Water Croft, Tumbler, Soap & tooth Stand
1 Small Hot Water Jug

Red Bedroom

1 4 Post Bedstead & Curtains
3 Blankets. 2 Pillows. 1 Bolster.
1 Quilt
1 Bedside Carpet
1 Bedside Chamber Stand.
1 Window Curtain
1 Night Stool
1 Cloathes Horse
1 Oak Wardrobe
1 Wash and Stand
6 Chairs
1 Arm Chair
1 Dressing Table Mahogany   *with Glass*
1 White *do*
1 Looking Glass Moveable
1 Blue Jug & Bason
1 Glass Water Croft & Tumbler
1 Hot Water Jug, 1 Glass for Soap
1 Chamber
1 Fender fire Irons & brush.

Closet to Bedroom

1 Mahogany Bookcase
1 Small Table & drawer
1 Chair
2 Bookshelves Mahogany.

Green Bedroom

1 4 Post bedstead & Curtains
1 Palliass. ~~2~~1 Mattrass~~es~~. 1 Featherbed.
3 Blankets
1 Quilt. 1 Bolster. 2 Pillows.
1 Bedside Carpet
1 Bedside Chamber Stand

2 Chambers
1 Cloaths horse
6 Chairs
1 Mahogany Table
1 Looking Glass at Mantle Piece
1 Ditto Moveable
1 Mahogany Wardrobe
2 Small Chests of Drawers
1 Fender & Fire Irons
1 White Table
2 China Basons & Jugs
1 China Soap Stand
1 Glass Water croft & Tumbler
1 Blue Hot Water Jug
1 Window Curtain
2 Chambers – add^d 8 March 1822

Closet to Bedroom

1 Dressing Table. 1 Night Stool.
1 Chair

Purple Bedroom

1 4 Post Bedstead & Curtains
1 Palliasse. 2 Mattrasses. 1 Feather bed.
1 Bolster. 2 Pillows
3 Blankets. 1 Quilt.
1 Bedside Carpet
1 Druggett Carpet
1 Bedside Chamber Stand
1 Cloaths horse
1 Indian Mat
1 Dressing Glass
1 Looking Glass (Pier.)
1 Ditto Mantle piece +
1 White Table
6 Arm Chairs
1 Mahogany Table with drawers
1 Biddey
2 Jugs & Basons blue
1 Hot water Jug
1 Glass Water croft & Tumbler
1 Glass for Soap
2 Window Curtains
1 Fender fire Irons & brush
4 Black Ornaments on chimney
1 Chamber added 8 March.

Newbridge House, County Dublin

Furniture ~ Upper Floor

Closet to Bedroom
Remarks

1 Drugget Carpet
1 Dressing Table
1 Wash and stand
1 Jug & Bason & Chamber
1 Night Stool
2 Chairs

Passage Room

6 Chairs
2 Couches Rush bottom
1 White Tent Bed with   *Buff Curtains &*
  Curtains 1 Palliasse 1 Pillow   *Small 4 Post bed with*
1 Feather bed 3 Blankets
1 Quilt   *Bolster & Pillow*
7 Prints on the Wall

Wash Hand Stand
1 White Jug Bason & Chamber

Bow Room

1 4 Post Bedstead & Curtains
1 Palliasse. 2 1 Mattrasses 1 Bolster
1 Feather bed. 3 2 Pillows
3 Blankets. 1 Quilt.
1 Bedside Carpet
3 Window Curtains
1 Mahogany Wardrobe
1 Mahogany Chest of Drawers
1 Large Baby House
6 Cane Bottom Chairs
1 Night Stool
1 Dressing table
1 Writing table with drawers
1 Small Table
1 Carpet
1 Hearth Rug
1 Fender fire Irons & brush
                                                1822
2 1 Jug 2 1 Bason 1 Water Croft   *1 Jug & Bason add.d 8 March*
  & tumbler   *1 Small Water Jug*
1 Soap & tooth Case
1 fire screen
1 Cloaths Horse
1 Couch with Palliass & Cover & Pillow
1 Indian Mat
5 China Chimney Ornaments
2 1 Chambers

White Bedroom.
Remarks

1 Tent Bedstead & White Curtains
1 Palliass. 1 Mattrass. 1 Feather bed
1 Bolster. 1 Pillow. 1 Quilt.
3 Blankets
8 Chairs & covers White
1 Carpet
2 Window Curtains
1 Rug
1 White Table
1 Small Chest of Drawers
1 Low Mahogany cloaths press
1 Mahogany Table with drawer
1 Looking Glass moveable
1 Pier *Ditto*
2 1 Jug & Basons 1 Tumbler.   *1 Water Croft 1 Soap Glass*
1 Chamber
1 Fender. & Fire Irons.

Children's Bedroom

1 4 Post Bedstead & Curtains
1 Feather Bed
3 Blankets
1 Bolster 1 Pillow
1 Oak Chest of Drawers
2 Childrens Bedsteads & Curtains
2 Mattrasses. 2 feather beds.
2 Bolsters. 2 Pillows
6 Blankets. 2 Quilts.
8 Chairs
1 Arm Chair
1 Dressing Table
1 Small Table
1 Pier looking Glass
1 Looking Glass Moveable
1 Peice of Carpet
1 Fender. 1 Poker & Tongs
2 White Basons 1 Jug
2 Chambers

Closet to Bedroom

1 Large White press . 1 night stool
1 Dressing Table . 1 Chair.
1 Jug & Bason Blue

1821   *Furniture ~ Upper Floor*

Nursery Bedroom

                                               Remarks

2   Oak 4 post Bedsteds & Curtains   *One removd to Passage*
2   Feather Beds   *Room   do*
1   Mattrass
2   Bolsters. 1 Pillow.   *1. Bolster remvd*
5   Blankets. 2 Quilts.   *2. do & 1 Quilt*
2   Childrens Bedsteds & Curtains
2   Mattrasses 2 feather beds
6   Blankets. 2 Quilts. 2 Pillows
2   Bolsters
1   Small Couch with Pillow & Bolster   *removd to James's Room*
2   Small Chests of Drawers
1   White Table
1   Mahogany Table with drawers
1   Round Table.
1   Cloaths Horse
1   High fender _ 1 low *do*
1   Set fire Irons & Brush
5   Chairs
7   Stools
1   Peice Carpet
1   Looking Glass Moveable
10   Chimney china ornaments
2   Chambers
5   Pictures on the walls

Closet to Nursery

1   White Press
1   Oak Wardrobe
1   Mahogany Table & drawers   *Removd to Passage Room*
1   Looking Glass   Moveable   *do*
1   Night Stool
1   Bedside chamber Stand
1   High childs chair
1   Chair. 1 Foot Tub, 1 Chamber

1821   *Furniture ~ Ground Floor*

Butlers Room

                                               Remarks

2   Tent Bedsteds & Curtains
2   Presses
1   Chest of Drawers
1   Mattrass
2   Feather Beds
2   Bolsters
2   Pillows
6   Blankets
2   White Quilts
4   Chairs
2   Tables
1   looking Glass
1   Carpet
1   Fender

Footmans Room

2   Tent Beds & Curtains
2   Palliasses
2   Feather Beds
2   Bolsters
6   Blankets
2   Rug Quilts
1   Chest Drawers
1   Press
4   Chairs
2   Basons 1 Jug   *1 Jug & Bason added 8 March*
2   Tables
1   Looking Glass
2   Chambers
1   Wash and Stand

Coachmans Room

2   4 Post Bedsteds & Curtains
2   Palliasses
2   Feather Beds
6   Blankets
2   Bolsters.
2   Rug Quilts
1   Tent Bedsted & Curtains
1   Palliasse
1   Feather Bed
1   Rug Quilt
2   Peices of Carpet
4   Chairs
1   Fender

Newbridge House, County Dublin

1821 *Furniture ~ Ground Floor*

1 Chest of Drawers   *Remarks*
1 Table
1 Looking Glass
2 Basons. 1 Jug.   *1 Jug & bason added 8 March*
3 Chambers.

Cooks Room

2 4 Post Bedsteds & Curtains
2 Mattrasses
2 Feather beds
6 Blankets
2 Bolsters 1 Pillow
2 White Quilts
1 Table
1 Looking Glass
2 Chests of Drawers
4 Chairs
2 Peices of Carpet
1 Jug 1 Bason 3 2 Chambers
1 Night Stool
1 Mirror fixture

Housemaids Room

2 4 Post Bedsteds & Curtains
2 Palliasses
2 Feather beds
5 Blankets
2 Rug Quilts
2 Chests of Drawers
1 Table
1 Looking Glass
1 Bason & Jug
2 Chambers
4 Chairs
1 Small Corner Press

Housekeepers Room

2 Large Presses
4 Tables
1 Chest of Drawers
1 Wooden Box for Cloaths
10 Chairs
1 Carpet
1 Fender & fire Irons
10 Small Pictures on the Walls.

Servants Hall

2 Long Tables
2 Long Forms
2 Small high Presses
2 Chairs
1 Large Wooden Box

Kitchen

1 Press
1 Dresser
1 Fire Skreen
1 Long Table
1 Small Table
1 Fender & Fire Irons
1 Fountain
6 Chairs
1 Pewter Dish
8 Pewter Plates
1 Wooden Salt Box
1 Large Fish Kettle & Strainer. Copper
1 Small   *Ditto*   & Cover   *Do.*
5 Tosspans & Covers ..   *Do.*
1 Soup Pot & Cover   *do.*
2 Stewing Pots & Covers   *do*
1 Frying Pan
1 Oval Ditto for Fish
1 Omlet Pan   *Copper*
2 Potatoe Pots & Covers
1 Pot Oven & Cover
2 Cleavers. 1 Saw.
1 Dutch Oven & Stand
1 Saucepan Strainer for Eggs.
1 Tin Egg Boiler
3 Seives
1 Pestle & Mortar
1 Spice Mill
1 Dredging Box
1 Chocholate Pot
1 Cheese Toaster
1 Large Copper Can
3 Copper Jelly Shapes
1 Tin Tourte Shape
1 Volevante Shape
4 Brown Pans
6 Iron Skewers
1 Bread Grater

3 Spits
2 Cradle Ditto
1 Large Ladle
1 Small Ditto
1 Flesh fork
1 Basting Ladle
1 Slice
6 Spoons
2 Tubs
1 Low Table
1 Plate Rack
1 Chicken Coop
3 Tripods
1 Dripping Pan
2 Gridirons
2 Smoothing Irons
2 Pewter Mugs for Measures
1 Wooden Coal Box
1 Tea Kettle.
1 Spit Coffee Roaster
1 Chopping Block
1 Salamander
2 Large Metal Saucepans & Covers
3 Small _ *Ditto* _ *Do* _
10 Tin Candlesticks
1 Sweeping Brush
1 Scouring Brush
1 Set Stilliards
2 Lead Skewers for ballancing
1 Carving Knife & fork
1 Callender
1 Brass Skellitt
1 House Bucket
2 Wooden Bowls
1 Pudding Pan Tin
6 Wooden Spoons
1 Egg Slice. 1 fish *do*
5 Tin Saucepans & Covers
1 Warming Pan
2 Brass Candlesticks
1 Spice Box
1 Coffee Mill
1 Pr Scales & Weights Copper
12 Mince Pie Patty pans
24 Tartelet _ _ *do* _
1 Set of Patty Cutters
2 Sets of Tin Pastry Cutters
1 Pr Sugar knippers
1 Sugar Mallett & Cleaver

1 Marble Pestle & Mortar
2 Larding Pins
2 Turnip Scoops
2 Small Pastry Cutters
1 Pr Beef Steak Tongs
1 Round Copper Cutlet Sheet
2 Scollop Shells
2 Tin high Candlesticks
1 Jelly Bag
1 Tammois
1 Ironing Blanket

Pantry

1 Long Table & Drawers
1 Short *do*
1 Small Press
3 Shelves fixtures

Crockery

7 Dishes		*3 bought add*d *19 Dec*r
6 Cushion *do* with Covers		
3 Baking Dishes		
50 Flat Plates		
2 Fruit Dishes		
7 Soup Plates		
1 Cheese Plate	china	
1 Oyster Dish	*do.*	
3 White Dishes		*6 added 8*th *March 1822*
22 White Plates		*6 added. do –*
12 Soup Plates		
1 Tureen		
1 White Jug		*2 added 8 March 1822*
1 Ladle 6 Spoons		
1 Black Tea Pot	*& Cream Jug*	
14 Large Cups & Sawcers		*Parlour now breakfast*
11 Small *ditto* . gold Edged		*Drawing Room Tea –*
18 Small plates		
8 Egg Cups		
1 Sugar Bowl		
1 Slop Bowle	Gold Edged.	
1 *Ditto* —— plain _		
8 Cups & 9 Saucers _ _ _		*Housekeepers Room*
1 Cream Ewer		
1 Tea Pot		
2 Blue Bowls *23 added 8 March*		*in the Nursery*

Newbridge House, County Dublin

3	Plates
1	White Mug
6	Small Mugs
1	Beer Jug
1	Black Pan
2	Cups & Saucers
1	Water Pitcher
3	Butter boats
1	White *Ditto* added 8 March 1822
1	Mustard Pot – *do* – *do*
1	Sallad Bowl – *do*

- 6 Small Mugs — *2 added March 8 1822*
- 1 Beer Jug — *2 added March 8 1822.*
- 3 Butter boats — *one of them broke in handle.*

Linen

12	Diaper Table Cloths
8	Small *Ditto*
8	P.r Sheets
3	P.r Small *do*
12	P.r Grey *do* for Servants
18	Pillow Cases
3	Long *do*
7	Servants Hall Table Cloths
6	Market Cloths
4	Doz Towells
6	Round Towells
1	Jelly bag
11	Damask Table Cloths
3	Small *Do*
2	Large Napkins
12	Best Napkins
11	Small *do* old.
12	Glass Cloths ×
3	Knife Cloths ×
6	Dusters
6	Kitchen Cloths ×
2	Pudding Cloths — *2 add.d bought: 19 Dec.r*

14 { (brace beside Damask Table Cloths / Small Do)

Plate

1	Silver Eperne
1	P.r Large Candlesticks
2	P.r Smaller *ditto*
2	Embossed Soup Toureens & Covers
2	Ladles for *ditto*
2	Small Toureens with Covers
2	Beef Steak Dishes
4	Round Salvers

1	Oval *Do*		
4	Square *do*		
2	Larger *do*		
4	Embossed Butter Boats		
1	Beer Mug ×		*Given away*
1	Cocoa Nut Mug Silver Mountd		
1	Tankard		
8	Butter Ladles		
2	Sugar Ladles	✓	
6	Salt Cellars & Spoons		
4	Doz & 5 Table Spoons		
9	Bottle labels	✓	
1½	Doz.n. Tea Spoons		
1	Doz. Egg Spoons		
2	Butter Trowells		
4	Doz Silver forks		
4	Gravy Spoons	✓	
1	Sallad fork	✓	
1	Bread Basket		
1	Fish Trowell		
2	Sconces for Candles		
2	Claret Jugs		
2	Large Wine Coolers with Covers		
4	Wine Coasters		
3	Cruet Stands different sizes		*1 Given away*
1	Pepper Castor		
1	Wine Funnell	✓	
6	Skewers	✓	
1	Marrow Spoon	✓	
1	Asparagus Tongs	✓	
1	Small Pan	✓	
2	Doz.n Silver handled Knives		
1	Coffee Pot		
1	Library Candlestick	✓	
1	*Ditto* Inkstand	✓	
1	Toast Rack	✓	
1	Tea Pot		
1	Cream Ewer		
1	P.r Sugar Tongs	✓	
1	Stand for Teapot		
1	Cayenne Pepper Spoon		
23	Desert Silver Knives & Forks with China Handles		
1	Silver Knife Fork & Spoon.		*Charles's*
2	Cocoa Nut Mugs silver mounted.		*childrens*
1	Silver Mustard Pot & Spoon		
1	Fork		*Thomas's*
2	Spoons & Forks		*Williams & Henry's*
4	Corks with silver Tops	✓	

Plated Articles

1 P.r Plated Candlesticks		*Remarks*
1 P.r *Ditto* with Branches		
4 Plated Coasters		
1 Gravy Spoons		
1 Cruet Stand		
2 Large Flat Dishes		
2 Smaller Ditto		
4 Cushion Dishes & Covers		
5 Flat Candlesticks & Extinguishers		
1 P.r Small Candlesticks . Bedchamber		

Glass

14 Coolers	
13 Finger Glasses	*6 Finger glasses*
11 Ale Glasses	*3 added.*
12 Champayne *do*	
12 Beer — *Do*	*12 added*
22 Wine Glasses for Coolers	
22 claret Glasses cut	
35 Wines Glasses *do.*	
6 Odd Wine Glasses	*Housekeepers Room*
2 Cut Goblets	*Childrens Cha.s & Toms*
2 Claret Decanters	
4 Wine Decanters	
1 Spirit Decanter	
2 Cut Water Jugs	

PLATE 52
Basket, *c.* 1749–51, maker's mark of John Hamilton (*fl.* 1709–*d.* 1751), silver. Known for introducing the rococo style into Irish silver, this basket is a fine example of this Dublin maker's style, with the rim chased with masks, scrolls and shell ornaments, and the handles cast in the shape of female terms. It is engraved with the Cobbe arms.

Newbridge House, County Dublin

1 Sugar Glass & Cover
1 Ditto & stand without Cover
1 Cut glass Sallad Bowl
1 Butter glass & stand Cut
1 Plain *do* – & stand
5 Cut Cruet Glasses
2 Glasses for Lamps
1 Salt Cellar   *Housekeepers Room*
2 Cruets   *Do*
4 Glasses for Pickles
1 Glass for Custard or Cream   *1 Cream Glass added 8 March*
1 Sweet Meat Glass   *1822*
28 Liquere Glasses . 1 Ale Glass.
7 Small Wine Decanters
8 Round flat Glass Plates
1 Set of Eperne Glasses
5 Odd Tops for Glass bowls
1 Glass for Flowers. 3 Lamp Shades
2 Jelly Stands Small
4 Chandiliers   *2 Broken & Imperfect*
1 Large Glass. Cut with the Battle of the Boyne

Sundries

1 Red Japan Spoon Tray
2 Red Coasters
1 Cork Screw
1 Pr Nut Crackers
1 Bottle Brush
3 Mahogany Trays
2 Knife Trays
2 Mahogany Candlesticks
1 Japⁿ Snuffer dish
5 Pr Snuffers large & small.
1 Plate Bucket
1 Bread Basket
1 Pail & Wooden Bowle
1 Tin Oil Pot
1 Tea Urn
1 Japan Tea Tray
3 Black Japan Trays
2 *Do* — – –   old
7 Carving Knives   Ivory Handles
45 Ivory Handled Knives   18 of them crested.
25 Small   *do*
9 Carving Forks
10 Small 3 pronged forks
6 Oyster Knives
7 Knives & Forks *12 added*   *Servants Hall.*

3 Horn Goblets   *Do* _
3 Small *Do*   *Do* _
1 Beer Can   *Do* _
1 Tea Tray   *Nursery use*
1 Foot Tub   *do* _
1 Tea Kettle   *do*
2 Smoothing Irons   *do*
1 Ironing Blanket   *do*
1 House bucket   *do*
1 Coal Scuttle   *do*
1 Saucepan _ 1 Sweeping broom   *do* .
1 Foot Tub   *Housemaids use*
1 House bucket   *do* _
1 Pail
1 Coal Scuttle
1 Sweeping brush
1 Carpet   *do*
1 Stair brush
1 Blacking brush 1 Whiting *do*
1 Dust Pan 1 Water Pitcher
1 Box for brushes
1 Popes head
1 Tin Bathing Tub
5 Earthen Pans for lards-.
1 Wooden salting tub

1821   ## China

                                  Revised May 1836

20 Dishes different sizes (Peacock)
2 Round Ditto   *do*   *1 broken. 2 reworked*
34 Soap Plates   *do*   *2 broken*
52 Flat Plates   *do*   *8. broken & 2. gone*
1 Butter boat   *do* .
6 Round Dishes   Cheese Set.
17 Plates _   — _ — *do* _
11 Round Dishes   Supper Set
24 Flat Plates
7 Baskets   Desert. (Peacock.
4 Baskets with Covers & Stands _ *do.*
2 Ice Pails Covers & Plates _   *do*
4 Sugar boats Covers & Plates _ *do*
4 Cream boats _ *do* _ *do* _ *do*
6 Oval Dishes
47 Flat Plates
4 Leaves _ for Fruit
4 Dolphins with Plates & Covers
10 Oval Dishes   (French Desert Set
1 Basket
2 Cream & Sugar Pails with Stands

2	Round Dishes
2	Heart Shaped Dishes.
24	Plates
13	Round Dishes _ (Common Set
7	Soup Plates
19	Flat Plates
6	Baskets & 8 stands *D°* match (odd sets
2	Baskets without stands _ *do*
23	Round Dishes different sizes *do*
2	Small Oval *do*
17	Round Blue & Gold Small Dishes
6	Blue & White Dishes round
1	Large Flat Dish Blue & White
2	Oval Deep Dishes _ *do*
2	Small flat Plates
1	Deep Coloured Sallad Dish
1	Teapot White & Gold
2	Cream Jugs
1	Sugar Bowl & Cover
12	Tea Cups & Saucers
8	Coffee Cups & Saucers
1	Slop Bowl
2	Plates
12	Custard Cups & Covers
1	Blue Sugar Bowl & Cover
1	Small *do_* without Cover
1	Blue Honey Pot
1	Blue flower Stand
	Ornamental China
2	Large Gold & Red Jars
2	High. *do* . *do*
3	Bottles *do* . *do*
2	Bowls with China Figures
2	*Ditto* _ Red & Gold.
1	Blue & Gold De Jurnè 4 Pieces
4	Pices Chelsea China
4̶2̶	Large figures 2 Small *do*
6	Odd Cups & Saucers
6	Tea Pots
1	Green Sugar bowl & Cover
1	Ink Stand Tray _ 5 Peices
2	Flowerd Cups 1 Cover
4	Coffee Cups
1	Sugar bowl Plate & Cover
2	Oyster Shells & 1 Stand
1	Cawdle Cup Cover & Stand
5	Blue Peices of China odd
1	Cream Jug 3 odd pieces
1̶	~~Large B~~

Revised and corrected
May 1836

1. gone – Cup.

1. do _ Cup.

1821 *Carriages & Harness*

1	Four Wheel Landau with Hindseat
1	Hammer cloth for *Ditto*
1	Set 2 Horse Harness Complete
1	*Do* – for Leaders _ _ *do*
4	Carriage Boxes
1	Pᵣ Spare Reins for Wheelers
1	Pᵣ Night Bridles with Bits (~~complete~~ *No Bridoons*
2	Spare Collars *1. with Mᵣ farington*
3	False Collars *1. with Mᵣ Sims*
2	Spare Belly bands
1	Curricle
2	Curricle Trunks
3	Curricle Boxes
1	Set Curricle Harness (Complete
1	Spare Curricle Bar
1	Caveason
1	Pᵣ Tandem Reins
1	Spare Britches
1	Jaunting Car & Cushions
1	Set of Harness to *Do* _ Complete
1	Basket to fit Jaunting Car
1	Running Martingale
1	Pᵣ Curricle Trunk Straps
5	Trunk Straps
1	Patent Chain *do*
1	Drag Chain
1	Circingle. ×
1	Large Bit for Hardmouth Carriage horse
2	Mouthing bits
1	Coat Belt ×
1	Saddle 3 Girths
1	Small Saddle Childrens 2 girths
2	Double Rein Bridles Complete
1	Single Rein Jointed Bit
1	Twisted Snaffle Mounted
2	Watering bridles *1 to Mᵣ William*
1	Brest plate
1	Martingale
	Curb Chains
3	Pᵣ Spare Stirrup Irons
2	Spare Cheek Bits unmounted
4	Snaffle bits unmounted.
2	Snaffle bridles complete
1	Childs Martingale & nose band.
1	Leather Girth
5	Winter Horse Sheets
2	Summer *do*

Newbridge House, County Dublin

5 Rollers

1 Hood 1 Breast Plate & 1 Pad Cloth

2 Exercise Pads

3 Double Shanked   Collars & chains

6 Pillar Reins

4 Back Reins

2 Long four Horse Whips   ×

1 Carriage   _   _ *do*   2 horse

2 Slips

1 Cover for Saddle travelling

1 Wheel Chair

1 Sheep Rug for Curricle

1 P.ʳ Saddle bags

Books

[For suggested identifications of books
listed in abridged form in the list below,
see Appendix IV, pp. 377–82.]

Divinity	VOLS
1 Large Prayer Book	1
2 Large Bibles	2
Bible in 4 Parts	4
Dialogues on Christianity Jackson	2 –
Small Prayer books & book of Psalms	3
Book of Prayers	1
Gilpin on the New Testament	2 –
Gilpins Lectures	1
Scotts Bible with Notes	6 –
Bible Explained	1
Hornes Letter on Infidelity	1
Robinsons scripture characters	5
Burders Village Sermons	1
Companion to the altar	1
Address to the Christian World	1 –
The Whole duty of Man	1
Trimmers Abridgement of the Bible	2
Do Explanations	2
Trimmers Sacred History	6
Doyleys History of the Life & Death of Christ	1
Paleys Sermons	1
Coopers Doctrinal Sermons	1
Coopers Practical Sermons	4
Knox's Sermons	1 –
Potts's Discourses	1
Sherlocks Discourses	1
Josephus History of the Jews	3

Hannah Mores Practical Piety	2
Christian Morals	2
Religious Tracts	5
Addisons Evidences of the Christian Religion	1
Paleys Thology	1
Watsons Apologies	1
Nelsons Devotions	1
Nelsons Festivals	1
Seckers Lectures	1
Trimmers Liturgy	1 –
Sturms Reflections	3
Soane Jennings's Evidences	1
Wells's Geography of the Bible	2
Fleurys Catechism	1
Flavells Saint Indeed	1
Thomas a Kempis	1
Bunyans Pilgrims progress	1
Gisbornes Sermons on Christian Morality	1
Faber on the Phrophices	2
Durhams Astro = Theology	1
Claphams Abridgement of Lincolns Theology	1
World without Souls	1
Porteus's Evidences of the Christian religion	1
Introduction to the Knowledge of Chrisⁿ religion	1
Dr Doddridges Rise & progress of religion & the Soul.	1
Venn's Sermons	2
Milners Church History	5
Porteus's Lectures	2
Bickerstaths Scripture Help	1
Thoˢ A Kempis Smalr. Ed.	1
Theron & Aspasio	2
Wilberforce Practical View of Christianity	1
Mores Essay on St Paul	2

Education	
Edgeworths Practical Education	2 –
Do ____ Professional	1
Ketts Elements of General Knowledge	2 –
Brooke's Gazetteer	1
Walkers Classicks	1
Johnsons Dictionary	2
Robertsons History of Greece	1
Students Dictionary	1
Geography	1
Do _ by Devis	1
Devis's Grammar	1
Do _ Miscellanies	1

Goldsmiths History of England	1 –
Memoria Technica	1
Mental Improvement	1
Locke on Education	1
Hints on Schools	1

History. Antiquities & Memoirs

Rollins's Ancient History	10
Ledwich's Antiquities	1
Lelands History of Ireland	3
Lemprieres Tour to Morrocco & Tangiers	1
Life of Col Hutchinson	1
Tully's Tripoli	1
Lord Littletons History of England	2 –
Survey of the Turkish Empire	1
Gardens Tacitus 1 missing	4
Robertsons Works	12 –
Sullys Memoirs	5
Sewards AnecDotes	4
Cœlebs in Search of a Wife	2
History of the Stage	1
Rules for an Army	1
Johnsons Works	6 –
Spectator	8 –
Gil Blas – 2 Sets	8
Novelists Magazine	1
History of Automathes	1
Tour to Cheltenham	1
Tales of the Genii	1
Swiftiana	2
Mavors Tourists	6 –
Miseries of Human Life	1 –
Tanzai & Neadarnè	1
Atala	1
Heroine	3 –
Junius's Letters	1 –
Idler	2 –
Persian & Turkish Tales	2 –
Travels thro' Africa	1 –
New Fairy Tales	2 –
Landlords friend	1
Leadbeaters Cottage Dialogues	1
Dialogues of Women	1
Penns Critical remarks and Plays	2 –
India Courier	10 –
The Mourner	1
Voltaire	1
Fathers Legacy	1

Fragments Miss Smith		1
Klopstocks letters	*do*	1
Kirk White		2
Belesarius		1
Pocket Library		1
Robinson Crusoe		1
Arabian Nights		3 –
Ossiàn		2 –
The World		1
Death of Abel		1
Raselas		1
Rural Philosophy E Bates		1 –
Velvet Cushion		1
Abridgement of Goldsmiths animated Nature		1
Economy of Human life		1 –
New Covering to Velvet Cushion		1 –
Easops fables prose by L Estrange		1
Voltaires Works		35 –
Campbells Voyage round the World		1 –
Odd Volume Thompsons Works & Plays.		1 –
Voyage to Senegal		1 –
Spirit of English Wit		1 –
Percey Anecdotes		22 –
Scrap book		1
Sketch Book		2
Guszman d Alfarache		2
Anastatius		3
Maws Gardning		1
Debretts Peerage		2
Whites Farriery		4
Sternes Sentimental Journey		1 –
Picture of Paris		1
Buxton on Prison Discipline		1 –
Book of Ranks		1
Domestic Cookery		1
Book on Cookery		1
Phillidore on chess		1
Book of Roads		1
Commons Journals appendex & Index		23 –
Sportsmans Dictionary		1
Burns Justice		5 –
New Bath Guide		1
Tablet of Memory		1
Dicksons Husbandry		2 –
Buchan's Domestic Medicine		1 –
Justice & Sheriffs Guide		1 –

Poems

Pope's Homers Illiad		1
Odissey		1
Horace		1
Virgil		1
Ovid		2 –
Collins		1
Milton		2 –
The Wreath	Reath	1 –
Rowe		1 –
Young		1
Shenstone		1
Akenside		1
Calliope		1
The Laurell		1
The to penny Post bag		1
Gays Fables		1
Æsops *do*		1
Popes Works		6 –
Bloomfields Poems		1
N. Bloomfields – *do*		1
Haleys Plays		1
Scottish Minstrel		1
Peter Pindar		1
The Selector		1
Priors Poems		2 –
Swifts Poems		2 –
The Nurse – Roscoe		1 –
Godsmiths Poems		1
Parnells		1
Cowpers		2
Mants		1
Montgomerys		1
Cunninghams		1
Butlers Hudibrass		2

Tomkins Selection	1
Churchills Poems	3
Dispensary Poems Garth	1
Oxford Prize Poems	1
Derricks Dryden	4
Littles Poems	1
Priors Poems	1

French Books

Les Trois Femmes	1
Bossuetts Histoire Universale	1
Histoire Ancienne	1
Romaine	1
De France	2
L Ami des Enfans	4
Chef dOeuvres dEloquence	1
Synoneme de Gerrard	2
Exercises de Chambaud	1
Ouvre de Boileaux	1
Vocabulaire	1
Testament	1
Le Duc de Lauzun	2 –
Grammar & Exercises by Chambaud	2
Do – *Do* – by Perrin	2
La Bonne Mere	1
Dictionaire de L Etenvilles	1
Odd Volume. Anecdotes Turkish	1
Waillies Grammar	1
Voyage Sentimentaile	1 –

For books added since this list was made,
see a Catalogue in the library, wherein all the
books are mentioned, distinguishing those
of my brothers & my own — C.C.

[Note written on the verso of folio 48]

Mr McCabe
Peter's Place
Mount St

Untitled list of plate to be given to Charles Cobbe [loose sheet]

26 March 1814

1 Soop Ladle
1 Salver
2 Waiters
4 butter boats
2 Ladles
4 Wine coasters
1 Egg Saucepan
1 Fish Trowel
6 Salts & Spoons
1 Marrow Spoon
1 Snuff pan
3 Gravy Spoons
18 Table Spoons
12 Desert Spoons
2 Dozen Silver handled knives
11 Desert Do. –
2 Carving knives & forks
1 Dozen Tea Spoons
2./2 4 pronged forks
1 Teapot
1 Sugar dish & tongs
2 Scallop dishes
1 Cream Pot
5 Egg Cups
6 Egg Spoons

all these things my son Charles
has given to me during my life
and at my death I desire he
may have them *A Cobbe*

Bath y^e: 26th: of March 1814

*A List of Plate
Given to Mrs Cobbe
March 1814 —
which she promised
to leave me —
C.C.*

List of Plate [loose sheet]

Novr 1821

1½ doz^n large Spoons
3 Gravy *do* ——
1 Doz Desert *do*
1 Breakfast *do*
4 Sauce spoons
1 Soup Ladle
13 Tea Spoons
2 odd *do* +
6 Egg *do*
1 Sugar *do*
1 Cream Ewer
1 Sugar bowl & Tongs +
1 Wine Funnel
1 Snuffer Stand
2 Small Waiters
1 Large do
5 Egg Cups
4 Butter boats & Covers
1 Tea Pot & Stand
6 Salts with Spoons
1 Fish Trowell
1 Marrow Spoon
2 Doz^n forks ×   30
2 Doz. Silver Handled Knives
2 Carving *do*. & forks
11 Small *do* ——   8
4 Plated handled Knives + *Plated*
1 Coffee Pot – Plated   *Feb/21*
1 Mustard —— *do*
1 Breadbasket – *do*
4 Coasters —— *do*
2 Cruets – —— – *do*
2 bed chamber Candlesticks *do*
1 Toast rack   *do*
1 Tea Urn   *do* ×
4 Salts   *do*
3½ Doz^n Forks   *do*
2 Knives   *do*
Cover dish   *do*
4 Pr Candlesticks   *do*
2 *do* —— *do*. with branches *do*
1 Egg Saucepan Silver.

List of Plate
Novr 1821
——
Bath ——

*[various calculations
of weight and cost
jotted in upside down]*

Newbridge House, County Dublin

PLATE 53
One of a set of four pincushion dishes, *c.* 1765,
maker's mark of John Laughlin (*fl.* 1745–75), silver
(see p. 347)

18

MOUNT STEWART,
COUNTY DOWN
1821

EDMUND JOYCE

THIS INVENTORY WAS CREATED in September 1821 for the second Marquess of Londonderry, better known as Lord Castlereagh (plate 48), just five months after the death of his father Robert Stewart, the first marquess, and eleven months before his own untimely and tragic death. The inventory is not a probate valuation but rather a list of the items *in situ* at Mount Stewart. Although Castlereagh did reside on a regular basis at Mount Stewart, particularly before the Union, he did not inherit it until near the end of his life. Most of his career was spent in England, either in his house in St James's Square, London, or his English country seat at North Cray, Kent.

In 1737 Alexander Stewart, a well-to-do merchant, of Stewart's Court and Ballylawn, County Donegal, married his cousin Mary Cowan, daughter of Alderman John Cowan of Londonderry. Mary Cowan, on the strength of a great inheritance acquired on the death in 1737 of her unmarried and childless brother Sir Robert Cowan, governor of Bombay (1729–34), had become a very wealthy heiress. The property on Strangford Lough in County Down was purchased in 1744, when her trustees invested a part of her fortune, said to be in the region of £42,000, in the two extensive manors of Newtownards and Comber. The Stewarts' purchase of this land (consisting in all of sixty townlands), the influential English marriages made by their son, Robert, and the family's increasing wealth and standing in County Down, brought about their elevation from merchants to marquesses in two generations.

Robert Stewart (1739–1821), first Marquess of Londonderry (plate 47), pursued a political career in Dublin and sat as an MP between 1771 and 1783. His achievements encouraged his eldest son, also Robert, to pursue a political career, which in his case became one of international importance. The founding Alexander Stewart lived in a house which was the centrepiece of the square in Newtownards, the principal town on his estate. His son, Robert, moved further along Strangford Lough, where numerous phases of development at Mount Stewart (originally called Mount Pleasant) and the surrounding landscape reflected the rising aspirations of the Stewarts. The first house built there by Robert Stewart was a modest affair. It is shown, from a distance, in two paintings of 1786 by Solomon Delane. But these were commissioned not to feature the house, but to show off the nearby and recently completed Temple of the Winds, which had been constructed to the drawings of James 'Athenian' Stuart on a rise of ground overlooking the lough.

Although James Wyatt had earlier produced a set of drawings for a new house and stable block, it was about 1804 before the first marquess took the actions needed to create a house worthy of his family status. He decided to retain the long, low,

325

whitewashed range represented in Delane's paintings, and to add a grand, comfortable wing complete with an imposing entrance and garden front. His son Robert, styled Lord Castlereagh from 1796, persuaded him to engage the services of George Dance the Younger. Much of these alterations by Dance appear in two drawings which are now housed in Sir John Soane's Museum (see frontispiece). The parade of rooms opening off an elongated central entrance hall complete with a grand stairwell portrays an elegant house befitting a marquess. The library at Mount Stewart, famed for its series of window shutters decorated with book spines, en suite with the '6 Mahogney Bookcases Inlayed and Full of Books' itemized in the inventory, dates from this period of development at Mount Stewart.

The inventory is of particular interest because it brings to life the day-to-day as well as the very elaborate items needed if a grand residence were to operate efficiently. For example, it includes '15 Londonderry Sola[r] grates' which adorned the rooms of the recently constructed wing at Mount Stewart. These grates, according to an advertisement in the *Belfast News-Letter* from 1813, were in fact the 'invention of the Right Honourable the Earl of Londonderry' and demonstrate his own practical bent and his active involvement with the new developments at Mount Stewart. Dictates of high fashion and high status were also obeyed. Of the numerous chairs disposed around the house, a total of 116 were made of the then fashionable bamboo. A bountiful collection of dining-tables, dinner wares and an extensive *batterie de cuisine* signify refined sociability and regular entertainment. The display of overt symbols of rank and status such as the set of eleven crested hall chairs, and of family portraits, supplemented with prints and busts of key figures such as Wellington, Napoleon and Princess Charlotte, assertively and stylishly promote the Londonderry lineage and political importance.

On Castlereagh's death in August 1822 the titles and estate passed to his half-brother, Charles William Vane (1778–1854). At his instigation, the extension by George Dance the Younger and the earlier house were transformed by William Vitruvius Morrison in the mid-1830s into the much grander house there today. Charles, third Marquess of Londonderry, married twice. His only son by his first marriage succeeded to his Irish titles and estates but died childless in 1872. His second marriage, in 1819, was to Frances Anne Vane-Tempest, the daughter and sole heiress of Sir Henry Vane-Tempest of Wynyard Park, County Durham. Their eldest son succeeded to British titles created to accompany the inheritance of the Vane-Tempest estates, but in 1872 succeeded as fifth Marquess of Londonderry as well. Thereafter, all the titles and estates descended to the eldest son in each generation, until the seventh marquess (1878–1949) broke with tradition and gave the Mount Stewart estate to his youngest daughter Lady Mairi. Mount Stewart is now managed by the National Trust, and Lady Rose Lauritzen, Lady Mairi's daughter, maintains the family connection and lives there with her husband, Peter.

This inventory is deposited at PRONI (the Public Record Office of Northern Ireland).

Mount Stewart, County Down
1821

An Inventory
of the Household
Furniture
belonging to The Most
Noble the Marquis of
Londonderry
Taken at Mount Stewart
Sept.   *1821*

Enterance Hall

A Marble Chimney piece Londonderry Sola Grate Fender Fire Shovle Tongues harth Brush and Harth Rugg

6 Dinning Tables of Different sizeses

1 Large dinning table under the stairs Old

11 Hall Chairs painted, Crest and Cor_^o net on

2 pedestals with Female bust's on

1 Bust of Walter James Esqre on Chimney piece

2 Lamps with 3 burners, one bottom cut Glass the other plate

1 Weather Glass

1 Footstool

1 Stepladder

3 pieces of Frize one with border all Round

2 pieces of Oil Cloth

2 Scarlet Curtains of Frize with frame and rods of Wood and 4 Brass pins

Billiard room

A Marble Chimney piece Londonderry sola Grate Brass mounted

A Green painted Fender Brass Top

A Billiard Table brown Holland cover and brush

13 Kews 6 maces and 6 Balls (long Kew and long mace broken

2 Markers Glazed one Glass broken

2 Rules of the Game framed and Glazed

A Mahogney side Table 4 Bust's, 3 marble and 1 plaster paris

2 Pedestals with busts, of Duke of Wellington, & Honble F. Stewart

A small bust of Bonaparte on Chimney piece

6 Mahogney Chairs with hair seats

3 Black painted Chairs with Cane seats

2 printed Cotton window curtains lyned white Callico

Drapery white Muslin lyned Blue Calico

White Fringe and Tossels

Rods and pole for drapery plain wood & 2 brass Curtain ^{pins}

Carpet Round the Table and 3 pieces scarlet Frize

2 Bell Ropes with rings

2 Coloured prints of views In Italy Guilt frames & Glazed

A small print of Duke Wellington in Rich guilt frame

Dinning room

A Marble Chimney piece Londonderry Sola Grate fender

Fire Irons bellows and hearth brush

2 Side Boards with high Backs brass Mounted and Inlayed

1 Mahogney wine Couper brass Mounted

2   *do*. plate Baskets   *do*   *do*

1 *D^o* dinning Table in 5 piece's 4 on Pillar and Claw

16 *D^o.* Chairs Morroco seats

14 Bamboo painted Chairs Cane seats

1 Mahogney plate warmer

1 Japan   *do*   *do*

1 Folding Japan Indie Screen 6 leaves

1 *do*. Scarlet screen black painted frame 7 leaves

1 *do*   *D^o* Frize *do*   *do*   7 *do*

1 *do*   *do do*   *do*   4 *do*

1 Small *do*. ^{one}_^ side painted *do*

1 Small *do* Scarlet, black_^ ^{painted} Fire screen 4 leaves

2 *D^o* Fire screen one Slyding

2 Chair back *D^o*

10 Large portrait Family painting's, all with rich guilt Frames

2 Small Busts 1 Figure 2 Urans of plaster paris

1 Lamp brass mounted 4 burners and plate Glass Cylinder

2 Side Board Lamps

4 Scarlet Merreen window Curtains bound with black Velvet,. Drapery Complete 8 Brass Curtains pins

1 Window seat Stuffed black painted frame with Cover the same as the Window Curtains

4 Linen Rola Blinds

A Large Square portieguies Mat

A printed Cloth basket, and harth Rug

2 Black and Scarlet Bell pulls with rings and Tossels

Music Room

A marble stove Londonderry sola grate Fender and Fire Irons

1 Soffa hair Squabe 4 Fether Cushions blue printed Cotton Covers

1 Black painted Chaise Longue hair Squabe and one pillow 2 Sets of Furniture one Scarlet Merreen the other Blue printed Cotton

1 Blue printed Cotton window Curtain lyned with yellow and yellow, Fringe, 2 Brass Curtain pins and Two Bell pulls with rings

4 Black painted Arm Chairs with Cane seats

1 music Stool Stuffed and Worked Cover

1 Footstool and 1 D.º Scarlet Cover

1 Old Mahogney Chair Stuffed seat and Back

8 Bamboo Chairs with Cane Seats

2 Mahogney Oval Tables covers Gray Cloth

2 do Small Square D.º

2 D.º Breakfast D.º with Folding leaves each

1 D.º oval with drawr and Inlayed

1 Beach Wood Round Table on pillar and Claw

1 Indie Cabnet with 5 drawrs Inlayed with Ivory on Black painted Stand

1 Black painted Music Stand

1 *do do* bookcase, 2 blue China Flower pots on Top

Green Carpet and Harth Rug

1 Letter Box

1 Lamp brass Mounted 3 Burners Cut Glass Cylinder

1 Writing Desk

1 Mahogney Fire Screen

1 Aulder *D.º*

2 pole *do*

1 Large Bust on Pedelstal

4 prints framed and Glazed Frames rich guilt, princess Charlotte, Duke Wellington, Marquis of Londonderry and Lord Stewart

Library

A marble Chimney piece Londonderry Sola Grate Fender
Fire Irons and harth brush

6 Mahogney Bookcases Inlayed and Full of Books

5 Busts Verious on Top and 7 Verious Ornaments plaster paris

4 Pedelstals with large Busts

1 Square mahogney Table Inlayed, game Box with 9 Holes and 9 Balls

1 Soffa Table Inlayed with 2 Folding leaves

1 mahogney writing Table Inlayed with Folding Top

1 *do* oval *do* on pillar and Claw

1 Small *do do do*

1 Beach Wood Round Table on pillar and Claw with ~~Cloth Cover~~ Scarlet Cloth Cover

1 Small do square *do. do*

2 Writing desks with Ink bottles

2 Soffas Stuffed hair Backs 4 Wool squabes 2 Fether pillows 2 Sets of Furniture for each of printed Cotton

1 Woolsack for the Center of the Room one hair cushion & 2 Fether pillows, and Two Sets of printed Cotton Furniture

2 Large Arm Chair Stuffed hair seats, 4 hair Cushions and 2 Sets of printed Cotton Furniture for each

12 Bamboo painted Chairs with Cane seats

3 Black *do do* with Fether Cushions and printed Cotton Covers

1 Mahogney Two Arm Chair with Scarlet Cloth Cushion and Back

1 Mahogney Footstoll Scarlet covers

2 Footstolls

1 Lamp brass mounted 4 Burners and Cut glass cylinder

2 Mahogney pole Screens brass mounted and Screens of White Worked Silk

2 mahogney pole screens painted

1 Ormelew Time piece with 2 Figures and Glass shade belong ing To the Dowager Marchioness

2 China Vaws for Chimney piece

2 D.º Match Cups

4 paper Hand Screens

2 Black Velvet Bell pulls

1 Mahogney Glazed 8 leafed screen 16 pains 2 Broke
A map of the County down
And Old Turkey Carpet, harth Rug, and large square portiegies Mat

6 printed Cotton Window Curtains Drapery the same with ~~the~~ blue ~~and~~ Cotton and muslin Drapery

12 Brass Curtain pins and 13 Brass Drapery pins
The painting of Lord Stewart in Uniform on Horseback in Rich guilt Frame blonging To Dowager Marchioness

Ante Room

A Marble Chimney piece Londonderry sola Grate Fender Fire Irons and bellows

1 Mahogney Table Scarlet Cloth Cover
2 Small *do. do* with drawrs each
1 Round *do do* on pillar and Claw
1 Small square Mahogney Top Table, on pillar and Claw. Aulder Wood
1 Indie Cabnet with drawrs and Marble pillars and Inlayed with Marble and other Verious Stones
1 *do* Cabnet with Indie Figures, blue and Gold China Jar on Top
1 Mahogney Cabnet Glazed with 2 drawrs 5 Shelves and Back Glazed with plate Glass, Full of Figures Shells &^c with 6 large Shells on Top, ~~bl~~ Belonging to Lady Emily or D. Marchioness
1 Female Bust
2 prints Framed and Glazed one guilt Frame the other Black and guilt
A painting of the Tomb, of the late Capt Tho [*indistinct letters scored through*] Stewart framed and Glazed Frame Rich guilt
1 Half Moon picture framed and Glazed, Frame rich guilt Glass Cracked
2 Back Gammon Boxes 1 set of Men 2 dice Boxes but on[e] dice
2 China Figures over Chimney piece with painted Glass shades in hand for Candles
1 Hand Screen
1 Small Braunes Uran mounted in Ormelew
1 Hand [*rubbed out*] Mahogney swing Bookcase full of Book and
1 Small Bust of Bonaparte on Top
1 Indie Japan Box containeing 4 Boxes with Motheraperral Counters for Cards and 12 Counter Tray's
1 Indie Broad Sword and Scabard
2 Bamboo painted Chairs Cane seats
1 ~~Ten~~ [*rubbed out*] Miniture Cabinet Inlayed with Ivory Containing Ten minitures
1 Set of Window Curtains printed Cotton with Drapery Complete
8 Brass Curtain pins
9 Transperencies in a mahogney Frame
1 Piece of Gray Frize with border all Round
1 *do   D^o*   for the Window
2 Bell pulls with rings

Drawing Room

A marble and Wood Chimney piece common grate

5 Bars Fender and Fire Irons bellow and harth brush
1 Small Square Mahogney Table Inlayed with black
2 mahogney Card Tables
1 *do* Side Table marble Top
1 *do do do* Folding Top
6 D.^o Bookcases with Books
1 D.^o music Stand
1 Large Folding 8 leafed screen Black Painted frame Covered with Caricaturo's and other pictures
2 Fire Screens one mahogney and the other painted
1 Beachwood writing desk covered with gray Cloth 2 Drawrs
1 Large mahogney Fire Screen
1 Bookstand Beachwood
2 mahogney seats 4 Hair Cushions
4   *do*   Chairs Stuffed hair seats and Backs
An Old Two Armed Chair leather cover brass Nailed and Two Cushions
12 Bamboo painted Chairs Cane seats
3 Foot Stools
3 printed Cotton window Curtains lyned Orange Coloured Cotton with printed Cotton Drapery white Fringe and Tossles
2 Large Looking Glasses guilt Frame
1 portrait painting of Lord Stewart over the Fire place
37 prints Verious Framed and Glazed Frames Guilt 2 Glasses Cracked
2 D.^o Framed and Glazed Frames Black and guilt
2 profoils Framed and Glazed
A Head of the Honble W^m pitt framed and Glazed
2 China Bottles, 2 Flower Pots Earthen Ware
1 Uran for Burning pastiles
2 paper hand Screens
2 Bell pull with Rings
A plated ~~Glass~~ Ink Stand with 3 Glasses
A Kiderminster Carpet with Green Border

Nurcery or Small parlour

A Marble and wood Chimney piece, Fender Fire Irons and Bellows

A mahogney Press bedstead doors Glazed Bust of The marquis of Londonderry on Top

A deal painted cupboard doors Glazed (2 pair Cracked Bust of master James on Top

1 Large Oval mahogney Dinning Table folding leaves
2 mahogney Card Tables
1 Side Board marble Top
1 Black painted Arm Chair Cane seat hair Cushion and Cover
2 mahogney Chairs with Hair seats
2 *do do* with leather *do*
10 Bamboo painted Chairs rush seats
1 Mahogney Fire Screen
2 Hand Screens
1 Portrait painting over the Chimney piece
5 prints Framed and Glazed, Frames Black and Guilt One Extruco Frame with Glass
2 *do, do* and Varnished
3 white Cotton Window Curtains with Fringe
2 Bell pull's Ivory K$_\wedge^{n}$obes
  A Kiderminster Carpet

Marquis of Londonderry's Bed Room

A Common Grate 4 Bars fender Fire Irons and harth Brush
A Four posted bedstead, mahogney Foot pillars Turned
printed Cotton Furniture lyned white Cotton Fether Bed bolster and pillow in Broad Striped Tick
2 Wool mattress blue and White Cover
1 pair of Blankets a Binder and white Cotton Counterpane
2 printed Cotton Window Curtains with ~~wh~~ White lyning
1 Mahogney Chest 5 Drawrs
1 Small Square Mahogney Table
1 Folding down   *do* Dressing *do.*
1 Swing *do,* Dressing Glass
~~1 *D^o* Comb, Tray with Drawr~~
1 *D^o* Bedside Cupboard one White Utensil
1 Square deal painted Table
White Wash hand bason and Ewer water Bottle Tumbler soap and Brush Tray
1 Square Fire Screen and one mahogney pole Screen
2 mahogney Chairs hair seats & backs and
                     printed Cotton Covers
2   *do do* Leather *do do do do*
2 Bamboo Painted Chairs Rush seats
1 Portrait Painting over Chimney piece, with guilt Frame
2 prints Framed and Glazed, Frames black and Guilt
  A Kidminster Carpet in 3 pieces

Study

A Common Grate 5 Bars Fender Fire Irons and bellows
1 mahogney wardrobe 4 drawrs
1 *D^o* Secretary with wardrobe Top and drawrs
1 *do, do do* Door plate Glass
1 Large *do,* Writing desk with drawrs and Covered with Green base
1 Small *D^o* on Top
1 *do do* writing Table with Folding Top and drawr
                  on pillar $_\wedge^{\&\,Claw}$
2 *do do* portable writing desks brass mounted
1 *do do* Table with 2 drawrs
1 Oak press
1 Large oak Chest
1 Small *D^o* brass mounted
4 mahogney Chairs hair seats
1 *do* Writing Stoll
1 *do* Case containing a Telliscope
1 *D^o* moroco supposed to contain weights & Scales
1 *D^o* Fire Screen
1 Large deal painted Bookcase doors glazed Full of Books
2 Gun cases and $_\wedge^{2\,Guns}$ one Silver-mounted ~~Gun~~
1 print framed and Glazed – Frame Guilt
1 Brass Taper Wax Candlestick
2 Set of window drapery
1 Bell pull with Brass ring
  A Kiderminster Crapet

Marchioness of Londonderry's bed Room

A Common Grate 4 Bars Fender Fire Irons and bellow
A Small Tent Bedstead, Fether Bed and bolster in Striped ^{Tick}
Down pillow hair mattress Blue and white Check Cover
2 Blankets and white Cotton Counterpane
1 Mahogney Chest 5 drawrs
1 *D^o* Secretary 5 drawrs and drawrs Inside
1 Small mahogney Reading desk 5 drawrs Covered
                with Scarlet ^{Cloth}
1   *D^o* Swing Dressing glass
1   *D^o* Fire Screen
1   *D^o* bedside Cupboard one white Utensil
1   *D^o* wash Hand Stand bason & Ewer brush
Tray One water bottle Chiped
1 Small Oval Beach wood Table
1 Square   *D^o*   *do*

2	*do*	Deal	*do*
4		*do*	Stool
1		*do*	Earing Horse
1		*do.* writing desk covered with Scarlet Cloth

1 mahogney Chamber bath Tin lyner
18 Deal Shelves and 1 Mahogney
1 print Framed and Glazed of the late Lord Camden
4 Bamboo painted Chairs Cane Seats
  A Kiderminster carpet
2 printed Cotton window Curtains printed Cotton Drapery with White Fringe
1 Bell pull and Brass ring
1 Camp Stool and 2 Straw Hassecks

Passage at Foot of Back Stairs

2 Eight day Clocks one in Black Case with plate Glass door
  The other in a Wainscott Case
1 Deal painted press with 2 drawrs
1 Bust
1 Peice of Oil Cloth from End To End
2 Shades for Lamps

Best Stair Case and lobby

1 Large Indie Chest Brass mounted
2 *do* Coloured Views of Shipping in Indie black Frames and Brass Ornaments
2 paintings of the Honble Alex^{dr} Stewart, house Ards, black frame & brass ornaments
1 View of Rocks near the above place black frame and brass ornaments
1 *D.º* of Mountains in a Black Varnished Frame *Dº do*
2 Black Oak seats, with Cane bottoms
10 Painted Chairs *do do*
1 Liverpool lamp brass mounted and Glass shade
1 *do do* in passage
1 Large Portuigues Mat
1 *D.º* Bust on Braget

Sky light bed Room

A Marble Chimney piece Common Grate 4 Bars fender Tongs and Shuvle
A Tent Bed Stead mahogney Tuned Foot pillars printed Cotton Furniture, with White lyning Fether Bed bolster and pillow in Striped Tick
3 Blankets and a printed Cotton Counter pane
1 Round Table on pillar and Claw

1 mahogney Swing looking Glass with drawr
  Glass Cracke
4 *D.º* Chairs Stuffed hair Seats and backs with Printed Cotton Covers
  A Kiderminster Carpet

North or Buff dressing Room

A Marble Chimney piece Londonderry Sola
Grate Fender
Fire Irons Bellows and harth Brush
A Tent Bedstead Mahogney Foot pillars white Cotton Furniture and Fringe Fether Bed bolster and Pillow in Striped Ticken
1 Pair of Blankets a Binder and White Cotton Counterpane
  White Dimity window Curtains with Fringe and Muslin Drapery
2 Brass Curtains pins
1 Long Mahogney Dressing Table with Knee hole and 11 Drawrs
1 *do* Small Dressing Table with frame for Glass wanting Top
2 Small *do.* Fly Table one with drawr
1 *do* Swing Dressing Glass
3 Bamboo painted Chairs Cane seats
  White wash hand bason and ewer blue and white Soap and Brush Tray Jug for warm water & Tumbler
1 Bell pull and ring
  A Kiderminster Carpet
  Brown Holland Rola Window Blind

North or Buff Bed Room

A Marble Chimney piece Londonderry sola
Grate Fender
Fire Irons bellow and harth Brush
A four posted bedstead Turned foot pillar printed Cotton Furniture lyned with Buff Fether bed bolster
2 Pillows in Striped Ticken
1 Hair Mattress In Striped Tick and 1 Straw palerwas
2 Blankets a Binder and white Cotton Counterpane
  A Small Tent Bedstead White Cotton Furniture with Fringe a Fether bed bolster and pillow in Striped tick
  Hair Mattress in blue and white Check Straw palerwas
1 Pair Blankets a Binder and white Cotton Counterpane
  Printed Cotton Window Curtains lyned, Drapery Buff Cotton Bound with black Velvet

Mount Stewart, County Down

6 Brass Curtain P̶i̶ and Bed pins and 3 Small *D⁰*
A Brown holland Rola blind
1 Mahogney wardrobe 2 drawrs and 3 deal Shelves
1 *D°.* chest of 5 drawrs
1 *D°.* dressing Table with Knee hole and 5 Drawrs inlayed
1 *D°.* Night *D°.*
1 *D°.* Chamber Bath white lyner
1 *D°* Bedside Cupboard white Utensil
1 *D°.* Swing Looking Glass
1 Green painted wash hand Stand white wash hand. Bason and Ewer blue and White Soap and Brush Tray Jug for warm water, Water bottle and Tumbler
1 pʳ.. White Earthen Candlestcks
2 Mahogney Chairs Stuffed hair seats and back printed Cotton Covers
1 Soffa, Back and side Stuffed hair Squabe
4 Fether pillows and printed Cotton Covers
2 painted arm Chairs with Cane seats
2 *do*   *do*   *do*   *do*
1 Mahogney dressing Stool printed Cotton Cover
2 Bell pulls and Rings
A Kiderminster Carpet and harth Rug

Best Dressing room

A Marble Chimney piece Londonderry Sola Grate Fender
Fire Irons and harth Brush
A Mahogney Canopy Bedstead on 4 Claws Hair ᴀ^Mattress
2 Fether Bolsters and hair Pillow printed Cotton Covers Printed Cotton Curtains lyned white Cotton and Silk Tossels
4 Brass Curtain pins and 2 Rings printed Cotton window Curtains and Drapery with Tossels, Curtains lyned white Cotton
2 mahogney Chairs Stuffed hair seats and Backs 2 Sets of Covers the one printed Cotton the other plain *D°.*
1 mahogney Dressing Stool Stuffed hair Seat and Covers
1 *D°.* Chest of 5 Drawrs
1 Mahogney dressing Table 2 drawrs
1 *D°.* Swing Dressing Glass 1 *do.*
1 *D°.* Wash hand stand Folding Top & 2 Drawrs
1 Brown w̶a̶s̶h̶ and white wash hand Bason & Ewer Blue and White Soap and Brush Tray and Jug for warm Water, Water Bottle and Tumbler
1 Bedside Cupboard one white Utensil
1 Small Square Mahogney Fly Table
1 Water Coloured painting of Fruit Framed & Glazed

Frame Black and Brass Ornaments
1 Mirror in guilt Frame
A Kiderminster Carpet and harth Rug
1 Bell pull & Ring

Best Bed Room

A Marble Chimney piece Londonderry sola Grate Fender Fire Irons bellows and hearth brush
A four posted Bedstead Mahogney foot pillars Turned and Inlayed a Canopy Cornish Frame mahogney Inlayed.
Drapery poles guilt five Ornaments on Top, Drapery lyned, of Cornish and head Cloth, blue Silk and Silk Tossles
Curtains and Canopy, Dickerwork Curtains lyned with white Cotton
1 Chaise Longues Stuffed hair Squabe 2 Fether pillows printed Cotton Furniture With Tossels
1 Fether Bed bolster and 2 pillows in Striped Ticken
2 Hair Mattress in Striped Tick and 1 Straw paleraws
2 Blankets a Binder 2 White Cotton Counterpanes one Dicker work the other one printed Cotton Counterpane with Fringe
3 Dicker work white Cotton Window Curtains with Dicker work Sowed on and Dicker work Drapery with Silk Fringe
3 Mahogney Inlayed Cornishes
6 Brass Curtain pins
3 Brown Rola Blinds
1 Mahogney Wardrobe: 3 ᴀ^Slyding Shelves and 4 drawrs
1 *D°.* Chest of 4 Drawrs Turned pillars and Feet
1 *D°.* Octagon Table with Folding leaves
1 *D°.* Square Fly Table with Drawrs and Inlayed
1 *D°.* Small Table with Frame and Feet Turned *D°.*
1 Writing Table
1 Mahogney wash hand Stand Inlayed with blue and white Hand bason and Ewer and a Chinee China wash hand Bason with Soap and Brush Tray, 2 China Jugs for Warm water, Water Bottle and Tumbler
1 Mahogney Chamber Bath with White lyner
1 *do* Bedside Cupboard Inlayed blue and white Utensel
1 *D°.* pair Bedside steps
1 *D°.* Night Stool white pan and blue and white Utensel
1 Large deal Toylet Table on Casters blue Cover and Worked Muslin Toylet
1 Swing dressing Glass with Three Drawrs

5 mahogney Chairs Stuffed hair seats and backs with
2 Sets of Covers the one white Cotton Dicker work
sowed on and the other plain White Cotton
2 mahogney ~~Chairs~~ Dressing stools with
Covers the same as the Chairs }
2 Bamboo painted Chairs Cane seats
1 Beach wood frame for Chaise Seat
1 mahogney pole screen painted Velvet
1 Deal Earing Horse
1 Water Coloured painting of Sheels and weeds framed
& Glazed Frame Mahogney
2 Indie China Bottles
2 Blue & White China Cups and Saucers
1 Cabnet China Cup
1 Indie D^o plate
2 China Match Cups / one Cracked
A Kiderminster Carpet and harth Rug
2 Bell pulls and Rings

White or Green dreesing Room

A marble Chimney piece Londonderry Sola Grate
fender, Tongs Shuvel Bellows and hearth brush
A Tent Bedstead Turned mahogney Foot pillars
White Dimity Furniture with white Cotton Fringe
Fether Bed Bolster and pillow in Striped Ticken Wool
mattress in Check and a Straw palerwas
1 pair Blankets a Binder and a White Cotton
Counterpane
White Cotton Window Curtains, Drapery blue
and Black Border, with Fringe and Tossells
2 Brass Curtain pins
Brown Holland Rola Blind
1 Beachwood Chest 4 Drawrs Inlayed
1 mahogney dressing table Folding Top
1 Square D^o Fly Table
1 D^o wash hand Stand high back white wash hand
Bason and Ewer, blue and White Soap and Brush tray
Jug for warm water, Water Bottle and Tumbler
1 mahogney Chamber bath white lyner Chiped
1 D^o Bedside Cupboard White Utensil
1 Pair white Earthen Candlesticks
4 Bamboo painted Chairs Cane seats
1 Print Varnished in Black frame brass ornaments
1 *do*. of Lord Byron Guilt Frame and Glazed
A Green Kiderminster Carpet and harth rug

White or Green Bed Room

A marble Chimney piece Londonderry sola Grate
Fender Fire Irons bellows and harth Brush
A four Posted Bedstead mahogney Turned foot pillars
Green and Black painted Cornish
White Cotton Furniture with Crimson Border and
do. Muslin Drapery with *do*. *do* and
do Cotton Fringe
Fether bed Bolster and 2 pillows hair mattress in
blue and White Check and Straw paleraws
3 Blankets and White Cotton Counterpane
A Small Tent Bedstead white Cotton Furniture
Fether bed bolster and pillow hair mattress in
Striped Tick
A Straw paleraws in Flannell
1 Pair Blankets a Binder and white Cotton Counterpane
2 White Cotton window Curtains with Crimson Border
white muslin and Cotton Drapery with D^o D^o
& white Fringe, Green and white painted Cornish
2 pieces of High Book cases mahogney Inlayed 6
Shelves each
1 mahogney Chest 5 drawrs Inlayed
1 *do.* *do* 3 *do* *do*
1 Mahogney Inlayed Night Stool white lyner Inlayed
1 D^o Bedside Cupboard White Utensel
1 *do* wash hand Stand blue and White wash hand
Bason and ewer, blue and White Soap and Brush
Tray, Jug for warm Water, Water Bottle and Tumbler
(bottle Cracked)
1 mahogney Chamber bath, Inlayed white Lyner
1 Small Square mahogney Fly Table
4 mahogney Chairs Stuffed hair seats and Back white
Cotton Furniture white Border and Fringe
2 Bamboo painted Chairs Cane seats
A Small Indie Japan Cabnet with 10 Drawrs on frame
A *do* *do* *do* Work Box
1 Black Painted pole Screen
2 paper painted hand D^o
1 Square deal Toylet Table
1 *do.* mahogney dressing Glass
1 *do* Oak *do* Stool with Cover
1 *do* *do* frame for Chair seat
1 print Framed and Glazed Frame Guilt
1 *do* *do* *do* of the Duches of Devonshire
2 Black wedgewood Inkstand
2 Bell pulls and Rings
A Kiderminster Carpet and harth Rug
2 Curtain Hooks
3 Rola and 2 Blinds

Mount Stewart, County Down

Pink dressing Room

A marble Chimney piece Londonderry sola Grate
Fender Fire Irons Bellow and harth Brush
A mahogney Bedstead on 4 Claws
Tea Coloured Furniture lyned white Cotton Fring
a Hair Mattress 2 Fether bolsters & pillow & Tossels)
     white Cotton furniture)
Tea Coloured window Curtains drapery lyned, Fringe)
     white, white Cotton)
A Large 2 Armed Oak Chair Stuffed hair sides and
Back with pink Cotton Cover

2 mahogney Chairs Stuffed hair seats and backs
white Cotton
Covers with White Cotton Fringe
1 mahogney dressing Stool Stuffed and covers
4 Bamboo painted Chairs Cane Seats
1 mahogney dressing Table Inlayed with Knee hole
       & 3 drawrs
1 *D°* Swing *D°* Glass
1 *do* Square Fly Table one drawr
1 *do* wash hand Stand Inlayed brown and white hand
bason and Ewer *do. do* Soap and Brush Tray *do.*
Figured Jug for warm water, Water bottle (Cracked)
and Tumbler
1 mahogney Chamber bath Inlayed and white lyner
1 *D°* Bedside Cupboard
1 yew pole Screen painted Velvet
1 Small mahogney Chest 4 drawrs Inlayed
1 Beach Frame for Coach seat
1 Deal painted Bookcase 4 Shelves
1 print of The Hon^{be} W^{m} pitt Framed and Glazed
frame guilt
A Kiderminster Carpet and harth Rug
2 large Brass Curtain pins
1 Linen Rola blind
1 Bell pull with Ring
1 White Earthen Foot pan

Pink Bed Room

A Marble Chimney piece Londonderry Sola Grate
Fender Fire Irons Bellows and hearth Brush
A fourposted Bedstead Mahogney Turned foot pillars
A Chevaux-de-Frise Cornish and Valences printed
Cotton Furniture and Drapery lyned with pink Silk
worsted Fringe and Tossels
A Fether Bed bolster and 2 pillows in Striped Tick

2 Hair mattresses one in Striped Tick the other in
       blue Check
1 Wool *do,* in   *do* *do* & Straw
      paleraws in *D°*
3 Blankets a printed Cotton Counterpane bound
with pink
4 printed Cotton Window Curtains lyned with pink
Drapery of *D°.* lyned pink Fringe and Tossles
8 Brass Curtain pins
4 Linen Rola Blinds
1 Deal Framed Couch, hair Squabe & 4 Fether pillows
with Covers to match the Bed Furniture
2 mahogney Chairs Stuffed hair seats and Back
with Covers *do. do*
1 painted dressing Stool hair Stuffed with pink
cotton Covers
6 Bamboo painted Chairs Cane seats
A mahogney Inlayed wardrobe 2 drawrs and
       3 deal Shelves
A *do* Pembrook Table Folding leaves 2 drawrs Gray
Frize Cover with black Fringe
1 Oval mahogney Fly Table
1 Deal Toylet Table with Toylet Cover of muslin &
Cotton Complete
1 mahogney Swing dressing glass 3 drawrs
1 *D°* Inlayed high Back wash hand stand Red & White
1 wash hand bason and Ewer and *D°. do.* soap &
Brush Tray water Craft and Tumbler, brown &
white Figured Jug for warm water
1 Pair of mahogney bedside Steps
1   *D°.* Night Stool white lyner
1   *D°.* Bedside Cupboard Red and white Utensel
1 yew pole paper Screen
1 Earing Horse
1 Black painted 4 leafed Screen Covered with
Caricatures &
2 Bell Ropes and Rings
1 print of the Earl of Malmesburry Guilt Frame &
       Glazed
1 *D°* Small
1 Straw work Box
1 China Cabnet Bason with covers and Stand, bason
& Stand cracked
1 Large Cabnet Cup with cover and ~~basoneer,~~ ^{Saucer} Cup
      ^{&} Cover Cracked
2 Small *do* *do* with Saucers one Saucer Cracked
2 China Tea Kiddys with China Stand
1 *D°.* Partridge Setting
1 Kiderminster Carpet

Boudouar

A Marble Chimney piece Londonderry sola Grate
fender and Fire Irons
A mahogney bedstead 4 Claws pink Cotton Furniture
Trimed with blue and Black printed Cotton with Eagle
and Ring to Support them
Fether Squabe 2 Bolsters and pillow with pink Cotton
Covers bound blue and black
1 Straw Hassick with pink Cotton Covers
Pink Cotton and White muslin window Curtains
with blue and black Cotton Triming, Drapery pink
Cotton and white muslin to match [*overwritten*]
With Triming to match
4 Brass Curtain pins
1 Brown Linen Rola Blind
1 Mahogney Inlayed Chamber bath with White lyner
1 Black painted Arm Chair Cane seats
1 *do*   *do   do   do*
1 Wedgewood Ware paste Still Uran Cracked
A Kiderminster Carpet

Bedrooms of the Old House N.º 1

A Common Grate 5 Bars fender Fire Irons &
harth brush
A 4 Posted bedstead, Mahogney Turned Foot pillars
White Dimity Furniture white Cotton Fringe Tester
and head cott [*overwritten*] cloth, lyned pink Cotton
Fether bed Bolster and 2 pillows in Striped Tick
One Wool and one hair Mattress in blue and white
Check and Straw paleraws in Striped Tick
3 Blankets and White Cotton Counterpane
A Small Turn up Tent ½ Tester Bedstead white Cotton
Furniture fether bed bolster and pillow in Striped tick
Hair mattress and Straw palerwas in   *D⁰   D⁰*
2 Small Blankets and white Cotton Counterpane
2 Dimity Window Curtains white Cotton Fringe
2 Linen Rola Blinds
8 Small Brass Curtain pins
1 Beach wood wardrobe with 2 drawrs and
3 deal Shelves
1 Mahogney Inlayed dressing Table Knee hole 5 drawrs
1 *do* Swing dressing Glass one drawr
1 *D.º* Inlayed High back wash hand Stand white bason
and Ewer Yellow and Black soap and Brush Tray
1 mahogney writing And *D.º* Jug for warm water,
water Craft and Tumbler
1 mahogney writing Desk with drawr Inside

1 *D.º* Inlayed Fly Table
1 *do* Chamber Bath with white lyner
1 Mahogney Bedside Cupboard white Utentsil
1 *do* pole paper Screen
1 *D.º* Footstool
1 *D.º* Night Table with White lyner
2 *D.º* Chairs Stuffed hair Seats Cotton Covers
2 Bamboo painted Chairs Cane seats
1 mahogney Dressing Stool with Cover
1 Beach Wood Earing Horse
1 Black painted swing bookcase 2 Shelves
A Kiderminster Carpet and harth rug

N.º 2

A Common Grate 4 Bars Fenders Fire Irons bellow
and harth brush
A Tent Bedstead printed Cotton Furniture Tester
and head both lyned white Cotton Fether Bed
Bolster and pillow in Striped Tick Wool mattress in
Blue and white Check
Straw paleraws in Sacken
1 pair Blankets a Binder and white Cotton Counterpane
White Dimity window Curtains lyned white Cotton
D⁰ Cotton Fringe and one Rola but no Blind
1 mahogney Chest of 7 Drawrs
1   *D.º*   Dressing Table
1 Square *do* Fly   *do*
1 *do* Dressing Glass
1 *D.º* Bedside Cupboard White Utensil
1 *do* Chamber Bath White lyner
1 Green painted wash hand Stand with high back
& Drawr
White bason and Ewer blue and white soap and
Brush Tray and *do D.º* Jug for warm water, water
Craft and Tumbler
A Painted dressing Stool Stuffed hair Seats
2 Bamboo painted Chairs Cane Seats
2 Green painted   *do* Stuffed hair seats with Covers
1 Beach Earing horse
1 paper hand Screen
A painted Bookcase with 3 shelves
1 Bell Pull
A Kiderminster Carpet

Mount Stewart, County Down

N.º 3

A Common Grate 4 Bars Fender Fire Irons and harth brush

A Tent Bedstead mahogney Foot pillars, Dimity Furniture Cotton Fringe, Fether Bed bolster and pillow in Striped Tick, Wooll mattress in Blue and white Check Straw palerwas in Sacken

3 Blankets and white Cotton Counterpane
  White Cotton Window Curtains white Fringe
1 mahogney Chest of 8 Drawrs
1 Square *do*, Table of 1   *D°*
1   *D.º* Folding Top Dressing Table with
                            Dressing Glass
1 Small Square *D°*   writing   *D°* with *D°*
1 *D°..* Bedside Cupboard white Utensel
1 Beach Earing Horse
2 White painted Chairs Stuffed hair seats white
                            Cotton Covers
1 Bamboo *do.*   *do*   Cane Seats
3 deal Book Shelves with a few Books
  Green Rola Blind
  White Bason and Ewer blue and white Soap & Brush tray
  Jug for warm water, Water Craft and Tumbler
1 Bell Pull and Ring
  A printed Woolen Carpet

N.º 4

A Common Grate 4 Bars Fenders Fire Irons (no Shuvle) and harth Brush

A Tent bedstead mahogney foot pillars printed Cotton Furniture Fether bed bolster and pillow in Striped Tick

A Small ½ Tester bedstead Striped Tick Hangings White Cotton, window Curtains, Fether bed Bolster and Pillow in Striped Tick, hair mattress in blue & White Check

2 Blankets Binder and white Cotton Counterpane
2 Old Chest of Drawrs
  painted swing dressing Glass with drawr
1 mahogney Fly Table with drawr
1 *do* Arm Chair Stuffed hair seats with Cotton Covers
3 *do*   *do*   *do*   *do*   *do*   *do*
  White Bason and Ewer Soap Dish and white Utensil
  A piece of Old Brussels Carpet

N.º 5

A Common Grate 4 Bars fender Fire Irons and harth Brush

A Tent Bedstead mahogney foot Pillars
White Dimity Furniture Fringe and Tossels
Fether bed bolster and pillow in Striped Tick
Hair mattress in Blue and white Check & Staw paleraws

3 Blankets and white Cotton Counterpane
  printed Cotton Window Curtains lyned white, and white Cotton fringe
2 White Cotton Rola Blinds
1 mahogney Chest 5 Drawrs
1 *D.º* Inlayed dressing Table Knee Hole and 5 Drawrs
1 Swing   *do* Glass
1 Small Square mahogney Fly Table
1 mahogney Bedside Cupboard White Utensel
1 *D.º* Chair Stuffed hair Seat white Cotton Cover
2 Bamboo painted Chairs Cane seats
1 Deal painted wash hand Stand high Back White Bason and Ewer Jug for warm water Blue & white Soap and Brush Tray
  Bell pull and Ring
  A Kiderminster Carpet

N.º 6

A Common Grate 4 Bars Fender and Fire Irons
A Tent Bedstead white Cotton Furniture fither bed Bolster and pillow in blue Tick Hair mattress Check in blue & white

1 pair Blankets a Binder and white Cotton Counterpane printed Cotton window Curtains lyned, white Rola no Head
1 mahogney Chest 5 drawrs
1 Small *D.º* dressing Table 2 drawrs and Slyding leaf
1 Square *do*   *do*   *do*   1   *do*
1 *D.º* Swing looking Glass with *do*
1 *D°* Bedside Cupboard white Utensil
1 *do* Chair Stuffed hair Seats and printed Cotton Cover
2 White painted Chair stuffed hair Seats
              and white   *D°*   *D°*
1 Bell pull
  A Kiderminster Carpet
  White Bason and Ewer Jug warm water soap dish & tumbler

N.º 7

A Common Grate 4 Bars fender fire Irons and Harth brush

1 Secretary with 4 Drawrs 8 *do* Inside & 2 Bookcases over with 2 Shelves

1 mahogney Dressing Table with Folding Top and Frame for looking Glass and 2 drawrs

A mahogney Top Soffa Table Inlayed with 2 drawrs on pillar and Claw Beach wood

A Square Mahogney Fly Table painted deal frame

1 Small Square Mahogney work Table with drawer

1 Square deal Table painted frame 2 drawrs & Green Case Cover

1 painted reading desk Covered with Green base

1 Deal Framed Couch wool Squabe 4 Cushions with printed Cotton Furniture

1 mahogney 2 armed Chair Stuffed hair seats cotton furniture

2 *do* *do* *do* *do* *do* *do*

2 Bamboo painted *D.º* Cane seats

1 Footstool

1 mahogney paper screen

1 Beach pole *D.º* *D.º*

2 paper hand *D.º*

1 Small painting framed and Glazed

1 *do* Bookcase 4 shelves

1 Indie picture painted on Glass Cracked

Dimity Window Curtains lyned white Cotton

White muslin Drapery Cotton Fringe and Tossells

2 Green Rola Blinds

A Kiderminster Carpet

A List Harth Rug

4 Small Brass Curtain pins

1 Bell pull and Ring

N.º 8

A Common Grate 4 Bars fender Fire Irons bellow and harth brush

A 4 posted bedstead Mahogney foot Pillars printed Cotton Furniture Curtains Lyned pink Valences Trimed white fringes

Fether Bed bolster and 2 pillows in Striped Tick Wool mattress in blue and white Check and Straw palerwas in Tick 3 Blankets and white Cotton Counterpane

printed Cotton window Curtains lyned Red Cotton white Cotton Fringe

4 Small Curtains Rings

2 Green Rola Blinds

1 mahogney Chest of 5 Drawrs

1 Square *do.* Dressing Table with 1 Drawr

1 Swing *do* *D.º* Glass with 1 *do,*

1 Suqare *do* *do* Table Beach Wood draw and Frame

1 *D.º* Bedside Cupboard White Utensil

1 *D.º* deal painted Table white Bason and Ewer blue and white

Soap and Brush Tray water Bottle and Tumbler

1 mahogney Chair Stuffed hair seat Cotton Cover

2 painted *do* *do* *do* *D.º* *D.º*

2 Bamboo painted Chairs Cane seats

A Two leafed Folding paper Fire Screen

A Black painted pole *D.º*

2 Painted Swing bookcases 4 Shelves each some Books

1 *do* *do* 2 *D.º* and 1 Drawr

1 Bell Pull and 2 Rings

1 Beach Earing horse

1 Straw Hassick covered Red Cloth

A Kiderminster Carpet and harth Rug

N.º 9

A Common Grate 4 Bars fender Fire Irons bellows & harth brush

A Tent Bedstead White Cotton Furniture fether Bed bolster and pillow in Striped Tick Hair mattress in Brown holland

3 Blankets and White Cotton Counterpane

printed Cotton window Curtains lyned White

4 Small Brass Curtain window pins

An Old Secretary 4 drawrs inside, Bookcase over

A Oval Table 2 folding leaves (one broke)

1 Square mahogney Fly Table

1 *D.º* wash hand Stand white Bason and Ewer soap and brush Tray Jug for warm water Water Bottle and Tumbler

1 mahogney Bedside Cupboard White Utensil

1 *D.º* Night Stool White Lyner printed Cotton Cover

~~2~~ 1 *D.º* Chair Stuffed hair Seat *do* *do* *do,*

2 White painted Chairs Stuffed hair seats

printed ^White *D.º* *D.º*

2 Bamboo painted Chairs Cane Seats

1 Old Oak Chest 5 Drawrs

1 Green Painted Dressing Table

1 Swing Dressing Glass

1 Painted Bookcase 3 Shelves

1 Bell pull and ring

A water Coloured Drawing Varnished and Frame

A Kiderminster

Nº 10

A Common Grate 4 Bars fender Fire Irons and hearth brush
A Small Tent Bedstead printed Cotton Furniture Fether bed bolster And pillow in Striped Tick
Printed Cotton Window Curtains 2 Brass pins
3 Blankets and White Cotton Counterpane
A mahogney Chest of 5 drawrs
An Old Chest 7 do.
1 Samall Square mahogney Fly Table with drawr
2 Green Painted Chairs Stuffed hair seats Cotton Covers
1 Bamboo painted Chair Rush seats
1 Swing painted Bookcase 3 Shelves
A White Utensil, soap, dish, white Bason Ewer and Tumbler
A piece of Kiderminster Carpet

Nº 11

A Common Grate 4 Bars Fire Shuvle and poker
4 posted Bedstead fether bed bolster and pillow in Striped ^Tick
1 pair Blankets a Binder and White Cotton Counterpane
3 Old Chairs Stuffed hair seats
1 painted D.º Rush seat
An old deal Chest 5 drawrs
1 Long do Table Green Cover
A Old Square Table
A Dressing Glass
A piece of Carpet

Nº 12

2 Barrick Bedsteads 2 Fether pillows Two Beds and 1 Bolster In Striped Ticken
2 pair of Blankets 2 Binders & White Cotton Counterpane
A mahogney Chest of 4 drawrs
A Old Deal Table with 2 Shelves
4 Chairs and a Piece of Carpet

Nº 13 or Store room

Containing Shelves Cupboards & &c

Bed Room passage

Covered with Gray Frize and Gray Cloth from End to End
At East End Deal presses Fixed
3 half Window Blinds Green Sarge
1 Liverpool Lamp

West End House Maids Closet

4 Small New Tea Kettles for bed Rooms
1 do do do do Tin
1 Copper warming pan
3 painted Tin shades for rush lights
4 Swinging frames for Looking Glasses
1 Carpet Broom &c &c

Back Stair Case

A Kiderminster Stair Carpet with Border & 22 Rods

Bath Room

1 Chair
1 Earing horse
1 Thermometer

Cabin bed Rooms Nº 1

A Common Grate 4 Bars fender fire Irons bellows & harth brush
Small Tent Bedstead printed Cotton Furniture
Fether Bed Bolster and Pillow in Striped Tick
Wool matress in Blue and White Check
1 pair Blankets a Binder and White Cotton Counterpane
4 mahogney Chairs Stuffed hair Seats printed Cotton Covers
1 Chest of 5 drawrs
1 Small mahogney Chest of 6 Drawrs
1 Deal Dressing Table with drawr frame painted
1 mahogney swing dressing Glass 3 drawrs Glass Cracked
1 Small Square Fly Table deal Top
1 Dº Earing horse
1 Dº painted Bookcase 2 drawrs
One White Utensil Bason & Ewer soap and Brush Tray Water Craft and Tumbler
A piece of Kiderminster Carpet

Nº 2

A Common Grate 4 Bars fender Fire Irons

4 Posted Bedstead printed Cotton Furniture lyned white Fether Bed Bolster and 2 pillows in Striped Tick Hair mattress in Blue and White Check

2 Blankets and white Cotton Counterpane
A half Tester Turn up Bedstead fether Bed bolster and Pillow in Striped Tick
Wool mattress in Blue & White Check and 2 Blankets

2 Printed Cotton Window Curtains lyned
4 Chairs Stuffed hair seats printed Cotton Covers
1 mahogney Chest of 5 drawrs
1 Large painted deal press
1 *do do* drawrs
1 Small Deal Chest
1 Square *do* dressing Table
1 mahogney Swing *Dº* Glass
4 deal Shelves
1 White Utensil Bason and Ewer
A piece of Carpet and harth Rug

Nº 3

A Common Grate 4 Bars Fender and Tongs
a Small Tent Bedstead printed Cotton Furniture Fether Bed Bolster and pillow in Striped Tick and hair Mattress in Brown holland
printed Cotton Window Curtains lyned white

2 mahogney Chairs Stuffed hair seats and Backs
1 *Dº* leather Cover Stuffed hair Seats
1 Large Oak Chest 2 drawrs
2 deal presses
4 Deal Shelves
1 Square Deal Dressing Table
1 Small mahogney Fly *Dº*
White Utensil Bason and Ewer Jug for warm water &ᶜ
A piece of Kiderminster Carpet

Nº 4

A Common Grate 4 Bars Fender and Fire Irons
A Tent Bedstead printed Cotton Furniture Fether bed bolster and pillow in Striped Tick wool mattress in blue and white Check

2 Blankets a Binder and printed Cotton Counterpane
1 Oak Wardrobe with 2 drawrs
1 *do* Chest with with 1 *do*
An Old *Dº* Secretary with 4 *do*
A mahogney Chest with 5 *do*

1 Small Square deal dressing Table
1 mahogney Chair Stuffed hair seat
4 Chairs Verious *Dº Dº Dº*
1 mahogney Swing dressing Glass broke
2 Deal Shelves
1 Painted Swing Bookcase
1 White Utensil 2 Basons 1 Ewer Soap and Brush Tray and Tumbler
3 pieces of Carpet

Bed Rooms, over the Servants Hall

2 Bedsteads with blue and white Furniture
2 Fether Beds and bolster in Striped Tick
2 pair Blankets 2 Binders and 2 Cotton Counterpanes
1 Small Square dale Table
2 Old Chairs and one leather Trunk
1 Small Looking Glass
1 White Utinsil and Bason
4 Stump Bedsteads 4 Fether Beds 5 Bolsters in Striped Ticken
4 Pair Blankets 4 Binders and 4 Rugs
2 Large Wooden Chests
2 Trunks
2 Square Dale Tables

Butler's pantry and Bed Room

A Common Grate 5 Bars Fire Irons
Mahogney Bedstead fether bed bolster and pillow in Striped Tick
Wool mattress in Blue & White Check a pair of Blankets a Binder and White Cotton Counterpane

6 mahogney hair bottomed Chairs
1 *Dº* leather seat hair Stuffed
1 *do* swing dressing Glass and Drawr
2 *do* Dinner Trays
1 Japan *Dº*
4 Painted deal presses
1 *do do* dinning Table 2 leaves
2 Long Dressing *do do* 2 Drawrs each
1 Small Square *Dº Dº*
3 Coats of Arms plaster of Paris
1 Coloured print framed and Glazed
1 Family Crest in Stained marble
2 deal Knife Trays
4 Japan Tin Spoon Trays
1 Peat Basket
2 Square Japan Candlesticks with Snuffers and Extinguishers
2 Round *Dº Dº* with 2 Snuffers & 1 *Dº*

1 Large white water Jug
2 Cut wine Decanters
11 plain *D°*   *D°*
2 — water Crafts
10 Cut Wine Coolers
21 plain *do*   *do*
6 Cut Finger Glasses
7 plain *D°*   *D°*
8 Cut Rummers
2 Dozen 3 [*overwritten*] & 3 Large Cut wine Glasses
1   *D°* and 7 Small   *D°*   *D°*
1 Cut Tumbler with the likeness of prince Blucher
1 Wedgewood Beer mug mounted with Silver plate
1 Very large ale Glass
6 Small   *D°.* *D°*
36 Lamp Glasses Verious
5½ lb of Wax Candles Short Sixes
2½ lb of *D°.*   *D°.*   *D°* foures and one Wax Taper
   Two Blunderbusses and 2 Pistoles
1 Brass Lamp

Breakfast Pantry

A Common Grate 5 Bars hanging Foot man Tongs
Shuvle Brush and Tosting Fork
1 Coffee mill
1 Large deal press with Slyding leaves
1   *do*   Table with Drawr
2   *do*   dressers
1 Wooden Bole

Kitchen

A Common Grate 5 Bars 3 Rosting Dogs and
hinging Bar
and Crain Fender Fire Irons and Bellows
A Wind up Jack and Chair
2 Large deal Tables
1   *do*   *do* Dresser with 2 Shelves
1 Small Square *do*
2 Oak Chairs and 2 Old deal *do*
2 Deal presses
1 Hot Closet 2 Shelves lyned with Tin
1 Large marble mortar 2 pistols on pedelstal mortar
   Cracked
1 Chopping Stool
2 deal Salt boxes and a Spoon Box with 6 Wooden
   Spoons
1 Ovan 2 Rosters with Racks &*c*
1 Brass Lamp

2 Boilers Fixed, one Copper Cover
1 Tea Boilers
2 pepper mills
1 Dripping pan baster and ladle
1 Large oval Copper Soupe pot with Cover
3 Small Round *D°.*   *do*   *do* with 2 Covers
1 Oval ~~Dripping~~ *D°.* Frying pan
1   *do*   *D°* Stue   *D°*

Size 1ˢᵗ 4   large Round Copper S~~auce~~ Stue pans no Covers
2.. 4   Large   *do*   *do*   *D°*
~~2~~ 1   *do*   *do*   *D°*   with Covers
3.. 3   *do*   *do*   *do*   no *D°*
4 6   *d°*   *d°*   *do*   *D°*
4 6   *D°*   *D°*   *do*   with Covers
4 7   *do*   *do*   *do* Two with Covers
6 Large Copper Sauce   pans   wanting Covers
3   *do*   *do*   *do*   one with   *D°*
2   *do*   Sottee   *do*
3   *do*   omelet   *do*
4   *do*   pudding *do* Plain
4   *do*   ornamented Jelly molds
7   *do*   ladles
3   *do*   Skewers
2   *do*   Spoons
1   *do*   Tea Kettle
1 Oval   *D°*   Fish   *D°* no Cover
1   ~   *do*   mug
1 Tin Sugar ~~Box~~ [*rubbed out*] Canister with 2 Scopes
1   *do* Spice Box and *do* pepper and Salt Box
3   *do* Drudging Boxes one Wanting Cover
3   *do* mugs
2   *do* Cullendors
2   *do* Bread Graters
1   *do* Dutch Ovan
7 Tin Ornamented Jelly molds
1   *do* Tartlet pan
1 Size 24   Tin Oval   Tartlet pans
2 = 17 *do* *do*   *D°..* *D°*
3 = 7   *do* *do*   *do.* *D°*
x — *x* *do* *do.*   *do.* *D°*
1   4   *do* Round   *D°.* *D°*
2   7   *do* *do*   *do* *do*
1 Box of 5 Tin paste Cutters Fluted
1   *do* of 11 *do*   *do* Sheel Shaped
1   *do* of 12 *do*   *do* Round
4 Tin Ornamental Cutters Verious
1 *D°* Water Can
1 Large meat Saw

1 *do* Beff fork
1 Pair Stake Tongs
3 Iron Fish Kettles 2 Wanting Covers 2 Drainers
17 Iron Sauce pans Verious & 1 Iron Tea Kettle
12 *Dᵒ Dᵒ Dᵒ* Covers Verious
1 *D͟ᵒ͟* pan
2 Iron Gridirons
2 *Dᵒ* Spits
1 Coffie Roster
2 Large Iron Skewers
29 Small *do do* on hooks Verious
3 Large Iron Spoons
3 Small *Dᵒ Dᵒ*
1 Tosting Fork
2 mincing Boards and 3 Knives
1 Hatchet and 1 Chopper
3 Root Scoopes
4 Larding pins
1 Paste pricker
1 Salamander
1 Peat Basket

Cooks Pastery

1 Long deal paste Board
1 *Dᵒ D͟ᵒ͟* Dressers with Shelves
2 Deal Hinging Shelves
6 Small *do do*
1 meal and Salt Bin
1 Flour tub with beam Scales weights and Flour Scoupe
1 Pair Short Steps Roling pin and lemon Squeezers
1 Frame for Jelly Bag
1 High Stool

Cooks pantry

Best blue Dinner Service

	2	Soupe Tureens and one Covers
1 Size	2	Dishes
2 —	1	*do*
″ —	2	Tureens 2 Covers and one Stand
3	4	Dishes
4 —	6	*Dᵒ*
5 —	10	*do*
6 —	2	*do*
		One Vegatable Dish Complete
	5	pie Dishes
	1	Fish Drainer
	2	Sallet Boles
	4	Dozen and 9 dinner plates

14 Soupe plates
18 pudding *do*
20 Cheese *do*
1 Dresser with 2 Covers under and 5 deal Shelves
21 Dishes Verious
2 Vegetable Dishes with Covers
10 pie *do*
1 potting *do* with Cover
2 Raised pie *do* one Cover and 1 lyner
32 Dinner plates
16 Soupe *Dᵒ*

White Ware

9 Dishes Verious
1 Fish Drainer
2 pudding Basons
2 *do* molds
14 Plates
3 Deep Browns Pans
2 Shella *Dᵒ Dᵒ*
14 Brown Jars and 11 Covers

Sculery

1 Large Water Boiler
1 Stone Sink
1 Large Deal Table
1 *do do* Dresser and 2 Shelves
1 *do do* plate Rack
3 Dish Tubs 2 Round and one oval
2 Water pales

Cold Meat Ladder [*recte* larder]

1 Deal Dresser
4 *Dᵒ* Shelves

Servant's Hall

A Common Grate 4 Bars
1 Deal Corner Cupboard
1 Long Deal Table
6 *do* Furmes
1 *do* Dresser
1 Large Chest
1 Row Coat pins
1 pair of Iron Fly Candlesticks
3 Beer Coppers
3 Hornes
3 Pewter Salts

Mount Stewart, County Down

Housekeeper's room

A Common Grate 4 Bars Swing ₍Trivet₎ Fender Fire Irons bellows and harth brush
A Large deal Linnen press with 8 drawrs
A Large Oval mahogney dinning Table 2 leaves
A Small *do*   *do*   *do* 2 *do*
A Camp   *do*   *do* Folding top & Drawr
A   *D?* side Board ~~do~~ one Drawr
A Round   *do* Tea Table on pillar and Claw
10   *D²* Chairs hair Seats
 2 Bamboo Painted   *D?* Rush *D°*
 1 Large Indie Japan Tea Tray
 1   *do*   *do do*
 1 Tin   *do*   *do do*
 1 Looking Glass Cracked
 4 Prints Framed and Varnished
 3 Female painting on Glass Framed
 2 Oil Painting in guilt Frames
 2 Chimney Ornaments
  Blue and White Window Curtains
 3 Wedge Wood Tea pots
19 Breakfast Cups and Saucers Verious
12   *D?*   *D°*   *D°*
 1 Slap Bason and one White Sugar Bason
10 Blue & White Jars
 6 Cut Glass Salts and 1 muster pot
10 plain Tumblers
 3 Wine Glasses
 6 Black handled Knives and forks
 9 *D°*   *do*   *do*   *do*
 6 *D°*   *D°*   *do*
 4 Green *do*   *do*
 3 *D²:* Carving Knives and 2 Forks

Store Room

A Common Grate 4 Bars Fender Fire Irons and harth Brush
 2 Bamboo painted Chairs Rush seats
 1 Sugar & Tea Kiddy
 1 Dresser with Cupboard under
 2 Small *do, do,*   *do.*   *do*
 2 Cupboards Wire Fronts
 5 Shelves
 1 Large Glass Jar
 4 Small   *D°*
11 Green Glass pickling Bottles
 4 Indie *D?*   *D°*
  Preservings pots Verious
 1 pair Copper Weights and Scales

Still Room

A Common Grate 4 Bars & Bellows
 3 Small Deal Tables one with drawr
 4 Bamboo Painted Chairs rush seats
 8 Deal Shelves
 4 Copper preservings pans 2 Bought new
 1 *do*   Sugar   *D°*
 5   Freezers   one Bought New
 4   Ice *do*   *do.. do*
 4   *do* Shattles
 1   *do* Tub
 2   *do* Freezing pales   Bought New
 1 Brass pickling Kettle   *do   do*
 1 Pewter Inkstand
 1 Jocklet Pot and mace
 2 Coffie Pots
 2 Pair of Wafer Irons
13 Bisket Shapes
10 Japan hand Candlesticks Verious 5 pʳ.. Snuffers & 7 Extinguisher
 1 pair Brass   *D°* Snuffers and Tray
 1 Sugar nipers   Bought new
 1 *D²:* Chopper
 2 Hair Sives   Bought new
 2 Lawn *D°*   *D°*
 1 Japan Water Can

Bake House

A Brick Ovan 2 Flour Bins
 1 Kneeding Trough and [*overwritten*] — Flour and Bread pricker &ᶜ
 2 Wooden Stooles
 1 Dresser with Drawr
 2 Wooden pales New
 7 Role Shapes New
 5 Bakeing Sheets *D°*
 1 Peel and how Rake
  Beam Weights and Scales

Thomas Bowman's Room

A Grate
A Ten Bedstead Fether Bed bolster and pillow
Pair Blankets a Binder and Rug
 1 Bamboo Painted Chair Rush Seat
 1 Painted Chest of Drawrs
 1 *D°*   Dressing Table
 1 *D?*   *D°*   Glass

Temple
Dinning Room

A marble Chimney piece An Old Fashioned Steel Grate
4 mahogney Dinning Tables 2 folding leaves each
12 *D.º* Chairs hair Seats
1 Oil painting of the Temple
1 Vaws plaster of paris

Drawing ~~room~~ [rubbed out] Room

A marble Chimney piece as above
8 Bamboo painted Chairs Cane seats
3 Figures and 2 Vaws plaster pair

Kitchen

1 Kitchen Range
4 Cupboards under windows
 Dresser in the Center with Cupboards under
1 Deal Dresser and Shelves
2 painted Chairs hair Seats

Dairy

2 Fether Beds 2 Bolsters & 5 Blankets

Laundery

A Common Grate a Fixed Stove and 2 Earing Closets
6 Flat Smoothing Irons

2 Stands for *D.º*
1 Mangle & 3 Rolers
1 Ironing Dresser
4 Drawrs and 2 Cupboards under
3 Deal Table
2 Old Earing Horses
8 Wash Tub & Sundry *D.º*
1 Water pale and 2 Old *Dº*
1 Cooler
2 Deal presses
5 Clothes Baskets

Garden Room's

3 Grates Fender and Fire Irons bellows and harth brush
 A Tent Bedstead Cotton Furniture
2 Fether Beds 2 Bolsters and 1 pillow
2 pair Blankets 2 Binders and white Cotton
 Counterpane and Rug
1 painted Chest of 6 Drawrs
2 Deal presses One painted
2 Tables with 2 Folding leaves each
1 Round mahogney *Dº* on pillar and Claw
3 Deal Table Verious
1 mahogney Chair hair seat
1 *D.º* Dressing Glass
1 Oak Two armed Chair
6 *Dº*   Small   *D.º*

Septr 1821

An Inventory of China & Cut Glass
at Mount Stewart belonging to
The Most Noble The Marquis of Londonderry

Red & gold	Size's					
Indea Round	1	5	Dinner	Dishes		
	2	5	*Ditt.º*	*Dtº*	1 cracked	
	3	5	*Dtº*	*Dtº*		
	4	5	*Dtº*	*Dtº*		
	5	3	*Dtº*	*Dtº*		
Dittº Octagon	1	5	*Dtº*	*Dtº*	1 Riveted	
	2	4	*Dtº*	*Dtº*		
	3	4	*Dtº*	*Dtº*	2 Riveted	
	4	2	*Dtº*	*Dtº*		
	5	3	*Dtº*	*Dtº*		
Dittº Round Desert	1	4	Desert	Dishes		
	2	4	*Dtº*	*Dtº*		
	3	2	*Dtº*	*Dtº*		

Mount Stewart, County Down

		2	Shell *Dt?* *Dt?*	
		7	Round Dinner Plates	17 *Ditt?* *Dtt?* diformt [1 Riveted]
		37	Octagon *Dt?* *Dt?*	20 Riveted
		13	Round Desert *Dt?*	
Ditt? Coloured	1	2	Dinner Dishes	1 Cracked
& Gold[G]Edge	2	2	*Dt?* Dishes	
	3	2	*Dt?* *Dt?*	1 *Ditt?*
	4	1	*Dt?* *Dt?*	*Dt?*
		11	*Dt?* Plates Various	1 *Dt?*
		16	Soup *Dt?*	3 *Dt?*
Coloured & Gold	1	15	Dinner Dishes Various	1 *Dtt?*
		33	*Ditt?* Plates *Dt?*	2 *Dt?*
		18	*Dtt?* *Dt?*	
Coloured & Gold	1	4	*Ditt?* Dishes	1 Riveted
Edge	2	5	*Dt?* *Dt?*	2 *Ditt?*
	3	5	*Dt?* *Dt?*	4 *Dit?*
		23	*Dt?* Plates Various 13 *Dit?*	
Dresden China		10	Round Dinner Dishes of 3 Sizes 1 . 4 . 5	
		3	Oval Desert *Dt?* Handles Broken	
		2	Shell *Dt?* *Dt?* 1 Handle *Dt?*	
		15	Dinner Plates 7 Chipt	
Chelsea		2	Ice Pails to match not Dresden	
Bird Patern		5	Desert Dishes Various 2 . 2 . 1	
		37	Plates *Dt?* 1 . 2 . 4 . 30	
Coloured & White		11	Desert Dishes *Dt?* 1 Cracked	
		2	Old Tureens both Crack, 1 Cover	
		1	Large Punch Bowl Piece out	
		2	Flower or fruit Baskets 1 hand[le] off	
		2	Stands for *Dt?* *Dt?* 1 *Dt?* *Dt?*	
		1	White & Gold Fruit or flower Basket With Stand to match 1 Piece out of Basket	
		1	Small Marble vases	
		1	Imitation *Dt?* *Dt?*	
		8	Old Chimney Ornaments 6 Broken	
		1	Cock [?] *Dtt?*	
		5	Small Cabinet Tea Cups & 12 Saucers 3 Chip[d] [1 Cup Crack]	
		8	Cabinet Coffee Cups & 5 Saucers 1 Cracked	
		1	*Dt?* *Dt?* *Dt?* & Saucer Dresden	
		1	Old fashioned Bason With cover & Stand	
		1	Blue & White, Painted & Gold Ink Stand Broken	
		2	Green Leave Dishes	
Old Blue & White		23	Round Dishes various 12 Cracked & 2 Chipd	
China		17	Oval *Dt?* *Dt?* 1 *Dt?* *Dt?*	
		2	Dinner Plates & 1 Soup *Dt?*	
		18	Water *Dt?*	
		1	Tureen Cracked with Cover	
White Green		8	Oval Dishes	
& Gold Desert		4	Shell *Ditt?*	
Service New		1	Deep *Dt?* with Handles for center of Table	
		37	Small Plates 1 Very Small	

	21	Breakfast *Dt?*
	19	*Dt?* Cups & Saucers
	23	Tea *Dt?* & 29 *Dt?*
	29	Coffe Cup's & Saucers
	3	Sugar Bason's with Covers
	3	Muffin Plates with *Dt?*
	2	Bread & Butter Plates
	3	Egg Cups
White & Gold	2	Cups & 11 Saucers
Breakfast &	10	Tea Cups & 2 *Dt?*
Tea Service	7	Coffe *Dt?* 2 Cracked no Saucers
	1	Slop Bason
	2	Honey Potts with Stands & Covers
	2	Egg Cups
	29	Breakfast Plates 1 Cracked, some chipid
	1	Bread & Butter Plate
Supper Dishes &^C	3	Dishes & 4 Covers
	1	Center with Cover & Liner Egg Cups & frame
Cut & Engraved Glass	1	Large Triffle Bowl with Foot & Ladle
	1	Oval Glass for Platow
	8	Sweet Meat Shealls
	18	Engraved *Dt? Dt° Dt?*
	1	Large Round Butter Glass — 1 Stand & 2 Covers
	2	Oval *Dt? Dt?* 3 Stands & 2 Covers
	1	*Dt? Dt? Dt?* 2 Stands no Cover
	2	Oval Sugar Glasse's
	1	Round *Dt?* Bason
	3	Cream Pails 1 Wanting Handle
	2	Cream & 1 Milk Pott
	11	Japan Tea Trays & Waiters
	1	Brown Tea Urn

Septr 1821

*An Inventory of Table & Home Linen
at Mount Stewart belonging to
The Most Noble The Marquis of Londonderry*

	Size's				
Damask	1	7	Table	Cloths	
	2	1	*Ditt°*	*Dt?*	
	3	12	*Dt?*	*Dt?*	
	4	2	*Dt?*	*Dt?*	
	5	5	*Dt?*	*Dt?*	
	6	1	*Dt?*	*Dt?*	very fine
	7	4	*Dt?*	*Dt?*	
	8	4	*Dt?*	*Dt?*	
	9	8	*Dt?*	*Dt?*	
	10	5	*Dt?*	*Dt?*	
	11	3	*Dt?*	*Dt?*	

Mount Stewart, County Down

	12	2	Dt?. Dt?.	
Ditt? Lay Overs	1	4	Double Lay Overs	
	2	2	Single Dt?. Dt?.	very Long
	3	2	Dt?. Dt?. Dt?.	
Ditt? Napkins	1	12	Dinner Napkins	
	2	7	Ditt? Ditt?	
	3	2	Dt?. Dt?.	
	4	25	Dt?. Dt?.	
	5	4	Dt?. Dt?.	
	6	17	Dt?. Dt?.	
	7	17	Dt?. Dt?.	
	8	20	Dt?. Dt?.	
	9	47	Dt?. Dt?.	
Ditt? Breakfast	1	20	Breakfast Napkins	
	2	19	Dt?. Dt?.	very old
Diaper	1	9	Table Cloths	
	2	12	Ditt? Dt?	
	3	7	Dt?. Dt?.	
	4	14	Dt?. Dt?.	
	5	16	Dt?. Dt?.	
Ditt? Common for Hall	1	3	Large Dt?. Dt?.	
	2	6	Dt? Dt?. Dt?.	
	3	6	Dt?. Dt?.	
Ditt? Napkins	1	19	Breakfast Napkins	
	2	8	Waiting Dt?.	
Fine Sheets	1	3	Pair's of Large Sheets	
	2	6	Ditt?. of Dt?.	
	3	24	Dt?. of Dt?.	6 p?s quite new
	4	24	Dt?. of Dt?.	
Coarse	1	3	Dt?. of Dt?.	quite new
	2	12	Dt?. of Dt?.	
	3	13	Dt?. of Dt?.	
	4	4	Dt?. of Dt?.	
Froiled	1	8	Dt?. of Dt?.	all very old
		25	Fine Pillow Case's Frilld	
		36	Dt?. Dt?. Dt?. Plain	
		8	Coarse Dt?. Dt?.	
		9	Dimity Table Covers Frilld	
		1	Dt?. Dt?. Dt?. Plain	
		7	Doz?. & 2 Fine Chamber Towls	
		5	Doz?. & 5 Coarse Ditt? Dt?.	
		6	Round Towls quite New	
		12	Dt?. Dt?. various very old	
		24	House Maids Dusters quite New	
		6	Kitchen Rubbers Dt?. Dt?.	
		24	Knife Cloths Dt?. Dt?.	
		18	Coloured Doily's	
		18	Cloths & Rubbers all very old	

An Inventory of plate belonging % The Most
Noble the Marquis of Londonderry taken at
Mount Stewart Sept.ʳ,   *1821*

Size	Nº					Inches Inches
1	2	Oval Tureen				12½ by 9½
1	1	Large round dish		Diameter		19½
2	1	*D.º,, do,,*		*do*		17½
3	2	*do,, do,,*				13½
4	4	*do,, do,,*		*do,,*		11½
		2 — *Wanted 2 23 In for top & bottom*				
1	1	Large Oval *do*	*1 to match for*	*do,,*		21½ by 16
		Covers wanted	*top & bottom*			
2	1	*do,, do,,*	*1 to match for*	*do*		19½ by 14½
			removes			
3	2	*do,, do,,*	*flanks*	*do*		16¼ by 12½
		Covers wanted				
4	4	*do, do,,*		*do*		14¼ by 11
		2 *oval wanted for flanks sec.ᵈ Course*				
5	4	*do do,* *Covers wanted*		*do*		12½ by 9¼
1	4	Pincushions *do*	*sec.ᵈ Course*	Square		9¾
1	4	Corner or Shell *do,*	*Do + d ·*			12½ 9
1	4	Large Butter ewers				
2	4	Small *do. do.*				
1	4	Dozen plates	*more plates wanted*	Diameter		9¾
1	6	Oval Salts		*do,*		5 by 3¾
2	4	Round *do*				
1	6	Bottle stands		Diameter		5¼
2	6	*do, do,*		*do*		4¾
1	1	Large Round Salvers		*do*		22
2	2	*do, do,*		*do*		11
3	4	*do, do,*		*do,*		6½
4	1	*do, do,*		*do,*		7¾
5	2	*do, do,*		*do*		5½
1	1	Bread Basket				14¼ by 11
2	1	*do do.*				12 by 10¾
,,	1	Eppyrn in 24 pieces Complete				
	1	Crewet Stand One Glass Crewet wanting & Top				
	1	Muster pot and spoon with Tin lyning				
	1	Silver Ring wrought for Round Dish				8
1	4	Fluted dinner Candlesticks mahogney Bottoms				
2	2	*do, do*				
3	4	Wrought *do, do,*				
4	6	Card Table *do* 3 nausels Wanting				
1	4	Flat hand *do* 3 Extinguishers				
2	4	*do do* *do* 2 *D.º* one wanting a handle				
	2	Snuffers Trays both wanting handles				
	1	Coffie pot				
	2	Pint muggs				
	2	Goblets				

1	Tumbler
1	Wine Funnell
3	Soup ladles
2	Fish Slices
6	Gravy Spoons handle of one Broken
47	Table *do*, *12 Left out*
22	Desert *do*,
8	Sauce ladles
2	Sugar *D?*
2	Cream *do*,
2	Marrow Spoons & one Silver scewer
1	Asperagus Tongues
1	Butter Knife
29	Tea Spoons *7 Left out*
12	Salt *do*, of three different kinds Viz 6,, 4,, & 2 *4 Left out*
47	Dinner forkes
23	Desert *do*
4	pair Sugar Tongues *1 Left out*
14	Wine lables of sundry paterns *one chain wanted*
45	Silver handled Knives and 23 *do* different
22	*do. do.* Forkes patern of the 23 above
22	Desert *do, do,* Knives Two Extraw handles
1	Silver Sauce pan (Broken)

Plated Artic[l]es

2	pair Dinner Candlestick with one pair of Branches *2 p^r Left out*
14	Hand Candlesticks 11 Extinguishers 1 nausel wanting, 3 p^r. Snuffers
1	Crewet stand Complete (Viz 7 Crewet *Left out*
1	pair Candlesticks for pantry *Left out*
4	Heaters for pincushion Dishes
6	Oval dish Covers
2	Round *do do* and one Round Waiter *Waiter Left out*
4	pincushion dish Covers
2	White handled Carving Knives and Forks 3 Extraw Forks
4	pair of large Steel Snuffers and 2 pair of Doubters
1	Small Taper Candlestick
4	Dozen & 2 Ageket handled knives of Different Sizeses
1	Butter Knife
1	Asperaugus Tongs
1	Plato in 3 pieces painted Velvet Guilt Wood $_\wedge$frame plate glass one Glass Broke
1	*D?* $_\wedge$Sqr with plated framed and Silvered plate Glass

Glossary

Items are listed in alphabetical order with their modern spelling (where applicable) in roman, and unusual names or spelling variations are shown in italic. Definitions are given where appropriate and according to context, with short titles of sources given here in parentheses and full titles given in the bibliography (pp. 390–1).

ABBREVIATIONS (as used in some of the inventories):

₡ (C struck through with two lines), used to denote a hundredweight (112 lb).

℔ (lb for *libra* or pound] struck through as here, is said to have evolved into the # or hash symbol. Used at Kilrush House to denote a pound (see the bed at 'Nº 6 In the Yellow Room', p. 150).

ꝑ (a crossed p), used to denote the Latin word *per* [by].

pwt (*dpt*; *dwt*; *pwtt*) pennyweight, a twentieth of a troy ounce.

∼ (tilde), diacritic mark used in the inventory of the bishop of Elphin's books (pp. 95–103) and in that of Dublin Castle (p. 72) to denote a missing <ti> as in *observaõnes* [observationes], *conscienæ̃* [conscientiæ] or *justiã* [justitia]; also at Elphin to denote a missing <t>.

vizᵗ, **videlicet**, Latin word for 'namely', 'that is to say', 'to wit'; from *vide*, stem of *videre* to see and *licet* it is permissible.

yᵉ the; **y**ᵐ them; **y**ᵗ that: vestigial use of the Old English letter thorn <þ>, here represented by the letter y; the letter has since been replaced in English by the digraph <th>.

agate *agatt*; *ageket*; *aget*; *aggot* 'A precious stone of several Sortes' (Bailey).

airing horse *earing horse See also* clothes-horse.

airwood *See* harewood.

allumette A match or spill for lighting something (borrowing of the French *allumette*, from the verb *allumer*, to set alight).

alphabet An alphabetized filing system of drawers or pigeonholes often in a cupboard or table.

andiron *and iron*; *hand iron*; *handiron* The Kilkenny Castle 1705 inventory itemizes both andirons and [fire] dogs in the drawing-room (p. 33) and in Lady Harriet's room (p. 39), perhaps implying a distinction between two terms usually deemed synonymous. The French have two terms also: *chenet* [fire dog] and *hâtier* [andiron]. The latter replaces the obsolete French term *landier*. *Chenet*s (literally small dogs) are the two dogs on which logs are put in a fireplace; *landiers* were large fire dogs with notches for spits and with a receptacle on top for heating up liquids. Our word andiron stems from the Old French *andier* that agglutinated with the definite article to form *landier*. According to the *Le Grand Robert* dictionary, the word *andier* derives from the Gallic word *andéros*, meaning a bull, after the animal heads that adorned early andirons.

antechamber *anti chamber*; *anty chamber* A waiting-room to a principal room or bedroom.

antherine *anterne*; *anterine* A light stuff made from wool and silk mixed, or of mohair and cotton.

apirn *See* epergne.

argentee From the French *argenter* to coat with silver-leaf, the term is used to describe the finish of candlesticks. Perhaps the nozzle and base were silver-plated.

asparagus-tongs *asparagus tongues*; *asperaugus tongs*

aurora *arora* Of an orange hue like the dawn sky.

Axminster carpet Knotted pile carpet made at the Axminster factory in Devon established in 1755 by Thomas Whitty. By the 1790s the term Axminster meant English knotted-pile carpets in general.

baby house A doll's house.

Bacchanals *Bachonells*; *Backonells* 'A festival in honour of Bacchus' (OED).

backband Strap or chain fastened to a draught-horse's straddle (q.v.) that is used to keep up the shafts of a cart.

back-chair *back chaire*; *backt chaire*; *bak chaire* A chair with a back.

backgammon table *back gammon —*; *backgamon —* A games table or board for the game of backgammon.

back-stool *back stole*; *back stoole*; *backt stoole* A stool or chair with a back, but without arms.

baize *baces*; *baise*; *base*; *bayes* A heavy woollen cloth, raised and napped on both sides. Commonly used as a table or carpet covering. For linings and occasionally for cushions and seat upholstery.

baker A baking dish.

baking *bakeing*; *beaking*

351

bale A bundle or package; also a measure of quantity. *See also* swinging bale.

bandle A coarse unbleached linen cloth.

barm can A vessel for the fermenting agent (barm) in brewing.

barrack A plain building or range of buildings in which a number of people are housed.

barrack bedstead *barrick bedstead* A kind of portable, folding bed.

barrel *barrell* A measure of capacity for liquids and dry goods.

base *bace* Support for a bedstead.

basin *bason*; *basong*; *beason*

basset-table *bassett* — A card-table for the gambling game of basset (*bassetta*).

bed carpet Either a rug or small carpet placed on one side of the bed, or a carpet, made of three relatively narrow strips, which is placed on three sides of the bed. *See also* bed-round.

bedding 'Includes beds and mattresses of all kinds, whatever they may be stuffed with, also the bolster, pillows, sheets, blankets, and counterpane' (Webster).

bed-furniture *beds ffurniture*; *furniture* 'Comprises the curtains which generally inclose [*sic*] the bed or which are suspended from the canopy or top'. 'The *drapery of beds* or *bed furniture* includes curtains, valances and headcloth' (Webster).

bed-hangings *hanings* Bed-drapery. The term is sometimes used to describe bedding.

bed-round *bedround carpet*; *carpet bedround*; *carpet round the bed* 'The name of a breadth of carpet which went round three sides of the bed, leaving the remainder of the floor bare ' (Caddy). There are surviving examples in the state bedrooms at Blickling Hall, Norfolk, an Axminster from the second half of the 18th century, and at Osterley House, Middlesex, a bed-round by Thomas Moore to a design of February 1779 by Robert Adam.

bedside carpet *bed side carpet*; *bedside carpett*; *bid side carpit*; *sid bed carpet*; *side bed carpet*

bedside cupboard A cupboard or set of drawers by bed, often with room for a chamber pot or utensil (q.v.).

bedstead *beadstead*; *bed stead*; *bed-stead*; *bed.stead*; *bed:stead*; *bed=stead*; *beddstead*; *bedsted*; *bedsteed* The frame of a bed upon which a mattress is placed.

bedtick *bed tick* 'A large flat quadrangular bag or case, into which feathers, hair, straw, chaff, or other substances are stuffed to form a bed' (OED). *See also* tick.

beef-tree *beef tree* A cambrel, which is defined by Bailey as 'a crooked stick with Notches on it, on which Butchers hang their Meat'.

bell-metal *bellmettle* An alloy of around four parts copper to one of tin.

bench A long seat, usually with a back.

bergère *berger* A large easy chair, or a tub-chair.

Berlin[e] *Berliene* A four-wheeled covered carriage, sometimes with a separate hooded back seat for a footman.

bidet *biddy*; *biddey*; *bidee*; *bidée*

bijou box *bouzu box* A jewellery casket, probably.

billiard-mace A shaft with flat-faced head used to push the cue ball into contact with the other balls on the billiard-table.

bin *binn*

bird's eye *bird eye* Indicates any fabric woven in a design consisting of a small diamond with a centre dot.

blancmange *blamonge* An opaque white jelly made with milk that is set in a mould and served as an intermess (q.v., and *see also* in François Massialot's *The Court and Country Cook: Giving new and plain direction*, the duc d'Orléans's bill of fare for dinner, Easter day, 26 March 1690), or as a sweetmeat.

blotting-book *blotting book* Either a book of leaves of blotting-paper to blot letters written in ink, or a notebook to record transactions.

blue-and-white ware Earthenware with blue-and-white glaze; may also refer to porcelain adorned with a blue-and-white pattern.

blunderbuss 'A short Brass Gun of a large Bore' (Bailey).

boiler *boyler*; *boylor* May indicate either a movable vessel or a tank affixed to the kitchen grate.

bomb-cart A cart for carrying ordnance.

bookplate A label often gummed inside the front cover of a book to show to whom the book belongs, often adorned with a crest or other decorative device.

boot-jack *boot jack*; *jack* A device for pulling off a boot.

botting tool Probably a bott stick to force the 'bott', or refractory clay plug, into a tap hole to stop the flow of molten iron in a foundry.

bottle cooper A wine-cooper; a basket for six or twelve bottles used in a wine-cellar.

bottle drain *bottle drane*; *bottle drean*

bottle slider *botle slider* Bottle coaster.

boudoir *boudouar*

Boyle linen Although the town of Boyle carried on some weaving, this linen is more likely to have been manufactured by a maker or sold by a draper of that name.

bracket *brackett*; *braget* 'A small (usually ornamental) shelf, or set of two or three shelves, for the wall of a room' (OED).

branch The word 'branch' was often used to denote a chandelier or candelabrum, but also used to describe the arm supporting a candle, extending from a mirror frame, the mirror serving to magnify illumination.

brazier *brizier* A pan on a footed base for braising or broiling.

breeches *britches*; *britchers* Possibly breeching (horse strap enabling the animal to pull backwards).

brewer's sling A device for lifting heavy casks at a brewhouse.

brocatelle *bockadell*; *brocadell*; *brockadell*; *brockadella* A woven patterned fabric with contrasting warps and wefts, often in different fibres, especially linen and silk. Often with a large foliate pattern, the surface with relief or *repoussé* effect, it is used for both upholstery and hangings. A coarse brocade.

bronze *braunes*

Brussels carpets Introduced from Tournai in Belgium, they were made initially in England to the same technique at Wilton and later at Kidderminster.

buckram A coarse fabric of hemp or linen stiffened with gum and calendered before being dyed in a variety of colours. Used for linings to curtains, bed valances and wall-hangings.

buff A dull light yellow.

bureau *beaureau*; *beawrow*; *beurow*; *bewrow*; *buero*; *burew* A writing desk.

bushel Vessel for dry goods; as a measure of capacity typically containing four pecks or eight gallons.

butt A large cask; as a measure of capacity the equivalent of half a tun.

butter ewer A vessel for pouring melted butter at table; possibly an Irish term.

cabinet cups Possibly large cups for display.

caddow Coarse woollen rug or coverlet.

caddy *cadea*; *kiddy See* tea-caddy.

caffa A rich silk cloth like damask; but by the 18th century, the name given to a painted cotton cloth imported from India.

caffoy *caffoiy*; *caphoy*; *cofoy*; *coifoy*; *cuffoy* A patterned woollen fabric with a pile. Used in seat upholstery, bed- and wall-hangings and wallpaper.

calamanco *calamencoe* A wool or wool and silk cloth with a glossy surface and a twilled weave on the right side only. Plain and also patterned in stripes or flowers. Used for wall- and bed-hangings, window-curtains and chair-covers.

calico *calicoe*; *callico*; *callicoe* A cotton plain weave cloth which was printed, coloured and dyed. First made in India and later in the West. Commonly used in clothing and for window-curtains, bed-hangings, linings and chair-covers. The name derives from Calicut (now Kozhikode), a town on the coast of Malabar discovered by the Portuguese in 1498, whence this cloth was first imported.

calico chintz Printed calico imported by the East India Company until manufacturing of it began in England in the late 17th century.

cameo (sulphur) A cast made in sulphur from a carved precious stone.

camlet *camblet*; *camblett*; *camblette*; *chamlet* A plain weave worsted cloth of silk or wool, or of mixtures of these, sometimes with goat's hair. It may be watered to give a glossy surface or pressed under rollers to give a waved pattern. Used for bed-hangings, window-curtains and chair-covers.

camp-bedstead Portable, folding bed often for camp or barrack use; a stretcher-bedstead.

camp chair, armchair or stool Lightweight folding portable furniture. Usually with x-frame stretchers and a wooden or leather seat.

can *canne* Cylindrical drinking vessel.

cane *cain*, *kane* A hollow, jointed woody stem of particular reeds and grasses such as bamboo used for seating, and sometimes painted.

cannel coal *kennel coal* Bituminous hard coal that burns with a bright flame.

Canterbury A tray, made to stand by a table at dinner or supper. Later an open-topped stand with partitions to hold sheet music, music books and the like.

cantoon Narrow curtain hung at the corners of a bed that closed the gaps between the main curtains.

canvas Hempen cloth.

caparison An ornamented covering for a horse's saddle or harness.

caple Horse, corresponding to the Irish *capall*, a horse or mare.

capriole A horse-drawn two- or four-wheeled carriage. Term seems to be an Irish usage.

car *carr* Farm cart, carriage, or wagon.

carbine 'A sort of short Gun, between a Musket and a Pistol, used by Horsemen' (Bailey).

carding-table A table for carding wool or cotton?

carpet 'A sort of covering, worked either with the needle, or on a loom, to be spread on a table, trunk, an estrade, or even a passage, or floor' (Chambers).

cart-sole *cart soal* The beam of a cart.

case Protective case curtains to hang around a four-poster bed or loose covers for furniture and upholstered furniture.

cask A vessel for liquids or dry goods; a measure of capacity varying according to commodity.

caudle A confection of wine or ale, sugar and spices served in a basin or a cup.

cavesson *caveason* A kind of horse's nose-band that works on the nasal bone and is used especially in training.

cedar An aromatic, reddish-brown softwood used for furniture and panelling. Used for chests for storing textiles as a natural insect repellent.

cellaret *cellar* 'A case of cabinet-work made to hold wine bottles' (OED). *See also* gardevine.

centre (**dish**) *centre* Decorative dish for the centre of the dining-table.

chafing-dish *chaffing —*; *chaifeing —*; *cheafing —* A portable grate that is filled with burning charcoal for heating food in a dining-room.

chamber Chamber pot.

chamber airer A bedroom frame for airing clothes.

chamber horse Exercise chair.

chamber utensil Chamber pot.

chamber vase Urine pot (?)

chandelier *chandeleer*; *chandilier*; *shambileire*; *shandelier* A branched candlestick often hung from a ceiling or roof, but it was also a term

Glossary

353

for a candelabrum. From the French for a candlestick.

chased *cheas'd* Silver the surface of which has been adorned with embossing.

check[ed], checker[ed] or **chequer[ed]** *checard; cheque; chequer'd* A fabric made of any fibre of plain weave, with coloured warp and weft stripes intersecting at right angles to form squares. Checks may also be printed.

Chelsea *Chelsea china* Soft-paste porcelain manufactured at the Chelsea porcelain factory between 1748 and 1770.

chest of drawers *chist of drawers* See also nest of drawers.

cheval fire screen A low screen comprising a panel that can be raised or lowered within a frame standing on transverse feet.

cheval-glass A free-standing framed mirror that may be tilted about pins halfway up its sides.

chevaux-de-frise Decorative jagged pattern with spiking.

chimney Chimney-piece.

chimney-glass A fireplace overmantel mirror. Many are rectangular, tripartite, with central arched plates and have a variety of decorated frames, such as carved and gilt or *verre églomisé* borders. Some examples incorporate a painting *en suite* with the mirror.

china *Chania; Cheny; Chinah; Chinea; Chinee; Chynah* This may refer either to Asian export ceramic ware, much of it from China and imported through the East Indian companies or to European porcelain. Loosely speaking, the term is used for all ceramic ware: porcelain as well as earthenwares. At Mount Stewart a wash-hand basin is described in 1821 as 'Chinee china', in other words, made of porcelain imported from China or through the East India companies.

china-ware 'Ware made of china or porcelain' (OED).

chintz *chince; chints* A cotton fabric which is painted or block printed in colours with generally large-scale pattern, often floral. First imported into England by the East India Company, and later manufactured in England. An extremely fashionable material used for bed-hangings and window-curtains.

chocolate pot/cup *chocholate pot; chockolet pot; chocolat pott; jacolet cupp; jocklet pot*

churn-dash A long-handled plunger that is worked up and down when making butter in a churn (Kinmonth, pp. 440–1).

cistern *cester'n; cestern; cesterne; cestorn; cestron; cistorn; cistern* A large vessel for water or other liquids. Also, a container filled with ice to cool wine bottles.

clamb A kind of clamp.

claw-table A one-legged table with claw feet.

close-stool *cloas stool; cloce stool; cloose stoole; close-stoole; closestoole; closetoole* A chair with a hinged padded or wooden seat over an elliptical hole, concealing a shelf with a chamber pot.

closet *cossett* 'A small Apartment in a Room' (Bailey).

cloth Plain-wove woollen fabric.

clothes-horse *cloath horse; cloase horse; close horse*

cloths (*for cleaning*) *cloas; cloase; cloaths; close; clothes*

clouded stuff *Chinée, clouded silk, clouded satin.* 'Chiné, a fancy silk material in which the patterns are printed on the warp threads, before weaving' (Tweney & Hughes).

cock A tapped spout with a valve for controlling the flow of liquids.

coffee biggin *coffee bigon* A kind of coffee-pot containing a strainer.

coffee-dish Coffee-cup.

Colebrookdale ware *Coalbrook Dale* Hard-paste porcelain from this Shropshire manufactory.

coloured *colered; colord; coulourd; cullard*

comfort and ease See ease-and-comfort.

commode *comode* A French furniture form. A decorative, heavy-bodied chest, with three or more tiers of drawers, set on four short legs. Used both in bedrooms and drawing-rooms. Also a name given to a close-stool.

composition [stone] Compo, an artificial stone with varied ingredients.

concordatum An Irish historical term for an 'order in Council relative to the disposal of money set apart for particular purposes of state; a special payment under such an order' (OED).

condition A selection of comments made by the inventory compilers on the state of items they list is given in the main index under the heading 'condition'. There can be found instances of wear and tear, as well as repair, and some items are said to have been nearly new. But nature has also intervened. The corn crop at Elphin, described as 'worst I have ever seen', may reflect the calamitous weather and poor harvests in Ireland in 1740.

cooler See keeler.

coop A small basket or cage for carrying or keeping fowls. Later a pen for chickens; a henhouse.

copper A ductile and malleable metal used in the making of kitchen utensils; a furnace or boiler to provide hot water for brewing, for laundry or general use; also a mug or vessel for liquor. The domestic copper for hot water was often made of cast iron; the brewing copper had a convex bottom.

coral *coralle* Corn chaff, here wasted in brewing; from the Old French *curail*, chaff.

corkscrew (Copley style) A folding corkscrew in which the steel shaft is hinged and folds back inside a bow, often made of silver. Named after John Singleton Copley, who painted a *trompe l'œil* of a corkscrew hanging on a nail in the late 1760s. The

354

painting is now at the Museum of Fine Arts, Boston.

cornice *cornish* A moulded architectural trim.

corporation box An engraved box presented on behalf of civic corporations to honour the benevolence, achievement or patronage of an individual.

couch *coutch*

counter 'Counting-Board in a Shop' (Bailey).

counterpane *counterpain*; *counter paine*; *counterpaine*; *counter pan*; *counterpan*; *counter pane*; *counterpann*; *counterpayne*; *counterpin*; *cownterpen* An elaborately decorated bed-cover, usually embroidered or decorated with applied trimmings. Often shaped to fit around the posts at the foot end and over the bolsters at the head. The word is a corruption of counterpoint, a word that in turn derives from the Old French *contrepointe* and ultimately from the Latin *culcita puncta* [quilt stitched through], referring to the technique of sewing through the wadding to keep it in place.

couteau 'A large knife used as a weapon' (OED); a term frequently used in the 18th century.

cover Loose cover for chairs, stools, settees and tables; a term widely used also for the lid of a vessel.

coverlet *coverlid* A quilt or counterpane as uppermost covering on a bed.

crackle/craquelé *crackley*; *crackly* China characterized by a crazed glaze surface.

crane An upright axle with a horizontal swivelling arm for hanging a pot or kettle over the fire.

crock Earthenware vessel; often to hold buttermilk in the dairy (Kinmonth, p. 439).

croft *craft* Carafe, often listed as a 'water croft'.

Cromaboo linen Possibly armorial linen of the FitzGerald family, who from 1766 became the dukes of Leinster. Their war-cry, and later

their motto, was 'Crom-a-boo', which has been translated as 'Crom for ever' (referring to Croom Castle, Co. Limerick), or, taking 'boo' to derive from the Gaelic *buaidh*, as 'Crom to victory'.

cross chair *x chair* Possibly a chair with a cross splat to the back or with cross-stretchers to the legs.

cross seat Probably a cross-framed stool or chair.

cross stand *x stand* A folding stand for trays; also perhaps a dish cross, with two centrally pivoted arms and adjustable feet, often fitted with a burner and wick at the centre to keep dishes warm.

cross stool *x stool* Probably a cross-framed stool or chair.

crub Short crook for a packhorse.

cruets *crewet*; *crewett*; *cruit*; *cruite*

crystal *cristiall*

cue *kew*; *queue* Billiard-cue.

cullender *collender*; *cullendor* Colander (or cullender).

cup (bed finial) *cupp*

curricle 'A light two-wheeled carriage usually drawn by two horses abreast' (OED).

curry-comb A comb for rubbing down or dressing a horse.

cushion *cushon*; *cuson*; *cussion*; *cution*

cut (of glassware) Cut glass.

damask *Damascus* A woven fabric with patterns created in satin weave. Of different fibres including silk, wool and linen. Used for bed- and wall-hangings and seat upholstery as well as for table-cloths and napkins. Some inventories seem to call this cloth Damascus; the Castlecomer inventory uses both words.

Danzig oak *Dansick oake* Oak timber grown in the Danzig region.

deal *dale* A sawn board cut from European softwoods, especially yellow pine and fir. Often used for the carcass of veneered furniture and for utilitarian furniture that is sometimes painted.

Decca work *dicker work*; *dickerwork* Embroidered silk made in the

Deccan, southern India. Deccan derives from the Sanskrit *dakṣiṇā*, one meaning of which is south. Also, the name given to floral embroidery probably derived from Indian patterns; a design based on this also found printed on cotton.

deception commode A close-stool. The term seems only to have been used in Ireland.

déjeuner *de jurnè*; *déjeuné* A breakfast-service.

delft *delf*; *delfe*; *delph* Tin-glazed earthenware originally produced in the Dutch town of Delft, but also made in Ireland and Britain.

desk *desque* A piece of furniture for writing or reading with either a flat or sloping top; it may also be a moveable table-top desk.

dessert *desart*; Desert

diaper *deaper*; *diap*^{r}; *diap*^{t} A linen fabric, woven with lines crossing to form diamonds with the spaces filled with a motif. Used mostly for table linens. 'Linen cloth woven with flowers, and other figures. . . . A napkin' (Johnson). Beck suggests the word may derive from the town of Ipre [Ypres] in Flanders, known for its linen manufactures, but there is no etymological foundation for that. The OED gives a derivation from the Byzantine Greek δίασπρος, which may have meant 'thoroughly white' or 'pure white'.

dicker work *See* Decca work.

dimity *dimety*; *dimitty* A woven cotton cloth, of different qualities, sometimes corded or patterned or embroidered. Most examples are white. Used mainly for bed-hangings but also for window-curtains, chair-covers and clothing.

dish-ring Stand for hot dish at table in Ireland, France and Britain, often with openwork. Sometimes given the misnomer of potato ring.

dog *dogg* *See* fire dog.

doily A small decorative mat of paper or cloth often placed under food;

Glossary

355

a small ornamental dessert napkin. Named after a linen draper in the Strand, London.

door *dore*

doré dore Gilt. French borrowing.

dornick *darnix* A silk, worsted, woollen, or partly woollen fabric, used for hangings, carpets, vestments; fabric originated in the Walloon town of Tournai, called Doornik in Dutch.

douter *dowter* An implement either in the shape of a hollow metal cone on the end of a handle to snuff the flame of a candle, or, in the plural, a pair of flat-ended tongs to pinch the wick.

doving pan and cover Possibly a drawing-pan and lid.

Dowlas linen A coarse linen originally woven in Brittany, named after the town of Daoulas [Daoulaz in Breton] that lies south-east of Brest. In the 19th century, a strong calico was made in imitation of linen and was called Dowlas.

drab 'A grey or dull brown colour like drab cloth' (Beck).

drab cloth A thick, strong grey cloth (Beck); a woollen cloth (Bailey).

dredging-box *drudging box*; *druging box* Sprinkler or dredger for flour.

Dresden Hard-paste porcelain, produced at the factory founded in 1710 by Augustus the Strong at Meissen near Dresden.

dripping-pan A pan to catch the drips from meat being turned on a spit.

Drogheda linen Linen woven at Drogheda in the Boyne Valley.

dropper *droper* Perhaps the device for removing the trub from the wort in brewing?

drugget *druggett*; *druggitt* A thin, tough cloth of wool or wool and linen, used for wall- and bed-hangings in the early 18th century. By 1800 it had come to mean a coarse wool and linen cloth for protecting table tops and carpets.

dumb-waiter *dumb waitor* Stand of two or more circular tiers with central post support on three or four short legs. Used as a serving table in the dining-room.

Dutch chair A ladder-back chair with a rush or leather seat.

Dutch oven *Dutch ovan* A cooking utensil heated by radiated heat from the grate. Joseph Merlin filed his patent application for a type of Dutch oven with mechanical jack that he dubbed a 'rôtisseur' on 29 January 1773.

earthen Made of baked clay as in earthenware.

ease-and-comfort *comfort and ease* A leg-rest.

economist Housekeeper.

eider down *eyder* — Soft feathers from the breast of an eider duck.

ell A measure of length, employed for textiles. Approximately 45 inches.

epergne *apirn*; *eperne*; *eppyrn* A tiered, ornate centrepiece for the table, usually of silver.

equipage Service (e.g., in china, porcelain, earthenware or glass).

ewer *yewre*; *yore*

eye cup 'A small vessel with a rim shaped to fit the orbit of the eye, used to wash or apply medication to the eye' (OED); an eyebath.

falling leaf A drop leaf of a table; a falling table comprising a board hinged to the wall at one end and supported on one or two hinged legs at the other (Kinmonth, pp. 375–85).

fast Of furniture, fixed, built in, set.

field bed[stead] *feild bed*; *feild bedstead*; *field bed stead* A bed, usually with a shaped top, designed to be easily dismantled and portable. Often used when travelling. Some had elaborate hangings while others were used by servants.

filemot *ffillomatt*; *fillomatt* From the French *feuille-morte*, it is 'a Colour like that of a faded Leaf' (Bailey).

filigree Openwork decoration.

fireback Plate (often in cast iron) lining the back of a fireplace.

fire dog *dogg. See also* andiron.

fire peel *fire piele See* peel.

fire shovel *ffireshoell*; *ffireshouell*; *fireshovell*; *fireshovle See also* shovel.

fixed *fixt* Fitted or built in.

flag-bottomed *flagg bottom'd* With seats in flag or reed or rush.

flagon *flaggon*

flasket *fflaskett* 'Long shallow basket' (Johnson); 'a sort of great basket' (Bailey); also a tub for washing clothes.

flat candlestick Chamber candlestick on a dish base, with a handle, and with the extinguisher held in a socket on the handle.

flint-glass Originally a lustrous glass made from lead oxide, alkali, and ground flint stone to provide the siliceous ingredient.

flock/flox Wool or cotton waste used for stuffing. Flox is a variant spelling of the plural 'flocks' but is used in the singular.

floorcloth 'A fabric for covering floors; chiefly applied to substitutes for carpeting' (OED).

fly candlestick Possibly a candlestick of which some components have been cut in metal using a fly press.

footman Stand placed near the fireplace to support kettle or cooking vessel.

forest-work 'A decorative representation of sylvan scenery' (OED); fruits, flowers and foliage.

form *ffoarme*; *forme*; *forum*; *fourm*; *furme* A bench or long stool with a plain oak, walnut, cane or upholstered seat; long seat without back.

freezer In the context of Mount Stewart (1821), it is likely to have been a container used in ice-cream making.

French Either imported from France or made using French techniques and design.

frieze *frise*; *frize* A kind of coarse woollen cloth, with a nap, usually on one side only. Beck states that it appears to have been a distinctive Irish product very early.

frilled *froiled*; *frilld*

fringe 'An ornamental border of hanging threads or plaited work' (Beck).

fuller A tool for making a groove in metal; also the name given to the groove in a metal surface, notably on a horseshoe.

furbelow[ed] *furbuloed* 'Furbeloe, plaited or ruffled Trimming for Women's Petticoats, Scarves, &c' (Bailey). An ornamental strip of stuff gathered and sewn to the skirt of a lady's dress, or to a curtain; a flounce.

furniture calico, cotton or **linen** Fabrics possibly of upholstery grade or printed with large pattern repeats. In the late 18th century there was the Irish Furniture Cotton and Linen Warehouse on Werburgh Street, Dublin, presumably making fabrics for soft furnishings.

fusee or **fusil** *fusie* A light musket.

fustian *fustain* A twill weave cloth with linen warp and cotton weft, later all cotton, which could be printed or embroidered. Used for bed-hangings and chair-covers.

gad A rope, band or tie made from the fibres of a twisted twig or of several; a withe.

gadrooned *gadd* Inverted fluting or beading seen in furniture, metalwork and textiles. Also known as knurling and nulling.

gallon Measure of capacity.

gardevine 'A case or closet for holding wine-bottles' (OED). *See also* cellaret.

gaufrier *goffrey* French word for waffle-iron.

Genoa damask *Genoway damask* As late as the 17th century, Genoa supplied nearly all Europe's damask (Beck).

gilt *guilt* A technique for ornamenting wood, metal, glass and ceramics with gold leaf. Includes honey gilding, lacquer gilding, mercury gilding, ormolu, party gilt and size gilding.

gimlet *gimblet* A boring tool with very sharp point, threaded tip and corkscrew-like shaft.

gouge *gauge* In the context of a woodturning lathe, this is likely to be a gouge rather than a gauge.

grater *greater*

green May refer to green cloth. *See also* baize.

green-work Representation of trees and foliage on tapestries, verdure.

greycloth *gray cloth* 'Unbleached or undyed cloth' (OED).

gridiron *grediron* Platform of iron bars on short feet and with long handle for cooking meat over a fire.

gudgeon Pivot on which a wheel turns.

gyle vat Tub in which the wort (or gyle) ferments in brewing.

gymp or **gimp** Coarse lace formed by twisting threads around a coarse foundation of wire or twine. Made in varying quantities of silk, wool or cotton, it is used chiefly in upholstery (Beck).

hair Animal hair; often horsehair; goat's hair was sometimes used in weaving camlet (hair camlet). Curled horsehair with its natural springiness was used for stuffing mattresses.

haircloth *hair cloth* Coarse open fabric.

hair silk Silk thread.

halberd *halbert* A weapon combining battle-axe and spear.

half-headed bed Bedstead with medium height back, short corner posts and no canopy.

hames Curved lengths of wood forming part of draught-horse's collar.

hand board A tray, especially a tea-tray.

harewood *airwood* 'A variety of sycamore . . . richer in figure and sometimes striped' (Holtzapffel).

harnum *Haarlem*; '*Haerlem*' (KC 1717) Thought to be a corruption of the name of the linen-weaving town of Haarlem in the United Provinces, thus Haarlem linen.

harpsichord *harpsecale*; *herpsicord*

harrateen or **harateen** *harriteen* A worsted fabric, available either plain or watered or with a waved pattern. Used for bed-hangings and window-curtains, occasionally for chair-covers and for linings.

hassock *hasseck*; *hassick* A firm cushion, originally stuffed with rushes or straw, used as a foot rest or a kneeler.

haulm *halm* Possible interpretation of a word used to describe a chaff-filled bolster at Carton House, with the conjectured meaning there of 'straw'.

hay-tedder Hay tether.

hazard table Table for playing the gambling game of hazard with two dice.

hod A 'sort of Tray for carrying Mortar, in Use with Bricklayers' (Bailey); 'The Hod is a kind of three square trough made up at one end and open at the other, haveing a staffe fixed to its bottom' (Holme).

hoe (kitchen utensil) *how* Possibly a griddle or flat plate for cooking flatbreads known as hoe cakes.

hogshead *hg'sh'ds*; *hhead* A measure of liquid containing 63 gallons. Also used generically to describe any large barrel.

Holland A fine quality linen cloth, imported from Holland, which could be white or brown and occasionally patterned. Used for spring curtains, blinds and bed sheets. 'The principal mart or staple of this cloth is at Haerlem [sic], whither it is sent from other parts as soon as wove, there to be whitened the ensuing spring' (Chambers).

horse (frame) Clothes-horse.

huckaback Highly absorbent linen towelling with raised figures.

hundredweight *cwt* An avoirdupois weight of 8 stones, or 112 pounds.

hunting-chair Armchair with sliding leg rest (Sheraton).

India *Indea*; *Indian*; *Indie*; *Indien* Imported from Asia, notably from India, China or Japan, through the East India Company, or made in imitation of such imports.

intermess[es] 'Courses set on a Table between other Dishes' (Bailey); name also given to the dishes on which they are served.

iron See urn.

Glossary

jack 'An engine which turns the spit' (Johnson); a roasting-jack. *See also* boot-jack; leather jack; smoke-jack.

japanned *japan*; *japand*; *japin*; *jappan'd*; *jappand* Lacquered in imitation of oriental lacquer-work.

japanning A European imitation of oriental lacquer, used to decorate furniture, boxes and wall-panelling. *See also* lacquer[ed].

jorum *juren* A large drinking-bowl, especially for punch.

keeler *cooler* Vessel for cooling liquids; also a household shallow tub.

keeve or kive *kieve* 'A tub or vat; specifically, a vat for holding liquid in brewing and bleaching' (OED).

kennel-pot *kennal pot* A large kettle (q.v.)

kettle *ketle* An open cooking pot or pan; later a handled vessel with spout for boiling water.

Kidderminster *Kedermast^er*; *Kidermaster*; *Kidminster*; *Kidminster*; *Kittermast*; *Kittermaster*; *Kitterm^r* A worsted cloth, sometimes with a woven geometric or striped pattern, named after the town of Kidderminster, a centre of worsted spinning and weaving. Used for wall- and bed-hangings and for window-curtains. Also, a floor-covering of flat woven reversible double cloth like Scotch carpet (q.v.).

kiddy See tea caddy.

Kildare linen Possibly linen associated with the subsidiary title of the FitzGerald family before the conferment of the dukedom of Leinster.

kish A wicker basket < Irish *cis*, used chiefly for carrying turf.

lacquer[ed] *lackered*; *lakerd* Asian varnish used as finish on Chinese and Japanese furniture. *See also* japanning.

lading-pail Bucket used for draining out liquid.

lancewood A tough, elastic wood imported from the West Indies, possibly the Jamaican *Oxandra virgata*.

landau A four-wheel carriage with a top in two parts that may be opened. When open the back part may be folded while the front part removed. Named after the German town where the carriage was first made.

landscape *landskip*

lantern *lanthorn*; *lanthorne*; *lantron*

larder *lawrder*

lath *lat*

lathe *leath*

laundry *lawndrea*

lava ware A stoneware made with a semi-vitreous finish that has the appearance of lava.

lawn-sieve A sieve of a fine linen like cambric.

lay-over *lay over* A cloth laid over a tablecloth.

leather jack *lither jack* A large leather can for small beer, or, more generally, a jug or bottle made of leather.

leno A type of cotton gauze.

Liège *Leige* Possibly a kind of quilting woven in the Walloon city of Liège.

lime screen Apparatus for sifting lime.

linen Production in Ireland was directly stimulated by the arrival of Huguenot refugees seeking shelter, many of whom settled in the neighbourhood of Lisburn, Co. Antrim/Co. Down, and soon made its brown linen famous. Among them was Louis Crommelin (1652–1727), who was appointed overseer of the Royal Linen Manufacture of Ireland. As the 2nd Duke of Ormonde wrote, 'Louis Crommelin and the Huguenot colony have been greatly instrumental in improving and propagating the flaxen manufacture in the north of the kingdom, and the perfection to which the same has been brought in that part of the country has been greatly owing to the skill and industry of the said Crommelin' (as quoted by Beck).

list 'Selvage, border or edge of a cloth, usually of a different material from the body of the cloth' (OED). The border of a stuff, or that which bounds its width on either side.

Liverpool lamp An oil lamp that evolved around 1800, with a disc to adjust illumination and with a globular shape to lower part of the chimney.

Londonderry Solar Grate Invented by Robert Stewart, Earl of Londonderry, later 1st Marquess of Londonderry (see plate 47), this grate throws the heat equally 'into every part of the room, as the radii of a circle proceed from its centre'. Advertised thus in the *Belfast News-Letter*, 15 October 1813, p. 3.

looking-glass *lookinglass*

losset Wooden tray or kneading trough < the Irish *losaid*, used for making bread or cakes.

lotto box A box for the cards and counters of the game of chance called lotto, forerunner of bingo.

lustre *luster* A glass pendant used to ornament a chandelier. Also a candlestick of cut glass, ornamented with drops.

lutestring (lustring) *lewtstring*; *luetstring* A silk taffeta with a special glossy finish achieved by applying gum to the fabric and heating it. Mostly plain and used for curtains, linings and covers for toilet tables. Assimilated with 'lute string', the word, however, derives either from the French *lustrine* or the Italian *lustrino*.

madder An Irish wooden drinking vessel, or one for measuring liquids; a mether. 'The "madder," so often mentioned in Irish song, is a wooden tankard, made square; there were then no tools for turning. Wooden noggins and wooden dishes were universal; they are still much used in country parts' (Morgan). The madder is celebrated in Laurence Whyte's poem *Critical Annotations*, published in 1742.

mahogany *mahog.*; *mahogney*; *mahog^y*; *mah^y*; *mah^y*; *mohoganey*; *mohogany*; *mohogony*; *mohog^y*

mahogany lock *mohoganey. lock* An Irish front-door-lock or stock-lock where the rim-lock mechanism is housed in a dug-out block of mahogany.

mandrel *mandrell*; *mandrill* 'A (more or less) cylindrical rod round which metal or other material is forged, cast, moulded, or otherwise shaped' (OED).

mangle A device for squeezing water out of linen and clothes and for pressing after washing.

marrow spoon A spoon designed for scooping out bone marrow.

Marseilles *Marseills*; *Marsellas*; *Marselles* A bed-cover made of layers of fabric sewn together with an all-over embroidered pattern, named after the French city of Marseilles, which specialized in such quilting. Subsequently developed as a machine-woven technique.

martingale A strapping device that is designed to prevent a horse from rearing or throwing its head back. The word is said to derive from the town of Martigues in south-eastern France. Note the intrusive <n> before the <g> as in Portingale (q.v.).

mash-tub For mashing the hops in brewing beer.

matted Woven or plaited with rushes.

mattress *matreess*; *matress* A quilted cushion, or sort of quilted bed stuffed with wool, horsehair etc.

Merlin chair A kind of invalid chair invented by John Joseph Merlin that the occupant propels by turning the rear wheels by hand. In the context of Newbridge House, it is not clear whether the chair itself was manufactured by Merlin or whether the proper name was being used generically.

metal May perhaps indicate either iron or bell-metal.

mignonette A plant of the family Resedaceae, with fragrant yellow flowers.

mohair *mohare*; *moheare* Highly durable and expensive cloth made from the wool of the Angora goat, and also a mixture of Angora goat wool and silk. Originally imported from the Levant but later manufactured in England, using coarse English wool. Often used as upholstery material.

monteith *montaafe* A punchbowl with a removable scalloped rim 'to let drinking glasses hang there by the foot so that the body or drinking place might hang in the water to coole them' (Andrew Clark [compiler], *The Life and Times of Anthony Wood, Antiquary, of Oxford, 1632–1695, Described by Himself*. Oxford, Oxford Historical Society, 1984, vol. III, p. 84).

moreen *marine*; *merine*; *merreen*; *morine* A worsted cloth with a watered finish, created by pressing under rollers, and then glazed. Used for seat upholstery, bed- and wall-hangings and window-curtains.

morone *marone* Maroon.

mother-of-pearl *pearl*; *motheraperral*

mule 'Beast ingender'd between an Ass and a Mare, or a She-Ass and a Horse' (Bailey).

multiplying wheel A device added to a roasting-jack in order that the machine may run much longer without winding.

muslin A fine transparent cotton textile imported originally from India.

mustard *muster*

nankeen A type of Chinese porcelain made in, or shipped from, Nanking, and later copied in Europe.

nest of drawers An 18th-century term for a small chest of drawers.

niggar *nigger*; *niggard* False side or bottom to grate, in iron or firebrick.

noggin *naggin* A small drinking vessel; a measure of alcoholic liquor.

north country The region in Britain north of the river Humber.

nozzle *nosell* Socket on a candlestick or sconce into which a candle is inserted.

office Of the service rooms of the household, especially the kitchen. At Borris House, term used for the library.

ogee *O. G.* A moulding with an S-shaped section; 'A Member of a Moulding consisting of a Round and a Hollow' (Bailey).

oilcloth Coarse hempen or flaxen fabric laid down as a floor-covering, the durability of which was greatly enhanced by paint or oil.

old-fashioned *oldfashined*; *old fashon* Of a design from an earlier period, deemed outmoded.

ombre *umbro*; *vmber* A trick-taking card game for three players.

omelette *omelet*; *omilet*; *omlet*

organ barrel Barrel possibly from either an organ or an organ clock.

ormolu *ormelew*

ottoman *otta* Low upholstered seat without arms or back, typically serving also as a storage box with hinged seat for the lid.

ounce (troy) The standard measure of weight used for silver and other precious metals and precious stones.

oven stopper A stout iron sheet *to cover the mouth* of an *oven; it is lifted and put in* position with handles (*Report and Transactions – The Devonshire Association for the Advancement of Science, Literature and Art*, 1902, vol. 34, p. 98).

oyster table A table inlaid with mother-of-pearl, or a table with an oyster or whorled veneer. May also be a table with a hidden box for diners' discarded oyster shells.

palampore *palampoe*; *pallampoe*; *pallempore* A richly patterned cloth, originally made in India. Also the name given to a hanging, shawl, or bedspread made from this cloth.

pallet *pallat bedstead* A lowly bedstead often with a straw-filled bed.

palliasse *paleraws*; *palerwas*; *paliass*; *pallyass* A mattress, often of sacking, stuffed with straw; it may also be of plaited straw without covering (Kinmonth, pp. 311–12). Word borrowed from Middle French *paillasse*.

papillote *papiliotte*; *papillotte* Curl paper for the hair.

Glossary

359

paragon *paragin* A fine worsted cloth. Plain and embroidered. Used in curtains, hangings, upholstery but seldom in clothing.

parlour Term used for a room for dining or supping (as at Killadoon).

pastille urn *paste still uran* Pastille burner.

pastry Building or place where pastries are made.

patent lamp Possibly an Argand Oil Lamp, patented 1784 in England by the Swiss inventor Aimé Argand, with a cylindrical wick and chimney.

patty *pattee*; *petty* A small pie or pasty, or occasionally the dish it is baked in.

pear tree Pearwood.

peck Vessel for dry goods, with capacity equivalent to a quarter of a bushel.

peel A broad thin board, or metal sheet, with a long handle for putting bread in and out of the oven. A shovel.

Pembroke table Small table with drop-leaf on either side. Probably named after Henry Herbert, 9th Earl of Pembroke, son of Philip Herbert, the 8th earl, who was lord-lieutenant of Ireland, 1707–8.

pennyweight *dwt*; *pennw*ᵗᵗ; *pwt*; *pwtt* A twentieth of a troy ounce.

Persian A thin soft silk for linings.

Persian carpet *Percian carpett*

pestle *pistle*

pewter *putter*

phaeton 'A type of light four-wheeled open carriage, usually drawn by a pair of horses, and having one or two seats facing forward' (OED).

pier A wall between two openings or windows.

pier-glass *pear —*; *peer —*; *piear —* A looking-glass hung on a pier wall between two windows, often elaborately framed.

piggin *piggen* A small, staved pail with one stave longer than the rest to serve as a handle.

pillion 'A kind of soft saddle for women to ride on' (Bailey). The word is of Irish origin (*pillín*, also *pilliún*), a pack-saddle, a small cushion.

pincushion dish *pincushen —* Salad dish similar in shape to a pincushion [dish].

pinery Place where pineapples are grown.

pipe As a measure of capacity, typically equivalent to two hogsheads.

plate *pleat*

plateau *plato* A tray or flat dish.

plate-basket A basket for plate and china.

plated May refer to plated silver (base metal coated with silver foil) or to Sheffield plate (q.v.).

plate drain *plate draen*

plate-trunk A trunk for storing and transporting plate [silver].

plumeau A feather duster.

poker *pocker*; *poke*

pole glass A dressing glass mounted on an upright rod.

pole-screen A screen mounted on an upright rod.

pomatum *pomatom* A scented ointment for the skin and hair originally made with apples (from *pomatum*, post-classical Latin for cider). This toilet requisite was kept in an often-ornate box or pot.

pool Pool dish, for stakes at a game of cards, especially quadrille.

pope's head brush A cleaning brush with bristles set in a sphere and fitted to a long handle for dusting ceilings.

poplin *popling* A mixed material of silk and worsted. According to Beck, Irish weavers had a high reputation for their poplin in the 18th century.

porcelain Although the term is not used in any of the inventories in this book, much of the so-called china referred to is European-made porcelain ware rather than export china ware. Unlike earthenware, porcelain is vitrified and so does not need to be glazed to be impermeable.

porphyry *porphery* A hard stone with crystals of white, red or purple that can be highly polished. Quarried in Egypt in antiquity.

Portingale Portugal or Portuguese; this version of the word derives from the Middle French, with an intrusive <n> before the <g>, a phenomenon found also in late Middle English, e.g., nightingale (*nehtægale* in Old English) and martingale (q.v.).

Portugal mat *portieguies —*; *portingale matt*; *Portuigues mat* Woven reed mat often with decorated border.

powdering tub A tub for salting or pickling meat or fish.

press A simple wooden cupboard, usually shelved; sometimes two-tiered with hinged doors, and sometimes with inside drawers.

press bed[stead] A cupboard concealing a fold-down bed.

print 'A printed (usually cotton) fabric' (OED).

pritch A goad.

pritching Possibly another name for a pritchel, a tool for punching or enlarging holes in horseshoes.

pudding *pudden*

pulpatoon *pulpetoon* A game dish baked with a forcemeat crust.

puzzling-pin (or peg) A short tapering peg of wood (sometimes of dogwood, ash or oak) fastened securely to a hunting dog's collar and round its lower jaw behind the tusks to force the animal to keep its head up while on the scent.

quadrille box A box to hold the playing cards for the game of quadrille.

quilt A bed cover consisting of two pieces of fabric, stuffed with a layer of wool or down, joined together with stitches or lines of stitches. Can be decorative or plain.

register grate A domestic grate with a device for regulating the draught of the fire.

remove A dish served in place of one that is removed within a course at a meal (cf. *relevé* in French, a dish that follows another).

ribbery A lath forming part of the groundwork for thatch on some dwellings in Ireland. *See* Roberta Reeners *A Wexford Farmstead: The conservation of an 18th-century farmstead at Mayglass* (Kilkenny, 2003), p. 44.

ridder A kind of sieve, perhaps here for cleaning wheat.

riddle 'A sieve, an oblong Sort of Sieve to separate the seed from the corn' (Bailey). 'A coarse-meshed sieve … generally consisting of a circular rim with a base formed of strong wires crossing each other at right angles' (OED).

roller A broad strap wrapped around a horse's body used especially to hold a saddle or blanket in place; a rolling pin; a garden roller.

roller blind *rola blind*

Roman chair An armchair inspired by classical Roman design, probably modelled on the *sella curulis*, with a series of cross-framed s-shaped legs held together by a bolt through their crossing point, and possibly with a leather seat.

Roman Charity The picture of an 'old man suckin' listed at Kilkenny Castle may well depict the Roman legend, known as Roman Charity, of the aged Cimon in prison awaiting execution without food, who, in an act of filial piety, is suckled by his visiting daughter Pero.

rubber Hard cloth for cleaning.

rug (as in 'rug quilt') 'A kind of coarse woollen cloth, frequently of Irish manufacture' (OED).

rummer 'A broad mouth'd large drinking Vessel' (Bailey).

rushlight A cheaper form of lighting using the pith of a rush dipped in tallow or some other grease.

Russia leather *rushey —*; *Rushy —*; *Russian —* Named after country of origin. Calf-skin or cowhide, tanned and dressed so that it resists water and deters insects. Used for chair covers.

sackcloth *sacken*

sacking A cloth of either flax or hemp that is stretched across the frame of a bed to support a mattress.

sad colour A 'deep or dark colour' (Bailey).

salad *sallad*; *salled*; *sallet*

salamander *salimander*; *sallamander*

A browning iron with a long handle used to brown or toast the surface of roasts or pastry; 'A circular iron plate which is heated and placed over a pudding or other dish to brown it' (OED).

sally desk A wickerwork desk of willow wood or perhaps a table-top desk of solid willow < Irish *saileach*: cf. *salix* in Latin.

sarcenet *sarsnet*; *sasnett* A fine, thin woven silk and dyed in a range of colours, or in black. Commonly used for protective furniture cases. Name said to derive from having first been made by the Saracens, probably in Spain.

sarcophagus *sarophagus* Wine-cooler with feet (late 18th century).

satin *saten*; *sattan*; *satten*; *sattin*; *satting* 'A kind of silken stuff, very smooth and shining, the warp whereof is very fine and stands out, the woof coarser and lies underneath: on which depend that gloss, and beauty, which gives it its price' (Chambers).

saucer *saser*

sauté pan *sottee pan*; *soutier* (?)

say 'A light, twilled woollen fabric resembling serge, used for aprons, bedding, curtains, etc., and (from the 17th cent.) commonly green in colour' (OED); 'A thin sort of Stuff' (Bailey).

scalloped *scollop*[d] Ornamented or trimmed in the shape of a scallop-shell.

scantling *scantlen* A length of timber some two to four inches thick and of similar width.

scoop *scope*; *scoupe*

Scotch carpet[ing] A flat woven reversible double-cloth floor-covering, produced in various centres in Scotland.

Scotch pint A measure of capacity equivalent to approximately three imperial pints.

screen *screin*

screw reading desk Desk with threaded adjustable central support.

scrutoire *screwtore*; *scruitore*; *scrutore* An escritoire: a desk, writing cabinet or writing box.

scuffle[r] Horse-hoe.

seascape *sea skip*

secrétaire/secretary Writing-desk or bureau.

serge *sarge*; *searge* A twilled cloth with worsted warp and woollen weft, middleweight, inexpensive and durable, ranging in quality.

server Salver.

set Fitted, fixed, built in.

settee *sattee*; *settea*; *settiee*; *stettee* Seating furniture with arms to accommodate two or more people.

seu See sieve.

shallow *shella*

shambileire; *shandelier* See chandelier.

sheep-crook Shepherd's crook.

Sheffield plate, old Plate made of silver-coated copper using a process invented by Thomas Boulsover in 1743 and brought to perfection in Sheffield to fuse the two metals together. Old Sheffield plate was sold at a fraction of the cost of its solid-silver counterparts. Further cost reduction resulted from the use of die-cutting and of fly presses.

shoeing tool *shewing tool* A name for a number of tools used for shoeing a horse.

shovel *shovell*; *shovle*; *shuvle* See also fire shovel.

sieve *sive*

silver lace Braid woven with silver strip, wire or silver thread (silver strip wound round a core of fibre, usually silk).

silver tabby Watered silk with threads of silver. See also tabby.

silver wash A film of silver deposited from a solution on to another metal.

sive Conjunction for 'or' before the subtitle of a book in Latin.

skeleton desk A movable sloping desk to put on a table.

skewer *scewer* A loaded skewer or skiver seems to be one with a lead head for balancing.

Glossary

skiver *sciver*

smoke-jack *smoak jack* Like the common jack, a smoke jack turns the spit. However, it is driven not by the smoke of the fire but by the draught of rarefied air acting on a fan in the chimney.

Smyrna carpet *Smyrnah carpett* Originally carpets woven in the Turkish *vilayet* or province of Aidin, of which Smyrna was the capital.

snaffle 'A sort of Bit for a Horse' (Bailey).

snuffer-pans *snuffer panes*

sofa *saffoiy*; *soffa*

soup-plate *soap —*; *soop —*; *soupe —*

Spanish table A table with folding iron legs.

spider-table An occasional table with spider-like legs.

spinet *spinnete*; *spinnett*

sponge *spung*; *spunge*

squab *scqob*; *squob* 'A soft stuffed Cushion or Stool' (Bailey).

Staffordshire ware Lead-glazed or salt-glazed earthenware, or creamware, stoneware etc., from Staffordshire; but can also be dinner wares of porcelain or blue-and-white lead-glazed earthenware.

stained marble Possibly a description of scagliola, i.e., Italian plasterwork done in imitation of stone.

standing bed or bedstead 'High bedstead' (OED).

standing clock Long-cased clock.

steelyard *stilliard*.

stew-hole 'A small stove in a kitchen-hearth on which anything is put to boil or stew' (Neuman & Baretti).

sticks Candlesticks.

stilling or stillion *stelling* A stand for a cask (OED); stillion is also a vessel in which to catch yeast.

still-room *still room* Originally a room for distilling cordials; later a room where preserves were kept.

stock lock A lock in a wooden case, usually fitted to an outside door.

stone Either made of stone or of stoneware.

stool *stoll* It may mean a seat (and not just a stool in the modern sense of the word).

straddle A small saddle or pad put on the back of a carriage-horse, to support the shafts of the carriage.

strainer *streaner*

straining-frame *strainein —*; *straineing —* Frame on which a picture on canvas or paper etc. is stretched.

strapper 'The cow is termed a tidy cow the year she drops her calf and if she gives milk a second year she is called a strapper cow.' In letter written by Nathaniel Nisbett of Lifford to James Hamilton, 8th Earl of Abercorn (Gebbie).

stripped damask Probably striped damask, where 'striped' has been corrupted to 'stripped'.

Studdert linen Possibly linen associated with a manufacturer or draper of that name.

stuff A general term for worsted cloths.

stuffed Filled with padding to provide a yielding support.

stump bedstead A bedstead without tester or posts, sometimes with a very low headboard.

sumpter cloth *sumpture cloath* Used to cover luggage carried by a horse or mule, it is a cloth richly embroidered as a mark of status.

surcingle *circingle* Girth for a horse.

sweet oil *sweel* [with uncrossed t] *oil* Olive oil.

swing[ing] bale *swinging beal* Sometimes made of hollowed wrought iron, it was a hanging device used to separate horses in their stalls.

swingletree A pivoted crossbar in a carriage, plough or harrow, to which the traces are fastened, giving freedom of movement to the draft-animal and balancing the pull.

syllabub *silly bub* A drink or dish made of milk curdled with wine or cider or other acid.

tabby A plain weave silk, slightly heavier than lutestring, and stronger and thicker than taffeta. 'A kind of silk taffety watered or waved' (Bailey).

tablecloth *table clothe* See also lay-over.

taffety *tafty* A variant of taffeta. A wide variety of silk and silk/cotton goods originally imported from Bengal but later woven in Europe. 'A kind of fine, smooth, silken stuff; having usually, a remarkable lustre, or gloss' (Beck, quoting Chambers).

tambour-frame Drum-shaped frame for stretching material for embroidery. Much in vogue in the latter half of the 18th century, the embroidery and sewing of muslin, including on tambour-frames, gave employment to many women in Ireland and western Scotland (Beck).

tambour writing-desk/table Roll-top desk/table with sliding top of slats on a canvas backing.

tamis *tammois* Sieve or strainer. In modern French *tamis* is a flat drum-shaped sieve with fine mesh.

Tangier mat *Tangeer Matt*

tapestry A decorated textile fabric.

tarrier Auger used by the cellarman to bore a barrel.

tassel *tasell*; *tassel*; *tossel*; *tossell*; *tossle*

tea-caddy *tea kiddy*

tea-canister Tea-caddy.

tea-dish Tea-cup.

tea-kitchen Tea-urn.

tea-table Small table or tray designed primarily for a tea service.

tester *teaster* The horizontal upper section of a bed, sitting on the posts, and usually made of carved wood, or of wood covered with a fabric; a canopy over a bed.

thread damask *thrid damask* Sort of damask made in Normandy, whereof the woof and warp are of thread (Fleming & Tibbins).

tick/ticken; *ticking*; *tickeing*; *tikein* A strong, closely woven linen twill in a variety of colours and stripes. Used for feather beds, mattresses, bolsters, pillows and some men's clothing such as waistcoats and breeches. *See also* bedtick.

tierce Measure of capacity, equivalent to a third of a pipe.

tin Most likely to be sheet iron coated with tin.

tissue A rich silk, often woven with silver and gold thread.

toilet/toilette *toylet*; *toilet cover* Dressing table drapery.

tomahawk In the context of the duke's study at Carton House, this may refer either to a North American Indian stone axe or to a metal-bladed hatchet produced by Europeans for trade with North American Indians.

tongs *tonges*; *tongues*

tortoiseshell/turtleshell *tartle shell* The shell of certain turtles, notably the hawk's-bill turtle.

tourte Pastry pie baked in a pan.

traveller A graduated wheel with handle designed to measure the perimeter of an object, especially that of a wheel.

tray *trea*

trellis *trelace*

trencher case Possibly a case for storing trenchers (wooden plates).

trestle *tressell*; *trussell*

trippet or **trivet** *trevitt*; *tripet* A stand (often three-legged) for utensils before a fire or fastened to the front of the fire grate.

trou-madame (or troll-madam) **table** A table for playing the game *trou-madame* (like bagatelle).

troy weight *trea w^t See* ounce (troy).

tumbrel *tumbler* A farm cart that can be tipped to empty the contents.

tumrell Possibly a tumbler, where 'tumbrel', here corrupted, has been used for the word 'tumbler', rather than vice versa, where 'tumbler' is sometimes used in dialect to refer to tumbrel, meaning a farm cart.

tun Large cask (as measure of capacity, usually the equivalent of 4 hogsheads); in brewing a vat; also name given to a chest for storage.

Tunbridge ware A form of inlay, consisting of minute squares cut from strips or rods of different coloured woods, assembled to create a design similar to a mosaic. Named after Royal Tunbridge Wells, Kent.

tundish A shallow vessel with a tube at the bottom used as a kind of funnel in brewing; term also used to describe a wine funnel.

tunning tub *tuning tubb*

tureen *terreen*; *toureen*; *turine*; *turreen* A deep vessel with a lid, usually oval. Placed upon a matching platter and used for serving soup.

Turkey leather Goatskin dressed with galls to make a fine binding leather. 'Leather tawed with oil, the hair side not being removed until after the tawing' (OED).

Turkey stone Turquoise.

Turkey work/worked *Turky*; *Turky work*; *Turky worke*; *Turky-work't* A woollen pile fabric made in imitation of Turkish carpets, for use as upholstery and table and floor carpets.

Turk's cap *Turks cap* Small round cake-tin or mould in the shape of a tulip or perhaps as if writhen like a turban.

twill A kind of weave producing a diagonal effect in the finished cloth.

umbrello 'A wooden Frame covered with Cloth or Stuff to keep off the Sun from a Window' (Bailey).

umbro. See ombre.

urn *iron*; *uran*

utensil In the context of the bedroom, this may refer to a chamber utensil or pot.

valance *valence*; *vallans*; *vallen*; *vallence*; *vallens* A strip of fabric, suspended below the tester of a bed to conceal the curtain-rod and below the frame of the bed stock to conceal the gap underneath, or hung above a window to conceal the curtain-rod.

valuation Among the inventories compiled for valuation purposes published in this book there are some with puzzling features. At Dublin Castle (1707), both the Irish and English pewter to be shipped back to London on behalf of the 2nd Duke of Ormonde are listed but valued according to differing rates per pound weight of 12 pence or 13 pence (12d and 13d) respectively. At Kilrush House (1750), for example, values expressed in pounds, shillings and pence (£ s d) are quite often multiples of 6½d, sometimes, but not always, based on a rate for particular goods quoted within the inventory. Further multiples of 6½d are to be found in the valuation of goods and chattels at No. 10 Henrietta Street (1772) with some of the silver valued at 6s 6d per ounce and some at 6s. There are further instances to be found at Morristown Lattin (1773) and Castlecomer (1798) of amounts divisible by 13, although that division of some of these amounts may be coincidental. These values would seem on many occasions to be associated with the exchange rate set at the time between Irish and British currency (both expressed in pounds, shillings and pence) of '8 1/3l. per Cent' [£8⅓ per cent], or at a ratio of 13/12 or 6 ½d/6d (Draper, pp. 229–30). The rules applied when there was a need to convert British rates to Irish ones for local appraisal of certain goods have yet to be established. Interestingly, it is clearly stated that the valuations of goods at the bishop's house at Elphin are expressed in sterling. *See* the conversion table on page 364.

vase *vace*; *vaws* In the context of the bedroom, this may refer to a chamber vase or pot.

vat *fatt* A vessel or cask for storing liquids or foodstuffs such as cheese, or for boiling.

verd-antique A marble-like breccia, mostly serpentinite, mixed with calcite and dolomite.

voider *voidore*; *voyder* 'A tray, basket, or other vessel in which dirty dishes or utensils, fragments of broken food, etc., are placed in clearing the table or during a meal' (OED);

Irish £ s d	Sterling £ s d	Sterling guineas	Possible instances occur at
6½d	6d		
1s 1d	1s 0d		Morristown Lattin
2s 2d	2s 0d		
2s 8½d	2s 6d		
5s 5d	5s 0d		Castlecomer; Morristown Lattin
6s 6d	6s 0d		Morristown Lattin
8s 1½d	7s 6d		Morristown Lattin
10s 10d	10s 0d		Morristown Lattin
11s 4½d	10s 6d	½ guinea	Morristown Lattin
13s 0d	12s 0d		Castlecomer; No. 10 Henrietta Street
13s 6½d	12s 6d		
16s 3d	15s 0d		Morristown Lattin
18s 11½d	17s 6d		
£ 1 1s 8d	£ 1 0s 0d		
£ 1 2s 9d	£ 1 1s 0d	1 guinea	Kilrush
£ 1 14s 1½d	£ 1 11s 6d	1½ guineas	Morristown Lattin
£ 2 5s 6d	£ 2 2s 0d	2 guineas	Kilrush; No. 10 Henrietta Street
£ 2 16s 10½d	£ 2 12s 6d	2½ guineas	Morristown Lattin
£ 3 8s 3d	£ 3 3s 0d	3 guineas	Castlecomer
£ 4 11s 0d	£ 4 4s 0d	4 guineas	Kilrush
£ 6 16s 6d	£ 6 6s 0d	6 guineas	Borris House; Kilrush
£ 13 13s 0d	£ 12 12s 0d	12 guineas	Kilrush
£ 18 4s 0d	£ 16 16s 0d	16 guineas	

Table showing Irish values after conversion from sterling. *See* 'valuation' on previous page.

'a Table-basket for Plates, Knives, &c. a wooden painted Vessel to hold Services of Sweet-Meats' (Bailey).

wainscot *wainscoate*; *wainscott*; *winscott* High quality oak, often imported from the Baltic region. Mainly used for panelling and furniture.

waiter A salver or small tray.

walnut *wallnut*; *wallnutt*; *wallnut tree*; *wallnuttree*; *wall nutt tree*; *wallnutt tree*; *walnutree*; *walnut tree*

Walpole china Perhaps oriental blue-and white china, as in the collection of Horace Walpole (1717–1797).

wash-ball A ball of soap for washing the hands and face or for shaving.

wash-hand stand *wash and stand*

water croft *See* croft.

water plate A warming plate for food with reservoir for hot water.

Wedgwood Pottery made by Josiah Wedgwood (1730–1795) and his successors at Etruria, Staffordshire.

wether *weather* (Castrated) ram.

wheel car Farm cart.

white ware Possibly white-glazed earthenware or stoneware.

window-shuts Window shutters.

window stool Window bench, window-seat or windowsill.

Windsor chair A wooden chair with a saddle seat and a bent spindle back, produced in a variety of styles.

wine-cooper *cooper* Wine bottle basket.

wine labels *wine labbles*

winkers A bridle with blinkers.

Worcester porcelain Worcester china.

worked Embroidered, adorned with needlework.

worsted *wosted* Wool cloth that has been combed to remove all the short fibres, with a tightly twisted yarn, giving a smooth hard surface. The name is derived from the village of Worstead, near Norwich.

wort pump Pump used in brewing to force the wort (new ale) from the drainer to the cooler.

wrenching-tub *wrenching tubb* A laundry tub for wringing water out of clothes; also for washing plate.

wrought *wraught* A decorative finishing technique. In textiles, especially silk, decorated as with needlework, embellished or embroidered. In metals, beaten out or shaped by hammering or handwork.

Wyatt cornice Cornice moulding after Gothic revival design by the architect James Wyatt.

yellow ware *yellow stone ware*. Possibly cream-ware, an earthenware or stoneware with a creamy glaze.

yore See ewer.

APPENDIX I

Buyers at Captain Balfour's town house sale 1741/2

See inventory on pp. 108–21

Acton, Miss: table, deal, 110
Adams, Mrs: silver, cream saucepan, 117; —, tankard, 117
Asdle, Mr: cabinet, walnut, 110
Atkins, Mrs: butter cups, silver, 117
Bags, Mrs: quadrille box, 119
Baillie, Mr: silver, candlesticks, 117; —, cruet stand and castor, 117; —, tea-dish, 117
Baker, Mrs: cups, saucers and bowl, 119; porringer, 119
Baldwin, Mr: tallboy, mahogany, 109
Barlow, Mrs: tablecloths, 114
Barnwell, Mr: ticking, 120
Bell, the maid: blankets and underblanket, 109; candlesticks, high, 111; plates, pewter, 112; saucepan, copper, 112; sheets, 115, 116; —, coarse, 114; tea kettle, copper, 112
Bligh, Mrs: tablecloths, 113
Bolton, Mr: hall lantern, 110; kettle-stand, mahogany, 109; spoons, silver, 118; Turkey carpet, 109; watch and chain, gold, 118
Bonnom, or Bomrom, Mr: dish stand, silver, 117; tablecloths, 114; tea-pot, silver, 117
Brooks, Mr: chocolate cups and saucers, 118
Brown, Mr: lay-overs, 115; napkins, 114; sheets, 115; tablecloths, 113
Brown, Mrs: fish pan, copper, 112; plate warmer, brass, 112; skillet, brass, 112; window-curtains, scarlet, 108
Burton, Mrs: tablecloths, 114; sheets 115
Bush, Mr: blankets, underblanket, quilt and mattress, 110; oilcloth, for the stairs, 110; tallboy, mahogany, 110

Bush, Squire: table, marble, on carved frame, 109
Butler, Sir Richard: box of counters, 119; tea-chest, mahogany, 119
Byrne, Mr: butter casks, 113
Byrne, Mrs: towels, 114
Calahan, Mr: silver, candlesticks and sockets, 117; —, slop-bowl, 117; jug, glass, 119; towels, 114
Carr, Mrs: feather-bed, bolster, blankets and rug, 111; tablecloths, 114
Cash, Mr: coffee-cups, tea-cups, hearty cup, 118
Caterwood, Mr: pistol, Highland, 120; ring, gold, 118; sheets, 115, 116; tablecloth, 115; tea-pot, china, 118; towels, 114
Caufield, Mr: punch-ladle, silver, 117
Chapman, Mr: pictures, hunting-pieces, 108
Clifton, Mr: soup spoon, silver, 117
Cole, Squire: chimney-piece, marble and coving stones, 109
Coope, Mrs: branches, brass, 110
Coppin, Dean: pot, iron, 113; tea-bell, glass, 119
Coppinger, Mrs: blankets and Manchester quilt, 109
Corker, Mrs: candlestick, silver, 118; sheets, 115, 116; towels, 114
Creagh, Mr: pictures, fruit-pieces, 108
Croaker, Mrs: tea-cups and saucers, 118
Cromie, Mr: globe and iron, 112; knife basket, copper, 112
Delahunty, Mr: bucket, 111
Demsey, Mr: bed- and window-curtains, camlet, 109; dining-table, mahogany, 108; feather-bed, bolster and pillows, 109
Dogan, Mr: window-curtains, 110
Dogan, Mrs: bedstead, feather-bed,

bolster, blankets and quilt, 111; dressing glass, 110; flock-bed, bolster, blankets and quilt, 111
Dwire, Mr: bed, calamanco, 110
Easte, Mrs: towels, 114; —, French, 114
Ewing, Mr: bed, blue cloth, 111; table, deal, 110
Fairbrother, Mr: chimney-piece, marble, and coving stones, 109
Feild, Mr: pillowcases, 114; salvers, silver, 117
Fenlon, Mr: coal boxes, 111
FitzGibbon, Mrs: knives and forks, silver, 117
French, Miss: saffron pot and saucer, 119
Gardiner, Luke (*c.* 1690–1755) [prob.]: bed and counterpane, wrought-work, 109; chairs, rush-bottomed, 109; prints of the fortifications, 108
Gash, Mrs: swords, broad, 121
Gibbons, Mrs: cruets, 120; decanters, 120; —, glass, 120; glass baskets, 119; plate and salver, glass, 120
Gledstones, Mr: bowl and dish, 118; dishes and plates, 119
Gooding, Mr: cans, silver, 117; tablecloths, 114
Gorge, Mrs: coffee-cups, 119; custard cups, 119; decanters, 120; jar, china, 118; jug and mug, 120; punchbowl, 119; soup-plates, 119; sweetmeat glasses, 119; water bottles, 120
Gormon, Mr: blankets and rug, 111; gun, bullet, 120; knife-basket, 112; knives and forks, ivory-handled, 112; pasty pan, grater and rolling pin, 112; plates, pewter, 112; tables, deal, 110, 113; tea-kettle, copper, 112
Gormon, Mrs: sheets, 114, 115, 116; tablecloth, 114

365

Groves, Miss: jug, glass, 119
Hamilton, Mrs: Turkey carpet, 108
Hannel, Mr: dressing glass, 109; maps, 109
Harmon, Mrs: napkins, 113, 114; tablecloth, 114
Harvey, or Harvy, Mrs: blunderbuss; 121; gun, 121
Hasale, Mr: grate (moving) and furniture, 109
Hearne, Daniel (archdeacon of Cashel): clock, 110; cupboard, shelved, 108; window-curtains, scarlet camlet, 108
Hearne, Mrs: blunderbuss, 121; cushions for kneeling, velvet, 109; pistols, case of, 121
Helsham, Mrs: napkins, 113
Hoey, Mr: hand board, Indian, 119; pictures: the Seeches [?], 108; —, landscapes for overdoors, 108; sales [unspecified], 118
Hunt, Mr: silver, coffee-pot, 117; —, monteith, 116; —, punch-ladle, 117; —, salver, 117; —, sauce-boats, 117; —, saucers, 117; —, spoon tray, scalloped, 118; —, sugar-bowl, 117
Hutchinson, Mrs: cheese-toaster, copper, 112; smoothing-irons, 111
Hutchinson, Samuel (dean of Dromore) [poss.]: bottle drain, 111; pictures: still-life flower-pieces, 108
Ivres, Mr: sword, silver-hilted, 121
Ivres, Mrs: sword, mourning, 121
Johnson, Mr: plates, 119
Johnson, Mrs: chest, walnut, 109; dressing table, oak, 110
Kenedy, Mr: pictures (figure-pieces): *The Kiss Returned* [two pictures], 109
Kenton, Mrs: napkins, 113, 114; tablecloth, 114
Lee, Mr: branches and shades, 108
Levison, Captain: coffee-pot, copper, 112; cruet-frame, 120; dishes, 119; mortar, brass, 111; napkins, 113; tablecloth, 113; tea-board, mahogany, 120; teaspoons, silver, 116
Longfield, Mr: napkins, 114; tablecloths, 114
Mane, Mr: ring, Turkey stone, 118; shoe and knee buckles, silver, 118; snuff-box, mother-of-pearl, 118

Marshal, Mr: colander, copper, 112; crane and hooks, 111; dishes, pewter, 113; dredging-box and basting ladle, copper, 112; hanging rack, 120; kettle, copper, and cover, 112; mortar, brass, 112; napkins, 113; —, diaper, 113; niggars, 111; pillion and shag cloth, 120; rings, diamond, 118; roasting-jack, 111; saucepan and cover, copper, 112; scales, pair of, 112; sheets, 115, 116; snuffbox, gold, 118; soup-dishes: pewter, 113; —, silver, 117; stewpan, copper, and cover, 112; tablecloths, 113, 114; —, diaper, 113; trunk for plate, 120
Maude, Elizabeth, *née* Cornwallis, Baroness: plates, china, 119
Maude, Miss: toaster, ebony, 118
McMullan, Mrs: napkins, diaper, 113; tablecloths, 114; —, diaper, 113
Moore, Mr: bed, blue cloth, 111; blankets and quilt, 110; branches, gilt, 108; candlesticks, flat, 111; chairs, elbow, and stools, 109; chest of drawers, deal, 111; chimney-glass, gilt-framed, 108; cistern, mahogany, 108; close-stool, 110; dresser, deal, 111; dripping-pan, iron, and frame, 112; feather-bed, bolster, blankets and rug, 111; grate (moving), with brass fender and irons, 108; —, with furniture, 110; ladle and skimmer, brass, and flesh fork, 112; ladle, copper, and skimmer, brass, 112; locks, iron, 110, 111; press, 108; sconce, gilt-framed, 108; Scotch carpet, 108; warming-pan, 112
Moorehead, Mr: sheets, 115, 116
Moorel, Mr: knocker and handle, brass, rolling stone and bin, 120
Murry, Mr: chicken coop, 111; chopper and salt-box, 113; dishes, pewter, 112; forms, 113; gridiron and frying-pan, 112; plate drain, 113; powdering tub, 113; roasting-jack spits, 111; sheets, 114, 115, 116; standing racks, 111; tongs, fire shovel and poker, 111; trays and bowl, 113
Nenoe, Mr: chest of drawers, oak, 110; coconut cups, silver-mounted, 118;

desk, oak, 109; plates, pewter, 112; table tops, marble, 109; tea-chest, mahogany, 119; washing-tubs and pail, 113
O'Hara, Mrs: shoe and knee buckles, silver, 118; stock buckles, silver, 118; tablecloths, 114
Owens, Mrs: dressing table, oak, 109
Parsons, Squire: quadrille box, 119
Parsons, Sir Laurence: box of counters, 119; decanters, glass, 120; memorial glass, 'The Glorious Memory', 13, 120; wine-glasses, 120
Pearson, Miss: china, broken, 119
Peters, Mrs: plates, pewter, 112
Preston, Mr: lay-overs, 114; tablecloths, 114; teaspoons, silver, 116
Preston, Squire: gilt work: chimney-glass, 108; —, sconce, 108; silver, candlesticks, 117; —, chamber pot, 116; —, cup and cover, 116; —, marrow spoon, 117; —, snuffers and dish, 117; —, tea-kettle and lamp, 116
Putland, Miss: water tumrels [?], 119
Putland, Mr: silver, cup and cover, 116; – scalloped dish, 117; wine-glasses, 120
Reeves, Mr: chairs and elbow chair, rush-bottomed, 110; door-locks, mahogany-cased, 110; water casks, 111
Reilly, Catty: dressing glass, 111
Reily, Mr: dining-table, oak, 109
Ribton, Mr: blunderbuss, 121
Rieves, Mr: sword, silver-hilted, 121
Roberts, Miss: tablecloth, 113
Rogers, Mr: crocks, 113
Rudgate, Mrs: castors, 120; decanters, glass, 120
Sands, Mrs: sheets, 115
Sanford, Mrs: jug, glass, 120; napkins, 113
Saurin, Louis (dean of St Patrick's Cathedral, Ardagh) [poss.]: chairs with leather seats, 108
Scofier, Mr: print, 108
Seamor, Mr: knife-box, copper, 112
Shouldam, Mr: beer-glasses, 120
Smith, Councillor: chairs and armed chairs with tapestry seats, 108; picture, landscape, 108

Smith, Mr: basin-stand, mahogany, 109; bellows, 112

Spring, Mr: bed, four-post, and window-curtains, 110; carpets, 111; salts and salt-spoons, silver, 116

Staples, Mrs: strainer, silver, 117

St Leger, Elizabeth, Lady: dishes, china, 119

Stradwell, Mr: couteau, 121

Stuard, Mrs: stand and lamp, silver, 116

Tayler, Mr: cups, agate, 118; ewer, china, with silver spout, 118; fire screen, 2-leafed, 108; plates, 119

Thomas, Mr: branches, brass, 109

Townly, Mr: gun, 121

Troy, Mrs: blankets, 110; chairs, rush-bottomed, 110; dressing glass, 109; feather-beds, bolsters and pillow, 110; powdering tub, 113; sheets, 116; tea-tongs, silver, 116

Vandeleur, Mrs: gallon, copper, 111; lamp, copper, 111; napkins, 113; sheets, 114; towels, French, 114

Walker, Mr: cane with gold head, 118; china-ware, canisters, 118; —, punchbowl, 119; —, tea-pots, 118; diamond jewellery: buckle, 118; —, ring, 118; household linen: napkins, 116; —, sheets, 115, 116; —, tablecloths, 114; silver, candlesticks, hand, 117; —, castors, 117; —, coconut cups (silver-mounted), 118; —, cream ewer, 117; —, extinguisher, 117; —, knives, forks and spoons, 117; —, saucepan, 117; —, spoons, 117

Walsh, Mr: mug, glass, 120; sword, silver-hilted, 121

Walsh, Mrs: salts and salt-spoons, silver, 116; tablecloths, 113

Warburton, Mrs: beer-glasses, 120; canisters, sugar mallet and hammer, 120; card-table, mahogany, 109; chairs, oak, 113; chest, walnut, 110; coal, 120; —, cannel, 120; decanters, 120; —, silver, 116; dining-table, mahogany, 108; door-locks, brass, 120; dressing box, 110; feather-beds, bolsters and pillows, 109, 110; fish-plate, pewter, 112; flasket, twig, 111; forms, 113; glass-basket, 112; grate (moving): with brass fender and irons, 109; —, with furniture, 110; gun, screw-barrel, 120; lay-overs, 115; napkins, 113, 115; pot, iron, 113; powdering tub, 113; quilt, damask, 120; quilting, French, 116; rummer, glass, 119; saucepan, copper, 112; sheets, 115, 120; sideboard table, mahogany, 108; sweetmeat glasses, 119; sweetmeat stands, glass, 119; tablecloths, 113, 114, 120; —, diaper, 113; tapestry-hangings, 109; tea napkins, 115; tea-table, mahogany, 109; towels, 114; trippets, 113; water glasses, 119, 120; —, with bowl and salts, 120; water tumrels [?], 119

Ward, Mr: shoe and knee buckles, silver, 118; supper table, mahogany, 108; tablecloths, 114; towels, 114

Wesbit, Mr: picture, sea-piece, 108

White, Mrs: silver, salvers, 117; —, soup-ladle, 117

Wilcocks, Mr: napkins, 115

Woulfe, Mr: coconut cup, 119; cups, saucers and delft bowl, 119

APPENDIX II

Books in the second Duchess of Ormonde's closet at Kilkenny Castle, 1705

The titles shown below were all first published by 1705 and are given as suggested identifications of books listed in abridged form in the inventory. See p. 36.

Allestree, Richard (attrib.): *The Art of Contentment*; *The Causes of the Decay of Christian Piety*; *The Government of the Tongue*; *The Ladies Calling*; *The Lively Oracles Given to Us*

Assheton, William: *A Seasonable Apology for the Honours and Revenues of the Clergy*; *The Cases of Scandal and Persecution*

Bible, in quarto, in 2 parts

Book of Common Prayer, The [several copies]

Cotton, Charles: *The Wonders of the Peake*

Cross, Nicholas: *The Cynosura: or, A saving star that leads to eternity discovered amidst the celestial orbs of David's Psalms, by way of paraphrase upon the Miserere*

Evelyn, John: *Silva: or, A discourse of forest-trees and the propagation of timber*

Gunning, Peter: *The Holy Fast of Lent Defended against All its Prophaners: or, A discourse shewing that Lent-fast was first taught the world by the apostles*

Hyde, Edward (1st Earl of Clarendon): *Animadversions upon a Book, Intituled,* Fanaticism Fanatically Imputed to the Catholick Church, by Dr Stillingfleet, and the Imputation Refuted and Retorted by S. C. [Serenus Cressy] *by a Person of Honour*

Littleton, Adam: *Sixty-one Sermons Preached Mostly on Publick Occasions*

Lloyd, David: *Dying and Dead Men's Living Words: or, Fair warnings to a careless world*

Lucy, William: A *Treatise on the Nature of a Minister* [poss.]

Mendoza, Antonio Hurtado de (transl. from the Spanish by Sir Richard Fanshawe): *To Love Only for Love Sake: A dramatick romance* [*Querer por Solo Querer*]

Morley, George: *A Sermon Preached at the Magnificent Coronation of the Most High and Mighty King Charles the II*[d.]

Mossom, Robert (bishop of Derry): *Sion's Prospect in it's* [sic] *First View: Presented in a summary of divine truths, consenting with the Faith profess'd by the Church of England* [poss.]

Mountagu, Walter: *Miscellanea Spiritualia: or, Devout essays*

Patrick, Symon: *The Parable of the Pilgrim: Written to a friend*

Sall [or Saul], Andrew: *A Sermon Preached at Christ-Church in Dublin, before the Lord Lieutenant and Council* [poss.]; *True Catholic and Apostolic Faith Maintain'd in the Church of England*

Seignior, George: *God, the King, and the Church: (To wit) Government both civil and sacred together instituted*

Taylor, Jeremy: *A Discourse of the Nature, Offices, and Measures of Friendship: With rules of conducting it*

Temple, William: *Observations upon the United Provinces of the Netherlands*

Trial of Mr Morden, The [work not identified]

Woodford, S.: *A Paraphrase upon the Psalms of David*

APPENDIX III

Books in the study at the bishop's mansion house, Elphin, County Roscommon, 1740

PLATE 54
Title page from Bernhard Varen's *Descriptio Regni Japoniæ*, Amsterdam, Elzevir, 1649

The titles shown below were all first published by 1740 and are given as suggested identifications of books listed in abridged form in the inventory. See pp. 95–103. Numbers in parentheses refer to the numbering of the books in the inventory.

Adam, Melchior: *Vitæ Germanorum Medicorum* (287), 101; *Vitæ Germanorum Philosophorum* (159), 98

Addison, Joseph: *The Free-holder* [prob. the Dublin edition, first published in 1716 by the bookseller George Grierson, of *The Free-holder: or, Political essays* (the book edition of essays published as issues of Addison's periodical the *Free-Holder*)] (140), 97

Aldrovandi, Ulisse: *De Piscibus libri 5: et De cetis lib. unus* [poss.] (244), 100

Allestree, Richard (attrib.): *The Whole Duty of Man: Laid down in a plain and familiar way, for the use of all, but especially the meanest reader* (89), 96

Amelot de la Houssaie, Abraham Nicolas (Nicolas Amelot de la Houssaye): *Mémoires historiques, politiques, critiques, et littéraires* [poss.] (62), 96

Ames, William: *Bellarminus Enervatus a Guilielmo Amesio S.S. Theologiæ Doctore in Academia Franekerana in Quatuor Tomos Divisus* (16), 95; *Bellarminus Enervatus, sive, Disputationes Anti-Bellarminianæ* [variant title] (366), 103

Anacreon of Teos: *Odæ et Fragmenta* (318), 102

Anonymous: *A Lady's Religion: In a letter to the Honourable Lady Howard* ['By a Divine of the Church of England'] (304), 101

Anonymous: *Law Quibbles: or, A treatise of the evasions, tricks, turns and quibbles commonly used in the profession of the law* [published by Thomas Corbett at Addison's Head without Temple-Bar]: (174), 98

Anonymous: *The Several Acts for the Improvement of the Hempen and Flaxen Manufactures in this Kingdom* [published in Dublin by Andrew Brooke, prob.] (308), 101

Appian of Alexandria: *Appiani Alexandrini Romanarum Historiarum* (173), 98

Aquinas, Thomas: *Summa Theologica* (254), 100

Aristoteles (Aristotle): *Poetics* (52), 96

Athenaeus (Isaac Casaubon, ed.): *Deipnosophistæ* [prob.] (253), 100

Athenagoras [of Athens]: *Libellus pro Christianis. Oratio de resurrectione cadaverum* (57), 96

Augustine, Saint (Aurelius Augustine, bishop of Hippo): [book not specified] (328), 102

Aulus Gellius: *Noctes Atticæ* [prob.] (317), 102

Ausonius, Decimus Magnus, from Burdigala [Bordeaux]: *Opera* (345), 102

Bacon, Sir Francis: *The Essays: or, Councils, civil and moral, of Sir Francis Bacon, Lord Verulam, Viscount St. Alban* (312), 102; (104), 97; *Of the Proficience and Advancement of Learning, Divine and Humane* (201), 99

Baglione, Giovanni: *Le vite de' pittori, scultori, architetti, ed intagliatori* [poss.] (217), 99

Baronius, Caesar (Cesare Baronio): *Annales Ecclesiastici* (44), 95

Barrow, Isaac: *The Works of the Learned Isaac Barrow, D.D. Late Master of Trinity College in Cambridge. Published by the reverend Dr. Tillotson, dean of Canterbury* (263), 100

Bellarmino, Cardinal Roberto: *De Scriptoribus Ecclesiasticis* (90), 96

Bellori, Giovanni Pietro: *Le vite de' pittori, scultori, architetti, ed architetti moderni* [poss.] (217), 99

Belon, Pierre (du Mans): *Les Observations de plusieurs singularitez et choses memorables, trouvées en Grèce, Asie, Judée, Egypte, Arabie, & autres pays estranges* (207), 99; *Petri Bellonii Cenomani, Plurimarum Singularum et Memorabilium Rerum in Græcia, Asia, Ægyto, Judæa, Arabia, aliisq. Exteris Provinciis ab Ipso Conspectarum Observationes* (transl. into Latin by Carolus Clusius [Charles de l'Écluse]) (380), 103

Bennet, Thomas: *A Defence of the Discourse of Schism* (55), 96; *An Essay on the Thirty Nine Articles of Religion* (176), 98

Berkeley, George (later bishop of Cloyne) (attrib.): *The Ladies Library: Written by a lady* (published by Richard Steele, 1714) (65), 96

Béroalde de Verville, François: *Le Moyen de parvenir. Œuvre contenant la raison de tout ce qui a esté, est, et sera* (127), 97

Beveridge, William (bishop of St Asaph): *The Church-Catechism Explained: For the use of the Diocese of St. Asaph* (305), 101

Bibles: (226), 99; (248), 100; in Latin (377), 103; *Biblia, ad Vetustissima Exemplaria Castigata* [a Latin edition of the Vulgate Bible, edited by Hentenius (Johnannes Henten)] (379), 103; Biblia Græca (237), 100; New Testament [in French] (70), 96; New Testament in Greek and Latin (Desiderius Erasmus, ed., with his revision of the Latin Vulgate): *Novum Instrumentum Omne ab*

Erasmo Roterodamo Recognitum et Emendatum (368), 103. See also Mill, John

Blankaart, Steven: *Lexicon Medicum Græco-Latinum* (18), 95

Blount, Thomas: *Fragmenta Antiquitatis: or, Antient tenures of land and jocular customs of some mannors made publick for the diversion of some, and instruction of others / by T. B. of the Inner-Temple, Esquire* (98), 97

Boate, Gerard: *Ireland's Natural History: Being a true and ample description of its situation, greatness, shape and nature . . .* (301), 101; — (et al.): *Natural History of Ireland* (211), 99

Boccaccio, Giovanni: *Le Decameron de maistre Jean Bocace Florentin. Traduict d'italien en françoys par maistre Antoine Le Maçon, conseiller du roi, & tresorier de l'extraordinaire de ses guerres* [poss.] (93), 96; *La geneologia de gli dei de Gentili* (178), 98

Böhm, Johannes: *Mores, Leges et Ritus Omnium Gentium* (319), 102

Boileau-Despréaux, Nicolas: *Œuvres diverses du Sieur Boileau Despreaux : avec* Le Traité du sublime*, ou du merveilleux dans le discours, traduit du grec de Longin* (19), 95

Bolton, Sir Richard: *A Justice of Peace for Ireland* (256), 100

Borel, Pierre: *Historiæ et Observationes Medico-Physicæ* (154), 98

Botero, Giovanni: *Mundus Imperiorum* [Latin transl.] (382), 103; *Le relationi universali* (213), 99

Boxhorn, Marcus Zuerius van: *Historia Universalis Sacra et Profana* (215), 99

Briet, Philippe: *Acute Dicta Omnium Veterum Poetarum Latinorum* (8), 95

Bull, George: *Vindication of the Church of England from the Errors and Corruptions of the Church of Rome* (160), 98

Burnet, Gilbert: *Burnet's Travels: or, A collection of letters to the Hon. Robert Boyle, Esq: Containing, an account of what seem'd most remarkable in travelling thro' Switzerland, Italy,*

some parts of Germany, &c. in the years 1685, and 1686 (5), 95; *A Discourse of the Pastoral Care* (100), 97; *An Exposition of the Church Catechism: For the use of the diocese of Sarum* (157), 98; *An Exposition of the Thirty-Nine Articles of the Church of England* (260), 100

Butler, Charles; *Monarchia Fœminina, sive, Apium historia* [translation into Latin by Richard Richardson of *The Feminine Monarchie: or, The historie of bees*] (298), 101

Butler, Samuel: *Hudibras* (190), 99

Buxtorf, Johann (the elder): *Thesaurus Grammaticus Linguæ Sanctæ Hebrææ* (86), 96

Cabassut, Jean: *Notitia Ecclesiastica Historiarum, Conciliorum et Canonum Invicem Collatorum* (259), 100

Caesar, Caius Julius: *Inuictissimi Īperatoris Cōmentaria: Seculorū iniuria antea difficilia: & valde mēdosa* [poss.] (360), 103; *Opera cum notis variorum* [Frans van Oudendorp, ed., poss.] (188), 99

Calvin, Jean: *Institution de la religion chrestienne* (138), 97

Camden, William: *Camdenus Illustratus, sive, Græca grammatica luculenta* [poss.] (281), 101; *Institutio Græcæ Grammatices Compendiaria in Usum Regiæ Scholæ Westmonasteriensis* (6), 95

Cardano, Girolamo [or Geronimo]: *Arcana Politica, sive, De prudentia civil* (333), 102; *De Subtilitate* (60), 96

Castellio, Sebastian (Sébastien Châteillon): *Liturgia, seu, Liber precum communium, et administrationis sacramentorum, aliorumque rituum et ceremoniarum in ecclesia anglicana receptus* (275), 101

Cato, Marcus Porcius: *De Agricultura, sive, De re rustica, liber* (303), 101

Caussin, Nicolas: *La Cour sainte ou Institution chrétienne des grands* (92), 96

Cave, William: *Scriptorum Ecclesiasticorum Historia Literaria* (252), 100

Celsus, Aurelius Cornelius: *De Re Medica* (285), 101

Cheyne, G.: *An Essay of Health and Long Life* (132), 97

Chillingworth, William: *The Works of William Chillingworth, M.A.* (204), 99

Cicero, Marcus Tullius: *De Officiis* (139), 97; *De Philosophia* (356), 103; *Epistulæ* (320 and 330), 102; *Epistulæ ad Familiares* (351), 103; *Opera* [odd vol. of *Epistulæ*] (364), 103; *Opera* [poss.] (243), 100; *Orationes* (146a), 98; *Philosophicorum*, vol. 1 (47), 96

Clenardus, Nicolaus (Nicolaas Cleynaerts): *Institutiones Linguæ Grecæ* (68), 96

Clerke, Francis: *Praxis in Curiis Ecclesiaticis* (published by Thomas Bladen, printer and bookseller, also chaplain to James Butler, 1st Duke of Ormonde) (131), 97

Cocker, Edward: *The Young Clerk's Tutor Enlarged: Being a most useful collection of the best presidents [sic] of recognizances, obligations, conditions, acquittances, bills of sale, warrants of attorney, &c.* (12), 95

Coke, Sir Edward: *The First Part of the Institutes of the Laws of England: or, A commentary upon Littleton: not the name of the author only, but of the law itself* (4), 95

Conybeare, John: *A Defence of Reveal'd Religion against the Exceptions of a Late Writer, in His Book, Intituled, Christianity as Old as the Creation, &c.* (199), 99

Corranza, Bartolomé: *Summa Conciliorum Summorunque Pontificum a Sancto Petro usque ad Julium Tertium* (91), 96

Corvinus, Johannes Arnoldi [born Joannes Arnoldsz. Ravens]: *Digesta per Aphorismos Strictim Explicata* (346), 102

Coster, Franciscus: *Apologia Catholica* (117), 97

Council of Trent: *Catechismus ad Parochos ex Decreto Concilii Tridentini Editus: Et Pii V. Pont. Max. Jussu Promulgatus* (46), 96

Court of Exchequer: *The Arguments of Sir Richard Hutton, Knight, One of the Judges of the Common Pleas, and Sir George Croke, Knight, One of the Judges of the Kings Bench* (291), 101

Cumberland, Richard: *De Legibus Naturæ Disquisitio Philosophica: In qua earum forma, summa capita, ordo, promulgatio & obligatio è rerum natura investigantur quinetiam elementa philosophiæ Hobbianæ cùm moralis tum civilis, considerantur & refutantur* (103), 97; (195), 99

Curio, Johannes: *Medicina Salernitana: id est, Conservandæ; bonæ* (336), 102

Della Porta, Giovanni Battista: *Fisonomia dell'uomo e la celeste* (137), 97

Demosthenes: *Orationes* [in English] (316), 102

Diodati, Giovanni: *Annotationes in Biblia* (238), 100

Dopping, Anthony (bishop of Meath): *Tractatus de Visitationibus Episcopalibus* (326), 102

Duncombe, Giles: *Tryals Per Pais: or, The law of England concerning juries by Nisi Prius, &c.* (180), 98

Dupin, Louis Ellies [also Du Pin]: *A Compendious History of the Church: From the beginning of the world to this present time* [transl. from the French] (315), 102; *A Complete Method of Studying Divinity: or, A regular course of theological studies, digested into a new method* [transl. from the French] (156), 98

Dutton, Matthew: *The Law of Masters and Servants in Ireland* (182), 98

Eachard, John: *The Grounds and Occasions of the Contempt of the Clergy and Religion Enquired into: In a letter written to R. L.* [prob. Sir Roger L'Estrange] (297), 101

Ellis, John: *Articulorum XXXIX Ecclesiæ Anglicanæ Defensio* (279), 101

Erasmus, Desiderius: *Colloquia* (162), 98; *Erasmi Roterodami Colloquia Familiaria* [poss. edition by Guillaume Binauld, bookseller, Dublin] (74), 96; *De Duplici Copia Verborum ac Rerum Commentarii . . . Addita sunt nunc recens in usum studiosa juventutis doctissima commentaria à M. Veltkirchio conscripta* [poss.] (2), 95; *Stultitæ Laus* [The Praise of Folly] (130), 97; — (preface by): *Historiæ Romanæ Scriptorum Latinorum Veterum* (247), 100

Estienne, Charles: *Dictionarium Historicum, Geographicum, Poeticum* (210), 99

Estienne, Henri: *Apologie pour Hérodote. Ou traité de la conformité des merveilles anciennes avec les modernes* (51), 96

Estienne, Robert: *Hebræa, Chaldæa, Græca & Latina Nomina Virorum, Mulierum, Populorum, Idolorum, Urbium, Fluviorum, Montium, Cæterorúmque Locorum quæ in Bibliis Leguntur . . .* (361), 103

Euripides: *Tragedies* (362), 103

Eustachius a Sancto Paulo (Eustache Asseline): *Ethica, sive, Summa moralis disciplinæ, in tres partes divisa* (3), 95

Fanzini, Federico: *Descrittione di Roma antica, e moderna* [poss.] (321), 102

Fleetwood, William: *Four Sermons* [prob.] (105), 97

Florio, John (compiler): *A Worlde of Wordes, or, Most copious and exact dictionarie in Italian and English* (272), 101

Foster, James: *Sermons* (232), 100

Fuller, Thomas: *Church History of Britain, from the Birth of Jesus Christ until the Year MDCXLVIII* (257), 100

Gaguin, Robert: *Rerum Gallicarum Annales* (348), 102

Gale, Thomas: *Opuscula Mythologica Physica et Ethica Græce et Latine* (229), 100

Garthwait, Henry: *Monotessaron, the Evangelical Harmonie* (381), 103

Gastrell, Francis: *The Certainty and Necessity of Religion in General: or, The first grounds and principles of humane duty establish'd in eight sermons preach'd at S. Martins in the Fields* [poss.] (165), 98

Geddes, Michael: *A Tract Proving the Adoration of Images, Purgatory etc., Were Unknown in the Spanish Church in the 8th Century* (151), 98

Gerberon, Gabriel: *La Règle des mœurs contre les fausses maximes de la morale corrompuë* (335), 102

Gibson, Edmund: *Synodus Anglicana* (168), 98

Gibson, Thomas: *Anatomy of Humane Bodies Epitomized* (153), 98

Godwin [Godwyn], Thomas: *Moses and Aaron: Civil and ecclesiastical rites, used by the ancient Hebrewes* (234), 100

's Gravesande, Willem Jacob (transl. from the Latin by John Theophilus Desaguliers): *Mathematical Elements of Natural Philosophy Confirmed by Experiments: or, An introduction to Sir Isaac Newton's philosophy* (170), 98

Gray, Thomas: *Bibliotheca Parochialis, etc.: or, A Scheme of such theological and other heads, as seem requisite to be perus'd, or occasionally consulted, by the reverend clergy* (27), 95

Grew, Nehemiah: *The Anatomy of Plants* (203), 99

Grotius, Hugo: *De Jure Belli ac Pacis* (231), 100; *De Veritate Religionæ* (365), 103

Hanmer, Meredith (transl.): *The Ancient Ecclesiasticall Histories of the First Six Hundred Years after Christ: Written in the Greek tongue by three learned historiographers, Eusebius, Socrates, and Evagrius* (369), 103

Harrington, James: *The Oceana* [poss. 1737 Dublin edition, called, *The Oceana of James Harrington, Esq; and His Other Works . . .* (268), 100

Harvey, William: *Exercitatio Anatomica de Circulatione Sanguinis* (309), 102

Haunold, Christoph: *Controversiarum de Justitia et Jure Privatorum Universo* [prob.] (87), 96

Hederich, Benjamin: *Lexicon Manuale Græcum. Omnibus sui generis lexicis, quæ quidem exstant, longe locupletius, eaque ratione in tres partes . . . divisum* [poss.] (270b), 101

Helwig, Christoph: *Theatrum Historicum* (372), 103; [poss.] (133), 97

Hierocles of Alexandria: *Hieroclis Philosophi Alexandrini Commentarius in Aurea Carmina* [poss.] (58), 96

Hieronymus, Eusebius Sophronius. *See* Jerome, Saint

Hildebrand, Friedrich: *Antiquitates Potissimum Romanæ è Rosino aliisque in Compendium Contractæ, et juxta ordinem alphabeti dispositæ* (95), 96

Hippocrates: *Aphorismi Græce et Latine* (310), 102

Horatius (Louis Desprez, ed.): *Opera: Interpretatione & Notis* [In usum serenissimi Delphini series] (224), 99

Hunt, Edward: *An Abridgment of all the Statutes in Ireland, in the Reigns of Queen Anne and King George* (148), 98

Huygens, Christiaan: *Celestial Worlds Discover'd: or, Conjectures concerning the inhabitants, plants and productions of the worlds in the planets* (323), 102

Jansen, Cornelius: *Paraphrasis in Omnes Psalmos Davidicos* (375), 103

Jerome, Saint: *Opera* [perhaps edited by Marianus Victorius Reatinus] (241), 100

Jewel, John: *Apologia Ecclesiæ Anglicanæ* (347), 102; *The Apology of the Church of England* [translation of the *Apologia* by Thomas Cheyne] (123), 97

Johnson, John: *The Clergy-Man's Vade Mecum: or, An account of the antient and present Church of England the duties and rights of the clergy and of their privileges and hardships* (273), 101

Jonson, Ben: *Comedies and Tragedies* (43), 95

Juvenalis, Decimus Junius: (John Dryden *et al.*, transl.): *The Satires of Decimus Junius Juvenalis* ['Translated into English verse by Mr. Dryden and several other eminent Hands'] (10), 95; — *and Aulus Persius Flaccus* (Louis Desprez, ed.): *Satiræ: Interpretatione ac notis* [In usum serenissimi Delphini series] (225), 99

Kettlewell, John: *The Measures of Christian Obedience* (194), 99

King, William (bishop of Derry, later archbishop of Dublin): *De Origine Mali* (146b), 98

Lactantius, Lucius Caecilius Firmianus: *Opera* (85), 96

Lambarde, William: *A Perambulation of Kent: Conteining the description,*

hystorie, and customes of that shyre (126), 97

Le Clerc, Jean: *A Supplement to Dr. Hammond's* Paraphrase and Annotations on the New Testament (230), 100

Le Grand, Antoine: *Historia Sacra a Mundi Exordio ad Constantini Magni Imperium Deducta* (111), 97; *Philosophia Veterum e Mente Renati Descartes, More Scholastico Breviter Digesta* (110), 97

Leusden, Johannes: *Clavis Græca Novi Testamenti* (280), 101; *Compendium Græcum Novi Testamenti* (277), 101

Lewis, John: *The History of the Life and Sufferings of the Reverend and Learned John Wicliffe, D.D.* (191), 99

Lipsius, Justus: *Tractatus Peculiares Octo: Ad cognoscendam historiam romanum apprime utiles* (14), 95

Littleton, Adam (compiler): *Linguæ Romanæ Dictionarium Luculentum Novum: A new dictionary in five alphabets* (249), 100

Livius, Titus (Livy): *Decadis* [with annotations by Marcus Antonius Coccius Sabellicus] (261), 100

Locke, John: *An Essay Concerning Humane Understanding* (255), 100

Lower, Richard: *Tractatus de Corde: Item de motu & colore sanguinis, et chyli in eum transitu* (354), 103

Lucretius (Titus Lucretius Carus): *Of the Nature of Things* (Thomas Creech, transl.), (196), 99; *De Rerum Natura* (101), 97; (271), 101

Lunadoro, Girolamo: *Relatione della corte di Roma e dei riti da osservarsi in essa, e de' suoi magistrati, & officii, con la loro distinta giurisdittione* (54), 96

Lundorp, Michael Caspar: *Continuationis Joannis Sleidani* De Statu Religionis et Reipublicæ: *Tomus tertius* (41), 95

Lyons, Israel: *The Scholar's Instructor: An Hebrew grammar* [poss.] (341), 102

Machiavelli, Niccolò: *Discorsi sopra la prima deca di Tito Livio* (29), 95; *Machivel's Discourses upon the First Decade of T. Livius* (45), 95; *Florentini Disputationum, de Republica, quas*

*Discurs Nuncupavit, Libri III...
Ex italico latini facti* (11), 95;

Macrobius, Ambrosius Aurelius
Theodosius: *Opera* (122), 97

Manzini, Giovanni Battista: *Il trionfo
del pennello. Raccolta d'alcune
compositioni nate à gloria d'un ratto
d'Helena di Guido* (282), 101

Marcus Aurelius, Emperor of Rome:
De Seipso seu Vita sua (338), 102

Matthiæ, Christian: *Theatrum
Historicum Theoretico-Practicum*
[poss.] (133), 97

Maurice, Henry: *A Defence of Diocesan
Episcopacy: In answer to a book of
Mr. David Clarkson, lately published,
entituled,* Primitive Episcopacy
(166), 98

Maynwaring, Everard: *The Frequent,
but Unsuspected Progress of Pains,
Inflammations, Tumors, Apostems,
Ulcers, Cancers, Gangrenes, and
Mortifications Internal* (383), 103

Mela, Pomponius: *De Situ Orbis* (325), 102

Melanchthone, Philipp, and Kaspar
Peucer: *Chronicon Carionis* [Johann
Carion's *Chronicles* revised] (67), 96

Melander, Otho: *Jocorum atque Seriorum
cum Novorum, tum Selectorum atque
Memorabilium* (331), 102

Meriton, George: *An Exact Abridgment
of all the Publick Printed Irish Statutes
now in Force: From the third year of
the reign of King Edward the Second,
to the end of the last sessions of
Parliament, in the tenth year of His
present Majesty's reign, King William
the Third* (149), 98

Merula, Paulus: *Antiquitates
Romanorum: De sacrificiis,
sacerdotibus, legibus, comitiis et
præmiis quæ militiam sequebantur*
(214), 99

Mill, John (ed.): *Novum Testamentum
Græcum, cum Lectionibus
Variantibus . . .* (274), 101

Milton, John: *Paradise Regain'd* (339), 102

Molière (Jean-Baptiste Poquelin):
Œuvres de Molière (337), 102

Molloy, Charles: *De Jure Maritimo et
Navali: or, A treatise of affairs
maritime and of commerce* (192), 99

Molyneux, William: *The Case of Ireland's
Being Bound by Acts of Parliament in
England, Stated* (322), 102

Montaigne, Michel de: *Essays of
Michael Seigneur de Montaigne*
['made English by Charles Cotton,
Esq.'; this edition poss.] (370), 103

Mornay, Philippe de, seigneur du
Plessis-Marly: *The Mysterie of
Iniquitie: that is to say, The historie of
the papacie* ['Englished by Samson
Lennard'] (371), 103

Newton, Sir Isaac: *The Chronology of
Ancient Kingdoms Amended* (300), 101

Nicolson, William (bishop of Derry):
*The Irish Historical Library: Pointing
at most of the authors and records in
print or in manuscript which may be
serviceable to compilers of a general
history of Ireland* (175), 98

Officium Clerici Pacis: *A Book of
Indictments, Informations, Appeals
and Inquisitions* (221), 99

Origen (William Spencer, ed.): *Contra
Celsum* (208), 99

Ovid (Publius Ovidius Naso): *Epistulæ
ex Ponto* (332), 102

Panciroli, Guido: *Rerum Memorabilium*
(212), 99

Parsons, Robert: *Leicester's Common-
Wealth: Conceived, spoken and
published with most earnest
protestation of dutifull goodwill and
affection towards this realme* (311), 102

Pascal, Blaise: *The Mystery of Jesuitism:
Discovered in certain letters, written
upon occasion of the present differences
at Sorbonne between the Jansenists
and the Molinists, displaying the
pernicious maximes of the late
Casuists* [anonymous English
translation of *Les provinciales*]
(116), 97

Pasor, Georg: *Lexicon Græco-Latinum
in Testamentum Novum Domini
Nostri Jesu Christi* [prob.] (276), 101

Patrick, Simon: *The Devout Christian
Instructed how to Pray, and Give
Thanks to God: or, A book of devotions
for families, and for particular persons,
in most of the concerns of humane
life* (1), 95

Pausanias: *Græciæ Descriptio* (267), 100

Pearson, John: *An Exposition of the
Creed* (107), 97; (251), 100

Pemberton, Henry: *A View of Sir Isaac
Newton's Philosophy* [poss. a Dublin
printing in 1728] (218), 99

Petronius (Titus Petronius Arbiter)
(Pieter Burmann, ed.): *Petronius
Arbiter: Cum notis variorum et
burmanni* (114), 97

Petty, Sir William: *Political Arithmetick:
or, A discourse concerning the extent
and values of lands, people, buildings
husbandry, manufacture, commerce,
fishery, artizans, seamen, soldiers . . .*
(118), 97

Philo of Alexandria ('Philonis Judæ
Scriptoris Eloquentissimi, ac
Philosophi Summi'): *Lucubrationes
omnes quotquot haberi potuerunt*
(40), 95

Philosophical Transactions [of the
Royal Society]: no issue details
given (30), 95

Plat, Sir Hugh: *The Jewel House of Art
and Nature: Containing divers rare and
profitable inventions, together with
sundry new experiments in the art of
husbandry* (299), 101

Platina, Bartholomeo: *Historia B.
Platinæ de Vitis Pontificum
Romanorum* (206), 99

Plato (John North, ed. [prob.]): *Platonis
De Rebus Divinis: Dialogi selecti Græce
et Latine* (141), 97

Plautus: *Les Comédies de Plaute* [transl.
into French by Mademoiselle
Le Fèvre or Nicolas Gueudeville
(poss.)] (77), 96

Pliny the Younger: *Epistulæ* (177), 98

Plutarch: *Moralia* (61), 96

Polybius of Megalopolis (transl. into
Latin from the original Greek by
Niccolò Perotti): *Polybii
Megalopolitani Historiarum* (355), 103

Pratt, Samuel (dean of Rochester
[decanus roffensis]): *Grammaticæ
Latinæ in Usum Principis Juventutis
Britannicæ Compendium* (128), 97

Procopius of Caesaria: *Arcana Historia,
qui est liber nonus historiarum*
(262), 100

Appendix III

Purchas, Samuel: *Purchas his Pilgrimage: or, Relations of the world and the religions observed in all ages and places discovered, from the creation unto this present* (373), 103

Quincy, John: *Medicina Statica: Being the Aphorisms of Sanctorius, translated into English, with large explanations* (197), 99; *Pharmacopœia Officinalis & Extemporanea: or, A complete English dispensatory* (189), 99

Rapin, René: *Hortorum Libri IV* (284), 101; *Reflexions sur la poëtique d'Aristote, et sur les ouvrages des poëtes anciens et modernes*, or 2nd edition 'reveuë & augmentée': *Reflexions sur la poëtique de ce temps, et sur les ouvrages des poëtes anciens et modernes*, and [prob.] —: *Reflexions sur l'usage de l'éloquence de ce temps* (120), 97

Rastell, John: *Expositiones Terminorum Legum Anglorum (Exposicions of yᵉ termys of yᵉ law of England)* [poss.] (187), 99; Statutes (abridged in English by J. Rastell) [poss.] (179), 98

Ray, John: *The Wisdom of God Manifested in the Works of the Creation* (72), 96; — (ed.): *A Collection of Curious Travels and Voyages* (97), 97

Repertorie of Letters, The [unidentifed work, perhaps a letter-writing manual] (99), 97

Ricci, Bartolomeo: *Apparatus Latinae Locutionis: Ex M. T. Cicerone, Caesare, Sallustio, Terentio, Plauto, ad Herennium, Asconio, Celso, ac De Re Rustica* [poss.] (236), 100

Rice, Stephen: *The Great Law of the Crown: or, A sure guide for all persons concerned in the bishop's courts* (283), 101

Richer, Edmond: *Historia Conciliorum Generalium* (82), 96

Robbins, N.: *An Exact Abridgment of all the Irish Statutes: From the first session of Parliament in the third year of the reign of King Edward II. to the end of the eighth year of His Present Majesty King George II, or else: An Exact Abridgment of the Ecclesiastical*

Statutes in Force in Ireland (269), 100

Rogers, Thomas: *Faith, Doctrine and Religion, Professed and Protected in the Realm of England, and Dominions of the Same Expressed in Thirty Nine Articles* (169), 98

Rohault, Jacques: *Jacobi Rohaulti Physica: Latinè vertit, recensuit, et adnotationibus ex illustrissimi Isaaci Newtoni* (transl. of *Traité de physique* into Latin and notes by Samuel Clarke) [prob.] (193), 99

Rous, Francis: *Mella Patrum* (136), 97

Saint-German, Christopher: *Two Dialogues in English, between a Doctor of Divinity, and a Student in the Laws of England, of the Grounds of the Said Laws and of Conscience* (9), 95

Sanctius, Franciscus Brocensis (Francisco Sánchez de las Brozas): *Minerva, sive, De causis latinæ linguæ commentarius* (83), 96

Sanctorius, Sanctorius: *De Medicina Statica Aphorismi* (313), 102

Sanderson, Robert: *De Juramenti Promisorii Obligatione Prælectiones Septem* (69), 96; *De Obligatione Conscientiæ: Prælectiones secem Oxonii in schola theologica* (307), 101; (352), 103; (359), 103

Sanford, John: *A Grammer [sic] or Introduction to the Italian Tongue* [poss.] (88), 96

Sansovino, Francesco: *Du gouvernement et administration de divers estats, royaumes & republiques [sic], tant anciennes que modernes* [transl. from the Italian] (53), 96

Sarpi, Paolo (pseud.: Pietro Soave Polano): *Historia del Concilio Tridentino* (209), 99; *The History of the Council of Trent* (transl. by Nathaniel Brent, prob.) (265), 100

Scaliger, Joseph Justus (1540–1609): *Catulli, Tibulli, Propertii Nova Editio* (94), 96

Scaliger, Julius Caesar (1484–1558): *De Causis Linguæ Latinæ* (363), 103; (75), 96

Scapula, Johan[nes]: *Lexicon Græco-Latinum: E probatis auctoribus*

locupletatum, cum indicibus, et Græco & Latino, auctis, & correctis (245), 100

Schindler, Valentin: *Lexicon Pentaglotton, Hebraicum, Chaldaicum, Syriacum, Talmudico-Rabbinicum, Arabicum* (250), 100

Schola Medica Salernitana (attrib.): *Regimen Sanitatis Salernitanum* [poss.] (73), 96

Schrevel, Cornelis: *Lexicon Manuale Græco-Latinum et Latino-Græcum* [poss.] (270b), 101

Scot, Alexander: *Apparatus Latinæ Locutionis in Usum Studiosæ Juventutis* [poss.] (236), 100

Selden, John: *De Dis Syris, Syntagmata II* (71), 96; *Jani Anglorum Facies Altera* (349), 102; *De Synedriis et Præfecturis Juridicis Veterum Ebræorum* (289), 101

Senault, Jean-François: *De l'usage des passions* (358), 103

Severus, Sulpicius: *Historia Sacra* (293), 101

Shakespeare, William: *Works* (25), 95

Sheppard, William: *The Court-Keeper's Guide for the Keeping of Lawdays and Courts Baron* (13), 95; *The Parson's Guide: or, The law of tithes* (278), 101

Shipton, James: *Pharmacopœiæ Collegii Regalis Londini Remedia Omnia Succinctè Descripta* (15), 95

Sigonio, Carlo: *Historiarum de Occidentali Imperio Libri XX* (378), 103

Simmler, Josias: *Helvetiorum Respublica: Diversorum autorum quorum nonnulli nunc primum in lucem prodeunt* (329), 102

Simon, Richard: *The History of the Original and Progress of Ecclesiastical Revenues* [transl. from the French] (96), 97

Sleidan, Johann: *Galliæ Descriptio* [poss. as supplement to Philippe de Commines's *De Rebus Gestis Ludovici eius Nominis Undecimi, Galliarum Regis, & Caroli, Burgundiæ Ducis*] (78), 96

Smith, Sir Thomas: *De Republica Anglorum Libri Tres* (296), 101

Solleysell, Jacques de (Sir William Hope, transl.): *The Compleat Horse-Man: or, Perfect farrier* (155), 98

Sophocles: *Tragediæ* (367), 103

Spanheim, Ezekiel: *Dissertationes de Præstantia et Usu Numismatum Antiquorum* (222), 99

Sparrow, Anthony: *A Collection of Articles, Injunctions, Canons, Orders, Ordinances and Constitutions Ecclesiastical, with Other Publick Records of the Church of England, Chiefly in the Times of K. Edward VI., Q. Elizabeth, K. James, and K. Charles I ...* (22), 95

Spelman, Henry: *Concilia, Decreta, Leges, Constitutiones, in Re Ecclesiarum Orbis Britannici* (270a), 100; — (et al.); *Tithes too Hot to be Touched: Certain treatises, wherein is shewen that tithes are due* (376), 103

Spencer, John: *De Legibus Hebræorum Ritualibus* (374), 103

Spenser, Edmund: *The Faerie Queen* (233), 100

Steell, Robert: *A Treatise of Conic Sections* (102), 97

Stella, Didacus (Diego de Estella): *Contemptus Vanitatum Mundi* (135), 97

Stellato, Marcello Palingenio: *Zodiacus Vitæ: hoc est, De hominis vita, studio, ac moribus optimè instituendis, libri XII* (7), 95

Stillingfleet, Edward: *A Discourse Concerning the Unreasonableness of a New Separation, on Account of the Oaths: With an answer to the history of passive obedience, so far as relates to them* (219), 99; *Irenicum; a Weapon-Salve for the Churches Wound: or, The divine right of particular forms of church-government* (112), 97; *Origines Britannicæ: or, The antiquities of the British churches* (205), 99; *Origines Sacræ* (125), 97

Strabo: *Strabonis Geographica* (202), 99

Strada, Famiano: *De Bello Belgico* (109), 97; *Prolusiones Academicæ, Oratoriæ, Historicæ, Poeticæ* (343), 102

Strauch, Aegidius (Richard Sault, transl.): *Breviarium Chronologicum: or, A treatise describing the terms and most celebrated characters, periods and epocha's us'd in chronology* (227), 99

Sturm, Johann Christoph: *Mathesis Enucleata: or, The elements of the mathematicks* (228), 99; *Mathesis Juvenilis* (186), 99

Suetonius [Gaius Suetonius Tranquillus]: unspecified work (353), 103

Swinburne, Henry: *A Briefe Treatise of Testaments and Last Wills* (220), 99

Sydenham, Thomas: *Observationes Medicæ circa Morborum Acutorum Historiam et Curationem* (124), 97

Tacitus, Gaius Cornelius: *Opera* [In usum serenissimi Delphini series, poss.; Julien Pichon, ed.] (66), 96; unspecified work (334), 102

Tanner, Thomas: *Notitia Monastica: or, A Short history of the religious houses in England and Wales* (198), 99

Tasso, Torquato: *L'Aminte du Tasse. Pastorale* ['Traduite de l'italien en vers françois'] (306), 101

Taylor, Jeremy (bishop of Down, Connor and Dromore): *A Discourse of the Liberty of Prophesying* (20), 95; *A Dissuasive from Popery* (106), 97; *Holy Living and Holy Dying* (115), 97; *Sacred Order and Offices of Episcopacie by Divine Institution, Apostolicall Tradition, and Catholique Practice* (235), 100

Taylor, John: *Thesaurarium Mathematicæ: or, The treasury of the mathematicks* (152), 98

Theocritus: unspecified work (42), 95

Thou, Jacques Auguste de (Thuanus): unspecified work (286), 101

Tindal, Matthew: *A Defence of the Rights of the Christian Church* (150), 98

Torriano, Giovanni: *The Italian Reviv'd: or, The introduction to the Italian tongue* [poss.] (88), 96

Torsellini, Horatio: *Ristretto dell' historie del mondo* (56), 96

Totti, Pompilio (and/or Filippo de' Rossi): *Ritratto di Roma antica* (79), 96

Tyrrell, James: *A Brief Disquisition of the Law of Nature* (164), 98

Ussher, James, archbishop of Armagh: *An Answer to a Challenge Made by a Jesuite in Ireland: Wherein, the judgement of antiquity in the points questioned is truly delivered, and the noveltie of the now Romish doctrine plainly discovered* (324), 102; *Britannicarum Ecclesiarum Antiquitates* (290), 101; *Polycarpi et Ignatii Epistolae ... Dissertatio* (28), 95

Varen, Bernhard: *Descriptio Regni Japoniæ* (344), 102; *Geographia Generalis: In qua affectiones generales telluris explicantur* (142), 97

Vaughan, Rice: *A Discourse of Coin and Coinage: The first invention, use, matter, forms, proportions and differences, ancient and modern* (327), 102

Vaure, Claude: *La Cour de Rome la saincte. Ou traité des cérémonies & coustumes qui s'observent dans la ville de Rome ...* (121), 97

Venator, Daniel: *Analysis Methodica Juris Pontificii* (134), 97

Veneroni, Giovanni de: *Le Maître italien dans sa dernière perfection* (302), 101

Vergil, Polydore, of Urbino: *De rerum inventoribus* (350), 102; (59), 96

Virgil (Publius Vergilius Maro): *Opera* (342), 102

Voltaire (François-Marie Arouet): *The History of Charles XII; King of Sweden* (200), 99

Wake, William: *The Principles of the Christian Religion Explained: In a brief commentary upon the church-catechism* (158), 98

Walker, Obadiah: *Of Education: Especially of Young Gentlemen. In Two Parts* (49), 96

Ward, John: *A Young Mathematician's Guide: Being a plain and easy introduction to the mathematicks* (21), 95

Ware, Sir James: *The Antiquities and History of Ireland* (264), 100

Weissmann, Christian Eberhard: *Introductio in Memorabilia Ecclesiastica Historiæ Sacræ Novi Testamenti* (216), 99

Welchman, Edward: *XXXIX Articuli, Ecclesiæ Anglicanæ* (171), 98

Wells, Edward: *The Young Gentleman's Astronomy, Chronology, and Dialling* (129), 97

Appendix III

Wheare, Degory: *Relectiones Hyemales, de Ratione & Methodo Legendi utrasq[ue] Historias, Civiles & Ecclesiasticas: Quibus historici probatissimi, non solùm ordine quo sunt legendi catenatim recensentur, sed doctorum etiam virorum de singulis judicia subnectuntur . . .* (50), 96

Whiston, William: *Prælectiones Physico-Mathematicæ Cantabrigiæ in Scholis Publicis Habitæ: Quibus philosophia illustrissimi Newtoni mathematica explicatius traditur, & facilius demonstratur: cometographia etiam Halleiana commentariolo illustratur* (163), 98

Wilkins, John: *Mathematical Magick: or, The wonders that may be performed by mechanical geometry* (76), 96

Willet, Andrew: *Synopsis Papismi, that is, A generall view of papistrie* (266), 100

Willis, Thomas: *Cerebri Anatome; cui Accessit Nervorum Descriptio & Usus* (340), 102; *Pharmaceutice Rationalis, sive, Diatriba de medicamentorum operationibus in humano corpore* (17), 95

Willughby, Francis: *De Historia Piscium Libri Quatuor* [poss.] (244), 100

Wolleb, Johannes: *The Abridgment of Christian Divinitie: So exactly and methodically compiled, that it leads us as it were by the hand to the reading of the Holy Scriptures, ordering of common-places, understanding of controversies, clearing of some cases of conscience* ['faithfully translated (from Latin) into English, and in some obscure places cleared and enlarged, by Alexander Ross'] (357), 103

Womack, Laurence: *The Result of False Principles: or, Error convicted by its own evidence* (292), 101

Wood, Thomas: *An Institute of the Laws of England: or, The laws of England in their natural order, according to common use* (258), 100

Wood, William: *A Survey of Trade: In four parts* (181), 98

Wynne, John: *An Abridgment of Mr. Locke's Essay Concerning Human Understanding* (167), 98

Xenophon: [school edition, work not specified: *Historia Græca* perhaps] (223), 99; *Memorabilia Socratis* (113), 97

Zouch, Richard: *Elementa Jurisprudentiæ Definitionibus, Regulis & Sententiis Selectioribus Juris Civilis Illustrata* (294), 101

APPENDIX IV

Books at Newbridge House, County Dublin, 1821

The titles shown below were all first published by 1820 and are given as suggested identifications of books listed in abridged form in the inventory. See pp. 320–2.

Addison, Joseph: *The Evidences of the Christian Religion*, 320

Æsop: *Æsop's Fables*, 322; Sir Roger L'Estrange's version in English, 321

Akenside, Mark: *The Pleasures of Imagination* [Suttaby edition, poss.], 322

Alemán, Mateo: *Guzman de Alfarache* [poss. in translation]: *The Rogue: or, The Life of Guzman de Alfarache*, 321

Allestree, Richard: *The Whole Duty of Man, Laid down in a Plain and Familiar Way, for the Use of All, but Especially the Meanest Reader*, 320

Anonymous: *Anastatia: or, The memoirs of the Chevalier Laroux* [written by a lady: edition published 1797 in Dublin, perhaps; *see also* Thomas Hope's *Anastasius*], 321

Anonymous: *Arabian Nights Entertainments: Consisting of one thousand and one stories . . .* [translated into English from the French version of Antoine Galland, poss.], 321

Anonymous: *Calliope: Collection of Poems, Legendary and Pathetic* [poss.], 322

Anonymous: *The Laurel: Containing various branches of poetry*, 322

Anonymous: *Spirit of English Wit: or, Post-chaise companion*, 321

Anonymous: *A Sure Guide for His Majesties Justices of Peace: Plainly shewing their office, duty, and power, and the duties of the several officers of the counties, hundreds, and parishes, (viz.) sheriffs, county-treasurers, bridewell-masters, constables, overseers of the poor, surveyors of the high-wayes, and church-wardens, &c.* [poss.], 321

Barrett, Eaton Stannard: *The Heroine: or, Adventures of Cherubina*, 321; *Women: A poem*, Henry Colbourn, London, 1818, 2nd edition [though not 'dialogues', poss.], 321

Bates, Ely: *Rural Philosophy: or, Reflections on Knowledge, Virtue, and Happiness*, Longman and Rees, London, 1804, 3rd edition, 321

Beattie, James (*et al.*): *The Wreath: containing The Minstrel and other favorite poems* [Suttaby & Corrall edition, poss.], 322

Beresford, James: *The Miseries of Human Life: or, The groans of Samuel Sensitive, and Timothy Testy*, 321

Berquin, Arnaud: *L'Ami des enfans*, 322

Bibles, 320; [prob. incl. folio edition of 1723, John Baskett, with extra titles and illustrations provided by Richard Ware], 320

Bickersteth, Edward: *Scripture Help, Designed to Assist in Reading the Bible Profitably*, 320

Blair, Hugh: *A Companion to the Altar: Shewing the nature and necessity of a sacramental preparation, in order to our worthy receiving the Holy Communion*, 320

Bloomfield, Nathaniel: *An Essay on War, in Blank Verse; Honington Green, a Ballad; The Culprit, an Elegy; and Other Poems...* [poss.], 322

Bloomfield, Robert: *Poems* [book not specified], 322

Boileau-Despréaux, Nicolas: *Œuvres de Boileau Despréaux* [poss.], 322

Book on Cookery: not identified, poss. Hudson and Donat's *The New Practice of Cookery, Pastry, Baking, and Preserving*, first pub. 1804, 321

Bossuet, Jacques-Bénigne: *Discours sur l'histoire universelle*, 322

Bourdaloue, Louis et al.: *Chefs-d'œuvre d'éloquence chrétienne, ou sermons de Bourdaloue, Bossuet, Fénélon et Massillon*, 322

Brooke, Henry (attrib.): *A New System of Fairery: or, A collection of fairy tales entirely new*, printed by S. Powell, Dublin, 1750, 321, 378 [*illus.*]

Brooke, Richard: *The General Gazetteer: or, Compendious geographical dictionary*, 320

Brown, Thomas, the Younger [pseudonym for Thomas Moore, poet]: *Intercepted Letters: or, The Twopenny Post-Bag*, 322

Buchan, William: *Domestic Medicine*, 321

Bunyan, John: *The Pilgrim's Progress*, Sowler and Russell, Manchester, 1795, 320

Burder, George: *Village Sermons*, 320

Burn, Richard, et al.: *The Justice of the Peace, and Parish Officer*, 321

Butler, Samuel: *Hudibras*, 322

Buxton, Thomas Fowell: *An Inquiry, whether Crime and Misery are Produced or Prevented, by Our Present System of Prison Discipline*, 321

Campbell, Archibald: *A Voyage round the World from 1806 to 1812: In which

377

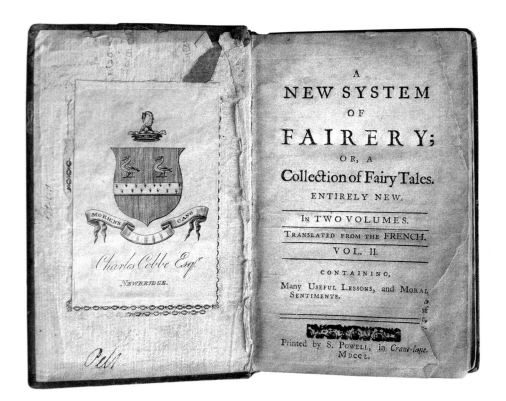

PLATE 55
Henry Brooke (attrib.): *A New System of Fairery*, book published in Dublin in 1750: title page of volume II; with Charles Cobbe's bookplate on facing page

Japan, Kamschatka, the Aleutian Islands, and the Sandwich Islands were visited..., 321

Chambaud, Lewis: *Exercises to the Rules and Construction of French-Speech* [edition published in Dublin in 1762 by James Potts and Samuel Watson, poss.], 322; *A Grammar of the French Tongue*, 322

Charrière, Isabelle de: *Les Trois Femmes. Nouvelle de l'abbé de la Tour*, 322

Chateaubriand, François-René de: *Atala*, 321

Chetwood, William Rufus: *A General History of the Stage: From its origin in Greece down to the present time* [poss.], 321

Churchill, Charles: *The Poetical Works of Charles Churchill* [Dublin 1780 edition, perhaps], 322

Clapham, Samuel (George Pretyman, ed.): *An Abridgment of the Lord Bishop of Lincoln's Elements of Christian Theology, for the Use of Families*, F. C. and J. Rivington, London, 1804, 2nd edition, 320

Collins, William: *The Poems of William Collins* [Suttaby & Corrall edition, poss.], 322

Cooper, Edward: *Practical and Familiar Sermons: Designed for parochial and domestic instruction*, T. Cadell and W. Davies, London, 1811, 2nd edition, 320; *Sermons Chiefly Designed to Elucidate Some of the Leading Doctrines of the Gospel*, T. Cadell and W. Davies, London, 1810, 4th edition, 320

Cowper, William: *Poems by William Cowper* [or his translation of Homer's *Illiad*, perhaps], 322

Crébillon, Claude-Prosper Jolyot de: *Tanzaï et Néadarné : Histoire japonoise*, 321

Crossman, Henry: *An Introduction to the Knowledge of the Christian Religion*, 320

Cunningham, John: *Poems, Chiefly Pastoral* [poss.], 322; *The Poetical Works of John Cunningham* [poss.], 322

Cunningham, John William: *A World without Souls*, 320; *The Velvet Cushion*, T. Cadell and W. Davies, London, 1815, 8th edition, 321

Damberger, Christian Frederick: *Travels through the Interior of Africa, from the Cape of Good Hope to Morocco ... between the Years 1781 and 1797* (poss.), 321

Debrett, John: *Debrett's Correct Peerage of England, Scotland and Ireland*, 321

Defoe, Daniel: *The Life and Most Surprising Adventures of Robinson Crusoe, of York, Mariner* [title of the c. 1818 Dublin edition], 321

Deletanville, Thomas: *A New French Dictionary, in Two Parts*, 1 vol., 322

Derham, William: *Astro-Theology: or, A demonstration of the being and attributes of God, from a survey of the heavens*, 320

Devis, Ellin: *The Accidence: or, First rudiments of English grammar: Designed for the use of young ladies*, 320; *An Introduction to Geography: For the use of Mrs. Devis's little society*, 320; *Miscellaneous Lessons,*

Designed for the Use of Young ladies: On a new plan, 320

Dickson, Adam: *The Husbandry of the Ancients*, 321

Doddridge, Philip: *The Rise and Progress of Religion in the Soul*, 320

Dodsley, Robert (transl.): *The Economy of Human Life: Complete in two parts: Translated from an Indian manuscript*, 321

D'Oyley, Catherine: *The History of the Life and Death of Our Blessed Saviour*, 320

Dryden, John (incl. life and notes by Samuel Derrick): *The Miscellaneous Works of John Dryden, Esq: Containing all his original poems, tales, and translations*, J. and R. Tonson, London, 1763, 4 vols, 322

Edgeworth, Maria and Edgeworth, R. L. [Richard Lovell]: *Practical Education*, J. Johnson and Co., London, 1811, 3rd edition, 320

Edgeworth, Richard Lovell: *Essays on Professional Education*, 320

Eton, William: *A Survey of the Turkish Empire*, 321

Faber, George Stanley: *A Dissertation on the Prophecies, that Have Been Fulfilled, Are now Fulfilling, or Will hereafter Be Fulfilled*, 320

Flavell, John: *A Saint Indeed: or, The great work of a Christian opened and pressed*, 320

Fleury, Claude: *A Short Historical Catechism: Containing an abridgement of sacred history, and of the Christian doctrine. Taken from the French of Abbé Fleury*, 320

Florian, Jean-Pierre Claris de: *La Bonne Mère, comédie en un acte et en prose*, 322

Garth, Samuel: *The Dispensary: A poem: In six cantos*, 322

Gay, John: *Fables*, 322

Geography: work not identified, 320

Gessner, Salomon: *The Death of Abel* [translated from the German], 321

Gilpin, William: *Exposition of the New Testament*, 320; *Lectures on the Catechism of the Church of England*, 320

Girard, Gabriel: *Synonymes françois* [poss.], 322

Gisborne, Thomas: *Sermons Principally Designed to Illustrate and to Enforce Christian Morality*, T. Cadell and W. Davies, London, 1813, 3rd edition, 320

Goldsmith, Oliver: *Goldsmith's History of the Earth and Animated Nature, Abridged: Containing the natural history of animals, birds, fishes, reptiles, & insects*, 321; *The History of England: An abridgement of the history of England: From the invasion of Julius Caesar to the death of George II* [perhaps this single volume], 321; *The Poetical Works of Oliver Goldsmith* [Suttaby & Corrall edition, poss.], 322

Gordon, Thomas (ed.): *The Works of Tacitus: With political discourses upon that author, by Thomas Gordon, Esq*, 321

Gregory, John: *A Father's Legacy to his Daughters*, 321

Grey, Richard: *Memoria Technica: or, A new method of artificial memory*, 321

Grosvenor, Benjamin: *The Mourner: or, The afflicted relieved*, 321

Haley, William: *Three Plays: With a preface, including dramatic observations of the late Lieutenant-General Burgoyne* [poss.], 322

Hamilton, Elizabeth: *Hints Addressed to the Patrons and Directors of Schools* [with reference to the Plan of Education by Johann Heinrich Pestalozzi], 321

Harrison & Company: *The Novelists' Magazine*, 321

Hervey, James: *Theron & Aspasio: or, A series of dialogues and letters, upon the most important and interesting subjects*, 320

Histoire de France: book not specified, 322

Histoire romaine: book not specified, 322

Hope, Thomas: *Anastasius: or, Memoirs of a Greek*, John Murray, London, 1820, 3rd edition (poss.), 321

Horne, George: *Letters on Infidelity*, 320

Hutchinson, Lucy: *Memoirs of the Life of Colonel Hutchinson: Governor of Nottingham Castle and town*, 321

Hwass, Christian (fils): *Voyage sentimental en Suisse*, 322

Jackson, Mrs John: *Dialogues on the Doctrines and Duties of Christianity: Intended for the instruction of the young*, Rivington, *et al.* London, 1806, 320

Jenyns, Soame: *A View of the Internal Evidence of Christian Religion*, 320

Johnson, Samuel: *A Dictionary of the English Language; In which the words are deduced from their originals, and authorized by the names of the writers in whose works they are found. Abstracted from the folio edition, by the author, Samuel Johnson, A.M. To which is prefixed, a grammar of the English language*, J. F. and C. Rivington, L. Davis, W. Owen, T. Longman *et al.*, 2 vols, London, 1786, 320; *The History of Rasselas, Prince of Abyssinia: A Tale*, 321; *The Idler*, 321; *The Works of Samuel Johnson, LL.D: A new edition in six volumes: with an essay on his life and genius, by Arthur Murphy, Esq.*, Luke White, Dublin, 1793, 321

Josephus, Titus Flavius: *Antiquities of the Jews* [poss., in abridgement], 320

Journals of the House of Commons, 321

Junius: *The Letters of Junius* [Suttaby edition, poss.], 321

Keatinge, Henry S. (publisher): *The Holy Bible Explained: or, The Old and New Testament digested and illustrated*, 320

Kempis, Thomas à: work not specified, 320

Kett, Henry: *Elements of General Knowledge: Introductory to useful books in the principal branches of literature and science*, 320

Kirkby, John: *The Capacity and Extent of the Human Understanding: Exemplified in the extraordinary case of Automathes; a young nobleman who was accidentally left upon a desolate island and continued nineteen years in that solitary state separate from all human society*, 321

Appendix IV

Klopstock, Friedrich Gottlieb (Klamer Schmidt ed.): *Klopstock and His Friends: A series of familiar letters, written between the years 1750 and 1803*, 321

Knox, Vicesimus: *Sermons: Chiefly intended to promote faith, hope, and charity*, 320

La Croix, François Pétis de [transl. into English by William King from the French version]: *The Persian and Turkish Tales, Compleat* [Watson's British Classics edition perhaps], 321

Ladies' Pocket Library, The [published by John Archer, Dublin, 1790, poss.], 321

Lamb, Charles (attrib.): *A Book Explaining the Ranks and Dignities of British Society, The* [published by Tabart and Co, London, in their Juvenile Library], 321

Leadbeater, Mary: *Cottage Dialogues among the Irish Peasantry*, 321; *The Landlord's Friend*, 321

L'Écluse des Loges, Pierre Mathurin de l' (ed.): *Memoirs of Maximilian de Bethune, Duke of Sully, Prime Minister of Henry the Great* ('Newly translated from the French edition of M. de L'Ecluse'), 321

Ledwich, Edward: *The Antiquities of Ireland*, 321

Leland, Thomas: *The History of Ireland*, 321

Lempriere, William: *A Tour from Gibraltar to Tangier, Sallee, Mogodore, Santa Cruz, Tarudant, and Thence over Mount Atlas to Morocco*, 321

Le Sage [Lesage], Alain René: *The Adventures of Gil Blas of Santillane* [poss. Tobias Smollett's translation], 321

L'Estrange, Sir Roger: *Fables of Æsop and Other Eminent Mythologists*, 321

Little, Thomas [pseudonym for Thomas Moore]: *Poetical Works of the Late Thomas Little, Esq.* [prob.], 322

Locke, John: *Some Thoughts Concerning Education*, 321

Lyttelton, George: *The History of England: From the earliest dawn*

of authentic record to the ultimate ratification of the General Peace of 1802, 321

Macpherson, James: *The Works of Ossian &c: Containing the poetical works of James Macpherson Esq*, 321

Mant, Richard: poetical work not specified, 322

Marmontel, Jean-François: *Belisarius* [poss.], 321

Mavor, William Fordyce: *The British Tourists: or Traveller's pocket companion, through England, Wales, Scotland, and Ireland*, 321

Mawe, Thomas and Abercrombie, John: *Every Man his Own Gardener*, 321

Milner, Joseph & Milner, Isaac: *The History of the Church of Christ*, T. Cadell and W. Davies, London, 1812, 3rd edition, 320

Milton, John: Poetical works not specified, 322

Mirone, Mr. de [pseudonym for Pierre Lambert de Saumery]: *Anecdotes vénitiennes et turques: ou, Nouveaux mémoires du Comte de Bonneval depuis son arrivée à Venise jusqu'à son exil dans l'isle de Chio, au mois de mars*, 322

Mitchell, Archibald: *India Courier*, 321

Molesworth, Robert: *Short Course of Standing Rules for the Government and Conduct of an Army* [poss.], 321

Montgomery, James: poetical work not specified, 322

More, Hannah: *Christian Morals*, T. Cadell and W. Davies, London, 1813, 4th edition, 320; *Coelebs in Search of a Wife*, 321; *An Essay on the Character and Practical Writings of Saint Paul*, T. Cadell and W. Davies, London, 1815, 4th edition, 320; *Practical Piety: or, The influence of the religion of the heart on the conduct of the life*, 320

More, Hannah (*et al.*): *Cheap Repository Tracts* [poss.], 320

Moreau, Simeon: *A Tour to Cheltenham Spa: or, Gloucestershire Displayed*, 321

Morell, Sir Charles [pseudonym for James Ridley]: *The Tales of the Genii* [in Walker's British Classics edition perhaps], 321

Mortimer, Thomas: *The Student's Pocket Dictionary*, 320

Nelson, Robert: *A Companion for the Festivals and Fasts of the Church of England*, 320; *The Practice of True Devotion*, 320

New Bath Guide, The: or, Useful pocket companion, 321

Owen, William: *Book of Roads: or, A description of the roads of Great Britain*, 321

Oxford Prize Poems: Being a collection of such English poems as have at various times obtained prizes in the University of Oxford, 322

Paley, William: *Natural Theology: or, Evidences of the existence and attributes of the Deity, collected from the appearances of nature*, 320; *Sermons and Tracts*, 320

Park, Mungo: *Travels in the Interior Districts of Africa* [poss.], 321

Parnell, Thomas: *Poems by Thomas Parnell, D.D.* [poss.], 322

Penn, John: *Critical, Poetical, and Dramatic Works*, 321

Percy, Sholto and Reuben: *Percy Anecdotes: Original and select*, 321

Perrin, John [Jean-Baptiste Perrin]: *A Grammar of the French Tongue: Founded on the decisions of the French Academy*, 322; *Instructive and Entertaining Exercises, with the Rules of the French Syntax* [poss. 1789 or 1796 edition published in Dublin], 322

Philidor, A. D. [pseudonym for François André Danican]: *Analysis of the Game of Chess*, 321

Pindar, Peter [pseudonym for John Wolcot]: *The First Part of Peter Pindar's Poems* [poss. 1791 Dublin edition], 322

Pope, Alexander: *Imitations of Horace* [poss.], 322; *Messiah: A sacred eclogue, in imitation of Virgil's* Pollio [poss.], 322; *Pope's Poetical Works* [Walker's British Classics edition perhaps], 322; Work as translator: *Illiad of Homer, The*, 322; *Odyssey of Homer, The*, 322; co-translator: *Metamorphoses* by Ovid [poss.], 322

Porteus, Beilby: *Lectures on the Gospel of St. Matthew: Delivered in the parish church of St. James, Westminster*, T. Cadell and W. Davies, London, 1815, 14th edition, 320; *Summary of the Principal Evidences for the Truth and Divine Origin of the Christian Revelation, A*, 320

Pott, Joseph Holden: *Elementary Discourses, Designed for the Use of Young Persons after Confirmation*, 320

prayer books, 320

Prior, Matthew: *The poetical works of Matthew Prior* [poss.], 322

psalms, book of [*Psalms of David as Sung in Newtown Barry Church*, John Watlen, London, 1811 (poss.)], 320

Reynolds, John: *A Compassionate Address to the Christian World*, 320

Riccobuoni, Luigi: *A General History of the Stage: A general history of the stage, from its origin* [poss.], 321

Robertson, William: [transl. of *Abrégé de l'histoire grecque* by Pons-Augustin Alletz]: *The History of Ancient Greece, from the Earliest Times Till It Became a Roman Province*, 320; *The Works of William Robertson … To which is prefixed an account of his life and writings by the Rev. Alex. Stewart* [prob.], 321

Robinson, Thomas: *Scripture Characters: or, A practical improvement of the principal histories in the Old and New Testament*, Mathews and Leigh, London, 1808, 320

Rollin, Charles: *The Ancient History of the Egyptians, Carthaginians, Assyrians, Babylonians, Medes and Persians, Macedonians, and Grecians*, 321; *Histoire ancienne des Egyptiens, des Carthaginois, des Assyriens, des Babyloniens, des Mèdes et des Perses, des Macédoniens, des Grecs …* [poss.], 322;

Rowe, Elizabeth: *The Poetical Works of Mrs Elizabeth Rowe* [Suttaby & Corrall edition, poss.], 322

Rundell, Maria Eliza (*née* Ketelby) [anon.]: *A New System of Domestic Cookery: Formed upon principles of economy; and adapted to the use of private families: By a lady* [poss.], 321

Sartory, Madame de (*née* Wimpffen): *Le duc de Lauzun*, 322

Savigny, J. B. Henry, and Corréard, Alexander: *Narrative of a Voyage to Senegal in 1816: Undertaken by order of the French government, comprising an account of the shipwreck of the Medusa, the sufferings of the crew, and the various occurrences on board the raft, in the desert of Zaara, at St Louis, and at the camp of Daccard* (London, 1818, 2nd edition), 321

Scott, Thomas: *The Holy Bible, containing the Old and New Testaments with original notes, practical observations, and copious marginal references* [edition not specified], 320

scrap-book, 321

Secker, Thomas: *Archbishop Secker's Lectures on the Catechism, Arranged in Questions and Answers, for the Use of Schools and Families*, 320

Selector, The: Containing the Beauties of Gray, Goldsmith, Falconer, & Somerville [Suttaby & Corrall edition, poss.], 322

Seward, William: *Anecdotes of Some Distinguished Persons: Chiefly of the present and two preceding centuries*, 321

Shenstone, William: *The Poetical Works of William Shenstone* [poss. and in Suttaby & Corrall edition], 322

Sherlock, Thomas: *Discourses Preached on Several Occasions*, 320

sketch-book, 321

Smith, Elizabeth: *Fragments in Prose and Verse*, 321

Smith, Robert A. (ed.): *The Scotish* [sic] *Minstrel: A selection from the Vocal Melodies of Scotland, Ancient & Modern, Arr. for the Piano Forte* [poss.], 322

Spectator, The, 321

Sportsman's Dictionary, The: or, The Gentleman's Companion; for Town and Country, 321

Sterne, Laurence: *A Sentimental Journey through France and Italy*, 321

Sturm, Christoph Christian [transl. from German]: *Reflections on the Works of God, and on His Providence in the Regions of Nature, and in the Government of the Universe*, 320

Styles, John [anon.]: *A New Covering to the Velvet Cushion*, 321

Swift, Jonathan: *The Poetical Works of Jonathan Swift* [edition not specified], 322

Tansillo, Luigi (transl. from the Italian by William Roscoe): *The Nurse: A poem*, 322

Thomson, James: *The Works of James Thomson* [poss.], 321

Tomkins, E. (compiler): *Poems on Various Subjects: Selected to enforce the practice of virtue, and to comprise, in one volume, the beauties of English poetry* [poss.], 322

Trimmer, Sarah: *An Abridgment of the New Testament*, 320; *An Abridgment of Scripture History*, 320; *A Companion to the Book of Common Prayer*, 320; *Sacred History, Selected from the Scriptures*, 320; *A Scripture Catechism: Containing a familiar explanation of the lessons selected from the writings of the four Evangelists*, 320

Tronchet, Louis: *Picture of Paris: Being a complete guide to all the public buildings and curiosities in that metropolis* [prob.], 321

Trusler, John: *The Tablet of Memory, or historian's guide: Wherein every remarkable occurrence in our history, such as battles, sieges, conspiracies, rebellions, invasions, tryals, executions, fires, earthquakrs* [sic]*, storms, revolutions, births, marriages, deaths and every other memorable event that has happened in England and Ireland to the present time are accurately recorded…*, Peter Hoey, Dublin, 1782, 321

Tully, Miss: *Narrative of a Ten Years' Residence at Tripoli in Africa*, 321

Venn, John: *Sermons*, J. Hatchard, London, 1816, 2nd edition, 320

Villon, François: *Le Testament* [poss.], 322

Vocabulaire: work not identified, 322

Voltaire [François-Marie Arouet]: work not identified, 321; *Works*, 321

Wailly, Noël-François de: *Abrégé de la grammaire française*, 322

Wakefield, Priscilla: *Mental Improvement: or, The beauties and wonders of nature and art*, P. Wogan, Dublin, 1800, 1st edition, 321

Walker's Classics published by Walker and Edwards: volumes not specified, 320

Watson, Richard: *Two Apologies, One for Christianity, in a Series of Letters Addressed to Edward Gibbon, Esq.; the Other for the Bible, in Answer to Thomas Paine*, 320

Wells, Edward: *An Historical Geography of the Old and New Testament*, 320

White, Henry Kirk: work not specified, 321

White, James: *A Complete System of Farriery, and Veterinary Medicine Containing a Compendium of the Veterinary Art*, 321

Wilberforce, William: *A Practical View of the Prevailing Religious System of Professed Christians, in the Higher and Middle Classes in this Country: Contrasted with real Christianity*, 320

Wilson, Charles Henry: *Swiftiana*, 321

World, The [perhaps the weekly produced by Edward Moore, assisted by Horace Walpole, R. O. Cambridge, the Earl of Chesterfield, and others], 321

Young, Edward: *Night Thoughts* [poss. and in Suttaby & Corrall edition], 322

List of inventory sources

Inventories transcribed and printed with kind permission of their owners. The transcribers, Jessica Cunningham (JC), Rebecca Campion (RC) and John Adamson (JA), are shown by their initials.

BARONSCOURT, Co. Tyrone, 1782 (JC): Abercorn Papers, PRONI MS D623/D/4/1, courtesy of the Deputy Keeper of the Records, the Public Record Office of Northern Ireland.

BISHOP'S MANSION HOUSE, ELPHIN, Co. Roscommon, 1740 (JC): National Library of Ireland, Wicklow Papers, NLI MS 38,597/22 and NLI MS 38,639/25 (books in the study).

BORRIS HOUSE, Co. Carlow, 1818 (RC): Kavanagh Collection.

CAPTAIN BALFOUR'S HOUSE, 1741/2 (JC): National Library of Ireland, Townley Hall Papers, NLI MS 10,279.

CARTON HOUSE, Co. Kildare, 1818 (RC): The Carton House Inventory, 1818 (PP/CAR/1), courtesy of Castletown Foundation and OPW/Maynooth University Archive Research Centre.

CASTLECOMER HOUSE, Co. Kilkenny, 1798 (JC): National Library of Ireland, Prior-Wandesforde Papers, NLI MS 35,542 (1).

DUBLIN CASTLE, Dublin, 1707 (JC): National Library of Ireland, Ormonde Papers, NLI MS 2521.

HILLSBOROUGH CASTLE, Co. Down (JC), inventory of 1746, PRONI MS D607/B/1C; inventory of 1777, PRONI MS D607/B/13, courtesy of the Deputy Keeper of the Records, the Public Record Office of Northern Ireland.

KILKENNY CASTLE, Co. Kilkenny, 1705 (pp. 1–54: JC; pp. 55–82: JA): National Library of Ireland, Ormonde Papers, NLI MS 2524.

KILLADOON, Co. Kildare, inventories 1807–29 (JC): Clements Archive.

KILRUSH HOUSE, Freshford, Co. Kilkenny, 1750 (JC): St George family at Kilrush House.

LISMORE CASTLE, Co. Waterford, 1702/3 (JC): National Library of Ireland, Lismore Estate Papers, NLI MS 43,762.

MORRISTOWN LATTIN, Co. Kildare, 1773 (JC): National Library of Ireland, Mansfield Papers NLI MS 38,357/1; and undated supplementary document to 1773 household inventory.

MOUNT STEWART, Co. Down, 1821 (JC); china, cut glassware, linen and plate (JA): PRONI MS D654/S1/1: courtesy of the Deputy Keeper of the Records, the Public Record Office of Northern Ireland.

NEWBRIDGE HOUSE, Co. Dublin, 1821 (RC): Cobbe Papers, Hugh Cobbe Division.

NO. 10 HENRIETTA STREET, Dublin, 1772 (JC): National Library of Ireland, Gardiner Papers, NLI MS 36,617.

ST JAMES'S HOUSE, London, c. 1710 (JC): National Library of Ireland, Ormonde Papers, NLI MS 2521.

SHELTON ABBEY, Co. Wicklow, 1816 (RC): National Library of Ireland, Wicklow Papers, NLI MS 38,574/20.

List of plates

PLATE 1

Samuel Alken (1756–1815), after a drawing by Thomas Sautelle Roberts (*c.* 1760–1826): *Lismore Castle, County Waterford*, 1795, aquatint. This image is reproduced courtesy of the National Library of Ireland, NLI ET B253.

PLATE 2

Attributed by Baumstark & Delmarcel to the Gouda workshop of Pieter de Cracht (*c.* 1600–1662), woven from designs by Sir Peter Paul Rubens (1577–1640): *Marcus Valerius consecrates Decius Mus. c.* 1648, linen and wool, 164⅛ × 165¾ in. (417 × 421 cm). Courtesy of the Office of Public Works, Kilkenny Castle.

PLATE 3

Title inscribed on the front page within the bound volume of manuscripts containing the 1705 inventory of Kilkenny Castle (see pp. 31–53). This image is reproduced courtesy of the National Library of Ireland, Ormonde Papers, NLI MS 2524.

PLATES 4 and 5

Francis Place (1647–1728): *Kilkenny Castle and Saint Canice's Cathedral*, 1699, ink and wash on paper (and detail), 4¹⁵⁄₁₆ × 15⅜ in. (12.5 × 39 cm), NGI.7525. National Gallery of Ireland Collection. Photograph © The National Gallery of Ireland.

PLATE 6

Charles Brooking: *A Map of the City and Suburbs of Dublin*, 1728: detail showing a view of Dublin Castle (Maps.aa.188.72.1). Reproduced by kind permission of the Syndics of Cambridge University Library.

PLATE 7

Unknown artist, said to be after Carlo Dolci (1616–1686): *Madonna and Child*, oil on canvas, 53 × 39 in. (135 × 99 cm). Courtesy of the Office of Public Works, Kilkenny Castle.

PLATE 8

Sutton Nicholls (*fl.* 1680–1740): *St James's Square, c.* 1725, engraving, 12¾ × 17¹⁵⁄₁₆ in. (32.4 × 45.6 cm), R. H. Stephenson Bequest (E612-1929). © Victoria and Albert Museum, London.

PLATE 9

John Michael Wright (1617–1694): *Sir Neil O'Neill as an Irish chieftain*, 1680, oil on canvas, support: 91⅝ × 64¼ in. (232.7 × 163.2 cm); purchased with assistance from the Art Fund, 1957 (T00132). Tate Images, London. Note the Japanese *dō-maru* (胴丸) armour lying at O'Neill's feet. A Japanese *dō-maru* armour was sent to James I by Shōgun Tokugawa Hidetada in 1613 (now at the Royal Armouries, Leeds). We owe this reference to Joe Earle.

PLATE 10

John Brooks (*fl.* 1730–56): *Right Reverend Dr Robert Howard (1683–1740), Lord Bishop of Elphin (1730–40)*, mezzotint after a painting by Michael Dahl (1656/1659–1743). RCB Library, Dublin, Portraits of Archbishops, Bishops, Dignitaries bequeathed by Rev. Wm. A. Reynell, B.D., 1906.

PLATE 11

John Rocque (*c.* 1704–1762) (cartographer), Andrew Drury (engraver): *An Exact Survey of the City and Suburbs of Dublin, 1756*, GE DD-2987 (2657 B); detail showing the area around St Stephen's Green, Dublin. Bibliothèque nationale, Paris.

PLATE 12

Robert Furze Brettingham (1750–1820): Hillsborough Castle, drawing of the west front, 1788. Hillsborough Castle (PRONI D671/P/8/22/12). Courtesy of the Deputy Keeper of the Records, Public Record Office of Northern Ireland.

PLATE 13

Michael Dahl (1656/1659–1743) (attributed to): *Charles Boyle, 2nd Earl of Burlington and 3rd Earl of Cork (c. 1662–1704)* (detail), oil on canvas. Bridgeman Images/ Chiswick House, London. *See* plate 57 on page 387.

PLATE 14

Sir Godfrey Kneller (1646–1723): *James Butler, 2nd Duke of Ormonde (1665–1745)*, oil on canvas, 57 × 91 in. (145 × 231 cm). Oxford Portraits: University of Oxford.

PLATE 15
Artist unknown, follower of Michael Dahl (1656/1659–1743): *Mary Butler* (née *Somerset*) (*1665–1733*), *2nd Duchess of Ormonde*, oil on canvas, 39 × 25 in. (99 × 63 cm). Courtesy of the Office of Public Works, Kilkenny Castle. Photography by Vicky Comerford.

PLATE 16
Pompeo Batoni (1708–1787): *Wills Hill, 1st Earl of Hillsborough, later 1st Marquess of Downshire* (*1718–1793*), 1766, oil on canvas. Signed and dated on base of altar: POMPEIUS BATONI PINXIT/ROMÆ ANNO 1766, oil on canvas, 89½ × 63½ in. (227 × 161 cm). Collezione Ugo e Chiara Pierucci – Rome.

The Countess Margaretta (*b.* 1729) died on 19 January 1766. The earl is here depicted gazing at his late wife's likeness.

PLATE 17
Sir Joshua Reynolds, PRA (1723–1792): *Luke Gardiner, the Younger, later 1st Viscount Mountjoy* (*1745–1798*), half-length, in a beige, fur-trimmed coat, white stock and striped red waistcoat, oil on canvas, 30⅛ × 24⅝ in. (76.7 × 62.7 cm). © 2010 Christie's Images Limited.

PLATE 18
Thomas Gainsborough (1727–1788): *James Hamilton, 8th Earl of Abercorn* (*1712–1789*), 1778, oil on canvas, 87 × 57¼ in. (221.2 × 145.4 cm), 14479. bpk-Bildagentur|Bayerische Staatsgemäldesammlungen – Neue Pinakothek, Munich.

PLATE 19
Frank Lydon (1836–1917): *Baronscourt* (*c.* 1876), from Rev. F. O. Morris: *The County Seats of the Noblemen and Gentlemen of Great Britain and Ireland*, vol. IV, printed by Benjamin Fawcett, ink on paper. Private collection.
The plates in Morris's book were drawn by Alexander Francis Lydon and printed from coloured woodblocks using eight or more overlays from separate wooden blocks by Benjamin Fawcett (1808–1893) of Driffield, Yorkshire. While the retirement on 6 December 1876 of the 1st Duke of Abercorn as lord lieutenant of Ireland is stated in *Burke's Peerage* 1878, it is not mentioned in the quotation from Burke's in the passage on Baronscourt in Morris's book. Volume IV of the book, in which Baron's Court is featured, was therefore probably published in 1876 or 1877.

PLATE 20
Hugh Douglas Hamilton, RHA (1739–1808): *Susan Frances Elizabeth (Anne) Butler* (née *Wandesford*), *Countess of Ormonde* (*1754–1830*), oil on canvas, 50 × 39 in. (127 × 99 cm). Courtesy of the Office of Public Works, Kilkenny Castle.

PLATE 56
Richard Cooper II: *Madonna and Child*, engraving dated 1763, after a painting wrongly attributed to Antonio Allegri, called Correggio. The engraving has the following legend: 'To the Queen / This plate is humbly inscribed; / by Her Majesty's most devoted, and most obedient, humble servant / Rich.d Cooper. / From the Original painting of Corregio [*sic*], formerly in the Ormond collection, and now in the possession of John Butler Esq.r / Sold for the Author, at D: Wilson's Bookseller, near York Buildings, in the Strand London. ⸺ according to Act of Parl.t'

List of plates

PLATE 21
John Brooks (*fl.* 1730–56) (engraver), mezzotint after a painting by Francis Bindon (*c.* 1690–1765): *Brigadier General Richard Saint George of Woodsgift, County Kilkenny* (*d.* 1755), 1744, mezzotint sheet: 14 5/16 × 10 9/16 in. (36.6 × 26.8 cm), plate: 13 5/8 × 10 in. (34.7 × 25.3 cm), NGI.10044. National Gallery of Ireland Collection. Photograph © National Gallery of Ireland.

PLATE 22
John Brooks (*fl.* 1730–56): *Richard St George when major general*, mezzotint after a painting by Stephen Slaughter of 1744 (1920,0420.158). © The Trustees of the British Museum.

PLATE 23
Mountjoy House, No. 10 Henrietta Street, Dublin, engraving from the *Dublin Penny Journal* (Q900.b.30.2; p. 257: 1st page of issue no. 189, vol. IV, February 13, 1836). Reproduced by kind permission of the Syndics of Cambridge University Library.

PLATE 24
John Rocque (*c.* 1704–1762) (cartographer), Andrew Drury (engraver): *An Exact Survey of the City and Suburbs of Dublin*, 1756, GE DD-2987 (2657 B); detail showing the area around Henrietta Street, Dublin. Bibliothèque nationale, Paris.

PLATE 25
John Brooks (*fl.* 1730–56): *The Right Honble Luke Gardiner Esq.*, mezzotint after a painting by Charles Jervis (1902,1011.308). © The Trustees of the British Museum.

PLATE 26
M. J. Smith (draughtsman); J. Cooke (lithographer): *South Front of Morrastown, Lattin. Co. Kildare*, lithograph (44.81 P1). Irish Architectural Archive, Dublin. Photography: Commandant Con Costello, 1984.

PLATE 27
(i) 'Butlers Pantree Continued: Plate'; (ii) 'Kitchen'. Pages from the Baronscourt inventory of 1782, PRONI D623/D/4/1, ff. 8v, 9r. Courtesy of the Deputy Keeper of the Records, Public Record Office of Northern Ireland.

PLATE 28
'Castlecomer House', frontispiece engraving to McCall, Hardy Bertram (ed.), *Story of the Family of Wandesforde of Kirklington & Castlecomer* (McCall). Courtesy of the Syndics of Cambridge University Library, classmark 496.b.90.6.

PLATE 29
One of a set of Irish George III mahogany hall chairs, painted with the crest of the Clements family. Sotheby's Archive.

PLATE 30
Antoine-Marie Melotte (1722–1795): *Battle of the Amazons*, battle-piece relief in wood after a painting attributed to Sir Peter Paul Rubens (1577–1640). Sotheby's Archive.

PLATE 31
Henry Bone (1755–1834), after unknown artist: *Nathaniel Clements, 2nd Earl of Leitrim (1768–1854)*, 1813, pencil squared in ink for transfer (NPG D17713). © National Portrait Gallery, London.

PLATE 32
Front page of the Shelton Abbey inventory, 1816, Wicklow Papers, NLI MS 38,574/20. This image is reproduced courtesy of the National Library of Ireland.

PLATE 33
Allen & Townsend and Clarke, Delahunt & Co. (auctioneers): Shelton Abbey, Arklow, catalogue for an auction sale, 16 October – 3 November 1950. Courtesy of Fonsie Mealy Auctioneers.

PLATE 34
John Preston Neale (1780–1847) (draughtsman); William Radclyffe (engraver) (1783–1855): *Borris House, County Carlow*, 1819, engraving. Published in Neale, 1822–3, no. 50. Private collection.

PLATE 35
Madame de Beaurepaire [Françoise-Cunégonde Chacheré de Beaurepaire] (*c.* 1763–1856): *Walter Kavanagh*, 1808, pastel. All rights reserved.

PLATE 36
Morgan's Cabinetmakers and Upholders label. Kavanagh Collection.

PLATE 37
The Carton library bookplate showing the arms of the dukes of Leinster, pasted on the inside front cover of a copy of John Rocque's *A Survey of Kilkea: One of the Manors of the Right Honble Iames Earl of Kildare*, 1760. Courtesy of Robin Halwas Limited, London.

PLATE 38
Sir Richard Morrison (1767–1849): Engraved plan and elevation of the garden front at Carton after Morrison's additions of *c.* 1815 (0096/068-2/4/05). Guinness Collection, Irish Architectural Archive, Dublin.

PLATE 57
Michael Dahl (1656/1659–1743) (attributed to): *Charles Boyle, 2nd Earl of Burlington and 3rd Earl of Cork* (c. 1662–1704) *with the 1st Duke of Kingston-upon-Hull* (1655–1726) (left) *and the 3rd Baron Berkeley of Stratton* (1663–1697) (right), 1690s (?), oil on canvas. *See* plate 13 for detail in colour on page 129.

PLATE 58

John Brooks (fl. 1730–56): *Dr Hugh Boulter, archbishop of Armagh (1672–1742)*, engraving. The likeness of Robert Howard, bishop of Elphin (plate 10, page 86) was altered, possibly by James McArdell, Brooks's pupil.

PLATE 39

Mack, Williams & Gibton (attributed to): Rosewood-banded mahogany dining-table, *c.* 1815, probably commissioned by Augustus Frederick FitzGerald, 3rd Duke of Leinster (1791–1874) for the newly built dining-room at Carton House. Although now with seven pedestals, this table might well be the 'Sett of Mahogany Pillar Tables (Consisting of 8 [ )]' in the Carton House inventory of 1818 (see under 'Dining Room' on p. 273). Sotheby's Archive.

PLATE 40

Pompeo Batoni, Italian, 1708–1787: *Robert Clements, later 1st Earl of Leitrim (1732–1804)*, 1754, oil on canvas, 39¾ × 28¾ in. (101 × 73 cm). Hood Museum of Art, Dartmouth, New Hampshire: purchased through a gift from Barbara Dau Southwell, Class of 1978, in honour of Robert Dance, Class of 1977, a gift of William R. Acquavella, and the Florence and Lansing Porter Moore 1937 Fund.

PLATE 41

Pompeo Batoni (1708–1787): *Ralph Howard, later 1st Viscount Wicklow (1726–1786)*, 1752, oil on canvas, 39⅛ × 29³⁄₁₆ in. (99.4 × 74.1 cm), purchase, Museum Art Fund 1960.8. Collection of the Speed Art Museum, Louisville, Kentucky.

PLATE 42

John Preston Neale (1780–1847) (draughtsman); William Radclyffe (engraver): *Shelton Abbey*, 1820, engraving. Published in Neale, 1822–3, no. 57. Private collection.

PLATE 43

Artist unknown: *Portrait of Walter Kavanagh (d. 1818) of Borris House, County Carlow*, oil on canvas. On the reverse: 'Brought from Gracefield Queens County. W Kavnagh [*sic*], Borris brother in law Alicia Kavanagh (nee Grace)', *c.* 14 × 12 in. (36 × 30 cm). Kavanagh Collection. Photograph by Roger Jones.

PLATE 44

Charles Robertson (1759–1821): *Charles Cobbe (1781–1857)*, miniature in watercolour on ivory, 2⅜ × 2 in. (6 × 5 cm). Cobbe Collection, courtesy Alec Cobbe.

PLATE 45

Hugh Douglas Hamilton, RHA (1739–1808): *Lady Louisa Conolly (1743–1821)* 1785, pastel on paper, 9 × 7½ in. (23 × 19 cm). Castletown Foundation. Davison & Associates, Office of Public Works.

PLATE 46

Gédéon Gaspard Alfred de Grimaud [Alfred Guillaume Gabriel], comte d'Orsay (1801–1852) (after an original work attributed to): *Augustus Frederick FitzGerald, 3rd Duke of Leinster (1791–1874)*, 1830s, lithograph after drawing attributed to Orsay; image on sheet 11⅞ × 9½ in. (30 × 24.2 cm). This image is reproduced courtesy of the National Library of Ireland, NLI EP LEIN-AU (2) II.

PLATE 47

Hugh Douglas Hamilton, RHA (1739–1808): *Robert Stewart, 1st Marquess of Londonderry, MP (1739–1821)*, oil on canvas, 29 × 24 in. (73.7 × 61 cm), NT 1221352. The Discretionary Trust, Mount Stewart.

PLATE 48

Sir Thomas Lawrence PRA (Bristol 1769–London 1830): *Robert Stewart, Viscount Castlereagh, later 2nd Marquess of Londonderry, KG, GCH, MP (1769–1822)*, c. 1814, oil on canvas, 49 × 39 in. (124.5 × 99.1 cm), NT 1542307. The Estate of the Marquess of Londonderry.

PLATE 49

William van der Hagen (*fl.* 1720–1745): *An extensive view of Carton House, County Kildare, with Maynooth in the distanc*e, oil on canvas, 42⅜ × 52⅝ in. (107.6 × 133.6 cm). © 2017 Christie's Images Limited.

PLATE 50

Unknown lithographer: *New Bridge, Co. Dublin*, c. 1860, lithograph after a drawing by Frances Power Cobbe (1822–1904). Cobbe Collection, courtesy Alec Cobbe.

PLATE 51

Frances Power Cobbe (1822–1904): *The Drawing Room at Newbridge House*, 1840s, ink on paper. Cobbe Collection, courtesy Alec Cobbe.

PLATE 52

Basket, c. 1749–51, maker's mark of John Hamilton (*fl.* 1709–*d.* 1751), silver. Cobbe Collection, courtesy Alec Cobbe.

PLATE 53

One of a set of four pincushion dishes, c. 1765, maker's mark of John Laughlin (*fl.* 1745–75), silver, width, 9⅜ in. (24 cm). Mount Stewart, County Down. Photography: National Trust Images/Bryan Rutledge.

PLATE 54

Title page from Bernhard Varen's *Descriptio Regni Japoniæ*, Amsterdam, Elzevir, 1649. Koninklijke Bibliotheek, The Hague/Proquest.

PLATE 55

Henry Brooke (attributed): *A New System of Fairery*, book published in Dublin in 1750: title page of volume II; with Charles Cobbe's bookplate on facing page. Cobbe Collection, courtesy Alec Cobbe.

PLATE 56

Richard Cooper II's engraving dated 1763 of the painting said to be after Carlo Dolci, wrongly attributed to Antonio Allegri, called Correggio, 'formerly in the Ormond Collection'. Courtesy of the Office of Public Works, Kilkenny Castle.

PLATE 57

Whole of triple portrait (detail in plate 13) showing Charles Boyle, 2nd Earl of Burlington and 3rd Earl of Cork with the 1st Duke of Kingston-upon-Hull (1655–1726) (left) and the 3rd Baron Berkeley of Stratton (1663–1697) (right), 1690s (?), oil on canvas, 56⅝ × 72 in. (144 × 183 cm). Chiswick House, London/Bridgeman Images.

PLATE 58

Engraving of Dr Hugh Boulter, archbishop of Armagh (1902,1011.313). © The Trustees of the British Museum. This likeness uses the engraving of Robert Howard, bishop of Elphin (plate 10), with face and wig altered; new background introduced; and inscription erased and replaced. See *British Mezzotinto Portraits* (John Chaloner Smith, London, 1884). Perhaps James McArdell, Brooks's pupil, did the alterations to the Howard original (Gordon Godwin: *British Mezzotinters: James McArdell*, 1903).

List of plates

Bibliography

Bailey, N. (Bailey), *A Universal Etymological Dictionary* (4th edn, London, 1728)

Barnard, Toby, *A Guide to Sources for the History of Material Culture in Ireland, 1500–2000* (Dublin, 2005)

—— *Making the Grand Figure: Lives and possessions in Ireland, 1641–1770* (New Haven and London, 2004)

—— and Jane Fenlon (eds), *The Dukes of Ormonde, 1610–1745* (Woodbridge, 2000)

Baumstark, Reinhold, and Guy Delmarcel, *Rubens: Subjects from history. The Decius Mus series*, Corpus and Rubenianum Ludwig Burchard, part XIII, vol. 2 (London and Turnhout, 2019), p. 86, no. 17

Beck, S. William (Beck), *The Drapers' Dictionary: A manual of textile fabrics. Their history and applications* (London, 1886 edn)

Bennett, Douglas, *Irish Georgian Silver* (London, 1972)

Cabinet Makers' Society: *Rules & Orders of the Cabinet Makers' Society*; with scale of prices pasted in (London, *c.* 1830), online at the British Library <https://www.bl.uk/>

Caddy, Florence (Caddy), *Household Organization* (London, 1877)

Chambers, E. (Chambers), *Cyclopædia: or, An universal dictionary of arts and sciences* (5th edn, London, 1741)

Cobbe, Alec, *Birds, Bugs and Butterflies: Lady Betty Cobbe's Peacock China. A biography of an Irish service of Worcester porcelain* (Martlesham, Suffolk, 2019)

—— and Terry Friedman, *James Gibbs in Ireland: Newbridge, his villa for Charles Cobbe, archbishop of Dublin* (Bookham, Surrey, 2005)

Collins, Brenda, *Flax to Fabric: The story of Irish linen* (Lisburn, 1994)

Committee of Master Cabinet Makers, *The Prices of Cabinet Work, with Tables and Designs, Illustrating the Various Articles of Manufacture* (London, 1797), online at the Hathi Trust <https://www.hathitrust.org/>

Cornforth, John, 'Hillsborough Castle, Co. Down – II', *Country Life*, vol. 188, no. 31, 4 August 1994

Crawford, W. H., *The Irish Linen Industry* (Belfast, 1987)

Dolan, Terence Patrick (Dolan), *A Dictionary of Hiberno-English* (Dublin, 2004)

Draper, John: *The Young Student's Pocket Companion, or Arithmetic, Geometry, Trigonometry, and Mensuration* (Whitehaven, 1772)

Fenlon, Jane, *Goods & Chattels: A survey of early household inventories in Ireland* (Kilkenny, 2003)

—— *The Ormonde Picture Collection* (Dublin, 2001)

ffolliott, Rosemary, 'Captain Balfour's auction, 15th March 1741-2', *The Irish Ancestor*, vol. XVI, no. 1 (1984), pp. 21–31

FitzGerald, Alison, *Silver in Georgian Dublin: Making, selling, consuming* (London, 2019)

—— (ed.), *Studies in Irish Georgian Silver* (Dublin, 2020)

FitzGerald, Desmond (The Knight of Glin) and James Peill, *Irish Furniture: Woodwork and carving in Ireland from the earliest times to the Act of Union* (New Haven and London, 2007)

—— *The Irish Country House* (New York and London, 2010) (includes a chapter on Killadoon)

Fleming, Charles, and J. Tibbins (Fleming & Tibbins), *Royal Dictionary: English and French and French and English* (Paris, 1846)

Ford, Alan, James McGuire and Kenneth Milne (eds), *As by Law Established: The Church of Ireland since the Reformation* (Dublin, 1995)

Foster, Sarah, 'Going shopping in eighteenth-century Dublin' in *Things*, vol. IV (1996)

Francis, Peter, *Irish Delftware: An illustrated history* (London, 2000)

Gebbie, John H. (Gebbie), *An Introduction to the Abercorn Papers, as Relating to Ireland, 1736–1816* (Omagh, 1972)

Guinness, Desmond, *Georgian Dublin* (London, 1979)

Hearne, John M. (ed.), *Glassmaking in Ireland: From the medieval to the contemporary* (Dublin, 2010)

Holme, Randolph (Holme), *The Academy of Armory, or, A storehouse of armory and blazon* (Chester, 1688)

Ince, William, and John Mayhew, *The Universal System of Household Furniture* (reprinted with a preface by Ralph Edwards) (London, 1960)

Jackson-Stops, Gervase, 'Baronscourt, Co. Tyrone – I', *Country Life*, vol. 166, no. 4279, 12 July 1979, pp. 86–9

—— 'Mount Stewart, Co. Down – I & II', *Country Life*, vol. 167, no. 4313, 6 March 1980, pp. 646–9; no. 4314, 13 March 1980, pp. 754–8

Jervis, Simon Swynfen, *British and Irish Inventories: A list and bibliography of published transcriptions of secular inventories* (Leeds, 2010)

Johnson, Samuel (Johnson), *A Dictionary of the English Language (abstracted from the Folio Edition)* (9th edn, London, 1790)

Joyce, Edmund, *Borris House, Co. Carlow, and Elite Regency Patronage*, Maynooth Studies in Local History Series (Dublin, 2013)

Kinmonth, Claudia (Kinmonth), *Irish Country Furniture and Furnishings, 1700–2000* (Cork, 2020)

Laffan, William, and Christopher Monkhouse, with Leslie Fitzpatrick (eds), *Ireland: Crossroads of art and design, 1690–1840*, exh. cat., Chicago Art Institute, 17 March – 7 June 2015 (New Haven and London, 2015)

MacGregor, Arthur (ed.), *The Cobbe Cabinet of Curiosities: An Anglo-Irish country house museum* (New Haven and London, 2015)

Malcomson, A. P. W. (ed.), *The Clements Archive* (Dublin, 2010)

McCall, Hardy Bertram (ed.) (McCall), *Story of the Family of Wandesforde of Kirklington & Castlecomer: Compiled from original sources; with a calendar of historical manuscripts* (London, 1904)

Morgan, Sydney (Morgan), *Lady Morgan's Memoirs: Autobiography, diaries and correspondence* (London 1863)

Murdoch, Tessa (ed.), *Noble Households: Eighteenth-century inventories of great English houses. A tribute to John Cornforth* (Cambridge, 2006)

Neale, John Preston (Neale), *Views of the Seats of Noblemen and Gentlemen, in England, Wales, Scotland, and Ireland* (vol. VI) (London, 1822–3)

Neuman, Henry, and Giuseppe Baretti (Neuman & Baretti), *A New Dictionary of the Spanish and English Languages* (New York, 1842 edn)

O'Brien, Jacqueline, and Desmond Guinness, *Great Irish Houses and Castles* (London, 1992)

Oxford English Dictionary (OED online) (OED) (Oxford)

Pollard, M., *A Dictionary of Members of the Dublin Book Trade, 1550–1800* (London, 2000)

—— *Dublin's Trade in Books, 1550–1800* (Oxford, 1989)

Purcell, Mark, *The Big House Library in Ireland: Books in Ulster country houses* (Swindon, 2011)

Rothwell, James, 'Silver at Mount Stewart: Dazzling across Europe', in *National Trust Historic Houses & Collections Annual*, 2017, pp. 40–5

Sambrook, Pamela, *Country House Brewing, 1650–1950* (London 1996)

Sheraton, Thomas (Sheraton), *The Cabinet Dictionary* (London, 1803)

Sinsteden, Thomas, 'Household plate of the dukes of Ormonde', *Silver Studies*, vol. xxiii (2008), pp. 123–34

Sotheby & Co. (Sotheby): *Catalogue of a selected portion of the Library at Shelton Abbey, the property of the Rt. Honble. The Earl of Wicklow*, sale catalogue, 11 and 12 December 1950

Sotheby's, London, *Royal & Noble*, sale catalogue, 21 January 2020 (includes property from Killadoon and a dining-table from Carton House)

Tweney, C. F., and L. E. C. Hughes (eds) (Tweney & Hughes), *Chambers's Technical Dictionary* (London and Edinburgh, 1900)

Webster, Thomas (Webster), assisted by Mrs William Parkes, *An Encyclopedia of Domestic Economy* (London 1844)

Westropp, M. S. Dudley; Mary Boydell (ed.), *Irish Glass: A history of glass-making in Ireland from the sixteenth century* (Dublin 1978)

Other Inventories Consulted

Kilkenny Castle, Co. Kilkenny, inventory of 7 October 1717 (KC 1717), Fortified Estates Commission FEC 1/876 The National Archives, Kew

Killadoon, Co. Kildare, inventory of 1836 (K 1836), Clements Archive

St James's Square, London, inventory of 17 April 1719 (St James 1719), Fortified Estates Commission FEC 1/880, The National Archives, Kew

Index of personal names

Page numbers in italics refer to illustrations.

Unless otherwise stated, attributions for works of art featuring in the inventories here transcribed are those given in the inventories themselves or in other inventories from the same houses and may not reflect current scholarship. Other inventories are referred to here under short titles with their full details shown on page 391 in the Bibliography. For other works of art not featuring in the inventories, artists' and craftsmen's names are given where known. Unless mention in an inventory is quite specific, identification of sitters in portraits is based on circumstantial evidence and dating and therefore conjectural.

Abercorn, James Albert Edward Hamilton, 3rd Duke of, 124

Abercorn, James Hamilton, 7th Earl of: and Baronscourt, 177

Abercorn, James Hamilton, 8th Earl of, 177, 178; and Baronscourt, 177; and Duddingston House, near Edinburgh, 177; inventory of Baronscourt, 179–85; portrait by Gainsborough, *134*

Abercorn, James Hamilton, 2nd Marquess (later 1st Duke) of: and Baronscourt, 178

Abercorn, John Hamilton, 1st Marquess of, 178

Allen & Townsend (Dublin auctioneers), 235

Anne, Queen: portraits, full-length, 76; —, half-length, 84

Annesley, James: portrait, 125

Arlington, Elizabeth Bennet (*née* Isabella van Nassau-Beverweerd), Lady: portrait (half-length), 38

Arran, Charles Butler, 1st Earl of (2nd creation): portrait (half-length) (poss.), 38

Arran, Mary Butler (*née* Stuart), Countess of: portrait, 35

Arran, Richard Butler, 1st Earl of (1st creation): portraits, 76; —, [by Smith, KC 1717], 35; —, half-length (poss.), 38

Assheton, William (chaplain to 1st Duke of Ormonde), 36

Balfour, Captain, 105; account of his goods sold by auction, 108–21. *See also* Appendix I, pp. 365–7, for buyers at the auction

Barlow, Francis, 77

Batoni, Pompeo: portraits; Clements, Robert, later 1st Earl of Leitrim, 201, *257*;

Hillsborough, Wills Hill, 1st Earl of, *132*; Howard, Ralph, later 1st Viscount Wicklow, 227, *258*

Baxter, Martin (at Kilkenny Castle), 42

Beaufort, Henry Somerset, 1st Duke of: portraits, 70; —, half-length, 76

Beaufort, Henry Somerset, 2nd Duke of: portrait (half-length), 76

Beaurepaire, Madame de (Françoise-Cunégonde Chacheré de Beaurepaire): portrait of Walter Kavanagh, *243*

Belfour[t], Captain. *See* Balfour, Captain

Bermingham, Mary, mother of Mary Clements, Countess of Leitrim: portrait drawing 'of M^{rs}. B.' (prob.), 218; needlework by (prob.), 216

Beverweerd, Lord. *See* Nassau, Lodewijk van

Bindon, Francis, 147; portrait, St George, Richard, when brigadier general, 147; —, mezzotint by Brooks after Bindon, *146*

Blücher, Prince Gebhard Leberecht von, Prussian field marshal: likeness on cut-glass tumbler, 340

Bohemia, Elizabeth Stuart, Queen of: portrait, 37

Bolger, Bryan, 248

Bolton, Charles Paulet, 2nd Duke of: portrait (full-length), 159

Bolton, Alderman Thomas (Dublin goldsmith), 29, 72

Bonaparte, Napoleon: portrait busts, 326, 327, 329

Bone, Henry: portrait of Leitrim, Nathaniel Clements, 2nd Earl of, *222*

Bosschaert, Thomas Willeboirts (poss.): *The Persecution* (picture), 73

Boulter, Hugh (archbishop of Armagh), *387*

Boulton, Matthew, 12, 13

Boylan, Patrick (wallpaper-maker), 306

Boyle, Charles. *See* Burlington, Charles Boyle, 2nd Earl of, and 3rd Earl of Cork

Boyle, Richard. *See* Cork, Richard Boyle, 1st Earl of

Bracker, Thomas, 162

Brettingham, Robert Furze: architectural drawing of Hillsborough Castle, *122*

Brisco, John (shipmaster): *Betty* galley, 70; *Pearle of Chester*, 72

Broadwood, John, & Sons: grand pianoforte, 273; pianoforte, 271

Brooke, Henry (attrib.): *A New System of Fairery*, 306, *378*

Brooking, Charles: *A Map of the City and Suburbs of Dublin* (illus. Dublin Castle), 54

Brooks, John: mezzotint portraits, Gardiner, Luke (after Jervis), *163*; Howard, Robert, bishop of Elphin (after Dahl), 86; St George, Richard; —, when brigadier general (after Bindon), *146*; —, when major-general (after Slaughter), 153

Burlington, Charles Boyle, 2nd Earl of, and 3rd Earl of Cork, 19; inventory of goods at Lismore Castle, 20–3; portrait attrib. to Dahl, *384*; —, detail, *129*

Burlington, Richard Boyle, 3rd Earl of, and 4th Earl of Cork, 20

Butler, James. *See* Ormonde, James Butler, 1st Duke of, or 2nd Duke of

Butler, Lady Amelia: her apartment at London, St James's Square, 77; portrait, 82

Butler, Lady Elizabeth (poss.): her room at Kilkenny Castle, 39

Butler, Lady Frances (*née* Touchet) (full-length) [copy after van Dyck, KC 1717], 37

Butler, Lady Harriet: portrait, 75

Butler, Lady Mary (later 3rd Baroness Ashburnham): portrait (poss.), 75

Butler, Sir Richard, 5th Baronet: at Balfour house sale (poss.), 119

Byron, George G., 6th Baron: portrait print, 333

Calderwood, Robert, 156, 161; plate received by, 161–2

Camden, Charles Pratt, 1st Earl: portrait print, 331

Canova, Antonio (after): bust of Venus, 217

Capell of Hadham, Arthur Capell, 1st Baron: portraits, 70, 75 (or perhaps same picture)

Caravaggio, Polidoro da: long pieces, 34, 36

Casey, Christine, 12

Castlereagh, Robert Stewart, Viscount, later 2nd Marquess of Londonderry: portrait by Lawrence, *263*. *See also* Londonderry, Robert Stewart, 2nd Marquess of

Catherine of Braganza (queen of Charles II): portrait, full-length by Huysmans [KC 1717], 37

Cavendish, Lady Elizabeth (*née* Cecil): portrait (full-length), 53

Chambers, Ephraim: *Cyclopædia*, 87

Chambers, Sir William (1723–1796), 12, 177

Charlemont, Anne Caulfeild (*née* Bermingham), Countess of, 201; portrait busts, 202; —, cast of bust by Joseph Nollekens [K 1836], 215, 218

Charles I: portraits, 37; —, equestrian [St James 1719], 77; —, full-length, 82; —, in needlework, 35; —, of his three children, 38; —, with Henrietta Maria, his queen consort (full-length), 37

Charles II: portraits, 36; —, full-length, 52, 82; —, full-length after Lely [KC 1717], 37; —, head [KC 1717], 33

Charlotte Augusta, Princess of Wales: portraits, bust, 326; —, print, 328

Chesterfield, Elizabeth Stanhope (*née* Butler), 2nd Countess of: portraits, 31, 53, 76; —, by Lely [KC 1717], 37

Chesterfield, Philip Stanhope, 4th Earl of: portrait bust in bronze, 202, 203, 205, 214

Clarke, Delahunt & Co. (auctioneers, Wicklow Town), 235

Clements, Mary, later 2nd Countess of Leitrim. See Leitrim, Mary Clements (*née* Bermingham), 2nd Countess of

Clements, Nathaniel, the Elder, 202

Clements, Nathaniel, the Younger. *See* Leitrim, Nathaniel Clements, 2nd Earl of

Clements, Robert, 201, portrait as a young man by Batoni, 201, *257*

Cobbe, Anne Power (*née* Trench) (*d.* 1835): inventory (1814) of silverware to be given to Charles Cobbe, her son, 323

Cobbe, Charles (1686–1765) (archbishop), 305, 306

Cobbe, Charles (1781–1857), 305; his bookplate, *366*; his dressing room at Newbridge House, 307, 310; inventories for Newbridge House, furniture, 308–22; —, books, 320–2; —, silver at Bath, 1821, 323; portrait miniature by Robertson, *261*. *See also* Appendix IV, pp. 377–82, for mostly conjectured identification of his books

Cobbe, Charles (1811–1886): his coconut mug with silver mounting, 316

Cobbe, Elizabeth (*née* Beresford), Lady (1736–1806), 305

Cobbe, Frances (*née* Conway) (1777–1847), 307; her bedroom at Newbridge House, 307, 310

Cobbe, Frances Power (1822–1904), 305; *The Drawing Room at Newbridge House* (drawing), *309*; *New Bridge, Co. Dublin* (lithograph after drawing by), *304*

Cobbe, Henry (1817–1898): his spoon and fork, 316

Cobbe, Rev. Henry William (1785–1823), 306

Cobbe, Thomas (1733–1814), 305, 306

Cobbe, Thomas (1813–1882): his fork, 316

Cobbe, William (1816–1911), 319; his spoon and fork, 316

Congreve, Mrs Mary (*née* Browning), 19; her room at Lismore Castle, 21

Congreve, Colonel William, 19, 23; his room at Lismore Castle, 21

Conolly, Louisa-Augusta (*née* Lennox), Lady: portrait miniature by Hamilton, 248, *261*, 273

Cooke, J.: lithograph of Morristown Lattin, *164*

Cooper, Richard, II (engraver): *Madonna and Child* (stated on engraving to be after Correggio), *385*

Cooper, Sir William, 1st Baronet: portrait (half-length), 140

Cork, Richard Boyle, 1st Earl of (the Great Earl), 19

Cornforth, John, 11

Correggio, Antonio Allegri da: *Madonna and Child* (attrib.), *69*, *70*, 385

Cowper, George Nassau Clavering-Cowper, 3rd Earl (prob.) (Wedgwood portrait medallion), 271

Crace, John Gregory, 20

Cracht, Pieter de: *Marcus Valerius consecrates Decius Mus* (modern attrib. of tapestry), *24*

Cranborne, James Gascoyne Cecil, Viscount (later 1st Marquess of Salisbury): his dressing room at Hillsborough Castle, 138

Cranborne, Mary-Amelia Cecil (*née* Hill), Lady (later 1st Marchioness of Salisbury), 15; her bedroom at Hillsborough Castle, 124, 138

Crommelin, Louis, 358

Crosley, Mrs (at Hillsborough), 14, 125

Cutts, John, 1st Baron Cutts (commander-in-chief in Ireland), 68

Dahl, Michael: portraits; Burlington, Charles Boyle, 2nd Earl of (attrib.), *129*; Howard, Robert, bishop of Elphin (mezzotint after Dahl), *86*; Ormonde, Mary Butler (*née* Somerset), Duchess of (by follower of Dahl), *131*

Dance, George, the Younger, 326; *Designs for alterations to Mount Stewart*, architectural drawing of portico elevation (detail), *frontispiece*

Delane, Solomon, 325

Delany, Mary (*née* Granville) (letter writer and artist), 15, 123

Desmond, Richard Preston, 1st Earl of: portrait (full-length), 37

Devonshire, Mary Cavendish (*née* Butler), 1st Duchess of: portraits, by Lely [KC 1717], 31; —, print, 333

Devonshire, William and Elizabeth Cavendish, 3rd Earl and Countess of: portrait by Lely [KC 1717], 38

Devonshire, William George Spencer Cavendish, 6th Duke of, 20

Digby, Simon (artist and chaplain to Thomas Butler, 6th Earl of Ossory, 1668, later bishop of Elphin): portrait, Butler, Thomas, 6th Earl of Ossory (watercolour) [KC 1717], 35

Dixon, Samuel (Dublin artist and picture dealer), 15

Dolci, Carlo: *Madonna and Child* (attrib.), 69

Dorset, Mary Sackville (*née* Compton), 6th Countess of: portrait (poss.), 75

Downshire, Wills Hill, 1st Marquess of, 123

Duffe, Thomas. See Ormonde, Thomas Butler, 10th Earl of

Dungannon, Arthur Hill-Trevor, 1st Viscount: portrait (half-length), 140

Dunne, Bryan (appraiser), 14, 174

Dyck, Sir Anthony van: painting unspecified [in KC 1705 and KC 1717], 37; portraits, Butler, Lady Frances (*née* Touchet) (full-length) [copy after, KC 1717], 37; —,

Pembroke, Philip Herbert, 4th Earl of [copy after, KC 1717], 31; —, Richmond and Lennox, James Stuart, 1st Duke of (full-length) [KC 1717], 37; —, Richmond and Lennox, Mary Stuart (*née* Villiers), 1st Duchess of (full-length) [KC 1717], 37; —, Strafford, Thomas Wentworth, 1st Earl of [copy after, KC 1717], 32

Ecklin, Robert (lieutenant-general), 68

Eeckhout, Gerbrand van den: Melchizedek and other figures [KC 1717], 38

Elizabeth I: portrait (half-length), 84

Ellis, Joseph, 157

Este, Susanna (wife of Charles Este, bishop of Ossory, and widow of Robert Clements): at Balfour house sale, 106

Fairford, Arthur Hill, Viscount (courtesy title), later 2nd Marquess of Downshire, son of Wills Hill: his room at Hillsborough Castle, 138–9

Fawcett, Benjamin: print of Baronscourt, *135*

Felster, George (Dublin picture dealer), 67

Fenlon, Jane, 12, 27

Ferguson, William Gouw: pictures, ruin, 77; —, unspecified, 76

ffolliott, Rosemary, 11, 105; her transcript of the Balfour house auction sale, 13

Finckley, Stephen (upholsterer), 65, 66, 67

FitzGerald, Desmond, Knight of Glin, 12, 15, 201

FitzGerald family, 247

Fitzpatrick, Elizabeth (*née* Butler), Lady (poss.): portrait, 31

Fountaine, Sir Andrew: his room at Dublin Castle, 66, 67

Fox, Charles James: portrait bust, 203, 214

Fox, Luke (chief justice of the common pleas) (poss.): portrait print, 272

French, John (upholsterer), 65, 66, 67

Frobenius, Johannes [Johann Froben] (Swiss scholar-printer): portrait, 38

Gainsborough, Thomas: portrait, Abercorn, James Hamilton, 8th Earl of, *134*

Gardiner, Charles (1720–1769), 155, 156, 161; inventory of plate received from, 161–2

Gardiner, Luke (*c.* 1690–1755), 155, 156, 157; at Balfour house sale (prob.), 107, 108, 109; inventories, goods at Dublin, No. 10 Henrietta Street, 157–61; —, plate weighed at house, 162; portrait by Jervis, mezzotint by Brooks, *163*

Gardiner, Luke, the Younger, later 1st Viscount Mountjoy (1745–1798), 155, 162; portrait by Reynolds, *133*

Gardiner, Sackville, 155, 162

Gascar(s), Henri: portraits, Charles II (head) [KC 1717], 33; James II (head) [KC 1717], 33; —, Ormonde, Elizabeth Butler (*née* Preston), 1st Duchess of [KC 1717], 35; —, Ormonde, James Butler, Ist Duke of, with René Mezendier [KC 1717, NGI 4198*], 33

Geminiani, Francesco, 105

George I: portrait (full-length), 159

Gibbs, James, 12, 305

Gorge, Mrs (poss. Katherine Gorges, *née* Keating, widow of Hamilton Gorges of

Rathbeale Hall, Swords): at Balfour house sale, 118, 119, 120

Grafton, Henrietta Fitzroy (*née* Somerset), 2nd Duchess of, 155

Grafton, Isabella Fitzroy (*née* Bennet), 1st Duchess of: portrait, 82

Grantham, Henrietta de Nassau d'Auverquerque (*née* Butler), 1st Countess of: portrait, 82

Grigg, Richard (poss.): eight-day clock, 183

Guinness, Desmond, 7

Hagen, William van der: view of Carton House, 247, *264*

Hamilton of Donalong, Baroness Mary (*née* Butler): portrait (prob.), 38

Hamilton, Hugh Douglas: portraits, Conolly, Louisa Augusta (*née* Lennox), Lady, *261*; —, Londonderry, Robert Stewart, 1st Marquess of, *262*; —, Ormonde, Susan Frances Elizabeth (Anne) Butler (*née* Wandesford), Countess of, *136*

Hamilton, James Hamilton, 1st Duke of: portrait (poss.), 37

Hamilton, John (Dublin silversmith): bread basket (silver, with maker's mark), 316, *317*

Hearne, Daniel, archdeacon of Cashel: at Balfour house sale, 106

Helsham, Mrs (prob. Jane Helsham, widow of Richard Helsham, previously Widow Putland, *née* Rolton): at Balfour house sale, 113

Henrietta Maria of France: portraits (full-length), 82; —, with Charles I, 37

Henry, Prince: portrait (full-length), 37

Hester, William (Dublin clock-maker, son of Henry Hester, London clock-maker), 68

Hill, Arthur: portrait (half-length), 140

Hill, Marcus: portrait (half-length), 140

Hill, Michael (MP and Wills Hill's paternal grandfather): portrait (half-length), 140

Hill, Sir Moses (Moyses) and Lady Hill: portrait (half-length), 140

Hill, W.: portrait (half-length), 140

Hillsborough, Margaretta Hill (*née* FitzGerald), Countess, 15

Hillsborough, Mary Hill (*née* Rowe), Viscountess (Wills Hill's mother): portrait (half-length), 140

Hillsborough, Wills Hill, 1st Earl of, later 1st Marquess of Downshire, 123; his bedchamber at Hillsborough, 139; inventory of his lodge at Hillsborough, 137–45; his library at Hillsborough, 140; portrait (full-length) by Batoni, 123, *132*, 140. *See also* Hillsborough, Wills Hill, 2nd Viscount

Hillsborough, Wills Hill, 2nd Viscount, later 1st Earl of Hillsborough, 123; his bedchamber at Hillsborough, 126; inventory of his house at Hillsborough, 125–8. *See also* Hillsborough, Wills Hill, 1st Earl of

Hobbema, Meindert: landscape, 306

Hobbs, Mr: his portrait head on copper, 38

Hogarth, William: prints, 140; —, 'Rake's Progress' and 'Four Times of Day', 15, 125

Holland, Henry Vassall-Fox, 3rd baron: portrait print, 272

Hondius, Abraham (poss.): hunting-pieces, 73, 76

Hope, Thomas, 202; *Anastasius: or, Memoirs of a Greek*, 321

Howard, Hugh, 227

Howard, Patience (*née* Boleyn), 87, 93, 94

Howard, Ralph, later 1st Viscount Wicklow, 88; portrait by Batoni, *258*. *See also* Wicklow, Ralph Howard, 1st Viscount

Howard, Ralph, physician, 88

Howard, Robert, bishop of Elphin, 87, 88, 89, 227; inventories, of household goods, 89–94; —, of books in his study, 95–103; mezzotint portrait by Brooks after Dahl, *86*. *See also* Appendix III, pp. 369–76, for conjectured identification of his books

Huguenots: Crommelin, Louis (linen manufacturer), 358; La Coudrière, Jean Rabault (chevalier seigneur), 67; Le Clerc, Jean (temporary assistant at the London Savoy French Church in 1682), 100; Mezendier, René (servant to 1st Duke of Ormonde) (poss.), 33; Perrin, John [Jean-Baptiste Perrin] (French teacher in Co. Kilkenny), 322; Rocque, John (cartographer), map of Dublin (details), *104*, *154*; —, map of Ireland (after), 10; Roumieu, David or his brother Paul Roumieu (Dublin silversmiths) (prob.), 67; Saurin, Louis (dean of St Patrick's Cathedral), 108; Seignior, George (chaplain to the 1st Earl of Burlington), 36

Huntingdon, Elizabeth Hastings (*née* Lewis), 7th Countess of (prob.): portrait, 37

Hutchinson, Samuel (dean of Dromore): at Balfour town house sale, 108, 111

Huysmans, Jacob: portrait of Catherine of Braganza (full-length) [KC 1717], 37

Hyde, Lady Catherine: portrait, 77

Inchiquin, William O'Brien, 3rd Earl of, 66, 67

Ingoldsby, Richard, Major General, 247

James II: portrait head by Gascar [KC 1717], 33

James, Sir Walter-James: portrait bust, 327

Jervas, Charles. *See* Jervis, Charles

Jervis, Charles: portrait of Gardiner, Luke, mezzotint by Brooks after Jervis, *163*

Johnston, John (architect): Castlecomer House, 1802, *186*

Jordaens, Jacob (after) (poss.): portrait head, 84

Kavanagh, Elizabeth (*née* Butler), Lady, 239

Kavanagh, Thomas: letter of 1818 to, 239

Kavanagh, Walter, 237, 238; inventory for Borris House, 239–43; portraits, by Beaurepaire, *243*; —, by unknown artist, *260*

Kennedy Gardner, John, 147

Kildare, Lady Emilia FitzGerald (*née* Usher St George) (poss.): her room at Hillsborough Castle, 139

Kirchoffer, John, 157

Kneller, Sir Godfrey: portraits; Ormonde, James Butler, 2nd Duke of, *130*; Ormonde, Mary Butler, 2nd Duchess of, with her son Thomas, Earl of Ossory [KC 1717], 31

La Coudrière, Jean Rabault (chevalier seigneur; or perhaps his son Guillaume): his room at Dublin Castle, 67

Lattin, George, 165; inventory on his death, 166–75

Laughlin, John (Dublin silversmith): salad-dishes (silver, with maker's mark), *324*, 347

Lawrence, Thomas: portrait of Castlereagh, Robert Stewart, Viscount, later 2nd Marquess of Londonderry, *263*

Leinster, Augustus Frederick FitzGerald, 3rd Duke of, 247; inventories for Carton House, 249, 252–6; 265–301; —, for Waterstown, 301–3; portrait by the comte d'Orsay, *261*

Leitrim, Mary Clements (*née* Bermingham), 2nd Countess of, 201; at Killadoon; her bed chamber, 217, 218; —, her bedroom, 206

Leitrim, Nathaniel Clements, 2nd Earl of, 201; inventories for Killadoon, from 1807, overlaid with 1812, 203–13; —, from 1812, revised in 1829, 214–25; at Killadoon, his attic storey room, 209; —, his dressing room, 205, 206, 217; —, his room, 221; portraits, bust, 202, 215; —, in pencil by Henry Bone, 222

Leitrim, Robert Clements, 1st Earl of: portrait as young man by Batoni, 201, *257*

Leitrim, William-Sydney Clements, Viscount (later 3rd Earl of Leitrim): Gibraltar rock, 214, 216

Lely, Sir Peter: portraits, Charles II; full-length [copy after Lely; KC 1717], 37; —, Chesterfield, Elizabeth Stanhope (*née* Butler), Countess of [KC 1717], 37; —, Devonshire, Mary Cavendish (*née* Butler), 1st Duchess of [KC 1717], 31; —, Devonshire, William and Elizabeth Cavendish, 3rd Earl and Countess of [KC 1717], 38; —, Ormonde, James Butler, 1st Duke of (full-length) [KC 1717], 37; —, Ossory, Thomas Butler, 6th Earl of (full-length) [KC 1717], 37; —, Richmond and Lennox, Frances Theresa Stuart, 3rd Duchess of (full-length) [KC 1717], 37; —, York, Anne Stuart (*née* Hyde), Duchess of (half-length) [KC 1717], 37

Leysted, William, 162

Lilly, Alexander (silversmith), 162

Llandaff (*née* Coghlan), Countess of, third wife of 1st Earl of Llandaff (prob.): cameo sulphur portrait, 214

Locker, John (silversmith), 162

Londonderry, Amelia Stewart (*née* Hobart), Marchioness of: her bedroom at Mount Stewart, Co. Down, 330

Londonderry, Charles Vane (*né* Stewart), 3rd Marquess of, 326

Londonderry, Frances Stewart (*née* Pratt), Marchioness Dowager of, 328, 329

Londonderry, Robert Stewart, 1st Marquess of, 325; inventor of the Londonderry Solar Grate, 358; portrait by Hamilton, *262*

Londonderry, Robert Stewart, 2nd Marquess of, 325, 326; his bedroom at Mount Stewart, 330; inventories for Mount Stewart, china and cut glass, 343–5; —, household furniture, 327–43; —, linen, 345–6; —, plate, 347–8; portraits, glazed bust, 329; —, print, 328. *See also* Castlereagh, Robert Stewart, Viscount

Longfield, Ada (later Leask), 11
Longford, Anne Aungier (*née* Chichester, widow of John Butler, 1st Earl of Gowran), Countess of: portrait by Smith [KC 1717], 35
Lorrain, Claude: landscape, 204
Lucey, Conor, 12
Lydon, Frank: drawing of Baronscourt, *135*
Lyon, Peter (London mangle-maker), 144
Mack & Gibton (furnishers, Dublin), 306
Mack, Williams & Gibton (cabinet-makers, Dublin), 238
MacMurrough Kavanagh family, 237
Mainwaring, Sir Phillip: portraits with Strafford, Thomas Wentworth, 1st Earl of, at Kilkenny Castle [KC 1717], 37; —, at Dublin, No. 10 Henrietta St (full-length) (prob.), 159
Malmesbury, James Harris, 1st Earl of: portrait print, 334
Manby, George, 87, 91, 93
Marlborough, Duchess of: portrait (half-length), 14, 140
Mary, Princess Royal and Princess of Orange (*née* Stuart): portraits, 33; —, half-length, 75
Mary, Queen of Scots: portrait, 77
Mary II: portraits, 159; —, full-length, 76
Masclary, Major Henry, 71
Master James (bust), 329
Maude, Elizabeth (*née* Cornwallis), Baroness: at Balfour house sale, 106, 116, 119
Mazarin, Hortense de la Porte de la Meilleraye (*née* Hortensia Mancini), duchesse de: portrait, 82
McDonnell, Joe, 12
McKercher, Mr: portrait, 125
Melotte, Antoine-Marie: battle-piece reliefs in wood, one of which after *Battle of the Amazons* (attrib. to Rubens), 214, *215*
Merlin, John Joseph: Dutch oven, 356; scales (weighing), 217; wheel-chair, 308
Mezendier, René: portrait with Ormonde, James Butler, 1st Duke of [by Gascar, KC 1717; unatrrib. NGI 4198*], 33
Midleton, Anne Brodrick (*née* Trevor), Viscountess: portrait (half-length), 140
Miller, Philip: *The Gardiners Dictionary: Containing the methods of cultivating and improving the kitchen, fruit and flower garden …*, 300
Montaigne, Michel de (chevalier de l'Ordre de Saint-Michel): *Essays*, 103; portrait head, 82
Morgan's (Lewis and Anthony Morgan), cabinet-makers and upholders, Dublin, 229, 234, 238, 245; label, 239, *245*; letter of 1818 to J. Kavanagh, 239
Morris, Rev. F. O.: *The County Seats of the Noblemen and Gentlemen of Great Britain and Ireland*, 135
Morrison, Sir Richard, 178, 228, 237, 238, 248; plan and elevation drawing of Carton House, *250–1*
Morrison, William Vitruvius, 178, 228, 237, 238, 326
Mountjoy, 1st Viscount. *See* Gardiner, Luke, the Younger

Murray, Sir Mungo: portraits (full-length), by Wright, 82; —, ['in highland dress'; KC 1717], 37
Nash, John, 12
Nassau, Lodewijk van, Lord Beverweerd: portrait (half-length), 38
Neale, John Preston (draughtsman): Borris House, *236*; Shelton Abbey, *259*
Nicholls, Sutton: engraving of St James's Square, London, *74*
Nollekens, Joseph: portrait bust of Charlemont, Anne, Countess of [K 1836], 215, 218
Northumberland, Catherine Fitzroy (*née* Wheatley), duchess of: portrait (half-length), 75
Ogilby, John (Bible illustrator), 32
O'Neill, Sir Neil, 2nd Baronet: portrait as an Irish chieftain (full-length) by Wright, 82, *83*
Orange, Amalia of Solms-Braunfels, Princess of: portrait (full-length) (poss.), 52
Orange, Princess Mary of. *See* Mary, Princess Royal and Princess of Orange
Orange, Prince William of. *See* William III
Ormond, Earl of: portrait (half-length), 82
Ormond, James Butler, 12th Earl of. *See* Ormonde, James Butler, 1st Duke of
Ormond, James Butler, Earl of: portrait of 9th or 12th earl [?], 37
Ormond, Thomas Butler, 10th Earl of, 27; portraits, 37; —, in Scottish armour, 37
Ormond, Walter Butler, 11th Earl of, 27
Ormonde, Anne Butler, Countess of. *See* Ormonde, Susan Frances Elizabeth (Anne) Butler, 17th Countess of
Ormonde, Elizabeth Butler (*née* Preston), 1st Duchess of: portraits, by Gascar [KC 1717], 35; —, full-length, 75
Ormonde, James Butler, 1st Duke of, 27; portraits, 33; —, in crayon [KC 1705] (in watercolour by Digby [KC 1717]), 35; —, full-length, 53, 82; —, half-length, 76; —, by Lely (full-length) [KC 1717], 37
Ormonde, James Butler, 2nd Duke of, 27, 358; his apartment at London, St James's Square, 81; inventories, Kilkenny Castle, 31–53; —, Dublin Castle, 55–68; —, goods on board the *Pearl of Chester*, 72; —, pictures and furniture on board the *Betty* galley, 70–1; —, pictures to Kilkenny Castle, 73; —, plate sold to Thomas Bolton, 72; —, at London, St James's Square, 75–85; portraits, 75; —, by Kneller (full-length), *130*; —, by van Traight (full-length), 73
Ormonde, John Butler, 17th Earl of, 187
Ormonde, Mary Butler (*née* Somerset), Duchess of: books in her closet, 36; portraits, 71, 76, 82; —, by follower of Dahl, *131*; —, by Kneller [KC 1717], 31. *See also* Appendix II, p. 368, for conjectured identification of her books
Ormonde, Susan Frances Elizabeth (Anne) Butler (*née* Wandesford), 17th Countess of, 187; inventories for Castlecomer, china, 195; —, copper wares, 195; —, furniture and effects, 189–94; —, linen, 195; —, plate, 196–8; —, wines, 199; portrait by Hamilton, *136*

Ormonde, Thomas (Duffe) Butler, 10th Earl of: portrait, 70
Ormonde children: portrait, 70
Orsay, Gédéon Gaspard Alfred de Grimaud, comte d': portrait of Augustus, 3rd Duke of Leinster, *261*
Ossory, Emilia Butler (*née* van Nassau-Beverwaard), Countess of: portrait as 'Lady Dowager' (half-length), 37
Ossory, Thomas Butler, 6th Earl of: portraits, 37, 70, 75; —, in crayon [KC 1705] (in watercolour by Digby [KC 1717]), 35; —, full-length, 82; —, full-length [Lely; KC 1717], 37; —, by Lely [KC 1717], 37
Ossory, Thomas Butler, Earl of (*d.* 1689): portrait with his mother by Kneller [KC1717], 31
Overkirk, Lord (monsieur d'Auverquerque) [Hendrik van Nassau-Ouwerkerk]: portrait (half-length), 77
Paget, Frances (*née* Rich), 5th Baroness: portrait of her daughter (poss.), 37
Parsons (squire, at Balfour house sale), 119
Parsons, Sir Laurence (3rd Baronet): at Balfour house sale, 119, 120; memorial glass for William III, 13, 120
Pearce, Sir Edward Lovett, 155
Peill, James, 12, 201
Pembroke, Philip Herbert, 4th Earl of: portrait [copy after van Dyck, KC 1717], 31
Pembroke, Thomas Herbert, 8th Earl of (lord lieutenant of Ireland, 1707–8), 63, 65, 67
Perrin, John [Jean-Baptiste Perrin] (Huguenot French teacher in Co. Kilkenny), 322; *A Grammar of the French Tongue: Founded on the decisions of the French Academy*, 322; *Instructive and Entertaining Exercises, with the Rules of the French Syntax*, 322
Pitt, William, the Younger: portraits, head, 329; —, print, 334
Place, Francis (1647–1728): drawing of Kilkenny Castle and Saint Canice's Cathedral, *52–3*; —, detail, *30*
Poyntz, Sir Nicholas: portrait, 38
Preston & Son Ltd (cabinet-makers, Dublin), 238
Preston, Elizabeth, Lady. *See* Ormonde, Elizabeth Butler (*née* Preston), 1st Duchess of
Preston, Squire (of Gormanston): at Balfour house sale, 108
Princess Royal. *See* Mary, Princess Royal and Princess of Orange
Pugin, Augustus Welby Northmore, 20
Putland, John (poss.): at Balfour house sale, 106, 116, 117, 120
Radclyffe, William (engraver): Borris House, *236*; Shelton Abbey, *259*
Raleigh, Sir Walter, 19
Rawdon, Lady Helena (*née* Perceval) (poss.): her room at Hillsborough Castle, 126
Rembrandt Harmenszoon van Rijn: painting of an old man's head; ['Rindbrand'; KC 1717], 38
Reynolds, Joshua: portrait of Luke Gardiner, the Younger, *133*

Index of personal names

395

Ribera, Jusepe de (called Lo Spagnoletto): chimney-piece painting (poss.), 31

Ricciardelli, Gabriele, 227

Richmond and Lennox, Frances Teresa Stuart, Duchess of: portrait, full-length by Lely [KC 1717], 37

Richmond and Lennox, James Stuart, 1st Duke of: portrait, full-length by van Dyck; KC 1717], 37

Richmond and Lennox, Mary Stuart (née Villiers), Duchess of: portraits, full-length by van Dyck; KC 1717], 37; —, (poss.), 35

Roberts, Thomas Sautelle: drawing of Lismore Castle, 18

Robertson, Charles: portrait of Charles Cobbe (1781–1857), 261

Robertson, William, architect, 148

Rochester, Henrietta Hyde (née Boyle), countess of, 82

Rochester, Laurence Hyde, 1st Earl of, 67; portrait, 70; room of his page, Mr Young, 68

Rocque, John (map-maker): An Exact Survey of the City and Suburbs of Dublin, detail, Henrietta Street, 154; —, St Stephen's Green, 104; map of Ireland (after Rocque), 10; Survey of the Kildare estates: Manor of Kilkea, 1760, 385

Roe, Sir Thomas: portrait, 14, 125

Rosamund ['Fair Rosamond' (St James 1719), poss. Rosemary Clifford, 12th-century beauty]: portrait (half-length), 84

Roumieu, Mr: David or his brother Paul Roumieu (Dublin silversmiths) (prob.): his room at Dublin Castle, 67

Rowe, Anthony (Wills Hill's maternal grandfather): portrait (half-length), 140

Rowe, Colonel Henry: portrait (half-length), 140

Rowe, Sir Henry: portrait (half-length), 140

Rowe, Sir Thomas: portraits (half-length), 140; —, with Lady Rowe, 140

Rubens, Sir Peter Paul: battle-piece Battle of Amazons (relief after), 214; Decius Mus tapestry design, 24; history piece [KC 1717], 33

Ruyter, Michiel Adriaanszoon de, Lieutenant-Admiral: portraits, 70, 73

Saurin, Louis (dean of St Patrick's Cathedral, Ardagh): at Balfour sale (poss.), 108

Schalcken, Godfried (poss.): portrait by candlelight, 159

Scott, Thomas (Bible commentator), 320

Seignior, George: chaplain to the 1st Earl of Burlington, 36

Sinsteden, Thomas, 28, 106

Slaughter, Stephen: portrait, St George, Richard, when major-general, mezzotint by Brooks after Slaughter, 153

Smith, George, 202

Smith, John (1652–1743) (mezzotint artist): portraits, Arran, Richard Butler, 1st Earl of (of the 1st creation) [by Smith, KC 1717] (poss.), 35; —, Longford, Anne Aungier (née Chichester), Countess of [by Smith, KC 1717] (poss.), 35. See also Smitz, Gaspar

Smith, M. J.: drawing of Morristown Lattin, 164

Smitz, Gaspar (c. 1635–Dublin, 1707): portraits, Arran, Richard Butler, 1st Earl of (of the 1st creation) [by Smith, KC 1717] (poss.), 35; —, Longford, Anne Aungier (née Chichester), Countess of [by Smith, KC 1717] (poss.), 35. See also Smith, John

Soane, Sir John: and Baronscourt, 178; Sir John Soane's Museum, 326

Somerset, Elizabeth Seymour (née Percy), Duchess of: portraits, 70, 77; —, half-length, 76

St George, Richard, 147, 149, 152; inventory, 149–52; portraits; —, when brigadier general by Bindon, 147; —, when brigadier general by Brooks after Bindon, 146; —, when major-general by Brooks after Slaughter, 153

St Leger, Elizabeth, Lady: at Balfour house sale, 106, 119

Steuart, George, 177

Stewart, Alexander, 325; portrait painting, 331

Stewart, Charles, later 3rd Marquess of Londonderry: portraits, 329; —, equestrian, 328; —, print, 328. See also Londonderry, Charles Vane, 3rd Marquess of

Stewart, Emily-Jane, Lady, 329

Stewart, Hon. F.: portrait bust, 327

Stewart, Captain Thomas (eldest son of Lieutenant-Colonel William Stewart of Ballylawn, and great uncle of Lord Castlereagh, poss.): painting of his tomb, 329

Strafford, Thomas Wentworth, 1st Earl of, 187; portraits, 32; —, full length in armour, 37; portraits with Sir Philip Mainwaring, at Kilkenny Castle [KC 1717], 37; —, at Dublin, No. 10 Henrietta St (full-length) (prob.), 159

Synge, Edward, bishop of Elphin, 88, 93, 94

Talbot, Charlotte Chetwynd-Talbot (née Hill), Countess: her room at Hillsborough Castle, 137–8

Thomason, Edward, 238

Thornton, Peter, 11

Thurles, Elizabeth Butler (née Poyntz), Viscountess: portrait, 31

Titian: chimney-piece of several figures [copy after, KC 1717], 32; Venetian senators [copy after, KC 1717], 37

Tompion, Thomas (clockmaker): standing clock (longcase clock), 68

Traight, Walter van: portrait, Ormonde, James Butler, 2nd Duke of, 73; likenesses of ladies ['Family Picture', KC 1717], 34

Tromp, Cornelis Maartenszoon, Lieutenant-Admiral: portraits, 70, 73

Tyrconnell, Richard Talbot, Earl (and Jacobite Duke) of (lord deputy of Ireland, 1687–91), 247

Vallance, James (Dublin auctioneer), 306

Vane, Charles William. See Londonderry, Charles Vane (né Stewart), 3rd Marquess of

Varen, Bernhard, Descriptio Regni Japonia, 369

Victors, Jan: Jacob (Old Testament) (painting) (prob.), 73

Walker, Thomas (Dublin silversmith) (poss.): at Balfour house sale, 106, 114, 115, 116, 117, 118, 119

Walpole, Sir Robert, 148

Wandesford, Susan Frances Elizabeth (Anne). See Ormonde, Susan Frances Elizabeth (Anne) Butler

Wandesford, John, 1st Earl, 187

Warburton, Mrs: at Balfour house sale, 106

Wedgwood, Josiah, 12

Wellington, Arthur Wellesley, 1st Duke of: portraits, bust, 326, 327; —, prints, 327, 328

Westmorland, Catherine Fane (née Stringer), Countess of: portrait, 76

Wicklow, Eleanor Howard, née Caulfeild, 3rd Countess of (prob.): her bedchamber at Shelton Abbey, 231

Wicklow, Ralph Howard, 1st Viscount, 227, 228; inventory for Shelton Abbey, 229–34. See also Howard, Ralph, later 1st Viscount Wicklow

Wicklow, William Howard, 4th Earl of, 228

Wijk, Jan: boar-hunting scene (prob.), 77; figure-pieces, 84

William III (William of Orange), 27, 187; memorial glass for, 13; portraits, 159; full-length, 82

Wright, John Michael: portraits, Murray, Sir Mungo (full-length), 37, 82; —, O'Neill, Sir Neil, as Irish chieftain (full-length), 82, 83

Wyatt, James, 12, 325, 364; Wyatt-style window cornices (prob.), 292

York, Anne Stuart (née Hyde), Duchess of: portraits, full-length, 37; —, half-length (poss.), 76, 84; —, half-length by Lely [KC 1717], 37

York, James Stuart, Duke of: portrait (full-length), 37

* NGI 4198: Held at the National Gallery of Ireland, where it is catalogued as Double Portrait of Two Gentlemen by an unknown artist, c. 1690, oil on canvas

General index

Page numbers in italics refer to illustrations; those in boldface to entries in the Glossary (pp. 351–64). Boldface is also used within some of the index entries to help readability of subheadings. Other inventories are referred to here under short titles with their full details shown on page 391 in the Bibliography.

This is not an exhaustive index and some items recurring often at the houses but with minimal descriptions are marked *passim*. Items for which one or more characteristics are given may often be found under their common (and descriptive) names as well as under what they are made of, and in many cases under their colour also. Distinction between archaic terms and modern equivalents is maintained, for example: 'armed chairs' and 'elbow chairs' are listed as well as armchairs. Mistaken descriptions in the inventories, such as 'stripped damask', presumably for 'striped damask,' are also preserved.

In the inventories, there is a recurring problem in the use or absence of the word 'covered'. A ticken mattress is one covered with ticken; a leather squab is one covered in leather, but a feather mattress is one filled with feathers, and a hair cushion could be either filled or covered with hair. There is added confusion when an item has a covering and a protective cover as well. It is not always possible to be sure which is being referred to. This ambiguity also applies to tables where 'covered' can mean either with a fabric/leather inset covering, or else a loose cover laid on the table. When indexing such items, there has been at times an element of interpretation about whether something has a covering or a cover, or is stuffed with a particular material. Where it is impossible to tell with any degree of certainty, the entries are purposely left ambiguous.

Abbey Leix, Co. Laois, 7
Act of Union, The (1800), 13, 187, 247
Æsop's Fables: Sir Roger L'Estrange's version in English, 306
agate, 351; cups, 36, 118; knife-handles, 348; picture support, 35
airers. *See* airing horses; bed airers; chamber airers; clothes airers; clothes-horses
airing horses, 334, 338, 343; beech-wood, 335, 336, 337; deal, 331, 333. *See also* clothes-horses
alabaster: bowl, 71; salver, 71; table tops, 217; vases, 216
alarm: clock, 189
alder: fire screen, 328; pillar-and-claw support for mahogany table, 329; poles, 92
ale, 93, 194
ale cellars, 93, 285
ale glasses, 234, 286, 317, 318, 340
allumette cases, 216, 217, 218, 219, 220, 221, **351**; china, 216
almanac, perpetual, 140
almond-paste pots and covers, 218, 219
alphabet press, 219
alphabets, 351; deal, 290, 297
alphabet tables, 217; mahogany, 206
anchor: iron, 168
andirons, 31, 32, **351**; brass, 32, 33, 39, 40, 42; garnished with brass and gilt, 35; lacquered, 34; marble, 33, 37; silver, 71, 72; steel, with brasses, 36; wrought, 31. *See also* fire dogs
antherine, 351; window-curtains (striped), 77
antiques, 204; dish, round, 278; lamp in bronze, 204; spurs, 272
Antwerp: tapestry-hangings, 33, 42, 51; wall-hangings, 42
anvils, 272; blacksmith's, 295
apple trees, 173
aprons: butcher's, 299; cook's, 281
arable farming: corn, 93; oats, 152; wheat, 152
Ards House, Letterkenny, Co. Donegal: painting, 331; view of rocks nearby, 331
argentee: 351; candlesticks, 128
armchair-back: scarlet cloth, 328
armchair bottoms: mohair, 210, 211, 224; rush, 206, 210, 212, 220, 223, 224. *See also* armchair seats
armchair cases: damask, 31; serge, 31
armchair coverings: damask, 267, 268, 269, 270, 271, 272; leather, 193, 216, 229, 233, 271; silk, French, 79; tapestry, 206, 216, 219, 255, 256, 266, 267, 309

armchair covers: calico, 203, 229, 239; chintz, 204; cotton, 336; Damascus, 210, 212, 219, 223; flannel and Damascus, 206
armchairs: bamboo, 271; cane, 43, 47; deal, 90; gilt, 254, 265; gilt-framed, 267, 268, 269, 270, 271, 272; Grecian-style, 204; mahogany, 211, 224, 229, 328, 336; oak, 89, 90, 211; painted, 332; —, black, 328, 330, 335; —, green, 203. *See also* armed chairs; elbow chairs
armchair seats: cane, 239, 328, 332, 335; leather, 240; stuffed hair, 328, 336
armed-chair bottom: cane, 139. *See also* armed-chair seats
armed-chair cases: hair camlet, 42; stuff, 33
armed-chair coverings: brocatelle, 40, 41; damask, 33; leather, 140, 329; serge, 47; velvet, 56; —, figured, 33, 53
armed chairs, 39, 140, 141, 142; black-framed, 33; cane, 47, 151; with carved and gilt frames, 33; Chinese, 139; japanned, 41; mahogany, 337; oak, 334, 343; painted, 138; sycamore, 145. *See also* armchairs; elbow chairs
armed-chair seats: leather, 108; stuffed hair, 337; tapestry, 108
armed-chair sides and back: hair, 334
arms: brass, 125; —, gilt, 125; glass, 90. *See also* coats of arms
ash: ash-tree, 173; axle-trees, 92; cart shafts, 172; timber, 172
asparagus-tongs, 351; silver, 316, 348; silver-plated, 348
auction sales: Captain Balfour's household goods (1741–2), 108–21; Shelton Abbey furniture and books (1950), 228, *235*
audience room: at Baronscourt, 186
augers, 168, 296
aurora, 351; aurora and white, bed-furniture, 38
awl blades, 298
axe, 302. *See also* felling axes; pickaxes
axle-trees, 166, 172; ash, 92; iron, 166
Axminster carpets, 203, 204, 215, 306, **351**
baby house, 307, 312, **351**
backbands: iron, 166
back-chair cases: damask, 38, 42; serge, 37; stuff, 33; taffety, 38
back-chair coverings: damask, 33; velvet, figured, 33, 37
back-chair covers: Damascus, 224
back-chairs, 84, **351**; black-framed, 33; gilt-framed, 42; stuffed, 37
backed chairs. *See* back-chairs

backgammon: **boxes**, 291, 309, 310, 329; —, morocco, 272; **tables**, 139, 140, 189, 274, 310, **351**; —, mahogany, 123, 125, 283
back-stool cases: hair camlet, 42
back-stool chairs, 179
back-stool coverings: damask, 180, 181; velvet, 56
back-stool covers: linen, 180
back-stools, **351**; backed stools, 42
bacon house: Carton House, 290
bags for feathers: linen, 294
baize, **351**; chair cases, 38; chair-covers, 53; curtains, 32; screens, 157; table covers, 204, 308. *See also* green baize; green cloth
bakehouses: at Baronscourt, 184; at Carton House, 289–90; at Kilkenny Castle, 48; at Mount Stewart, 342
bakers: blue-and-white ware, 274; china, 34, 36, 274, 278; japanned wood, with loose pewter insides, 37
baking-dishes, 278, 315; china, 128; copper, 158; delft, 233; silver, 162; yellow stoneware, 183
baking pan: tin, 171
baking-plates: copper, 142
baking sheets, 342; copper, 195
balances. *See* beams; scales; steelyards
bales, **352**; of calico, 282; of line, 282
Balfour town house: inventory of goods belonging to Captain Balfour, sold 1741/2, 108–21
ballrooms: at Carton House, 303; at Dublin, No. 10 Henrietta St, 159
balls, black, 34. *See also* billiard-balls
bamboo: armchair, with stuffed seat, 271; chairs, 270, 328; —, with stuffed seats, 271, 276
bamboo (painted): **chairs**, cane-seated, 327, 328, 329, 331, 333, 334, 335, 336, 337, 343; —, rush-seated, 330, 338, 342
bandle, **352**; sheets, 23; tablecloths, 23
barometers, 216, 230, 271, 308. *See also* weather-glasses
Baronscourt, Co. Tyrone: inventory, 1782, 179–85; print by Fawcett of drawing by Morris, *135*
barrack, **352**; at Carton House, 290–2
barrack bedsteads, 338
barrack mattresses, 125, 126
barrel organ, 308
barrel racks, 285
barrels, 23, 128, 166, **352**; of malt, 93; of oats, 93; of potatoes, 93; of wheat, 93; half-barrels, 23; Parliament, 93
bases (bed), **352**; damask, 31, 40, 43; hair camlet, 42; mohair, 33; sarcenet, 39; satin, clouded, 41; serge, 47; silk, 35; —, Indian, 41
basins: blue ware, 269, 270, 271, 290; brown-edged ware, 272, 278; china, 37, 128, 183; —, old-fashioned, 344; —, with cover and stand, 344; —, with covers, 34; —, with handles, 34; earthenware, 46; green-edged ware, 268; nankeen china, 183; pewter, 22, 171, 286; red-edged ware, 270; red-striped, 278; white ware, 46, 254, 255, 256, 265, 269, 275, 276, 277, 278, 288, 339. *See also* basins and ewers; caudle basin; shaving-basin; slop-basins; sugar basins; wash-hand basins

basins and ewers, 217, 221, 253, 266, 267, 276, 289, 291, 308, 330; blue-and-brown ware, 218; blue-and-white ware, 219, 220; silver, 217; white ware, 253, 275, 287, 335, 336, 337, 338, 339; white-and-gold ware, 218, 219; yellow ware, 220, 221. *See also* bottles and basins; hand basins; jugs and basins; wash-hand basins
basin-stands, 169, 209, 217, 219, 220, 229, 230, 231, 244; and ware, 241, 242, 244; **deal**, 274; **mahogany**, 109, 140, 190, 191, 206, 207, 208, 209, 229, 230; **oak**, 221
basin-table, with drawer, 217
basket cloths (for laundry), 280
baskets, 268, 287, 293; for flower-pots, 205; for foul linen, 139; for glasses, 23, 67, 112, 119; for jaunting-car, 319; for potatoes, 298; **china**, 318, 319; —, with ormolu handles, 216; —, with stands, 233, 319; **tinned**, 66, 67; **Worcester porcelain**, with covers and stands, 318. *See also* clothes-baskets; flaskets; flower baskets; fruit baskets; glass-baskets; knife-baskets; laundry baskets; meal baskets; peat-baskets; plate-baskets; straw basket; table basket; turf baskets; wine-bottle baskets; work-basket
basket stands: for flower-pots, 205
basketwork: screen, 303; servers, 273. *See also* wickerwork
basset-table (leaf), 33, **352**; covering for, in say, 33
baster for dripping-pan, 340
basting ladles, 127, 171, 183, 315; copper, 112, 142, 284; iron, 284
bath: tin, 223
bathing-tubs, 45, 66; lead-lined, 32; tin, 318
bath-stoves, 220, 221
bayonets, 158, 289
beams (balance), 67, 279, 293, 341, 342; iron, 166; wooden, 48; **scale bottoms**, in copper, 279; —, in wood, 285. *See also* scales; steelyards
bed airers, 254, 275
bed canopies, 241; mahogany, round, 221
bed carpets, 137, 206, 208, 220, 223, 224, 254, **352**; Brussels, 207, 218; Scotch carpeting, 190; Turkey-work, 31; Venetian, 266. *See also* bedside carpets; bed-rounds
bed-case: paragon, 75. *See also* case curtains
bedchamber ware: delft, 231
bed commodes, 213, 217, 218, 219, 220, 221, 223, 224
bed-cords, 90
bed-curtain linings: calico, 190, 191; cotton, 332; sarcenet, 39; silk, 139; —, Venetian, 33; silk green, 21
bed-curtains: calico, 191, 202, 208, 209, 210, 212, 219, 220, 221, 223, 229, 230, 231, 241, 255, 268, 270; —, striped, 267; **check**, 210, 211, 212, 213, 223, 224, 231, 232, 267, 275, 276, 289, 290; **chintz**, 125, 160, 207, 208, 209, 210, 221, 223, 265, 275, 310; **chintz and calico**, 254; **chintz calico**, 217, 218, 220, 255, 256, 265, 266, 267; **chintz palampore**, 190; **cloth**, 48, 50, 79, 81; **cloth and brocatelle**, striped, 43; **cotton**, 138, 141,

169; —, printed, 332, 337; **Damascus**, 191, 212; —, 'stripped', 210, 224; **damask**, 38, 40, 43, 70, 77, 79; **Decca work**, 332; **dimity**, 139, 190, 209, 221, 268; **drugget**, 38, 39, 40, 42, 44, 80; —, striped, 36; **furniture cotton**, 190, 191; **furniture linen**, 191, 192, 193; **green cloth**, 46, 49; 'harnum', 49; —, damask, 42; **harrateen**, 125, 126; **Kidderminster**, 48, 50; **linen**, 138; **matted**, 242; **mohair**, 33; **moreen**, 192, 231, 274, 275, 289, 291; **palampore**, 282; **paragon**, 192, 193, 194; **Persian**, 84; **plaid**, 78, 84; **satin**, clouded, 41; —, Indian, 39; **serge**, 20, 21, 43, 47, 50, 80; **silk**, Indian, 41; **silk damask**, 138, 139; **stuff**, 21, 89, 145, 225; —, clouded, 20; —, Irish, 47; —, printed, 43, 46, 68, 81; —, striped, 80; **tabby**, 39; **worsted**, 126
bed-drapery: calico, 219; chintz calico, 217, 218; cotton, printed, 334; muslin, 333; silk, 332
bed-drapery linings: silk, 334
bed finials. *See* cup finials
bed-furniture, **352**: **blue-print**, 55, 58, 59, 60, 61, 62; **camlet**, 79, 80, 109, 143; **camlet stuff**, 182; **check**, 137, 142, 143, 144, 145, 184; **chequer**, 185; **chintz**, 126, 138, 180, 182; **cotton**, 137, 141, 142, 331, 333, 334, 335, 336, 337, 343; —, printed, 330, 331, 334, 335, 336, 338, 339; **damask**, 31, 34, 38, 40, 43, 76, 78, 79, 84, 126, 181; —, Genoa, 56; —, worsted, 57; **dimity**, 333, 335, 336; **drugget**, 39, 40, 42; **drugget plaid**, 79; **hair camlet**, 42; **harrateen**, 80, 126; **Kidderminster**, 58, 59; **mohair**, 33; **moreen**, 181, 182; **paragon**, 78; **plaid**, 57, 61, 62, 80; **print**, 59, 60, 61; **satin**, clouded, 41; **serge**, 58; **striped textile**, 181, 182; **stuff**, 57, 58, 60, 62, 109, 141, 182, 184; —, chequered, 58, 60, 61, 79; —, Indian (figured), 57; —, printed, 58; —, striped, 47; **taffety**, flowered, 144. *See also* bed-hangings
bed-furniture linings: cotton, 330, 334; Persian (striped), 57; silk, 334; —, lutestring, 137; stuff, 61; —, worsted, 61; taffety, 42
bed-hangings: Kidderminster, 61; stuff, clouded, 20; tick, striped, 336
bed-linen, 179; Boyle, 281. *See also* bolster cases; bolster covers; pillowcases; pillow covers; pillows; sheets
bed-lining: sarcenet, 41
bedpans, 254, 275; pewter, 22. *See also* night pans
bed-pillars: fluted, 254; **mahogany**, 241, 265, 270; **oak**, 256, 265. *See also* bedstead foot pillars
bed-posts: mahogany, 190, 191; —, fluted, 190; **oak**, 191, 192, 193; —, fluted, 190; Venetian silk cases for, 33
bedroom vases. *See* chamber vases
bed-rounds, 188, 229, 230, **352**; Turkey, 182; Venetian, 255, 256, 266, 267, 268, 269, 270; Wilton, 230
beds: boarded, 171; deal, 211, 213, 225; four-post, 225; French, mahogany, 221; half-headed, **357**; oak, 288; swing, 209, 221; turn-up, mahogany, 213; wagon, 230, 231,

398

242, 244; wagon-roof, 220, 229. *See also* bedsteads; canopy beds; children's furniture; field beds; press beds; settee-bed; settle beds; sofa-beds; wardrobe-bed

beds (bedding): calamanco, 110; chaff-stuffed, 296, 298; feather-stuffed, *passim*; flock, 23, 40, 42, 43, 44, 46, 47, 48, 49, 50, 58, 59, 60, 62, 66, 81, 91, 111; straw, 43; stuff, 89; ticken, 50, 296. *See also* feather-beds

bed-sheets, 280

bedside carpets, 137, 138, 139, 141, 142, 170, 180, 181, 182, 185, 231, 242, 244, 276, 310, 311, 312; Scotch, 181; Turkey, 182

bedside chamber stands, 310, 311, 313

bedside commodes, 241, 242, 244, 266; with 1 drawer, 266; mahogany, 230, 266

bedside cupboards, 332, **352**; mahogany, 330, 332, 333, 334, 335, 336, 337; —, inlaid, 332

bedside stands, 241, 242

bedside steps: mahogany, 332, 334. *See also* bed-steps

bedstead bottoms: cord and mat, 32, 40, 41, 42, 43, 44, 46, 47, 48, 49, 50, 60; corded, 49, 50, 66; of laths, 43; sackcloth, 31, 38, 39; sacking, 33, 39, 40, 41, 42, 48, 70, 189, 194

bedstead cornices: *chevaux-de-frise*, 334, **354**; deal, 270, 271; **mahogany**, 241; —, carved, 270; —, inlaid, 332; —, ogee, 292; **painted**, green and black, 333; silk, 332

bedstead feet: claw, 332, 334, 335; cross-footed, 38; gilt, 31, 38, 40, 42, 52

bedstead foot pillars: mahogany, 331, 336, 337; —, turned, 330, 331, 333, 334, 335; —, turned and inlaid, 332; turned wood (unspecified), 331

bedsteads, 47, **352**; deal, 143, 145, 275, 288, 298, 299; —, painted, 253; iron, 291, 292, 300; mahogany, 334, 335, 339; **bookcase**, 269; in a **box**, 142; **children's**, 312, 313; **cradle**, in painted deal, 253, 254; **folding**, 42, 194; —, with canopy, 38; **four-post**, *passim*; —, with canopy, 265; —, children's, 209; —, deal, 143; —, mahogany, 138, 139, 160, 217, 218, 219, 223; —, oak, 138, 142, 143, 144, 145, 313; **frame**, 294; **French**, 255; **half-headed**, 43, 44, 46, 48, 49, 50, 60, 62, 68; **half-tester**, 336, 339; **high**, 20, 21; **low**, 21, 23; **low-post**, 267; **sloping**, 289; **standing**, 232; **state bed** (Kilkenny Castle), 70; **table**, 31, 36, 82; **tall**, 77; **tallboy**, oak, 192; **turn-up**, 339; —, oak, 286; **two-posted**, 171. *See also* beds; barrack bedsteads; box bedsteads; camp-bedsteads; canopy bedsteads; field bedsteads; pallet bedstead; pillar bedstead; press bedsteads; stump bedsteads; truckle bedstead

bed-steps, 217, 218, 219, 241, 242; with calico, 207; with carpet covering, 207; with chintz, 207; mahogany, 207, 255, 267, 268, 269, 270, 292. *See also* bedside steps

bed table: oak, 291

bedticks, 296, 303, **352**

bed-valances: calico, 220; —, striped, 221; chintz, 223; chintz calico, 220; cloth, 50; Damascus, 'stripped', 224; dimity, 221; green cloth, 46, 49; hair camlet, 42; serge, 42, 47

bed-valances (inner or inward): damask, 31, 40; silk, Venetian, 33

bed-warmer: copper, 268

beech-wood: airing horses, 335, 336, 337; bookstand, 329; chairs, 128; chaise-longue frame, 333; chest, with 4 drawers, inlaid, 333; coach-seat frame, 334; drawer to dressing table, 337; frame to dressing table, 337; pillar-and-claw support for mahogany table, 337; pole-screen, paper, 337; tables, oval, 330; —, round, 328; —, square, 328, 330; wardrobe; with 2 drawers, 3 deal shelves, 335; writing desk, with 2 drawers, 329

beef axe, 168

beef forks, 341; iron, 142

beef saws, 299

beef-steak dishes. *See* steak-dishes

beef-tree, 299, **352**

beef tub, 284

beehives, 93, 300; bee stand, 300

beer, 194; March beer, 93; table beer, 92

beer cans, 286, 318

beer cellars: at Carton House, 285; at Elphin, the bishop's house, 92; at Morristown Lattin, 167

beer coppers, 142, 341

beer-glasses, 91, 120, 183, 234, 283, 317

beer jug, 316

beer mugs: silver, 316; silver-mounted, 340; Wedgwood, 340

beer stands, 285

bell-lamps, 158, 308, 310

bell-metal, **352**; mortar, 45

bellows: *passim*; chamber, 277; forge, 295; fumigating, 277; spar (painted), 204

bell-pulls, 335, 336; brass-handled, 215; with ivory knobs, 330; with rings, 327, 328, 329, 331, 332, 333, 334, 336, 337; —, in brass, 330, 331; with tassels, 221; velvet, 203, 204, 214, 328

bell-ropes: with rings, 327, 334

bells, 32, 91, 183; and pulleys, 67; glass, 169; —, hall, 189; —, staircase, 189; metal, 277; silver, 161

bell-weights: brass, 203, 214

belly-bands, 319

benches, 194, **352**; deal, 192; long, 192, 193

bench vice, 297

bergères, **352**; leather covered, 205

berlin (carriage), **352**; trunk, 84

Betty galley (owner John Brisco), 70

Bibles, 36, 99, 100, 320; Biblia Græca, 100; in Latin, 103; New Testament [in French], 96; New Testament [in Greek and Latin] (Desiderius Erasmus ed.), 103; Ogilby's Bible, 32; Scott's Bible, 320

bibs, 268; point lace, 268

bidets, **352**; mahogany, 191, 210, 230, 256, 272; —, with delft pan, 255, 256, 265, 266, 267, 268, 269, 270, 292; —, with leather covering, 206, 207, 208

bijou box [?], **352**; silver, 198

bill-hooks, 168, 298, 300, 302, 303

billiard-balls, 192, 308, 327

billiard-cues, 192, 327; press for, 274

billiard-maces, 192, 327, **352**

billiard-markers, 192; brass, 274; glazed, 327

billiard-rooms: at Carton House, 274; at Castlecomer House, 192; at Mount Stewart, 327

billiard-table brush, 327

billiard-tables, 123, 140, 274, 308, 327; mahogany, 192; **covers for**, 308; —, brown Holland, 327; —, English stuff, 192; —, ticken, 274

bindings: chintz, 281; **lace**, 282; **velvet**, to window-curtains, 327; —, to window-drapery, 331

bins, 289; corn, 92; deal, 91; flour, 342; for oats, 49, 50, 158, 167, 292, 293; meal and salt, 341; salt, 284

birch: brooms, 298

birdhouse, 294. *See also* coop

bird's eye, **352**; tablecloths, 141; **diaper**, towels, 280, 282; **damask**, napkins and tablecloths, 282

biscuit: figural group, 219

bistre: drawings, 214

bits (for horses), 319; cheek, 319

black: fire-screen frames, 327; **leather-work**, armchair coverings, 193, 271; —, armed-chair covering, 140; —, chair coverings, 125; —, chair seat, 126; —, library-table coverings, 217, 272; —, library-table lining, 271; —, reading-chair covering, 272; —, table covers, 39, 210; **velvet**, bell-pulls, 203, 204, 214, 328; —, window-curtain bindings, 327; —, window-drapery bindings, 331; —, writing-desk covering, 33

black-and-scarlet: bell-pulls, 327

black-and-yellow: dessert china, 233

black fixtures: chimney-pieces, 125; —, marble, 194

black frames: armed chairs, 33; back-chairs, 33; cabinets, 33, 269; chairs, 32; fire-screens, 32, 76; folding-screens, 327, 329; looking-glasses, 41, 56, 75, 78, 126; stools, 34; window seat, 327. *See also* picture frames; print frames

black furniture: armchairs, 328, 330, 335; balls, 34; —, for footstool, 217; bookcase, 328; cabinet stand, 328; chairs, 221, 327, 328; chaise longue, 328; chest with frame (Indian), 75; chests, japanned, 71, 76; chests of drawers, japanned, 56, 57; clock case, 331; clock pedestal, 125; flower table, 216; inkstand, 221; music stand, 328; play table, 33; pole-screens, 333, 337; screens, 334; —, japanned, 67; stand, 79; stools, 31, 55; swing bookcase, 335; tables, 78; —, japanned, 76; —, square, 82, 84; tables and stands, 38, 41, 42; —, japanned, 75; tea-stands, 82; trays, japanned, 318

black inlay: table, mahogany, 329

blacksmith's shop, 295–6

blacksmith's tools: anvils, 295; bellows, 295; bench, 295; botting tools, 295, **352**; mandrels, 295; punches, 295; tinman's shears, 295; tongs, 295; vices, 295; wrenches, 295. *See also* farrier's tools

black ware: butter pots, 127; cream ewers, 283; crocks, 284; pan crocks, 294; pickling crock (prob.), 277; pitchers, 288; tea-pots, 278, 300, 315

blancmange, 352; cups, 175; moulds for, in copper, 184

blankets: English, 56, 169, 170, 253, 255, 256, 265, 266, 267, 268, 269, 270, 274, 275, 276, 286, 289, 290, 294; Irish, 170, 171, 253, 254, 266, 275, 276, 289, 301; silk, 46; stitched, 70, 84

blinds: caned, with mahogany frames, 271; linen, 270, 271, 272, 274; serge, 338; spring, 217, 218, 219, 271, 274; Venetian, 203, 204, 205, 206, 214, 215, 217, 294; white Holland, 273. *See also* roller blinds

blinds (for horse mill), 298

bloodstone (upon a pedestal), 36

blotting-books, 218, 219, 220, **352**; morocco-bound, 203, 204, 214, 215

blue: bell-pulls, 221; **calico**, bolster and pillow covers, 219; —, window-curtains, 77; —, window-drapery lining, 327; **camlet**, bed-furniture, 143; —, window-curtains, 125; **check**, bed-curtains, 275, 289; —, bed-furniture, 145; —, chair- and elbow-chair covers, 180; —, festoon window-curtain, 290; —, mattresses, 334; —, remnants, 282; **cloth**, chair coverings, 204; **damask**, back-chair cases, 42; —, bed-furniture, 79; —, chair coverings, 31; —, window-curtains, 138; **frieze**, table cover, 169; **harrateen**, bed-curtains, 125; **Indian silk**, window-curtains, cornices and valances, 82; **Kidderminster**, bed-curtains, 50; —, bed-furniture, 58; —, headcloths, 50; —, testers, 50; —, wall-hangings, 20; **lutestring**, chair-backs and seats, 80; **mohair**, window-curtain furniture, 82; **mohair and silk**, window-curtains, 144; **moreen**, bed-furniture, 181; **paragon**, bed-furniture, 78; —, curtains, 157; **plush**, bookbinding, 32; **print** (fabric), bed-furniture, 59, 61; **satin**, window-curtains, 56; **serge**, bed-curtains, 21; —, quilts, 211, 286; —, window-curtain linings, 39, 42, 56; **silk**, bed-curtain linings, 139; —, bedstead cornice and headcloth, 332; —, chair coverings, 39, 53; —, stool coverings, 53; —, window-curtains, 84; **silk damask**, window-curtains, 138; **stuff**, bed-furniture, 141, 182, 184; —, chair coverings, 181, 182; —, wall-hangings, 57; **stuff** (clouded), bed-curtains, 20; **tabby**, bed-furniture, 39; —, quilt, 39; **taffety**, window-curtains, 42; **tick**, pillow, 336; **Turkey leather**, bookbinding, 32, 36; **velvet**, armed-chair coverings, 56; —, chair coverings, 52; —, window cushions, 76; **velvet** (figured), armed-chair coverings, 33, 53; —, back-chair coverings, 33; —, elbow-chair coverings, 47; —, table carpet, 33

blue-and-black: cotton, bed-furniture trimmings, 335; —, window-curtain trimmings, 335

blue-and-brown ware: basins and ewers, 218; night vases, 218, 223; toothbrush tray, 218; wash-ball stands, 218

blue-and-gold china: dishes, small, 319; jar, 329

blue-and-gold Indian china: broth basins and covers, 218

blue-and-grey china: vase, 205

blue-and-pink: calico: bed-curtains, 202, 208, 219

blue-and-white: calico (striped), bed-curtains and valances, 221; —, window-curtains, 221; **check**, bed-furniture, 144, 145; —, mattresses, 331, 333, 335, 336, 337, 338, 339; —, pillow cover, 330; —, remnant, 144; **drugget**, bed-furniture, 39; **linen**, bed-curtains, 138; **plaid**, bed-furniture; **serge**, quilts, 211

blue-and-white china, 233; basin, 37; dessert dishes, 128; dinner-plates, 344; dishes, 175; —, flat, 319; —, large, 36, 37; —, oval, 344; —, round, 319, 344; flower-pots, 205, 206; pot-pourri pots, 205; punchbowls, 36; soup-plate, 344; tea-pots, 118, 128; vase, 205; water plates, 344. *See also* china-ware

blue-and-white English china: flower-pots, 220

blue-and-white Indian china: flower-pots, 220

blue-and-white ware: baker, 274; basins and ewers, 219, 220; chamber utensils, 332; cream-jug, 276; dishes, delft, 175; hand basin and ewer, 332; jars, 342; jugs, 332, 335; jugs and basins, 208; mugs, 208, 217, 219, 220; night vases, 218, 219, 220; plates, 217, 219; punchbowl, 119; slop-bowl, 175; soap-and-brush trays, 331, 332, 333, 335, 336, 337; soap boxes, 219, 220; soap stands, 219, 220; toothbrush trays, 219, 220; wash-hand basin and ewer, 333

blue-and-yellow: stuff (chequered), bed-furniture, 79

blue china: bakers, 278; basin, with handles, 34; cups and saucers, 218; dessert-plates, 195; flower-pots, 328; soup-plates, 195; tureen and cover, 195; vases with saucers, 215

blue furniture: chairs, 139, 221; footstool, 221

blue glass-ware: finger glasses, 234

blue porcelain: mug, Colebrookdale, 206

blue-print (fabric): bed-furniture, 55, 58, 59, 60, 61, 62; cushions, 328; wall-hangings, 57, 60

blue stone-china: ewers, 273

blue ware: basins, 269, 270, 271, 290; bowls, 278, 283; butter boats, 282; chamber vases, 269, 270; cups and saucers, 283; dishes, 278; —, oval, 278; hot-water jug, 311; jugs, 270, 282, 300; jugs and basins, 310, 311, 312; plates, 278, 300; salad bowl, 282; slop-bowls, 300; tea-cups and saucers, 300

blunderbusses, 46, 121, 140, 286, 340

boat rest, 300

boilers, 45, 151, 152, 299, 341, **352**; with covers, 183, 340; copper, 286, 288; fixed, 340; iron, 144, 288; metal, 284, 293; set, 184. *See also* kettles

bolster cases: calico, 203, 205, 221; furniture calico, 271

bolster covers: brown linen, 220; calico, 203, 218, 219, 223, 239; cotton, 335

bolsters: feather-stuffed, 84, 296, 332, 334; filled with curled hair, 35; flock, 43, 49;

hair, 269, 271; haulm-chaff-stuffed, 296; Holland, 61; tick, 301, 336; —, cotton, 253, 254; —, linen, 254; —, striped, 34, 330, 331, 334, 335, 336, 337, 338, 339; ticken, 50, 275; —, striped, 331, 332, 333, 338, 339; ticking, Flanders, 33, 48, 56

bolts, 90; sticking, 297; to doors, 90

bookbinding: plush, 32; Turkey leather, 32, 36

bookcase doors: glass, 140, 160, 209, 271, 310, 330; looking-glass, 160; —, panels, 270; panel work, 271, 276; trellis-work, 220; wirework, 271

bookcases, 220, 244, 308, 337; of dictionaries, 203, 215; with 2 shelves, 337; with 4 shelves, 337; **mahogany**, 138, 139, 180, 191, 221, 234, 311, 329; —, with 2 drawers, 208, 220; —, with 6 shelves, 333; —, desktop, 270, 276; —, with glazed doors, 160, 209, 271; —, inlaid, 326, 328, 333; —, with looking-glass doors, 160; —, with looking-glass panels, 270; —, with trellis-work doors, 220; —, with wire and panelled doors, 271; **oak**, with glazed doors, 140; **twig**, 303. *See also* bookcases (painted); pier bookcase; swing bookcases

bookcases (painted): with 2 drawers, 338; with 3 shelves, 335, 337; with 4 shelves, 334; black, 328; deal, 330, 334; with glazed doors, 330

Book of Common Prayer, The, 32, 36

bookplates, **352**; Carton House library, *246*; Charles Cobbe (1781–1857), *366*

books: at Elphin, in the bishop's study, 95–103; at Kilkenny Castle, in the Duchess of Ormonde's closet, 36; —, in the Duke of Ormonde's closet, 42; at Mount Stewart, 326, 328, 330; at Newbridge House, 320–2; on board the *Betty* galley, 71; on board the *Pearle of Chester*, 72. *See also* Bibles; Book of Common Prayer, The

bookshelves, 190, 218, 219, 220; **deal**, 336; **harewood**, with drawers, 271; **inlaid**, 206; —, with 1 drawer, 217; **mahogany**, 191, 206, 208, 276, 311; **oak**, 126; **satinwood**, with 1 drawer, 204. *See also* hanging bookshelf

bookstands, 203; with 2 shelves, 1 drawer, 215; **beech-wood**, 329; **harewood**, with drawers, 271; **rosewood**, 215

boot-and-shoe rack, 310

boot-jacks, 208, 219, 220, 277, 308, **352**; **mahogany**, 255, 256, 265, 266, 267, 269, 270, 272, 291

borders: linen tick, to bolster, 253; —, to feather-bed, 253; velvet, to stool, 33

boring-block, 296

Borris House, Co. Carlow: engraving by Radclyffe of drawing by Neale, *236*; inventory, 1818, 239–45

bottle cloths, 280

bottle coopers, 296, **352**; japanned, 286; **mahogany**, 233, 234; —, octagonal, 273. *See also* wine-coopers

bottled beer: ginger spruce, 287

bottle-drainer, 287

bottle draining rack: deal, 45

bottle drains, 92, 111, 174, **352**

bottled wines: Burgundy, 194, 199;

'Calcavella' (Carcavelhos, prob.), 199; champagne, 194, 199; ginger, 287; graves ('vins de graves'), 199; Hermitage, red and white, 199; hock, 199; Madeira, 199; Malaga, 199; port, 199; 'Ravesatt' (Rivesaltes, prob.), red and white, 199; sherry, 199

bottle labels: silver, 316

bottle rack, 143

bottles: for seltzer-water, 194; **china**, 180, 181, 309, 319, 329; —, ornamental, 218; —, square, 34; **cut-glass**, 218; —, eau-de-Cologne, 216; **glass**, 219; **Indian china**, 333; **stoneware**, 90

bottles and basins, 180, 181, 185

bottle sliders, 180, **352**

bottle stands, 216; deal, 285; mahogany, 125; silver, 183, 347

bottle stoppers: glass, 218, 219; silver-plated, 206

bottle tickets: silver, 183

bottle tops: silver, 198, 217

bottle tray: mahogany, 125

boudoir: **352**; at Newbridge House, 335

bowls: for cold cream, with stand and cover, 218; for wine, 91; **alabaster**, 71; **blue ware**, 278, 283; **china**, 91, 274, 278; —, and covers, 271; —, with Chinese figures, 319; **delft**, 119, 175; **French china**, 208; —, with cover and saucer, 204; **glass**, 91; **Indian china**, with cover and stand, 220; **porcelain**, 277, 278; **wooden**, 92, 166, 279, 283, 284, 285, 288, 294, 302, 303, 315, 318, 340; **Worcester porcelain**, with cover and basin, 206. *See also* butter bowl; punchbowls; salad bowls: slop-bowls; sugar-bowls

box-barrows, 166, 167

box bedsteads: deal, 157

boxes: with composition-stone panels, 272; for counters, 119; —, china, 310; for eggs, 48; for fat, 143; with partitions, 44, 45; pomatum, in silver, 198; quadrille, 119; **cut-glass**, 197; —, with silver top, 197; **deal**, 52, 142, 193, 272, 287, 298; —, long, 51; **gold**, enamelled, 198; —, French, 198; **japanned**, 70; —, Indie, 329; —, tin, 272; **mahogany**, 139, 272; **spar**, 207; **walnut**, 126; —, brass-garnished, 36; —, on frame, 40; **wooden**, 296, 314; —, for clothes, 314; **yew**, 273. *See also* candle-boxes; coal boxes; corporation boxes; dredging-boxes; dressing boxes; lotto box; packing boxes; pepperboxes; salt-boxes; snuff-boxes; strongboxes; workboxes

box irons. *See* smoothing-irons

box of drawers: mahogany, 311

boxwood: candlesticks, 303

Boyle linen, 281, **352**; bed-linen, 281

Boyne, The Battle of the (1690), 83; memorial glass, 318

braces, 290; and bits, 295

brackets, 75, 77, 82, 191, 219, **352**; for clocks, 203, 214; **carved**, 76; **deal**, for lights, 274; **gilt**, 310; **inlaid**, 206; **iron**, for sideboards and table, 159; **mahogany**, 193, 206; **walnut**, 82

braise kettle, with plate and cover, 183

branches, 108, 270, **352**; brass, 52, 109, 110,

158, 256, 267; crystal, 37; gilt, 108; silver, 196; silver-plated, 241, 272, 348; tin, 'for lights', 303

branch lamps: brass, 287

brandiron, 23. *See also* gridirons; trivets

brass mountings: bucket, round, 157; chests, 330, 331; chests of drawers, 218, 219, 267, 268, 270; fire irons, 274; fireguards, wire, 255, 256, 265, 266, 267, 268, 269, 270, 271, 272; grate, 327; hall lantern, 274; lamps, 327, 328; —, Liverpool, 331; plate-baskets, 327; plate bucket, 205; sideboards, 327; vase, marble, 272; wine-cooper, 327; writing-desks, portable, 330

brass-work: at Hillsborough Castle, 143; at Lismore Castle, 22; **andirons**, 32, 33, 36, 39, 40, 42; —, garnishing, 35; **arms**, 125; **bell-pull handles**, 215; **bell-pull rings**, 330, 331; **bell-weights**, 203, 214; **billiard-markers**, 274; **box**, garnishing, 36; **branches**, 52, 109, 110, 158, 256, 267; **branch lamps**, 287; **brewing pan**, 23; **cabinet frame garnish**, 35; **cabinet garnishings**, 33; **candlesticks**, 22, 46, 50, 66, 77, 78, 79, 81, 127, 128, 273, 276, 284, 288, 289, 296, 301, 315, 342; —, 4-light, with ormolu, 286; —, flat, 22, 67, 128, 143, 232, 276, 288; —, hand, 81, 85, 91; —, high, 143; —, long, 290; —, to reading desks, 204; —, standing, 67; —, tall, 91, 276; —, taper, 330; **chafing-dish**, 127; **chest** (Indian), raised decoration, 274; **clasps**, to writing-case, 217; **cocks**, 64, 93, 284, 285, 287, 288; —, to cistern, 32; **colander**, 45; **cranes** (birds on plinths), 274; **curtain pins**, 270, 327, 328, 329, 331, 332, 333, 334, 335, 337, 338; **curtain-rods**, 35, 219, 270, 271, 292; **dishes**, 45; **door-locks**, 89, 90, 120; **drapery pins**, 328; **extinguishers**, 276, 284; **fenders**, 40, 90, 108, 109, 157, 233, 239, 269, 272, 273, 274, 277, 310; —, top to, 327; —, wire treillage to, 206, 208; **figure-sculpture**, 179; **fire-dog ornament**, 43; **fire-pan**, brass knobs to, 40; **fire peel**, 64; **fire shovels and tongs**, 31, 32, 33, 40, 41, 42; —, knobs to, 31, 32; **footman**, 289; **grate**, 272; —, facing, 194; **grater**, 283; **handles**, to chest of drawers, 221; —, to writing-table, 221; **hat hooks**, 274; **hearths**, 82; —, Dutch, with handles and balls in brass, 52; **honeysuckle pins**, 216; **inlay**, 273; **kettles**, 22, 45; —, Welsh, 22; **knocker**, 120; **ladles**, 22, 45, 112; **lamps**, 340; —, 1-burner, 287; —, 2-burner, 287; —, 6-burner, 287; **latticework**, to library-table doors, 272; **locks**, 89, 90; **looking-glasses**, 35; —, frame garnishing, 31, 38; **marble table-top borders**, 159; **mortars**, 111, 112, 183; —, with pestle, 91; **patent lamp**, with 2 lights, 205; **pattypan**, 45; **pepperbox**, 91; **pepperpot**, 22; **pickling kettle**, 342; **picture frames**, with ebony, 214, *215*; —, ornaments to, 331, 332, 333; —, with tortoiseshell, 214; **plate stand**, 90; **plate warmer**, 112; **plinths**, 274; **poles** to fire screens, 272, 273; **punchbowl** (china) garnishing, 36; **scales**, 79, 284; **scale weights**, 79, 279; **sconces**, 32, 45,

90; —, with silver wash, 31; **screen stands**, 218; **sets of drawers**, garnish, 207; **skillets**, 112, 158, 171, 279, 288, 315; **skimmers**, 22, 45, 91, 112; **snuff-dish**, 22; **snuffer-frames**, 46; **snuffer-pan**, 77; **snuffers**, 22, 46, 77, 78, 79, 85, 127, 128, 276, 284, 342; **snuffer-trays**, 276, 342; **stair-rods**, 231; —, and screw staples, 189; **stove-grate**, 137; **surveyor's chain**, 297; **table-and-stand**, garnishing, 38; **table ornament** (fish), garnish, 278; **tongs**, 31, 32, 33, 38; **trellis-work**, bookcase, 220; **umbrella stand**, 214; **upholstery nails**, 253, 254, 329; **warming-pans**, 22, 47; **window rods**, 272

brass-work (silvered): nozzles and pans to sconces, 76

braziers and covers, **352**; oval, copper, 195

bread: ring for, 45

bread-and-butter plates: china, 345

bread-baskets, 303, 318; silver, 347; —, maker's mark of John Hamilton, 316, *317*; silver-plated, 241, 323; yellow stoneware, 183

bread-box, 232

bread colander: tin, 284

bread-graters, 314; tin, 340

bread-pans, 278

bread pricker, 342

bread-rasps, 90, 284

breakfast cloths, 141, 280; diaper, 195; square pattern, 179

breakfast-cups and saucers, 342; china, 233, 345

breakfast knives, 282

breakfast napkins, 141, 280; damask, 346; diaper, 346; Dutch matted pattern, 280

breakfast-parlours: at Castlecomer House, 189; at Dublin, No. 10 Henrietta Street, 156, 158; at Shelton Abbey, 229

breakfast plates: china, 128, 345; porcelain, 277

breakfast-rooms: at Baronscourt, 180; at Hillsborough Castle, 15, 123, 139; at Morristown Lattin, 165, 170; at Newbridge House, 315

breakfast services: at Carton House, rosebud, 277; —, blue-edged, 278

breakfast spoon: silver, 323

breakfast tablecloths, 141

breakfast-tables: claw, 125; mahogany, 189; —, with drawers, 270; —, with folding leaves, 328

breast-plates, 319, 320

breeches, 298, 319, **352**

brewhouses: at Baronscourt, 184; at Carton House, 289; at Elphin, the bishop's house, 92; at Hillsborough Castle, 128, 144; at Kilkenny Castle, 51; at Kilrush House, 151; at Lismore Castle, 23; at Morristown Lattin, 166

brewing: barm can, 166, **352**; boilers, copper, 144, 166, 289; brewing pans, 23; —, brass, 23; brewer's slings, 166, 285, 287, **352**; cocks, copper, 166; coolers, 128, 151, 166; —, and spout, 144; —, fixed, 51; coppers, 92, 128, 354; —, fixed, 51, 92; —, set, 184; coral

General index 401

waste tub, 23; dropper, 93, **356**; furnace, 151; gutters, wooden, 51; gyle-room, 92; gyle-tub, 151, **357**; keeves, 23, 92, 128, 151, 166, **358**; keeve stool, 92; kennel-pot, 166, **358**; lading-pails, 23; malt bin, 166; malt mill, 151; mashing shovels, 166; mash-tub, 144, **359**; oars, 51; pipes, 285; pump, leaden, 289; shovel, 289; sieves, 166; standing tub, 92; stillions, 23, 166, 285; streamer, wooden, 166; trough, 51; tundishes, 92; —, wooden, 166; tunning tubs, 23, 128; tuns, fixed, 51; washing-tubs, 92; wheat-mill (steel), 92; wort pumps, wooden, 51, **364**; wort sieve, 128

bridle-bits: snaffle, 319

bridles, 299; night, 319; snaffle, 167, 293, 319; twisted snaffle, 319; watering, 167, 319; winkers, 298

brocatelle, 352–3; armed-chair coverings, 40, 41; carpets, 36; chair coverings, 47, 53

broiler: sheet iron (for beef), 284; broiling plate, 183

bronze: candlesticks, 203, 204, 214; figures, 204; —, with lamp, 308; lamps, 203, 204, 214; paperweight handle, 214; paperweights, 203, 214; —, head-shaped, 204; patent lamps, 273; urn, 329; watch-stand, 221

bronze and gold: inkstand, 204; table frames, 273

bronzed work: buffalo, 279; figure-sculpture, 274; lion, 279

bronzes (sculptures): boar, 216, 274; bull, 274; dogs, 274; figures, 203, 214; —, in groups, 204, 273; —, with lamp, 308; Hercules, 273; lions, 205, 216, 274; Venus and Adonis, 273. *See also* Index of personal names, pp. 390–4

brooms, 92, 292; birch, 298; carpet, 288, 338; hair, 125, 126; hearth, 31, 125, 126; sweeping, 318

broth basins: china, 277; Indian china, 220; —, and covers, 218

brown: stuff, bed-furniture, 126

brown-and-white ware: hand basin and ewer, 334; jugs (figured), 334; soap-and-brush tray, 334; wash-hand basin and ewer, 332

brown china: tea-pot, 128

brown-edged ware: basins, 272, 278; jugs, 278

brown Holland, 357; billiard-table cover, 327; mattresses, 337, 339; roller blinds, 331, 332, 333

brown linen: bolster covers, 220; cushion-covers, 220; pillow covers, 220; roller blinds, 335

brown pans, 314; deep, 341; shallow, 341

brown ware: jars and covers, 341; pan crocks, 284; tea-urn, 345

brushes: billiard-table, 327; blacking, 318; bottle, 318; carpet, 318; —, of twig, 278; crevice, 288; dry rubbing, 278; dust, 288; dusting, 278, 288; foot, 203, 205, 214, 274; hand, 126; heads for, 90; painting, 278; paste, 142, 284; pope's head, 318, **360**; scrubbing, 278, 288; stair, 278, 288, 318; sweeping, 288; table, 288; vegetable, 284; whiting, 318. *See also* brooms; hearth brushes; shaving brush

brush trays, 256, 265, 266, 267, 268, 269, 270, 271, 272, 275, 276, 278, 330. *See also* toothbrush trays; soap-and-brush trays

Brussels, 353; bed carpets, 207, 218; carpets, 204, 208, 228, 229, 255, 336; floor carpets, 207, 218; quilts, 289; —, worsted, 275, 290, 291, 292

buckets: brass-mounted and round, 157; copper, 171; leather, 293; mahogany, 169; —, square, 157; wooden, 302, 303. *See also* fire-buckets; house buckets; pails; stable buckets

buckles: diamond, 118; silver, shoe and knee, 118; —, stock, 118

buckram, 353; remnant, 282

buff, 353; Mount Stewart, Buff Bedroom, 331–2; —, Buff Dressing Room, 331; bed-curtains, 256, 312; bed-furniture lining, 331; **chintz**, festoon window-curtains, 267; —, window-curtains, 256, 266; **chintz calico**, bed-curtains, 254, 256, 265, 266, 267; —, festoon window-curtains, 255, 265; —, window-curtains, 266, 267; **cotton**, window-drapery, 331; **furniture calico**, length of, 281

bull and bullocks. *See* livestock

bullock scrapers, 298

bullock yard: at Carton House, 299

bureaux, 67, 180, **353**; mahogany, 125, 126, 137, 138, 139; oak, 141; wainscot, 185; walnut, 160

bushels, 293, 299, **353**

busts: on brackets, 233; female figure, 329; **cast**, Apollo Belvedere, 221; **marble**, 273, 327; —, Medusa, 216; —, Venus (after Canova), 217; **plaster of Paris**, 327; —, bronzed, 274. *See also* portraits (busts)

butlers' pantries: at Baronscourt, *176*, 183; at Borris House, 240; at Castlecomer, 192–3; at Dublin, No. 10 Henrietta St, 157; at Hillsborough Castle, 141; at Killadoon, 205, 224; at Mount Stewart, 339–40; at Shelton Abbey, 234

butlers' rooms: at Killadoon, 211, 213; —, butler's bedroom, 224; at Newbridge House, 313

butter boats, 175, 282, 316; blue ware, 282; china, 233; delft, 233; silver, 316, 323; —, and covers, 323; Worcester porcelain, 318

butter bowls, 127, 173

butter buckets, 294, 302

butter casks, 113

butter coolers: cut-glass, 286

butter crocks, 173, 294

butter cups: silver, 117

butter ewers, 353; silver, 347

butter glasses and stands: cut-glass, 318; —, oval, 345; —, round, 345

butter knives: silver, 240, 348; silver-plated, 348

butter ladles: silver, 316

butter pail and cover: white ware, 278

butter pan: delft, 294

butter plates: silver, 197

butter pots, black, 127

butter saucepan: copper, 195

butter scales, 294

butter slices: wooden, 284

butter trowels: silver, 316

butts, 353; of Madeira, 199; of oil, 287

cabinet basin: china, with cover and stand, 334

cabinet coffee-cups and saucers: china, 344; Dresden porcelain, 344

cabinet cups, 353; china, 333; with saucer and cover, 334

cabinet doors: glass 329

cabinet frames, 41; black, 33, 269; brass-garnished, 35; with carved work, 34

cabinet mouldings: silver, 274

cabinets: brass-garnished, 33; with composition-stone panels, 271; for miniatures, 329; **ebony**, with black frame, 33; **inlaid**, 274; —, with tortoiseshell, 33; —, Tunbridge ware, 206, 220; **japanned**, 34; **mahogany**, 126, 190; —, with drawers inside, 273; —, glazed, with 2 drawers, 5 shelves, 329; **walnut**, 110; —, on frame, 41

cabinets (Indian), 36, 138, 309, 310; on a frame, 269; scarlet, 269; **inlaid**, 329; —, with 5 drawers, 328; —, with drawers, 329; **japanned**, 276; —, with 10 drawers, on a frame, 333

cabinets of curiosities, 273, 307; at Newbridge House, 305

cabinet stand: black-painted, 328

cabinet tea-cups and saucers: china, 344

caddows, 21, 23, 40, 42, 43, 44, 46, 47, 48, 49, 50, **353**; silk, 50

caddy, 353. *See* sugar caddy; tea-caddies

caffa, 353; cushions, figured, 32; —, long for the church, 32

caffoy, 353; carpets, 79; chair coverings, 75, 82; cushions, 66; panel work, 150; settee-bed covering, 150; wall-hangings, 82; window-curtains, 82

cake dishes: porcelain, 277

cake pans: copper, 195

cake plates: china, 233; porcelain, 277, 278

calamanco, 353; bed, 110

calico, 281, 353; armchair covers, 203, 229, 239; bed-curtain linings, 190, 191; bed-curtains, 191, 202, 208, 209, 210, 212, 219, 220, 221, 223, 229, 230, 231, 255, 268, 270; bed-curtain trimmings, 208, 209, 221; bed-drapery, 219; bed-step adornment, 207; bed-valances, 220; bolster cases, 203, 205, 221; bolster covers, 203, 218, 219, 223, 239; bookshelf back covering, 271; chair cases, 270, 271; chair-cover linings, 191; chair-covers, 191, 203; curtains, 38; cushion cases, 203, 205, 221, 270; cushion-covers, 203, 206, 207, 218, 219, 220; cushions, 52; dressing-stool covers, 217, 218, 219, 220; hunting-chair cover, 217; mattress case, 221; mattress cover, 223; ottoman cover, 216; pillowcases, 203, 205, 221, 269; pillow covers, 203, 206, 216, 218, 219; quilts, 21, 78, 80, 84, 90, 209; remnants, 281, 282; seat-back cushion covers, 239; sofa covers, 229, 239; squab cases, 221; squab cover, 216; tester, 41; window-curtain linings, 189, 190, 191, 327; window-curtains, 21, 39, 40, 41, 77, 79, 189, 191, 203, 208, 209, 214, 219, 220, 221, 230, 231, 232, 233, 242, 271;

window-curtain valances, 208, 209, 220, 221; window-drapery, 203, 214, 219, 233, 271; window-drapery lining, 327; window-stool covers, 203. *See also* furniture calico

calico (Indian): curtains, 32; valance, 32; wall-hangings, 32, 42

calico (printed), 281

calico (striped): bed-curtains, 267; bed-valances, 221; festoon window-curtains, 267, 269; window-curtains, 221

calico and muslin: toilet-table covers, 207

calico chintz, **353**. *See also* chintz calico

callipers, 297

cameo (sulphur), **353**; portrait of Llandaff, Countess of, 214

camlet, **353**; bed-furniture, 79, 80, 109, 143; length of, 144; window-curtains, 80, 109, 125. *See also* hair camlet

camlet stuff: bed-furniture, 182

camp-armchairs, 256, 267

camp-beds, 169, 170, 210, 212, 224

camp-bedsteads, 242, 256, 276

camp-chairs, 70, 81, 231, **353**; with Russia leather coverings, 81

camp-stools, 81, 331

camp table: mahogany, with folding top and 1 drawer, 342

candelabra, painted, 228, 229

candle-boxes, 92, 279; deal, 52, 90

candle chests, 21, 32, 45, 157

candle-shades: for branches, 108; painted glass, 329; plated silver, 203, 214; tin, 204

candle stands: elm, 255; mahogany, on pillars and claws, 272; silver-plated, 203, 214

candlestick bottoms: mahogany, 347

candlestick cloths: grey linen, 280

candlesticks: *passim*; **argentee**, 128; **boxwood**, 303; **brass**, *passim*; **bronze**, 203, 204, 214; **china**, 204, 216, 256, 267; —, monkey-shaped, 220; —, with silver sockets, 71; **Colebrookdale**, 204, 219; **copper**, hall, 195; **delft**, 219, 303; —, gilt-edged, 255, 256, 265, 266, 267; **earthenware**, 332, 333; **iron**, 48, 171; **mahogany**, 318; **ormolu**, 273; —, 4-light, and brass, 286; **silver**, 117, 118, 162, 196, 283, 316; —, with branches, 317, 323; —, chamber, 198; —, library, 316; —, small, 161; silver-plated, 183, 198, 241, 275, 317, 323, 348; **spar**, 207; —, Derbyshire, 218, 220; **steel**, 288; **tin**, 46, 127, 276, 277, 284, 288, 289, 290, 291, 292, 293, 315; —, with stand, 80; **Wedgwood**, 207, 208, 218; **white ware**, 332, 333

candlesticks (bedchamber): silver-plated, 241, 317, 323

candlesticks (card-table): silver, 347

candlesticks (dinner): silver, fluted, 347; —, wrought, 347; silver-plated, 348

candlesticks (flat), 80, 111, 234, **356**; brass, 22, 67, 128, 143, 232, 276, 288; copper, 195; silver, 347; silver-plated, 317; tin, 144, 283, 287

candlesticks (fly), **356**; iron, 341

candlesticks (French): gilt, 219

candlesticks (hand), 79, 80; brass, 81, 85, 91; japanned, 342; silver, 117; silver-plated, 183, 348

candlesticks (high), 111; brass, 143; iron, 232; tin, 315

candlesticks (long): brass, 290; iron, 285

candlesticks (pillar), 180

candlesticks (reading), 203, 214; brass, 204; silver-plated, 204

candlesticks (round): japanned, 339

candlesticks (square): japanned, 339

candlesticks (standing): brass, 67

candlesticks (tall): brass, 91, 276

candlesticks (taper): brass, 330; silver-plated, 348

candlestick sockets: silver, 71, 117

cane, **353**; armchairs, 43, 47; armchair seats, 239, 328, 332, 335; armed-chair bottom, 139; armed chairs, 47, 151; chair bottoms, 170, 296, 312, 331; chairs, 20, 21, 31, 67, 78, 79, 80, 81, 203, 204, 206, 207, 214, 217, 218, 219; —, painted, 208, 229; chair seats, *passim*; —, child's, 265; easy chair, 78; elbow-chairs, 20, 21, 22, 78, 79; sashes, 82; seat bottoms, 331; squab bottoms, 34; stools, 21, 22; table, square, 78

canisters, 120, 126; china, 118; Chinese composition, 271; tin, 276, 289. *See also* coffee canister; sugar canisters; tea-canisters

cannel coal, 120, **353**

canoes, 291; model of one, 273

canopies, 38, 42, 43, 265, 332; Decca work, 332; 'harnum' damask, 42

canopy beds, 208, 209, 220, 221

canopy bedsteads, 190; mahogany, 332. *See also* canopy beds

cans, **353**; with funnel, 64; **copper**, 127, 314; —, 5-, 2- and 1-gallon, 285; **japanned**, 275; **silver**, 117, 161, 197; **tin**, 283, 288, 293, 294; —, 2-gallon, 286; **wooden**, 23

Canterburys, 216, **353**; dinner, 274; mahogany, 205; —, supper, 240; partitioned stands in satinwood, 272

cantoons, **353**; damask, 31, 38, 40; mohair, 33; satin, clouded, 41; —, Indian, 39

canvas, **353**; chair coverings, 52; fire screens, 180, 182; mattress, 50; for needleworking, 268; quilt, 35; sieve, 278; for stuffing, 268; tapestry linings, 31, 41, 42, 51; wall-hanging linings, 51

caparisons, 71, **353**

caple rope, 90, **353**

caprioles, 167, **353**

caps, 268. *See also* nightcap; Turk's caps

carafes. *See* crofts

caravan, 293

carbine, 301, **353**

carding-tables, 66, 67, **353**

card racks, 203, 214

card-table covering: velvet, 33

card-tables, 66, 89, 90, 140, 150, 168, 179, 193, 203, 214, 239, 308, 309, 310; mahogany, 109, 125, 139, 160, 189, 229, 230, 233, 273, 275, 303, 329, 330

caricatures: prints, 192; on screen, 329; screen coverings, 329, 334

carnations, 301

carpenter's workshop, 296

carpet-brooms, 288, 338

carpet-brushes: twig, 278, 288

carpet coverings: bed-steps, 207; —, Brussels carpet, 255, 267, 268, 269, 270, 292; dressing stool, 265; footstools, 265, 273; stools, 271

carpet covers: green baize, 229, 310

carpets, **353**; Axminster, 203, 204, 215, 306; brocatelle, 36; Brussels, 204, 208, 255, 336; caffoy, 79; carpet strips, 170; carpet-slips, 203, 204, 215; cloth, 41; cloth and brocatelle, striped, 43; drugget, 39, 40, 42, 309, 310, 311, 312; —, striped, 36; gilt-leather, 50, 51; green cloth, 42; Irish, 267; Kidderminster, 329, 330, 331, 332, 333, 334, 335, 336, 337, 338; leather, 51; Nymphs, 51; Pallas, story of, 51; Persian, 33, 51; Scotch, 108, 189; for sideboards, 169; Smyrna, 51; stool covering, 273; Turkey, 108, 109, 179, 180, 181, 182, 189, 205, 211, 216, 224, 272, 273, 292, 328; Turkey-work, 44, 51, 66, 79; velvet, 32; —, French, 38; Venetian, 265, 269, 287; woollen, printed, 336. *See also* bed carpets; bed-rounds; bedside carpets; stair-carpeting; table carpets

carriage accessories: trunk covers and straps, 293

carriages: berlin, 84; caprioles, 167; chariot, child's, 293; curricle, 319, **355**; horse break, 293; jaunting-cars, 293, 319; landau, 319; phaeton, **360**; —, child's, 293; snow, 293; summer, 293; tilbury, 293; carriages and harness at Newbridge House, 319–20

Carrick-on-Suir, Co. Tipperary, 12

cars, **353**; car sides, 172; car slats, 172; car wheels, 166

cart house: at Morristown Lattin, 166–7

Carton House, Co. Kildare: architectural drawing by Sir Richard Morrison, *250–1*; inventory of 1818, 249–56 and 265–303; view by Hagen, 247, *264*; Waterstown (Shell Cottage), 301–2

cartoons, 159

carts: bomb-carts, 297, **352**; drays, 297; mule carts, 297. *See also* cars

cart-soles, 172, **353**

carved work: armed chair, 145; armed-chair frames, gilt, 33; battle-pieces, 214, *215*; bedstead cornices, 270; box tops, 273; brackets, 76; cabinet frames, 34; chair frames, gilt, 34, 38; chairs, 45; chimney-glass frame, 271; headboards, gilt, 52; —, washed, 41; looking-glass frames, 125; —, gilt, 81, 138; —, silvered, 34; picture frames, 32; —, gilt, 33, 38; pier-glass frames, 126, 159; —, gilt, 138; ram's-head decoration, 37; sconces, gilt, 35, 37, 82; slab-table frames, 274; stamps for pastry cook, 284; table stand and silver-leafed, 34; table frames, 109, 159; tester, 34; wild boar ('sangolier' [*sanglier*]), 79; writing-table legs, 221

carving-forks, 318

carving-knives: ivory-handled, 318

carving-knives and forks, 128, 234, 282, 285, 315, 342; silver, 323; silver-plated, 348

case-curtain rods, 31, 33, 40, 41
case curtains: damask, 76; lutestring, 70; paragon, 78; serge, 31, 33, 39, 40, 41
case furniture. *See* cabinets, chests, chests of drawers; cupboards, presses, secretaries, wardrobes
casement frames: iron, 51
cases: mahogany, 272; for dirk, 270; of pistols, 121, 270, 303; for telescope, 330; for weights and scales (morocco), 330
cases (textiles), **353**. *See* armchair cases; armed-chair cases; back-chair cases; back-stool cases; bed-cases; bolster cases; chair cases; cushion cases; elbow-chair cases; mattress case; pillowcases; stool cases
cases of drawers, 231, 241, 244; mahogany, 229, 230, 231, 242, 244; oak, 232; walnut, 231
casks, 92, 151, 166, 167, 287, **353**; butter, 113; vinegar, 23, 143; water, 111
casserole dishes and covers: silver, 196
Castlecomer House, Co. Kilkenny, *186*; inventories, 1798, 189–99
castors (vessel): silver, 117, 161; —, castor urns, 197; wooden, 120
castors (wheel and swivel): bedsteads, fourpost, 217, 218, 219; chairs, 221; chess table, 273; claw-tables, 218, 219; clothes-horse, 220; dressing tables, 267, 269; Pembroke table, 218; sofa table, 273; toilet table, 332; writing-table, 221
cattle, 93, 152. *See also* livestock
caudle basin, **353**; with stand and cover, 218
caudle cups: china, with cover and stand, 319; with saucers and covers, 218
cauliflower boxes, 300
cavesson, 319, **353**. *See also* noseband
cayenne-pepper spoon: silver, 316
cedar, **353**; chests, 144; table drawers, 190; trunk, 192; wardrobe shelves, 190
cellar (cabinet), **353**: mahogany, lead-lined, 189
cellars, 285; at Carton House, 285, 287; at Dublin Castle, 64; at Elphin, the bishop's house, 92–3; at Kilkenny Castle, 45; at Lismore Castle, 23. *See also* ale cellars
centre dishes, 278, **353**; china, 345; —, dessert, 344
centrepiece: ewer, 273. *See also* centre dishes; epergnes
chaff: bed stuffing, 296, 298
chaff cutter, 293
chafing-dishes, 79, 184, **353**; brass, 127; copper, 90; iron, 172
chair-backs: Chinese, 270; hair, 329, 330, 332; lutestring, 80; satin, clouded, 51; silk, French, 80; stuffed, 190, 192, 210, 224, 289, 328; stuffed hair, 331, 332, 333, 334, 339; upholstered, 231
chair bottoms: board, 36, 39, 40, 42, 44, 50; —, black, 39, 40, 42; cane, 170, 296, 312, 331; curled-hair stuffing, 189, 190; flag, 21, 22; hair, 216, 220, 339; hair-stuffed, 190; leather, 90, 168, 180, 290; matted, 46, 126; mohair, 209; rush, *passim*; silk and worsted (worked), 268; stuffed, 190, 191, 192; wooden, 144. *See also* chair seats
chair cases: baize, 38; calico, 270, 271; cloth and mohair, 33; Damascus, 276; damask,

34, 40, 56; false, 41; paragon, 75; satin, 41; serge, 33, 34, 40, 41, 51, 75, 77
chair coverings: brocatelle, 47, 53; caffoy, 75, 82; canvas, 52; chintz, 125; cloth, 47, 50, 204, 309; cotton, 137; damask, 31, 70, 125; gilt-leather, 32, 40, 41, 43, 44, 47, 48, 49, 50; greycloth, 43; hair silk, 189; haircloth, 233, 287; leather, 40, 44, 48, 49, 50, 80, 125, 205, 216, 291; Russia leather, 46, 47, 66; serge, 20, 21; silk, 39, 53, 180, 253, 254; silk brocatelle, 41, 46, 52; stuff, 56, 181, 182; tapestry, 203, 204, 215, 217, 291; Turkey leather, 81; Turkey-work, 20, 21, 22, 32, 50; velvet, 38, 52, 53, 55, 56, 78, 84; worked, 168
chair-cover linings: calico, 191
chair-covers: baize, 53; calico, 191, 203; check, 125, 126, 180; cotton, 138, 139, 190, 332, 333, 334, 335, 336, 337, 338, 339; —, and Decca work, 333; —, printed, 330, 331, 332, 334, 336, 338; Damascus, 191, 192, 193; —, 'stripped', 210; damask and gold colour, 70; dimity, 139, 190; flannel and chintz, 204; leather, 339; needleworked worsteds on canvas, 192; palampore, 282; serge, 41, 76; silk, clouded, 204
chair frames: black, 31; carved and gilt, 38; mahogany, 168
chair furniture: cotton, 337
chairs: low, 21; **bamboo**, 270, 271, 276, 328; —, painted, 327, 328, 329, 330, 331, 333, 334, 335, 336, 337, 338, 342, 343; **beech-wood**, 128; **black-framed**, 31, 32; **cane**, 20, 21, 31, 67, 78, 79, 80, 81, 203, 204, 206, 207, 214, 217, 218, 219; —, painted, 208, 229; **carved** (frames), 34; **cherry-wood**, 299, 300; **deal**, 211, 225, 303, 340; **Dutch**, 78, 79; **gilt**, 291, 292; **gilt-framed**, 34, 38, 52, 203, 204, 215; **Gothic-style**, 204; **mahogany**, 160, 161, 190, 191, 192, 205, 209, 213, 224, 233, 240, 269, 270, 272, 287, 308, 309, 310; —, and cane, 204, 205; —, cane-seated, 273; —, fashionable, 189; —, hair-bottomed, 216, 220, 339; —, hair-seated, 327, 330, 342, 343; —, leather-seated, 330, 339; —, morocco-seated, 327; —, old-fashioned, 211, 212, 223, 224; —, with stuffed bottoms, 189; —, with stuffed seats, 300, 335, 336, 337, 338, 339; —, with stuffed seats and backs, 192, 328, 329, 331, 332, 333, 334, 339; **mahogany-framed**, 190; **oak**, 67, 89, 90, 91, 92, 93, 113, 128, 171, 211, 224, 289, 300, 310, 340; —, fold-up, 223; —, with stuffed bottoms, 192; **old-fashioned**, 212, 213, 223, 224; **painted**, 31, 138, 139, 206, 255, 256, 265, 266, 267, 331, 337, 338, 343; —, black, 221, 327, 328; —, blue, 139, 221; —, blue and white, 138; —, green, 203, 204, 207, 209, 210, 211, 215, 335, 338; —, white, 139, 336, 337; —, yellow, 208; **porter's**, 274; **Roman**, 203, 214, **361**; **rosewood-stained**, 216; **wainscot**, 31, 126; **walnut**, 137; **walnut-framed**, 42; **wooden**, 44, 46, 48, 50, 142, 145, 184, 185; —, carved, 45; **wrought**, 89. *See also* armchairs; armed chairs; back-chairs; camp-chairs; children's furniture; easy

chairs; elbow-chairs; hall chairs; night-chairs; study chair; Windsor chairs
chairs (with reading desks), 203, 214
chair-seat frame: oak, 333
chair seats: cane, *passim*; damask, 126; hair, 327, 330, 332, 339, 342, 343; hair-stuffed, 339; leather, 108, 126, 240, 330, 339; lutestring, 80; morocco, 327; needlework, 161; rush, 229, 230, 231, 232, 253, 254, 276, 289, 330, 338, 342; satin, clouded, 51; silk, French, 80; stuffed, 192, 270, 271, 289, 328; stuffed hair, 329, 331, 332, 333, 334, 335, 336, 337, 338, 339; tapestry, 108; upholstered, 230, 231, 241. *See also* chair bottoms
chair seats and backs: old-fashioned, 51
chaises longues, 205, 332; beech-wood framed, 333; black-painted, 328
chamber airers, 275, 296, **353**; mahogany, 255, 256, 265, 266, 267, 268, 269, 270, 271, 274, 292; —, with 2 folds, 279
chamber-bath liners: tin-ware, 331; white ware, 332, 333, 334, 335
chamber baths: mahogany, 331, 332, 333, 335; —, inlaid, 333, 334, 335
chamber chests, 231; mahogany, 270
chamber horse, **353**; mahogany, 272
chamber pots, 308, 310, 311, 312, 313, 314; earthenware, 46; pewter, 93; silver, 116, 161; white ware, 20, 46, 312. *See also* chambers; chamber utensils; chamber vases
chambers, 308, **353**. *See also* chamber pots
chamber tables, 241; mahogany, 242
chamber utensils, **353**; blue-and-white ware, 332; red-and-white ware, 334; white ware, 330, 332, 333, 335, 336, 337, 338, 339
chamber vases, 206, 253, 254, 255, 256, 265, 266, 267, 268, 269, 270, 275, 276, 277, 278, 286, 289, 291, **353**; blue ware, 269, 270; green-edged ware, 268; white ware, 253, 254, 275, 287, 290, 291, 292, 301
champagne-glasses, 175, 234, 317
chandeliers, 79, 81, 318, 353, **353–4**; crystal, with 10 branches, 33; glass, 75; writing, 140. *See also* branches
chandelier sockets: gilt, 33
chaplain's room: at London, St James's Square, 79
charcoal: charcoal pan, 33; grate for, 31; half-barrel, 298
chart frame, 292
check, **354**; Hillsborough Castle, Blue Checked Room, 137; armed-chair covers, 128; bed-curtains, 210, 211, 212, 213, 224, 231, 232, 267, 275, 276, 289, 290; chair-covers, 125, 126, 180; curtain, 289; cushion-covers, 138, 144; elbow-chair coverings, 182; elbow-chair covers, 180; festoon window-curtain, 290; length of, 144; mattresses, 125, 331, 333, 334, 335, 336, 337, 338, 339; mattress quilt, 84; pillow covers, 125, 330; quilts, 144, 171, 276; remnants, 282; settee covers, 125; window-curtains, 140, 231, 232. *See also* chequer-work
checker work. *See* check; chequer-work

cheese dishes: Worcester porcelain, round, 318

cheese-making: cheese press, 23; cheese vats, 92, 127

cheese plates: china, 315; pewter, 22; porcelain, 341; Worcester porcelain, round, 318

cheese slice: silver-plated, 240

cheese-toasters, 314; copper, 112, 158; silver, 161

Chelsea porcelain, 344, **354**; dessert dishes (bird-pattern), 344; flower-pots, 205; ornaments, 319; plates (bird-pattern), 344

chequer-work: bed-furniture, 185; quilts, 50, 253, 254. *See also* check

cherry (colour): sarcenet, bed-lining, 41

cherry-wood: chairs, 299, 300; table, folding, oval, 125; timber, 173

chessboard, 309

chessmen, 273

chess-tables, 274; mahogany, with claw feet and castors, 273; morocco lining to, 273

chest frames, 71; gilt, 76

chestnut shovel: 278

chest-of-drawers top: marble, French, 219

chests, 82, 193; for bacon, 285; for oats, 299; **beech-wood**, with 4 drawers, inlaid, 333; **brass-mounted**, 274, 330, 331; **cedar**, 144; **deal**, 91, 171, 276, 294, 339; —, for church cushions, 142; —, for paper hangings, 142; with frames, 75, 76; **iron**, 171, 217, 244, 308; **iron-bound**, 144, 171; **japanned**, 76; —, with silver furniture, 71; **leather-covered**, 76; **mahogany**, 150, 205; **oak**, 91, 125, 145, 171, 255, 330, 339; —, with 2 drawers, 339; —, with 5 drawers, 337; —, for blankets, 139; **walnut**, 109, 110; —, bedchamber, 230; **wooden**, 339. *See also* candle chests; chamber chests; chests; linen-chest; plate-chests; spice chest; store chests; sugar-chest; tea-chests

chests of drawers: *passim*; **brass-mounted**, 218, 219, 267, 268, 270; **deal**, 111, 141, 291; —, with 5 drawers, 338; **elm**, 274; **japanned**, 56, 57, 192; **lancewood**, 255; **mahogany**, 137, 138, 181, 190, 219, 220, 221, 256, 271, 275, 310, 312; —, with 3 drawers, 333; —, with 4 drawers, 332, 334, 338; —, with 5 drawers, 330, 332, 333, 336, 337, 338, 339; —, with 6 drawers, 338; —, with 7 drawers, 335, 338; —, with 8 drawers, 336; —, banded and strung, 255, 265; —, inlaid, 333, 334; **oak**, 89, 110, 137, 139, 149, 160, 194, 221, 223, 256, 266, 267, 274, 275, 276, 290, 312; **painted**, 225, 342; —, with 6 drawers, 343; **wainscot**, 184, 185; **walnut**, 161, 181. *See also* box of drawers; cases of drawers; chest with drawers; nests of drawers; sets of drawers

chest with drawers: mahogany, 275

cheval dressing glasses, 218, 219, 256, 269, 270

cheval fire screen, 296, **354**

cheval-glasses, 267, 268, 269, **354**; mahogany-framed, 267, 268, 269

chevaux-de-frise, **354**; cornice, 334

chicken coops, 111, 294, 315. *See also* coop; poultry coops

children's bedding: blankets, 212; mattress, 212

children's furniture: beds, 209, 221; 334—, swing, 209, 221; bedsteads, 312, 313; —, four-post, 209; chairs, 216, 309; —, cane-seated, 265; —, mahogany and cane, 205; cot, 265; high chair, 313; night-chairs, 209, 221; tables, 216, 273, 309

chimney-glasses, **354**; *passim*; with 2 diamond plates; black-framed, 75; gilt-framed, 76, 82, 108, 160, 270, 271; glass-framed, 82; oval, 139; pearwood-framed, 56, 283

chimney-ornaments, 308, 309; black, 311; china, 312, 313, 344; spar, 269, 270

chimney-pieces, 189, 296; coving stones for, 109; flowered carving on, 148, 149; marble, 109, 125, 149, 327, 328, 329, 331, 332, 333, 334, 335, 343; —, black, 194; —, and wood, 329. *See also* pictures (figure-pieces)

chimney sconces, 55

china, **354**; allumette cases, 216; bakers, 34, 36, 274, 278; baking-dishes, 128; basins, 37, 128, 183; —, with cover and stand, 344; —, with covers, 34; —, with handles, 34; baskets, 318, 319; —, with ormolu handles, 216; —, with stands, 233, 319; bottles, 180, 181, 309, 319, 329; —, ornamental, 218; —, square, 34; bowls, 91, 274, 278, 319; —, and covers, 271; boxes for counters, 310; bread-and-butter plates, 345; breakfast-cups and saucers, 233, 345; breakfast plates, 128, 345; broth basin, 277; butter boats, 233; cabinet basin, with cover and stand, 334; cabinet coffee-cups and saucers, 344; cabinet cups, 333; cabinet tea-cups and saucers, 344; cake plates, 233; candlesticks, 204, 216, 256, 267; —, monkey-shaped, 220; —, with silver sockets, 71; canisters, 118; caudle cup, cover and stand, 319; centre dishes, dessert, 344; —, with cover and liner, 345; cheese plate, 315; chimney-ornaments, 312, 313, 344; chocolate cups and saucers, 128; cock (bird), 344; coffee-cups, 91, 145, 319, 345; —, and saucers, 319, 345; coffee-dishes, 128; cream-jugs, 319; cream-pails, 318; cups, 271; —, with handles, 269; cups and covers, 36, 277, 319; —, and saucers, 206, 216; —, and stand, 271; cups and saucers, 145, 175, 270, 271, 272, 333; —, gilt, 271; custard cups and covers, 277, 319; déjeuner, 319; dessert dishes, 128, 344; —, oval, 344; —, shell, 344; dessert-plates, 128, 195, 233; dessert service, 277; dinner dishes, 128, 344; dinner-plates, 233, 344; dishes, 37, 175, 183, 233, 278; —, enamelled, 158; —, flat, 319; —, gilt, 233; —, heart-shaped, 319; —, large, 34, 36, 37, 91; —, octagonal, 278; —, oval, 319, 344; —, round, 233, 277, 278, 319, 344; —, shell, 277; —, square, 277; dog pan, 279; egg-cups, 277, 345; —, with frame, 204, 216; extinguishers, 204, 216; figures, 194, 216, 310, 329; flagons, 34; flower or fruit baskets with stands, 344; flower-pots, 34, 205, 206, 207, 216, 310, 328; flower-stand, 319; fruit-dishes, 183; handles to knives and forks, 316; honeypots, 319; —, with covers and stands, 345; ice-pails, 277, 344; inkstands, 203, 215, 216, 319, 344; jars, 34, 76, 118, 179, 180, 203, 214, 216, 273, 309, 310, 319, 329; —, with covers, 34, 76, 274; —, lesser, 36; —, with saucers, 203, 214; —. with silver-topped lids, 36; jugs, 193, 332; —, and basins, 311; match cups, 277, 328, 333; match-stands, 273; muffin dishes and covers, 277; muffin plates and covers, 345; mugs, 128, 175, 193; ornaments, 194, 203, 214, 215, 274; oyster dish, 315; oyster shells, 319; papillote case, 203; plates, 33, 71, 91, 233, 277, 278, 319; —, flat, 319; —, small, 344; pot-pourri pots, 205; pots, high and round, 34; punchbowls, 36, 119, 128, 344; salad bowls, 233, 277; salad-dishes, 128, 319; sauce-boats, 233, 277; saucers, 256, 277; slop-basins, 145, 345; slop-bowls, 233, 319; soap-and-brush tray, chinée, 332; soap stand, 311; soup-dishes, 128; soup-plates, 128, 195, 233, 319, 344; sugar-basins, with covers, 345; sugar-bowls, 233, 277, 319; —, and covers, 319; sugar cup, 33; sugar dishes, with covers, 145; sugar-pails, 318; sugar stands, 233; supper dishes, 128; —, and covers, 345; tea caddies and stand, 334; tea-cups and saucers, 33, 91, 319, 345; —, gilt, 128; tea-kettles, 34; tea-pots, 34, 118, 128, 145, 180, 233, 277, 319; tureens, 233; —, and covers, 195, 344; urns, 273, 303; vases, 205, 216, 217, 273, 328; —, and covers, 205, 216, 217; —, with saucers, 215; wafer tray, 204; wash-hand basins, 128; —, chinée, 332; water plates, 344; wine-coolers and cups, 277. *See also* French china; Indian china; *see also under* Chelsea; Colebrookdale; Dresden; nankeen; Staffordshire; Worcester

china (*craquelé*): ornaments, 203, 204; vases, 204

china cloths: grey linen, 280

china rooms: at Dublin, No. 10 Henrietta Street, 158; at Kilrush House, 148, 150; at Newbridge House, 305, 306, 310; at Shelton Abbey, china closet, 233

china-ware, 34, **354**; at Captain Balfour's house, 118–19; at Castlecomer House, 195; at Elphin, the bishop's house, 91; at Hillsborough Castle, in 1746, 128; —, in 1776, 145; at Kilkenny Castle, 34, 36; at Morristown Lattin, 175; at Mount Stewart, 343–5; at Newbridge House, 318–19

Chinese: figure, 279; saucer, gilt, 255; stone ornaments, 279

Chinese composition: canisters, 271

Chinese furniture: armed chairs, 139; commode, painted, 139; tables, 255; —, painted, 310

Chinese porcelain: dolphins, 318

Chinese rose, 301

chintz, **354**; Hillsborough Castle, 'Great Chince Room', 123, 125; —, 'Little Chince room', 123, 126; armchair covers, 204; bed-curtains, 125, 160, 207, 208, 209, 210, 221, 223, 265, 275, 310; bed-curtain trimmings, 207, 208; bed-furniture, 126, 138, 180, 182; bed-steps, 207; bed-valances, 223;

General index

405

chair coverings, 125; counterpanes, 139, 180; cushion-covers, 139, 204, 206, 207; elbow-chair covering, 125; festoon window-curtains, 255, 267; hunting-chair covers, 204; pillow covers, 204, 207; quilt, 224; sofa cover, 204; window-curtains, 125, 126, 160, 206, 207, 208, 210, 223, 256, 266; window-drapery, 207

chintz calico: bed-curtains, 217, 218, 220, 254, 255, 256, 265, 266, 267; bed-drapery, 217, 218; bed-valances, 220; festoon window-curtains, 255, 256, 265; sofa cover, 217; window-curtains, 218, 220, 266, 267; window-drapery, 218

chintz palampore: bed-curtains, 190; window-curtains, 189, 190

chisels, 295, 297, 298, 302. *See also* pruning chisels

chocolate cups, 175, 354; and saucers, 118; —, china, 128

chocolate pots, 82, 91, 128, 314, 342, 354; copper, 142; with stick, 184

choppers, 113, 283, 299, 341

chopping-blocks, 22, 45, 142, 143, 167, 184, 232, 315

chopping stool, 340

christening robe, satin with sarcenet lining, 268

churn-dashes, 173, 293, 303, 354

churn drainer, 294

churns, 92, 127, 128, 144, 293, 303; child's, 294; delft, 294; wooden, 294

cider, 194; cider press, 300; cider trough, 300

ciphers: on cups and cream ewers, 277; on ivory cups, 272

cisterns, 37, 354; copper, 45, 66; leaden, 32, 45, 84, 297; mahogany, 108, 140; wooden, 67

cistern stands, 216; mahogany, 205

claim for compensation: Castlecomer House, 187

clambs, 298, 354

claret: cut-glass glasses for, 317; glass decanters for, 317; in hogsheads, 199

claret-jugs: silver, 316

claw feet: bedsteads, 39, 332, 334, 335; breakfast-table, 125; chess table, 273; clothes airer, 230; sofa tables, 273; tables, 141, 145; —, round, 139, 140

claw-tables, 203, 214, 216, 354; round, 203, 214; inlaid, 204; mahogany, 141, 145, 204, 205, 210, 224; —, on castors, with marble top, 218, 219; —, reading, 216; —, round, 140

cleavers, 22, 91, 184, 314; —, for sugar, 315; iron, 45, 64, 127

clipping-shears, 300, 302

clock cases: black with plate-glass door, 331; glass, 274; mahogany, 189, 274; wainscot, 331

clocks: chamber, 244, 273, 274, 310; —, with alarm, 189; double movement, 82; eight-day, 158, 189, 232, 274, 283, 284, 290, 294, 300, 301, 331; —, by Richard Grigg (poss.), 183; —, chamber, 139; —, on pedestal, 125; French, with figures on stand and glass shade, 216; monthly, 140; organ clock, barrel from [?], 296; ormolu, 205, 274; —, with 2 figures and glass shade, 328; pendulum, 32; repeating, and stand, 76;

standing or longcase, 362; —, by Thomas Tompion, 68; wooden, 303

close-stool chair, 170

close-stool pans: delft, 170; earthenware, 59; pewter, 89, 169; white ware, 59

close-stools, 20, 21, 39, 67, 89, 110, 169, 180, 181, 185, 354; gilt-leather covered, 33, 42; leather-covered, 33, 39; oak, 48; wainscot, 57, 84, 126

closet, 354; medicine closet, 194

cloth, 354: armchair-back, 328; bed-curtains, 48, 50; bed-valances, 50; carpet, 41; chair coverings, 47, 50, 204; curtains, 40, 310; cushions, 328; hassock covers, 337; headpiece, 50; reading-desk cover, 330; stool coverings, 309; table covers, 271, 328, 329; tester, 50; wall-hangings, 51; window-curtains, 308; writing-desk covering, 331; writing-table top lining, 244. *See also* green cloth

cloth and brocatelle (striped): bed-curtains, 43; carpet, 43

cloth and mohair: chair cases 33

clothes airers, 242; mahogany, 230

clothes-baskets, 90, 91, 127, 284, 288, 343; long, 144; round, 144

clothes-chests, 126; Indian, with leather cover, 138; mahogany, 160

clothes-horses: *passim*; folding, 144; deal, 232, 275, 276, 286, 289; mahogany, 221, 223, 224, 230, 255, 308; —, with boot-jack, 255, 256, 265, 266, 267, 269, 270, 272; —, folding, 209; with leaves, 220; —, for night clothes, 139; —, upright, 209; oak, 223. *See also* airing horses; horses (frames)

clothes-presses, 80, 171, 185, 311; deal, 78; mahogany, 241, 244, 312; —, on drawers, 244; oak, 139, 274

cloths (for cleaning), 354

clouded stuff, 354

coach and horses, 65

coach-houses: at Carton House, 293; at Elphin, the bishop's house, 92; at Morristown Lattin, 167

coachman's cloths, 281

coach-pole, 167

coach-seat frame: beech-wood, 334

coal boxes, 111, 288; copper, 274, 288, 289, 293, 301; deal, 289; iron, 90, 286, 289; wooden, 293, 315. *See also* coal scuttles

coal hammer, 51

coal rakes, 51; iron, 45

coal scuttles, 283, 318; copper, 180, 276; iron, 275, 288

coal shovels, 286, 288, 295

coasters, 318; silver, 197; silver-plated, 317, 323

coat pins, row of, 341

coats of arms: Charles Cobbe, *366*; dukes of Leinster, *246*; plaster of Paris, 339; Royal Hanoverian, 239, *245*. *See also* crests (heraldry)

cock (bird): china, 344

cocks (harvesting): hay, 92; straw, 92

cocks (plumbing), 354; brass, 64, 93, 284, 285, 287, 288; —, to cistern, 32; copper, 143

cocoa pot and cover, japanned, 282

coconut cups, 119; silver-mounted, 118

coconut mugs, silver-mounted, 316

coffee biggin, 354; silver, 197

coffee canisters, 276

coffee cans, 175, 302; fluted, 175; porcelain, 277, 278

coffee-cups: china, 91, 145, 319, 345; —, and saucers, 319, 345; coloured, 119; porcelain, with saucers, 277

coffee-dishes, 354; china, 128

coffee-mills, 171, 182, 284, 286, 315, 340

coffee-pots, 91, 128, 184, 342; copper, 112, 142, 171, 287, 289, 290; —, and cover, 195; porcelain, 277; silver, 117, 161, 196, 316, 347; silver-plated, 323; —, and stands, 240; tin, 232, 284, 287

coffee-roasters, 91, 142, 171, 315, 341

coffee-urn: silver-plated, 240

colanders, 315; brass, 45; copper, 63, 112, 142, 195, 283; pewter, 91, 183; tin, 22, 127, 171, 279, 340. *See also* bread colander

cold-cream bowl, 218

Colebrookdale ware, 354; candlesticks, 204, 219; flower-pots, 204; inkstand, 204; mugs, 206, 217; papillote cases, 204; pen trays, 204, 219; wafer trays, 204

coloured glass: bottle, 216

colours and dyes. *See* aurora; bistre; black; blue; buff; cherry colour; crimson; drab colour; filemot; fringe colours; green; grey; mahogany; olive; orange; pink; sad colour; scarlet; straw; tea colour; white

commode covers: leather, 204

commode doors: plate glass, 215

commodes, 140, 191, 354; for boots and shoes, 217; dressing-room, 270; inlaid, 203, 204; —, French, 215; mahogany, 180, 190, 191, 192, 206, 207, 208, 209, 210, 255; painted (Chinese), 139; rosewood, with marble tops and plate-glass doors, 215. *See also* bedside commodes; corner commodes; deception commodes; night commode

commode stands, 242

commode tops: marble, 215; —, dove, 219

compasses, pair of, 295

composition [stone], 354: box panels, 272; cabinet panels, 271; figures, 233; table tops, 274; vase, 279

compote dishes and covers: silver, 196

concordatum, 65, 354

condition, 354; basin, china, 'a piece of it wanting', 37; bed finials, 'much decayed', 39; books, 'not worth 2ᵈ' [book by Jacques-Auguste de Thou], 101; —, 'miserably abus"d' [book by John Pearson], 100; carpeting, 'but a few months in use', 189; —, 'never been in use', 193; —, 'very little used', 189; carpets, 'very foule & bad', 51; chair-bottom embroidery, 'unfinished', 268; chairs, 'motheaton' [moth-eaten], 53; —, 'quite new', 191; cream-pail, 'wanting handle', 345; crop of winter corn, 'the Worst I Ever Saw', 93; cup, footed, 'cracked and mended', 36; curtains, 'much damaged & torn', 91; —, 'much too scant', 32; —, 'much worne & broken', 44; dinner-plate, 'riveted', 344; dishes, china, 'bit of it broken off', 37; —, 'broke and

mended', 36; **dressing glass**, 'very much cracked', 209; **dressing table**, 'top split', 265; **fender**,'very shabby', 209; **flower-piece**, 'verry foule', 43; **fringe** in gold and silver to bed-furniture, 'much tarnished', 34; **jack**, 'useless till mended', 91; **kettle**, 'ye bottom worne out, quite Useless', 45; **looking-glass glass**, 'mildewed', 35; **lumber**, 'only fit to be burnt', 53; **napkins**, 'worne out', 23; **paintings**; 'all of them wants cleaneing', 53; **patchwork quilt** in silk, 'unfinished', 281; **picture**, landscape, 'mildyed' [mildewed], 38; **quilt**, 'much decayd', 41; **rakes**,'unfinished', 296; **snuffer trays**, 'wanting handles', 347; **table**, 'shabby', 211; **table stands**, 'wants mending', 41; **tester**, 'wore quite out', 44; **towels**, round, 'quite New', 346; **wall-hangings**, 'very much worne out and broken', 42; —, 'very old and decayed', 40; **wash-house pump**, 'not in Order', 51; **weather-glass**, 'not in Order', 31; **window-curtains**, 'a very few Months in use', 189; —, 'not more than a year up', 189
confectioner's belongings: at Dublin Castle, 64
confectioner's office utensils: at Dublin Castle, 64, 65
confectioner's room: at Kilkenny Castle, 46
console-table: mahogany, 308
conversation seats: deal, 303; matted, 303
conversation stools, 189
convex glass, 234
cooks' rooms: at Baronscourt, 185; at Killadoon, 211, 225; at Newbridge, 314
coolers, 343; for water, 127; glass, 317. *See also* wine-coolers
coop, 22, **354**. *See also* chicken coops; poultry coops
cooper's tools: auger, 296; mace, 296; stake, 296
cooper's workshop, 296; hoop iron, 297
copper, **354**; baking-dish, 158; baking plates, 142; baking sheets, 195; basting ladles, 112, 142, 284; bed-warmer, 268; beer coppers, 142; blancmange moulds, 184; boilers, 166, 286, 288, 289; braziers and covers, 195; bucket, 171; butter saucepan, 195; cake pans, 195; candlesticks; —, flat, 195; —, hall, 195; cans, 127, 285, 314; chafing-dish, 90; cheese-toasters, 112, 158; chocolate pot, 142; cisterns, 45, 66; coal boxes, 274, 288, 289, 293, 301; coal scuttles, 180, 276; cocks, 143, 166; coffee-pots, 112, 142, 171, 287, 289, 290; —, and cover, 195; colanders, 63, 112, 142, 195, 283; cutlet sheet, 315; dishes, 65, 195; —, oval, 195; dishing spoons, 283; dredging-boxes, 112, 143, 283; dripping-pans, 63, 142, 283, 340; Dutch oven, 63; fire peels, 64; fish boats, 63; fish-kettles, 283, 314; —, and covers, 142, 158; —, oval, 340; fish pans, 63, 112; fish-slices, 283; freezers, 342; frying-pan, 340; gallons, 111, 283, 285; grater, 183; half-gallon, 285; ice-pails, 286; ice pans, 342; ice shuttles [?], 342; ice tub, 342; jelly-moulds, 340; jelly shapes, 314; jorum, 63;

kettle pots, 91; kettles, 45, 112, 224, 255, 256, 265, 266, 267, 268, 269, 270, 271, 272, 287; —, and covers, 158; knife-basket, 112; knife-box, 112; ladles, 112, 142, 283, 340; lamp, 111; *melonnière*, 127; moulds, 143; mug, 340; omelette pans, 314, 340; pails, 66; paintings on copper, 35, 273; pan, 284; pattypans, 63, 143; plate warmers, 169, 183; —, capuchin, 157; pots, with covers, 63; preserving pans, 279, 342; pudding-pans, 91, 340; saucepan covers, 284; saucepans, 63, 91, 112, 142, 171, 279, 340; —, and covers, 112, 340; sauté pans, 340; scale weights, 315, 342; scallop-shells, 143; shapes, 195; skewers, 340; skillets, 213, 225; soup-pot covers, 195; soup-pots, 195, 314; —, oval, 142, 340; —, round, 340; spoons, 340; stewing pots and covers, 314; stewpan covers, 195; stewpans, 63, 112, 142, 195, 284; —, oval, 195, 340; —, round, 195, 340; strainer, 314; sugar pan, 342; table and stand, finish to, 34; tea-kettles, 112, 142, 144, 209, 210, 340; tea-kitchens, 142, 195; toss-pans, 91, 171, 284; —, and covers, 314; warming-pans, 91, 172, 338; watering pot, 167
coppers, 44, 127, 128, **354**; and covers, 171; boiling, 143; division with 3 covers, 184; fixed, 44, 45, 48, 51, 92; set, 184; for water, 143. *See also* beer coppers
copper thread: fringe to window-curtains, 34
copper wares: at Castlecomer House, 195; at Dublin Castle, 63; at Hillsborough Castle, 142; taken to Kilkenny Castle from Castlecomer House, 195; at Mount Stewart, 340; at Newbridge House, 314; at Shelton Abbey, 232
coral, **354**
corks, 90; silver-topped, 316. *See also* economist's corks
corkscrews, 318; hammer, for bottling wine, 290; silver-bowed (Copley style?), 197, **354–5**
corn: spring, 93; winter, 93; bin for, 92; **corn screen**, 93; **corn weeder**, iron, 297; —, wood, 297
corner cabinets: inlaid, 274
corner commodes, 217; inlaid, 207, 219; mahogany, 206
corner-cupboards, 71, 78, 291, 301, 303; fast to wall, 285; with glazed doors, 84; **deal**, 144, 283, 289, 341; **japanned**, and frame, 76; **walnut**, 158
corner presses, 192, 287, 300, 314; deal, 192; mahogany, 209, 223
corner-shelf: mahogany, 271
corner-stands: mahogany, 125
corner-table, 160
cornices, **355**; Wyatt, **364**. *See* bedstead cornices; curtain cornices; door cornices; window cornice; window-curtain cornices
corporation boxes, **355**; gold, 198; —, Waterford, 198; oak, carpenter's, 271
cot, 265; **cot-curtains**, dimity, 265
cotton: armchair covers, 336; armed-chair covers, 138, 139, 144, 334; bed-curtain linings, 332; bed-curtains, 138, 141, 169; bed-furniture, 137, 141, 142, 331, 333, 334, 335, 336, 337, 343; bed-furniture linings,

330, 334; bolster covers, 335; chair coverings, 137; chair-covers, 138, 139, 190, 332, 333, 334, 335, 336, 337, 338; chair furniture, 337; counterpanes, 139, 330, 331, 333, 335, 336, 337, 338, 339, 343; cushion-covers, 139; dressing-stool covers, 333, 334; fringes, bed-furniture, 333, 334, 335, 336; —, chair covers, 334; —, window-curtains, 335, 337; —, window-drapery, 334; hassock cover, 335; headcloth lining, 335; lengths of, 144; mattresses, 137, 138; pillow cover, 335; quilts, 137, 138, 141, 142, 143, 144, 145, 157, 169, 170, 211, 212, 223, 224, 253, 254, 275; roller blinds, 336; rugs, 137, 138, 343; seating furniture, 333; squab covers, 335; tester lining, 335; trimming to window-curtains, 335; window-curtain linings, 137, 332, 334, 335, 337; window-curtains, 137, 144, 190, 330, 333, 336; window-drapery, 335. *See also* buff; calico; chintz; furniture calico; furniture cotton
cotton (printed): bed-curtains, 332, 337; bed-drapery, 334; bed-furniture, 330, 331, 334, 335, 336, 338, 339; bed-furniture trimmings, 335; chair-covers, 330, 331, 332, 334, 336, 338, 339; counterpanes, 331, 332, 334, 339; cushion-covers, 328; cushions, 337; dressing-stool cover, 332; night-stool cover, 337; pillow covers, 332, 334; seating furniture, 328, 332; window-curtains, 327, 328, 329, 330, 331, 332, 334, 336, 337, 338, 339; window-drapery, 329, 331, 334
cotton (tufted): counterpane, 125; quilt, 170
cotton and muslin: window-curtains, 335; window-drapery, 328, 335; window-drapery trimming, 335
cotton and Decca work: chair-covers, 333; counterpanes, 332; window-curtains, 332
couch-bed covering: satin, 180
couch-beds, 125, 270
couch bottoms: rush, 312
couch coverings: grey linen, 272; plaid, 56; satin, 180
couches, 21, 272, 274, 312, 313; Grecian-style, 271; couch frame, 47; framed (deal), 334, 337; gilded, 35
council chamber: at Kilkenny Castle, 41
counter, **355**; with drawers, 290
counterpane frame, 70
counterpanes, **355**; *passim*; **chintz**, 139, 180; **cotton**, 139, 330, 331, 333, 335, 336, 337, 338, 339, 343; —, with Decca work, 332; —, printed, 331, 332, 334, 339; —, tufted, 125; **damask**, 31, 38, 40, 43, 76, 84; **dimity**, 139, 209, 221; **drugget**, 39, 40, 42; —, striped, 36; **Indian work**, 34; **Marseilles**, 268, 269; **satin**, 268; —, Indian, 39; **serge**, 20, 49; **silk**, 35; —, Venetian, 33; **silk damask**, 138; **stuff**, 21; —, clouded, 20
counters (for card games), 193; mother-of-pearl, 329; trays for, 329
couples, pair of (brace or leash), 299
couteau, 121, **355**
cover dish: silver-plated, 323
coverlets, 184, 185
covers (textiles), **355**. *See* armchair covers; armed-chair covers; back-stool covers;

bolster covers; chair covers; cushion-covers; easy-chair cover; elbow-chair covers; mattress covers; pillow covers; settee covers; stool covers; window-seat covers

cows. *See* livestock. cow-yard, 167

crackle, **355**. *See* china (*craquelé*)

cranes, 111, 127, 152, 340, **355**; and hooks, 111

cranes (birds on plinths): brass, 274

cream boats, covers and plates: Worcester porcelain, 318

cream ewers, 300, 315; with cipher and coronet, 277; black ware, 283; porcelain, 277, 278; silver, 117, 240, 316, 323

cream glass, 318

cream-jugs, 315; blue-and-white ware, 276; china, 319; silver, 197; Wedgwood, 277

cream-ladles: silver, 348

cream-pails: china, 318; cut-glass, 345

cream-pots: cut-glass, 345; glass, 145; silver, 323

cream saucepan: silver, 117

cream spoons: silver, 197

cream tub, 173

crests (heraldry): at Killadoon, on hall chairs, 200, 205, 214; at Mount Stewart, on hall chairs, 326, 327; —, in stained marble, 339; at Newbridge House, on hall chairs, 308; —, on ivory-handled knives, 318; at Shelton Abbey, on hall chairs, 233. *See also* coats of arms

cribs, 299

crimson: **caffa**, church cushions, 32; **caffoy** carpets, 79; **damask**, armchair and stool cases, 31; —, back-stool coverings, 180; —, bed-furniture, 43, 84, 126; —, chair coverings, 70; —, counterpane, 84; —, stool coverings, 70; —, window-curtains, valance and cornices, 75; **lutestring**, window-curtains, 82; —, window-curtains and cornices, 81; **moreen**, bed-curtains, 231; —, cushions, 291; **paragon**, bed-case, 75; —, bed-furniture, 78; —, chair cases, 75; —, window-curtains, 158; **serge**, armchair and stool cases, 31; —, case curtains, 31; —, chair cases, 51; —, curtains, 33; **stuff**, festoon-curtain lining, 282; **taffety**, curtains, 33; **velvet**, carpet, 38; —, chair coverings, 38, 53, 84; —, cushions, 32; —, sofa covering, 84; —, stool coverings, 84; —, wall-hangings, 84

crimson-and-gold: damask, bed-furniture, 40, 76

crimson-and-white: damask, bed-furniture, 31; —, wall-hangings, 35

crockery: at Newbridge House, 315–16

crocks, 113, **355**; black ware, 284. *See also* butter crocks; pan crocks; *see also under* pickle-making

crofts (carafes), **355**; *passim*; cut-glass, 269, 270, 272, 277, 286; glass, 183. *See also* water crofts

Cromaboo linen, **355**; napkins, 279, 280; tablecloths, 279

cross chairs ('x chairs'), **355**; mahogany, 274

cross-cut saws, 296, 297, 302

cross-footed bedstead, 38

cross seats, **355**; mahogany, 274

cross stands, **355**; mahogany, 240; silver, 161

cross-stitch (wrought): cushion, 33

cross stool ('x stool'), **355**; mahogany, 290

crow-bars, 296, 298

crows, 142; iron, 91

crubs, 167, **355**

cruet-frames, 120; silver, 161

cruets, 91; cut-glass, 318; glass, 183, 347; silver-plated, 323

cruet-stands: silver, 117, 316, 347; silver-plated, 241, 317, 348. *See also* cruet-frames

crystal: branches, 37; chandelier, 10-branched, 33; glass with cover, garnished, 34

cuffs, 268; point lace, 268

cullenders. *See* colanders

cupboards: fast in wall, 288; fast to wall, 289; with glazed doors, 329; wire-fronted, 342; for plate (silver?), 45; **deal**, 276, 296; **lancewood**, 254; **mahogany**, for chamber pot, 125. *See also* corner-cupboards; presses; press-cupboards

cupboards (painted), 287; deal, 329

cup finials (for beds), 31, 39; gilt, 42, 52; with plumes, 43; with sprigs, 38, 40, 42; —, satin-covered, 41

cups: agate, 36, 118; china, 271; —, with handles, 269; —, rice-patterned, on stand, 219; **earthenware** (footed), 36; **French china**, 208; —, belonging to ice-pails, 278; —, with basket handles, 204; **glass**, 278; **ivory** (ciphered), 272; **silver**, 161, 196; **stone**, 272, 273; **white ware**, 290. *See also* breakfast-cups; butter cups; cabinet cups; caudle cups; chocolate cups; coconut cups; coffee-cups; tea-cups

cups and covers: **china**, 36, 319; —, and saucers, 206, 216; —, and stands, 271, 277; **gold**, 198; **silver**, 71, 116; **silver-gilt**, 162

cups and saucers: blue ware, 283; china, 145, 175, 270, 271, 272, 333; —, gilt, 271; French china, 204, 219; Indian china, 218, 220; nankeen china, 183; porcelain, 277, 278; Walpole china, 183; wooden, 303. *See also* chocolate cups

curb-chains, 319

curricle, 319

curricle accessories: bar, 319; boxes, 319; harness, 319; sheep rug, 320; trunks, 319; trunk straps, 319

curry-combs, 292, **355**

curtain-cornices: damask, Indian, 75

curtain pins, 272; brass, 221, 270, 327, 328, 329, 331, 332, 333, 334, 335, 337, 338

curtain-rods: brass, 35, 219, 270, 271, 292; lacquered, 37, 40; wooden, 327. *See also* case-curtain rods; window rods; stair rods

curtains: baize, 32; calico, 38; —, Indian, 32; check, 289; cloth, 40; damask, 291; —, Indian, 75; drugget, striped, 36; frieze, 327; harrateen, 128; linen, 44; moreen, 290; muslin, 207, 215; paragon, 157; —, false curtains, 56; plaid, 81; serge, 33, 40, 44, 81; stuff, 81; —, printed, 41; taffety, 33. *See also* bed-curtains; case-curtains; window-curtains

cushion cases: calico, 203, 205, 221, 270; dimity, 269; furniture calico, 271

cushion-covers: brown linen, 220; calico, 203, 206, 207, 218, 219, 220; check, 138, 144; chintz, 139, 204, 206, 207; cotton, 139; —, printed, 328; Damascus, 206, 219; silk, clouded, 204

cushion dishes with covers, 315; silver-plated, 317. *See also* pincushion dishes

cushion frames: gilt, 35

cushions: blue-printed, 328; caffa, figured, 32; caffoy, 66; calico, 52; cloth, 291, 328; cotton, printed, 337; cross-stitch (wrought), 33; damask, 33, 41, 47, 78, 291; drugget, 39, 40; —, striped, 36; feather-stuffed, 169–70, 328; flox-filled, 52; hair, 139, 270, 274, 291, 328, 329, 330; 'harnum', 41; Indian silk, striped, 52; leather, 204, 214; —, Indian, 272; mohair, 79; moreen, 291; quilted, 52; quilting, 46; sarcenet, 39; satin, 52; silk, 35; silk damask, 138, 139; stuff, 43; tabby, 39; ticking, 52; Turkey-work, 21; velvet, 32

cushions (church), 142; caffa, 32

cushions (to kneel upon): velvet, 109

custard cups: china, and covers, 277, 319; coloured, 119; porcelain, 277

custard glass, 318

cut glass: bottles, 218; —, eau-de-Cologne, 216; boxes, 197; —, with silver tops, 197; butter coolers, 286; butter glasses and stands, 345; —, oval, 345; —, round, 345; claret glasses, 317; cream-pails, 345; cream-pots, 345; crofts, 269, 270, 272, 277, 286; cruets, 318; decanters, 286, 340; dinner glasses, 286; finger glasses, 340; goblets, 317; lamp cylinder, 328; lustres, 140, 229; milk pot, 345; patent lamp, with brass-work, 205; plateau glass, oval, 345; rummers, 340; salad bowl, 345; salts, 342; sugar glasses, oval, 345; sugar-basin, round, 345; sweetmeat dishes, 278; sweetmeat shells, 345; trifle bowl, footed, with ladle, 345; tumblers, 218, 268, 269, 270, 272, 340; wash-hand glasses, 286; water-jugs, 317; wine-coolers, 340; wine glasses, 318, 317, 340

cut glass-ware: at Mount Stewart, 345; at Newbridge House, 317

cutlet beater, 283

cutlet sheet: copper, 315

dairies: at Carton House, 293; —, summer, 294; —, winter, 294; at Elphin, the bishop's house, 92; at Hillsborough Castle, 127, 144; at Morristown Lattin, 173

Damascus, 195, **355**; armchair covers, 210, 212, 219, 223; back-chair covers, 224; bed-curtains, 191, 212; chair case, 276; chair-covers, 191, 192, 193, 224; cushion-covers, 206, 219; sofa case, 276; window-curtains, 191, 193. *See also* damask

Damascus ('stripped'): back-chair covers, 210; bed-curtain trimmings, 210; bed-curtains, 210, 224; bed-valances, 224; window-curtains, 205

damask, **355**; Baronscourt, Damask Bed Chambers, Green, Yellow, 181; Hillsborough Castle, 'Blue Damask Room',

138; —, 'Red Damask room' 126; armchair cases, 31; armchair coverings, 267, 268, 269, 270, 271, 272; armed-chair coverings, 33; back-chair cases, 38, 42; back-chair coverings, 33; back-stool coverings, 180, 181; bases (bed), 31, 40, 43; bed-curtains, 38, 43, 70, 77, 79; bed-furniture, 31, 34, 38, 40, 76, 78, 79, 126, 181; bed-valances (inward), 31, 40; breakfast napkins, 346; cantoons, 31, 38, 40; case curtains, 76; chair cases, 34, 40, 56; chair coverings, 31, 125; chair seats, 126; counterpanes, 31, 38, 40, 43, 76, 84; curtains, 291; cushions, 33, 41, 47, 78, 291; dinner napkins, 346; easy-chair covering, 76; elbow-chair cases, 38; elbow-chair coverings, 43, 75, 181; elbow-chair covers, 76; elbow-stool coverings, 181; festoon curtain, 282; headboard, 40; headcloths, 31, 38, 40, 43; lay-overs, 141, 195, 346; napkins, 141, 179, 280; —, dessert, 195; —, dinner, 195; quilt, 120; settee coverings, 75, 125; sofa covering, 292; stool bottoms, 34; stool cases, 31; stool coverings, 43, 75, 76, 126; tablecloths, 141, 179, 195, 279, 316, 345; tea napkins, 179; testers, 31, 38, 40, 43, 81; towels, 179; wall-hangings, 34, 35, 70; window-curtain cornices, 75; window-curtains, 33, 35, 38, 40, 56, 70, 75, 76, 77, 78, 125, 126, 138, 272; —, draw-up, 34; window-curtain valances, 35, 75, 76; window-seat coverings, 76.
See also Genoa damask
damask (bird's eye): napkins and tablecloths, 282
damask (flowered): elbow-chair coverings, 77; festoon window-curtains, 274
damask (Indian): curtains, valance and cornices, 75; window-curtains, 33
damask (star pattern): lay-over, tablecloth, 141
damask (worsted): bed-furniture, 57; door- and window-curtains, wall-hangings, 77; quilt, 57
damask and gold: chair-covers (colour), 70; tester and headcloth, 70
Danzig oak, 355; hazard table, 33
deal, 355; airing horses, 331, 333; **alphabets,** 290, 297; **armchair,** 90; **basin-stand,** 274; **beds,** 211, 213, 225; **bedstead cornices,** 270, 271; **bedsteads,** 143, 145, 288, 298, 299; —, four-post, 143; **bin,** 91; **boards,** 92, 168, 292; **bookshelves,** 336; **bottle-draining rack,** 45; **box bedsteads,** 157; **boxes,** 142, 193, 272, 287, 298; —, long, 51; **brackets,** for lights, 274; **candle-boxes,** 52, 90; **chairs,** 211, 225, 303, 340; **chests,** 91, 171, 276, 294, 339; —, for church cushions, 142; —, for paper hangings, 142; **chests of drawers,** 111, 141, 291; —, with 5 drawers, 338; **clothes-horses,** 232, 275, 276, 286, 289; **clothes-press,** 78; **coal box,** 289; **conversation seats,** 303; **corner-cupboards,** 144, 283, 289, 341; **corner press,** 192; **couch frames,** 334, 337; **cover,** 40; **cupboards,** 276, 296; **desks,** on a frame, 300; —, sloping, with drawers, 276; **door,** 298; **dressers,** 51, 91, 111, 284, 301, 303, 340, 341; —, with drawers, 293; —, with 2

shelves, 340, 341; —, with shelves, 303, 341, 343; —, square, 340; **dressing tables,** 90, 125, 126, 139, 212, 229, 265, 269; —, with 1 drawer, 338; —, with 2 drawers, 267; —, with drawers, 276; —, on castors, 267, 269; —, square, 339; **fire screen,** 158; **fireguard,** 290; **forms,** 128, 141, 145, 158, 192, 211, 224, 275, 303, 341; **hall-table,** 149; **hanging shelves,** 284, 289, 341; **harp case,** 274; **horses,** 212, 294; —, folding, 288; **jelly stand,** 142; **kitchen-tables,** 142, 300, 302, 340; **knife-basket,** 283; **knife-trays,** 339; **laths,** for napkin drying, 51; **linen-press,** with 8 drawers, 342; **nests of drawers,** 276, 290; **office stool,** 274; **office table,** with book rack and shelves, 275; **packing boxes and cases,** 52; **panel work,** 290; **pasteboard,** 341; **plank,** 168; **plate rack,** 341; **press beds,** 157, 205, 224; **presses,** *passim;* —, fast to wall, 290; —, fitted to wall, 285, 292; —, fixed, 338; —, with folding doors, 192; —, for groceries, 91; —, with sliding leaves, 340; **racks,** 285; —, ceiling, 51; **salt-boxes,** 340; **scales,** for butter, 294; **scantling,** 168; **seats,** 158; **set of drawers,** 212; **settle bed,** 294; **shelves,** 91, 276, 279, 302, 331, 339, 341, 342; —, hanging, 284, 289, 341; —, to table, 212; **side table,** 141; **sideboard leaf,** 285; **soap chest,** 142; **sofa,** 158; **spider-tables,** 265, 276; **stand,** 302; **step-ladders,** 276, 290; **stools,** 274, 301, 331; **store press,** 193; **stump bedsteads,** 292, 296; **supper tables,** 224; **tables,** *passim;* —, with 1 drawer, 141, 144, 145, 210, 223, 274, 275, 276, 290, 300, 303, 340; —, with 2 drawers, 300, 337; —, with 3 drawers, 141; —, with 8 drawers, 142; —, with drawers, 192, 223, 275, 276; —, fixed, 279; —, with flaps, 140; —, large, 158, 192, 275, 340; —, long, 48, 51, 211, 224, 287, 338, 341; —, with 1 shelf, 212, 224; —, with 2 shelves, 338; —, short, 48; —, small, 110; —, square, 331, 337, 339; **table tops,** 294, 338; **toilet tables,** 190, 334; —, on castors, 332; —, square, 333; **trestle-table,** 293; **twine box,** 284; **wardrobe shelves,** 332, 334, 335; **wash-table,** 272; **window-curtain cornices,** 269; **writing-desks,** 192, 331
deal (painted): bedsteads, 253; **bookcases,** with 4 shelves, 334; —, with glazed doors, 330; **cradle bedsteads,** 253, 254; **cupboard,** 329; **dining-table,** with 2 leaves, 339; **dressers,** 284, 302; —, with drawers, 300; **dressing tables,** 255, 256, 265, 266, 267; —, with 1 drawer, 253; **presses,** 211, 224, 253, 254, 275, 339, 343; —, with 2 drawers, 331; **shelf,** 302; **table frames,** 337; **tables,** 308; —, with 1 drawer, 253, 254; —, with drawers, 253; —, square, 330, 337; **wardrobes,** painted mahogany colour, 191, 193; **wash-hand stand,** 336
death's head, 35
decanters, 193, 234, 283, 286; **cut-glass,** 340; —, for wine, 340; —, pint, 286; —, quart, 286; **glass,** 91, 120, 221, 286; —, for claret, 317; —, for spirits, 317; —, for water, 183; —, for wine, 183, 317, 318, 340; **silver,** 116

Decca work, 355; **bed-curtains,** 332; **canopy,** 332; on **cotton,** for chair-cover set, 333; —, for counterpane, 332; —, for curtains, 332; **window-drapery,** 332
deception commodes, 241, 268, **355;** mahogany, 242
déjeuners, 355; china, 319; Wedgwood, 218
delft, 355; baking-dishes, 233; bedchamber ware, 231; bidet pans, 255, 256, 265, 266, 267, 268, 269, 270, 271, 292; bowls, 119, 175; brown-edge delftware, 233; butter boats, 233; butter pan, 294; candlesticks, 219, 303; —, gilt-edged, 255, 256, 265, 266, 267; churn, 294; close-stool pan, 170; dishes, 175; —, round, 175; —, square, and covers, 233; fish boats, 233; fruit baskets, 175; ice-pail, 278; jugs, 193, 286; —, and covers, 175; milk pans, 173, 294; mugs, 175, 193; plates, 175, 233; salad-dish, 233; sauce-boats, 233; shapes, 278; soup-plates, 233; strainer, 294; sweetmeat stand, 175; tourte dish cover [?], 175; tubs, 283; tureen, 233; urns and covers, 294
delftware: at Morristown Lattin, 175
Derbyshire spar: candlesticks, 218
desks: with drawers, 44; skeleton, 271; **deal,** on a frame, 300; —, painted, 301; **inlaid,** 191; **mahogany,** 160, 191, 208, 212, 213, 216, 224, 272; **oak,** 109, 192, 193; **sally-wood,** 191, **361;** walnut, 160. *See also* reading desks; scrutoires; secrétaire; secretaries; writing-desks
desks (sloping): with drawers, 289; **deal,** with drawers, 276; **mahogany,** 276, 290; —, with drawers, 267, 269, 270, 276, 300; —, on a frame, 275
dessert baskets: Worcester porcelain, 318
dessert dishes: Chelsea porcelain (bird-pattern), 344; **china,** 128, 344; —, oval, 344; —, shell, 344; **Dresden porcelain,** oval, 344; —, shell, 344; **Indian china,** round, 343, 344; —, shell, 344
dessert-forks: silver, 348; —, with china handles, 316
dessert-knives: silver, with china handles, 316; silver-handled, 323, 348
dessert-plates: china, 128, 195, 233; Wedgwood, 195
dessert services: at Carton House, 302; —, china, 277; —, rosebud, 277
'**dessert-spoon forks':** silver, 197
dessert-spoons: silver, 162, 183, 197, 240, 323, 348
diamond: buckle, 118; hoop-ring, 118; rings, 118
diaper, 355; breakfast cloths, 195; breakfast napkins, 346; dinner-cloths, 195; —, coarse, 195; lay-overs, 195; napkins, 23, 113, 179, 280; sideboard cloths, 47; tablecloths, 23, 47, 113, 179, 195, 301, 316, 346; —, Dutch matting, 280; —, striped, 280; towels, bird's eye, 280, 282; waiting napkins, 346
dice-boxes, 329
dicker work. *See* Decca work
dictionaries: at Carton House, *The Gardiners Dictionary: Containing the methods of cultivating and improving the kitchen, fruit*

and flower garden . . . (Philip Miller), 300; at Elphin, the bishop's house, 100, 101; at Killadoon, 203, 215; at Newbridge House, 320, 321, 322

dimity, 355; bed-curtains, 139, 190, 209, 221, 268; bed-furniture, 333, 335, 336; bed-valance, 221; chair-covers, 139, 190; cot-curtains, 265; counterpanes, 139, 209, 221; cushion cases, 269; length of, 281; mattresses, 125, 126; pillowcase, 269; stool covers, 139; table covers, frilled, 346; —, plain, 346; window-curtains, 139, 190, 207, 219, 269, 331, 335, 337; window-drapery, 269

dining-chair bottoms: mohair, 211, 224

dining chairs, 179; mahogany, 211, 224

dining-parlours: at Castlecomer House, 189; at Newbridge House, 306, 307, 308. *See also* parlours

dining-rooms: at Baronscourt, 179; at Borris House, 240; at Captain Balfour's house, 109; at Carton House, 248, 273–4; at Hillsborough Castle, in 1777, 140; at Kilkenny Castle, 32; at Killadoon, 205; at London, St James's Square, 75, 81; at Mount Stewart, 327; —, Temple of the Winds, 343; at Shelton Abbey, 233. *See also* dining-parlours; parlours; supping room

dining-table (square), 339

dining-tables, 216; with 4 leaves, 233; deal, painted, with 2 leaves, 339; mahogany, 108, 125, 159, 168, 169, 179, 180, 192, 205, 239, 308, 310; —, with 2 leaves, 139, 343—, in 3 parts, 140; —, in 5 parts, on pillars and claws, 327; —, with cants, 192; —, Imperial, 240; —, Northumberland, 189; —, set of eight, on pillars, 273; —, with rosewood banding, 252; oak, 109, 141, 224; walnut, with cants, 192

dining-tables (oval), 229; mahogany, with 2 leaves, 342; —, with folding leaves, 330; oak, 210

dining-tables (round): mahogany, 125, 140

dinner-cloths: diaper, 195; —, coarse, 195

dinner dishes: china, 128, 344; Dresden porcelain, round, 344; Indian china, 344; —, octagonal, 343; —, round, 343

dinner forks, 282; silver, 348

dinner glasses: cut-glass, 286

dinner knives and forks, 282

dinner-napkins: damask, 346

dinner-plates, 282, 341; china, 233, 344; Dresden porcelain, 344; Indian china, octagonal, 344; —, round, 344; pewter, 285; porcelain, 341; Staffordshire, 278

dinner services: best blue at Mount Stewart, 341; Staffordshire at Carton House, 278

dinner trays: mahogany, 339

dirk: silver-mounted, 270

dish-covers, 232; pewter, English, 63; silver-plated, oval and round, 348; tin, 44, 286

dishes: blue ware, 278; —, oval, 278; brass, 45; china, 37, 175, 183, 233, 278; —, enamelled, 158; —, flat, 319; —, gilt, 233; —, heart-shaped, 319; —, large, 34, 36, 37, 91; —, octagonal, 278; —, oval, 319, 344; —, round, 233, 277, 278, 319, 344; —, shell, 277;

—, square, 277; copper, 65, 195; —, oval, 195; delft, 175; —, square, and covers, 233; —, round, 175; earthenware, 289; French china, oval, 278, 318; —, round, 278; —, square, 278; pewter, 22, 44, 127, 171, 184, 193, 195, 277, 283, 284, 314; —, English, 63, 113; —, Irish, 63; porcelain, 341; —, oval, 277; —, round, 277; —, shell, 277; —, square, 277; silver, corner, 347; —, gadrooned, 196; —, large, 347; —, oval, 72, 162, 347; —, round, 72, 162, 347; —, shell, 347; —, square, 162; silver-gilt, large, 71; silver-plated, covered, 241; —, covered, with stands, 240; —, flat, 317; Staffordshire, oval, 278; —, square, 278; Wedgwood, 195; white ware, 277, 278, 282, 315, 341; wooden, 287, 303; Worcester porcelain, 318; —, oval, 318; —, round, 318; yellow stoneware, 183; —, large, 183; —, round, 183; —, second-course, 183. *See also* dessert dishes; dinner dishes; salad-dishes; scallop dishes; tea-dishes; tundishes; vegetable dishes

dishing spoons: copper, 283

dish kettle, 183

dish-rings, 355; pewter, English, 63; silver, 183, 347

dish stand: silver, 117

dish trays: mahogany, 286

dish tubs: round and oval, 341

dog beds: wooden, 299

dog kennel: at Carton House, 299

dog muzzle, 299

dog pan: china, 279

dogs. *See* fire dogs

dog trough: wooden, 167

doilies, 346, 355–6

doll's house. *See* baby house

dolphins [sea monster dishes]: Chinese porcelain, 318

door cornices: silver tabby, 32

door covering: green cloth, 189

door-curtains, 84; damask, worsted, 77; green baize, 308; plaid, 56; silver tabby, 32; stuff, 56

door-handles: lacquered, 189

door-locks: *passim*; brass, 89, 90, 120; iron, 89, 90, 111; mahogany-cased, 106, 110; stock-locks, 89, 90, 91, 92, 93

doors: deal, 298; iron, 303

door springs, 189

door-valances: tabby, 32

dornick, 356; window-curtains, 41

dough: dough troughs, 48; doughing knife, 48

douters, 356; silver, 183; silver-plated, 203, 214, 348. *See also* extinguishers; snuffers

doving pan, 356

Dowlas linen, 281, 356; dusters, 280, 281; remnants, 281, 282

down: pillow, 330. *See also* eider down

drab colour: broth basin and saucer, 220; moreen, length of, 281; —, window-cornices, 274; —, window-curtains, 273, 274, 282; —, window-drapery, 273

drab cloth, 356; ease-and-comfort covering, 271; footrest coverings, 273; library-chair coverings, 273; sofa coverings, 273

drapery, 203, 214. *See also* bed-drapery; window-drapery

drapery pins: brass, 328. *See also* rose pins

drapery poles: gilded, 332

drawing board: horn, 291; mahogany (horse), 292

drawing-boxes, 191, 271

drawing-pan [?], 142

drawing-rooms: at Baronscourt, 179; at Borris House, 239; at Castlecomer, 189; at Dublin, No. 10 Henrietta Street, 159; at Dublin Castle, 56, 57, 67; at Elphin, the bishop's house, 90; at Hillsborough Castle, in 1746, 125; —, in 1777, 139; at Kilkenny Castle, 33–4; at Killadoon, in 1807, 204–5; —, in 1812, 203–4; —, in 1829, 214–16; at London, St James's Square, 76, 82; at Mount Stewart, 329; —, Temple of the Winds, 343; at Newbridge House, in 1821, 309; —, in the 1840s, *309*; at Shelton Abbey, 229

drawings, 206; bistre, 214; in crayon, 216; gilt-framed, 218; pastel, *243*; watercoloured, 337

dredging-boxes, 171, 314, 356; copper, 112, 143, 283; tin, 279, 340

Dresden porcelain, 356; cabinet coffee-cups (and saucer), 344; dessert plates, oval, 344; —, shell, 344; dinner dishes, round, 344; dinner-plates, 344; figures, 207; flower-pots, 207

dressers: *passim*; with 5 shelves, 341; fixed, 45, 144; ironing, 343; deal, 51, 91, 111, 284, 301, 303, 340, 341; —, with drawers, 293; —, with 2 shelves, 340, 341; —, with shelves, 303, 341, 343; —, square, 340; deal, painted, 284, 302; —, with drawers, 300

dressing boxes, 71, 110, 138, 169, 310; fir, 138; japanned, 139

dressing glasses: *passim*; and stand, 76; cheval, 256, 269, 270; oval, 138, 139; mahogany, 161, 206, 343; —, with 1 drawer, 209; —, hanging, 277; —, square, 333, 335; painted, 342; spar, 207; walnut, 160. *See also* looking-glasses; swing dressing glasses

dressing-glass frames: cheval, 218, 219, 269; gilt, 277; Indian, 217; japanned, 76, 206, 208, 277; mahogany, 206, 207, 208, 209, 210, 221, 256, 269

dressing-stool bottoms: rush, 206, 207, 208, 209, 210, 224

dressing-stool case: taffety, 32

dressing-stool covering: carpet, 265

dressing-stool covers: calico, 217, 218, 219, 220; cotton, 333, 334; —, printed, 332

dressing stools, 276; Grecian-style, 217; rush-bottomed, 220; mahogany, 332, 333, 335; —, with stuffed seats, 332, 334; oak, square, 333; painted, with stuffed seats, 334, 335

dressing-stool seats: hair, 332, 334, 335

dressing tables, 169, 191, 192, 241, 242, 244, 276; with 1 drawer, 217, 218, 219, 223; with 2 drawers, 219, 220, 339; deal, 90, 125, 126, 139, 212, 229, 265, 269; —, with 1 drawer, 338; —, with 2 drawers, 267; —, with drawers, 276; —, with 1 shelf, 224; —, on

castors, 267, 269; —, square, 339; **deal, painted,** 255, 256, 265, 266, 267; —, with 1 drawer, 253; **elm,** 255, 266, 269; —, with 1 drawer, 265; —, with drawers, 255, 268, 270; —, with leaves, 270; **fir,** 138; **mahogany,** 137, 138, 139, 159, 160, 181, 191, 207, 224, 241, 256, 266, 267, 301, 311, 330, 331, 335; —, with 1 drawer, 208, 221, 256, 336; —, with 1 drawer, 1 shelf, 205, 206, 209, 210, 221; —, with 2 drawers, 208, 332; —, with 2 drawers and sliding leaf, 336; —, with 5 drawers, 269; —, with drawers, 190, 220; —, with beech-wood drawer and frame, 337; —, with 1 shelf and divisions, 209; —, square, with 1 drawer, 337; **mahogany and ebony,** with 2 drawers, 207; **oak,** 89, 90, 109, 110, 137; —, with 1 drawer, 220, 221; **painted,** 310, 342; —, green, 337; **walnut,** 137
dressing tables (folding top): **mahogany,** 333, 336; —, with 2 drawers, 337
dressing tables (knee-hole): **mahogany,** with 11 drawers, 331; —, inlaid, with 3 drawers, 334; —, inlaid with 5 drawers, 332, 335, 336
drinking-horns, 127, 141; silver, and cover, 161
dripping-pans, 127, 171, 183, 315, **356;** copper, 63, 142, 283, 340; iron, 45, 112; tin, 22
Drogheda linen, 280, **356;** kitchen rubbers, 281; knife cloths, 281; remnant, 281
drugget, 356; Kilkenny Castle, 'Drugitt Room', 40; bed-curtains, 38, 39, 40, 42, 44, 80; bed-furniture, 39, 40, 42; carpets, 39, 40, 42, 309, 310, 311, 312; counterpanes, 39, 40, 42; cushions, 39, 40; floor carpet, 273; headcloths, 39, 40, 42, 44; rug, 309; testers, 39, 40, 42, 44; wall-hangings, 38, 39, 40, 42; window-curtains, 42, 52
drugget (striped): bed-curtains, 36; carpet, 36; counterpane, 36; curtains, 36; cushions, 36; wall-hangings, 36
drugget plaid: bed-furniture, 79
drum and sticks, 272
Dublin: Dublin Castle, 12, 27, 29; engraving by Brooking, *54;* inventory of 1707, 55–73; **Henrietta Street,** 147; —, as on Rocque's map, *154;* —, Mountjoy House, engraving of, *154;* **No. 10 Henrietta St;** inventories, 1772, 157–62; **Leinster House,** 247, 279; **Marino,** 12; views of (on fire screens), 214; **St Stephen's Green,** as on Rocque's map, *104*
Dublin Society, The, 13
dumb-waiters, 216, 274, 308, **356;** mahogany, 140, 189, 205, 233, 240. *See also* Canterburys
dung drags, 298
dung forks, 297, 300, 302
dung knife, 298
Dunmore House, Co. Kilkenny, 12, 27, 38, 53, 73; pictures from, 53
dusters, 281, 316; Dowlas linen, 280, 281
dustpans, 278, 288, 318
Dutch chairs, 78, 79, **356**
Dutch diaper: tablecloths, 47
Dutch matted pattern: breakfast napkins, 280; napkins, 280
Dutch ovens, 64, 127, **356;** and stand, 314; copper, 63; tin, 340

eagle: Eagle [Dressing] Room, Killadoon, 202, 208, 219; eagle and brass ring for drapery, 202, 208, 219, 335; table support, 179
earthenware, 356; at Elphin, the bishop's house, 90; basins, 46; candlesticks, 332, 333; chamber pots, 46; close-stool pan, 59; dish, 289; flower-pots, 329; foot pan, 334; footed cup, 36; jar, 38; milk pans, 92; pans, 46, 48; —, for lards, 318; tea-pot, 33. *See also* blue-and-white ware; blue ware; brown-and-white ware; brown-edged ware; green-edged ware; white ware
ease-and-comforts, 356; drab-cloth-covered, 271; green-cloth-covered, 272
easy-chair cover: serge, 76
easy-chair coverings: damask, 76; velvet, 41
easy chairs, 70, 77, 84, 160, 169, 231; cane, 78
ebony: cabinet, 33; picture frames, with brass, 214, *215;* table, 43; toaster, 118
ebony and tortoiseshell: looking-glass frame, 42
economist's corks, 356; silver, 197. *See also* corks
edge tools, 167–8. *See also* woodworking tools
edging iron, *297*
edging shears, 300
eel nets, 291
egg boiler: tin, 314
egg-cups, 300, 315; china, 277, 345; porcelain, 278; silver, 197, 323
egg saucepans: silver, 323
egg slice, 315
egg-spoons: silver, 240, 316, 323
egg-stand: silver-plated, 240
Egyptian granite, 'porphyry pedestals' (k 1836), 214
Egyptian-style: footstool, 204; sofa, 204
eider down, 356; quilt, 217
elbow-chair bottoms: leather, 126; rush, 110
elbow-chair cases: damask, 38; serge, 37, 75; taffety, 38
elbow-chair coverings: check, 182; chintz, 125; damask, 43, 75, 76; —, flowered, 77; leather, 125; mohair, 77; silk, 180, 181; —, flowered, 82, 181; —, French, 77; velvet, 78, 81, 82; —, figured, 37, 47
elbow-chair covers: check, 180; needleworked worsteds on canvas, 192; serge, 76, 79, 82
elbow-chairs, 161, 179, 182, 184, 185; cane, 20, 21, 22, 78, 79; folding, 43; gilt-framed, 76; mahogany, 160, 161; stuffed, 37. *See also* armchairs; armed chairs
elbow-stool coverings: damask, 181
ell (measure), **356;** of camlet, 144
elm: candle stand, 255; chest of drawers, 274; dressing tables, 255, 266, 269; —, with 1 drawer, 265; —, with drawers, 255, 268, 270; —, with leaves, 270; forks, 173; spider-tables, 255; —, with 1 shelf, 271; tables, 191, 244, 269, 284, 285, 290; —, narrow, 270; voider tables, 255, 266, 287
Elphin, Co. Roscommon: inventories of the bishop's mansion house, 1740, 89–103
embroidery: fringe, to bed-furniture, 33, 38; —, to mantle in gold and silver, 268; —, to silk tester, headboard and counterpane, 33

enamel-work: box, 198; china dishes, 158; portraits, 203, 214
encoignure. See corner cabinets
English china: flower-pots, 220. *See also under* Chelsea; Colebrookdale; Staffordshire; Worcester
engravings, 229, 231, 233
entrance halls: at Killadoon, 205; at Newbridge House, 308. *See also* halls
epergnes, 356; glasses for, 318; silver, 162, 196, 316, 347; silver-plated, 241
equipages, 356; tipped with silver and cut glass, 128
escritoire. *See* scrutoire
Etruscan style: flower-pot stands, 218; vases, 203, 204, 214, 215
ewers, 179, **356;** china, with silver spout, 118; French china, 208; glass, 217; stone-china, 273. *See also* basins and ewers; butter ewers; cream ewers; jugs; jugs and basins; water ewers; water-jugs
extinguishers, 288; brass, 276, 284; china, 204, 216; japanned, 339, 342; plated, 268; silver, 117, 347; silver-plated, 183, 317, 348; steel, 204; tin, 276, 290. *See also* douters; snuffers
eye cups, 255, 268, 269, 270, **356**
falling leaves, 356; falling table (prob.), oak, 274; tables, drop-leaf, 45, 276
farming equipment: at Carton House, 297–9; at Elphin, the bishop's house, 92
farrier's tools: fullers, 295, **357;** pritchel, 295, **360;** shoeing tools, 295, **361;** Solleysell's book: *The Compleat Horse-Man; or, Perfect farrier,* 98; White's book: A *Complete System of Farriery,* 321
feather-beds: *passim;* bordered, 254, 255, 256, 265, 266, 267, 269, 270, 275, 276, 289; **Holland,** 61; tick, 301, 336; —, cotton, 253, 254; —, linen, 254; —, striped, 34, 330, 331, 334, 335, 336, 337, 338, 339; **ticken,** striped, 331, 332, 333, 338, 339; **ticking,** Flanders, 33, 48, 56
feathers: bolster stuffing, 84, 296, 332, 334; cushion stuffing, 169–70, 328; hand screens, 216; pillow stuffing, 253, 269, 270, 328, 332, 334; squab stuffing, 335
feeding bags, 298
feeding-tube, 298
felling axes, 167, 298
fenders: with wirework, 189, 190, 206, 207, 208, 209, 210, 224, 229, 240, 287, 289, 300; **brass,** 40, 90, 108, 109, 157, 233, 239, 269, 272, 273, 274, 277, 310; **brass-topped,** 327; **iron,** 21, 22, 32, 49, 303; **steel,** *passim;* **tin,** 125, 126, 128, 137, 138, 139, 144, 169, 289, 290, 300
festoon curtain: damask, 282
festoon curtain lining: stuff, 282
festoon pillows, 265, 267
festoon window-curtains, 268; calico, striped, 267, 269; check, 290; chintz, 255, 267; chintz calico, 255, 256, 265; damask, flowered, 274
field beds, 356; *passim;* sacking-bottomed, 57
field bedsteads, 21, 57, 60, 61, 70, 79, 185, 211, 212, 229, 265, 266, **356;** with mahogany posts, 191; with oak posts, 193

General index 411

figures: biscuit, 219; brass, 179; bronze, 203, 204, 214; —, in groups, 204, 273; —, with lamp, 308; —, Hercules, 273; —, Venus and Adonis, 273; bronzed, 274; china, 194, 216, 310, 329; composition stone, 233; Dresden porcelain, 207; French china, 271, 273; marble, 272, 308; —, Jupiter, 308; —, Marcus Aurelius, 309; ormolu, 274; plaster of Paris, 343; wax, children and dog, 273; Wedgwood, 203, 214

filemot, 356; counterpane, 62; Kidderminster bed-furniture, 59

files, 295; flat, 296

filigree-work, 356; bijou box, 198; toothpick case, 198

finger glasses: cut-glass, 340; glass, 317, 340

fir: dressing boxes, 138; dressing tables, 138; tables, 141, 142; writing-desk, 142

firearms: blunderbusses, 46, 121, 140, 286, 340; carbine, 301; fowling-piece, inlaid with pearl, 270; fusees, 85; guns, 71, 121, 128, 140; —, and bayonet, 289; —, half-stock, 140; —, screw-barrel, bullet, 120; —, silver-mounted, 330; muskets, 23, 46, 158; pistols, 71, 121, 340; —, brass-barrelled, 289, 303; —, brass-mounted, 140, 290; —, cases of, 121, 270; —, Highland, 120; —, silver and steel, 140; —, silver-mounted, 270; repeaters, 158

firebacks, 356; iron, 20, 21, 22, 31, 32, 33, 35, 38, 39, 40, 82

fire-buckets, 91; leather, 298

fire dogs, 39, 67, 71, 75, 76, 77, 81, 356; with brasses, 43; iron, 21, 39; with plate [silver] tops, 71; silver, 76; silver-garnished, 33. See also andirons

fire engine, 293

fire-fork: iron, 22

fire grates: iron, 303

fireguards, 217, 220, 221; deal, 290; steel, 209; wire, 272, 292; —, brass-mounted, 255, 256, 265, 266, 267, 268, 269, 270, 271, 272

fire irons: passim; brass-mounted, 274; steel, 221, 239, 268, 269, 272, 273, 274

fire pans, 38; with brass knobs, 40

fire peels, 356; brass, 64; copper, 64

fire-screen bases: mahogany, 272, 273

fire-screen frame: black-painted, 327

fire screens, 77, 84, 125, 140, 168, 170, 180, 203, 216, 270, 271, 308, 310, 312, 314; cheval, 296; Indian, 76; lined, 283; sliding, 327; —, moreen, 240; square, 330; with views of Marino, Dublin, 202, 214; alder, 328; canvas, 180, 182; deal, 158; mahogany, 139, 328, 329, 330; mahogany and silk, 204; mahogany and stuff, 205; needlework, 82, 159; —, black-framed, 32; painted, 229, 329; silk, 229; tapestry, 309; tin-lined, 183; wrought, black-framed, 76. See also fire screens (folding); pole-screens

fire screens (folding): with 2 leaves, 108, 337; with 4 leaves, scarlet, 287; paper, 271, 337; —, Indian, 75. See also folding-screens

fire shovels: passim; for griddle, 51; brass, 31, 32, 33, 40, 41, 42; brass-knobbed, 31, 32; iron, 64, 296; silver-garnished, 33, 71

fire tongs: blacksmith's, 295

firewood, 297

fish boats: copper, 63; delft, 233

fish drainers, 341; porcelain, 341; white ware, 341; yellow stoneware, 183

fish frying-pan, oval, 314

fishing-nets: casting, 291; draught-net, 291; eel, 291; landing, 291; silk, 291

fishing-rods, 291

fish-kettles, 127; brass bottom for, 45; copper, 314; —, and covers, 142, 158, 283, 314; —, oval, 340; iron, 341; oval, 183

fish ornament: brass-mounted, 278

fish pans: copper, 63, 112

fish-plates, 65, 171; pewter, 112; round, 184; silver, 162

fish shears, 142

fish-slices, 65, 315; copper, 283; silver, 348. See also fish trowels

fish trowels: silver, 240, 316, 323

fixed furniture, 356; corner-cupboard, 285; corner presses, 287; cupboards, 40, 289; dressers, 45, 144, 286; falling leaves, oak, 274; nests of drawers, 275, 276, 290; night tables, 290, 292, 338; presses, 192, 193, 285; —, deal, 290, 292, 338; —, painted, 224; showcases, 307; sideboard, 31; tables, deal, 279, 302; —, mahogany, 182; —, oak, 51

flag: chair bottoms, 21, 22

flagons: china, 34; silver, 71

flails, 297

flannel: palliasse, 333; Welsh, 282; window-curtains, 206

flannel and chintz: chair-covers, 204

flannel and Damascus: armchair covers, 206; sofa covers, 206

flaskets, 356; clothes, 21; twig, 111

flat-irons. See smoothing-irons

flat pan and cover, 283

flesh-forks, 45, 112, 127, 171; iron, 22, 64, 296, 315

flint-glass, 356; water bottles, 64

flock, 356; bolsters, 43, 49; mattresses, 33, 38, 39, 143, 212, 223, 224; picture, 33

flock-beds, 23, 40, 42, 43, 44, 46, 47, 48, 49, 50, 58, 59, 60, 62, 66, 81, 91, 111

flocking: window-curtains, 20

floor carpets, 139, 181, 207, 220; Brussels, 207, 218, 228, 229; drugget, 273; 'planned to room', 221; Scotch, 125; Turkey, 125; Venetian bed-rounds, 255, 256, 266, 267, 268, 269, 270; Wilton, 139

floor-cloths: frieze, 327, 329, 338; green baize, 224; greycloth, 338; oilcloth, 189, 216, 224, 269, 308, 331; —, for the stairs, 110

flouncing: pillowcases, 280

flour-box [?], 184

flour scoop, 341

flour tubs, 67, 279, 284, 296, 341

flower baskets, 145; china, with stands, 344

flower-pattern china: pot-pourri pots, 205; vases, 205

flower-pot basket and tin, 205

flower-pots, 278, 301, 302; —, with carnations, 301; —, with marjoram, 300; Chelsea porcelain, 205; china, 34, 205, 206, 207, 216, 310, 328; Colebrookdale, 204; Dresden porcelain, 207; earthenware, 329; English china, 220; Indian china, 220

flower-pot stands: Etruscan-style, 218; painted, 206

flower-stands, 216, 233, 308; painted, 273; china, 319

flower table: black-stained, with tin centre, 216

flox, 356; cushion filling, 52

fly-tables, 179; deal top, square, 338; mahogany, 331, 339; —, with 1 drawer, 331, 334, 336, 338; —, inlaid, 335; —, oval, 334; —, square, 332, 333, 335, 336, 337, 338; —, square, inlaid, with drawers, 332

folding-screen frames: black-painted, 327, 329

folding-screens, 144; with 4 leaves, frieze, 327; with 6 leaves, japanned, Indie, 327; with 7 leaves, 327; with 8 leaves, caricature covering, 329; mahogany, 210; silk, 218. See also firescreens (folding); screens

folding-screen stands: brass, 218

folding-tables, 144; oval, 79, 125; round, 78; square, 79; writing-table, 84; cherry-wood, 125; mahogany, 125, 139; walnut, 138

food: bacon, 91, 194; beef, 194; hams, 194

footboards, 242; mahogany, 241, 270

footman's cloths, 281

footmen, 210, 224, 287, 340, 356; brass, 289; iron (swing), 223

footmen's rooms: at Hillsborough Castle, 142; at Killadoon, 211, 213; at London, St James's Square, 81; at Newbridge House, 313; at Shelton Abbey, 225; footman's pantry, at Castlecomer, 194

foot pans, 218; earthenware, 334; japanned, 255, 287, 292; tin, 212; —, japanned, 255, 256, 265, 266, 267, 268, 269, 270, 271; white ware, 209, 334; yellow ware, 206, 207, 209, 217, 219, 221

footrests: drab-cloth-covered, 273

footstool coverings: carpet, 265; gilt-leather, 43; green-cloth, 205

footstool covers: scarlet, 328

footstools, 203, 214, 217, 221, 327, 328, 329, 337; carpeted, 273; Egyptian-style, 204; mahogany, 328, 335; round, 203, 205, 206, 214; square, worked by Mary Bermingham (prob.), 216

foot tubs, 313, 318; white ware, 310

forest-work, 356

forge: at Carton House, 295–6

forks: 3-pronged, 318; elm, 173; iron, 48, 166; —, with wooden handle, 48; silver, 240, 316, 323, 348; —, 3-pronged, 162; —, 4-pronged, 323; silver-plated, 323. See also dessert-forks; dinner forks; flesh-forks; salad forks; toasters; toasting forks

forks (farming): dung forks, 297, 300, 302; hay-forks, 297; potato forks, 297; sling forks, 297; thatching fork, 298

forms, 356; passim; in servant maids' hall, 285; in servants' halls, 91, 141, 158, 184, 192, 211, 224, 232, 285, 314, 341; deal, 128, 141, 145, 158, 192, 211, 224, 275, 303, 341

fountains, 314; marble, 294

fowling-piece: gun, inlaid with pearl, 270

fowling piece (picture), 38

freedom boxes. See corporation boxes

freezers, 356; copper, 342

freezing pails, 342

French ceramic ware: basin, ewer and cup, 218

French china: at Carton House, 278; bowl, cover and saucer, 204; bowl, ewer and cup, 208; cups, belonging to ice-pails, 278; —, with basket handles, 204; cups and saucers, 204, 219; dishes, oval, 278, 318; —, round, 278; —, square, 278; figures, 271, 273; inkstand, 204; plates, 278; tureens, 278

French furnishings: carpet, crimson, 38; castors to bedsteads, 217, 218, 219; quilting, 116; towels, 114; window-curtains in striped calico, 221

French furniture: bed, mahogany, 221; bedstead, 255; cabinets, inlaid, 274; candlesticks, gilt, 219; chests of drawers, brass-mounted, 218, 219, 267, 268, 270; —, with French marble top, 219; claw-tables, mahogany, 218, 219; clocks, ormolu, 274; —, with figures on stand and glass shade, 216; commode, inlaid, 215; corner cabinets, inlaid, 274; lavabos, mahogany, 218, 219; table, inlaid, 217; weather-glass, 290

French horn, 291

French jewellery: gold box, 198

French kitchen: at Kilkenny Castle, 45

French silk: armchair coverings, 79; chair-backs and seats, 80; elbow-chair coverings, 77

French silver: dish-ring, 183; marrow spoon, 183

frieze, 356; curtains, 327; floor-cloths, 327, 329, 338; table covers, 169, 334

fringe, 357; **bed-curtains**, silk, 43; **bed-furniture**, cotton, 333, 334, 335, 336; —, embroidery, 33, 38; —, gold and silver, 34; —, silk, 35, 40, 41; —, velvet, 35; —, worsted, 47, 334; **carpet**, crimson, 32; **chair cases**, gold and silver thread, 34; **chair covers**, cotton, 334; **counterpane**, silk, 268; **curtains**, silk, 34, 44; **door-furniture**, 32; **mantles**; gold, silk, 268; **remnants**, 282; **stool bottoms**, edging fringe, 34; **wall-hangings**, copper thread, 34; —, silk, 35; **window-curtains**, copper, silver and gold thread, 34; —, cotton, 335, 336, 337; —, silk, 35, 272, 273; —, thread, 32; **window-curtain trimmings**, 189; **window-drapery**, cotton, 334, 337; —, silk, 332

fringe and gymp trimmings (knotted): bed-curtains, chair-covers and window-curtains, 190

fringe colours: black, table cover, 334; black and scarlet, remnants, 282; black and yellow, bed bases and cushions, 39; black, blue and white, chair cases, 38; crimson, carpet, 32; crimson, black and white, bed-furniture, 31; green, bed-furniture, 35; —, door-furniture, 32; —, wall-hangings, 35; —, window-curtains, 35; red, counterpane, 268; white, bed-furniture, 333, 334, 335, 337; —, chair-covers, 334; —, remnant, 282; —, seating-furniture, 333; —, window-curtains, 335, 336; —, window-drapery, 327, 329, 331, 334; yellow, window-curtains, 328

fruit baskets, 302; china, with stands, 344; delft, 175

fruit bowls, 302

fruit-dishes, 233, 302, 315; china, 183; silver, 196

frying-pans, 64, 91, 112, 171, 183, 284, 301, 314; copper, oval, 340; iron, 22, 64, 127, 142

funnel, 64. *See also* wine funnels

furbelows to window-curtains, 57, 357; in satin, 56

furniture calico, 357; bolster case, 271; cushion case, 271; length of, 281; pillowcases, 270, 271; window-curtains, 270, 282

furniture cotton, 357; bed-curtains, 190, 191

furniture linen, 357; bed-curtains, 191, 192, 193; window-curtains, 191

fusees, 85, 357

fustian, 357; mattress, 268; mattress quilt, 84; pillows, 33, 57, 268, 269; for pillows, 195, 282

gads, 92, 357

gallons, 357; of arrack, 199; cistern capacity, 37; copper, 111, 283, 285; for milking, 92

game box, 328

gaming-tables. *See* backgammon tables; basset-table; card-tables; hazard tables; ombre tables; *trou-madame* tables

garden chairs, portable, 205

gardener's house: at Carton House, 300; at Kilkenny Castle, 50

gardener's room: at Elphin, the bishop's house, 93

garden mats, 290, 291, 296

garden rakes, 302

garden seats, 166, 167, 298, 302

garden seeds, 93

garden shears, 167

garden tools, 93, 167, 300, 302

gardevine, 357; mahogany, 286

gate lodge: at Carton House, 303.
See also guardhouse; porters' lodges

gates, 303; double, 303; iron, 297, 303

gaufrier, 284, 357

Geminijany's Room (prob. Geminiani's Great Room, Spring Gardens, Dame Street, Dublin), 105, 107, 121

Genoa damask, 357; bed-furniture, 56

Gibraltar rock: paperweight, 214, 216

gilding, 357; andiron garnishing, 35; armchair frames, 267, 268, 269, 270, 271, 272; armchairs, 254, 265; armed-chair frames, carved, 33; back-chair frames, 42; bedstead feet, 31, 38, 40, 42, 52; brackets, 310; branches, 108; candlesticks, 219; chair frames, 52, 203, 204, 215; —, carved, 34, 38; chairs, 291, 292; chandelier sockets, 33; chest frame, 76; chimney-glass frames, 82, 108, 160, 270; —, with carved fretwork, 271; couch, 48; cup finials, 42, 52; cushion frames, 35; drapery poles, 332; dressing-glass frame, 277; elbow-chair frames, 76; headboard, carved, 52; hearth, 72; looking-glass frames, 35, 37, 168, 180, 206, 207, 210, 224, 231, 268, 329; —, carved, 81, 138; mirror frames, 228, 229, 332; pedestals, for

carving of rams' heads, 37; —, for china, 35, 37, 53; picture frames, *passim*; —, black and gilt, 125, 329, 330; —, carved, 33, 38; pier-glass frames, 76, 138, 139, 189, 204, 206, 207; pier-table frames, 291; punchbowl (china) garnishing, 36; sconce frames, 75, 108; sconces, carved, 35, 37, 82; scrutoire, 75; settee frames, 76; sofa frame, 216; squab feet, 34; stands, 37, 71, 82; table, 36; table frames, 76, 82, 159, 269, 270, 273; trunk nails, 192; upholstery nails, 189, 191; window-curtain cornices, 204, 215, 272, 273, 292

gilt leather-work: carpets, 50, 51; chair coverings, 32, 40, 41, 43, 44, 47, 48, 49, 50; close-stool coverings, 33, 42; footstool covering, 43; pieces, 51; screens, with 6 leaves, 160; —, church, 291; sideboard coverings, 51; stool coverings, 47, 50; table carpets, 32; wall-hangings, 32, 41, 43, 47, 49, 50, 51

gimlets, 290, 357

gimp. *See* gymp; fringe and gymp; muslin and gymp

ginger. *See* bottled wines; bottled beers

girths, 293, 319

glass: bookcase doors, 140, 160, 209, 271, 310, 330; cabinet doors, 329; corner-cupboard doors, 84; cupboard doors, 329; press doors, 78

glass-baskets, 23, 67, 112, 119, 303

glass bucket, 286

glass cases: for clock, 274; for shell-work, 15, 138

glass-cloths, 281, 282, 316

glasses: comfit, 64; cream, 64, 318; crystal, garnished, with cover, 34; custard, 318; finger, 234, 317, 340; for epergnes, 318; memorial, Battle of the Boyne, The (1690), 318; —, William III, 13, 120; ratafia, 64; sweetmeat, 91, 119, 318; whipped syllabub, 91. *See also* ale glasses; beer-glasses; champagne glasses; jelly glasses; rummers; sugar glasses; tumblers; water glasses; wine-glasses

glasses (mirrors). *See* cheval glasses; chimney-glasses; dressing glasses; hanging-glasses; looking-glasses; mirrors; pier-glasses; toilet glasses

glass-trays: mahogany, 283, 286; silver, 183

glass-ware, 234; at Baronscourt, 183; at Captain Balfour's house, 119–20; at Elphin, the bishop's house, 91; at Morristown Lattin, 175; at Newbridge House, 317; bell, 169; bottle, 219; bottle stoppers, 218, 219; bowl, 91; cream-pots, 145; crofts, 183; cruets, 183, 347; cups, 278; decanters, 91, 120, 221, 286, 340; —, claret, 317; —, spirit, 317; —, water, 183; —, wine, 183, 317, 318; ewer, 217; glass with tin foot, 175; ink-bottles, 206; jars, 278; jugs, 119, 120, 206; lamp, 211; mug, 120; mustard pot, 183; pickling bottles, 342; plates, round, 318; punchbowl, 175; rummer, 119; salts, 175, 183; salvers, 46, 120; sweet bottles, painted, 36; sweetmeat stands, 119; tea-bell, 119; tumblers, 119, 175, 183,

General index   413

208, 217, 218, 219, 220, 221, 290; wine-coolers, 234, 286, 340. *See also* cut-glass; glasses

glass-work: candle-shades, painted, 329; **chandelier** with glass drops, 75; **coolers**, 317; **frames** for, chimney-glass, 82; —, hanging-glass, 82; —, looking-glass, 76; —, pier-glass, 75; **globe** for candle, 205; **lanterns**, 32, 46, 77, 84, 85, 89, 125, 139, 141, 285, 286, 287, 301; **sconces**, 66, 71, 75, 77, 79, 82, 84, 85; —, gilt-framed, 76; —, with silver frames and nozzles, 76; **still**, 292

globes, 221; glass, 205; globe and iron, 112; terrestrial, 308

gloves: point lace, 268

glue-pot, 297

goblets: cut-glass, 317; horn, 318; silver, 347; silver-plated, 283

gold: corporation boxes, 198; cup and cover, 198; enamelled box, 198; French box, 198; medal, 198; ring, 118; snuff-box, 118

gold-and-white china: tea-pot, 118

gold lace: trimmings to bed-furniture, 84

gold thread: fringes, bed-furniture, 34; —, chair cases, 34; —, window-curtains, 34; lacework to, seating furniture coverings, 84 —, wall-hangings, 84; pincushion tissue, 71; **trimmings**, bed-curtains, 70; —, chair coverings, 70; —, wall-hangings, 70

goldwork: at Castlecomer House, 198

Gothic Revival style: Hillsborough church, 123; Lismore Castle, 20; Shelton Abbey, its transformation to, 227; chairs, 204; window-cornice (Wyatt), 292

gouges, 297, **357**

granaries: at Carton House, 293; at Elphin, the bishop's house, 93; at Morristown Lattin, 174

grape scissors, 300

grass barrows, 299, 302

grass pickers, 297

graters, 112, 142, 282, **357**; brass, 283; copper, 183; tin, 171, 279

grates: brass, 272; with brass facings, 194; brass-mounted, 327; with cheeks, 47, 48; cradle, 37, 53; fixed, 43, 45, 46, 47, 49, 50, 78, 79, 80, 81, 85, 137, 138, 139, 140, 141, 145, 180; half-round, 36, 42, 43, 48, 53; iron, 33, 44, 48, 49, 51, 90, 140; Londonderry Sola[r] Grate, 326, 327, 328, 329, 331, 332, 333, 334, 335; **358**; loose, 44; moving, 108, 109, 110, 143, 168, 169, 300; set, 180, 181, 182, 183, 184, 185; standing, 79; steel, old-fashioned, 343; for wood or charcoal, 31. *See also* register grates; sarcophagus grate; stove-grates

gravy-pan, 127

gravy spoons, 282; silver, 197, 240, 316, 323, 348; silver-plated, 317

grease-boxes, 298

Grecian style: armchairs, 204; couch, 271; dressing stool, 217; lamps, 273; sofas, 203, 214, 215

green: caffoy, chair coverings, 75; **calamanco**, bed, 110; **calico**, bed-curtains, 270; —, remnants, 282; —, window-drapery, 271; **Damascus** ('stripped'), bed-curtains

and valances, 224; **damask**, bed-curtains, 77; —, bed-furniture, 34, 78, 181; —, chair cases, 34; —, chair coverings, 125; —, settee coverings, 125; —, stool coverings, 126; —, wall-hangings, 34; —, window-curtains, 34, 125, 272; **drugget**, wall-hangings, 38; **furniture calico**, bolster case, 271; —, cushion case, 271; —, pillowcases, 270, 271; —, window-curtains, 270, 282; **Kidderminster**, carpets, 333; —, wall-hangings, 32; **leather-work**, armchair coverings, 229; —, sofa covering, 229; **lutestring**, bed-furniture lining, 137; **mohair and silk**, window-curtains, 144; **moreen**, bed-curtains, 231, 289; —, bed-furniture, 182; —, curtain, 290; —, window-curtains, 189; **paragon**, case curtains, 78; Persian, length of, 282; —, window-curtain linings, 272; **print** (fabric), bed-furniture, 59, 60, 61; —, wall-hangings, 58; **say**, table coverings, 33, 49; **serge**, bed-curtains, 80; —, bed-furniture, 58; —, blinds, 338; —, chair cases, 75; —, quilts, 275; —, window-curtains, 21, 46, 47; **silk**, elbow-chair coverings, 181; —, fire screens, 204, 229; —, folding-screens, 218; —, settee covering, 182; **silk** (clouded), chair-covers, 204; —, window-curtains, 204; **silk damask**, cushions, 139; **stuff**, bed-curtains, 145, 225; —, wardrobe-curtains, 223; —, window-curtain cornices and valance, 75; —, window-curtains, 75, 144; **stuff** (printed), bed-curtains, 43, 46; —, bed-furniture, 58; —, curtains, 41; —, headcloth, 43, 46; —, tester, 43; **velvet**, writing-table covering, 75; **worsted**, bed- and window-curtains, 126

green-and-black: bedstead cornices, 333; carpet, 221

green-and-blue china: bottles, ornamental, 218

green and gold: damask, armed-chair and back-chair coverings, 33; —, stool coverings, 75

green-and-white: check, length of, 144; —, window-curtains, 140; **drugget**, bed-furniture, 40, 42; —, wall-hangings, 38

green-and-white furniture: chairs, cane, 206, 207; wash-hand table, 221

green-and-yellow: cloth, table cover, 271

green baize: carpet covers, 229, 310; coverings for, reading-desk, 337; —, writing-desk, 330; door-curtain, 308; floor-cloth, 224; quilt, 171; screens, 308, 309; table cover, 337; wardrobe hangings, 190. *See also* green cloth

green china: cup, cover and saucer, 216; dishes, 37

green cloth, **357**; bed-curtains, 46, 49; bed-valances, 46, 49; carpet, 42; door covering, 189; ease-and-comfort coverings, 272; footstools, 205; headcloth, 49; length of, 273; library-chair coverings, 272; library-table lining, 272; ombre-table coverings, 33, 76; table carpet, 84; table coverings, 205, 216; table covers, 168, 203, 214, 338; testers, 46, 49; writing-table covering, 89. *See also* green baize

green-edged ware: basins, 268; bowl, 302; chamber vases, 268; cup, 278

green furniture: chairs, 144, 170, 182, 207, 209, 210, 212, 215; stools, 203, 214

greenhouse plants, 301

green-red-and-blue china: vases and covers, 205

green-work, 357

grey: drugget, floor carpet, 273; frieze, floor-cloths, 338; marrow-bone cloths, 281; window-cornice, 233

greycloth, 357; chair covering, 43; floor-cloth, 338; table covers, 328; writing-desk covering, 329

grey linen: candlestick cloths, 280; china cloths, 280; couch covering, 272; housemaids' cloths, 280; knife cloths, 280; remnants, 281, 282; sheeting, 281; sheets for servants, 316; towels, 280

griddles, 171, 284

gridirons, 22, 45, 64, 91, 112, 127, 183, 195, 283, 301, 315, **357**; double and single, 142; iron, 341

grinding-stones, 166, 297; grindstone, 302

groceries, 193; storage for, 91

groom of the chamber's cloths, 281

guard. *See* fireguards

guardhouse: at Kilkenny Castle, 50. *See also* gate lodge; porters' lodges

gudgeons: 357; iron, 166

gun-cases, 128, 330; mahogany, 271

guns, 71, 121, 128, 140; and bayonet, 289; bullet, 120; —, screw-barrel, 120; half-stock, 140; silver-mounted, 330

gymp, 357. *See also* fringe and gymp; muslin and gymp

Haarlem, 357. *See also* 'harnum'; 'harnum' damask

hair, 357; armchair seats, 328, 336; armed-chair seats, 337; armed-chair sides and backs, 334; bolsters, 269, 271; chair bottoms, 216, 220, 339; chair-bottom stuffing, 190; chair seats, 327, 329, 330, 331, 332, 333, 334, 335, 336, 337, 338, 339, 342, 343; chair-backs, 329, 330, 331, 332, 333, 334, 339; chair-seat stuffing, 339; cushions, 139, 270, 274, 291, 328, 329, 330; dressing-stool seats, 332, 334, 335; mattresses, *passim*; pillows, 271, 332; sofa-back, 328; squabs, 328, 332, 334; trunk bindings, 80, 84, 126, 142, 171

hair (curled): bolster stuffing, 35; chair-bottom stuffing, 189, 190; mattresses, 190, 241

hair-brooms, 125, 126

hair camlet: armed-chair cases, 42; back-stool cases, 42; bed-furniture, 42

haircloth, 275, 357; chair coverings, 233, 287; parlour-chair coverings, 273

hair-line, 91

hair-sieves, 91, 278, 284, 288, 342

hair silk, 357; chair coverings, 189

halberds, 85, 291, 357

half-barrels, 166; for charcoal, 298

half-gallon: copper, 285

half-pint: pewter, 290

hall chairs: mahogany, crested, 200, 202, 203, 205, 214, 233, 308, 326; **oak**, 287; **painted** and crested, 327

halls: at Borris House, 240; at Castlecomer House, 189; at Dublin, No. 10 Henrietta Street, 158; at Hillsborough Castle, 125; at Killadoon, 205, 214; at Kilrush House, 149; at Morristown Lattin, 169; at Mount Stewart, 327; at Shelton Abbey, 233. *See also* entrance halls

hall-table: deal, 149

hames, 92, 166, **357**

hammer-cloth, 319

hammers, 90, 295, 298, 300; cart, 298; coal, 51; pavier's, 298; set, 295; stone, 298; sugar, 120

hampers, 278, 285, 294, 296

handbarrows, 92, 297, 298, 302

hand basins and ewers: blue-and-white ware, 332; brown-and-white ware, 334. *See also* wash-hand basins (and ewers)

hand-bell, 180

hand board, 357; Indian, 119

handles: brass, to bell-pulls, 215; —, to chests of drawers, 221; —, to writing-table, 221; bronze, to verd-antique paperweight, 214

handsaws, 168, 275, 302

hand screens, 90, 125, 203, 214, 329, 330; feather, 216; mahogany and fluted silk, 214; paper, 218, 328, 329, 333, 335, 337; with transparencies, 203, 204

hanging bookshelf: 290

hanging-glasses: glass-framed, 82; walnut-framed, 149

hanging lock, 166

hanging shelves, 36, 40, 45, 286, 287; deal, 284, 289, 341; mahogany, 190

harewood, 357; bookshelves, with drawers, 271; bookstand, with drawers, 271; spider-table, 273; writing-tables, 255; —, tambour, 269

harewood (inlaid): worktables, 272; writing-table, tambour, 271

harness racks, 293

harness room: at Carton House, 298

harnesses: 1-horse, 167; 2-horse, 319; cart, 298; coach, 293; for a coach and six, 121; curricle, 319; gig, 293; head collars, 299; plough, 298; —, for mules, 298; trace, 298

'harnum', 357; bed-curtains, 49; cushion, 41; headcloth, 49

'harnum' damask: breadths of, 52; bed-curtains, 42; canopy, 42

harp case: deal, 274

harpsichords, 173; 'harpsicle', 70; with stand, 179

harp-string box: japanned tin, 272

harrateen, 357; bed-curtains, 125, 126, 128; bed-furniture, 80, 126; window-curtains, 125

harrows, 92, 297; break, 298; bush, 297; double, 298; iron chains for, 92; leather traces for, 92; Scotch, 298

hassock covers: cloth, 337; cotton, 335

hassocks, 214, 217, 218, **357;** straw, 331, 335, 337; worsted, 219, worked, 204

hatchets, 167, 290, 299, 300, 341

hat hooks: brass, 274

hat stand, 308

haulm, 357; haulm chaff, bolster, 296

hay, 65, 67; hay-forks, 297; hay-knives, 93,

298; hay-rakes, 92, 297; hay sweep, 297; hay-tedder, 298, **357;** hay-yards, 49, 50, 92, 172

hazard tables, 67, **357;** mahogany, 205; oak, Danzig, 33

head (over bookcase), 180

headboards: carved, 41; damask, 40; deal, 275; hair camlet, quilted, 42; satin, Indian, 39; silk, Venetian, 33

headcloth lining: cotton, 335

headcloths: damask, 38, 40, 43; —, gathered, 31; damask and gold, 70; drugget, 39, 40, 42, 44; green cloth, 49; hair camlet, 42; 'harnum', 49; Irish stuff, 47; Kidderminster, 48, 50; satin, clouded, 41; —, Indian, 39; serge, 42, 47; silk, 332; —, Indian, 41; —, Venetian, 33; stuff, printed, 43, 46; tabby, 39

headpiece: cloth, 50

hearth brushes: *passim*; inlaid, 204

hearth frame: silver, 76

hearth-rugs: *passim*; list, 337; scarlet, 203, 214

hearths: brass, 82; Dutch, with brass handles and balls, 52; gilt, 72; iron, 77, 81, 84; —, silver-framed, 76; steel, 67, 75, 82

hearth-stone: marble, 149

heaters, 294; for box smoothing irons, 91, 128; for pincushion dishes, 348; for stew pans, 283; for tea kitchen, 195. *See also* chafing-dishes

hedge shears, 298

hemp: mat, 308; rugs, 204, 308

henhouse, 294

high stool, 341

Hillsborough Castle, Co. Down: architectural drawing by Brettingham, *122*; inventories, of 1746 (Viscount Hillsborough's house), 125–8; —, of 1777 (Hillsborough Lodge), 137–45

hob-nob glasses, 234, 286

hods, 296, **357**

hoes (farming or gardening tool), 167, 303; draw, 300, 302; thrust (pushing), 300

hoes (kitchen utensil), 342, **357**

hogsheads, 128, 151, 167, 285, **357;** iron-bound, 128; for meal, 172, 173; measures of, ale, 93; —, claret, 199; —, port, 199; —, table beer, 92; —, wine, 68; for vinegar, 287

hog-tub, 127

holdfast, 296

Holland, 357; bolster, 61; feather-bed, 61; mangle cloths, 288; mattress, 268; mattress quilt, 84; pillow, 61; quilts, 31, 38, 40, 41, 43, 56, 57, 70, 75, 77, 80. *See also* brown Holland; white Holland

holsters, 293

honey-bowl: porcelain, and cover, 278

honeypots: china, 319; —, with covers and stands, 345

honeysuckle pins: brass, 216

hoop-ring: diamond, 118

horn: deers' horns, 272, 303; drawing board, 291; goblets, 318; lining to silver-plated plate, 198

horn brands, 299

horns, 184, 341; for powder, 290, 301. *See also* drinking-horns

horse-collars, 292, 298, 299, 319, 320

horse-gear: at Newbridge House, 319–20

horses (animal), 93

horses (frames), 225, **357;** for brushing clothes, 185; reading stand, 271; wet, 144; **deal,** 212, 294; —, folding, 288; **mahogany,** 209; —, drawing board; —, folding, 206, 207, 208; **oak,** 212; painted, 210. *See also* airing horses; clothes-horses

horse-sheets, 319

horse-trees, 92. *See also* swingletree

horsewhips: 2-horse, 320; 4-horse, 320; wagoner's, 298

hot closet, 340

hot plate, 283

hot-water jugs, 310, 311; blue ware, 311. *See also* warm-water jugs

house buckets, 284, 288, 315, 318

house clearance sale: at Captain Balfour's town house, 105–21

housekeeper's cloths, 281

housekeepers' rooms: at Baronscourt, 184; at Carton House, 276; at Castlecomer House, 193; at Killadoon, 210, 223, 224; at Mount Stewart, 342; at Newbridge House, 314; at Shelton Abbey, 232

housemaids' cloths, 281; grey linen, 280

housemaids' dusters, 346; Dowlas linen, 280

housemaids' rooms: at Baronscourt, 184; at Carton House, 275, 288; at Kilkenny Castle, 40; at Killadoon, 211, 225; at Mount Stewart, 338; at Newbridge House, 314

huckaback, 357; towels, 141, 179, 280

hundredweight, 232, 285, 293, 295, 299, **357**

hunting-chair covers: calico, 217; chintz, 204

hunting-chairs, 204, 217, 218, **357**

ice mallet, 298

ice moulds, 279; pewter, 279

ice-pails, 282; china, 277, 344; copper, 286; cups belonging to, 278; delft, 278; porcelain with covers, 277; —, Worcester, 318; silver-plated, 198, 240

ice pots, 193; pewter, 79

ice shuttles [?]: copper, 342

ice tub: copper, 342

iconography of ornament: crocodile (teapot lid), 220; eagle, ring for drapery, 208, 219; —, on table support, 179; griffin (table frame), 159; monkeys (candlesticks), 220; pigeons (vase), 216; rams' heads (pedestal), 37

Indian china: bottles, 333; bowl, with cover and stand, 220, **broth basins,** 220; —, and covers, 218; **cups and saucers,** 218, 220; **dessert dishes,** round, 343, 344; —, shell, 344; **dinner dishes,** 344; —, octagonal, 343; —, round, 343; **dinner-plates,** 344; —, octagonal, 344; —, round, 344; **flower-pots,** 220; **plates,** 333; **soup-plates,** 344; **sponge plate,** 217; **sponge saucer,** 220

Indian furnishings: cushion, leather, 272; mats, 203, 215, 311, 312; picture frames, black, with brass ornaments, 331; quilts, 55, 56, 61; wall-paper, 189, 192

Indian furniture: box, japanned, 329; **cabinets,** 36, 138, 309, 310; —, on frame, 269; —, inlaid, 328, 329; —, japanned, 276,

333; —, scarlet, 269; —, trunk, 310; **chests**, 82, 268; —, brass-mounted, 331; —, with frames, 75, 76; —, japanned, 76, 269; —, with raised brass-work, 274; **clothes-chest**, 138; **corner-cupboards**, 71, 78; —, japanned with frame, 76; **dressing-glass frame**, 217; **dressing-table ornaments**, 269; **fire screen**, folding, 75; **folding-screen**, japanned, with 6 leaves, 327; **hand board**, 119; **screens**, 70; —, with 6 leaves, 205, 216; **tea-table**, 76; **workbox**, japanned, 333

Indian silk: cushions (striped), 52; window-valance, 82

Indian weaponry: broad sword and scabbard, 329

Indian work: counterpane and pillows, 34. *See also* Decca work

ink-bottles, 203, 204, 217, 218, 219, 220, 272, 328; glass, 206; with plated tops, 221

inkstands, 206, 207, 208, 216, 217, 218, 219, 220, 300, 302; black-stained, 221; bronze and gold, 204; china, 203, 215, 216, 319, 344; Colebrookdale, 204; French china, 204; marble, 215; marble and ormolu, 203; pewter, 342; plated, 329; silver, 203, 204, 214, 272, 273, 316; Wedgwood, 333; yew, with 1 drawer, 272

inlaid work: bedside cupboard, 332; **bedstead cornice and foot pillars**, 332; **bookcases**, 326, 328, 333; **bookshelves**, 206, 217; **brackets**, 206; **cabinets**, French, 274; —, ivory, 328, 329; —, marble, 329; —, tortoiseshell, 33; —, Tunbridge ware, 206, 220; **chamber baths**, 333, 334, 335; **chest**, 333; **chests of drawers**, 333, 334; **claw-table**, 204; **commodes**, 203, 204; —, French, 215; **corner commodes**, 207, 219; **desk**, 191; **dressing tables**, 332, 334, 335, 336; **fly-tables**, 332, 335; **fowling-piece**, inlaid with pearl, 270; **hearth brush**, 204; **letterboxes**, 273; —, brass and tortoiseshell, 214; **looking-glass frames**, 56, 80; **nightstool**, 333; **oyster table**, inlaid with mother-of-pearl, 84; **pier tables**, 189; **scrutoire**, 75; **set of drawers**, 207; **sideboards**, 327; **sofa table**, 328; **stands**, inlaid with tortoiseshell, 42; **table tops**, 337; —, alabaster with black marble inlay, 217; **tables**, 56, 190, 203, 214; —, with 1 drawer, 205; —, with 1 shelf, 1 drawer, 218; —, brass, 273; —, French, 217; —, oval, 328; —, square, 328, 329; —, tortoiseshell, 310; **wardrobe**, 334; **wash-hand stands**, 332, 334, 335; **window-curtain cornices**, 332; **writing-desk**, 55; **writing-tables**, 75, 138, 328; —, tambour, 255, 271

intermesses, 44, **357**; lesser, 44

Irish: carpet, 267; sheets, 47. *See also* blankets, Irish; underblankets, Irish

Irish Georgian Society, 7

Irish plaid: wall-hangings, door- and window-curtains, 77

Irish Rebellion of 1641, 19

Irish Rebellion of 1798, 237

Irish stuff: bed-curtains, 47; —, striped, 80; headcloth, 47; stool, 47; tester, 47; window-curtains and valances, 31

Irish terms, inventions and conventions; caple [capall], 90; capriole, 167, **353**; concordatum, 65, **354**; corkscrew, bowed (Copley style), 197, **354–5**; gad, 92, **357**; kish, 298, **358**; losset, 289, **358**; madder (wooden tankard), 303, **358**; mahogany-cased door-lock, 110, **358–9**; pillion, 120, **360**; ribbery, 172, **360**; rug (cloth), 313; sally (willow), 191, **361**. *See also* Glossary, pp. 351–64

Irish tower-house furnishing, 148

iron furniture: at Dublin Castle, 64; at Hillsborough Castle, 142

ironing blankets, 144, 225, 288, 315, 318. *See also* smoothing blankets

irons. *See* smoothing-irons

ironware: at Lismore Castle, 22; basting ladle, 284; bedsteads, 291, 292, 300; beef forks, 142; candlesticks, 48, 171; —, fly, 341; —, high, 232; —, long, 285; chafing-dish, 172; chests, 171, 217, 244, 308; cleavers, 45, 64, 127; coal boxes, 90, 286, 289; coal rake, 45; coal scuttles, 275, 288; corn weeder, 297; dripping-pans, 45, 112; fire-fork, 22; fire shovels, 64, 296; fish-kettles, 341; flesh-forks, 22, 64, 296, 315; forks, 48, 166; frying-pans, 22, 64, 127, 142; kettle, 23; kitchen fork, 64; ladles, 45, 171; mattocks, 168; mincing knife, 64; oven stopper, 45; pan, 341; pestle, 45; pickaxes, 168; plate-warming stand, 66; poker ('firepoke'), 45; potato shovel, 299; pots, 22, 47, 90, 113, 127, 143, 294, 296; rakes, 167, 298, 300; rasps, 48; safe, 290; saucepans, 22, 341; scale weights, 67; shovel, 294; skewers, 127, 284, 314, 341; skivers, 91, 142; sledge, 168; slicers, 45; spoons, 285, 286, 341; steak-tongs, 142, 341; stewpan, 22; table frames, 294; tea-kettle, 341; tongs, 142; trivet, 45

ironwork: anchor, 168; axle-trees, 166; backbands, 166; boilers, 144, 288; broiler, 284; casement frames, 51; chest binding, 171; crow, 91; door-locks, 89, 90, 111; doors, 303; fenders, 21, 22, 32, 49, 303; firebacks, 20, 21, 22, 31, 32, 33, 35, 38, 39, 40, 82; fire dogs, 21, 39, 71; fire grates, 303; footman, swing, 22; gates, 297; grates, 33, 44, 48, 49, 51, 90, 140; gridirons, 341; gudgeons, 166; hearths, 77, 81, 84; hogshead binding, 128; hoop iron, 297; kitchen-ranges, 45, 142; locks, 110; pot hangers, 22; racks, 22, 45, 90, 171; rod iron, 297; screen stand, 39; sideboard brackets, 159; spit racks, 142; spits, 341; square-section iron, 297; stands for bars of grates, 207, 209; table brackets, 159; trunk binding, 47

ivory: bell-pull knobs, 330; carving-knife handles, 318; cups, ciphered, 272; fork-handles, 66, 90, 112; inlaid work on cabinets, 328, 329; knife-handles, 66, 90, 112, 318

jacks, 111, 152, **358**; and chains, 91, 195; draw-up jack, 50; multiplying wheels, 143, 183; weights for jacks, in lead, 143; —, in metal, 158; wind-up jack and chain, 340. *See also* boot-jacks; leather jacks; skewers; skivers; smoke-jacks; spits

jack (vessel for liquor), **358**. *See also* leather jacks

japanned goods, **358**; armed chair, 41; bakers, 37; bottle coopers, 286; boxes, 70; —, Indian, for counters, 329; cabinets, 34; —, Indian, 276, 333; can, 275; candlesticks, hand, 342; —, round, 339; —, square, 339; chests, black, 71; —, Indian, 269; —, Indian, black, on gilt frame, 76; chests of drawers, 192; —, black, 56, 57; cocoa pot and cover, 282; corner cupboard, Indian, and frame, 76; dressing boxes, 139; dressing-glass frames, 76, 206, 208, 277; extinguishers, 339, 342; folding-screen, with 6 leaves, Indian, 327; foot pans, 255, 287, 292; —, tin, 256, 265, 266, 267, 268, 269, 270, 271; knife, 283; lamps, 287; looking-glass frames, 32, 55, 84; night lamp, 218; pint can, 128; pints, 285; plate warmers, 233, 274, 327; screens, black, 67; —, church, 291; snuffer-dish, 318; snuffers, 285, 290, 339, 342; snuffer-trays, 219, 221, 285, 290; spoon-trays, red, 318; —, tin, 339; squabs, 34; stands, 75; tables, 31, 138, 179; —, black, on gilt frame, 76; —, square, black, 76, 84; tables and stands, 32, 40; —, black, 75; tea-boards, 140; tea-canister, 283; tea-kettle, 128; tea-pot, 278; tea-table, 33; tea-trays, 283, 289, 318, 342, 345; —, Indian, 342; —, tin, 342; tea-urn, 283; trays, 193, 234, 277, 279, 339; —, black, 318; trunk, 191; waiters, 140, 345; water-can, 318; workbox, Indian, 333; writing-table, 75

japanned leno: window-curtains, 221

jars: blue-and-white ware, 342; china, 36, 76, 118, 179, 180, 273, 310, 329; —, with covers, 34, 76, 274; —, deep, 34; —, high, 319; —, large, 34, 203, 214, 216, 274, 309, 319; —, long, 309; —, round, 34; —, with saucers, 203, 214; —, with silver-topped lids, 36; earthenware, 38; glass, 278, 342; porphyry, 273; stone, 299; —, ormolu-mounted, 273

jars and covers: brown ware, 341

jaunting-cars, 293; basket, 319; cushions, 293, 319; harness, 293, 319

jelly-bags, 315, 316; frame for, 341

jelly-glasses, 64, 91, 182, 278; and stand, 175

jelly-moulds: copper, 340; elephant, 284; fluted, 284; melon, 284; plain, 284; tin, 340

jelly shapes, 284; copper, 314; partridge, 284

jelly stands, 91, 128, 278, 284, 318; deal, 142

joint-stools, 40, 44, 46, 49

jorum, **358**; copper, 63

joss, Indian, 319

jugs: blue ware, 270, 282, 300; brown-edged ware, 278; china, 193; delft, 193, 286; —, and covers, 175; glass, 119, 120, 206; porcelain, 278; silver, and covers, 161; stoneware, 286; white ware, 275, 277, 300. *See also* jugs and basins; ewers; claret-jugs; cream-jugs; hot-water jugs; warm-water jugs; water-jugs

jugs and basins, 266, 267, 312, 313, 314; blue-and-white ware, 208; blue ware, 310, 311, 312; china, 311; white ware, 254, 256, 268, 270, 271, 272, 290, 291, 312; yellow ware, 209, 210. *See also* basins and ewers

keelers, 23, 92, 173, 294, **358**; wooden, 302
kegs, 287; for oil, 296
kettle pots: copper, 91
kettles, **358**; for heating lead, 288; **brass**, 22, 45; —, Welsh, 22; **copper**, 45, 112, 224, 255, 256, 265, 266, 267, 268, 269, 270, 271, 272, 287; —, and covers, 112, 158; **iron**, 23; **metal**, 276, 285, 288, 294, 301; **silver**, and stand, 197; **tin**, 206, 207, 208, 218, 279, 301, 310, 338; —, and stand, 302. *See also* boilers; coppers; fish-kettles; kettle pots; tea-kettles; tea kitchens
kettle-stands, 287; mahogany, 109. *See also* footmen
Kidderminster, **358**; bed-curtains, 48, 50; bed-furniture, 58, 59; bed-hangings, 61; carpets, 329, 330, 331, 332, 333, 334, 335, 336, 337, 338, 339; headcloths, 48, 50; stair-carpet, 338; testers, 48, 50; wall-hangings, 20, 32, 48; window-curtains, 48; worsted, 44, 49. *See also* Scotch carpeting
Kildare linen, **358**; napkins, 280; tablecloths, 279
Kilkenny Castle, Co. Kilkenny, 12, 27, 73; inventory of 1705, 31–53; drawing by Place, *52–3*; detail, *30*
Kilkenny marble: sideboard tops, 159
Killadoon, Co. Kildare: inventory of 1807, overlaid with that of 1812, 203–13; inventory of 1812, revised in 1829, 214–25
Kilrush House, Freshford, Co. Kilkenny: inventory of 1750, 149–52
kish, 298, **358**. *See also* turf keshes
kitchen cloths, 316
kitchen fork: iron, 64
kitchen knives, 283
kitchen-ranges, 183, 343; iron, 45, 142
kitchens: at Baronscourt, 183–4; at Captain Balfour's house, 111–12; at Carton House, 283–4, 300, 302; at Dublin, No. 10 Henrietta Street, 158; at Elphin, the bishop's house, 91; at Hillsborough Castle, in 1746, 127; —, in 1777, 142–3; at Kilkenny Castle, 45; —, French, 45; —, housekeeper's, 47; at Morristown Lattin, 171–2; at Mount Stewart, 340–1; —, at the Temple of the Winds, 343; at Newbridge House, 314–15; at Shelton Abbey, 232
kitchen seat, 302
kitchen-tables, 22, 127, 152, 183, 314; deal, 142, 300, 302, 340; oak, 283
kitchen vessels: wooden, 22
kneading-trough, 342. *See also* losset
knife-baskets, 112, 128; copper, 112; deal, 283; mahogany, 283
knife board, 301
knife-boxes, 183, 193, 286; copper, 112; mahogany, 157; wooden, 285
knife-cases, 157; mahogany, 233
knife cloths, 281, 316, 346; Drogheda linen, 281; grey linen, 280
knife-hafts: silver, 161
knife-rests, 278
knife-trays, 308, 318; deal, 339
knives: agate-handled, 348; ivory-handled, 318; japanned, 283; silver, 197; silver-handled, 71, 72, 316, 323, 348; silver-plated,

323; with silver-plated handles, 323; wooden, 303. *See also* carving-knives; dessert-knives
knives and forks: green-hafted, 193; ivory-handled, 66, 90, 112; silver, 117, 183, 197; —, and spoons, 316
knocker: brass, 120
lacework trimmings: bed-furniture, 79; toilet-table furniture, 190; window-furniture, 75, 76, 81, 82
lacquer-work, **358**; andirons, 34; curtain-rods, 37, 40; door-handles, 189; picture frames, 77; —, black, 41, 42; sconces, 31, 32. *See also* japanning
ladders, 93, 298, 300. *See also* library ladder; slating ladders; step-ladders
lading-pails, 144, **358**
ladles, 127, 315; for dripping-pan, 340; **brass**, 22, 45, 112; **copper**, 112, 142, 283, 340; **iron**, 45, 171; **silver**, 323; **wooden**, 166. *See also* basting ladles; punch ladles; sauce-ladles; soup-ladles; tureen ladles
lamp cloths, 281
lamp room: at Carton House, 287
lamps: 1-burner, 217; —, brass, 287; 2-burner, brass, 287; 3-burner, brass-mounted, 328; —, and cut-glass bottom, 327; —, and plate [silver] bottom, 327; 4-burner, brass-mounted, 327, 328; —, tin, 192; 6-burner, brass, 287; globe, 140; Grecian-style, 273; lamp with green glass, 211; sideboard, 327; brass, 340; bronze, 203, 204, 214; copper, 111; glazed, 289; japanned, 287; tin, 192; —, painted, 287. *See also* branch lamps; Liverpool lamps; night lamp; oil lamps; patent lamps; reading lamp
lamp-shades, 331; glass, 318, 331
lamp trays, 296; tinned, 287
lancewood, **358**; chest of drawers, 255; cupboard, 254
landau, 319, **358**
lanterns, 90, 128; glass, 32, 46, 77, 84, 85, 89, 125, 139, 141, 285, 286, 287, 301; green, 285; hall, 110; —, brass-mounted, 274; round, 46; rushlight, 268; side, 179, 185; tin, 289, 298
larders: at Baronscourt, 184; at Carton House, 284–5; at Elphin, the bishop's house, 90; at Hillsborough Castle, 127, 143; at Kilkenny Castle, 45; at Mount Stewart, 341
larding-pins, 142, 283, 315, 341
laths: bedstead bottom, 43; in deal for napkin drying, 51; for plastering, 172
lattice-work: brass, 272. *See also* treillage; trellis-work
laundries: at Baronscourt, 184; at Carton House, 288–89; at Hillsborough Castle, 127, 143–4; at Kilkenny Castle, 48; at Killadoon, 213, 225; at Mount Stewart, 343. *See also* wash-houses
laundry baskets, 213, 225
laundry maids' rooms: at Baronscourt, 184; at Kilkenny Castle, 48; at London, St James's Square, 80
lavabos: mahogany, 218; —, with marble top, 219
lava ware: wafer stand, 214
lawn-sieves, 278, 342, **358**
lay-overs, 115, 141, 279, 280, **358**; bird-eyed,

141; damask, 141, 195, 346; —, star pattern, 141; diaper, 195
lead: bathing-tub lining, 32; cisterns, 32, 45, 84, 297; kettles for heating lead, 288; pipes, 288; pump, 51; scale weights, 67; in sheets, 194; skewers for balancing, 315
lead-house: at Carton House, 297
leather jacks, 67, 127, 184, **358**; blackjacks, 45
leather-work: armchair coverings, 193, 216, 229, 233, 271; armed-chair coverings, 140, 329; armed-chair seat, 108; bergère coverings, 205; bidet coverings, 206, 207, 208; buckets, 293; carpets, 51; chair bottoms, 90, 168, 180, 290; chair-cover, 339; chair coverings, 40, 44, 48, 49, 50, 80, 125, 205, 216, 291; chair seats, 108, 240, 330, 339; chest cover, 76; close-stool coverings, 33, 39; clothes-chest cover, 138; commode covers, 204; cushions, 204, 214; —, Indian, 272; elbow-chair bottom, 126; elbow-chair covering, 125; fire-bucket, 298; letter bags, 290; letterbox, 203; library-table coverings, 214, 217, 272; library-table lining, 271; music-stool upholstery, 189, 191; pianoforte covers, 203, 204, 271, 275; reading-chair covering, 272; sofa covering, 229; stool covering, 32; table covering, 76; table covers, 39, 41, 81, 140, 210; trunk bindings, 84, 142, 171, 192, 231, 293, 339; wall-hangings, 51. *See also* gilt leather-work
leaves for fruit: Worcester porcelain, 318
Leinster House, Dublin, 247; linen from, 247, 279
Leixlip Castle, Co. Kildare, 7; doll's house at, 307
lemon squeezers, 278, 341
lemon strainer: silver, 197
leno, **358**; window-curtains, 221
letter bags: leather, 290
letterboxes, 214, 328; brass and tortoiseshell inlaid, 214; leather, 203; yew, 271; —, inlaid, 273
libraries: at Borris House (called the office), 244; at Carton House, large, 272–3; —, small, 272; at Elphin, the bishop's house, 'books in yᵉ Studie', 87, 95–103; at Hillsborough Castle, in 1777, 140; at Killadoon, 214; at Mount Stewart, 326, 328; at Newbridge House, 320–2; at Shelton Abbey, 227, 233–4
library-chair coverings: drab-cloth, 273; green cloth, 272
library desk, 291
library ladder, 291
library-table coverings: leather, 214, 217, 272
library-table doors: panel- and lattice-work, 272
library-table linings: green cloth, 272; leather, 271
library tables, 203, 214; with drawers, 271, 214; 217; **leather-covered**, 214; —, square, with 2 knee-holes and 18 drawers, 217; **mahogany**, with panelled doors on one side, 272; **rosewood**, 204; **satinwood**, round, on pillar and claws, 272
Liège, **358**; quilts, 231
light boxes for garden frames, 302

lime, powdered, 239; lime riddle, 174; lime screen, 299, **358**

line, bales of, 282

linen (cloth), 195, **358**; back-stool covers, 180; bed-curtains, 138; blinds, 270, 272; Boyle, 281; Cromaboo, 280; curtains, 44; Dowlas, 280, 281, 282; —, remnants, 281; Drogheda, 280, 281; —, remnant, 281; dusters, 280; feather bags, 294; Kildare, 280; length of, 280; mattress, 126; quilts, 126, 137, 138; roller blinds, 241, 270, 271, 327, 334, 335; spring blinds, 271, 274; Studdert, 280. *See also* brown Holland; brown linen, furniture linen; grey linen; Holland; white Holland

linen (household): at Balfour town house, 113–16; at Baronscourt, 179; at Carton House, 279–82; at Castlecomer House, 195; at Hillsborough Castle in 1777, 141; at Kilkenny Castle, 47; from Leinster House, Dublin, 279; at Lismore Castle, 23; at Mount Stewart, 345

linen calico: window-curtains, 229

linen-chest, 21

linen-presses, 45, 47, 79, 140; deal, 342

lion (over bookcase), 180

liqueur glasses, 286, 318

Lismore Castle, Co. Waterford: aquatint by Alken, *18*; inventory of 1702/3, 20–3

list, **358**; hearth-rug, 337

Liverpool lamps, 338, **358**; brass-mounted, 331

livestock: bull, 93; bullocks, 93; heifers, 93; milk cows, 93; strappers, 93, **362**

lobbies: at Castlecomer, 189; at Elphin, the bishop's house, 89; at Kilkenny Castle, 31, 32; at Killadoon, 208; at Morristown Lattin, 170; at Mount Stewart, 331; at Newbridge House, 310

lobby-carpet: Scotch carpeting, 189

lockers, 192, 193, 290

locks: brass, 89, 90; **iron**, 90, 110; 'mahogany locks', 110, **358–9**; box, 272; chest, 268; drawer, 89, 141, 205, 212, 217, 218, 219, 220, 221; gate, 303; press, 211, 212, 253, 254, 255, 279. *See also* door-locks; hanging lock; padlocks; tumbler locks

London: St James's Square, detail after John Rocque's map of London, 1746, *10*; —, engraving by Nicholls, *74*; —, inventory of 2nd Duke of Ormonde's house, *c.* 1710, 75–85

looking-glasses: *passim*; with glass arms, 90; hand, 140; hanging, 76, 79, 81; mantelpiece, 311; oval, 138, 140, 180, 273. *See also* cheval glasses; chimney-glasses; dressing glasses; hanging-glasses; looking-glasses (movable); pier-glasses; toilet glasses

looking-glasses (movable), 311, 312, 313. *See also* swing looking-glasses; swing dressing glasses

looking-glass frames: black, 41, 56, 75, 78, 126; black and tortoiseshell, 46; brass-garnished, 31, 35, 38; carved, 125; carved and gilt, 81, 138; ebony and tortoiseshell, 42; gilt, 35, 37, 168, 180, 206, 207, 210, 224, 231, 268, 329; glass, 76; inlaid, 56, 80; inlaid counterfeit stone, 33; japanned, 32, 55, 84; mahogany, 210, 212, 337; silver-garnished,

33; silver-leafed, 34; walnut, 125; white, 223, 224

lopping shears, 300

losset, 289, **358**

lotto box, 189

lumber, 292, 296, 297, 298

lumber-box, 279

lumber yard, 297

lustres, **358**; cut-glass, 140; —, 3-armed, 228, 229

lutestring, **358**; bed-furniture lining, 137; case curtains, 70; chair-backs and seats, 80; stool covers, 70; window-curtain trimmings, 189; window-curtains, 82; window-curtains and cornices, 81

mace (spice), 342

mace (tool), 296. *See also* billiard-maces

madders, 303, **358**

mahogany: alphabet tables, 206; armchairs, 211, 224, 328, 336; —, with leather upholstery, 229, 240; armed chair, 337; **backgammon tables**, 125, 283; basin-stands, 109, 140, 190, 191, 206, 207, 208, 209, 229, 230; **bed**, turn-up, 213; **bed canopy**, round, 221; **bed-pillars**, 241, 265, 270; bed-posts, 190, 191; —, fluted, 190; bedside commodes, 230, 266; bedside cupboards, 330, 332, 333, 334, 335, 336, 337; bedside steps, 332, 334; **bedstead cornices**, 241; —, carved, 270; —, ogee, 292; **bedstead foot pillars**, 330, 331, 336, 337; —, turned, 331, 333, 334, 335; **bedsteads**, 334, 339; —, four-post, 138, 139, 160, 217, 218, 219, 223; bed-steps, 207, 255, 267, 268, 269, 270, 292; bidets, 191, 210, 230, 256, 272; —, with delft pan, 255, 256, 265, 266, 267, 268, 269, 270, 271, 292; —, with leather covering, 206, 207, 208; **billiard-table**, 192; bookcases, 138, 139, 180, 191, 221, 234, 276, 311, 329; —, with 2 drawers, 208, 220; —, with drawers, 244; —, with glazed doors, 160, 209, 271; —, with looking-glass doors, 160; —, with panelled doors, 271; —, pier, 308; —, swing, 329; —, with trellis-work doors, 220; —, with wirework doors, 271; **bookshelves**, 191, 206, 208, 276, 311; **boot-jacks**, 255, 256, 265, 266, 267, 269, 270, 272, 291; **bottle coopers**, 233, 234, 273; **bottle stands**, 125; **bottle tray**, 125; **boxes**, 139, 272; **box of drawers**, 311; **brackets**, 193, 206; **breakfast-tables**, 189; —, with drawers, 270; —, with folding leaves, 328; **buckets**, 169; —, square, 157; **bureaux**, 125, 126, 137, 138, 139; **cabinets**, 126, 190; —, with drawers inside, 273; —, glazed, with 2 drawers, 5 shelves, 329; **camp table**, with folding top and 1 drawer, 342; **candle stands**, on pillars and claws, 272; **candlestick bottoms**, 347; **candlesticks**, 318; **canopy bedstead**, 332; **Canterburys**, 205; —, supper, 240; **card-tables**, 109, 125, 139, 160, 189, 229, 230, 233, 273, 275, 303, 329, 330; **case**, 272; **cases of drawers**, 229, 230, 231, 242, 244; **cellar**, lead-lined, 189; **chair frames**, 168, 190; **chairs**, 160, 161, 204, 205, 213, 223, 224, 233, 240, 269, 287, 308, 309, 310; —, cane-seated, 267, 268,

269, 270, 272, 273; —, children's, 205; —, hair-backed, 330; —, hair-bottomed, 216, 220, 339; —, hair-seated, 327, 330, 342, 343; —, leather-seated, 330, 339; —, mohair-bottomed, 209; —, morocco-seated, 327; —, old-fashioned, 211, 212, 223, 224; —, stuffed, 192; —, with stuffed backs and bottoms, 190; —, with stuffed bottoms, 189, 190, 191; —, with stuffed seats, 300, 335, 336, 337, 338, 339; —, with stuffed seats and backs, 192, 328, 329, 331, 332, 333, 334, 339; **chamber airers**, 255, 256, 265, 266, 267, 268, 269, 270, 271, 274, 292; —, with 2 folds, 279; **chamber baths**, 331, 332, 333, 335; **chamber chest**, 270; **chamber horse**, 272; **chamber table**, 242; **chess table**, 273; **chests**, 150, 205; **chests of drawers**, 137, 138, 181, 190, 220, 221, 256, 271, 275, 310, 312; —, with 4 drawers, 332, 338; —, with 5 drawers, 330, 332, 336, 337, 338, 339; —, with 6 drawers, 338; —, with 7 drawers, 335, 338; —, with 8 drawers, 336; —, banded and strung, 255, 265; —, with French marble top, 219; **chest with drawers**, 275; 205; **cheval-glass frames**, 267, 268, 269; **cisterns**, 108, 140; **cistern stand**, 205; **claw-tables**, 140, 141, 145, 204, 205, 210, 219, 224; **clock case**, 274; **clothes airers**, 230; **clothes-chest**, 160; **clothes-horses**, 139, 209, 220, 221, 223, 224, 230, 255, 308; —, with boot-jack, 255, 256, 265, 266, 267, 269, 270, 272; **clothes-presses**, 241, 244, 312; —, on drawers, 244; **commodes**, 180, 190, 191, 192, 206, 207, 208, 209, 210, 255; **console-table**, 308; **corner commodes**, 206; **corner presses**, 209, 223; **corner-shelf**, 271; **corner-stands**, 125; **cornice of organ**, 292; **cross chairs**, 274; **cross seats**, 274; **cross stand**, 240; **cross stool**, 290; **deception commode**, 242; **desks**, 160, 191, 208, 212, 213, 216, 224, 272; —, sloping, 275, 276, 290; —, sloping, with drawers, 267, 269, 270, 300; **dining chairs**, mohair-bottomed, 211, 224; **dining-tables**, 108, 125, 159, 168, 169, 179, 180, 192, 205, 239, 240, 308, 310; —, with 2 leaves, 139, 343; —, in 3 parts, 140; —, with cants, 192; —, Northumberland, 189; —, oval, 2 leaves, 342; —, oval, with leaves, 330; —, on pillars and claws, 327; —, round, 125, 140; —, with rosewood banding, 252; **dinner trays**, 339; **dish trays**, 286; **door-lock casing**, 1 10; **drawing board** (horse), 292; **dressing glasses**, 161, 206, 343; —, with 1 drawer, 209; —, hanging, 277; —, square, 333, 335; **dressing-glass frames**, 206, 207, 208, 209, 210, 221, 256, 269; **dressing stools**, 332, 333, 335; —, stuffed, 332, 334; **dressing tables**, 137, 138, 139, 159, 160, 181, 191, 207, 224, 241, 256, 266, 267, 301, 311, 330, 331, 335; —, with 1 drawer, 208, 256, 336, 337; —, with 1 drawer, 1 shelf, 205, 206, 209, 210, 221; —, with 2 drawers, 208, 332, 336, 337; —, with 5 drawers, 269; —, with 11 drawers, 331; —, with drawers, 190, 220; —, with folding top, 333, 336, 337; —, knee-hole, 331; —, with 1 shelf and divisions, 209; —, with

mahogany continued

sliding leaf, 336; —, square, 337; **dumb-waiters**, 140, 189, 205, 233, 240; **elbow-chairs**, 160, 161; **fire-screen bases**, 272, 273; **fire screens**, 139, 204, 205, 328, 329, 330; **fly-tables**, 331, 339; —, with 1 drawer, 331, 334, 336, 338; —, oval, 334; —, square, 332, 333, 334, 335, 336, 337, 338; **folding-screen**, 210; **folding-tables**, 125, 139; **footboards**, 241, 270; **footstools**, 328, 335; **frames for blinds**, 271; **French bed**, 221; **gardevine**, 286; **glass-trays**, 283, 286; **gun-cases**, 271; **hall chairs**, 200, 205, 214, 233, 308, 326; **hand screens**, 214; **hanging shelves**, 190; **hazard table**, 205; **horses**, 209; —, folding, 206, 207, 208; **kettle-stand**, 109; **knife-basket**, 283; **knife-box**, 157; **knife-cases**, 233; **lavabos**, 218; —, with marble top, 219; **library table**, 272; **looking-glass frames**, 210, 212, 337; **music stands**, 189, 329; **music stools**, 189, 191; **night box**, 220; **night-chairs**, 190, 207, 208; —, children's, 209, 221; **night commode**, 255; **night-stools**, 137, 274, 289, 332, 334, 337; **night tables**, 138, 139, 229, 230, 231, 256, 265, 267, 269, 276, 332, 335; **office chair**, 271; **organ casing**, 189; **panel doors**, to wardrobe-bed, 267; **parlour chairs**, 276; —, slatted, 273; **pedestals**, 233, 240; —, tin-lined, 273; **Pembroke tables**, 180; —, with 1 drawer, 218; —, with 2 drawers, 334; **picture frame**, 333; **pier tables**, 189, 229, 233, 239, 240; **pillar tables**, 161, 204, 273; —, round, 159; **plate-baskets**, 327; **plate buckets**, with brass hoops, 205; —, square, 205; **plate tray**, 125; **plate warmer**, 327; **pole-screens**, 274, 328, 330, 333, 335; **press beds**, 223, 225; **press bedsteads**, 191, 329; —, in form of a desk, 189; **presses**, 244, 266; —, for billiard cues, 274; —, with drawers and nests, 194; **reading desks**, 204; —, with 5 drawers, 330; —, on pillar, 204; —, screw, 310; **reading stand**, 271; **reading table**, claw, 216; **row of pegs**, 220; **sarcophagus**, 240; **screens**, with 6 leaves, 217; —, with 8 leaves and glazed, 328; —, paper, 337; **screw press**, 192; **scrutoire**, 126; **seats**, 329; **secrétaire**, 218; **secretaries**, 190, 230, 234, 330; —, with 5 drawers, 330; **sets of drawers**, 206, 207, 208, 210, 211, 213, 224; **settees**, stuffed, 192; —, with stuffed bottoms, 190; **shelves**, 138, 168, 331; —, to table, 206, 207, 209; **shutters**, 203, 205, 214; **sideboards**, 139, 180, 189, 240, 308; —, with 1 drawer, 342; **sideboard tables**, 108, 125, 140, 205, 233; **side tables**, 327, 329; —, with folding top, 329; **sofa**, leather upholstered, 229; **sofa frames**, 231, 273; **sofa tables**, 239; —, with claw feet on castors, 273; **spider-tables**, 190, 191, 204, 208, 209, 212, 224, 229, 230, 231, 232, 244, 256, 266, 268, 273, 276; **squabs**, 161; **stack seats**, 220; **stand**, railed, for loose papers, 204; **step-ladders**, 205, 274; **stools**, 179; —, round, with stuffed seat, 190; **study-tables**, 308; **sugar-store frame**, 189; **supper stand**, 205; **supper table**, 108; **swing dressing**

glasses, 223, 224, 330, 331, 334, 339; —, with 1 drawer, 332, 335, 337, 339; —, with 3 drawers, 334, 338; **swing looking-glasses**, 332; —, with 1 drawer, 331, 336; **table frames**, 273; **tables**, 126, 139, 181, 182, 189, 191, 193, 205, 206, 208, 211, 212, 240, 268, 283, 290, 300, 301, 309, 310, 311, 329; —, with 1 drawer, 205, 207, 208, 209, 210, 212, 216, 220, 223, 308, 312, 336; —, with 1 drawer, 1 shelf, 207; —, with 2 drawers, 330; —, with drawers, 206, 311, 313, 329; —, with 1 leaf, 269; —, with 1 leaf, with drawers, 276; —, with 1 shelf, 209; —, children's, 273; —, circular, 179, 230, 239, 240; —, folding down, 330; —, for lamp, 308; —, octagonal, 208; —, octagonal, with folding leaves, 332; —, oval, 149, 240, 269, 274, 276, 286, 287, 293, 328; —, painted, 309; —, on pillar and claws, 239; —, round, 90, 139, 180, 269, 270, 275, 283, 309, 329, 343; —, square, 214, 328, 329, 330, 336; —, three-piece set, 205; **table stands** (supports), 217; **table top**, 329; **tallboys**, 109, 110, 126, 160, 184, 191; —, half, 190, 191, 287; **tea-boards**, 120, 141; **tea-chests**, 90, 119, 205, 308; **tea-kettle stand**, 142; **tea store**, 239; **tea-tables**, 90, 109, 303; —, round, 160, 342; **tea-trays**, 211, 224; **telescope case**, 330; **toilet-glass frames**, 253, 269; **transparency frames**, 329; **trays**, 193, 234, 240, 279, 318; —, square, 157; **tubs**, 308; **voider tables**, 229, 244, 273, 276; —, with 1 drawer, 271; **wardrobes**, 190, 191, 205, 206, 207, 230, 310, 311, 312; —, with 2 drawers, 3 shelves, 332; —, with 4 drawers, 330; —, with 4 drawers, 3 sliding shelves, 332; —, with 4 drawers, 5 trays, 221; —, on drawers, 242; —, with drawers in wings, 241; —, with panelled doors, 255, 268; —, with wire doors, 255; —, with wirework doors, 268; **wash-hand stands**, 126, 138, 308, 330, 333, 337; —, with folding top, 2 drawers, 332; **wash-hand table**, 269; **weighing machine**, 206; **whatnots**, 273; **window-curtain cornices**, 332; **wine carrier**, 308; **wine-coolers**, 232, 233; **wine-coopers**, 189, 205, 327; **wine tables**, 274; **workboxes**, 190; **worktables**, 291; —, square, with 1 drawer, 337; **writing-case**, 217; **writing-desks**, 141, 335; —, with drawers, 330; —, portable, 330; —, tambour, 270; **writing-desk table**, with folding top, 267; **writing stool**, 330; **writing-tables**, 137, 139, 140, 205, 233, 244, 308; —, with 1 drawer, 206, 221; —, with 6 drawers, 205, 217, 221; —, with drawers, 138, 140; —, with folding top, 330; —, square, 336

mahogany (colour): wardrobes (painted), 191, 193

mahogany (inlaid): bedside cupboard, 332; bedstead, four-posted with corniced canopy and turned foot pillars, 332; bookcases, 328, 333; bookshelves, 206; chamber baths, 333, 334, 335; chests of drawers, with 3 drawers, 333; —, with 4 drawers, 334; —, with 5 drawers, 333; dressing tables, with 3 drawers, 334; —,

with 5 drawers, 332, 335, 336; —, knee-hole, 332, 334, 335, 336; **fly-tables**, 335; —, square, 332; **night-stool**, 333; **pier tables**, 189; **table top**, 337; **tables**, with drawers, 190; —, oval, 328; —, square, 328, 329; with turned feet, 332; **wardrobe**, with 2 drawers, 3 deal shelves, 334; **wash-hand stands**, 332, 334, 335; **writing-table**, with folding top, 328

mahogany and ebony: dressing table, with 2 drawers, 207

mallets, 279, 291, 302; sugar, 120, 315

malt: bin for, 166; in barrels, 93; mills, 151; —, in steel, 144

Manchester quilt, 109

mandrels, 295, *359*

mangle cloths, 225; Holland, 288

mangles, 213, 225, 288, 343, *359*; for linen, 194; by Peter Lyon, 144

mantel shelf. *See* chimney-pieces

mantel slab, and gilt frame, 271

mantles: satin, embroidered with sarcenet, 268; scarlet velvet, lined with sarcenet, 268

maple: stand, 240

map rack, 290

maps and plans, 70, 72, 80, 109, 125, 126, 240, 290, 291; Cork harbour, 66; County Down, 140, 328; Eddystone Lighthouse (Devon), 66; England, Scotland and Ireland, 66; Flanders, 66, 79, 84; Great Britain, 66; Hounslow Heath, 79; —, *The Camp On Hounslow-Heath* (poss.), 80; Kildare, 271; Namur, 66; Rocque, John (map-maker), *Exact Survey of the City and Suburbs of Dublin*, details, Henrietta Street, *154*; —, St Stephen's Green, *104*; —, Ireland and London (after Rocque), *10*; rolled-up maps, 72; world map, 47, 85

marble: family crest, 339; inlay, 329; painting on, 272

marble and wood: chimney-pieces, 329

marble furnishings: andirons, 37; bookcase slab, 308; chest-of-drawers top, 219; chimney-pieces, 109, 149, 327, 328, 329, 331, 332, 333, 334, 335, 343; —, and slab, 125; —, and wood, 329; —, black marble, 194; chimney-piece urns, 270; commode tops, 215, 219; fountain, 294; hearth stone, 149; inkstands, 215; —, with ormolu, 203; lavabo top, 219; mortars, 64, 65, 183, 279, 340; —, and pestle, 315; paperweight, Gibraltar rock, 214, 216; pillars, on cabinet, 329; plinths, 273, 274, 279; sideboards, on frames, 179; sideboard table, 169; sideboard tops, 330; —, Kilkenny marble, 159; side-table tops, 233, 329; slab in larder, 285; stands, with gilt frames, 71, 82; stove, 328; table tops, 109, 158, 159, 218, 219, 269, 270, 273; —, with brass borders, 159; —, Italian marble, on white carved frame, 159; tables, 70, 75, 140, 308; —, brass-mounted, 272; —, with carved frame, 109; —, with frames, 179, 180; —, with gilt frame, 82; —, with griffin in gilt frame, 159; —, in imitation marble, 344; —, with walnut frames, 81; vases, 229, 271, 272, 344. *See also* verd-antique

marble sculptures: busts, 273, 327; figures, 272, 308; statues, 214; Jupiter, 308; Marcus Aurelius, 309; Medusa, 205, 216; Venus, after Canova, 217

marjoram, 300

market cloths, 316

maroon-and-yellow: calico: bed- and window-curtains, 241

marquee cover, 291

marrow-bone cloths, 281

marrow spoons, **359**; silver, 117, 162, 183, 197, 240, 316, 323, 348

Marseilles, **359**; counterpanes, 268, 269; quilts, 190, 191, 192, 206, 207, 208, 210, 217, 218, 219, 220, 223, 241, 255, 256, 267, 270, 282

martingales, 319, **359**; child's, 319

match cups: china, 277, 328, 333

match-stands: china, 273

mathematical instruments, in case, 271

mats: hemp, 308; Indian, 203, 215, 311, 312; portingale, 70; Portugal, 70, 203, 215, **360**; Portuguese, 327, 328, 331; sheepskin, 273, 274; Tangier, 33, 34, 40

matted work, **359**; bed-curtains, 242; chair bottoms, 46, 126; conversation seats, 303

mattocks, 298; iron, 168

mattress case: calico, 221

mattress cover: calico, 223

mattresses, **359**; brown Holland, 337, 339; canvas, 50; check, 125, 331, 333, 334, 335, 336, 337, 338, 339; cotton, 137, 138; dimity, 125, 126; flock, 33, 38, 39, 143, 212, 223, 224; fustian, bordered, 268; hair, *passim*; —, bordered, 255, 256, 265, 266, 267, 268, 270, 276; —, curled, 190, 241; Holland, 268; linen, 126; straw, 141, 142, 143, 144, 145, 209, 212; tick, striped, 331, 332, 333, 334, 335; wool, 126, 133, 138, 141, 209, 210, 212, 221, 223, 255, 276, 330, 333, 334, 335, 336, 337, 338, 339; wool and hair, 253. *See also* barrack mattresses

mattress quilts: check, 84; fustian, 84; Holland, 84; silk, 84

meal: hogsheads, 172, 173

meal baskets, 143

meal tub, 299

measures of capacity, 193; pewter mugs for, 315. *See also* barrels; bushels; casks; gallons; hogsheads; pecks; pipes; pints; quarts; Scotch pints; tierces; tuns; wine-measures

meat rack, 45

meat rail and hooks, 45

meat saws, 283, 340

meat trays: silver, 183

medal: gold, 198

medallions, 282; as design feature, 220; oval, 271; Wedgwood, 271

medicine chests, 194; —, and stand, 244

medicine closet, at Castlecomer House, 194

Meissen porcelain. *See* Dresden porcelain

melon frames: with sashes, 300

melon ground, 300

melon moulds, 143, 284

melonnière ['meloniere']: melon dish, copper, 127

Merlin chair, 308, **359**

Merlin scales, 217

messenger's boxes, 290; morocco, 271

metal, **359**; bell, 277; boilers, 284, 293; kettles, 276, 285, 288, 294, 301; oven, 283; pot-hooks, 171; pot-oven, 171; pots, 171, 286; —, and covers, 301; rollers, 297, 298, 302; saucepans, 284; —, and covers, 315; scale weights, 166; trellis-work, 272; troughs, 299

metronome (musical chronometer), 273

mignonette, **359**; mignonette boxes, 300; —, for forcing, 300

milk bowls: wooden, 92

milk jugs: porcelain, 277

milk-pails, 127, 173, 294

milk pans, 67; delft, 294; earthenware, 92, 127

milk pots, 76; cut-glass, 345

milk strainer, 92

milk tub, 173

milled yarn: oyster cloths, 281; sheets, 281; stable rubbers, 281

mills. *See* coffee-mills; peppermills; *see also under* malt; wheat

mincing boards, 341

mincing knives, 127, 142, 283, 341; iron, 64

minute glass, 274

mirrors: gilt-framed, 228, 229, 332. *See also* cheval glasses; chimney-glasses; dressing glasses; hanging-glasses; looking-glasses; pier-glasses; swing-glasses; toilet glasses

mohair, **359**; armchair bottoms, 210, 211, 224; bed-furniture, 33; chair bottoms, 209; cushions, 79; dining-chair bottoms, 211, 224; elbow-chair coverings, 77; valance, 79; wall-hangings, 51; window-curtain furniture, 82

mohair and silk: window-curtains, 144

monteith, **359**; silver, 116

mops, 285, 286, 287, 289, 294; mop handles, 287; mopheads, 272, 287; yarn for, 287

moreen, **359**; Baronscourt, 'Blue Morine Bed Chamber', 181, bed-curtains, 192, 231, 274, 275, 289, 291; bed-furniture, 181, 182; curtain, 290; fire-screen covering, 240; length of, 281; screen, with 6 leaves, 217; seat covering, 303; seating furniture, 328; server coverings, 273; stool covering, 291; window-curtain cornices, 274; window-curtains, 189, 216, 233, 271, 272, 273, 274, 282, 327; window-drapery, 216, 233, 271, 272, 273; window-seat cover, 327

morocco: backgammon box, 272; blotting-book binding, 203, 204, 214, 215; case for weights and scales, 330; chair seats, 272; chess-table lining, 273; messenger's box, 271

morone, **359**. *See also* maroon

Morristown Lattin, Co. Kildare: inventory, 1773, 169–75; lithograph by Cooke, *164*

mortar boards, 296

mortars: bell-metal, 45; brass, 111, 112, 183; marble, 64, 65, 183, 279, 340. *See also* pestles and mortars

mother-of-pearl: counters, 329; inlaid work on fowling-piece, 270; oyster-table inlay, 84; snuff-box, 118

moulding planes, 296

moulds, 92, 143, 172; blancmange, 184; copper, 143, 184; fruit, 184; pewter, 184; pudding, 143; ribbed, 143; round, 143; tin, 143; **shapes**: cherry; church; croquant, oval and round; grape; heart; melon; pig; snuff-box; thimble; Turk's caps, 143. *See also* ice moulds; jelly shapes; shapes

Mountjoy House, Henrietta Street, Dublin: engraving from *Dublin Penny Journal*, 154

Mount Stewart, Co. Down: architectural drawing by Dance, detail, *frontispiece*, 2; inventory of 1821, 327–48

muffin dishes and covers: china, 277

muffin plates: china, and covers, 345; porcelain, 278; —, and covers, 277

mugs, 316; blue-and-white ware, 208, 217, 219, 220; china, 128, 175, 193; Colebrookdale, 206, 217; copper, 340; delft, 175, 193; glass, 120; pewter (for measures), 315; silver, 347; silver-mounted coconut, 316; tin, 340. *See also* beer mugs; coconut mugs

mule carts, 297, **359**

mule cloths, 71, 79

mules, 298; metal rollers for, 298; plough harness for, 298

mullets, 296

multiplying wheels, 143, 183, **359**

music, 189; music books, 309; rack for, 203, 215

musical chronometer (metronome), 273

musical instruments, 29; barrel organ, 308; drum and sticks, 272; French horn, 291; harpsichords, 70, 173, 179; organs, 274; —, mahogany-cased, 189; pianofortes, 123, 139, 203, 209, 215, 309; —, Broadwood, 271, 273; —, grand, 189, 204; —, upright, 239; spinet, 70, 80; tambourine, 272; triangles, 272

music rooms: at Carton House, 269, 282; at Mount Stewart, 328

music stands, 309; black-painted, 328; mahogany, 189, 329

music stools: leather-upholstered, 189, 191; mahogany, 189; —, round, 191; stuffed, and needlework cover, 328

muskets, 23, 46, 158

muslin, **359**; bed-drapery, 333; counterpane trimmings, 209, 221; curtains, 207, 215; quilt, 139; toilet-table furniture, 190; window-curtains, 219; window-drapery, 327, 331, 337

muslin (worked): toilet, 332

muslin and cotton: toilet, 334; window-drapery, 328, 333

muslin and gymp: bed-curtain trimmings, 190; window-curtain trimmings, 190

mustard and pepper stand, 300

mustard castor: silver, 197

mustard pots, 282, 303, 316, 342; glass, 183; silver, 197, 316; —, tin-lined, 347; silver-plated, 323

mustard spoons: silver, 316, 347

nails: nail box, 297; parcel of, 90. *See also* upholstery nails

nankeen china, **359**; cups and saucers, basin and sugar-basin, 183

napkins, 113, 114, 115, 116, 279; bordered, 279; Cromaboo, 280; damask, 141, 179; —, bird's eye, 282; —, 'from Boyle', 280; —, Cromaboo, 279; —, dessert, 195; —, dinner,

195; diaper, 23, 113, 179, 280; Dutch matted pattern, 280; Kildare, 280. *See also* breakfast napkins; dinner napkins; tea napkins; waiting napkins

needlework: chair seats, 161; fire screens, 32, 82, 159; —, sewn pieces for, 268; music-stool cover, 328; portrait of Charles I, 35; quilt, 144; screens, 159, 160; stool, 33; stool coverings, 273, 276

needleworked worsteds on canvas: chair, elbow-chair and settee covers, 192

neoclassical architecture: Baronscourt, 177

nests of drawers, 275, 297, 301, **359**; deal, 276, 290; for groceries, 193

Newbridge House, Co. Dublin: drawings by Frances Power Cobbe, drawing-room, *309*; —, house, lithograph of, after, *304*; inventory of 1821, 308–22; list of plate to be given to Charles Cobbe, 1814, 323; list of plate, 1821, 323

niggars, 111, 152, **359**

night box: mahogany, 220

nightcaps, 280

night-chairs, 141, 160, 191, 219, 220, 223; corner, 219; **mahogany**, 190, 207, 208; —, children's, 209, 221; **oak**, 141, 190, 191, 192

night commode: mahogany, 255

night lamp: japanned, 218

night pans, 278. *See also* bedpans

night quilts: cotton, 138; silk, 138, 139

night-stool cover: cotton, printed, 337

night-stools, 138, 139, 229, 231, 232, 310, 311, 312, 313, 314; **mahogany**, 137, 274, 289; —, inlaid, 333; —, with white-ware liner, 333, 334, 337; —, with white-ware pan, 332

night tables, 180, 181, 218, 230, 242, 244; fixed, 139; **mahogany**, 138, 139, 229, 230, 231, 256, 265, 267, 269, 332; —, with white-ware liner, 335; **oak**, 138

night vases, 221; blue-and-brown ware, 218, 223; blue-and-white ware, 218, 219, 220

noggins, 294, **359**; pewter, 276; wooden, 302

north country cloth: sheets, 23

nosebag, 292

noseband, 319. *See also* cavesson

nose-ring for bull: iron, 93

nozzles and pans, **359**; to brackets, in silver, 76; to sconces, in silvered brass, 76

nurseries: at Borris House, 244; at Dublin, No. 10 Henrietta Street, 160; at Elphin, the bishop's house, 89; at Killadoon, 208, 209, 221–3; at Morristown Lattin, 171; at Mount Stewart, 329–30; at Newbridge House, 313; at Shelton Abbey, 232

nurse's room: at Kilrush House, 151

nursing chairs, 218, 220

nutcrackers, 318

oak: armchairs, 89, 90, 211; **armed chairs**, 343; —, with stuffed sides and backs, 334; **basin-stands**, 221; **bed-pillars**, 256, 265; **bed-posts**, 191, 192, 193; —, fluted, 190; **bed table**, 291; **beds**, 288; **bedsteads**, four-post, 138, 142, 143, 144, 145, 313; —, turn-up, 286; **blanket chest**, 139; **bookcases**, with glazed doors, 140; **bookshelves**, 126; **bureaux**, 141; **case of drawers**, 232; **chairs**, 67, 89, 90, 91, 92, 93, 113, 128, 171, 211, 224, 289, 300, 310,

340; —, fold-up, old-fashioned, 223; —, with stuffed bottoms, 192; **chair-seat frame**, 333; **chests**, 91, 125, 145, 171, 255, 330, 339; —, with 1 drawer, 339; —, with 5 drawers, 337; **chests of drawers**, 89, 110, 137, 139, 149, 160, 194, 221, 223, 256, 266, 267, 274, 275, 276, 290, 312; **close-stool**, 48; **clothes-horse**, 223; **clothes-presses**, 139, 274; **corporation box**, 271; **desks**, 109, 192, 193; **dining-tables**, 109, 141, 224; —, oval, 210; **dressing stool**, square, 333; **dressing tables**, 89, 90, 109, 110, 137; —, with 1 drawer, 220, 221; **falling leaves**, 274; **hall chair**, 287; **horse**, 212; **kitchen-tables**, 283; —, with drawers and shelves, 283; **night-chairs**, 141, 190, 191, 192; **night tables**, 138; **plate-chest**, 44; **posts**, 92; **press bed**, 223; **press bedsteads**, 144, 145; **presses**, 210, 255, 266, 289, 330; —, with 2 drawers inside, 265, 266; —, with drawers, 301; —, with deal shelves, 256; **ribberies**, 172; **seats**, cane-bottomed, 331; **secretary**, with 4 drawers, 339; **set of drawers**, 211; **settle bed**, 49; **shelves**, 139, 302; **side table**, 90; **skeleton desk**, 290; **spider-table**, 210; **table beds**, 89, 90; **tables**, 48, 49, 66, 79, 90, 91, 93, 128, 137, 141, 171, 193, 209, 211, 212, 240, 283, 284, 285; —, with 1 drawer, 209, 210, 221, 223, 289; —, with 2 leaves, 303; —, with leaves, 300, 303; —, fixed, 51; —, folding, 128; —, oval, 84, 211, 224, 290; —, round, 171, 308; —, square, 67; **tallboy**, 191; **tallboy bedstead**, 192; **timber**, 173; **wardrobes**, 311, 313; —, with 2 drawers, 339; **writing-tables**, 89; —, with 1 drawer, 221

oars, 173; for brewing, 51

oats: barrels of, 93; bins for, 49, 50, 167; sowing of, 152

office furniture: chair, mahogany, 271; stools, 290; —, deal, 274; table, deal, with book rack and shelves, 275

ogee, **359**

oil cans, 287, 298; tin, 289

oilcloths, **359**; *passim*; fitted, 271; floor-cloths, 308; hearth covers, 229, 230, 231, 233; in rolls, 292

oil lamps, 240, 279, 286. *See also* patent lamps

oil paintings, 206, 231, 234, 239, 240; gilt-framed, 218, 241. *See also* pictures

oil pans, 298

oil pot: tin, 318

oil tray: tin, 289

oil vessel: tin, and stand, 287

old-fashioned, **359**; basin, china, 344; chairs, 213, 224; —, mahogany, 211, 212, 223, 224; —, oak, 223; —, seats and backs, 51; grate, steel, 343

olive (colour): punchbowl, china, 36

olive wood: tables, 78; —, and stands, 39, 41, 78

ombre tables, with green-cloth coverings, 33, 76, **359**

omelette pans, 283; copper, 314, 340

orange: cotton, window-curtain linings, 329; print (fabric), wall-hangings, 57. *See also* aurora

orange-and-white: drugget, bed-curtains, 44; —, headcloth, 44; —, tester, 44

organ clock, **359**; barrel from (poss.), 296

organs, 274; cornice of, mahogany, 292; mahogany-cased, 189

ormolu: basket handles, 216; candlesticks, 273; —, 4-light, 286; clocks, 205, 274, 328; figures, 274; inkstand (with marble), 203; picture frames, 214

ormolu mountings: ewers, stone-china, 273; jars, stone, 273; urn, bronze, 329

Ormonde Castle, Co. Tipperary, 27

ornamental cutters: tin, 340

ornaments: Chelsea porcelain, 319; china, 194, 203, 214, 215, 274; —, *craquelé*, 203, 204; for dressing-table, Indian, 269; plaster of Paris, 328; shells as decoration, 273, 329; Wedgwood, 219. *See also* chimney ornaments; rice ornaments

ottomans, **359**; stuffed, 302; —, square, with lined calico cover, 216

ounce (troy), **359**; *passim*

ovens, 183, 302; brick, 342; metal, 283

oven sheets, 283

oven stopper, **359**; iron, 45

oyster cloths: milled yarn, 281

oyster dish: china, 315

oyster knives, 318

oyster shells: china, 319

oyster tables, **359**; inlaid with mother-of-pearl, 84; for oyster-eating, 307, 310

packing boxes, 144, 173; deal, 52

packing cases, 71; deal, 52

padlocks, 91, 303. *See also* hanging lock

page's room: at Kilkenny Castle, 80

pails, 113, 127, 128, 318, 343; copper, 66; freezing, 279, 342; water, 341; wooden, 342. *See also* butter pail; cream-pails; ice-pails; milk-pails

paint box, 290

painted furniture, 138; armchairs, 203; —, cane-seated, 328, 330, 332, 335; **armed chair**, 138; **bedstead cornice**, 333; **bedsteads**, deal, 253, 254; **bookcases**, 328; —, with 2 drawers, 338; —, with 3 shelves, 335, 337; —, deal, with 4 shelves, 334; —, deal, with glazed doors, 330; **cabinet stand**, 328; **candelabra**, 329; **chairs**, 31, 138, 139, 203, 204, 206, 207, 215, 221, 343; —, bamboo, cane-seated, 327, 328, 329, 331, 333, 334, 335, 336, 337; —, bamboo, rush-seated, 330, 338, 342; —, cane, 208, 229; —, cane-bottomed, 331; —, cane-seated, 221, 255, 256, 265, 266, 267, 327, 328; —, rush-bottomed, 138, 139, 208, 209, 210, 211; —, rush-seated, 338; —, with stuffed seats, 335, 336, 337, 338; **chaise longue**, 328; **chests of drawers**, 225, 342; —, with 6 drawers, 343; **commodes**, Chinese, 139; **cupboards**, 287; —, deal, with glazed doors, 329; **desk**, deal, 301; **dining-table**, deal, with 2 leaves, 339; **dressers**, deal, 284, 302; —, with drawers, 300; **dressing glass**, 342; **dressing stools**, with stuffed seats, 334, 335; **dressing tables**, 310, 337, 342; —, deal, 255, 256, 265, 266, 267; —, deal, with 1 drawer, 253, 338; **fire-screen frame**, 327; **fire screens**, 229, 329; **flower-pot stands**, 206; **flower-stand**, 273;

General index   421

folding-screen frames, 327, 329; **hall chairs**, 327; **horse**, 210; **music stand**, 328; **pier-glass frame**, 206; **pole-screen**, 333; **presses**, 211, 212, 223, 224; —, deal, 224, 253, 254, 275, 296, 331, 339, 343; **reading desk**, 337; **sets of drawers**, 210, 212, 223, 224; **showcases**, 307; **stool**, 205; **swing bookcases**, 339; —, with 2 shelves, 335, 337; —, with 3 shelves, 338; —, with 4 shelves, 337; **swing dressing glass**, with 1 drawer, 336; **tables**, 191; —, China, 310; —, deal, 256, 308, 330, 337; —, deal, with 1 drawer, 253, 254; —, deal, with drawers, 253; —, mahogany, 309; **wardrobes**, deal, 191, 193; **wash-hand stands**, 332; —, deal, with high back, 336; —, with high back, 1 drawer, 335; **wash-hand table**, with 2 shelves, 221; **window-curtain cornice**, 333; **window-seat frame**, 327

paintings: on ceilings, 77; on copper, 35, 273; without frames, 217; in gilt frames, 255, 267, 270, 342; on glass, 342; —, Indian, 337; on marble, 272. *See also* pictures

palampore, 359; bed-curtains, 282; chair-covers, 282; palampores, 192; —, Indian, 310; quilts, 255, 268, 281; window-curtains, 282. *See also* chintz palampore

Palladian-style architecture, 177; Carton House, 247; doll's house, 307; Elphin, the bishop's house at, 88; Newbridge House, 305

pallet bedstead, 66, 359

palliasses, 359; *passim*; bordered, 254, 255, 256, 265, 266, 267, 270, 275, 289, 290, 292; flannel, 333; sacken, 335, 336; straw, 209, 255, 275, 276, 289, 290, 331, 332, 333, 334, 335, 336, 337; tick, 337; —, striped, 335

pan crocks: black ware, 294; brown ware, 284

panel work: caffoy, 150; composition stone, on box, 272; —, on cabinet, 271; **deal**, 290; **mahogany**, bookcase doors, 271, 276; —, bookcase with looking-glass panels, 270; —, library-table doors, 272; wardrobe-bed doors, 267; —, wardrobe doors, 255, 268; **plaster of Paris**, 277; **wainscot**, 173

pans: copper, 284; earthenware, 46, 48, 318; iron, 341; pewter, oval, 184; —, round, 184; silver, small, 316. *See also* snuffer-pans

pantries: at Elphin, the bishop's house, 90; at Kilkenny Castle, 45; at Newbridge House, 315

paperweights: bronze, 203, 214; —, head-shaped, 204; Gibraltar rock, 214, 216; verd-antique, 214

paperwork: fire screens, folding, 271, 337; —, Indian, 75; hand screens, 218, 328, 329, 333, 335, 337; paper for making dessert boxes, 282; pole-screens, 334, 335, 337; screen, 337

papillote cases, 215, 359; china, 203; Colebrookdale, 204; Wedgwood, 204

paragon, 360; bed-case, 75; bed-curtains, 192, 193, 194; bed-furniture, 78; case curtains, 78; chair cases, 75; curtains, 157; false curtains, 56; window-curtains, 158, 170, 192

parlour chairs: mahogany, 276; —, slatted, with haircloth covering, 273

parlours, 360; at Captain Balfour's house, 108–9; at Carton House, 248; —, gardener's, 300; at Dublin, No. 10 Henrietta St, 159; at Elphin, the bishop's house, 88, 90; at Hillsborough Castle, 123, 125; at Killadoon, 216; at Kilrush House, 149; at Lismore Castle, 22; at Morristown Lattin, 168–9; at Newbridge House, 306, 307, 315; at Shelton Abbey, 229. *See also* breakfast-parlours

pasteboards, 284, 287; deal, 341

paste cutters, 143; tin, 143; —, boxed, 284; —, fluted, 340; —, round, 340; —, shell-shaped, 340

paste pricker, 341

pastille burners, 329; Wedgwood, 335

pastille urn, 360

pastries: at Carton House, 284; at Kilkenny Castle, 45; at Mount Stewart, 341

pastry, 360. *See also* pastries

pastry cutters, 315; tin, 315

pasty pans, 112; tin, 22

patent lamps, 203, 214, 216, **360**; —, 2-burner, 216, 217; —, 3-burner, 203, 216; bronze, 273; cut glass and brass, with 2 lights, 205

patties, 175, **360**

patty cutters, 315

pattypans, 65, 67, 127; **brass**, 45; **copper**, 63, 143; —, for mince pies, 315; —, ribbed, 143; —, for tartlets, 315; **tin**, 91

pea pot, 127

Pearle of Chester (owner Brisco), 72

pearwood: chimney-glass and looking-glass frames, 56

peat-baskets, 339, 341

pecks, 48, 93, 299, **360**; half-peck, 48

pedestals: for busts, 327, 328; gilt, for a carving, 37; —, for china, 35, 37, 53; mahogany, 233, 240, 273

peels, 144, 342, **360**; wooden, 45, 48. *See also* fire peels

pegs (row): mahogany, 220

Pembroke tables, 360; mahogany, 180; —, with 1 drawer and castors, 218; —, with 2 drawers, 334

pennyweight, 360; *passim*

pen trays, 203, 215; Colebrookdale, 204, 219

pepperboxes: brass, 91; silver-plated, 183; tin, 340

pepper castor: silver, 197, 316

peppermills, 340

pepperpot: brass, 22

Persian, 360; bed-curtains, 84; length of, 282; linings, bed-furniture, striped, 57; —, window-curtains, 272

Persian carpets, 33, 51, 360

pestles: glass, 279; iron, 45; wooden, 283

pestles and mortars, 90, 127, 172, 279, 283, 299, 314, 340; brass, 91; marble, 315. *See also* mortars

pewter: basins, 22, 171, 286; bedpan, 22; chamber pot, 93; cheese plate, 22; close-stool pans, 89, 169; colanders, 91, 183; dinner-plates, 285; dishes, 22, 44, 127, 171, 184, 193, 195, 277, 283, 284, 314; fish-plate, 112; fruit mould, 184; ice moulds, 279; ice pots, 79; inkstand, 342; measures, half-

pint, 290; —, pint, 279, 290; —, quart, 279, 285, 290; mugs, for measures, 315; pans, oval, 184; —, round, 184; pie plate, 22; plates, 22, 50, 112, 127, 171, 184, 195, 277, 301, 314; porringers, 22; quarts, 171; salt-cellars, 47; salts, 341; soup-dishes, 113, 171; soup-plates, 184, 285; stands, 22, 91; stills, 22, 90; tundish, 91; water plates, 286; wine measures, 276; writing stand, 89

pewter (English): dishes, 68, 113; dish-covers, dish-rings, plates, 63

pewter (Irish): dishes, plates, salts and stands, 63

pewterware: at Dublin Castle, 63; at Elphin, the bishop's house, 91; at Hillsborough Castle, 143; at Lismore Castle, 22; at Shelton Abbey, 232, 91

pianoforte covers: leather, 203, 204, 271, 275

pianofortes, 123, 139, 203, 215, 309; Broadwood, 271, 273; grand, 189, 204; small, 209; upright, 239

pickaxes, 298, 302; iron, 168

pickle glasses, 286, 318

pickle-making: pickle-stands and covers, 175; pickling bottles, 342; —, Indian, 342; pickling crocks, 277, 279, 287; pickling kettle (brass), 342; pickling pan, 277; pickling pots and jars, 193; pickling saucers, 233; pickling tub, 90

pickles, 193. *See also* preserves

picture frames: black, 35, 37, 39, 41, 42, 43, 77, 84, 180, 181, 217, 255, 256, 266, 267, 268, 270, 283; —, with brass ornaments, 331, 332, 333; black-and-gilt, 125, 329, 330; black-and-gold, 204; black and lacquered, 41, 42; brass and ebony, 214, *215*; brass and tortoiseshell, 214; carved, 32; carved and gilt, 33, 38; gilt, *passim*; half-moon, 329; lacquered, 77; mahogany, 333; ormolu, 214; oval, 35, 37, 53; —, gilt, 77; stucco, 330; —, varnished, 330

pictures: Indian, 78; in worked flock, 33. *See below* for pictures by category; *see also* drawings; engravings; paintings; portraits; prints. *See also* Index of personal names, pp. 392–6

pictures (allegorical): Air and Water (tapestry), 84; boys and grapes (painting), 267, 268; boys and music (painting), 269; Don Quixote (tapestries), 41; Fire, Earth and Air (tapestries), 75; Hudrastic, 125; old man sucking [Roman Charity], 37, **361**; prints by William Hogarth, 'Four Times of Day', 15, 125; —, 'Rake's Progress', 15, 123, 125; the Senses, 37; —, touch, 37; Vanity, being a woman playing on a bass viol, and a boy on the other emblems of Vanity, 38

pictures (animal): birds and bird-cages, 73; cock and cat, 73; cocks and hens, 77; hen at roost, 70; hens, 73; neat [cattle] herd, 73; sheep going over a bridge, 73; tiger, 73

pictures (battle-pieces), 77; Boyne, The Battle of the (1690) (glasswork), 318; Dutch massacre [?], 158; horse battle, 73; reliefs in wood (Melotte, one of which after *Battle of the Amazons*, a painting attrib. to Rubens ['battle of the amazons' in K 1836]), 214, *215*

422

pictures (biblical): Ahasuerus, king of Persia, painting, 34; —, tapestry, 46; Cyrus, king of Persia, painting, 37; —, tapestries, 42; David and Goliath (painting on copper), 35; Jacob, the story of (painting) [prob. by Jan Victors], 73; Judith and the head of Holofernes, 37, 77; Melchizedek and other figures [Gerbrand van den Eeckhout in KC 1717], 38; Samson, 181; scripture piece, 159; Susanna and the Elders (painting on copper), 35; *The Persecution* (Thomas Willeboirts Bosschaert, poss.), 73

pictures (Christian): Christ and the Virgin Mary, 35; Christ at the river Jordan, 35; Holy Family, the, 77; Madonna and Child, 73; —, attrib. to Correggio, 70, *385*; —, said to be after Dolci, 69; —, oil painting, 218; —, with St John the Baptist, 70; —, with 3 other figures, 38; Madonna, the, 82; Magdalen, the, 35, 82; Our Lady and Christ, 38; —, in a garland of flowers, 37; Our Lady and St Luke, 73; St Catherine, 35, 77; —, in silk, 35; —, marriage of, 77; St Francis's head, 38; St John, 77; —, and a Lamb, 42; St John the Baptist, 37; —, head portrait, 38

pictures (conversation pieces), 77, 159

pictures (figure-pieces), 35, 38; basketmaker and woman, 77; building with small figures, 35; chimney-pieces, 32; —, of robbery, or painting by Ribera [?], 31; collation and singing, 73; congratulatory speech on Duke of Ormonde's coming to Ireland, 73; Dutch, 33, 35, 37, 53; Dutch market, 159; Italian woman, 38; lady with fruit, 76; man in armour, 76; masquerade, 34; men on horseback (tapestries), 77; old men's heads, [one of which by Rembrandt (KC 1717)], 38; old woman, fleaing a shock dog, 38, 73; —, selling fruit, 73; paintings by Jan Wijk, 84; royal family, 82; *The Kiss Returned*, 109; young woman selling fruit, 73

pictures (history pieces), 53, 76, 82, 159; with 3 figures by Rubens (KC 1717), 33; with figures, unspecified, 35, 37, 73; Ahasuerus, king of Persia, painting, 34; —, tapestry, 46; Alexander the Great (tapestries), 80; Boyne, Battle of the (1690) (glasswork), 318; City of London in flames, 84; Cyrus, king of Persia, painting, 37; —, tapestries, 42; Decius Mus, Publius, Roman consul (tapestries), 40, 51; —, consecration of, *24*; Diogenes (tapestries), 33, 76; merchant of Venice [poss.], 37; Sophonisba (poss. the Carthaginian noblewoman at the time of the Second Punic War), 35; Titian and Aretino, 34; Venetian senators [copy after Titian (KC 1717)], 37. *See also* portraits

pictures (hunting-pieces), 108; boar and hounds, or hunting piece by Abraham Hondius, 73; boar-hunting (Jan Wijk), 77; falconer, 43; *Hern Hawking*, poss. etching after drawing by Francis Barlow of heron hawking; or a picture of Herne, the hunter of Windsor forest, 77; *Hunting the Wild*

Boar, 77; scene by Abraham Hondius, poss., 76; stag, 73

pictures (landscapes), 32, 33, 34, 35, 37, 38, 39, 40, 41, 42, 43, 53, 73, 75, 76, 77, 78, 79, 80, 82, 84, 85, 108, 137, 141, 158, 159, 271; with beasts, 41; with buildings, 35, 36; with cattle, 77; with church, 37; with figures, 34, 35, 77; fishing, 33–4; with fountain, 35; garden, 73; with geese, 77; 'One of yᵉ king's houses', 37; landscape by Claude, 204; with monument, 76; mountain view, 331; ruins, 77; —, castle ruin 'cut in wood', 273; —, by William Gouw Ferguson, 77; tapestries, 77; —, forest-work, 38, 41, 78, 79; —, green-work, 77; —, with small figures, 31, 51

pictures (maritime): 3 figures and a ship, 40; fishermen, 31; ruin with shipping, 77; sea fights, 70, 82; —, draughts of, 84; sea-pieces, 78, 108, 159; seascape of the port of Vigo (Spain), 73; ship, 37; —, print, 84; shipping in India, views, 331; ships unloading, 73; Turkish port, 77

pictures (mythological): Bacchanalia (tapestries), 34, 51; Ceres (poss.), 82; Cupid, winged, 37; Europa, 40; Flora, 77; —, and putti, 37; —, with sceptres and crowns, 77; Jupiter, with Juno, 73; —, sacrifice to, 34, 85; Mercury and the Sabaean woman, 37; Neptune, 37; Nymphs (carpet), 51; Pallas (carpet), 51; Phoebus and Phaethon, 73; Polyphemus (tapestries), 33; Venus, 82; —, and Adonis, 34; Vulcan, Venus and several Cupids trying armour, 38

pictures (still-life), 37, 70, 84; birds, 140; —, and flowers, 15, 138, 140; —, beasts, fruit and flowers, 140; carrots in a wheelbarrow, 73; flower-pieces, 33, 34, 38, 43, 70, 75, 76, 77, 80, 82, 84, 108, 159; —, screen, 32; fowling-piece, 38; fruit-pieces, 34, 35, 38, 108, 158; —, with monkey, 38; —, watercolour, 332; shells and weed (watercolour), 333

pictures (topographical): Ards House, Letterkenny, Co. Donegal (painting), 331; —, rocks near Ards House, 331; City of Kilkenny, 85; the fortifications, 108; Italy, views of (coloured prints), 327; Lakes of Killarney (prints), 256; Marino, Co. Dublin, views of (fire screens), 202, 214; Naples, views of, 15, 139, 227; Powerscourt Waterfall, Co. Wicklow, 159; prospect of a church, 35; river Thames, views of, 141; The Temple [of the Winds at Mount Stewart] (oil painting), 343; views (paintings), 269; Windsor Castle, 73

pie dishes, 341; porcelain, 341

pie plates, 44; pewter, 22

pier bookcase: mahogany, 308

pier-glasses, 82, 139, 140, 179, 180, 181, 192, 203, 215, 217, 308, 310, 311, 312, **360**; in carved frames, 126, 159; gilt-framed, 76, 139, 189, 204, 206, 207; —, rope twist, 189; glass-framed, 75; oval, in carved and gilt frame, 138; in red-and-gold frame, 159; in white-painted frame, 206

pier-table covers, 229

pier-table frames: gilt, 291

pier tables, 218; half-round, 309; square, with drawers, 309; **mahogany**, 189, 229, 233, 239, 240; **satinwood**, 229

pigeon house: at Elphin, the bishop's house, 93

pigeon paddock: at Carton House, 299

piggins, 127, 144, 294, **360**

pig yard: at Carton House, 299

pillar-and-claw table supports: alder, 329; beech-wood, 337

pillar bedstead, 31

pillars (on cabinet): marble, 329

pillar tables: mahogany, 161, 204, *252*; —, round, 159; —, set of eight, 273

pillion, 120, **360**

pillow boards, made of old sheets, 23

pillowcases: coarse, 346; frilled, 346; plain, 346; **calico**, 203, 205, 221, 269; **dimity**, 269; **furniture calico**, 270, 271

pillion cloth: shag, 120

pillow covers: brown linen, 220; calico, 203, 206, 216, 218, 219; check, 125, 330; chintz, 204, 207; cotton, 335; —, printed, 332, 334

pillows: down, 330; feather-stuffed, 253, 269, 270, 328, 332, 334; festoon, 265, 267; fustian, 33, 57, 268, 269; hair, 271, 332; Holland, 61; Indian work, 34; plaid, 56; satin-covered, 180; tick, 301, 336; —, linen, 254; —, striped, 330, 331, 333, 334, 335, 336, 337, 338, 339; ticken, 275; —, striped, 331, 332, 333, 338

pincers, 298

pincushion-dish covers: silver-plated, 348

pincushion dishes, **360**; silver, maker's mark of John Laughlin, *324*, 347; yellow ware, 183. *See also* cushion dishes

pincushions, 218, 219; christening, 268; in gold tissue, 71; trimmed, and with covers, 281

pineapple plants, 301

pinery, 301, **360**; pine-watering tubes (tin), 300

pink: bookshelf back covering, 271; **calico**, remnants, 281; **cotton**, armed-chair cover, 334; —, bed-furniture, 335; —, bolster covers, 335; —, dressing-stool covers, 334; —, hassock cover, 335; —, headcloth and tester linings, 335; —, pillow cover, 335; —, squab cover, 335; —, window-drapery, 335; **cotton and muslin**, window-curtains, 335; **linings** (unspecified), bed-curtains, 270, 337; —, bed-furniture, 334; —, headcloth and tester, 335; —, window-curtains, 270, 271, 334; —, window-draperies, 270, 271, 334; **silk**: bed-furniture linings, 334

pink china, 233

pint cans: japanned, 128; silver, 197

pints: bottles (empty), 93; decanters, 175, 234, 286; japanned, 285; of Madeira malmsey, 199; mugs, silver, 347; pewter, 279, 290

pipeclay saucepan, 272

pipes (measure), 128, 284, **360**

pipes (plumbing): leaden, 288

pistols, 71, 340; brass-barrelled, 289, 303; brass-mounted, 140, 290; cases of, 121, 270, 303; Highland, 120; silver and steel, 140; silver-mounted, 270

General index

423

pitch, 297
pitchers, 285; black ware, 288. *See also* water pitchers
pitchforks, 92
plaid: bed, 57; bed-curtains, 78, 84; bed-furniture, 57, 61, 62, 80; couch covering, 56; curtains, 81; door-curtains, 56; pillows, 56; stool coverings, 56; wall-hangings, 56; window-curtains, 56, 61; window-hangings, 61. *See also* drugget plaid; Irish plaid
plank table, 51
plastering: board, 298; laths, 172
plaster of Paris: busts, 327; —, bronzed, 274; coats of arms, 339; figures, 343; ornaments, 328; panel work, 277; urns, 327; vases, 343
plate: blue ware, 300. *See also* silver (plate inventories)
plateaux, 360; cut-glass oval for, 345; silver-plated, 348
plate-baskets, 91, 128, 283, 285, 308, 360; mahogany, brass-mounted, 327; tin-lined, 286
plate buckets, 193, 233, 318; mahogany, square, 205; —, with brass hoops, 205
plate-chests, 286; oak, 44; travelling, 144
plate cloths, 281
plate drainer, 143
plate drains, 113, 171, 284, 286, 302
plated silver. *See* silver (plated)
plate glass: to brass lamp, 327; cabinet back, 329; door to eight-day clock, 331; door to secretary, 330; plateau bottoms, 348
plate racks, 44, 143, 315; deal, 341
plate stand: brass, 90
plate tray: mahogany, 125
plate-trunk, 120, 360
plate warmers, 308; brass, 112; copper, 169, 183; —, capuchin, 157; japanned, 233, 274, 327; mahogany, 327
plate-warming stand: iron, 66
plates: blue-and-white ware, 217, 219, 220; blue ware, 278; Chelsea porcelain (bird-pattern), 344; china, 33, 71, 91, 233, 277, 278, 319; —, flat, 319; —, small, 344; delft, 175, 233; French china, 278; glass, round and flat, 318; Indian china, 333; pewter, 22, 50, 112, 127, 171, 184, 195, 277, 301, 314; —, English, 63; —, Irish, 63; porcelain, 277; silver, 162, 347; —, gadrooned, 196; silver-plated and horn-lined, 198; Wedgwood, flat, 195; white ware, 277, 293, 301, 315; Worcester porcelain, flat, 318. *See also* bread-and-butter plates; breakfast plates; cheese plates; dessert-plates; dinner-plates; muffin plates; soup-plates
play-table, black, 33. *See also* gaming-tables
play-table covering: velvet, figured, 33
plinths: brass, 274; marble, 273, 274
plough reins, 297
ploughs: drill, 298; moulding, 298; Scotch wheel, 298; scuffling, 298
plumeaux, 218, 360
plush: bookbinding, 32
point lace: bibs, 268; cuffs, 268; gloves, 268; trimmings, christening robe, 268; —, shirt, 268; —, toilet-table furniture, 190
pokers: *passim*; 'firepoke', iron, 45

pole glass, 181, **360**
poles: alder, 92; for drying large linen, 51
pole-screen bases: mahogany, 273
pole-screens, 229, 233, 272, 273, 303, 328, **360**; beech-wood, 337; black-painted, 333, 337; mahogany, 274, 328, 330, 333, 335; —, brass-mounted, 328; paper, 334, 335; velvet, painted, 333, 334; yew, 334
pomatum box, **360**; silver, 198
pools (for card games), 193, **360**
poplin, **360**; window-curtains and linings, 56
porcelain, **360**; bowls, 277, 278; breakfast plates, 277; cake dishes, 277; cake plates, 277, 278; cheese plates, 341; coffee cans, 277, 278; coffee-cups and saucers, 277; coffee-pot, 277; cream ewers, 277, 278; cups and saucers, 277, 278; custard cups, 277; dinner-plates, 341; dishes, 341; —, oval, 277; —, round, 277; —, shell, 277; —, square, 277; egg-cups, 278; fish drainer, 341; honey-bowl, 278; ice-pails, and covers, 277; jug, 278; milk jugs, 277; muffin plates, 278; —, and covers, 277; pie dishes, 341; plates, 277; pudding plates, 341; salad bowls, 277, 341; soup-plates, 341; soup-tureens and one cover, 341; steak-dish, 277; sugar-bowls, 277, 278; sweatmeat cups, stands and covers, 277; tea-pot, 277; tureens, 341; —, and covers, 277; tureen stand, 341; vegetable dish, 341. *See also* porcelain *under* Chelsea; Colebrookdale; Dresden; Staffordshire; Worcester; *also under* Wedgwood ware
porphyry, **360**; Egyptian (entered as granite), 214; jar, 273
porringers: coloured, 119; pewter, 22; silver-gilt, 161
porters' lodges: at Dublin Castle, 58; at Hillsborough Castle, 145; at Kilkenny Castle, 46; at London, St James's Square, 85. *See also* gate lodge; guardhouse
porter's staff, with silver head, 85
portraits, 29, 267, 268, 269, 271, 330; admirals of France (three-quarter-length), 82; black-framed, 270; boy's head, 38; by candlelight (by Godfried Schalcken, perhaps), 159; cameo (sulphur), 214; in crayon, 217, 223; enamelled, 203, 204, 214; family, 158, 327; head (after Jordaens?), 84; heads, painted on copper, 273; likenesses of ladies, 34, 70, 73, 80, 138, 159; miniatures, 329; old man's head, 38; profile, 329. *See also* Index of personal names, pp. 392–6
Portugal mats, 203, 215, 327, 328, 331, **360**; portingale, 70
post-chaise: wheels for, 167
potatoes: in barrels, 93; potato baskets, 298; potato forks, 297; potato pots and covers, 314; potato shovel (iron), 299; **potato pattern** on tablecloths and napkins, 141
pot hangers, 22, 152; iron, 22
pot-hooks, 127; metal, 171
pot-ovens: and cover, 314; metal, 171
pot-pourri pots: china, 205
pots: china, high and round, 34; copper, with covers, 63; iron, 22, 47, 90, 113, 127,

143, 294, 296; metal, 171, 286; —, oval, with cover, 301; tin, 284
potting dish, with cover, 341
poultry coops, 92. *See also* coop; chicken coops
poultry yard, 174
powder horns, 290, 301
powdering room (Baronscourt), 182
powdering tubs, 22, 113, 167, **360**; lead-lined, 143
preserves, 193; preserving glasses, 64; preserving jars, 193, 301; preserving pans, 64, 142, 195, 279, 342; preserving pots, 193, 342; sweatmeat pots, 278
press beds, 151, 171, 212, 232, **360**; deal, 157, 205, 224; **mahogany**, 223, 225; **oak**, 223
press bedsteads, 32, 141, **360**; mahogany, 191; —, in form of a desk, 189; —, with glazed doors, 329; **oak**, 144, 145
press-cupboard, 49
presses, 313, **360**; high, 314; in niches, 192, 193; **deal**, 42, 157, 158, 160, 192, 193, 211, 225, 276, 279, 285, 286, 287, 289, 290, 291, 292, 294, 297, 338, 339, 340, 343; —, fast to wall, 290; —, with glazed doors, 78; —, for groceries, 91; —, with sliding leaves, 340; **glass**, 84; —, for books, 82; **mahogany**, 244, 266; —, for billiard cues, 274; —, with drawers and nests, 194; **oak**, 210, 255, 266, 289, 330; —, with 2 drawers inside, 265, 266; —, with drawers, 301; —, with deal shelves, 256; **wainscot**, 43, 78. *See also* alphabet press; corner presses; store press; tool presses
presses (painted), 211, 212, 223, 224; deal, 211, 224, 253, 254, 275, 339, 343; —, with 2 drawers, 331
prick, 167. *See also* pritch
print (fabric), **360**; bed-furniture, 59, 60, 61, 62; wall-hangings, 57, 58, 60
print frames: black, 180, 255, 256, 266, 267, 268, 270; black and gilt, 125, 329, 330; gilt, 241, 267, 327, 328, 329, 330, 333, 334
prints: *passim*; caricatures, 192; Hogarth, William, 140; —, 'Four Times of Day', 15, 125; —, 'Rake's Progress', 15, 123, 125; Italy, views of, 327; Lakes of Killarney, 256. *For portrait prints, see* Index of Personal Names, pp. 390–4
pritch, 299, **360**
pritchel, 295, **360**
probate inventories, 11, 105, 325; Borris House, 1818, 236–45
prospect-glass, 71
Protestant ascendancy, 11, 165
pruning chisels, 300, 302
pudding basins: white ware, 341
pudding-cloths, 281, 316
pudding coppers, 127
pudding moulds: white ware, 341
pudding-pans, 283; copper, 91, 340; tin, 91, 315
pudding plates: porcelain, 341
pulpatoon pans, 127, **360**
pump house: at London, St James's Square, 84; pump room, at Killadoon, 223
pumps, 142, 143, 173; for wort, 51; leaden, 51
punchbowls: blue-and-white ware, 119; china, 36, 119, 128, 344; —, with brass and gilt garnish, 36; glass, 175

punches (tool), 295, 298
punch-glasses, 180
punch-ladles: silver, 117
purple: cloth and mohair, chair cases, 33; mohair, bed-furniture, 33; —, wall-hangings, 51; serge, case curtains, 33; —, chair cases, 34
purple-and-white: Hillsborough Castle, Purple and White Room, 137; cotton, length of, 144
puzzling-pins, 299, **360**
quadrille boxes, 119, **360**
quarts: bottles (empty), 93; decanters, 175, 286; pewter, 171, 279, 285, 290; tin, 171, 289
quilting: cushions, 46, 52; French, 116; headboard, 42; squab coverings, 34
quilt linings: Persian, striped, 57
quilts, **360**; Brussels, 289; —, worsted, 275, 290, 291, 292; calico, 21, 78, 80, 84, 90, 209; canvas, 35; check, 144, 171, 276; chequered, 50, 253; chequer-work, 254; chintz, 224; cotton, 137, 141, 142, 143, 144, 145, 157, 169, 170, 211, 212, 223, 224, 253, 254, 275; damask, worsted, 57; eider-down, 217; green baize, 171; Holland, 31, 38, 40, 41, 43, 56, 57, 70, 75, 77, 80; Indian, 55, 56, 61; Liège, 231; Manchester, 109; Marseilles, 190, 191, 206, 207, 208, 210, 217, 218, 219, 220, 223, 241, 255, 256, 267, 270, 282; needleworked, 144; palampore, 255, 268, 281; rug, 301, 313, 314; sarcenet, 41; serge, 211, 275, 286, 289, 301; silk patchwork (hexagon), 281; stuff, 145; —, quilted, 211, 213, 223, 224, 225; tabby, 39; taffety, flowered, 144.
quilts (tufted), 89, 169, 208, 209, 210, 212, 220, 221, 223; cotton, 170
quilts (white), 89, 110, 125, 126, 141, 232, 313, 314; calico, 78; damask, 120; linen, 126, 137, 138; Marseilles, 192; muslin, 139; satin, 70; —, for cradle, 268; silk, 80. *See also* night quilts
racks: for boots and shoes, 310; for cards, 203, 220; ceiling, 51; deal, 51, 285; hanging, 120, 288; iron, 22, 45, 90, 171; for music books, 203, 215; for plates, 44, 127; standing, 111
rack staves, 173
raised-pie dish, with cover and liner, 341
rakes, 296, 299, 342.; iron, 167, 298, 300; road, 298; wooden, 300, 302; —, with iron teeth, 167. *See also* coal rakes; hay-rakes (*under* hay); garden rakes
rasps: iron, 48. *See also* bread-rasps
reading-chair: leather-covered, 272
reading-desk cover: scarlet cloth, 330
reading-desk covering: green baize, 337
reading desks, 203, 244, 308; with leather cushion, 214; **mahogany**, 204; —, with 5 drawers, 330; **painted**, 337; —, on pillar, 204; —, screw, 310, **361**
reading lamp, 287
reading stands: horse frame, 271; mahogany, on pillar and claws, 271
reading table, mahogany, on sliding pillar and claws, 216

red: **baize**: chair-covers, 53; **caffoy**, cushions, 66; **check**, bed-curtains, 267; **cloth**, bed-curtains, 79, 81; —, chair coverings, 50; —, curtains, 310; —, hassock cover, 337; —, stool covering, 309; —, wall-hangings, 51; —, window-curtain, 308; **cotton**, window-curtain linings, 337; **damask**, bed-curtains, 79; —, bed-furniture, 79; —, chair seats, 126; **leather-work**, bergère coverings, 205; —, bidet coverings, 206, 207, 208; —, carpets, 51; —, chair coverings, 205, 216; —, close-stool coverings, 33, 39; —, letterbox, 203; **morocco**, backgammon box, 272; —, blotting-book binding, 203, 204, 214, 215; —, messenger's box, 271; **velvet**, stools, round, 33
red-and-white: **check**, bed-furniture, 144; —, cushion-cover, 144; —, elbow-chair covers, 180; **chequer-work**, bed-furniture, 185; **cotton**, armed-chair cover, 144; **drugget**, carpet, 40; —, cushions, 40; —, wall-hangings, 40; **stuff** (worsted): linings to bed-furniture, window-curtains and window-hangings, 61
red-and-white ware: chamber utensil, 334; soap-and-brush tray, 334; wash-hand basin and ewer, 334
red china: tea-pots, 118
red-edged ware: basins, 270
reels and lines, 167, 298, 300, 302
register grates, 203, 214, 216, 217, 218, 219, **360**; steel, 203, 214; stove, 224
reins, 319; back, 320; double-rein bridles, 319; pillar, 320; plough, 297; single-rein jointed bit, 319; tandem, 319
remnants: buckram, 282; calico, 281, 282; check, 144, 282; Dowlas linen, 281, 282; Drogheda linen, 281; fringe, 282; fustian (for pillows), 282; grey linen, 281, 282; ticken, 281
removes, 347, **360**
repeaters: firearm, 158
repeating clock, 76
ribands: 2-knot, 3-knot, 33
ribberies, **360**; oak, 172
rice ornaments: cup on stand, 219; for chimney-piece (trees and houses), 220
ridders, 298, **361**
riddles, 299, **361**; lime, 174; wire, 302
rings: diamond, 118; gold, 118; Turkey stone, 118
roasters, with racks, 340
roasting dogs, 340
roller blinds, 239, 241, 242, 332, 333, **361**; brown Holland, 331, 332, 333; brown linen, 335; cotton, 336; linen, 241, 270, 271, 327, 334, 335; white Holland, 273
rollers, **361**; straps for horses, 320; metal, 297, 298, 302; stone, 297, 302. *See also* rolling pins
rolling mill, 48
rolling pins, 22, 45, 112, 143, 279, 341
rolling stones, 93, 120, 161, 166; with iron handle, 166
Roman Charity (picture of an 'Old man Suckin'), 37, **361**
root scoops, 341
rope: caple, 90. *See also* gads

rope twister, 298
rose pins: brass, 221
rosewood: bookstands, 215; commodes, with marble tops and plate-glass doors, 215; library table, 204; musical-chronometer case, 273; sofa tables, with 2 drawers each, 204
rubbers, 282, 346, **361**; coarse, 47; cook's, 281; kitchen, 346; —, in Drogheda linen, 281; stable, 281; table, 281
rug quilts, 301, 313, 314, **361**
rugs: cotton, 137, 138, 343; drugget, 309; hempen, 204, 308; sheep, 203, 204, 214, 216, 308, 320; Turkey, 272, 273
rummers, **361**; cut-glass, 340; glass, 119
rush: armchair bottoms, 206, 210, 212, 220, 223, 224; chair bottoms, *passim*; chair seats, 229, 230, 231, 232, 253, 254, 276, 289, 330, 338, 342; couch bottoms, 312; dressing-stool bottoms, 206, 207, 208, 209, 210, 220, 224; elbow-chair bottom, 110; stool bottoms, 193, 211, 212, 216
rushlights, **361**; lanterns, 268; painted tin shades for, 338
Russia leather coverings, **361**; camp-chairs, 81; chairs, 46, 47, 66
sackcloth: bedstead bottoms, 31, 38, 39. *See also* sacking
sacken: palliasses, 335, 336
sacking: bedstead bottoms, 33, 39, 40, 41, 42, 48, 194; field-bed bottom, 57; press-bedstead bottom, 189; state-bed bottom, 70
sad colour: **361**; rug, 40
saddlebags, 320
saddle racks, 293
saddle room: at Carton House, 293
saddles, 167, 293, 299, 319; children's, 319; saddle-tree, 290; side-saddle, 293
safe: iron, 290
saffron pot and saucer, 119
salad bottle, 286
salad bowls, 316; blue ware, 282; china, 233, 277; cut-glass, 318; porcelain, 277, 341
salad-dishes: china, 128, 319; delft, 233; silver, 162; —, maker's mark of John Laughlin, *324*, 347; yellow stoneware, long, 183; —, round, 183
salad forks: silver, 197, 240, 316
salamanders, 127, 184, 284, 315, 341, **361**
sally-wood: desk, 191, **361**
salt-boxes, 45, 48, 91, 113, 142, 183, 289; deal, 340; tin, 340; wooden, 22, 314
salt-cellars, 318; pewter, 47; silver, 316; —, oval, 240; silver-plated, round, 241
salting-tubs: with covers, 127; wooden, 318
salts: flat, 175; **cut glass**, 342; **glass**, 175, 183; **pewter**, 341; —, Irish, 63; **silver**, 116, 161, 196, 323; —, oval, 347; —, round, 347; **silver-gilt**, basket-shaped, 196; **silver-plated**, 183, 323. *See also* salt cellars
salt shovels: silver, 161
salt-spoons: silver, 116, 183, 196, 240, 323, 348
salt tub, 143
salvers: alabaster, 71; **glass**, 46, 120; **silver**, 71, 117, 161, 323; —, large, 117, 316, 347; —, oval, 316; —, round, 196, 316, 347; —, square, 316; **silver-plated**, 240. *See also* servers

General index

425

sand-boxes, 203, 204
sandwich dishes, 278
sarcenet, 361; bases (bed), 39; bed-curtain linings, 39; bed-lining, 41; christening-robe lining, 268; cushions, 39; mantle lining, 268; quilt, 41; window-curtains, 39
sarcophagus, 361; mahogany, 240
sarcophagus grate, 203, 214
sashes, 174, 191, 290; cane, 82; for garden frames, 300, 302; hothouse, 297
satin: chair cases, 41; christening robe, 268; couch and couch-bed coverings, with gold and silver stuff, 180; counterpane, 268; cushions, 52; furbelow to window-curtains, 56; mantle, 268; pillow coverings, with gold and silver stuff, 180; quilts, 70; —, for cradle, 268; stool coverings, 39; —, with gold and silver stuff, 180; window-curtains, 56
satin (clouded): bed-finial cups, 41; bed-furniture, 41; chair backs and seats, 51
satin (Indian): bed-furniture and wall hangings, 39
satinwood: bookshelf, with 1 drawer, 204; Canterburys, 272; library table, round, on pillar and claws, 272; pier tables, 229
sauce-boats: china, 233, 277; delft, 233; silver, 117, 161, 196; silver-plated, with stands, 241; stoneware, 128
sauce bottles: yellow stoneware, 183
sauce-ladles: silver, 197, 348; Staffordshire, 278
saucepan covers: copper, 284
saucepans, 80, 81, 127, 294, 318; large with covers, 183; copper, 63, 91, 112, 142, 171, 279, 340; —, and covers, 112, 340; iron, 22, 341; metal, 284; —, and covers, 315; silver, 117, 279, 284, 348; tin, and covers, 315
saucepan strainer: for eggs, 314
saucers: china, 256, 277; silver, 117
sauce spoons: silver, 279, 284, 323
sauce-tureens: silver, and covers, 196; Staffordshire, 278
sauté pans: ('soutiers' [?]), 283; copper ('sottee'), 340
saws, 297, 314
say, 361; basset-table leaf covering, 33; table covering, 49
scabbard, Indian, 329
scalding tub, 144
scales, 112, 166, 193, 232, 315, 342; designed by John Joseph Merlin, 217; brass, 79, 284; deal, for butter, 294; wooden, 127. See also beams; steelyards
scale weights, 232, 285, 293, 294, 341, 342; brass, 79, 290; copper, 315, 342; iron, 67; leaden, 48, 67; metal, 166
scallop dishes: silver, 323
scalloped, 361; scalloping, on dish (silver), 117; —, on spoon-tray (silver), 118; —, on tea-table (mahogany), 109
scallop-shells, 315; copper, 143
scantling, 361. See also under timber
scarlet: folding-screen, 327; footstool covers, 328; hearth-rugs, 203, 214; camlet, window-curtains, 108; cloth, armchair-back, 328; —, cushions, 291, 328; —, reading-desk cover, 330; —, table covers, 328, 329; —, writing-desk covering, 331;

damask, bed furniture, 56, 57; —, quilt, 57; frieze, curtains, 327; —, floor-cloths, 327; —, folding-screens, 327; moreen, seating furniture, 328; —, server coverings, 273; —, window-curtains, 271, 272, 282, 327; —, window-drapery, 271, 272; sarcenet, mantle lining, 268; velvet, mantle, 268
scarlet-and-gold: china dishes, round, 278
scarlet furniture: cabinet (Indian), 269
schoolroom: at Borris House, 244
sconces: long, 55; oil, 289; oval, 55; brass, 32, 45, 90; —, with silver wash, 31; carved and gilt, 35, 37, 82; gilt-framed, 108; —, with silvered branches and nozzles, 75; glass, 66, 71, 75, 77, 79, 82, 84, 85; —, gilt-framed, 76; —, with silver branches and nozzles, 76; —, with silver frames and nozzles, 76; lacquered, 31, 32; silver, 71, 316; tin, 284, 286, 289, 292. See also chimney sconces
Scotch carpeting, 189, 361; bed carpets, 190; bedside carpets, 181; carpets, 108, 125; lobby and stair-carpets, 189. See also Kidderminster
Scotch pints, 194, 361
scouring-brush, 315
scrapers, 297
scrap iron, 93, 290
screen (sieve): wire, 300
screen frame: with 4 leaves, 51
screens: with 2 leaves, needlework, 160; with 4 leaves, caricature covering, 334; with 6 leaves, 203, 204, 215; —, gilt-leather, 160; —, Indian, 76, 82, 205, 216; —, mahogany and moreen, 217; —, painted, 32; with 8 leaves, mahogany and glazed, 328; baize, 157; basketwork, 303; green baize, 308, 309; Indian, 70; japanned (black), 67; mahogany and paper, 337; needlework, 159; painted, 239; silk, worked, 328; tapestry, 309; tin-lined, 142; wicker, with iron stand, 39. See also folding-screens; fire screens; hand screens; pole screens
screens (church): gilt leather, 291; japanned, 291
screw press: mahogany, 192
screw taps, 295
scrutoires, 67, 72, 77, 84, 85, 361; gilt, with glass doors, 75; mahogany, 126. See also bureaux, secretaries, writing-tables
scuffles, 299, 302, 361
sculleries: at Baronscourt, 184; at Carton House, 284; at Hillsborough Castle, 143; at Kilkenny Castle, 44; at Mount Stewart, 341
sculptures: Venus, reclining, 273; brass: figures, 179; bronzed, buffalo and lion, 279; —, figures, 279; marble, busts, 273, 327; —, figures, 272, 308; —, statues, 214; —, Jupiter, 308; —, Marcus Aurelius, 309; —, Medusa, 205, 216; —, Venus, bust of, 217. See also bronzes (sculptures); Index of personal names, pp. 392–6
scythes, 300, 302
sealskin: trunk binding, 192
seat-back cushion covers: calico, 239
seat bottoms: cane, 331
seat coverings: moreen, 303

seating furniture: cotton, 333; —, printed, 332, 328; moreen, 328
seats: deal, 158; mahogany, 329; oak, 331
secrétaire, 361; mahogany; with brass gallery, 218
secretaries, 232; with drawers; and bookcases over, 337; mahogany, 190, 230, 234; —, with 5 drawers, 330; —, with plate-glass door, 330; —, with wardrobe top and drawers, 330; oak, with 4 drawers, 339; walnut, 231. See also scrutoires; secrétaire; writing-desks
seltzer-water: bottles for, 194
serge, 361; armchair cases, 31; armed-chair covering, 47; back-chair cases, 37; bases (bed), 47; bed-curtains, 20, 21, 43, 47, 50, 80; bed-furniture, 58; bed-valances, 42, 47; blinds, 338; case curtains, 33, 39, 40, 41; chair cases, 33, 34, 40, 51, 75, 77; —, false, 41; chair coverings, 20, 21; chair-covers, 41, 76; counterpanes, 20, 49; curtains, 33, 40, 44, 81; easy-chair cover, 76; elbow-chair cases, 37, 75; elbow-chair covers, 76, 79, 82; headcloths, 42, 47; quilts, 211, 275, 286, 289, 301; settee covers, 76, 82; stool cases, 31; stool coverings, 21; stool covers, 76; tester, 47; window-curtain linings, 39, 42, 56; window-curtains, 21, 32, 37, 39, 40, 42, 43, 46, 47, 52; window-seat covers, 76
serge [garment?]: silk, 91
servants' halls: at Baronscourt, 184; at Carton House, 285; at Castlecomer House, 192; at Dublin, No. 10 Henrietta St, 158; at Elphin, the bishop's house, 91; at Hillsborough Castle, 141; at Killadoon, 211, 213, 224; at Mount Stewart, 341; at Newbridge House, 314; at Shelton Abbey, 232
servers, 361; basketwork, covered in scarlet moreen, 273
sets of drawers: deal, 212; inlaid and brass-work, 207; mahogany, 206, 207, 208, 210, 211, 213, 224; oak, 211; painted, 210, 212, 223, 224
settee-bed covering: caffoy, 150
settee-beds, 150, 184
settee coverings: damask, 75, 125; silk, 182
settee covers: check, 125; needleworked worsteds on canvas, 192; serge, 76, 82
settees, 82, 144, 145, 160, 361; half, 179; gilt-framed, 76; mahogany, stuffed, 192; —, stuffed bottoms, 190; walnut, 144
settle beds, 49, 50, 91, 158, 172, 296, 299, 301, 303; deal, 294; oak, 49
settle bedsteads, 48, 50
shades. See candle-shades; lamp-shades; rushlight-shades
shapes: for biscuits, 342; for rolls, 342; tourte, 314; vol-au-vent, 314; copper, oval, 195; —, round, 195; delft, 278; tin, 284. See also jelly shapes; moulds
shaving-basin: silver, 161
shaving brush: silver, 197
shaving glasses, 254, 255; frame for, 254
shaving pots: tin, 255, 265, 267, 268, 269, 270; —, and stands, 256, 267, 269
shaving stand: and ware, 244

shears, 296, 298. *See also* clipping-shears; edging shears; garden shears; hedge shears; lopping shears; tinman's shears

sheep-brands, 299

sheep-crook, 299, 361

sheep racks, 298

sheep rugs, 203, 204, 214, 216, 308, 320

sheepskin: mats, 273, 274

sheets: bandle, 23; best, 195; coarse, 114, 179, 195, 281, 346; —, Irish, 47; fine, 141, 281, 346; finer, 47; frilled, 346; linen, twilled, 280; north country cloth, 23; second best, 195; for servants, 141; —, coarse, 23; —, grey, 316; for upper servants, 179

Sheffield plate, old: at Borris House, 238, 240–1; at Castlecomer House, 188, 198; at Mount Stewart (prob.), 348

shelf lining (tin), 340

shells, 273, 303, 329; cocoa (coconut shell poss.), 303; Shell Cottage (Waterstown) at Carton House, Co. Kildare, 301–2; shell-work, 138. *See also* oyster shells; scallop-shells; sweatmeat shells

Shelton Abbey, Co. Wicklow, 87; engraving, *259*; inventory of furniture, 1816, 229–34; sale catalogue of auction of contents (1950), front cover, *235*

shelves, 21, 22, 44, 192; for basins, 206; **deal**, 91, 212, 276, 279, 294, 302, 331, 339, 341, 342; —, painted, 302; **mahogany**, 138, 168, 206, 207, 209, 331; —, corner-shelf, 271; **oak**, 139, 302. *See also* bookshelves; hanging shelves

shingles (house tile), 92

shoes: boot and shoe rack, 310; commode for, 217; shoe buckles, 118; shoe stand, 244

shovels: iron, 294; wooden, 48. *See also* chestnut shovel; coal shovels; fire shovels; salt shovels; *see also under* brewing

show-box and lamp, 271

showcases (painted), 307

shutters, 293; mahogany, 203, 205, 214; window-shutter panels, 307, 326

sideboard brackets: iron, 159

sideboard cloths, 23; diaper, 47

sideboard coverings: gilt leather, 51

sideboard leaf: deal, 285

sideboards, 216; brass-mounted, 327; inlaid, 327; mahogany, 139, 180, 189, 240, 308; —, with 1 drawer, 342; marble, on frames, 179

sideboard tables, 32, 150, 168; mahogany, 108, 125, 140, 205, 233; marble, 169

sideboard tops: marble, 330; —, on iron brackets, 159

side tables: with fly feet, 192; **deal**, 141; **mahogany**, 327, 329; —, with folding top, 329; **marble-topped**, 233, 329; **oak**, 90

sieve bottoms, 90

sieves, 128, 293, 298, 314; brass-wire, 278; canvas, 278; hair-sieves, 278, 284; lawn-sieves, 278; silk, 48, 275; slat sieves, 278; wire, 300. *See also* hair-sieves; riddles; strainers

silk: bases (bed), 35; bed-curtain linings, 139; bed-curtain tassels, 332; bed-drapery, 332; bed-drapery lining, 334; bed-furniture linings, 334; bedstead cornice, 332; blanket, 46; caddow, 50; chair coverings, 39, 53, 180, 253, 254; counterpane, 35; cushions, 35; elbow-chair coverings, 180, 181; fire screens, 204, 229; folding-screens, 218; fringe, bed-curtains, 43; —, bed-furniture, 35, 41; —, counterpane, 268; —, curtains, 34, 44; —, wall-hangings, 35; —, window-curtains, 35, 272, 273; —, window-drapery, 332; headcloths, 332; mattress quilt, 84; night quilt, 139; quilts, 80, 138; serge [garment?], 91; settee covering, 182; sieves, 48, 275; stool coverings, 53; table carpet, 39; tassels, 332; window-curtains, 84, 139, 203, 215. *See also* French silk; Venetian silk

silk (clouded): chair-covers, 204; cushion-covers, 204; window-curtains, 204

silk (flowered): elbow-chair coverings, 82, 181

silk (fluted): hand screens, 214

silk (Indian): bed-furniture, 41; wall-hangings, 42

silk (tufted): fringe to bed-furniture, 40

silk (worked): pole-screens, 328

silk and worsted: chair bottoms, 268

silk brocatelle: chair coverings, 41, 46, 52

silk damask: bed-curtains, 138, 139; counterpane, 138; cushions, 138, 139; window-curtains, 138

silk green: bed-curtain linings, 21

silk patchwork (hexagon): quilt, 281

silver: andirons, 71, 72; asparagus-tongs, 316, 348; baking dishes, 162; basins and ewers, 161, 217; beer mug, 316; bell, 161; bijou box [?], 198; bottle labels, 316; bottle stands, 183, 347; bottle tickets, 183; bottle tops, 198, 217; branches, 196; bread-baskets, 347; —, maker's mark of John Hamilton, 316, *317*; breakfast spoon, 323; buckles, shoe and knee, 118; —, stock, 118; butter boats, 316, 323; —, and covers, 323; butter cups, 117; butter ewers, 347; butter knives, 240, 348; butter ladles, 316; butter plates, 197; butter trowels, 316; candlestick sockets, 71, 117; candlesticks, 117, 118, 162, 196, 283; —, card-table, 347; —, chamber, 198; —, flat, 347; —, fluted, 347; —, hand, 117; —, large, 316; —, library, 316; —, small, 161; —, smaller, 316; —, wrought, 347; cans, 117, 161, 197; —, pint, 197; carving knives and forks, 323; casserole dishes and covers, 196; castors, 117, 161; castor urns, for sugar, mustard and pepper, 197; cayenne-pepper spoon, 316; chamber pots, 116, 161; cheese-toaster, 161; china-jar lid tops, 36; claret-jugs, 316; coasters, 197; coffee biggin, 197; coffee-pots, 117, 161, 196, 316, 347; compote dishes and covers, 196; cork tops, 316; corkscrew with silver bow (Copley style?), 197; cream ewers, 117, 240, 316, 323; cream-jug, 197; cream-ladles, 348; cream-pot, 323; cream saucepan, 117; cream spoons, 197; cross stand, 161; cruet-frame, 161; cruet-stands, 117, 316, 347; cups, 161, 196; —, and covers, 71, 116; decanters, 116; dessert-forks, 348; dessert-knife-handles, 323, 348; dessert-knives and forks (china-handled), 316; 'dessert-spoon forks' (poss. tined spoons), 197; dessert-spoons, 162, 183, 197, 240, 323, 348; dinner forks, 348; dish stand, 117; dishes, corner, 347; —, gadrooned, 196; —, large, 347; —, oval, 72, 162, 347; —, round, 72, 162, 347; —, shell, 347; —, dish-rings, 183, 347; douter, 183; drinking-horn and cover, 161; economist's corks, 197; egg-cups, 197, 323; egg saucepans, 323; egg-spoons, 240, 316, 323; epergnes, 162, 196, 316, 347; extinguishers, 117, 347; fire-dog garnish, 33; fire dogs, 76; fire shovel and tong garnish, 33, 71; fish-plates, 162; fish-slices, 348; fish trowels, 240, 316, 323; flagons, 71; forks, 240, 316, 323, 348; —, 3-pronged, 162; —, 4-pronged, 323; fruit-dish, 196; furniture to japanned chest, 71; glass sconce garnish, 71; glass-tray, 183; goblets, 347; gravy spoons, 197, 240, 316, 323, 348; hearth frames and knobs, 76; images for the firestead (wrought silver?), 71; inkstands, 203, 204, 214, 272, 273; —, library, 316; jugs and covers, 161; kettle and stand, 197; knife-hafts, 161; knife-handles, 71, 72, 316, 323, 348; knives, 197; knives and forks, 183, 197; —, and spoons, 117, 316; ladles, 323; lemon strainer, 197; looking-glass frame garnish, 33; marrow spoons, 117, 162, 183, 197, 240, 316, 323, 348; meat trays, 183; monteith, 116; mugs, pint, 347; mustard pots, 197, 316, 347; mustard spoons, 316, 347; nozzles and pans to brackets, 76; pan, small, 316; pepper castor, 316; pincushion dishes, maker's mark of John Laughlin, *324*, 347; plates, 162, 347; —, gadrooned, 196; punch-ladles, 117; salad-dishes, 162; —, maker's mark of John Laughlin, *324*, 347; salad forks, 197, 240, 316; salt-cellars, 316; —, oval, 240; salts, 116, 161, 196, 323; —, oval, 347; —, round, 347; salt shovels, 161; salt-spoons, 116, 183, 196, 240, 323, 348; salvers, 71, 117, 161, 323; —, large, 117, 316, 347; —, oval, 316; —, round, 196, 316, 347; —, square, 316; sauce-boats, 117, 161, 196; sauce-ladles, 197, 348; saucepans, 117, 279, 284, 348; saucers, 117; sauce spoons, 279, 284, 323; sauce-tureens and covers, 196; scallop dishes, 323; scalloped dish, 117; sconce branches, 76; sconce frames, 76; sconce nozzles, 76; sconces, 71, 316; shaving-basin, 161; shaving brush and case, 197; skewers, 197, 316, 348; skillet, 72; slop-bowls, 117, 197; snuffer-dishes, 117, 197; snuffer-pans, 183; snuffers, 117, 183; snuffer-stand, 323; snuffer-trays, 347; snuff-pan, 323; soup-dish, 117; soup-ladles, 117, 183, 197, 240, 316, 323, 348; soup spoons, 117, 162, 197; soup-tureens and covers, 196, 316; sponge box, 161; spoons, 117, 118, 294, 316; spoon tray, scalloped, 118; spout to china ewer, 118; staff head, 85; stand and lamp, 116; steak-dishes, 316; strainer, 117; sugar-bowls, 117, 323; sugar castors, 183; sugar dish, 323; sugar spoons, 240, 323; sugar strainer, 240; sugar-tongs, 316, 323, 348; sword hilt, 121; table covering, 36; 'tablespoon forks' (poss. tined spoons), 197; table-spoons, 162, 183, 197, 282, 316, 323, 348;

Silver continued

tankards, 72, 117, 197, 316; taper-stand, 217; tea-dishes, 117, 197; tea-kettles, 161; —, and lamp, 116; tea-kettle stand, 161; tea-pots, 117, 197, 240, 282, 316, 323; tea-pot stands, 316, 323; teaspoons, 116, 183, 197, 240, 316, 323, 348; tea-tongs, 116, 183; toasting-fork, 279; toast-rack, 316; toothpick case, 198; tooth-powder boxes, 197; tray, for foul plates, 183; tumbler, 348; tundish, 161; tureen ladles, 162, 197; tureens, and covers, 162, 316; —, oval, 347; waiters, 196, 323; —, large, 323; warming-pan, 78; wash-ball boxes, 161, 217; water ewers, 161, 217; wine coasters, 316, 323; wine-coolers and covers, 316; wine-funnel plate, 197; wine funnels, 240, 316, 323, 348; wine jugs, 197; wine labels, 197, 240, 348

silver (plated): asparagus-tongs, 348; bottle stoppers, 206; branches, 241, 272, 348; bread-baskets, 241, 323; butter knife, 348; candle-shades, 203, 214; candle-stands, 203, 214; candlesticks, 183, 198, 241, 275, 317, 323, 348; —, bedchamber, 241, 317, 323; —, with branches, 317, 323; —, dinner, 348; —, flat, 317; —, hand, 348; —, reading, with 2 branches, 204; —, taper, 348; carving-knives and forks, 348; cheese slice, 240; coasters, 317, 323; coffee-pots, 323; —, and stands, 240; coffee-urn, 240; cover dish, 323; cruets, 323; cruet-stands, 241, 317, 348; cushion dishes with covers, 317; dish-covers, oval, 348; —, round, 348; dishes, covered, 240, 241; —, flat, 317; dish-stands, 240; douters, 203, 214, 348; egg-stand, 240; epergne, 241; extinguishers, 183, 317, 348; forks, 323; goblets, 283; gravy spoon, 317; ice-pails, 198, 240; knife-handles, 323; knives, 323; mustard pot, 323; pepperbox, 183; pincushion-dish covers, 348; pincushion-dish heaters, 348; plateaux, 348; salt-cellars, round, 241; salts, 183, 323; salvers, 240; sauce-boats with stands, 241; snuffers, 241, 348; snuffer-stands, 241; steak-dishes and stands, 198; sugar-bowl, 240; tea-kettle with stand, 241; tea-pot, 240; tea-urns, 240, 323; toast-rack, 323; tureens with stands, 241; waiters, 183; —, round, 348; wine labels, 240

silver (plate inventories): at Baronscourt, *176*, 183; at Bath (belonging to Charles Cobbe), 323; at Borris House, 240; —, plated silver, 240–1; at Captain Balfour's house, 116–18; at Castlecomer House, 196–8; —, plated silver, 198; at Dublin, No. 10 Henrietta Street, 155; —, plate weighed at, 162; —, account of plate received from Charles Gardiner, 161–2; at Dublin Castle (sold by the 2nd Duke of Ormonde), 72; at Mount Stewart, 347–8; —, plated silver, 348; at Newbridge House, 316, 323; —, plated silver, 317

silver and green: silk, cushions, 35

silver chasing, 354; candlesticks, 162; fruit-dish, 196; salts, 196

silver embossing: butter boats, 316; soup-tureens, 316

silver gadrooning, 357; dishes and plates, 196

silver-gilt: cup and cover, 162; dish, large, 71; porringer, 161; salts, basket-shaped, 196

silvering: sconce branches and nozzles, 75

silver lace, 361; trimmings, armed-chair coverings, 56; —, back-stool coverings, 56; —, window-curtain cornices, 56

silver-leaf: looking-glass frame, 34; stands, 34; table and stands, 34

silver mountings: beer mug, Wedgwood, 340; cabinet mouldings, 274; coconut cups, 118; coconut mugs, 316; corkscrew, 197; dirk, 270; gun, 330; pistols, 270; sword, basket-handled, 270

silver plate. *See* silver (plate inventories)

silver tabby, 361; door-cornices, 32; door-curtains, 32; door-valances, 32. *See also* silver thread

silver thread: fringes, bed-furniture, 34; —, chair cases, 34; —, window-curtains, 34

silver top: cut-glass box, 197

silver wash, 361; sconces, brass, 31

sink: stone, 341

skeleton desks, 271, 361; oak, 290

skewers, 361; meat, 22; **copper**, 340; **iron**, 284, 314, 341; —, loaded, 127; **lead** (for balancing), 315; **silver**, 197, 316, 348. *See also* skivers

skillets, 79; brass, 112, 158, 171, 279, 288, 315; copper, 213, 225; silver, 72

skimmers, 64, 65, 92, 127; brass, 22, 45, 91, 112; wooden, 303

skimming dishes, 173

skivers: iron, 91, 142; —, lead-headed, 91; —, loaded, 142. *See also* skewers

skylight, 331

slabs: hearth, 125, 150; **composition stone**, for table tops, 274; **marble**, for table tops, 269, 270, 273, 308; —, for work tops (dairy), 294; —, in larder, 285. *See also* mantel slab

slashing hook, 302

slating ladders, 166

slat sieves, 278

slaughter-house: at Carton House, 299; cloths for, 281; door-lock, 92

sledges, 295, 298; iron, 168

slicers: iron, 45

sling forks, 297

slop-basins, 342; china, 145, 345

slop-bowls, 175, 315; blue ware, 300; china, 233, 319; silver, 117, 197

slop tub, 279

smoke-jacks and chains, 142, 283, **362**

smoothing blankets, 275, 288. *See also* ironing blankets

smoothing-irons, 80, 81, 111, 172, 232, 279, 288, 294, 315, 318; hanging iron for, 48; stands for, 144, 279, 288, 343; **box**, 91, 111; **flat**, 22, 91, 128, 343; **box irons**, 128, 144; **flat-irons**, 144

Smyrna carpet, 51, **362**

snaffles, **362**. *See* bridle-bits; bridles

snow-breaker, 297

snuff-boxes: gold, 118; mother-of-pearl, 118

snuff-dish: brass, 22

snuffer-dishes: japanned, 318; silver, 117, 197

snuffer-frames: brass, 46

snuffer-pans, 180; brass, 77; silver, 183

snuffers, 79, 180, 182, 217, 221, 283, 288, 318; brass, 22, 46, 77, 78, 79, 85, 127, 128, 276, 284, 342; japanned, 285, 290, 339, 342; plated, 268; silver, 117, 183; silver-plated, 241, 348; steel, 128, 219, 288, 348; tin, 127, 276, 287. *See also* douters; extinguishers

snuffer-stands, 217, 283; silver, 323; silver-plated, 241

snuffer-trays, 342; brass, 276, 342; japanned, 219, 221, 285, 290; plated, 268; silver, 347

snuff-pan: silver, 323

soap, 193; in bulk, 90

soap-and-brush trays, 330; blue-and-white ware, 331, 332, 333, 335, 336, 337; brown-and-white ware, 334; china, chinée, 332; red-and-white ware, 334; white ware, 337, 338, 339; yellow-and-black ware, 335

soap-and-tooth case, 312

soap boxes, 217, 279; blue-and-white ware, 219, 220. *See also* soap chest; wash-ball boxes; wash-ball stands

soap chest: deal, 142

soap dishes, 336, 338

soap glasses, 311, 312

soap pots, 256, 268, 290

soap saucer, 310

soap stands, 208, 221, 255, 256, 266, 267, 268, 269, 270, 275, 276, 308, 311; and covers, 271, 272; blue-and-white ware, 219, 220; china, 311

soap trays, 265, 278, 287

sod irons, 297

sofa backs: stuffed hair, 328

sofa-beds, 202, 208, 209, 210, 212, 219, 221, 223

sofa case: Damascus, 276

sofa couch, 310

sofa coverings: damask, 292; drab-cloth, 273; leather, 229; tapestry, 206, 216; velvet, 84

sofa covers: calico, 229, 239; chintz, 204; chintz calico, 217; flannel and Damascus, 206

sofas: *passim*; Egyptian-style, 204; Grecian-style, 203, 214, 215; spring, 216; **deal**, 158; **gilt-framed**, 216, 292; **mahogany**, 229; —, framed, 231, 273

sofa tables, 203, 215; with 2 drawers, 214; with drawers, 309; **inlaid**, with 2 folding leaves, 328; **mahogany**, 239; —, with 2 drawers, on beech-wood pillar and claws, 337; —, with claw feet on castors, 273; **rosewood**, with 2 drawers, 204

soup-dishes, 341; china, 128, 233; pewter, 113, 171; silver, 117; yellow stoneware, 183

soup-ladles, 127, 282; silver, 117, 183, 197, 240, 316, 323, 348

soup-plates, 119, 128, 282, 315; china, 128, 195, 233, 319, 344; delft, 233; Indian china, 344; pewter, 184, 285; porcelain, 341; Staffordshire, 278; Worcester porcelain, 318

soup-pot covers, 142, 183, 195, 283, 314, 340; copper, 195

soup-pots, 127, 183, 283; copper, 195, 314; —, oval, 142, 340; —, round, 340

soup spoons: silver, 117, 162, 197

soup-tureen covers: porcelain, 341; silver, 196, 316; Staffordshire, 278

soup-tureens, 282; porcelain, 341; silver, 196, 316; Staffordshire, 278. *See also* tureens

sowing-sheets, 298

spades, 167, 285, 302, 303; garden, 300

Spanish table, 41, **362**

spar: bellows, painted, 204; boxes, 207; candlesticks, 207; —, in Derbyshire spar, 218, 220; chimney ornaments, 269, 270; dressing glasses, 207

sphinxes: Wedgwood, 204

spice-boxes, 315; tin, 127, 284, 340

spice chest, 137

spice mill, 314

spicery: at Kilkenny Castle, 46

spider-tables, 170, 210, 220, 223, 229, 242, 244, **362**; **deal**, 265, 276; **elm**, 255; —, with 1 shelf, 271; **harewood**, 273; **mahogany**, 190, 191, 204, 208, 209, 212, 224, 229, 230, 231, 232, 244, 256, 266, 268, 273, 276; **oak**, 210

spinet, 70, 80; frame for, 70, 80

spinning-wheels, 276, 303

spirit-case, 307, 308

spits, 22, 64, 91, 127, 142, 158, 183, 296, 315; iron, 341; iron holdfasts for, 142; bird spits, 45; cradle spits, 283, 315; hand spits, 283; jack spits, 111; rod spit, 171; spit racks, 127; —, iron, 142. *See also* coffee-roasters; jacks

sponge box: silver, 161

sponge plate: Indian china, 217

sponge saucers, 217; Indian china, 220

spoon box, 340

spoons: copper, 340; iron, 285, 286, 341; silver, 117, 118, 316; —, for dairy, 294; wooden, 279, 283, 303, 315, 340. *See also* breakfast spoons; cream spoons; dessert-spoons; egg-spoons; gravy spoons; marrow spoons; scallop spoons; sugar spoons; tablespoons; teaspoons

spoon-trays: japanned, 318; japanned tin, 339; silver, scalloped, 118

spurs, antique, 272

squabs (cushions), 47, **362**; calico cases, 221; calico covers, 216; cotton cover, 335; feather-stuffed, 335; hair, 328, 332, 334; wool-stuffed, 328, 337

squabs (seats), **362**; cane-bottomed, 34; with gilt feet, 34; japanned, 34; mahogany, 161; with quilt coverings, 34; with stuffed hair back and side, 332; **squab frame**, 47

squirt: wooden, 46

stable buckets, 93, 292

stables: at Carton House, 49, 50, 292, 293, 299; at Dublin Castle, 62; at Elphin, the bishop's house, 92; at Hillsborough Castle, 128; at Morristown Lattin, 167

stack seats: mahogany, 220

staff, porter's, with silver head, 85

Staffordshire ware, **362**; dinner-plates, 278; dishes; —, oval, 278; —, square, 278; sauce-tureens, sauce-ladles, 278; soup-plates, soup-tureen and cover, 278

stained glass, 291

staining: black, clock stand, 216; —, flower table, 216; —, inkstand, 221; rosewood, chairs, 216

stair-carpeting, 170, 217; Kidderminster, with border, 338; Scotch, 189; Wilton, 231

stair-rods, 170; brass, 231; —, and screw staples, 189

stamps (carved) [for pastry cook], 284

stand and lamp: silver, 116

standing-bed bottoms: mat and cord, 60

standing beds, 55, 57, 58, 59, 60, 61, 62, 76, 78, 79, 80, 81, 89, **362**

standing bedsteads, 77, 78, 79, 80, 84, **362**

stands: for brushing coats, 223; deal, 302; gilt, 37, 71, 82; inlaid with tortoiseshell, 42; iron, for grates, 207, 208, 209; japanned, 75; mahogany, for loose papers, railed, 204; maple, 240; marble, 71, 82; pewter, 22, 91; —, Irish, 63; silver-leafed, 34; stone, counterfeit, inlaid, 33

star-pattern: tablecloths, 195

statues. *See under* sculpture

steak-dishes: porcelain, 277; silver, 316; silver-plated, with stands, 198

steak-tongs, 171, 284, 315; iron, 142, 341

steel: andirons, 35; candlestick, 288; extinguisher, 204; fenders, 203, 204, 205, 206, 207, 208, 209, 210, 211, 220, 221, 223, 224, 229, 277, 283; —, with wirework, 206, 207, 208, 209; fire irons, 221, 239, 268, 269, 272, 273, 274; fireguard, 209; hearths, 75, 82; malt mill, 144; register grates, 203, 214; snuffers, 128, 219, 288, 348; stove-grate, 140

steels (knife sharpeners), 142, 283; and pouch, 299

steelyards, 315

step-ladders, 143, 167, 239, 284, 288, 292, 293, 297, 299, 308, 327; deal, 276, 290; mahogany, 205, 274; short steps, 341; standing, 167

steward's office: at London, St James's Square, 85

steward's parlour: at Baronscourt, 180

stewards' rooms: at Carton House, 282–3; at Castlecomer, 192; at Hillsborough Castle, 141; at Kilkenny Castle, 32; at Killadoon, 211, 224; at London, St James's Square, 78

stew-holes, 45, 46

stewing pots and covers: copper, 314

stewpan covers, 142, 183, 284; oval, 283; round, 283, 340; copper, 195

stewpans, 127, 183, 284; oval, 283; round, 283; copper, 63, 112, 142, 195, 284; —, oval, 195, 340; —, round, 195, 340; iron, 22

stillions, 23, 45, 167, 194, 287, **362**

still-rooms, **362**; at Carton House, 287; at Kilrush House, 152; at Mount Stewart, 342

stills, 152; glass, 292; pewter, 22, 90; still tops, 47

stirrup-irons, 319

stitch-work: blankets, 70, 84; cushion (cross-stitch), 33

stock-locks, **362**. *See also under* door-locks

stock-pot, with cover, 183

stone: Chinese ornaments, 279; cups, 272, 273; flags, 279; jars, 273, 299; rollers, 297, 302; sink, 341; troughs, 294, 296, 299; **counterfeit stone**, inlaid, looking-glass frame, 33; —, stands, 33; —, table, 33. *See also* composition stone; stone china

stone-china: ewers, 273

stone slide, 297

stoneware: bottle, 90; jug, 286; sauce-boats, 128

stool bottoms: false in damask, 34; rush, 211, 212

stool cases: damask, 31; serge, 31

stool coverings: carpet, 271, 273; cloth, 309; damask, 43, 70, 75, 76, 126; gilt-leather, 47, 50; leather, 32; moreen, 291; needlework, 33, 273, 276; plaid, 56; satin, 39, 180; serge, 21; silk, 53; stuff, 55, 56; —, Irish, 47; Turkey-work, 20, 21; velvet, 33, 84; wrought, 66

stool covers: dimity, 139; lutestring, 70; serge, 76; velvet, painted, 268

stools, **362**; black, 31; cane, 21, 22; conversation, 189; deal, 274, 301, 331; folding-up, 216; mahogany, 179; painted, 205; round, 33, 78, 84; —, in mahogany, with stuffed seat, 190; —, with black frames, 34; rush-bottomed, 193, 216; square, 76; wooden, 48, 342. *See also* camp-stools; chopping stool; close-stools; footstools; high stool; night-stools; writing stool

storage for groceries: deal press, 91; nest of drawers, 193

store chests, 194

store press: deal, 193

stove-grates, 78, 82, 84, 224; brass, 137; steel, 140

stove holes, 45, 46, 47

stoves, 183, 283, 302, 308; fixed, 343; marble, 328

straddles, 92, 166; cart, 298

straight-edge, 295

strainers, 294; and stands, 173; copper, 314; delft, 294; silver, 117; wooden, 303. *See also* lemon strainer; milk strainer; sugar strainer; tamis

straining-frames, 38, 53, **362**

straining ladders, 279

straw: bed, 43; hassocks, 331, 335, 337; mattresses, 141, 142, 143, 144, 145, 209, 212; palliasses, 209, 255, 275, 276, 289, 290, 331, 332, 333, 334, 335, 336, 337; workbox, 334

straw (colour): taffety, bed-furniture linings, 42

straw basket, 298

strings and tassels (for draw-up curtains), 32

strongboxes, 70; with frame, 75

stucco: Kilrush House, Stucco Room, 150, 152; extruco [?], 330; picture frames, 330

Studdert linen, 280, **362**

studies: at Baronscourt, 186; at Carton House, 271–2; —, old, 272; at Elphin, the bishop's house, 95–103; at Hillsborough Castle, 126; at Killadoon, 216; at Lismore Castle, 22; at Mount Stewart, 330; at Newbridge House, 308

study chair, 308

study-tables: mahogany, 308

stuff, **362**; armed-chair and back-chair cases, 33; bed-curtains, 21, 89, 145, 225; bed-furniture, 57, 58, 60, 62, 126, 141, 182, 184; bed-furniture linings, 61; beds, 89; chair coverings, 56, 181, 182; counterpane, 21; curtains, 81; cushion, 43; door-curtains,

56; festoon-curtain lining, 282; fire screen, 205; quilt, 145; stool coverings, 55, 56; wall-hangings, 57; wardrobe-curtains, 223; window-curtain cornices and valance, 75; window-curtains, 32, 55, 56, 57, 75, 126, 144. *See also* Irish stuff

stuff (chequered): bed-furniture, 58, 60, 61, 79

stuff (clouded): bed-curtains, 20; —, and bed-hangings, 20; counterpane, 20; tablecloth, 20

stuff (English): billiard-table cover, 192

stuff (figured, Indian): bed-furniture and window-curtains, 57

stuff (flowered): wall-hangings, 57

stuff (printed), 80; bed-curtains, 43, 46, 68, 81; bed-furniture, 58; curtains, 41; headcloths, 43, 46; tester, 43

stuff (quilted): quilts, 211, 213, 223, 224, 225

stuff (striped): bed-furniture, 47; wall-hangings, 39, 47; window-curtains (Indian), 32

stuff (worsted): linings to bed-furniture, window-curtains and window-hangings, 61

stump bedsteads, 289, 290, 294, 339, **362**; deal, 292, 296

sugar-basins: china, with covers, 345; cut-glass, round, 345; nankeen china, 183; white ware, 342

sugar boats, covers and plates: Worcester porcelain, 318

sugar-bowls, 175, 286, 315; china, 233, 277, 319; —, and covers, 319; porcelain, 277, 278; silver, 117, 323; silver-plated, 240; Wedgwood, 277

sugar caddy, 342

sugar canisters, 193; tin, 189, 340

sugar castors: silver, 183, 197

sugar-chest, 216

sugar-chopper, 342

sugar cup: china, 33

sugar dishes: china, with covers, 145; silver, 323

sugar glasses: and cover, 318; and stand, 318; cut-glass, oval, 345

sugar-ladles: silver, 316, 348

sugar nippers, 275, 276, 315, 342

sugar-pails: china, 318

sugar pan: copper, 342

sugar scoops, 340

sugar spoons: silver, 240, 323

sugar stands: china, 233

sugar store: mahogany-framed, with 1 drawer, 189

sugar strainer: silver, 240

sugar-tongs, 282; silver, 316, 323, 348

sumpter cloths (armorial), 46, **362**

supper dishes: china, 128; —, and covers, 345

supper plates, 282

supper stand: mahogany, 205

supper tables: deal, 224; mahogany, 108; —, Canterbury, 240

supping room: at Kilkenny Castle, 31

surcingle, 319, **362**

surveyor's chain: brass, 297

sweeping-brushes, 278, 283, 286, 287, 288, 289, 294, 301, 315, 318

sweet bottles: painted glass, 36

sweetmeat cups, stands and covers: porcelain, 277

sweetmeat dishes: cut-glass, 278

sweetmeat glasses, 91, 119, 318

sweetmeat shells: cut-glass, 345

sweetmeat stands: delft, 175; glass, 119

sweet oil, 238, **362**

swing bookcases: mahogany, 329; **painted**, 339; —, with 2 shelves, 335, 337; —, with 3 shelves, 338; —, with 4 shelves, 337

swing dressing glasses, 190, 223, 232, 336, 337; with 3 drawers, 332; **mahogany**, 223, 224, 330, 331, 334, 339; —, with 1 drawer, 332, 335, 337, 339; —, with 3 drawers, 334, 338; **painted**, with 1 drawer, 336

swing-glasses, 126, 149. *See also* swing dressing glasses; swing looking-glasses

swinging bales (for horses), 172, **362**

swinging bars, 298

swingletree, 92, **362**

swing looking-glasses, 138, 193; frames for, 338; mahogany, 332; —, with 1 drawer, 331, 336

swords: blade, 270; broad, 121, 140; —, Indian, 329; mourning, 121; silver-hilted, 121; silver-mounted and basket-handled, 270

sycamore: armed chair, 145. *See also* harewood; maple

syllabub, 91, **362**

syringes, 300

tabby, **362**; bed-furniture, 39; cushions, 39; quilt, 39. *See also* silver tabby

table basket, 23

table beds: oak, 89, 90

table bedsteads, 31, 36, 82

table brackets: iron, 159

table carpets: gilt-leather, 32; green cloth, 84; silk, 39; velvet, figured, 33; Venetian, for dressing table, 268

tablecloths, 113, 114, 115; bird's eye, 141; starred, 195; **bandle**, 23; **damask**, 141, 179, 195, 279, 316, 345; —, bird's eye, 282; —, Cromaboo, 279; —, Kildare, 279; —, star pattern, 141; **diaper**, 23, 47, 113, 179, 195, 281, 301, 316, 346; —, Dutch, 47; —, Dutch matting, 280; —, striped, 280; **stuff**, clouded, 20

table coverings: green cloth, 205, 216; leather, 76; say, 49

table covers, 308, 309; baize, 204, 308; cloth, 271, 273; dimity, frilled, 346; —, plain, 346; frieze, 169, 334; green baize, 337; green cloth, 168, 203, 214, 338; greycloth, 328; leather, 39, 41, 81, 140, 210; scarlet cloth, 328, 329

table drawers: cedar, 190

table-end lengthener, 32

table frames, 293; with folding oval leaf, 45; with griffin in gilt frame, 159; beech-wood, 337; bronzed, 273; carved, 109, 159, 274; deal, painted, 337; gilt, 76, 82, 269, 270, 273; iron, 294; mahogany, 273; walnut, 81

table linen. *See* breakfast napkins; dinner napkins; lay-overs; napkins; sideboard cloths; tablecloths; tea napkins

tables: Chinese, 255; ornamental, 310; Spanish, 41; deal, *passim*; —, with 1 drawer, 141, 144, 145, 210, 223, 274, 275, 276, 290, 300, 303, 340; —, with 2 drawers, 300; —,

with 3 drawers, 141; —, with 8 drawers, 142; —, with drawers, 192, 223, 275, 276; —, with 1 shelf, 212, 224; —, with 2 shelves, 338; —, with flaps, 140; —, fixed, 279; —, large, 158, 192, 275, 300, 302, 340; **deal, painted**, 308; —, with 1 drawer, 253, 254; —, with drawers, 253; **ebony**, 43; **elm**, 191, 244, 269, 284, 285, 290; —, narrow, 270; **fir**, 141, 142; **gilt**, 36; **inlaid**, 56, 214, 217; —, with 1 drawer, 205; —, with 1 drawer, 1 shelf, 218; —, tortoiseshell, 310; **japanned**, 75, 76, 138, 179; **mahogany**, 126, 139, 181, 182, 189, 191, 193, 205, 206, 208, 211, 212, 240, 268, 283, 290, 300, 301, 309, 310, 311, 329; —, with 1 drawer, 205, 207, 208, 209, 210, 212, 216, 220, 223, 308, 312; —, with 1 drawer, 1 shelf, 207; —, with 2 drawers, 330; —, with drawers, 206, 311, 313, 329; —, 1 leaf, 269; —, 1 leaf, with drawers, 276; —, with 1 shelf, 209; —, folding down, 330; —, for lamp, 308; —, three-piece set and 2 leaves, 205; **mahogany, inlaid**, with cedar drawers, 190; —, with turned feet, 332; **mahogany, painted**, 309; **marble**, 70, 75, 140, 308; —, with carved frame, 109; —, with eagle-shaped support, 179; —, with frames, 179, 180; —, with gilt frame, 82; —, with griffin in gilt frame, 159; —, on walnut frames, 81; **oak**, 48, 49, 66, 79, 91, 93, 128, 137, 141, 171, 193, 209, 211, 212, 240, 283, 284; —, with 1 drawer, 209, 210, 221, 223, 289; —, with 2 leaves, 303; —, with leaves, 300, 303; —, fixed, 51; —, folding, 128; —, large, 90; —, in servant maids' hall, 285; —, in servants' hall, 285; **olive wood**, 78; —, and stands, 39, 41, 78; **painted**, 191; —, China, 310; **silver-covered**, 36; **stone**, counterfeit, inlaid, 33; **tortoiseshell**, with brass inlay, 273; **wainscot**, 57, 58; —, with 1 drawer, 56; **walnut**, 35, 158, 232, 234; —, and stands, 40;. *See also* alphabet tables; breakfast-tables; card-tables; claw-tables; dining-tables; fly-tables; Pembroke tables; pillar tables; plank table; sideboard tables; spider-tables; supper tables; tea-tables

tables (children's), 216; mahogany, 273

tables (circular), 232; mahogany, 179, 230, 239, 240

tables (long), 22, 314; deal, 48, 51, 211, 224, 287, 338, 341; in servants' halls, 91, 184, 211, 213, 224, 314, 341; with drawers, 315

tables (octagonal), 220; mahogany, 208; —, with folding leaves, 332

tables (oval), 55, 66, 67, 77, 78, 216, 220; with 2 folding leaves, 337; **beech-wood**, 330; **cherry-wood**, 125; **mahogany**, 149, 269, 274, 276, 286, 287, 293, 328; —, on pillars and claws, 240, 328; —, with 1 drawer, inlaid, 328; —, with 2 leaves, 342; **oak**, 84, 211, 224, 290; **wainscot**, 82

tables (round), 22, 203, 214, 313; claw, 139, 214; drop-leaf, 45; on pillar and claws, 331; **beech-wood**, on pillars and claws, 328; **mahogany**, 90, 139, 180, 309; —, claw, 204; —, on pillars and claws, 269, 270, 275, 283, 329, 343; **oak**, 171, 308

430

tables (square), 22, 66, 79, 80, 81, 214, 232, 338; with 1 drawer, 217; **beech-wood**, 330; —, on pillar and claws, 328; **black**, 82; **cane**, 78; **deal**, 331, 339; —, with 2 drawers, 337; **deal, painted**, 330, 337; **inlaid**, 203; **japanned**, 76, 84; **mahogany**, 214, 239, 328, 330; —, with 1 drawer, 336; —, on pillar and claws, 329; **mahogany, inlaid**, 328, 329; **oak**, 67; **olive wood**, 78; **wainscot**, 84; **walnut**, 82

tables (triangular), 210, 220

tables and stands: black, 38, 41, 42; brass-garnished, 38; carved, 34; japanned, 31, 32, 40; silver-leafed and partial copper finish, 34; cover for, in deal, 40

'tablespoon forks': silver, 197

tablespoons: silver, 162, 183, 197, 282, 316, 323, 348

table supports: eagle-shaped, 179; mahogany stands, 217. *See also* pillar-and-claw table supports; table brackets; table frames

table tops: alabaster, inlaid with black marble, 217; **composition** [stone], 274; **deal**, 338; —, with iron frame, 294; **mahogany**, 329; —, inlaid, 337; **marble**, 109, 158, 159, 233, 269, 270, 273, 308, 329; —, on carved frames, 159; —, dove, 218, 219; —, on iron brackets, 159

tabouret: window-curtains and drapery, 240

taffety, 362; back-chair cases, 38; bed-furniture linings, 42; curtains, 33; dressing-stool case, 32; elbow-chair cases, 38; window-curtains, 42

taffety (flowered): bed-furniture, 144; quilt, 144

tallboys, 128; mahogany, 109, 110, 126, 160, 184, 191; oak, 191; **half tallboys**, 190, 191, 287. *See also* bedsteads, tallboy

tambour-frames, 139, 268, 362

tambour writing-desk, 362; mahogany, 270

tambour writing-tables, 362; harewood, 269, 271; inlaid, 255, 271

tambourine, 272

tamis, 315, **362**

tandem chains, 298

Tangier mats, 33, 34, 40, **362**

tankards: silver, 72, 117, 197, 316.
See also madders

taper-stand: silver, 217

tapestry, 193, 269, **362**; armchair coverings, 206, 216, 219, 255, 256, 266, 267, 309; armed-chair seats, 108; chair coverings, 203, 204, 215, 217, 291; chair seats, 108; fire screens, 309; screens, 309; sofa coverings, 206, 216

tapestry-hangings, 21, 75, 77, 78, 80, 109, 150; Ahasuerus, king of Persia, 46; Air and Water, 84; Alexander the Great, 80; Antwerp, 33, 42, 51; Bacchanalia, 34, 51; Cyrus, king of Persia, 42; Decius Mus, Publius, Roman consul, 40, 51; —, consecration of, *24*; 40, 51; Diogenes, 33, 76; Don Quixote, 41; figured work, 78; Fire, Earth and Air, 75; forest-work, 41, 78, 79; —, with small figures, 38; green-work, 77; landscapes, 77; —, with small figures, 31, 51; men on horseback, 77; Polyphemus, 33.
See also wall-hangings

tapestry linings: canvas, 31, 41, 42

taps. *See* cocks (plumbing); screw taps

tap wrenches, 295

tar, 297; **tar pot**, 299

tarrier, 90, 362

tartlet pans: tin, 284, 340; —, round, 340; —, oval, 340

tassels: bed-curtains, 332; bed-furniture, 31, 41, 334, 336; bedstead-cornice and headcloth, 332; bell-pulls, 189, 221, 327; pillows, 35; seating furniture, 332; window-curtains, 32, 189, 333; window-drapery, 329, 334, 337

tawny cloths, 284

tea-bell: glass, 119

tea-boards, 145, 169, 183; for fruit, 183; japanned, 140; mahogany, 120, 141; oval, 140; square, India, 140

tea boiler, 340

tea-caddies, 289, 342; china, and stand, 334

tea-canisters, 193, 276, **362**; japanned, 283

tea-chests, 216, 309; mahogany, 90, 119, 308; —, on stand, 205

tea colour: bed-furniture and window-curtains, 334

tea-cups and saucers: blue ware, 300; china, 33, 91, 319, 345; —, gilt, 128

tea-dishes, 76, **362**; silver, 117, 197

tea-kettles, 91, 128, 172, 184, 315, 318, 338; china, 34; copper, 112, 142, 144, 209, 210, 340; iron, 341; japanned, 128; silver, 161; —, and lamp, 116; silver-plated, 241

tea-kettle stands, 160; mahogany, 142; silver, with lamp, 161; silver-plated, 241

tea-kitchens, 145, 182, **362**; copper, 142, 195; with heater, 195

tea napkins, 115; damask, 179

tea-pots: *passim*; black ware, 278, 300, 315; china, 118, 128, 145, 180, 233, 277, 319; —, garnished, 34; earthenware, 33; japanned, 278; porcelain, 277; silver, 117, 197, 240, 282, 316, 323; silver-plated, 240; Wedgwood, 220, 342; white ware, 290; wooden, 303

tea-pot stands: silver, 316, 323

tea-services, 76; at Carton House, coloured, 277; —, white, gold and scarlet, 277; at Mount Stewart, white and gold, 345. *See also* equipage

teaspoons: silver, 116, 183, 197, 240, 316, 323, 348

tea-stands, 82

tea store: mahogany, 239

tea-tables, 56, 66, 72, 76, 78, 90, 126, 149, 150, 151, 168, **362**; with 1 drawer, 309; Indian, 76, 82; japanned, 33; mahogany, 90, 109, 303; tea-table top, 72

tea-tables (round), 170; mahogany, 160; —, on pillar and claws, 342

tea-tongs: silver, 116, 183

tea-trays, 318; japanned, 283, 289, 318, 342, 345; —, Indian, 342; —, tin-ware, 342; mahogany, 211, 224. *See also* tea-boards

tea-urns, 234, 318; brown ware, 345; japanned, 283; silver-plated, 240, 323.
See also tea-kitchens

telescope, in a mahogany case, 330

tenon saw, 296

tent-bedsteads, 289, 312, 313, 330, 331, 333, 335, 336, 337, 338, 339, 342, 343; —, turn-up, half-tester, 335

tent-poles, 291

tester lining: cotton, 335

testers, 362; calico, 41; cloth, 50; damask, 40, 43, 81; damask and gold, 70; deal, 275; drugget, 39, 40, 42, 44; green cloth, 46, 49; hair camlet, 42; 'harnum', 49; Kidderminster, 48, 50; satin, clouded, 41; —, Indian, 39; serge, 47; silk, Venetian, 33; stuff, Irish, 47; —, printed, 43; tabby, 39

testers (rising), 31, 33, 38, 42; carved, 34; damask, 31, 38

thatching-fork, 298

thermometers, 203, 214, 217, 271, 338

thread damask, **362**; window-curtains, 31

tick, **362**; bolsters, 301, 336; feather-beds, 301, 336; palliasse, 337; pillows, 301, 336

tick (cotton): bolsters, 253, 254; feather-beds, 253, 254

tick (linen): bolster, 254; borders, bolster, 253; —, feather-bed, 253; feather-bed, 254; pillow, 254

tick (striped): bed-hangings, 336; bolsters, 330, 331, 334, 335, 336, 337, 338, 339; —, Flanders, 34; feather-beds, 330, 331, 334, 335, 336, 337, 338, 339; —, Flanders, 34; mattresses, 331, 332, 333, 334, 335; palliasse, 335; pillows, 330, 331, 333, 334, 335, 336, 337, 338, 339

ticken, 195, **362**; beds, 50, 296; billiard-table cover, 274; bolsters, 50, 275; pillows, 275; remnants, 281

ticken (striped): bolsters, 331, 332, 333, 338, 339; feather-beds, 331, 332, 333, 338, 339; pillows, 331, 332, 333, 338

ticking, 362; cushions, 52; lengths of, 120, 195

ticking (Flanders): feather-beds and bolsters, 33, 48, 56

ticking (striped): feather-bed and bolster, 38

tierces, **362**; of table beer, 92

timber: ash, 172; —, slats and board, 172; aspen, 173; bog oak, 173; cherry-wood, 173; deal, boards, 92, 168, 292; —, plank, 168; —, scantling, 168; elm, scantling, 168; fir-deal, 168, 173; oak, 173; —, scantling, laths, ribberies etc., 172. *See also* woods for furniture

timber truck, 297

timepieces. *See* clocks

tin, 362; baking pan, 171; basket lining, 66; bath, 223; bathing-tub, 318; branches, 303; bread colander, 284; bread-graters, 340; candle-shades, 204; candlesticks, 46, 127, 276, 277, 284, 288, 289, 290, 291, 292, 293, 315; —, flat, 144, 283, 287; —, high, 315; —, with stand, 80; canisters, 276, 289; cans, 283, 286, 288, 293, 294; chamber-bath liner, 331; coffee-pots, 232, 284, 287; colanders, 22, 127, 171, 279, 340; dish-covers, 44, 286; dredging-boxes, 279, 340; dripping-pan, 22; Dutch oven, 340; egg boiler, 314; extinguishers, 276, 290; fenders, 125, 126, 128, 137, 138, 139, 144, 169, 289, 290, 300; fire-screen lining, 183; foot pan, 212; graters, 171, 279; jelly-moulds, 340; kettles,

General index

431

206, 207, 208, 218, 279, 301, 302, 310, 338; lamps, 192; —, painted, 287; lamp trays, tinned, 287; lanterns, 289, 298; moulds, heart, pudding and round, 143; mugs, 340; mustard-pot lining, 347; oil cans, 289; oil pot, 318; oil tray, 289; ornamental cutters, 340; paste cutters, 143; —, boxed, 284; —, fluted, 340; —, round, 340; —, shell-shaped, 340; pastry cutters, 315; pasty pans, 22; pattypans, 91; pedestal lining, 273; pepperbox, 340; plate-basket linings, 286; pot, 284; pudding-pans, 91, 315; quarts, 171, 289; rushlight-shades, 338; salt-box, 340; saucepans and covers, 315; sconces, 284, 286, 289, 292; screen lining, 142; shapes, 284; —, tourte, 314; shaving pots, 255, 256, 265, 267, 268, 269, 270; shelf lining, 340; snuffers, 127, 276, 287; spice-boxes, 127, 284, 340; sugar canisters, 189, 340; tartlet pans, 284, 340; —, oval, 340; —, round, 340; toast pans, 284; tray, 284; tundishes, 279, 285, 290; vegetable cutter, 284; water dishes, 286; water-can, 340

tin (japanned): box for harp strings, 272; foot pans, 255, 256, 265, 266, 267, 268, 269, 270, 271

tin-ware: at Elphin, the bishop's house, 90; at Hillsborough Castle, 143; at Lismore Castle, 22

tissue, 363; pincushion, woven with gold thread, 71

toasters, 22; ebony, 118

toasting-forks, 340, 341; silver, 279

toast pans: tin, 284

toast-racks: silver, 316; silver-plated, 323

toilet, 363; muslin and cotton, 334; muslin, worked, 332

toilet glasses, 231, 253, 254; mahogany-framed, 253. *See also* toilette glasses

toilet press: oval, 276

toilet services: spar, 207

toilet-table covers: calico and muslin, 207

toilet-table furniture: muslin, 190

toilet tables: deal, 190, 334; —, on castors, 332; —, square, 333

toilette glasses, 255, 256, 265, 266, 267, 269, 270, 275, 286, 289, 290; —, mahogany-framed, 268, 269, 292. *See also* toilet glasses

tomahawk, 272, **363**

tongs: *passim*; kitchen, 91; stove, 278; **brass**, 31, 32, 33, 38, 40, 41, 42; **brass-knobbed**, 31, 32; **iron**, 142; **silver-garnished**, 33, 71. *See also* asparagus-tongs; fire-tongs; steak-tongs; sugar-tongs; tea-tongs; wafer-tongs

tool-chests, 272, 297

tool presses, 205, 213, 224

toothbrush case, 310

toothbrush stands, 217, 255; gilt, Chinese, 255

toothbrush trays, 206, 221; blue-and-brown ware, 218; blue-and-white ware, 219, 220

toothpick case: silver, 198

tooth-powder boxes: silver, 197

tortoiseshell, **363**; cabinet inlay, 33; inlay on stands, 42; looking-glass frame, with black and tortoiseshell, 46; picture frame, with brass, 214; table, with brass inlay, 273

toss-pans: copper, 91, 171, 284; —, and covers, 314

tourte dish cover [?], **363**; delft, 175

towels: chamber, coarse, 346; —, fine, 346; damask, 179; diaper, bird's eye, 280, 282; French, 114; grey linen, 280; huckaback, 141, 179, 280; round, 281, 282, 346

transparencies: mahogany-framed, 329

traps, 67; cat traps, 291, 299; kite trap, 291; mantraps, 291, 297; rat traps, 299

traveller for wheels, 295, **363**

trays: japanned, 193, 234, 277, 279, 339; —, black, 318; **mahogany**, 193, 234, 240, 279, 318; —, square, 157; **silver**, for foul plates, 183; **tin**, 284. *See also* bottle tray; brush trays; plate tray; soap-and-brush trays; tea-trays; toothbrush trays; wafer trays

tray stand, 268

treillage. *See* trellis-work; wirework

trellis-work: brass, 220; metal, 272

trencher case, 22, **363**

trenchers, 285, 303; wooden, 92, 283, 302

trestle-tables, 46; deal, 293; oval, 32

triangles, 272

trifle bowl: cut-glass, footed, with ladle, 345

trimmings: **armed-chair coverings**, lacework, silver, 56; **back-stool coverings**, lacework, silver, 56; **bed-curtains**, 206, 207; —, calico, 208, 209, 221; —, chintz, 207, 208; —, fringe and gymp, 190; —, muslin and gymp, 190; —, 'stripped Damascus', 210; —, thread, gold, 70; **bed-furniture**, cotton, printed, 335; —, lacework, 79, 84; **chair coverings**, thread, gold, 70; **chair-covers**, fringe and gymp, 190; **christening robe**, point lace, 268; **counterpanes**, muslin, 209, 221; **shirt**, point lace, 268; **toilet-table furniture**, lacework, 190; —, point lace, 190; **wall-hangings**, thread, gold, 70; **window-curtain cornices**, lacework, silver, 56; **window-curtains**, cotton, 335; —, fringe, 189; —, fringe and gymp, 190; —, lutestring, 189; —, muslin and gymp, 190; **window-drapery**, cotton and muslin, 335; **window-furniture**, lacework, 75, 76, 81, 82

tripods, 283, 296, 315

trippets, 91, 113, 171, **363**

trivets, 46, 47, 64, 127, 142, 342, **363**; iron, 45; square, 183; triangular, 183

troughs, 299; lead-covered, 45; metal, 299; stone, 294, 296, 299. *See also* cider trough; kneading-trough; losset; water troughs

trou-madame tables, 203, 214, 291, 308, **363**

trowels, 48, 298; weeding, 302. *See also* butter trowels; fish trowels

truckle bedstead, 77

trunk cabinet, Indian, 310

trunk nails: gilt, 192

trunks: black, 126; carriage, 192; cedar, 192; hair-bound, 80, 84, 126, 142, 171; iron-bound, 47; japanned, 191; leather-bound, 84, 142, 171, 192, 231, 293, 339; sealskin-bound, 192

tubs: delft, 283; mahogany, 308. *See also* bathing-tubs; beef tub; cream tub; dish tubs; flour tubs; foot tubs; hog-tub; ice tub; meal tub; milk tub; powdering tubs; salting tubs: scalding tub; slop tub; washing-tubs; water tubs; wrenching tubs

tufting: cotton counterpane, 125; quilts, 89, 169, 208, 209, 210, 212, 220, 221, 223; silk fringe, 40

tumbler locks, 217, 221

tumblers: *passim*; cut-glass, 218, 268, 269, 270, 272, 340; glass, 175, 183, 208, 217, 218, 219, 220, 221, 290; silver, 348

tumbrels (cart), 92; tumbrel box, 166

'tumrels', **363**; glass, 119

Tunbridge ware, **363**; cabinets, 206, 220

tundishes, 299, **363**; pewter, 91, 92; silver, 161; tin, 279, 285, 290

tuns, **363**; for brewing, 51; chest or large vessel, 37; of coal, 120

tureen ladles: silver, 162, 197

tureens, 315, **363**; china, 233; —, and covers, 195, 344; delft, 233; French china, 278; porcelain, and covers, 277, 341; silver, and covers, 162, 316; —, oval, 347; silver-plated, 241; yellow stoneware, 183. *See also* sauce-tureens; soup-tureens

tureen stands: porcelain, 341; silver-plated, 241

turf, 93; turf baskets, 139, 170; turf boxes, 168; turf keshes, 92; turf room at Hillsborough Castle, 128; turf yard at Morristown Lattin, 173

Turkey: bed-round, 182; bedside carpets, 182; carpets, 108, 109, 179, 180, 181, 182, 189, 205, 211, 216, 224, 272, 273, 292, 328; floor carpet, 125; rugs, 272, 273. *See also* Turkey work

Turkey leather, **363**; bookbinding, 32, 36; chair coverings, 81

Turkey stone ring, 118, **363**

Turkey work, **363**; bed carpet, 31; carpets, 44, 51, 66, 79; chair coverings, 20, 21, 22, 32, 50; cushions, 20, 21; stool covering, 21

Turk's-cap moulds, 143, **363**

turned work: pillars and feet on chest of drawers, 332

turning-chisels, 297

turning-lathes, 296, 297

turnips: turnip barrows, 298; turnip scufflers, 298; turnip-scoops, 143, 315

turnspits, 45; for chine of beef, 45. *See also* jacks

turnstiles, 166

twig: bookcase, 303; carpet-brushes, 278, 288; flasket, 111

twill, **363**; sheets, linen, 280

twine boxes, 271; deal, 284

umbrella stand: brass, 214

umbrello, 52, **363**

under-blankets, 89, 91; English, 169, 170, 253, 267, 274, 275; Irish, 170, 171, 253, 254, 255, 256, 265, 266, 269, 275, 276, 286, 301

undercap, 268

United Irishmen: uprising, 24 June 1798, 187, 189, 196

upholstery: chair-backs and seats, 231; chair seats, 230, 241; **hair silk**, chair coverings, 189; **leather-work**, armchairs, 229; —, music-stool, 189; —, sofa, 229

upholstery nails: brass, 253, 254, 329; gilt, 189, 191

urns, 180, 181; with brass figure decoration on covers, 37; bronze, mounted in ormolu, 329; china, 273, 303; delft, and covers, 294; Italian, for chimney-piece, 270; marble, 270; plaster of Paris, 327. *See also* pastille burners

utensils, **363.** *See also* chamber utensils

valances, **363;** calico, Indian, 32; damask, Indian, 75; mohair, 79. *See also* bed-valances; window-valances

valet de chambre's room: London, St James's Square, 84

valuations, **363;** Balfour town house, 1741/2, 108–21; Borris House, 1818, 239–45; Castlecomer House, 1798, 189–99; Dublin, No. 10 Henrietta St, 1772, 157–62; Dublin Castle, 1707, 55–73; Elphin, the bishop's house, 1740, 89–103; Kilrush House, 1750, 149–52; Morristown Lattin, 1773, 166–75; Shelton Abbey, 1816, 229–34

vases, **363;** Etruscan-style, 203, 204, 214, 215; Wedgwood, 205, 207, 216; **alabaster,** 216; **china,** 205, 216, 217, 273, 328; —, and covers, 205, 216, 217; —, *craquelé,* 204 —, with saucers, 215; —, very large, 205; **composition** [stone], 279; **marble,** 229, 271, 272, 344; —, brass-mounted, 272; —, imitation, 344; **plaster of Paris,** 343. *See also* chamber vases

vats, **363:** boiling, 284; cheese-making, 92. *See also* kieves

vegetable cutter: tin, 284

vegetable dishes: porcelain, 341; with covers, 341

velvet: armed-chair coverings, 56; back-stool coverings, 56; bell-pulls, 203, 204, 214, 328; border to stool, 33; card-table covering, 33; carpets, 32, 38; chair coverings, 38, 52, 53, 55, 56, 78, 84; cushions, 32; —, to kneel upon, 109; easy-chair covering, 41; elbow-chair coverings, 78, 81, 82; fringe to bed-furniture, 35; gilt-table covering, 36; sofa covering, 84; stool coverings, 84; stools, round, 33; mantle, 268; wall-hangings, 84; window cushions, 76; window-curtain bindings, 327; window cushions, 76; window-drapery bindings, 331; writing-desk covering, 33; writing-table covering, 75

velvet (figured): armed-chair coverings, 33, 53; back-chair coverings, 33, 37; elbow-chair coverings, 37, 47; play-table covering, 33; table carpet, 33

velvet (painted): plateau, 348; pole-screens, 333, 334; stool cover, 268

Venetian furnishings: bed carpet, 266; bed-rounds, 255, 256, 266, 267, 268, 269, 270; blinds, 203, 204, 205, 206, 214, 215, 217, 294; carpets, 265, 268, 269, 287; table carpet, for dressing table, 268

Venetian silk: bed-post cases, 33; bedstead tester, 33; bed-valance (inner), 33; counterpane, 33; curtain linings, 33; headboard, 33; headcloth, 33

verd-antique, **363;** paperweight with bronze handle, 214

verging iron, 300

vices, 272, 295

vinegar bottles: raspberry, 278

vinegar-casks, 23, 143

vinegar cruets, 282

voider, 23, **363**

voider tables, 244; elm, 255, 266, 287; mahogany, 229, 244, 273, 276; —, with 1 drawer, 271

wafer irons, 142, 342

wafers: cup and saucer for, 204

wafer saucers, 203, 215

wafer stand: lava ware, 214

wafer-tongs, 277, 284

wafer trays: china, 204; Colebrookdale, 204

wages and labour, 93, 152

wainscot, **364;** bureau, 185; chairs, 31, 126; chests of drawers, 184, 185; clock case, 331; close-stools, 57, 84, 126; panel work, 173; presses, 43, 78; tables, 57, 58; —, with 1 drawer, 56; —, oval, 82; —, square, 84; writing-table, 77

waiters, 145, **364;** japanned, 140, 345; silver, 196, 323; —, large, 323; silver-plated, 183; —, round, 348

waiting napkins, 280; diaper, 346

walking cane, with gold head, 118

wall-hanging linings: canvas, 51

wall-hangings, 76; Antwerp, 42; blue-print, 57, 60; caffoy, 82; calico, Indian, 32, 42; cloth, 51; damask, 34, 35, 70; —, worsted, 77; drugget, 38, 39, 40, 42; —, striped, 36; gilt-leather, 32, 41, 43, 47, 49, 50, 51; Kidderminster, 20, 32, 48; leather, 51; mohair, 51; plaid, 56; —, Irish, 77; print, 57, 58, 60; satin, Indian, 39; silk, Indian, 42; stuff, 57; —, flowered, 57; —, striped, 39, 47; velvet, 84. *See also* tapestry-hangings

wall-paper: Indian, 189, 192

walnut: boxes, 126; —, brass-garnished, 36; —, on frame, 40; brackets, 82; bureau, 160; cabinets, 41, 110; case of drawers, 231; chair frames, 42; chairs, 137, 141; chests, 109, 110; —, bedchamber, 230; chests of drawers, 161, 181; corner-cupboard, 158; desk, 160; dining-table, with cants, 192; dressing glass, 160; dressing table, 137; folding-table, 138; hanging-glass frame, 149; looking-glass frame, 125; secretary, 231; settee, 144; table frames, 81; tables, 35, 158, 232, 234; —, square, 82; —, and stands, 40

Walpole china, **364;** cups and saucers, 183

wardrobe-bed, with mahogany panel doors, 267

wardrobe-curtains: stuff, 223

wardrobe doors: glass, 223; panel work, 255, 268; wirework, 255, 268

wardrobe hangings: green baize, 190

wardrobes: with drawers, 206; white, with drawers, 209, 223; **beech-wood,** with 2 drawers, 3 deal shelves, 335; **deal,** painted mahogany colour, 191, 193; **mahogany,** 191, 205, 206, 207, 230, 310, 311, 312; —, with 2 drawers, 3 shelves, 332; —, with 4 drawers,

330; —, with 4 drawers, 3 sliding shelves, 332; —, with 4 drawers, 5 trays, 221; —, on drawers, 242; —, with drawers in wings, 241; —, with deception commode, 268; —, inlaid, with 2 drawers, 3 deal shelves, 334; —, with panelled doors, 255, 268; —, atop secretary, 330; —, with shelves, 190; —, with wire doors, 255, 268; **oak,** 311, 313; —, with 2 drawers, 339

wardrobe shelves: cedar, 190; deal, 332, 334, 335

warming-pans, 112, 140, 184, 315; brass, 22, 47; copper, 91, 172, 338; silver, 78

warm-water jugs, 331, 332, 333, 336, 337, 339; blue-and-white ware, 332, 335, 336; brown-and-white ware, figured, 334; china, 332; yellow-and-black ware, 335

wash-ball boxes, **364;** silver, 161, 217

wash-ball stands: blue-and-brown ware, 218

wash-hand basins: china, 128; —, chinée, 332

wash-hand basins and ewers: blue-and-white ware, 333; brown-and-white ware, 332; red-and-white ware, 334; white ware, 330, 331, 332, 333

wash-hand glasses, 183; cut-glass, 286

wash-hand stands, 220, 300, 311, 312, 313, **364;** with 2 leaves, 218; **deal,** painted white, 336; **mahogany,** 126, 138, 308, 330, 333, 337; —, with folding top, and 2 drawers, 332; **mahogany, inlaid,** 332, 334, 335; **painted** green, 332; —, with high back and drawer, 335

wash-hand tables, 219; mahogany, 269; painted, white and green, 2 shelves, 221

wash-houses: at Baronscourt, 184; at Hillsborough Castle, 144; at Kilkenny Castle, 48, 51; at Kilrush House, 151. *See also* laundries

washing-stand, 242

washing tables, 219, 241; and ware, 241

washing-tubs, 51, 113, 127, 288, 293, 294, 300. *See also* wash-tubs

wash-table: deal, 272

wash-tubs, 343

watch and chain: gold, 118

watchman's room: at Carton House, 289

watch-stand: bronze, 221

water barrels, 297, 299

water-barrows, 299; with barrel, 300

water bottles, 91, 120, 330, 332, 333, 334, 337; flint-glass, 64

water brushes, 292, 298

water-cans: japanned, 342; tin, 340

water casks, 111

water closets, 217, 271

water crofts, **364;** *passim*

water dishes: tin, 286

water engine: pipe belonging to, 85

water ewers, 255, 256, 265, 266, 267, 269, 270, 276, 277; and cover, 278; silver, 161

water glasses, 91, 119, 120, 175, 183, 286

watering barrow, 302

watering pots, 300, 302; copper, 167

watering tubs, 279

water-jugs: *passim*; cut-glass, 317; gilt, Chinese, 255; white ware, 340. *See also under* jugs

General index

433

water pitchers, 316, 318
water plates, 171, **364**; china, 344;
  pewter, 286
Waterstown (Shell Cottage), at Carton
  House, 301–2
water troughs, 295, 299
water tubs, 66, 143, 284
wax: figure, 273; wax candles, 52, 193, 340;
  wax taper, 340
weaponry: bayonets, 158; **blunderbusses**,
  46, 121, 140, 286, 340; **carbine**, 301;
  couteau, 121; **dirk**, silver-mounted, 270;
  fusees, 85; **guns**, 71, 121, 128, 140; —,
  half-stock, 140; —, screw-barrel, 120; —,
  silver-mounted, 330; **halberds**, 85, 291;
  muskets, 23, 46, 158; **pistols**, 71, 121, 340;
  —, brass-mounted, 140; —, cases of, 121,
  270; —, Highland, 120; —, silver and steel,
  140; —, silver-mounted, 270; **repeaters**,
  158; **swords**, basket-handled, 270; —,
  blade of, 270; —, broad, 121, 140, 329; —,
  mourning, 121; —, silver-hilted, 121;
  tomahawk, 272
weather-glasses, 31, 84, 170, 179, 240, 290,
  327; French, 290. *See also* barometers
Wedgwood ware, 12, **364**; beer mug, 340;
  candlesticks, 207, 208, 218; cream-jug,
  277; déjeuner, 218; dessert-plates, 195;
  dishes, 195; figures, 203, 214; inkstands,
  black, 333; ornaments, black, 219; papillote
  case, 204; pastille burner, 335; plates,
  flat, 195; portrait medallion, 271; sphinxes,
  204; sugar-bowl, 277; tea-pots, 342; —,
  red and black, 220; vases, 205, 216; —,
  black, 207
weighing machine: mahogany, 206
weights: 4 pounds, 285; frank, 273; half
  hundredweight (56 pounds), 285, 293,
  295, 299; half stone (7 pounds), 285;
  hundredweight (112 pounds), 120, 232;
  quarter (28 pounds), 90, 232, 293, 295;
  stone (14 pounds), 285, 299
Welsh kettle: brass, 22
wethers, 93, **364**
whatnots: mahogany, 273
wheat: barrels of, 93; screen, 174; sowing of,
  152; wheat-mill in steel, 92. *See also* chaff
wheelbarrows, 93, 294, 298, 299, 300, 302, 303
wheel cars, 92, **364**
wheel-chairs, 320; Merlin, 308
wheeler's shop, 296
wheeling pits, 296
whip-saw, 297
white: **calico**, bed-curtain linings, 190,
  191; —, bed-curtains, 208, 209, 220, 221; —,
  bed-valances, 220; —, chair-covers, 191; —,
  cushion-covers, 206; —, length of, 281; —,
  mattress case, 221; —, pillow-covers, 206;
  —, window-curtain linings, 189, 190, 191,
  327; —, window-curtains, 21, 79, 208, 209,
  221; —, window-curtain valances, 221;
  camlet stuff, bed-furniture, 182; **cotton**,
  bed-curtain linings, 332; —, bed-furniture,
  331, 333, 334, 335, 336; —, bed-furniture
  linings, 330, 334; —, chair-covers, 139, 333,
  336; —, counterpanes, 330, 331, 333, 335,
  336, 337, 338, 339, 343; —, headcloth lining,

335; —, roller blinds, 336; —, rugs, 137; —,
  seating furniture, 333; —, tester lining,
  335; —, window-curtain linings, 332, 335;
  —, window-curtains, 330, 333, 336; **cotton**
  (and Decca work), chair-cover, 333; —,
  counterpane, 332; —, window-curtains,
  332; **cotton** (printed), counterpane, 332;
  damask, window-curtains, 33, 34, 35,
  38, 40, 76; **damask** (Indian), window-
  curtains, 33; **dimity**, bed-curtains, 139,
  190, 209, 221; —, bed-furniture, 333, 335,
  336; —, bed-valances, 221; —, chair-covers,
  139, 190; —, counterpanes, 209, 221; —,
  stool covers, 139; window-curtains, 207, 331;
  flannel, window-curtains, 20; **flocking**,
  window- curtains, 20; **linen**, roller blinds,
  241; **muslin**, window-drapery, 327, 337;
  sarcenet, christening-robe lining, 268;
  satin, christening robe and mantles, 268;
  —, couch, couch-bed and stool covering, 180;
  serge, window-curtains, 43; **silk**,
  pole-screens, 328. *See also* quilts (white)
white-and-gold china: tea-pot, 319
white-and-gold ware: basins and ewers,
  218, 219
white-and-purple: mohair, cushions and
  valance, 79
white china: cups and covers, 36
white frames: looking-glasses, 220, 223,
  224; pier-glasses, 159, 206; pier-table, 291;
  table, 274
white furniture: chairs, 139, 336, 337; —,
  bamboo, 336; clothes press, 311; dressing
  tables, 310, 311; presses, 312, 313; stools,
  139; tables, 311, 312, 313; tent bed, 312;
  wardrobe, 209, 223; wash-hand stand, 336
white glass-ware: finger glass, 234
white Holland: blinds, 273; roller blinds, 273
white ware, **364**; basins, 46, 254, 255, 256,
  265, 269, 276, 277, 278, 288, 339; basins and
  ewers, 253, 275, 287, 335, 336, 337, 338, 339;
  butter pail and cover, 278; candlesticks,
  332, 333; chamber-bath liners, 332, 333,
  334, 335; chamber pots, 20, 46, 312;
  chamber utensils, 330, 332, 333, 335, 336,
  337, 338, 339; chamber vases, 253, 254, 275,
  287, 290, 291, 292, 301; close-stool pan, 59;
  cup, 290; dishes, 277, 278, 282, 315, 341;
  fish drainer, 341; foot pans, 209, 334; foot
  tub, 310; jugs, 275, 277, 300; jugs and
  basins, 254, 256, 268, 270, 271, 272, 290,
  291, 312; night-stool liners, 333, 334, 337;
  night-stool pan, 332; night-table liner, 335;
  plates, 277, 293, 301, 315; pudding basins
  and moulds, 341; soap-and-brush trays,
  337, 338; sugar-basin, 342; tea-pot, 290;
  wash-hand basins and ewers, 330, 331,
  332, 333; water-jug, 340
wickerwork: screen, 39. *See also* baskets;
  basketwork; kish; twig
wig-stands, 181
willow. *See* sally-wood; wickerwork
Wilton: bed-round, 230; floor carpets, 139;
  stair carpeting, 231
windlass, 293
window-cornice: Wyatt, gilt, 292
window-curtain bindings: velvet, 327

window-curtain cornices: damask, 75; deal,
  269; gilt, 204, 215, 272, 273; Indian silk, 82;
  inlaid, 332; lutestring, 81; mahogany, 332;
  mohair, 82; moreen, 274; painted, 270,
  333; stuff, 75
window-curtain linings: calico, 189, 190, 191,
  327; cotton, 137, 332, 335, 337; Persian,
  272; poplin, 56; serge, 39, 42, 56; stuff,
  worsted, 61
window-curtains: antherine, 77; **caffoy**, 82;
  calico, 21, 39, 40, 41, 77, 79, 189, 191, 203,
  208, 209, 214, 219, 220, 221, 230, 231, 232,
  233, 241, 242, 271; —, striped, 221; **camlet**,
  80, 108, 109, 125; **check**, 140, 231, 232;
  chintz, 125, 126, 160, 206, 207, 208, 210,
  223, 256, 266; **chintz calico**, 218, 220, 256,
  266, 267; **chintz palampore**, 189, 190;
  cotton, 137, 144, 190, 330, 333, 336; —, with
  Decca work, 332; —, lining, 334; —, printed,
  327, 328, 329, 330, 331, 332, 334, 336, 337,
  338, 339; **cotton and muslin**, 335;
  Damascus, 191, 193; —, 'stripped', 205;
  damask, 33, 35, 38, 40, 56, 70, 75, 76, 77,
  78, 125, 126, 138, 272; —, draw-up, 34; —,
  Indian, 33; —, thread, 31; —, worsted, 77;
  dimity, 139, 190, 207, 219, 269, 331, 335,
  337; **dornick**, 41; **drugget**, 42, 52; **flannel**,
  20; **flocking**, 20; **furniture calico**, 270,
  282; **furniture linen**, 191; **harrateen**, 125;
  Kidderminster, 48; **leno**, japanned, 221;
  linen calico, 229; **lutestring**, 81, 82;
  mohair and silk, 144; **moreen**, 189, 216,
  233, 271, 272, 273, 274, 282, 327; **muslin**,
  219; **palampore**, 282; **paragon**, 158, 170,
  192; **plaid**, 56, 61; **poplin**, 56; **sarcenet**, 39;
  satin, 56; **serge**, 21, 32, 37, 39, 40, 42, 43,
  46, 47, 52; **silk**, 84, 139, 203, 215; —,
  clouded, 204; **silk damask**, 138; **stuff**, 32,
  55, 56, 57, 75, 126, 144; —, Indian, figured,
  57; —, Indian, striped, 32; —, Irish, 31;
  tabouret, 240; **taffety**, 42; **worsted**, 126
window-curtain valances: calico, 208, 209,
  220, 221; damask, 75; stuff, 75
window cushions: velvet, 76
window-drapery: velvet, 204, 207, 208, 217, 330;
  calico, 203, 214, 219, 233, 271; **chintz**, 207;
  chintz calico, 218; **cotton**, 331, 335; —,
  printed, 329, 331, 334; **cotton and muslin**,
  328, 335; **Decca-work**, 332; **dimity**, 269;
  moreen, 216, 233, 271, 272, 273; **muslin**,
  327, 331, 337; **muslin and cotton**, 333;
  tabouret, 240
window-drapery bindings: velvet, 331
window-drapery lining: calico, 327
window-hanging linings: stuff, worsted, 61
window-hangings: mohair, 82; plaid, 61
window rods: brass, 272
window-seat coverings: damask, 76
window-seat covers: moreen, 327;
  serge, 76
window seats, 221, 232, 239; stuffed, with
  black-painted frame, 327
window-shuts, 172, **364**
window-stool covers, **364**; calico, 203
window stools, 204, 214
window-valances: damask, 35, 76; Indian
  silk, 82; stuff, Irish, 31

434

Windsor chairs, 125, 142, 183, **364**
wine-bottle baskets. *See* wine-coopers
wine carrier: mahogany, 308
wine cellar utensils, 65
wine coasters: silver, 316, 323
wine-coolers; china, 277; cut-glass, 340; glass, 234, 286, 340; mahogany, 232, 233; silver, and covers, 316. *See also* ice-pails; sarcophagus
wine-coopers, 169, 308, **364**; brass-mounted, 327; mahogany, 189, 205, 327. *See also* bottle coopers
wine decanters: glass, 317, 318
wine funnels: silver, 240, 316, 323, 348; —, plate for, 197
wine-glasses, 91, 120, 175, 180, 183, 234, 277, 283, 286, 300, 302, 317, 342; cut-glass, 183, 317, 340
wine jugs: silver, 197
wine labels: silver, 197, 240, 348; silver-plated, 240. *See also* bottle tickets
wine-measures: pewter; —, half-pint, 276; —, noggin, 276
wines: at Castlecomer House, 199; at Dublin Castle, 65
wine tables: mahogany, 274
winkers, 298, **364**
winnowing: cloth, 93; machines, 297, 298; sheets, 174, 293
wirework: bookcase doors, 271; on fenders, 189, 190, 207, 210, 224, 229, 240, 287, 289, 300; —, brass, 206, 208; —, steel, 209; sieves, 300; —, brass, 278; fireguards, 270, 272, 292; —, brass-mounted, 255, 256, 265, 266, 267, 268, 269, 270, 271, 272; wardrobe doors, 255, 268
wood (unspecified): baker (japanned), 37; beam (balance), 48; bowls, 92, 166, 279, 283, 284, 285, 288, 294, 302, 303, 315, 318, 340; boxes, 296, 314; buckets, 302, 303; butter slices, 284; cans, 23; chairs, 44, 46, 48, 50, 142, 145, 184, 185; —, carved, 45; chests, 339; churn, 294; cistern, 67; clock, 303; coal box, 293, 315; corn weeder, 297; cups and saucers, 303; curtain-rods, 327; dishes, 287, 303; dog beds, 299; dog trough, 167; keeler, 302; kitchen vessels, 22; knife-box, 285; knives, 303; milk bowls, 92; noggins, 302; pails, 342; peels, 45, 48; pestle, 283; racks, 290; rakes, 167, 300, 302; salt-boxes, 22, 314; salting tub, 318; scales, 127; skimmers, 303; spoons, 279, 283, 303, 315, 340; squirt, 46; stools, 48, 342; strainer, 303; tea-pot, 303; trenchers, 92, 283, 302
woods for furniture. *See* alder; ash; beech-wood; boxwood; cedar; cherry-wood; deal; ebony; elm; fir; harewood; lancewood; mahogany; maple; oak; olive wood; pearwood; rosewood; sally-wood (willow); satinwood; sycamore; wainscot; walnut

woodworking tools: augers, 168, 296; bench vice, 297; braces, 290; —, and bits, 295; chisels, 297, 302; cross-cut saws, 168, 296, 297, 302; felling axes, 167, 298; gimlets, 290; glue-pot, 297; gouges, 297; handsaws, 168, 275, 302; hatchets, 167; holdfast, 296; mallets, 302; moulding planes, 296; scrapers, 297; tenon saw, 296; tool-chests, 272, 297; turning-chisels, 297; turning-lathes, 296, 297; whip-saw, 297
wool: carpet, printed, 336; mattresses, 126, 137, 138, 141, 209, 210, 212, 221, 223, 255, 276, 330, 333, 334, 335, 336, 337, 338, 339; squab stuffing, 328, 337
wool and hair: mattress, 253
woolsack, 328
Worcester porcelain, **364**; bowl, with cover and basin, 206; at Newbridge House, 307: baskets, with covers and stands; butter boat; cheese dishes, round; cheese plates; cream boats; dessert baskets; dishes, flat, round and oval; plates, flat; ice-pails, covers and plates; leaves for fruit; soup-plates, 318
work-basket, 126
workbenches, 272, 296, with drawers, 295, 296
workboxes: japanned, Indian, 333; mahogany, 190; straw, 334
workshop: at the Duke of Leinster's office, 297
worktables, 310; harewood, inlaid, 272; mahogany, 291; —, square, 1 drawer, 337
worsted, **364**; bed-curtains, 126; fringes, bed-furniture, 47, 334; hassocks, 219; —, worked, 204; Kidderminster, nailed about bed, 44, 49; quilts, Brussels, 275, 290, 291, 292; window-curtains, 126
wrenching-tubs, 44, 51, **364**
writing-case: mahogany, with brass clasps, 217
writing-desk coverings: green baize, 330; greycloth, 329; scarlet cloth, 331; velvet-covered, 33
writing-desks, 66, 139, 191, 328; with cabinet, 71; **beech-wood**, with 2 drawers, 329; **deal**, 192, 331; **fir**, 142; **inlaid**, 55; **mahogany**, 141, 335; —, portable and brass-mounted, 330; —, with drawers, 330. *See also* tambour writing-desk
writing-desk table: mahogany, with folding top, 267
writing stand: pewter, 89
writing stool: mahogany, 330
writing-table coverings: green cloth, 89; velvet, 75
writing-tables, 140, 145, 180, 215, 217, 241, 242, 244, 332; with 1 drawer, 218, 219, 220, 223; with drawers, 78, 312; with 2 leaves, 138; folding, 84; **harewood**, 255; **inlaid**, 138; —, with drawers, 75; **japanned**, 75; **mahogany**, 137, 139, 140, 205, 233, 244, 308; —, with 1 drawer, 206, 221; —, with 6 drawers, 205, 217, 221; —, with drawers,

138, 140; —, inlaid, folding top, 328; —, on pillar and claws, with folding top, 330; —, square, 336; **oak**, 89; —, with 1 drawer, 221; **wainscot**, 77. *See also* tambour writing-tables
writing-table top: cloth-lined, 244
wrought-work, **364**; chairs, 89; counterpane, 109; cushion, 33; fire screen, 76; stools, 66. *See also* Decca work; Indian work
x chairs, x seats, x stands, x stool. *See each under* cross
yarn: for mops, 287
yellow: caffoy, chair coverings, 82; —, wall-hangings, 82; —, window-curtains, 82; **calico**, bed-curtains, 219; —, bed-drapery, 219; —, bed-step adornment, 207; —, cushion-covers, 207; **camlet**, bed-furniture, 109; —, length of, 144; —, window-curtains, 109; **damask**, back- and elbow-stool coverings, 181; —, bed-furniture, 181; —, tester, 81; **damask**, back-stool coverings, 181; —, bed-furniture, 181; —, elbow-stool coverings, 181; —, tester, 81; —, window-curtains, 38; **damask** (Indian), curtains, valance and cornices, 75; 'harnum', bed-curtains, headcloth and tester, 49; 'harnum' damask, breadths of, 52; **harrateen**, bed-curtains, 126; —, curtains, 128; **mohair**, elbow-chair coverings, 77; **Persian**, bed-curtains, 84; **poplin**, window-curtains and linings, 56; **print** (fabric), bed-furniture, 60; **sarcenet**, bases (bed), 39; —, bed-curtain linings, 39; **satin**, cushions, 52; —, stool coverings, 39; **satin** (Indian), bed-furniture and wall hangings, 39; **serge**, back-chair cases, 37; —, bed-curtains, 47, 50; —, bed-valance, 42; —, counterpane, 49; —, curtains, 44; —, elbow-chair cases, 37, 75; —, headcloth, 42; —, window-curtains, 37, 39, 42, 47, 52; —, window-seat covers, 76; **silk**, window-curtains, 139; **silk damask**, bed-curtains, 139; **stuff**, bed-curtains, 89; —, beds, 89; —, window-curtains, 126
yellow-and-black ware: jug, 335; soap-and-brush tray, 335
yellow stoneware: baking-dishes, 183; bread-baskets, 183; dishes, 183; —, large, 183; —, round, 183; —, second-course, 183; fish drainers, 183; salad-dishes; —, long, 183; —, round, 183; sauce bottles, 183; soup-dishes, 183; tureens, 183
yellow ware, **364**; basins and ewers, 220, 221; foot pans, 206, 207, 209, 217, 219, 220, 221; jugs and basins, 209, 210; pincushion dishes, 183
yew: boxes, with carved tops, 273; inkstand, with 1 drawer, 272; letterboxes, 271; —, inlaid, 273; pole-screens, 334

General index

Books —

Divinity

Prayer Book
Bibles
in 4 Parts
...ques on Christianity & book...
...er prayer books & book...
...he of Prayers
...on on the New Testament   19
...ons Lectures
...ts Bible with notes
...he Explained
...nes Letters or Ins...
...risons Scripture C...
...nders Village...
...mpanion to the ch...
...ildrep to the Christ...
...e Whole duty of...
...rimmers Abridgm...

Do — Sacred
...rimmers Sacred
Doyleys History
...lleys Sermons   20
Coopers Doctrinal
Coopers Practi...
Simons Serm...
Pottos Discour...
Sherlocks Di...
Josephus...
Hannah...

...he sa...
Eight Velvett Chair...
A looking Glass 41½ 9
with a black frame
a black Japan Chest...
a wainscott Table and...

Bed Cham...

A feild bed and Sacking
Col. & Scarlett worsted dam...
Persian, quilt of the sam...
& Fustian Pillow, a quilt
2 window Curtains & 5 Ch...
a black Japand Chest of I...
a wainscoate Close Stool

Drawing Room

Two window Curtains of...
Chaires, one Small Chest
Small wainscott Table